INSIDERS' GUIDE® TO
THE MAINE COAST

THIRD EDITION

ANDREW VIETZE

INSIDERS' GUIDE®

GUILFORD, CONNECTICUT
AN IMPRINT OF THE GLOBE PEQUOT PRESS

All the information in this guidebook is subject to change. We recommend that you call ahead to obtain current information before traveling.

INSIDERS' GUIDE®

Text design: Sheryl Kober
Maps: XNR Productions, Inc. © Morris Book Publishing, LLC
Layout artist: Maggie Peterson

ISSN 1547-8939
ISBN 978-0-7627-5039-9

Printed in the United States of America
10 9 8 7 6 5 4 3 2 1

CONTENTS

Directory of Maps

Maine Coast

South Coast

Greater Portland

Midcoast

Acadia Area

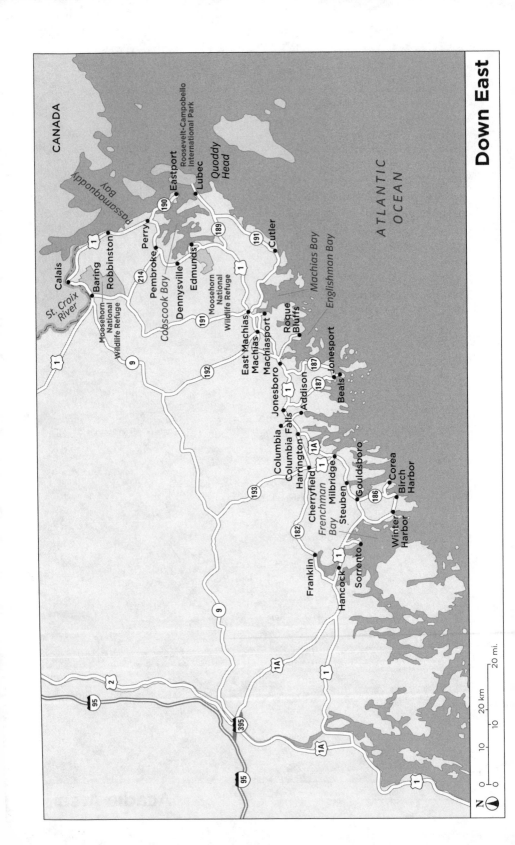

Down East

PREFACE

One of the nicest things about exploring the Maine coast is that it's just the right size. The state's grand waterfront is long enough at 280-some miles to be home to innumerable adventures, sights, and discoveries, but at the same time it's small enough that it's manageable—easy to travel and you can get to know it. If you had to, you could drive from one end to the other in five or six hours. But if you did so, you'd be missing out on so much.

If you started at Kittery and spent weeks meandering your way Down East, finally landing in Calais many days later, you'd happen upon all sorts of great stuff—waterfront restaurants, fine inns, exceptional meals, beautiful beaches, extraordinary trails, and scenery that has few rivals. And the nice thing is, if you were to return at some point and make the trip again (and of course you're going to want to), it would be the same—and entirely different. So many changes occur in the course of even one year here—new eateries, new B&Bs, new outfitters, new outdoor opportunities—that there is always something captivating and unexpected to be found in even those places you think you know. It makes poking about this great state a never-ending pastime.

Whole generations of people have found this to be the case, returning every summer. The first "summercators" began coming here in the late 19th century to escape the heat and noise of the city. They were hooked, and the tides of visitors haven't let up since, making this smallish state in the nation's northeasternmost corner into "Vacationland." Thanks to this annual influx, all the services you could need as a guest are there for you. A whole industry—one of Maine's largest—has been built to cater to your needs.

So get out there and explore.

ACKNOWLEDGMENTS

This book would never have come to your hands without the hard work and gracious assistance and support of Amy Lyons at The Globe Pequot Press; Paul Doiron, Dawna Hilton, Jeff Clark, Allister Timms, Clover McCallister, and Josh Moore at *Down East: The Magazine of Maine;* Losers/ Weepers Records, the afflictions, rural electric ("The Way Life Should Sound"), and the Oddfellows Orchestra for providing the soundtrack; everyone Down Point; the Maine State Office of Tourism; and all the parties listed inside.

Special thanks go to my Mom, principal archivist and number one fan, for all the afternoons watching the boy, and to my Dad, too. To Karin at Pen Bay Physical and Occupational Therapy, because the book would have read funny without any S, W, or Xs, and I needed the encouragement. And lastly to Lisa and Gus, with whom all my adventures begin and end.

HOW TO USE THIS BOOK

The Maine Coast—everyone has a different idea what those three words mean. To some the phrase conjures up resort communities on big white sandy beaches. To others it means little fishing villages far from the madding crowds. Still others think of it as cities like Portland or remote islands offshore. And they're all correct—beginning with beach and ending in cliffs, the state's coast is a rich and varied place, and it can be a lot of different things to a lot of different people.

But how exactly does one define the coast? How far inland does the term coast apply? (Maine weather forecasters, when they weren't predicting doom and posing in their sweaters, have spent years attempting to answer these questions.) For the purposes of this book, the counties with sea frontage will be considered coastal, and they'll be divided into five regions: South Coast, Greater Portland, Midcoast, Acadia Area, and Down East.

Each chapter will be arranged regionally, following the coast north by east, beginning at Kittery and ending up near Quoddy. So don't be confused when things are listed geographically rather than alphabetically. And also remember that while many people think heading to Eastport from Brunswick, say, is going north, it's actually east. Down East, for that matter. The farther you go, the better it gets.

This book will lay out the best in sites to see, things to do, dining, lodging, kidstuff, and more. Watch for the **i** —those Insiders' tips that let you in on the (shhh!) local secrets.

One of the nicer aspects about the state of Maine is that it functions like a big small town, and it also is always yielding new treasures to explorers. Doesn't matter how many times you've been to Waldo County, for example; every trip will reveal something unexpected and worthwhile, making travel here endlessly fun.

Over the years, thousands upon thousands of people have decided that they just don't want to leave when their vacation ends. Within these pages you'll also find plenty of resources if that describes you and you're relocating to the state. From private schools to area churches to hospitals to tax information, it's in here.

So whether you're on your first visit or are new Pine Tree State residents—Welcome to Maine.

AREA OVERVIEW

The Maine coast stretches for some 3,000 miles when all its islands and coves are included (some estimates even have it up over 5,000 miles). That's roughly the distance from Portland to Los Angeles, so it's no surprise that Maine is a widely varied place, beginning with miles of sandy beaches and resort communities and ending with rocky cliffs and tiny fishing villages. Along its length are a cosmopolitan city in Portland, vacation hot spots like the Kennebunks, Ogunquit, and Boothbay Harbor, suburbs like Cape Elizabeth and Falmouth, retirement meccas like Damariscotta and Topsham, enchanting islands like Monhegan, cottage communities like Bayside, national parks like Acadia, and hardscrabble Down East fishing villages like Jonesport and Lubec.

Because of this diversity, Maine means different things to different people. Some come for shopping, hitting the outlet towns of Kittery and Freeport, others for sun worshipping, setting up for vacation at a beachside motel in Old Orchard. Still others visit Maine to stay in an island inn, like the Chebeague Island Inn, to enjoy the old architecture of communities like Kennebunk and Belfast, to explore the wildlands on the shore at places like Cutler, or to kayak the isles and shoals of Muscongus Bay or Stonington.

Whatever you're looking for—small towns or big, the outdoors, great food, fairs and festivals—you'll surely find it here. In this chapter we'll walk up the coast, from Kittery to Calais, discovering each community on the way.

SOUTH COAST

Kittery Area

Maine's front door can be found in Kittery, a town most people associate with outlet shopping. The vast majority of visitors to the state drive up Interstate 95 from New Hampshire across the big green Piscataqua bridge and into this town of 9,400. Carved up a bit by highways and exits, Kittery is a pretty, old community that most people never discover, pulling off just to go to the 120 outlets that sprawl for a mile along U.S. Route 1 within view of I-95, temptingly flashing sale signs. This outlet row is where you'll find all of the big name brands—Banana Republic, Ralph Lauren, J. Crew, Old Navy, Tommy Hilfiger, Coldwater Creek, Gap, Timberland, Eddie Bauer, Hanna Andersson, and on and on—as well as local favorite Kittery Trading Post, an outfitter to rival L.L. Bean. Some amazing deals await in town—if you can remain patient enough to navigate the crowds.

But there's a lot more to Kittery than highways and half-priced shoes. Before the outlets arrived in the late 1970s and early 1980s, Kittery was known for its naval shipyard, which is still active on Seavey Island, spared by 2005 defense cuts. Because of its name—Portsmouth Naval Shipyard—and because of its location in Portsmouth Harbor, the yard has been the source of constant dispute between Maine and New Hampshire. (Taxes, you see. New Hampshire residents who work at the shipyard, repairing naval submarines, don't want to pay them to Maine.) Historic documents, maps, and the state border place the yard squarely in Maine, though, and the U.S. Supreme Court agreed, ruling in the Pine Tree State's favor when the dispute arose again a few years back. Regardless of where it is, visitors are welcome to tour the base's museum.

Kittery is also home to Kittery Point, one of scads of historic neighborhoods in the South Coast but with legitimate claims to being the oldest (York, just up the road, would argue, though). Kittery was settled in 1623 and has the architecture to prove it. Many distinctive colonials sit along the water in Kittery Point, some of which are owned by commuters who work in Boston, about an hour away. There are a couple neat old forts here, which once protected Portsmouth Harbor, as well as a pleasant strand down at Seapoint Beach, and a section of the Rachel Carson National Wildlife Refuge, an estuarine sanctuary for beasts but especially for migrating birds.

Inland from Kittery are the Eliots and the Berwicks, picturesque old communities that have north and south sections and sit on the Piscataqua River. Once shipbuilding and farming towns, they now have a suburban cast to them and send residents to work in Portsmouth, Portland, and Boston.

The Yorks

Many Maine towns are divided into villages—North Everytown, South Everytown, etc.—and are thus referred to in the plural, but the Yorks take the cake. Mark Twain used to spend a lot of time here, and he once quipped that you couldn't throw a brick in any direction without it hitting a postmaster. That's because there's one in York Village, York Harbor, York Beach, and Cape Neddick, all distinctly different villages and all in the town of York.

York is the first real beach community one comes to driving north in Maine, with four stretches of sands reaching out to embrace the cold waters of the Atlantic. About 13,000 people now call the area home, and the population quadruples come June with the arrival of all the summer people and tourists. This population swell is most evident in York Beach, which has the densely packed cottages, the taffy and T-shirt shops, the carousel, the arcades, the amusement park, the zoo, and the other sorts of superficial amusements you find in such places.

York Beach is a world away from York Village, the earliest chartered town in Maine (always challenging Kittery for the title). York Village was founded as Georgeana in 1640, taking its name

i For an inside look at a community, there's no better resource than the local paper. Most coastal communities in Maine have a weekly paper that details all the issues concerning residents, and it's usually published on Thursday. Find out more in the "Weekly Newspapers" section of the Arts and Entertainment chapter.

from Sir Ferdinando Gorges, who governed the area on behalf of the king of England. (It was renamed in 1652.) The architecture here is pure early American, with pretty gables and white clapboards everywhere, and the town has had the good sense to preserve it. About 50 buildings are listed on the National Register of Historic Places (a spooky old cemetery, the Old York Burying Ground, said to be haunted, holds the remains of many of their first residents). There are enough historic sites open to the public—the Old York Gaol (ca. 1653), the Old Schoolhouse (1745), the Emerson-Wilcox House (ca. 1740), and the Perkins House (1730)—to occupy a few afternoons.

York Harbor, likewise, wears its history well, only it was developed in an entirely different era, the late 19th century, when wealthy summercators discovered this shipbuilding center and began to transform it into a resort. Several neighborhoods of tidy Victorian cottages line lanes on the way down to the waterfront, and a lot of new summer places, part of the development boom York County has seen in the past few decades, are tightly squeezed in beside them. Between the two of them, York Harbor and York Village house much of the area's services, shops, and restaurants. Cape Neddick, also home to its share of old houses and cottages, is best known for Cape Neddick Light, affectionately known around town as the Nubble (see the Lighthouses chapter).

Ogunquit and Wells

Like many of the other resort communities on the South Coast, Ogunquit was built around its beach, which some claim is Maine's finest.

Its broad white sands cover more than 3 miles, and there's rarely a day when someone isn't out on them. Native Americans were the first to recognize the very obvious appeal of the strand, coming to frolic in the surf and giving Ogunquit its name, which means "beautiful place by the sea." Vacationers haven't let up since, regularly flocking here and overwhelming the 1,200 souls who call the town home.

The community has three principal areas: the beach itself; Perkins Cove, a fishing village on a narrow inlet at the south side of town that's been consumed by restaurants and boutiques; and downtown Ogunquit, a walkable Main Street of still more shops, inns, and eateries. A dozen art galleries can be found in town, testament to the community's rich history as an art colony, and there is an excellent local art museum as well as a summer theater that has welcomed some of Hollywood's biggest names over the years.

But it all started with the beach. Locals have made an effort to preserve the sanctity of these sands, and they've done a good job, keeping development several steps behind the grassy dunes at the edge of the beach. If you stand on the beach, back to town, all you see is glorious sea and surf, a wilderness of water. Lifeguards patrol in summer, when the sands are absolutely thronged with bikinis, umbrellas, beach balls, crying babies, coolers, and several acres of towels and blankets. Access is via Beach Street, right in the village, where there are changing rooms and restrooms; at Footbridge Beach, which is just north of downtown, and at Moody Beach, which is reached via Wells. All tend to be busy on a hot day—come early if you want a spot.

Perkins Cove, a mile down the coast, gets hopping, too, and parking is famously difficult at this little harbor. It's still a working waterfront—with Maine's only footpath drawbridge—but the activities of the local lobstermen based here have been eclipsed by all the boutiques and restaurants that have been retrofitted into old fishing shacks. Perkins Cove is connected to the rest of Ogunquit by the fantastic 1-mile walking path called the Marginal Way, which traverses rocks and shore, overlooking the open ocean and with

benches set up to enjoy the view. Paved and very easy going, the walkway is used by many people to get between town and cove, rather than trying to drive on congested Route 1. Some like to jump down to the tide pools below, others have a seat and survey the sea, and still others power walk while enjoying the views. The going is almost always elbow to elbow in midsummer. Best to show up early or late.

Marginal Way deposits you in downtown Ogunquit, a place of inns, B&Bs, resorts, restaurants, and hustle and bustle all crowded around a three-way intersection at the center of town. The community has become known as a gay-friendly place through the decades, with many businesses run by same-sex couples.

Like several other Maine towns, Ogunquit was "discovered" by artists in the late 19th and early 20th centuries, and once word got around, it became a veritable creative colony with some of the nation's biggest names in residence during the summer. The first to start throwing paint around here was Charles Woodbury, who arrived in Perkins Cove in 1888, calling it an "artist's paradise." Other painters were similarly impressed, and over the course of the next several decades he was joined by Walt Kuhn, Peggy Bacon, Elihu Vedder, Hamilton Easter Field, Yasuo Kuniyoshi, and Henry Strater. Their parties and hijinks were legendary. Strater would go on to found the Ogunquit Museum of American Art, a superb collection of works by these and other American greats, with a fine view of the water.

Ogunquit once was actually a village in the greater municipality of Wells, another beach town a few miles up Route 1 with a population of about 10,000. The pair split in 1980, and it's easy to see why, because they have very different personalities. While Ogunquit is relatively walkable and compact, Wells is a long, several-mile strip with no real town center. Like the one in Ogunquit, though, the town's beach is impressive—some 7 miles long. Also on the waterfront, sort of at odds with the Coppertone zone to its south and the commercial district to its north, are a couple of marshy spots dear to nature lovers and birds—the Wells National Estuarine Research

Reserve and the Rachel Carson National Wildlife Refuge (see the Green Space chapter).

Over the years Wells has become famous as a go-to place for antiques and used books, and some of the goods are even affordable. In more recent years, a couple of factory outlets have located here as well.

The Kennebunks

In high summer the Kennebunks—the name given to the villages of Kennebunk, Kennebunkport, Arundel, Cape Porpoise, and Goose Rocks—are as busy as Maine communities come. The population of 14,000 here probably quadruples in July and August as tourists, summer residents, and beach fans arrive to play on the wide sandy beaches, swim in the surf, shop boutiques, dine at some of Maine's best restaurants, stay in fun old inns, head out deep-sea fishing and whale watching, and maybe even catch a glimpse of the Bush family, who have summered here for ages.

The layout of the Kennebunks proves confusing to some as many people are unaware that Kennebunk has a waterfront. Because the town of Kennebunk Beach is closer to Kennebunkport than it is to the brick-lined downtown of Kennebunk, many people assume that it's part of the 'Port. Just remember that the Kennebunk River serves as the border between towns, and you'll know where you are. Better still to think of the place as one community, because that's largely how it functions.

The first European on the scene was likely Bartholomew Gosnold in 1602 or Martin Pring in 1603. Kennebunkport was settled a couple of decades later in 1629, Kennebunk in 1650, and in 1653 Kennebunkport incorporated as Maine's fifth town. This part of what is now Maine was particularly hard-hit during the French and Indian Wars, enduring many Indian attacks, but the colonists persevered, and in 1730 the community entered a prosperous time of shipbuilding. By the 19th century there were six shipyards along this stretch of coast, which combined to launch some 640 vessels. Trade with the West Indies was particularly important, and the seagoing success of these twin towns fueled a building boom of gracious sea captains' homes. (Kennebunk has more than 150 structures on the National Register of Historic Places and there's a fantastic walking tour of the finest streets.) Few Maine towns can rival its colonial revival and late Victorian architecture.

Tourism has been at the forefront of the economies of Kennebunk and Kennebunkport since at least the turn of the 20th century, when the Kennebunkport Sea Shore Company decided to position the community as a trendy summer resort the likes of Newport or Rhode Island. According to local historian Joyce Butler, the company saw to it that the place was kept neat and tidy, promoted it to the world, and attracted people in droves. Among the newcomers was the Walker family, who purchased the spit of land on Cape Arundel known as Damon's Park and Flying Point in the early years of the 20th century. The Walkers built a summer complex there that became known as Walker Point and was the summer playground for the young George Herbert Walker Bush, who'd go on to become the 41st president of the United States. Though not as popular as a tourist site now as it was during the first Bush presidency, Walker Point is still the subject of a lot of photographs and gawking—it's easily seen from Ocean Avenue—especially when word comes down that George Walker Bush, the 43rd president, is paying it a visit, which he may be doing more often these days. Why people bother is a good question, because the whole community is awash with Secret Servicemen, who, while just doing their job, make it difficult for everyday folks to travel from place to place.

The Kennebunks have quite the history of the famous and fortunate. The area became a popular retreat for artists, and several world-renowned authors have lived or summered here. The best known of these is probably Kenneth Roberts, a historical novelist and legendary curmudgeon who was born in Kennebunk and lived at Kennebunk Beach. His books of colonial and Revolutionary America—among them *Rabble in Arms, Arundel, Oliver Wiswell,* and *Northwest Passage*—were huge sellers in their day. Roberts can attribute some of his success to his friend, Pulitzer Prize–winning writer Booth Tarkington, who summered in Kennebunkport and helped the younger writer with his narrative structure.

Today many of the old homes in the Kennebunks have become inns and restaurants, and Dock Square, the small town center, has become a tourist haven with shops and boutiques and businesses hot for the summer dollars.

Biddeford and Saco

The twin cities of Biddeford and Saco stare across the Saco River at one another, and though they are distinctly different communities, their destinies have been entwined since the two were established in the 1630s. The larger of the pair, Biddeford has long been a manufacturing center, with Saco a more residential area. Neither has been a particularly big tourist draw, relative to the resorts to the south and Old Orchard Beach to the north, but each has its own summer enclave in Biddeford Pool and Camp Ellis. If visitors would take the time to explore a bit, they'd find enough to keep them occupied for a few days. Ferry Beach State Park, Saco Museum, the Saco Heath, and Camp Ellis Beach are in Saco, and the University of New England and East Point Sanctuary, and a cool museum in the streets walking tour are in Biddeford.

The English explored the Saco area when Captain John Smith sailed by in 1614 and took a look-see. Two years later, Sir Ferdinando Gorges sent the itinerant Richard Vines across the sea to do some prospecting in the area he had been granted. Homes started going up in 1630 or so, and the river and the village on its northside was originally called Pepperellboro, after Sir William Pepperrell, a large landowner. The name was changed in 1805 to Saco, after what the indigenous people called the Sawacatucke, which meant "burnt pine."

Factories emerged with the onset of the industrial age, and soon an ironworks was forging on the Saco side of the river. This development was followed by textile mills in Biddeford, which drew a large in-migration of French-Canadian workers. The twin cities have been a manufacturing center since, and many of the current 22,000 inhabitants of Biddeford can claim a Franco heritage. With a newly renovated theater downtown and some mills filled with upscale arts and retail, the gritty center is trying to change its image.

Old Orchard Beach

If your idea of fun is suntanning in a skimpy Speedo, playing arcade games, entering bikini contests, riding Ferris wheels, or shopping for two-dollar shot glasses, Old Orchard Beach is your kind of place—and you're in good company. The honky-tonk atmosphere of the town reels in vacationers in summer, making it into what might be Maine's largest city. Some 100,000 fun seekers have been known to be in town on any given weekend in August, turning the 7-mile beach here into one giant carnival. Fanning out from the old pier in the center of town are scores of hotels, motels, condos, pizza stands, and fried seafood shacks, as well as an arcade and an amusement park. You'll look a long time for parking and will probably never find the stand of apple trees that gave the town its name.

That orchard used to be a landmark to sailors, sitting high up above the beach. One of the first European settlers to see it was an Englishman named Thomas Rogers, who set up residence here in 1657, calling the place Garden by the Sea. He was rather quickly burned out by the Native Americans already living there. The territory here was considered part of the town of Saco until the 1880s, when it was incorporated and named Old Orchard (the Beach was added later). By then it was already a summer mecca. Back in 1837 an entrepreneurial gentleman named Staples had begun taking summer boarders on his farm for $1.50 a week, and his enterprise did well enough that he built the first inn in town. In 1847 trains began running from Boston to Portland right through Old Orchard's backyard, and that led to the development of a restaurant selling shore dinners. Six years later a connecting train was added to the route, bringing large numbers of Canadians down from Montreal. A resort was born.

After the Civil War things really started to boom, with trolley service to Saco and better train access. By the turn of the 20th century, Old Orchard had many of the same amusements that it does today, with roller skating, a merry-go-round and other rides, games of chance, and refreshment stands sprouting along the beach. A disastrous fire set things back a bit in 1907, but by the 1920s everything was rip-roaring again, with Guy Lombardo and Duke Ellington bringing their big-band acts to play for the masses.

And still they come. The 475-foot pier on the site today was built in 1980, and you can often hear French being spoken upon it in midsummer as Canadians continue to pour in for fun in the sun. The town has been attempting to broaden its appeal a bit by getting rid of some of the seedier elements that have crept in over the years and by adding beautifying things like flowers and landscaping in a quest to get families here.

There's certainly plenty to do. Old Orchard boasts Maine's largest waterslide, a gondola Ferris wheel and a roller coaster, championship miniature golf, championship real golf, Jet Ski rentals, parasailing, live music, karaoke, and more. Accommodations number in the hundreds, running the gamut from double-deck motels a la the Alouette Beach Resort to slightly more refined options like the Old Orchard Beach Inn, an 18-room hostelry that dates to 1730 and is on the National Register of Historic Places. And there are plenty of places to find eats as well. As Maine goes, Old Orchard is one of a kind.

GREATER PORTLAND

Mainers like to joke that the nice thing about Portland is that it's so close to Maine. The state's largest city is so much more cosmopolitan and urban than anywhere else Down East that it seems almost like another place—the metropolitan area here accounts for about a quarter of the population of the state. But there's actually still a lot of Maine left in it. First, the Portland Peninsula is small enough—just 3 miles across—that it's walkable and compact enough that it functions almost like a very big small town. People still know each other here.

Second, fishing remains a staple in the economy in Portland, just as it does in much of Maine. The waterfront is a working one, and the city's 64,000 residents have voted in the past to keep it that way, to keep the hip boots in and the high-rises out. Tourism long ago established a beachhead—vacationers flock to DiMillo's Floating Restaurant, to shops on the city side of Commercial Street, and to whale-watch boats—but it's still a fairly real place. In recent years, there's been talk of replacing the old Bath Iron Works dry docks, the victims of shipbuilding consolidation, with a hotel, but it hasn't happened yet.

The city also shares the architectural appeal of the rest of the state, being a treasure trove of Victoriana. The peninsula burned twice over the centuries, once during a punishing Revolutionary War bombardment and again as the result of a 19th-century warehouse fire. Many blocks were rebuilt immediately after that conflagration, so there are streets and streets lined with pretty old Victorian brick buildings, especially in the 6 blocks of the Old Port.

So with the sea, the fishermen, the small-town vibe, and the historic facade, the city remains rooted in Maine traditions even if people these days walk around with video phones and pink hair.

The first settlers in the area arrived in 1623. A gentleman by the name of Christopher Levett built a stone house on nearby Hog Island, but he returned to England to encourage others to come join him in this place he called Quack (from Casco, perhaps?), and whether he ever came back no one knows. After him came the notorious George Cleeve, who arrived in the 1630s, gained a small mandate from the patent holder of the area, and soon had tyrannical control over Casco Bay and its environs. He held onto it tightly until about 1658, when the district of Maine came under the control of Massachusetts and his influence waned.

In the years after Cleeve, the community here grew and prospered until a series of devastating Indian attacks emptied the town. When Samuel Moody was granted permission to set up a garrison here by the Massachusetts government, the site began to develop again, and soon it became an important port for trade with the West Indies and for shipbuilding.

The Revolutionary War years were tough on Portland, then called Falmouth. Locals were none too impressed with the British and their Stamp Act and threw their lot in with the Continental Congress and its militias. One fateful day, when a British sloop appeared in Casco Bay, a group of Mainers captured the vessel's captain, a man named Mowatt, and accused him of espionage. He was eventually released and would return to the city—with a vengeance. Mowatt came back on October 16, 1775, with four warships, and, when the colonists refused to give up their arms, he mercilessly opened fire, raining bombs. Remarkably no one was killed—despite Mowatt's order to "remove all human specie from the town"—but Falmouth was effectively wiped out. Two thousand people were left to face the oncoming winter homeless; 414 buildings were destroyed.

Though their town was a heap of wreckage, 700 people stayed on to rebuild, and by the 1780s the city—then known by its current name—was back in business, a hive of commercial activity. Portland became one of the largest cities in the young nation and boomed all the way up to the Civil War. During that conflict the staunchly abolitionist city sent 5,000 of its 25,000 residents to join the Union cause.

And then it burned again, this time due to a fire that began in a boat shop before sweeping across the peninsula. In this 1866 fire, little was spared. Most public buildings, many businesses, and scads of homes went up in a blaze worse than the 1775 bombardment. The city vowed to rebuild and did so with help from the rest of the nation. Many of the finest structures in town date back to this late-19th-century period of reconstruction, and there is enough of them that *National Geographic Traveler* called Portland's downtown one of the top historic places in the world.

This architecture, the surrounding sea, and the pleasant way of life in Portland have attracted all sorts of comers and earned accolades from countless magazines (the latest nods come from *U.S. News & World Report,* which called the city one of the best places to retire and *Organic Gardening,* which listed it among the nation's greenest cities). Portland has long been known as the Forest City, and while it's too developed now to have the kind of foliage it once did, it is still surprisingly green and pleasant, especially in its northernmost half. Parks sit on both flanks, overlooking Casco Bay and the harbor—the Eastern Promenade on one side and the Western Promenade on the other—and there are several woodsy areas spread about. The setting is further enhanced by the fact that the city is not even an hour and a half from Boston and less than that to the White Mountains, so getaways are easy.

But there's certainly enough to keep you busy here. In the past decade the city has been transforming Congress Street, the heart of the downtown and once Portland's principal retail corridor, into an arts district, anchored on one end by City Hall, home of Merrill Auditorium and the Portland Symphony Orchestra, and on the other by the I. M. Pei–designed Portland Museum of Art. In between are the Maine College of Art, the Maine Historical Society, the boyhood home of poet Henry Wadsworth Longfellow, several galleries, and a number of clubs, restaurants, and shops.

Retail has moved in large part to the Maine Mall in South Portland and, a few blocks down from Congress Street, to the Old Port, the distinctive shopping district retrofitted into old ship chandleries and Victorian warehouses just up from the waterfront. Six blocks of boutiques, specialty shops, and watering holes are located along the cobblestoned streets of the Old Port, and there are still more local establishments than chain stores among them. Portland is all about food—people like to say there are more restaurants per capita here than anywhere else in the country, save San Francisco—and this district is where a great many of them can be found.

The narrow, historic streets of the Old Port give way to Commercial Street and the waterfront, where boats come and go constantly and where the ferries that provide access to Casco

Bay's famed Calendar Islands (so named because there are allegedly more than 365 of them, one for every day). Several of these islands, such as Peaks and Long, have year-round populations, with people commuting across the bay on a daily basis and returning to their quiet seaside homes at night.

South of the city are the towns of Scarborough and Cape Elizabeth, which are both largely suburban areas that boast beaches and shopping centers. Scarborough begins to the west at Scarborough Marsh, a fantastic estuarine area that's the site of a popular Audubon sanctuary, and it ends in the congestion, chaos, and commercialism of the Maine Mall area near South Portland. Some of the state's best beaches line Scarborough's eastern front, which is also where Prouts Neck, a very exclusive summer community made famous by Winslow Homer, is located. Cape Elizabeth likewise has its own beaches as well as a pair of exceedingly popular state parks—Two Lights and Fort Williams. The latter is adjacent to Portland Head Light, Maine's best-known lighthouse.

South Portland, usually thought of as little more than a mall explosion, thanks to rampant chain development at the Maine Mall, is actually an interesting city with a personality all its own. With a population of about 23,000, it is Maine's fourth-largest urban area (behind Portland, Lewiston-Auburn, and Bangor) and is a diverse mix of industry, retail, and residential areas. Most of its appealing features are on the opposite side of the city from the scores of stores at the mall, where visitors will find a compact and attractive downtown, a network of greenways, Southern Maine Community College, Willard Beach, and Spring Point Ledge Light.

North of the city are the communities of Falmouth, Cumberland, and Yarmouth, each of which has a waterfront section of expensive homes and a more rural inland half. Housing development has been going great guns since the 1980s in all four, making way for more and more commuters. And to the west is the mill town of Westbrook, where the Sappi paper mill belches smoke from its location above the Presumpscot River. Much of the rest of the state's fifth biggest city is a mix of quiet suburban streets, big office buildings, and industrial park zones. Downtown Westbrook has enjoyed a renaissance of late, with an influx of arty businesses and restaurants.

Freeport

Usually getting cold feet puts an end to something, but in Freeport a pair of soggy boots was just the beginning. Leon Leonwood Bean went hunting one fateful afternoon and, not happy with his footwear, conjured up a design in his head. The Maine Hunting Shoe, better known as the "Bean boot," was launched in 1911, and the company Bean founded to sell them has never looked back, establishing a presence on Main Street in Freeport in its early years and leaving the door unlocked since. In these days of corporate scandals and cheap Chinese goods, the story of L.L. Bean is quite refreshing. From day one the young entrepreneur unconditionally guaranteed his products, most of which were hand-stitched on the premises, and he made customer service and shopping satisfaction the backbone of the company. It was—and still is—open 24 hours a day, every day, and it's filled with employees who know their stuff. (The company is one of the biggest catalog retailers in the world to boot.) You can still bring those old, hole-ridden Bean boots back with no questions asked—You Have Our Word.

Since the 1980s this great anchor store has attracted dozens of major retailers to downtown Freeport, creating one of the biggest outlet towns in the country. You want Anne Klein, Polo, North Face, and Banana Republic? You've got them, all in a pleasant downtown where you can walk rather than drive around. It may be a mall, for all intents and purposes, but it's all packaged up like a Maine village and is pleasant to walk around. That is, if you can find a place to park your car.

The 7,800 current residents of Freeport get a little tired of their community being defined by shopping (they should have thought of that when they let the stores flood in to begin with), and there is admittedly a lot more to the town. First, it has an important place in Maine history—

the papers that granted Maine statehood, certifying the split between Maine and Massachusetts, were signed in Freeport's Jameson's Tavern, which is now a restaurant (right near L.L. Bean). Second, it's a coastal community, a fact about which 90 percent of its visitors are probably unaware. South Freeport feels about as far from the bargain-bin bonanza as you could imagine, a genuine fishing village with a hardy lobster fleet and lobster in the rough available at Harraseeket Lunch and Lobster Company.

Down on the waterfront is where you'll also find a trio of fine parks. Wolfe's Neck Woods State Park is the largest, a 233-acre forest along the edge of Casco Bay. Then there's Winslow Memorial Park, a 90-acre, town-owned oasis on the bay in South Freeport with a small beach and picnic area. The third park is Mast Landing Sanctuary, a 140-acre site owned by the Nature Conservancy. Once a source of trees for Royal Navy masts, it's now a preserve well known for birding. There's a popular walking trail that clocks in at a little over a mile and a half.

On the north side of town is a real curiosity. People drive by the sign for Desert Road in Freeport all the time without thinking much of it. In fact there is a genuine expanse of sand in town, a tourist attraction known as the Desert of Maine that's just enough of a hoot to make it worthy of your time. A 300-acre farm until 1797, the site was overgrazed and overcleared until the topsoil had eroded completely away, revealing a sandy base. Now it looks like the Middle East, with vast sands and rolling dunes. Where there's an odd landmark, there are sure to be souvenirs, and that's the case here, too. A gift shop and information center on the premises will fill all your needs.

MIDCOAST

Brunswick

Brunswick is the state's largest town and dwarfs many of its cities, with 21,700 residents. (Population doesn't determine whether a community is a city or town in Maine; the type of municipal government does.) It sits at the point where Route 1 and I–295 diverge and has become a commercial and cultural center for the Midcoast. Two great institutions have come to define the town and have made the world at large aware of Brunswick, Maine—Bowdoin College and Brunswick Naval Air Station (BNAS).

Each has influenced the way the town has grown, Bowdoin and its 1,500 students have kept the downtown vibrant, and the navy and all its personnel helped spawn the retail development of Cooks Corner, an outpost of shopping centers on the eastern side of town.

Founded in 1794 as the first institution of higher learning in Maine, Bowdoin College has a long and rich history, filled with personalities of statewide, regional, and national note. Counted among its alumni are many of the most prominent Mainers of the past 300 years—from Henry Wadsworth Longfellow, to Civil War hero Joshua Chamberlain, to Arctic explorer Robert Peary, to Olympian Joan Benoit Samuelson, to distinguished senators and U.S. leaders including William Cohen and George Mitchell. A dozen Maine governors were educated here, as were writer Nathaniel Hawthorne, U.S. President Franklin Pierce, poet Robert Tristram Coffin, and scads of other national figures. The 110-acre campus itself is leafy and pleasant, with all the ivy and brick and granite a top-shelf liberal arts school is supposed to have and with a stand of pines that are among the oldest in the state. Many Brunswick residents have been known to take their lunch at the campus cafe and to use the bookstore as well. There are a pair of very good museums that are also open to the public (see Attractions chapter).

From Bowdoin's campus it's a half-mile walk down Maine Street, past the picture-perfect town green, to the center of Brunswick, several brick-lined blocks. This commercial corridor is the second-widest avenue in any New England town (behind Keene, New Hampshire), and the shops and restaurants here have a vitality to them that many other Maine downtowns have lost, thanks to all the students and the tourists who replace them in the summer. In the neighborhoods behind Maine Street are block after block of classic white-clapboard homes and pretty churches—138 buildings are in the National Register's Federal Street Historic District. At the end of Maine Street opposite Bowdoin, there is old Fort Andross, a mill building on the Androscoggin River.

For the impact it has on the local economy and for the number of pilots and sailors stationed just up the road from the shopping plazas of Cooks Corner, Brunswick Naval Station is a relatively quiet presence. And it's soon to get quieter—in 2005 BNAS was marked for closure by the Department of Defense. The base is the last active-duty airfield in the Northeast and the second-largest employer in Maine, with almost 5,000 people working there at its height, so the community is scrambling to figure out what to do next.

Across the tumbling Androscoggin River from Brunswick is Topsham (pop. 9,100), known for neighborhoods of attractive old homes and rampant development in the 1980s and 1990s. Shopping centers dominate one end of town, and they just seem to keep spawning more stores. Civic leaders have made efforts to keep the historic vibe downtown afforded by the homes on Elm Street and by the big Topsham Mill, now an office complex, by establishing a village center and by putting in a park. Shipbuilding and textiles were the main industries here in centuries past; today it's a bedroom to much bigger Brunswick.

Brunswick is also the jumping-off point to get to the magnificent Harpswells (pop. 6,000), eight distinct villages linked by bridges on an archipelago of 45 islands. The best known are Orr's and Bailey's Islands, popular cottage colonies exquisitely sited on Casco Bay. This is where you'll find a unique granite cribwork that lets the sea pass through, a curious span that's on the National Register of Historic Places. Cundy's Harbor is another Harpswell stunner, a fishing village on the briny New Meadows River.

Bath

Like its southerly neighbor Brunswick, Bath relies heavily on Defense Department dollars. While many Maine towns used to be shipbuilding centers, Bath still is one—and in a very large way. Navy contracts keep massive cranes and some 5,700 shipbuilders busy in the city on the banks of the Kennebec River. At any given time, big destroyers will be parked in the river, in full view of Route 1 motorists passing by on the tall and imposing Bath Bridge.

It's said that nearly half of the ships built in the United States in the second half of the 19th century were built in Bath. Today most of the shipbuilding in the city takes part at Bath Iron Works, founded in 1889. The yard lords over Bath, sprawling in a tangle of industrial buildings and high-rise–size cranes for about a mile along the Kennebec. At the moment BIW, a subsidiary of General Dynamics, is cranking out Aegis-class destroyers. Huge crowds turn out for launches in the summer.

You can learn all about the history of shipbuilding in Bath just up the road at the excellent Maine Maritime Museum (see Attractions chapter). Farther down the road from the museum is the Popham Peninsula, home of exceedingly popular Popham Beach. On a peninsula opposite Popham is another favorite beach at Reid State Park in Georgetown.

But there's more to the City of Ships than huge vessels. The community of 10,000 has a cool, historic downtown, which Mel Gibson fans might recognize from his 1993 movie *The Man Without a Face*, and some of the state's finest architecture in its armada of old sea captains' homes. The city is also something of a cultural center with its museums, excellent library, a handful of good restaurants, and the whimsical Chocolate Church, a gothic-spired former Congregational Church that is indeed painted chocolate brown and hosts a slate of concerts, dances, and arts shows.

Wiscasset

In recent years, Wiscasset has become known for its traffic tie-ups—they can go on for miles and miles on a hot August afternoon. But it would rather be known as the Prettiest Village in Maine, as a sign on Route 1 just below the village claims; some other communities like, say, Castine or Belfast, Monhegan or Stonington, might have a legitimate right to argue, there's no denying that Wiscasset (pop. 3,600), stacked up on a hill overlooking the Sheepscot River, is a good-looking place.

The downtown is pleasant, from the church and courthouse on a slight rise above Main Street to the rows of Victorian-era brick buildings that line it. Antiques stores fill many of them. But the really pretty parts of town are the neighborhoods that fan out from the town center. Many fine Federal and Greek Revival homes can be found here, once owned by the sea captains and merchants who flourished in the 19th century when Wiscasset was one of the largest shipbuilding centers north of Boston. Several small historic homes and history museums are popular draws in summer, and the town has made a name for itself as an antiques hot spot. An underappreciated gem of a park, Fort Edgecomb sits across the Davey Bridge in Edgecomb with great picnic grounds on a Sheepscot cove.

For decades the eyesore of the Maine Yankee nuclear power plant detracted mightily from this prettiest village, but it has since been removed. The town certainly enjoyed the taxes back when the plant was pumping out electricity, but it's making do thanks to all of the tourist dollars that wind up here, sucked in by the downtown—home of a pair of notable Midcoast eateries, Sarah's and Red's Eats—and to the businesses that line the approach to it on Route 1.

Just inland from Wiscasset are a pair of tiny communities that would hold their own in a prettiest village contest, Sheepscot and Head Tide, the latter in Alna, a fine pastoral town of hills and meadows on the Sheepscot River.

Boothbay Harbor

Boothbay Harbor was among the first places to be settled in Maine, and it's easy to see why people would have chosen to set up on this peninsula between the Damariscotta and Sheepscot Rivers. One of the deeper inlets on the coast, it is a very pretty place—that is, if you're standing on the harbor with your back to the land and looking out toward far away Damariscove Island, where those fishermen laid their claim before being driven off by Native Americans. If you turn around, you'll see the result of decades of barely restrained development, which in high season can turn the town into one big madding crowd.

Boothbay Harbor (pop. 2,347) has long been a resort community, one of the most popular in Maine. Shops, galleries, restaurants, B&Bs, and motels all fight for space downtown, and for anyone interested in shopping, day sailing, minigolf, or seafood, this is the place to be. (There is a wicked cool bowling alley, Romar Bowling Lanes, housed in a log cabin on the water, that's right out of a movie, established in 1946.) Where there isn't a motel in Boothbay Harbor there's a T-shirt shop. The harbor still has a fleet of lobstermen who try to eke out a living among all the pleasure craft and hurly-burly, and it is also home to Cap'n Fish's cruises, which are near legendary for whale watching and deep-sea fishing at this point (see the On the Ocean chapter). Many people enjoy strolling out onto Boothbay's famous 1,000-foot footbridge across the harbor to watch all the comings and goings.

If the throngs get to you, find one of the Boothbay Region Land Trust's excellent preserves. The busy conservationists have acquired 1,700 acres in the Boothbay region for use by the public and wildlife and turned them into 15 preserves. Some are woodsy, some are riverine—all are welcome after the bustle of the harbor. Or try visiting East Boothbay or Ocean Point, relaxed enclaves of summer homes.

The area was popular among fishermen from the get-go. They set up on Damariscove Island in the early 1600s, and year-rounders were here by the latter half of that century but were driven out by Indians. By 1729 white folks returned, in the form of 60 Scotch-Irish settlers, who called their neighborhood Townsend. Over the centuries residents here did a lot of fishing, even some whaling, and tried their hands at farming and woodcutting, too, supplying Boston with timber for a time. Shipbuilding was another profit maker, and in the late 1800s ice making and sardine canning were big. And while fishing remained a constant, and continues to this day, tourism has eclipsed just about everything else.

Damariscotta

The name of this community of 2,100, tucked alongside the Damariscotta River just below Route 1, has proven to be a tongue twister for many Maine visitors. The Abnakis named Damariscotta for the number of alewives they found in the river here. (The tiny herring still run in great numbers in springtime—you could walk across their backs, so numerous are they as they swim upstream—and are fun to watch in Damariscotta Mills. Ask around.) If you want to avoid embarrassment, pronounce it "Dam-uh-ri-Scott-uh." The small town of Newcastle is just across the river, and many people don't know where one begins and the other ends, so closely are the villages entwined.

Downtown Damariscotta is a historic village of well-preserved blocks that span the 19th century, and in its redbrick buildings are a mixture of tourist-oriented boutiques; good old Maine staples like Reny's, a discount department store; and a handful of restaurants. (The town is becoming known as an antiques hot spot, too.) Damariscotta is a service center for much of Lincoln County and has some cultural attractions as well, like the Round Top Center for the Arts.

Just inland from the saltwater Damariscotta River is Great Salt Bay, a broad swath of brine, and Damariscotta Lake, a long, skinny freshwater body ringed with cottages. The Damariscotta Shell Heaps are the famous site of ancient Abnaki oyster feasts, and a few years back the exceptional local conservation organization the Damariscotta River Association made a park in the area, a fantastic place for long walks in bayside meadows.

Pemaquid Peninsula

Damariscotta is the gateway town to the Pemaquid Peninsula, a long point of land that reaches down to the water like a lobster claw.

Two towns, Bristol and South Bristol, occupy the largest part of the peninsula, and they are divided into a half dozen villages. There's Walpole, which is hardly recognizable as its own entity, save for the Old Walpole Meetinghouse, a beautiful municipal gathering place built in 1772, and Bristol proper, a nifty community of older homes at the base of the Pemaquid River. Farther along are Round Pond, a summer colony that wraps around a cove on the east side of the peninsula; Christmas Cove, another enclave of vacation homes, which was "discovered" by Captain John Smith on Christmas Day in 1614; and the fishing village of New Harbor, which has a couple of great lobster wharves where you can grab some crustaceans fresh off the boats. Everyone loves the swinging bridge in South Bristol, which turns 45 degrees to make way for lobster boats passing through what is known as the Gut.

The real treat down in these parts, though, is Pemaquid itself, site of Pemaquid Light, Colonial Pemaquid, Fort William Henry, and Pemaquid Beach. The area practically drips with history, and Fort William Henry, a replica of a 1692 garrison that was originally built to beat back the Indians, the French, and a few pirates, too, is a good place to start looking for it. It has truly great vistas of Johns Bay. Not a quarter mile away is the Colonial Pemaquid Museum and a semipermanent archaeological site (see Attractions chapter).

Around the corner is one of the few sand beaches in the Midcoast, Pemaquid Beach, which arcs for 575 glorious yards on Johns Bay (see Beaches chapter). And no visit to Pemaquid would be complete without a walk on the rocks of Pemaquid Point. With fantastic views of the open Atlantic and of one of Maine's more distinctive lighthouses, it's a great place to picnic or smooch. Watch out during storms, though, because huge waves have been known to carry people off here.

Waldoboro

Waldoboro is one of the most underappreciated of Maine's towns, though its residents are probably happy about this fact. People typically cruise through on a fairly unattractive stretch of Route 1, full of convenience stores, pawnshops, and discount cigarette shops, and then stop at the top of the hill at now legendary Moody's Diner (see Restaurants chapter) for a bite before pushing on. That's a shame, because there's a lot more to this town of 5,000 than great pie and gas pumps.

Waldoboro was settled by a colony of Germans who migrated here before the Revolutionary War at the invitation of General Samuel Waldo, whose name the community bears. The good Saxons—40 families—thought that they were going to be settling in a prosperous city and were sorely disappointed to find only a raw pine forest at the head of the Medomak River. They persevered through rough winters and clashes with Indians and built the community they were looking for. The most obvious signs of this history are the Old German Meetinghouse, a fine structure that dates to the 1770s and still has its original box pews, and the nearby Old German Cemetery, where there are graves dating back to those early settlers.

Over the years Waldoboro became known as a shipbuilding center, and an industry was built around the incredible run of alewives, those small anadromous fish from the herring family. Today a lot of people make their living clamming out on the Medomak River, and others commute to larger towns for work. Besides Moody's, the other well-known local business is *Maine Antiques Digest*, a newspaper that got its start covering the growing antiques-dealing scene in Maine and now is a national monthly with subscribers around the globe.

Waldoboro's downtown is a small but fun place, perched on a hill overlooking the saltwater Medomak, where there is a handful of shops, restaurants, and banks. Many, many fine old homes and river vistas can be found if one takes the time to drive the roads that wander from here to places like Dutch Neck and Cove Road.

Travel far enough on one of these byways and you'll land in the gregarious-sounding town of Friendship. A working fishing village with a population of a little over 1,100, Friendship has two claims to fame. First, it's where the Friendship Sloop originated. These old sailing workboats are now valued as cruising vessels. Second, it's where Casper the Friendly Ghost made his home. Of course, when they filmed the 1995 movie about the spritely spirit, Hollywood producers determined that Friendship, as authentic as could be, with its active fleet of lobster boats and unspoiled vibe, didn't look enough like a Maine fishing village, so they chose to shoot much of the movie in the resort town of Camden. Their loss. The beautiful waters of Muscongus Bay spread out before Friendship, and since the late 1980s they've been discovered in a big way by kayakers.

Thomaston

Talk about reinventing your town. For more than 100 years, the stately community of Thomaston was dominated by the Maine State Prison, a dark dungeon of brick and cement and razor wire ominously set at one end of Main Street, right on Route 1 in full view of everyone passing through town. The state's maximum-security facility, full of lots and lots of bad guys, it was the inspiration for the prison in the 1994 film *The Shawshank Redemption* and had a reputation for being overcrowded and antiquated. No one was particularly sad to see it unceremoniously torn down in 2001 (though some area residents thought it might be great as a tourist site, maybe a quaint inn) and its inmates shifted to a new penitentiary on a back road in nearby Warren.

With the prison gone, the focus in Thomaston is squarely where it should be—on its historic brick downtown, filled with book stores, a cafe, and gift shops, and on the miles of fine Federal and Greek Revival homes built for the sea captains who ruled the town in the 18th and 19th centuries. The community was long ago called "the town that went to sea" because of the number of vessels built in shipyards on the St. George River and because of the merchants and sailors who shipped out of Thomaston's tiny waterfront.

Down on the water you'll find a plaque that commemorates the visit to the region paid by British explorer Captain George Waymouth in

1605. Not too long later, the spot became home to a trading post, and it really started to boom in the years after the American Revolution. The town was incorporated in 1777, named for war hero General John Thomas, and it was put on the map when George Washington's secretary of war, Henry Knox, set up in a mansion on a hill at the end of Main Street. Montpelier, a replica of that colonial showplace, was built on the site in the 1930s and is the most impressive structure in town now that the prison is gone.

Lime quarries were a staple of the economy for years, along with shipbuilding, brickmaking, and farming. Now townspeople do a lot of commuting. Some work at the imposing Dragon Cement plant, which sullies the view behind the Knox Mansion, while others head into the neighboring city of Rockland.

St. George River Area

The wide St. George River sweeps in between two communities on its way up to Thomaston—Cushing to the west, and St. George to the east. The latter pair were joined until 1803, when they split into a more manageable duo (they were already composed of almost a dozen distinct villages). This is the country that the Wyeth family of painters have made famous since early last century. A rural area of woods and fields, saltwater farms and fishing villages, the region first seduced N. C. Wyeth, a well-known illustrator, in the 1920s, when he set up household at Port Clyde.

His son Andrew would use an old, creaky Cushing farm—the Olson House—and the hardy couple that lived in it, Christina and Alvaro Olson, in a series of works, including *Christina's World*, one of the most famous American paintings of all time. Scores of his other paintings depict the area's windswept meadows, rolling hills, and tidal river. Wyeth fans routinely make the pilgrimage downriver to explore the countryside, especially now that the Rockland-based Farnsworth Museum has purchased the Olson House and opened it to tours (see Attractions chapter). Another artistic icon, sculptor Bernard "Blackie"

Langlais, lived down in Cushing as well, and many of his old wooden sculptures can still be seen in front of the house he shared with his wife.

The community took its name from a Massachusetts lieutenant governor, Thomas Cushing, back in 1789 when the town was incorporated (remember, Maine originally was part of Massachusetts). It was settled about 150 years prior to that by an English trader in 1634. The trader was chased out of the area by the French, who held this place until 1654 and who harassed English settlers until the French and Indian War drove them out. After the American Revolution there was a slow influx of residents drawn by farmland and fishing potential. Fishermen still work from various points down here, and the population has leveled at about 1,300.

Where Cushing is largely open and meadow strewn, the town of St. George is more woodsy and broken by a handful of villages—Port Clyde, Tenants Harbor, Martinsville, Spruce Head, Long Cove, and Clark Island. Granite quarrying became a huge industry here in the 19th century, and lots of old quarries remain (many, like those on Clark Island, make for great swimming holes).

Port Clyde, across the river from Cushing, is a stunner, a fishing village occupying a headland overlooking the Georges Islands. A cluster of homes and businesses make up the center of town right at the tip of the St. George Peninsula, among them the funky Port Clyde General Store, a 200-year-old gem with groaning floors, newspapers, pizza, and videos. The Dip Net Restaurant is behind the store, offering seafood with a fine view of the harbor.

The waterfront is a busy place in Port Clyde because it's here that vacationers and islanders catch the ferry to Monhegan. The Monhegan-Thomaston Boat Line sends the *Laura B.* and the *Elizabeth Ann* on the hourlong crossing a few times daily (see the next chapter, Getting Here, Getting Around).

Other attractions on this side of the St. George River are Marshall Point, home of Marshall Point Light (see Lighthouses chapter); Tenants Harbor; and the fishing community of Spruce Head. Bicycles might just be the best method of travel in these parts, and a local conservation group, the Georges River Land Trust, has put together a handful of routes and maps.

Monhegan Island

Many people have this idea that Monhegan Island makes for a great day trip, and it does, if that's all the time you have. But this 1-square-mile island 12 miles off the Midcoast is worth more than the six or eight hours you get between ferries. Everything good about the Maine coast can be found packed onto this bit of rock at sea. It has the woodsy heights, the surf crashing on the serrated coast, the blinking lighthouse, the miles of hiking trails, the old capes and cottages of weathered gray shingles, the classic New England inn, the small-town vibe, and the picture-perfect harbor with its lobster boats. (If you can't take a good photograph here, your camera must be malfunctioning.)

The island's history is particularly rich, too. Monhegan is generally regarded as the first place European explorers landed in the Gulf of Maine—they stopped by as early as 1497. Some say they even used the harbor here to repair vessels and wait out storms before Columbus ever made it to the New World. Native Americans were here first, of course, and the name Monhegan is thought to be a variation of a Maliseet or Micmac word for island. They likely traveled out here for the same purpose that early Europeans did—fishing. European fishermen began visiting in the early 17th century, sometimes staying, sometimes moving on, until about 1625, when a trading post was set up on the island. Permanent settlement followed in 1674.

Fishing remains one of the key elements of the local economy, and the Monhegan lobster-men have set up a program that has become a model in Maine, limiting their fishing to seven months of the year, between December 1 and June 25. They have a beautiful tradition of not heading out on day one of the season unless everyone is ready, and they make quite an effort to make sure everybody is, getting together in the weeks beforehand, repairing nets and boats and lending hands. The harbor is very active with fishing vessels through the winter and spring, and in summer several entrepreneurial islanders change their focus to the other economic force here—tourism.

The island is home to roughly 90 year-round-ers, and a few hundred others move in for the summer months. Thousands more arrive each week on the *Laura B.* and *Elizabeth Ann*, ferries from Port Clyde. Other mainland points send visitors, too. Many are day-trippers, some are arriving for a weekend at one of the excellent hostelries, and still more set up for a week at a rental cottage. Those in the know bring flashlights—electricity is limited out here—and wear good walking shoes, because there are no vehicles, save a few work trucks, on the island's dirt roads. The conveniences of modern life are few—no phones or TVs in your room—but that's really the point.

Art draws a lot of vacationers to the island, whether they're making it themselves, perusing the couple dozen galleries and artists' studios in town, or checking out sites made famous by all of the world-famous greats who have lived and worked on the island—from Robert Henri to Rockwell Kent to George Bellows to Edward Hopper to Jamie Wyeth.

Many others, though, come to enjoy the natural world. More than half of the island has been preserved as woods, and the vistas of crashing sea from atop cliffs are some of the best you're ever going to get. In the spring and fall, the island is known for birding—it's a real avian hot spot during these migratory periods. The trail network through these forests is rather extraordinary—that islanders have managed to blaze more than 17 miles of footpaths on little more than a mile and a half of island is something to wonder at.

Idyllic is the word on Monhegan. Those who schedule only a day trip to the island are often regretful when they board the 4 p.m. ferry back to the mainland.

Rockland

These are renaissance days for the city of Rockland. Once a down-at-the-heels fishing port known for its bikers and its smell, the burgh has reinvented itself since the early 1990s, thanks in large part to the success of the Farnsworth Art Museum downtown (see Attractions chapter). Long one of Maine's best art collections, the Farnsworth went through a major period of renovation and revival in the late 1990s, debuting the Wyeth Center, expanding display areas, and, perhaps most importantly, establishing a presence on Route 1 in the heart of downtown. Its new entrance on Main Street attracted other galleries to locate here and helped inspire the opening of a bunch of restaurants and shops and the restoration of the old Strand Theater into a showplace of movies and performances.

There's always been a lot to like about Rockland; it's just that the city's reputation got in the way. The location on the west side of Penobscot Bay is very nice, offering beautiful vistas from a variety of points (the best perhaps being the mile-long Rockland Breakwater, a wall of granite stones that protects the harbor). The 19th-century brick downtown, with its Greek, Italianate, and colonial revival blocks, looks like what a Maine downtown should look like, and there are streets of older homes in the neighborhoods beyond Broadway. You might recognize all this from the 2001 movie *In the Bedroom*, which was filmed at various points around town. The city boasts an excellent Carnegie library, too.

Lobsters have been a staple of the economy here as long as anyone can remember, and the city calls itself the Lobster Capital of the World, staking a mean claim to that title by processing millions of pounds of the tasty "bugs" a year. The lobster fleet shares space on the waterfront with a handful of schooners from the Maine Windjammer Association, graceful vessels that pretty up what's largely an industrial harbor. A resident Coast Guard station and Outward Bound's largest school also moor boats down here, and ferries come and go to the populated islands of Penobscot Bay on a regular basis. A mile-long boardwalk on the side opposite the breakwater is another good place to check out the waterfront.

Before the lobster industry became king in Rockland, the city was a big shipper of lime and

granite and, like so many other Maine ports, had its share of shipyards turning out vessels. Many of the city's 8,000 residents today are involved in the seafood business in one way or another, but plenty are also employed in retail and the service industry, at manufactories like Fisher Corporation, which makes snowplows; at PenBay hospital in Rockport; and at many stores and restaurants downtown.

Thanks to the Farnsworth Art Museum, the downtown is still a vital place where it can be difficult to find a parking spot in high summer, despite competition from two shopping plazas and a Wal-Mart on the edge of the city. On Main Street and in the blocks surrounding it are a handful of fine restaurants, many galleries, shops selling everything from high-end furnishings to yupscale women's clothes to used books, and, for some reason, at least a half dozen barber shops. Some in the city wonder if everything happened too fast and whether the population can support all these fancy restaurants—several are now shutting down for winter.

The joke used to be "Camden by the Sea, Rockland by the Smell," referring to the picturesque resort community up the road. But the city of Rockland continues to turn itself around. It can still stink on a hot August day, thanks to fish processing plants—but that's just keeping it real.

Penobscot Bay Islands

Poet Edna St. Vincent Millay, who grew up in Rockland and Camden, made her first impressions on the literary world with the poem "Renascence," in which she wrote: "All I could see from where I stood / were three long islands and a wood." She's referring to the isles of Penobscot Bay, several of which have year-round communities on them. These are romantic, windswept places, well worthy of poetry, and it's hard to visit without wanting to up and move to a cottage on one. The panoramas are spectacular almost anywhere you go on them, thanks to the fact that they're surrounded by the Atlantic Ocean and other islands and they overlook the Camden Hills and the mountains of Acadia. But there's something to the deep and rich sense of community that thrives on islands—everyone knows everyone, looks out for everyone, and all that good stuff—in a way that no longer happens in Any Suburb, USA. Plus, no Wal-Mart is going to move in and ruin the neighborhood any time soon.

Vinalhaven

This hardy isle of fishermen and artists is the largest of the 14 year-round islands of Maine, sitting right in the middle of the great inlet next to its sister island, North Haven. Lobstering is the mainstay of the economy, with shrimp, scallops, and urchins also contributing. Of Vinalhaven's 1,200 residents, 200 work on the water. The others do a little bit of everything, whatever it takes to be able to live on this 17-mile isle, an 80-minute ferry ride from Rockland. Many artists and writers have set up on Vinalhaven, the most notable being Robert Indiana—he of the love sign fame—and there are a few amenities for tourists. Libby House, Payne Homestead at the Moses Webster House, and the Tidewater Motel take in guests, and the latter rents bikes and cars (proprietor Phil Crossman is a hoot). A half dozen eclectic stores serve the islanders and sell T-shirts and take-out to visitors. And there is a good little museum in the old town hall that's run by the historical society, where you can learn a bit about the island's beginnings.

Archaeological evidence on the island suggests that the Red Paint People, an ancient Native American society known for its red ocher graves, visited Vinalhaven 5,000 years ago. Europeans didn't follow until the 1500s. English explorer Martin Pring sailed by in 1603, and supposedly the hungry captain witnessed gray foxes running about and named Vinalhaven and North Haven the Fox Islands. It wasn't until the 1760s that the island had a permanent resident, and the community began to build, becoming a town in 1789. Townspeople named the new municipality after John Vinal, a Boston lawyer who represented them in their 1785 bid to secede from Massachusetts. Early settlers like Thaddeus Carver of Marshfield, Massachusetts, who lent Carver's

Harbor his name, came looking for lumber and shipped plenty out, but what they discovered of real and unique value was granite—and lots of it. This discovery came at a time when the big cities of the northeast were building at a rapid rate, and granite from Vinalhaven quarries was used in such prominent structures as the Brooklyn Bridge, the Cathedral of St. John the Divine, and the U.S. Customs Houses and Post Office in New York; post offices in St. Louis, Kansas City, and Buffalo; the railroad station and the Board of Trade in Chicago; and the Washington Monument.

Vinalhaven has made a significant blip on the radar of tourism since, but it's still not overrun by any means. (Some local teens might feel it is, though—they've been known to insult visitors.) Day-trippers enjoy walking and biking the miles of roads, swimming in Lawson's and Booth's quarries, kayaking offshore, and playing in the island's several parks and preserves, places like Lane's Island, a breathtaking island of meadows, coves, and wildflowers linked to Vinalhaven by a bridge.

North Haven

You could almost jump across the Fox Island Thorofare from Vinalhaven to North Haven, so close are the two. Because of this proximity the early history of the two islands is very similar—they even claim the same gentleman as their first resident. But not long after granite was being discovered on Vinalhaven, the wealthy elite of Boston began discovering North Haven. The island became something of an exclusive enclave, which it remains to a certain extent. Tourist facilities are very limited—there are few bed-and-breakfasts and inns and only a single sit-down restaurant, the Coal Wharf.

North Haven is 12 miles off Rockland and about an hour by ferry. It's only 24 square miles and has two primary neighborhoods, North Haven Village and Pulpit Harbor (not including the intriguingly named hamlet of Sleepyville). The year-round population of 300 blooms in July and August to about 2,000 with the arrival of the summer people, many of whom are descendants of families that started coming here in the late 19th century.

Day-trippers will find excellent bicycling, a neat old golf course, pleasant walking, local artist Eric Hopkins's fine gallery, another art showplace at the North Haven Gift Shop, eats at a couple of restaurants, and a general store that stocks one of everything.

Matinicus

Twenty-two miles out into the drink, Matinicus is the farthest removed of Maine's populated islands. A local cottage rental company describes the isle as "extraordinary, but not for everyone." That is a very apt way of putting it. This rental agent continues, "If you would like to visit an island that is remote, a bit rustic, and that requires a sense of adventure, tolerance, independence and humor from its visitors, read on."

Enticing visitors to this 1.5-square-mile island, which isn't even on most maps, is an uphill battle. First is simply the time and distance. The ferry ride is 2 hours and 15 minutes long, and the ferry comes only three times a month in summer, less often than that in winter (but private boats are available—see www.matinicusexcursions.com or www.wildwoodcharters.com—as is air service). Second is the reputation of the place—it's generally considered the most insular of all of Maine islands, the East Coast's version of the Wild West. Simply put, many of Matinicus' 51 residents don't want to see outsiders.

But if you can deal with stony glances and a bit of rudeness, you'll find a lot to like on Matinicus. The natural world is the most obvious attraction. Walking trails squirrel here and there across the island and, unusual for a piece of rock at sea, there are two fine sand beaches. (The water's still cold, though.) Birding is exceptional—with boats available to take people out to see the puffin colony on Matinicus Rock—and many rare plant species inhabit the island as well. Simply strolling and looking around here is fun, like a walk back to the 1940s, corny as that may sound. This is also one of the few places anywhere where you can call and order a lobster dinner and have it delivered to your door. (Lobstering is the chief industry here.) Artists and photographers have long been drawn to Matinicus, dating back to the great George Bellows. If you make the effort, you'll see why.

Camden–Rockport Area

It would be hard to invent a better setting for a coastal Maine resort town than the one found in Camden. When he visited in 1605, Captain John Smith (yes, him again) was impressed, writing "under the high mountains of Penobscot, against whose feet the sea doth beat." And indeed Penobscot Bay laps picturesquely at the town's protected harbor, with a lighthouse-topped island sitting at the mouth and two round peaks looming imposingly above. A series of small summits—the Camden Hills—trundle inland from there past big Megunticook Lake. From the tops of Mounts Battie and Megunticook you think you can see forever out across the glistening expanse of the bay and over its spiny islands. Soaring cliffs, plenty of wildlife, rivers and streams, a waterfall—the area's got it all.

Which makes it too bad that so many people have discovered it. Camden is now notorious for the congestion that clogs its picturesque downtown, and it seems like every other week some magnate or other is moving into one of the gracious colonial revival homes that line High Street or sit above the harbor. Camden is one of the few places—perhaps the only spot in Maine—where Route 1, the highway up the Maine coast, yields to a local road. Hollywood sets up shop many a summer filming some picture or other—*The Man Without a Face* (1993), *Casper* (1995), *Thinner* (1996), and *In the Bedroom* (2001) in recent years.

The town has a year-round population of about 5,000 relatively affluent souls, and during June, July, and August they are joined by probably three times that number with the arrival of the tourists and summercators. People come for a variety of reasons, and many have similar aims—hiking or camping in Camden Hills State Park; shopping in the innumerable boutiques, specialty shops, and gift stores downtown; or heading out to sea on windjammers. The numerous eateries, kayak tours, grassy parks, and historic homes only add to the appeal. Two excellent auditoriums bring name acts to this wee town—the Camden Opera House and the Strom Auditorium at the impressive high school. Then there is the Camden Snow Bowl, which is everything a ski area should be: small, community-run, friendly, and inexpensive. Obviously a bigger draw in winter, it sees its share of hikers and bikers in the summer.

The sea built Camden. Shipyards were a mainstay of the economy for years (and still are, with huge Wayfarer Marine repairing yachts). Lime from area pits and wool from the Knox Woolen Mill employed many workers in subsequent years, and of course fishing fed many families. When East Coast business leaders discovered Camden in the 1950s, the summer trade began. The rich moved in, first for the summers and eventually for the remainder of the year, bringing their yachts with them. Camden Harbor is always awash in boats, from the majestic schooners like the *Mary Day* that anchor there to the raft of ostentatious yachts, colorful kayaks, and dinghies. A few hardy fishermen bravely navigate through the crowded basin on their way out in search of lobster.

Things are a little better in Rockport. Camden's sister town is also a haven for the affluent—many former CIA and Foreign Service workers among them—and has a busy little harbor, but it's not quite as overrun because there simply aren't as many touristy things to do here. The population here is 3,500, and in summer it too triples, with the influx of summer people and with students at the Maine Media Workshops, a world-class film and photography school that draws some of the top names in the field to Rockport.

Downtown are an arc of brick buildings and the pretty old Rockport Opera House, which sits on a hill above the harbor. Around the corner and up the road, the miles of summer homes and "cottages" begin. Some are neat old capes, some shingle-style, others the showy wannabe palaces of the nouveau Mainers.

The town's history is intertwined with Camden's, but it does have its own chapters, one of which is the life of Andre the Seal. Down on the waterfront in Rockport Marine Park is a monument to the beloved harbor seal, who jumped through hoops for audiences all summer long, shooting baskets, counting, singing, from the 1960s until late in his life. He was only a summer resident, swimming back to Boston Aquarium in the fall, and he was killed by a rival on the way in 1986.

Just northeast of Camden and Rockport is the town of Lincolnville, which is technically the southernmost municipality in character-laden Waldo County but behaves more like a suburb of Camden. Lincolnville is best known for its short sandy beach, along which a few restaurants, gift shops, and the always fun Beach Store are located. Bathers in the know travel another mile or so up the road to a tiny rock beach called Ducktrap, where the Ducktrap River empties into Penobscot Bay. There's better, more private swimming here. A skip up the road takes visitors to Tanglewood 4-H camp, which is filled with trails through the woods along the river. And several miles beyond that is Lincolnville Center, a swell village of old homes and vistas in the rolling Camden Hills.

Islesboro

Lincolnville Beach sends a ferry 3 miles across Penobscot Bay to the island of Islesboro several times daily. Like North Haven, Islesboro has an air of exclusivity about it, especially the village of Dark Harbor, which anchors one end of the skinny, 12-mile isle. Here the rich and famous built grand mansions in the Victorian era, many of which still exist. Back then the island's local population were the serving people for the wealthy. Today things are a little more real, though the social calendar of Dark Harbor is busy. John Travolta and Kirstie Alley have been some of the better known of the town's 600-some residents, but they have kept relatively low profiles.

The island was settled in the years before the American Revolution, with an influx of fishermen and farmers. When the War of 1812 gripped the mainland town of Castine, not too far away across East Penobscot Bay, the residents of Islesboro had a rough go of it, forced into cooperating with the British. Later in that century, they had to swallow their pride again after Jeffrey Bracket, a young, rich Boston fellow, visited the island and was smitten, and a few hundred wealthy people from the city moved in and colonization began. An informal caste system went into place that the island took more than a century to be rid of.

As on most of the other populated islands, lobstering is the big breadwinner on Islesboro. But there are also three boatyards turning out vessels, many islanders commute to jobs on the mainland since ferries are frequent and the crossing takes only 20 minutes, and others work from their homes, thanks to Internet connections, faxes, and e-mail.

Vacationers will find plenty to see and do and a few places to lay their head. Because the island is long and flat, it makes for great biking, and kayakers love all the coves and inlets and smaller satellite isles all around it. One of these islands is home to Warren Island State Park, an absolutely spectacular area if you have your own boat. There's a nice beach—called, originally enough, Town Beach—at Pendleton Point, and there are also a few shops and even a performing arts center that gets busy in July and August.

Belfast

In 2008 *Budget Travel* magazine labeled Belfast as one of the 10 Coolest Towns in the country. How cool is that? Not many other cities of 7,000 have their own vegetarian cafe, classes in African drumming and foil fencing, a professional theater company, another nationally known theater organization, a hip art deco movie cinema, a supermarket-size food co-op, a curling club, several art galleries, an art center in an old high school, an environmentally friendly department store, and naturopaths, homeopaths, and acupuncturists? Outside of California, that's a pretty hard place to find. (And maybe even in California.) As the shire town of wacky Waldo County, a

collection of cool rural towns with a lot of unique inhabitants, Belfast has become a truly amazing place.

The city underwent a profound and sometimes difficult change during the mid-1990s. The credit card giant MBNA built a massive headquarters here and buildings larger than anything found anywhere else in the Midcoast outside of Bath Iron Works, and then the company staffed them with 6,000 tie-and-dress–wearing telemarketers. This development was a bit difficult for many of the locals to swallow, since up to that point Belfast's populace was a mix of fishermen and back-to-the-land émigrés from the early 1970s, most of whom threw away their ties long ago. People stopped grousing a bit when MBNA started throwing money around to worthy causes, from the schools to the hospitals. And it was hard to argue that Belfast didn't need the jobs. Now that MBNA has been sold to Bank of America, those jobs are in question.

Named for Belfast, Ireland, the city was settled by a Scotch-Irish band of pioneers back in 1770. These tough folks had previously made their home in Londonderry, New Hampshire, and were bothered enough by the British that they upped and left. They liked what they found at this spot above the Passagassawaukeag River (that's Passy for short) and built a thriving little hamlet that grew and grew over the years as shipbuilding and lumbering prosperity moved in. You can walk around and literally see those good times written in wood and shingle—the city is well known in Maine for its distinctive Greek Revival, Federal, and Italianate homes (more than 200 structures in town are on the National Register). When Belfast burned in 1865 and again in 1873, the city rebuilt, and the result is a fine downtown of Victorian Gothic and Greek Revival brick. Some of these old buildings will cause crooks in your neck, you'll stare at them so long—they're that good-looking.

By the mid-20th century the focus of the economy changed from the water to the wings—of chickens. The city became for a while the biggest chicken processor in the world, and although this industry wasn't good for the harbor, which ran with blood, it kept the citizenry at work. Things got a bit down at the heels here when Frank Purdue and others proved they could produce and ship chickens quicker and the broiler industry went bust. So, many people were glad to see the green-and-tan empire of MBNA move in. Many civic leaders recognize the potential of tourism, but Belfast isn't the Maine summer theme park that is Camden down the road. Far fewer people explore Belfast, and it doesn't tart itself up for them.

The city is eminently walkable—at least the good parts are—and there's a stroller's tour all scripted and printed down at the Belfast Chamber of Commerce that will take you through the most attractive neighborhoods. The downtown has a handful of good restaurants—from the hip vegetariana of Chase's Daily to the cheap but good Bay Wrap—and the shopping is nothing if not eclectic. If you see something you like, buy it, because several of these stores won't be here on your next pass through town. These storefronts have quite the history of turnover. The city's park, right on Penobscot Bay, is worth a look, as is the harborfront park established by MBNA.

Plenty of accommodations are available, and you'd best give yourself more than one day. Make sure to travel into Waldo County, too, where you'll find innumerable treasures in towns like Searsmont, Freedom, and Liberty. The further you look into Belfast and Waldo County, the more unexpected delights you'll find.

Searsport

Searsport has two claims to fame: It's an antiques hot spot, and it has a rich maritime history, producing more sea captains per capita than anyplace else in the universe (or something like that) back in the days of tall ships. The former you can see evidence of just by driving around—there are antiques stores every half mile or so. The latter is less evident these days— you don't see mustachioed characters with muttonchops wandering around in gold-buttoned jackets—but you can find out everything you ever wanted to know about Searsport and the

sea at the Penobscot Marine Museum (see Attractions chapter).

Turns out 200 or so Searsport residents became ship captains—1 in 10 of all American heads of ship in the late 19th century. Shipbuilding was also booming by this period, with six shipyards spread across the city's waterfront on Penobscot Bay. The captains who went to sea returned with all sorts of exotic goods and experiences, and they built themselves impressive homes, like those found in Belfast and Thomaston. One family, the Nichols, had 35 members born at sea.

Searsport has one of the deepest ports in Maine, which it greatly benefited from in those early days and which in more recent years has made it one of a trio of ports—Portland and Eastport are the others—in the state's three-pronged cargo-shipping scheme. The waterfront in town remains a working one, but it is less about fishing and more about moving cargo—and, thanks to some big, ugly Irving and GAC plants—oil and chemicals. There's a great state park south of town off Route 1 at Moose Point.

Aside from the sea captains' homes, which can be truly impressive, like the homes of the Carriage House and Watchtide inns, the town is rather unassuming. Downtown is a hodgepodge of brick and wood storefronts—a National Register historic district that isn't quite as impressive as the one down the road in Belfast (a search for a good meal here will bring you back to Belfast, so you can compare. Convenience stores and flea markets are the main features as you head north. However, the past couple of years a real effort has been made to make the town more attractive to the millions of people headed past en route to Acadia—and it's working.

East of Searsport is Stockton Springs, another old shipbuilding port astride Route 1. Named Stockton after a seaside English town, the community added the Springs later when it was trying to make a name for itself in the bottled-water industry. The downtown has faded since that enterprise evaporated and others like poultry processing did, too.

Down on its waterfront, though, is Fort Point State Park and its attendant Fort Point Light, and up the road is the handsome hamlet of Sandy Point, where a handful of white clapboard historic homes flank a big white church—the very picture of a New England village. And tucked down an anonymous side street, unknpwn to most who pass by on Route 1, is a secret beach.

Bucksport

Witch tale, paper mill, imposing fort, vertiginous suspension bridge, and new marina—the Bucksport area has a little of everything. The town's situation at the head of Penobscot Bay, exactly the point where the Penobscot River descends to the sea, was ideally suited for the European settlers who made their way here in the 1760s. The Penobscot Indians came here to fish prior to that, seeking the river's famous salmon, but they were pushed out of the way by the English.

Colonel Jonathan Buck of the Massachusetts Bay Colony incorporated "Buckstown" in 1792 and opened a mill on the shore of the river. Quite aside from naming the community for himself and helping launch a shipping and trade industry here, Buck is remembered for an incident that occurred in the late 18th century. Everyone locally is tired of the story now, but it persists because of its creepy nature. Legend has it that while serving as a town magistrate, Buck sentenced a woman to die for witchcraft. She supposedly laid a curse on him, something to the effect that she'd follow him until he died and into the beyond, and now his tombstone bears the uncanny outline of a woman's leg—many consider this stripe a flaw in the granite, but it has reappeared every time it's been ground or buffed away. So the story goes. The grave is clearly visible from Route 1, but it's best to pull into the Hannaford parking lot and cross the street if you want to have a look.

The town would rather be known as an important Maine port and changed its name to Bucksport in 1817, remaining a vital shipping town because its of location on the river and thus on the route to Bangor. Fort Knox, the dramatic, medieval-looking bastion that hangs on a hill on the opposite side of the Penobscot, was built in the 1840s to protect the port and the river when

border tensions began to arise with the English. A few decades later, hunters and fishermen begin to discover the North Woods of Maine, and they often traveled to the area via Bangor, through Bucksport.

Today oil flows from Bucksport Harbor to Bangor, fueling homes and the Bangor airport, and the Verso Paper mill employs about 1,000 people. The latter produces glossy papers for catalogs like L.L. Bean and JCPenney and for magazines like *Time* and *Newsweek*. Cultural highlights are the Northeast Historic Film Archive, which resides in the Old Alamo Theatre and helps preserve old films—and regularly screens them, too. And in 2002 Bucksport opened a new 500-seat theater to bring drama and music to town. Several restaurants, inns, and B&Bs serve the community.

To reach Bucksport, you have to be prepared to drive over the soaring Penobscot Narrows Bridge, a dramatic, half-mile-long span that's known colloquially as the Bucksport Bridge. The soaring span narrow span rises 135 feet above the Penobscot, its steel suspension towers flying up another 300 feet. Newly rebuilt in 2007, the bridge has the highest public-bridge observatory in the world, which offers a look at the surrounding area from 420 feet up.

Blue Hill Peninsula

Though a lot of Mainers say the "real Maine" begins east of Ellsworth, many miles up the road, it's hard to improve on the Maine found on the Blue Hill Peninsula. This is the wide finger of land on which (or near) are located the villages of Blue Hill, Castine, Deer Isle, Stonington, Brooksville, Brooklin, Sedgwick, and Surry. It's an unhurried place where the vistas are drop-dead gorgeous, the roads are punctuated by fantastic old homes, the communities are just that—close-knit, small towns where people still wave at one another and the postal clerks know everyone—and it's still unsullied by chain development. Lobster fishing remains an important part of the economy, as does traditional boatbuilding, and yet there are all sorts of great cultural outlets and interesting populations of artists and writers. Very cool indeed.

With a population of just over 2,300, Blue Hill is the biggest town around, a place of stately old homes, a bustling downtown filled with shops and galleries, and a summer colony that gets things busy on August afternoons. The town had a big fight with the Rite Aid drugstore chain a few years back, not wanting what it considered an eyesore on its main drag, and it's easy to see what Blue Hill residents were keen on preserving. The community is uncommonly attractive, making a U around Blue Hill Harbor and backed up against the peak that gave the town its name. Points and peninsulas and coves are the norm around here, with many homes along them. The architecture is pretty fine, too, with 68 Federal and Greek Revival representatives on the National Register. The area has attracted enough artists, writers, and musicians (like Noel Paul Stookey of Peter Paul and Mary fame) and berthed the always popular and ever eclectic WERU, a community radio station well known in eastern Maine (89.9 FM).

According to the excellent local history put together by writer and resident Esther Wood, two men from North Andover, Massachusetts, migrated north to settle Blue Hill in 1762 (though they called it North Andover). Several villages sprouted over the ensuing years as people followed the pair—Head-of-the-Bay, the Neck, East Blue Hill, and North Blue Hill—each with its own school, store, and church. The current center of town developed around Head-of-the-Bay, and shipbuilding helped it prosper.

The first ship was built in 1792, and 132 more followed over the course of the next 90 years, resulting in a lot of nice homes in town. One of these houses belonged to Jonathan Fisher, parson of the local church. A true renaissance man, Fisher built his house, taught at the local Blue Hill Academy (now George Stevens Academy), and was also a poet, a scientist, a farmer, a painter, and a businessman. The Parson Fisher house, now a museum, is a fine place to learn about the rich history of the community.

When shipbuilding went to the wayside with the emergence of steel vessels and steam-

ers, another industry arose in Blue Hill, one that conflicts mightily with the genteel, artsy reputation the town has now—mining. The ground beneath Blue Hill seemed to contain a fair bit of copper and some zinc, too, and in the late 19th century, companies and individuals rushed in to extract the valuable minerals. A Canadian company attempted to resume operations in the 1970s to much local opposition.

Residents liked the emergence of arts as a cottage industry much better. Blue Hill has become known for its pottery and handcrafts and is home to several galleries worth visiting.

Castine

The flags of four nations have flown over the town of Castine. For two centuries years the British, the French, and the Dutch battled over the village, each occupying it for stretches at a time before being beaten on by the next country to move in. The French were the first to set up on the ax-head–shaped peninsula at the edge of Penobscot Bay. Explorer Samuel de Champlain, who sailed and mapped much of the Down East coast, sent a chart back to France for the perusal of King Henry IV in 1612 that showed the prime location of what's now Castine, overlooking Penobscot Bay and the entrance to the Penobscot River. Within a year the site was a French trading post.

Of course, Captain John Smith just so happened to cruise by in 1614 and included the headland on a map he was drawing of English territory. It would go back and forth from there, with the town changing hands numerous times. In 1667 the region was granted to the French officer Jean Vincent d'Abbadie de Saint Castin by the king of France, and the spot would ultimately take his name. Not 10 years later it would be bombarded by the Dutch, who occupied the peninsula twice, in 1674 and 1676, and then destroyed many buildings and forts in their wake.

The British moved back in and held the site, prompting colonial forces to attack from the bay in 1779 with a fleet of 18 warships and 24 personnel transports carrying 1,400 soldiers. It would go down as one of the worst, if not the worst, naval defeats in United States history as the British snuck up on the armada in the bay and wreaked havoc, and it would ruin the military career of officer Paul Revere. The British would hold Castine through the War of 1812 until finally it was liberated by the United States. We still own it today.

What's all this got to do with anything? The town of Castine is one of the finest-looking historic communities in Maine, with neat battlements and buried bastions all over the place, and a squillion 19th-century National Register homes (really, it's only 255). It's particularly comely, with street after street of fine Greek Revival and Federal buildings on the tidy grid on either side of it. More than 100 historic markers chronicle the town's turbulent history and make for a compelling walking tour. You can stop at several small historic-home museums while you're at it, and if you're up for a real walk, stop by Dyce Head Lighthouse. If ever there was a town for taking a constitutional, it's Castine.

Today you may see people walking about town in quasi-military–looking dress and wonder who's invading this time. These folks are cadets from Maine Maritime Academy, a college-level institution that prepares students for careers in the merchant marine, as well as in engineering and marine biology. The school's massive training vessel, the *State of Maine,* dominates the waterfront, and tours are available when it's in port.

Maine Maritime's 700 students, along with Castine's 1,300 residents, help keep the restaurants and inns busy during the cold winter months when the town's cottage owners are away.

Deer Isle

Deer Isle is the second-largest island on the Maine coast after Mount Desert, dangling between Penobscot and Blue Hill bays. To reach the island you pass before or over a couple of state landmarks—Caterpillar Hill, a gradual rise with an astonishing view of Eggemoggin Reach and East Penobscot Bay, and the Deer Isle Bridge,

a tall, arcing suspension span that strikes fear in a lot of people. When the state wanted to build a road across Eggemoggin Reach in 1939, connecting the island of Little Deer Isle to the mainland, islanders were not happy, afraid that they were losing their way of life.

Cruise the back roads of Deer Isle, and you'll understand what islanders wanted to protect. Split into three communities—Deer Isle, Little Deer Isle, and Stonington—it's a magnificent place. Because the island is so skinny, you're never far from a cove or a pocket beach or a headland. Jaw-dropping vistas of ocean and island are commonplace.

The bridge deposits you on Little Deer Isle, which is connected to Deer Isle proper by a winding causeway. The smallest of the three Deer Isle hamlets, it's home to a cottage community and Harbor Farm, a gift shop and housewares store, and the local chamber of commerce, which seems to be open only sporadically.

From there you cross the narrow causeway, which is frequently brutalized by storms, and then you hit the village of Deer Isle itself, where historic homes line the main drag and there can be found a thriving gallery and antiques scene, featuring the work of many graduates of the famed Haystack Mountain School of Crafts, which is located on the island. The school has converted so many of its students into island residents it's become a local joke. A dozen B&Bs, inns, and campgrounds cater to visitors needing a place to rest their head.

At the end of the road is the fantastically picturesque fishing village of Stonington, terraced on a hillside that looks out across Deer Island Thorofare and its constellation of small isles. Far from the nearest police station, Stonington had a reputation for lawlessness years ago, thanks to carousing fishermen. These days there are several fine inns, restaurants, and shops, and a couple of guide outfits thanks to Stonington's burgeoning reputation as a kayaking hot spot. Stonington also serves as the jumping-off point for Isle au Haut (Ile-a-HO), an idyllic, 4,700-acre gem that features a large and woodsy parcel of Acadia parkland (see Acadia chapter).

The Stone in Stonington comes from the granite on which the island rests. It's long been prized for its pink hue, and quarrying it was the principal industry here for more than a century. Before that and since, the town's been a fishing center. The rugged stone was extracted by an international cast of quarrymen, and it was shipped out to be used in the building of New York bridges, Rockefeller Center, the Boston Museum of Fine Arts, and the Smithsonian. The only active quarrying operation in Maine now is out on Crotch Island, a skip from Stonington across the harbor.

Ellsworth

Acadia's gateway town is Ellsworth, the point where travelers driving north on Route 1 have the option of following the coastal highway on its run Down East or breaking off onto State Route 3 toward Bar Harbor. Many Mainers consider this the exact point where the "real Maine" begins (after Ellsworth, that is). With three million tourists pouring past each year, you might imagine Ellsworth businesses popping up to lure them in, and you'd be right. The north half of this city of 6,400 is a strip-mall circus, one of the places Maine towns point to when they discuss out-of-control development and its negative effects on a town.

That's too bad, because as a community, Ellsworth otherwise has a lot going for it. The first local landmark one comes to traveling up Route 1 is the legendary Big Chicken Barn, an antiques and used books emporium that's worth half a day in itself. Traveling on you'll come to a steep hill that jogs left before heading down through some fine old homes to the Union River, which put Ellsworth on the map a couple of centuries ago. Then you hit a stoplight, and the city's historic downtown, a crux of brick buildings and attractive storefronts, spreads out before you. There's some nice shopping to be done here—from women's clothes to specialty foods to high-end cookware—and the city is also home to a couple of decent restaurants as well as an art deco theater that regularly shows films and schedules musical acts of regional repute.

The Penobscots and the Passamaquoddies were the first to make camp on the Union River, and they were followed by the French, who claimed most of the territory to the east. The English arrived and began to develop in 1763, when Benjamin Milliken built sawmills on the river powered by its 60-foot drop. The community grew and grew, becoming a center of shipbuilding and lumbering, before incorporating as a town in 1800, named for Oliver Ellsworth, a delegate to the Constitutional Convention of Philadelphia in 1787. Thirty-seven years later, Ellsworth would become the shire town of Hancock County.

An overwhelming fire decimated the downtown in 1855, but residents recovered and rebuilt and kept the wood and ships flowing. In 1868 the town became a city, with a population of about 5,000. Soon, though, the area's old-growth trees were gone and sailing ships out of vogue, and the city turned its attention to manufacturing, churning out shoes and bricks. Another inferno tore through town in 1933, leveling many buildings, but the city once again rose to the challenge. Today it is a thriving retail center for Hancock County, sucking in those tourists.

ACADIA AREA

Bar Harbor

Bar Harbor was originally named Eden, and the town and the island it resides on are certainly a garden of natural delights. Dozens of mountains rumble across Mount Desert Island, their round pates carved by ice age glaciers, their feet sticking into the chilly Atlantic. The sea relentlessly pounds the shore here, making spectacular displays, and lakes and woods occupy the isle's interior, filled with all manner of beasts and critters. Tempting indeed.

The town of Bar Harbor, on the northeast edge of Mount Desert, has a rich history—literally. Quite aside from its wealth of natural wonders, it became famous for being a summer home for the überaffluent. Curious scions of New York society came up to see the fabulously scenic island in the mid-19th century and found this Eden to be the apple of their eyes. So they told all their friends, and soon Bar Harbor had become the fashionable place to be in July and August, a resort of luxury and privilege where servants catered to the every wish of rusticators ensconced in "cottages" that would be called mansions anywhere else. If your last name was Rockefeller, Astor, Vanderbilt, or Carnegie, this was where you wanted to be.

People have been summering here for ages. The Native Americans were awestruck by this mountainous island and the excellent fishing grounds that encircled it, and they set up camp here during the warm weather months. (The excellent local Abbe Museum is a good place to learn about the island's earliest inhabitants.) French explorer Samuel de Champlain cruised past in 1604 on his way up the coast and labeled the spot I'lle de Monts Deserts, "island of bare mountains," on his charts. The name stuck.

Settled in 1786, Bar Harbor was a simple fishing town until Thomas Cole, a painter of the Hudson River school, showed up one day in the 1840s with his easel. His romanticized renderings of the island, its round peaks and thundering surf, attracted the attention of New York society, which, tired of sweltering in the summer heat of Manhattan, decided to migrate north. A few decades later, fancy magazines were comparing Bar Harbor to Newport, until then the queen of the social scene. Scores of mansion-size cottages went up—and alongside them grand hotels—and people were practically tripping over one another to get to croquet tournaments, garden parties, afternoon teas, and sumptuous soirees.

Then a couple of things happened: Acadia National Park opened in 1919, and in 1947 much of the island burned, taking 170 homes, 5 hotels, and 67 summer estates along with it. Acadia attracted a new type of person to the island—the camera-toting tourist. The fire just about killed the hoity-toity summercator scene in one fell swoop. (Although Martha Stewart, the heiress to all things Waspy and societal, bought the old Edsel Ford place in nearby Seal Harbor several years ago before she went to jail.)

These days Bar Harbor's grand age is an interesting historical footnote that middle-class moms and dads learn about at the historical society museum when they're in town to explore the park, play miniature golf, and go kayaking. Tourism is what Bar Harbor is all about now, and unfortunately, a lot of it is of the mainstream variety (T-shirt and sunglass shops, waterslides, go-kart rides, and knicknacks and gewgaws, that sort of stuff). But there's enough Eden remaining here—the beautiful Shore Path walkway, the blocks and blocks of distinctive old buildings, the cool College of the Atlantic, Bar Island, and, of course, Acadia—that it's most definitely worth your time, especially before June and after September.

Northeast Harbor

Discovered by rich summer people shortly after Bar Harbor, Northeast Harbor has a decidedly tony air when compared to the island's busiest town. First a haven for Philadelphians of means, who still show up in July and August every year, it has diversified a bit in recent years to include affluent summer residents from other cities on the eastern seaboard. There are only a couple places to stay for those not lucky enough to own a gray shingled manse overlooking Somes Sound, most notably the fine—and quite pricey—Asticou Inn. But the small village has enough to entertain anyone for an afternoon, especially if you enjoy gardens, offbeat museums, impressive yachts, and expensive boutiques.

Northeast Harbor (pop. 2,100) boasts one of the island's more accommodating harbors, so it's always had an appeal to visiting yacht owners. And because of the community's cachet, they often arrive in large and luxurious boats, so it can be fun just wandering around the harbor and gawking. Two of Maine's best public gardens—Asticou and Thuya—are located here, the former famous for its azaleas in springtime, the latter for its Oriental overtones, so you'll want to allow time to pay each a visit. The town also is home to a pair of unusual museums. One is Petite Plaisance, former home of famed French writer Marguerite

Yourcenar, and the other is the Great Harbor Maritime Museum, filled with boats and models.

Southwest Harbor

On the western or "quiet side" of the island, Southwest Harbor feels less like a playground and more like a real place than Bar Harbor or Northeast, which is because it is. While a lot of people do make it here in the summer to visit Acadia lands and there are plenty of seasonal homes, most here are year-rounders living peacefully in a very appealing, tight-knit community. Southwest (pop. 2,000) is also a working place, with a fishing fleet, a Coast Guard base, and several boatbuilding yards, most notably the headquarters of world-famous Hinckley Yachts. The small downtown is less tourist-oriented than some of its island neighbors, with a school, post office, library, a couple of restaurants, and some shops selling actual necessities.

But you'll find loads to do over here and, thankfully, a lot fewer people to compete with. The Southwest area—we're including Somesville, Manset, Bass Harbor, and the town of Mount Desert—has some of the best of Acadia's hiking trails, several nice inns, a couple of outing companies, freshwater swimming at picturesque lakes, great bicycling, and camping, too. Access for the sweet islands of Swans and Frenchboro is from Bass Harbor, and they are great fun to explore.

Many people in the know who prefer a slower, simpler vacation limit their time on the island to this western side and avoid the rush of Bar Harbor.

DOWN EAST

Schoodic Point Area

Traffic and tourism go from a scream to a sigh on Route 1 once you get past Ellsworth and the turnoff for Bar Harbor and Mount Desert. Though they have their own summer colonies and even a section of Acadia National Park, the next few peninsulas Down East couldn't be more different than the merry madness of MDI. Hancock Point is only a few miles down the road from Ellsworth,

and it is virtually unknown to day-trippers. Those who do come to stay at the pleasant Crocker House inn find themselves in an exclusive summer enclave of grand cottages and clay tennis courts. A Harvard historian, Frederick Jackson Turner, is said to have been the first to move in for the summer in the 1880s, and he was soon joined by a host of other scholars, giving the point a reputation as an intellectual and cultured retreat. According to a film about the hamlet—*A Century of Summers: The Impact of a Summer Colony on a Maine Coastal Town, 1886–1986*—prominent Bangor residents soon joined these professors, and Vassar and Princeton students had informal summer programs here as well. Famed conductor Pierre Monteux of the Metropolitan Opera and the Boston and London Symphonies set up a school for musicians in 1943, and it's still active. Today's summer residents include Senator Olympia Snowe and former senator and secretary of defense Bill Cohen.

Beyond Hancock Point is Gouldsboro, where author Louise Dickinson Rich spent her summers. She profiled the village of Corea, a part of the town of Gouldsboro (pop. 2,037), in her 1958 book *The Peninsula*. There are few amenities for tourists in Corea, but it rewards visitors with a look at an unspoiled fishing community. South of Gouldsboro is Winter Harbor (pop. 900), which is another little-known summer haven for the wealthy. A bunch of families with roots in Philadelphia occupy a spit of land called Grindstone Neck. The other notable resident of Winter Harbor is Acadia National Park, which owns the tip of land at the end of the Schoodic Peninsula (see Acadia chapter).

Milbridge

In 1890—at the height of the town's shipbuilding boom—Milbridge had a population of 1,963. Milbridge was one of the centers of boat construction Down East, thanks to loads of available timber and its fine situation on the Narraguagas River. Today there are 1,300 or so residents, dependent upon fishing, worming, gathering Christmas greens and trees, and, especially, blueberrying. (Washington County is the largest producer of wild blueberries in the nation, and one of the bigger processors, Jasper Wyman and Sons, is based in Milbridge.) If people knew better, they'd be descending upon Evergreen Realty and moving in like the wind. The town is amazingly appealing, with its old homes, pleasant Main Street, and truly exquisite scenery. The best time to pay a visit, if you want a dose of Americana, is during the town's popular festival, Milbridge Days, in July.

Just up the coast are the villages of Cherryfield, Harrington, Addison, and Columbia Falls, each of which is a historic, coastal gem.

Machias

It's a wonder, too, more people haven't discovered Machias. The Down East town of about 2,300 has just about everything people come to Maine to find—a magnificent stretch of coastline, pretty old architecture, an inviting downtown, friendly people, woods all around, and a host of natural delights in the surrounding area. The community makes for a great base for a Down East adventure. From here you can easily reach Jonesport, a rugged fishing village; Great Wass Island, famous for its wildflowers; and the Cutler public lands unit, a truly spectacular hiking and camping area.

That is, if you can bring yourself to leave Machias. The town straddles the Machias River and was named Mechises, which meant "bad little falls," by Native Americans. You can see why, driving into town, by stopping at Bad Little Falls Park and watching the churning, tumbling water and imagining a birchbark canoe going over. From here you pass a campus of the University of Maine system, with about 1,000 students, before hitting Court Street and downtown. Machias is the county seat for Washington County and thus has courts and federal buildings; they are joined by shops and a couple of good restaurants in a compact and attractive historic district.

British pirate Samuel "Black" Bellamy was one of the first to put Machias on the map. Famous for stealing the treasures of Spanish ships off the coast of the New World, the charismatic "pirate prince" attempted to set up a "pirates' republic" here in the 17th century, a sort of old folks' home for aging buccaneers. He was hanged in 1717 before it could ever happen.

The town was settled when a group of southern Mainers decided it was growing too crowded down there and decided to venture east in search of grazing lands for their cattle. They set up in what would become Machias in 1763, building a sawmill and getting right to work shipping timber, which became a huge industry hereabouts and helped build the town.

By the time of the American War of Independence, there were enough people in Machias to gather at Burnham Tavern, now a landmark and considered the oldest building east of the Penobscot, and discuss how they could help the colonies with the war effort. These early patriots gave the British a bit of what-for in 1775 when they attacked the *HMS Margaretta*, which was in town to protect area Loyalists. A small group of men boarded the vessel, fatally wounded its captain, and forced the surrender of the crew, giving the rebels their first naval victory. The British returned to burn neighboring Machiasport two years later, both as punishment for the taking of the *Margaretta* and because they suspected—rightly so—that the colonists were preparing an assault on English holdings in Nova Scotia.

Nothing quite as exciting as that has happened here since, but it's a nifty town.

Eastport

Welcome to Small Town X. When Fox TV producers were looking for the setting for their reality/mystery show *Murder in Small Town X*, broadcast in the summer of 2001, they chose tiny Eastport, Maine, to be the small town in question for a variety of reasons. First, it's terrifically photogenic, the very picture of what a small New England town should look like, with legions of fine old homes sitting on Moose Island overlooking a distinctive Victorian brick downtown and the fair waters of the bay beyond. Second, most of the town was available to be invaded by cameras and crews, with many storefronts empty downtown and several buildings elsewhere vacant after decades of downturn in the local economy. They named the faux town Sunrise, a reference to the fact that Eastport, being the most easterly city in the United States, sees the rays of the sun before any other city in the nation.

Despite the fact that Eastport is one of Maine's best-looking cities, it's so far off the proverbial beaten path—102 miles from Ellsworth at the farthest reaches of the Maine coast—most people can't imagine moving there. It's simply too remote. Such wasn't always the case. Back when ships were the primary mode of travel, the city was a prosperous place, a center of trade and fishing. Europeans used the deep channel here as a port as early as the 1600s, but settlement didn't come until 1772. The city was originally called Freetown, and its bailiwick included what's now called Lubec as well. Eastport was renamed when it incorporated in 1798.

In 1807, after the Embargo Act was passed limiting trade with foreign nations, the city of Eastport became a smuggling center, ferrying goods in and out of Canada. The War of 1812 clamped down on this activity, and in July 1814 the British invaded and occupied Eastport for four years. When they left, things began to pick up in the fishing industry, and in 1875 the process of canning was invented here, so that sardines could be packed and made to last. The city had its heyday during the late-19th-century sardine era.

That all crashed eventually, and the city fell on hard times. The 1960s brought the prospect of an oil refinery on the waterfront, an ugly idea that was rejected. A host of positive developments have popped up since the 1980s, though, from the advent of the aquaculture industry—those are salmon farms you see out in the bay—to the newly expanded commercial cargo port, to new crops of more adventuresome tourists, willing to make the drive Down East to see the "real Maine."

What these travelers find is a city that's all their own to explore, uncrowded and friendly. There are a few great places to stay, a few good restaurants, a hiking trail on Shackford Head, and a few great excursion boats. You can witness mustard being made the old-fashioned way, head out on a catered picnic in an old Woodie station wagon, cruise on a whale-watch schooner, or amble along on a self-guided walking tour through the historic districts downtown. If you're anything like other visitors, you'll find yourself keenly eyeing real estate ads, which show absolutely incredible deals—for example, a two-bedroom cottage with views to the bay for $82,000—for old homes with views of the water.

Lubec

If Eastport is the most easterly city in the United States, Lubec is the most easterly town, connected via the Franklin D. Roosevelt Memorial Bridge to New Brunswick, Canada's Campobello Island. (F.D.R. was a summer resident of the Canadian island, and there's an international park there in his honor.) The town is, in fact, the most easterly point in the nation. Once part of Eastport, Lubec has a similar history, which can be read by simply walking downtown, where many storefronts and buildings are vacant or boarded up. Sardine canning was the big deal here, just as it was in Eastport, and the aquaculture industry swept in about the same time as in Eastport to provide a few jobs. Even with the rough times it has seen, Lubec remains an appealing place; *Men's Journal* gave the town a nod in an August 2006 feature on affordable land in "paradise." The town has about 1,500 residents, a couple of neat B&Bs, a few shops, a new marina, and, of course, West Quoddy Head State Park.

Calais

Another border community, staring across the St. Croix River at St. Stephen, New Brunswick, Calais sits at the point where Route 1 takes a hard left, leaves the coast, and heads up toward the end of its run in Fort Kent. The city of 3,500 takes its name from the French port, a thank-you gesture for the help France gave to the colonists during the American Revolution. But you'll be real embarrassed if you say Calais the way the French would—here it's pronounced "callous." Sometimes called "the international city of Maine," the community enjoys a close relationship with its Canadian neighbor, offering mutual support for fires and other emergencies, sending a lot of shoppers across the border to take advantage of the exchange rate, and whooping it up together at the International Festival in August.

Driving into Calais on Route 1 along the St. Croix, there are several nice homes and a handful of gingerbread Victorian places that have an almost fairytale vibe. The downtown is a pleasant grid of streets that attest to the city's prosperous past as a thriving shipping port. The brick Main Street is a registered Historic District, and it's a sleepy place as most major industry has left town. The city is largely dependant upon the Domtar paper mill up the road in Woodland.

First a lumbering center and then a ship-building port, Calais was settled in 1779, but a French colony attempted to carve out a home on tiny St. Croix island in 1604. Famed explorer Samuel de Champlain led the party, and they made it through the winter—the first Christmas celebrated in the New World was right here—but had a rough go of it in the snow and ice and left for Nova Scotia in the spring. The National Park Service has set up a nifty interpretive walking trail that tells this story.

Shipbuilding began in earnest with the launch of the *Liberty* in 1801 and continued for much of the century. Farming and fishing were also substantial industries, and fishing remains an economic staple.

GETTING HERE, GETTING AROUND

It would be hard to use the old Maine expression "you can't get there from here" with a straight face these days. Getting to Maine—and getting around when you're here—has never been easier. The state is served by major airports in Portland and Bangor and by several smaller local airports in communities up and down the coast. High-speed train service between Portland and Boston is enjoying record-breaking ridership, giving the two bus companies that operate in Maine runs for their money. Ferries connect the state to its islands and to Canada. And the two principal automotive arteries—the Maine Turnpike and coastal U.S. Route 1—have undergone modernization in recent years in an effort to make driving simpler and safer. Not only can you get there from here but you can do so quickly and efficiently.

BY CAR

Getting around without a car in Maine is nigh impossible as public transportation is scarce outside the cities. The majority of visitors to Maine consequently arrive by automobile, driving across the big green bridge over the Piscataqua and breathing a sigh of relief once they do. (Maine is, as the sign says, the way life should be.) The bridge connects Maine to New Hampshire via Interstate 95 and connects to the Pine Tree State in Kittery, its southernmost town. From there, the highway proceeds up the coast as far as Portland before it begins to cut up into the interior of Maine toward Augusta. I–95, which is called the Maine Turnpike up to Portland, parallels Route 1 as it heads north, and these are the primary thoroughfares for accessing the Maine coast. To get where you're going quickly, stick to the fast-moving turnpike. For a more leisurely drive with a lot of local color and frequent stops, take Route 1.

The Maine Turnpike is a fairly straightforward piece of pavement—a modern four- and six-lane highway with a 65 mph speed limit—until it hits Greater Portland, where I–95 all of a sudden becomes I–295 and you have to start paying attention to signs. What you need to know is that most people heading up the coast leave the turnpike at exit 44 in Portland and follow

I–295 north for another 20 miles to the Route 1 Coastal Connector in the Brunswick area. Rest areas are uncommon on either I–95 or Route 1, so stop when you see one rather than waiting for the next.

Route 1 used to be called the Atlantic Highway and has a reputation as a scenic, seaside road. Don't be fooled. The two-lane highway does go through many picturesque villages, beginning in Kittery and following the coast to Calais, but ocean vistas are a rarity. Route 1 also has become known for traffic—if you visit in summer and don't want to sit for a bit in your car, avoid driving Route 1 north. If you're heading to the Midcoast, take I–95 to Augusta and cut back over to the coast on Route 17 or Route 3. These highways are just as big as Route 1 but don't become nearly as congested. Another option, if you're heading to Acadia or points Down East, is to take I–95 as far north as Bangor and cut over to Bar Harbor on U.S. Route 1A.

U.S. Route 1, Down East

From the point where most of the cars turn off Route 1—onto Route 3 en route to Bar Harbor—all the way to the end of the coast down near West Quoddy Head, this part of Maine is one epic scenic drive. Mainers like to call it the "real Maine" because it has yet to be overdeveloped or overrun.

ℹ️ Wondering where the bottlenecks are on any given day? Want to avoid the construction delays that pop up like spring flowers on Maine roadways? Visit the Maine Department of Transportation's well-done Web site at www.maine.gov/mdot. You can find the answers to these questions and more, from road advisories to scenic highways to traffic cams showing the current conditions at several locations.

BY AIR

Compared to airports in major metropolitan areas, the jetports at Portland and Bangor are real pleasures. Getting in and out is a fairly simple affair at either, but especially in Bangor, and parking is never too much of a problem. Portland has only 11 gates and two luggage carousels, so getting lost or waiting forever is unlikely, and Bangor has only a handful of gates. But just because they're on a smaller scale than most airports doesn't mean they are backward. Both have all the important amenities found elsewhere.

Portland International Jetport

The Portland International Jetport serves close to 1.4 million passengers annually and is perfectly sited for anyone who wants to visit southern Maine or coastal destinations as far north as Rockland. Flights come in and go out on a daily basis by several major carriers. Check out www.portlandjetport.org.

Commercial Airline Phone Reservation Numbers

Air Tran Airways	(800) 247-8726
Continental Airlines	(800) 523-3273
Delta Airlines	(800) 221-1212
Jet Blue	(800) 538-2583
Northwest Airlines	(800) 225-2525
United Express	(800) 864-8331
US Airways	(800) 428-4322

Car Rentals

Alamo	(207) 775-0855
Avis	(207) 874-7500
Budget	(207) 772-6789
Hertz	(207) 774-4544
National	(207) 773-0036

Bangor International Airport

Bangor International Airport bills itself as the "intelligent alternative" to other airports serving northern New England (Boston; Manchester, New Hampshire; and Portland), and in many ways it is. Travelers will be hard-pressed to find a simpler, friendlier way to fly the friendly skies than they will in this city-owned airport. It's especially easy and convenient if you're arriving intent on a visit to Acadia, Bar Harbor, the Down East coast, or even south as far as Camden or Rockland. Parking is a cinch, finding the terminal even easier, and just about everyone you encounter is pleasant and helpful. (If your plane is late they might even apologize. Imagine!) Check out www.flybangor.com.

Commercial Airline Phone Reservation Numbers

Allegiant air	(702) 505-8888
Continental Airlines	(800) 523-3273
Delta Airlines	(800) 221-1212
Northwest Airlines	(800) 225-2525
US Airways	(800) 428-4322

Car Rentals

Avis	(207) 947-8383
Budget	(207) 945-9429
Hertz	(207) 942-5519
National	(207) 947-0158

Other Air Options

A pair of smaller airports, both with daily airline service, provide further possibilities to travelers on the Maine coast.

Knox County Regional Airport

Knox County Regional Airport (207-596-0617; www.knoxcounty.midcoast.com/departments/

Close-up

Avoiding Traffic

On a busy August weekend, Maine's highways can get maddeningly crowded. Traffic here still doesn't amount to what one might expect on the way to Cape Cod, say, but things do get bumper-to-bumper at the tollbooths on the Maine Turnpike (I–95) and in touristy places like Wiscasset and Camden. And the lines can remain backed up for an hour or more on rare occasions. Mainers know better than to even try driving into certain communities in high summer and instead use some alternate routes. These can be handy to know. Here are a few tips and even a few secrets.

- To avoid traffic on the turnpike: Plan to arrive sometime other than a Friday afternoon, and try not to depart Sunday afternoon. Avoid driving on holiday weekends if at all possible.

- To avoid traffic in Greater Portland: Don't plan on passing through the city at rush hour. Congestion isn't really a problem in Portland except when commuters are traveling to and from work.

- To avoid traffic in Brunswick and Bath: Steer clear when the state's largest private employer—Bath Iron Works—lets out. The Bath Bridge, opened in 2000, has helped alleviate the traffic snarls that result when thousands of shipbuilders head home, but it still gets busy in both of these Midcoast communities around 3:30 p.m.

- To avoid traffic in Wiscasset: Take a left onto State Route 127 in Woolwich shortly after the Bath Bridge. Follow it 10 miles inland to Dresden Mills and cut back toward the coast on the Bog Road. Stay on this dirt road until it ends at State Route 218 in picturesque Head Tide, and then follow State Route 194 to Newcastle and take State Route 215 back to Route 1. This is a lengthy detour—and it's easy to get lost—but it's also quite pretty and can be quicker in the long run. A GPS unit would help, though.

- To avoid traffic in Rockland/Thomaston: Take a left off Route 1 onto State Route 90 in Warren and follow it to Rockport, skirting both of these Midcoast communities.

- To avoid traffic in the Camden/Belfast area: Grit your teeth and bear Route 1 through downtown Camden. Then take a left onto State Route 52 and follow it all the way to Belfast, bypassing a particularly slow stretch of Route 1.

- To avoid traffic en route to Bar Harbor: Route 1 can be a poky road, often backed up with convoys of RVs. Try heading first to Bangor and then taking Route 1A to Bar Harbor. There are fewer headaches that way.

airports) is served by Cape Air, a Cape Cod–based airline (800-352-0714) and Colgan Air (800-428-4322, a Virginia-based US Airways Express carrier, both of which offer regularly scheduled flights between Rockland and Boston. You can also book a flight to the islands of Penobscot Bay through Penobscot Island Air, a charter company based here. It's pricey, though. Call (207) 596-7500 for details. Another option at Knox County is Downeast Air, which offers charter services. Call (207) 596-5557.

Hancock–Bar Harbor Airport

Hancock–Bar Harbor Airport (207-667-7329; www.bhbairport.com), on Route 3 between Ellsworth and Bar Harbor, is another airport served by Colgan Air, connecting the Mount Desert Island area with Boston and the world. Car rentals are available through Hertz (207-667-5017) and Enterprise (207-664-2662). Local taxi service is also available. Local taxi service is available, and you can also connect with the Acadia area's exceptional Island Explorer bus fleet (www.exploreacadia.com).

BY TRAIN

Amtrak Downeaster

When a new passenger train service between Boston and Portland was first proposed in the late 1980s, naysayers pooh-poohed the idea, saying it would never see any sort of ridership. The train began rolling in December 2001, and within a month or so the Amtrak Downeaster had proved all its critics wrong. It was soon averaging 25,000 riders per month, and by the end of 2002 more than 300,000 passengers had taken to the rails. Revenues in its first year were up by 44 percent over projections, and the trend has been upward with 2008 strong as well. Everyone, it seems, loves the train.

There's a lot to like. It's a simple, efficient, and relatively inexpensive way of getting to Maine. (Parking, for example, is a miraculous $3 a day at the Portland Transportation Center.) The train makes five round-trip journeys between the two cities every day, beginning at 5:45 a.m. and rolling to a stop at 1:25 at a.m. The trip takes a little over two-and-a-half hours, because the train stops twice in Massachusetts and three times in New Hampshire before it makes its first station visit in Maine at Wells. Then it heads to Saco and Old Orchard Beach (between May and October only) before arriving at the Portland Transportation Center off Congress Street and I-295. Tickets are $24 one-way between Boston and Portland and are $6, $9, and $11, respectively, to Old Orchard, Saco, and Wells.

There are several options for ground transportation once you've arrived at the Portland Transportation Center (207) 828-1151. The Portland Explorer bus service connects the train station to the airport, the ferry terminal, the Maine Mall, and several hotels. One-way fare is $2.00. Call (207) 772-4457 for details.

The Greater Portland Transit District's METRO buses leave the train hub regularly for downtown Portland, the Maine Mall, and the airport. The fare is $1.25. Call (207) 774-0351 for more information.

Taxi fares from the train station to downtown Portland are about $9, and taxis are readily available. Car rentals can be handled at the airport.

For further information, call Amtrak at (800) USA–RAIL, call the local Northern New England Passenger Rail Authority at (207) 780–1000, or visit the Downeaster's site at www.thedowneaster.com.

Maine Eastern Railroad

The Maine Eastern starts its run in Brunswick and travels as far as Rockland with stops in Bath and Wiscasset. The train makes runs several times a day on weekends beginning in May; from June 25 through the autumn, the train chugs from Wednesday through Sunday, and there are foliage and holiday trips as well. Check the schedule at www.maineeasternrailroad.com or call (866) 637-2457 for details. Fares are $15 to $25, depending on your destination.

BY BUS

Concord Trailways

The sight of a Concord Trailways bus rolling down Route 1 with its windows all aglow from multiple TVs is a common one these days. The New Hampshire–based company provides daily service from Boston to 12 communities in Maine via its Maine Coastal Route. Express trips go straight from Boston to Portland and Bangor. Fares are $21 one-way, $35 round-trip. The Maine Coastal Route makes the following stops in Maine: Portland, Brunswick, Bath, Wiscasset, Damariscotta, Waldoboro, Rockland, Camden, Lincolnville, Belfast, Searsport, and Bangor. Fares range from $47 round-trip in Brunswick to $62 in Searsport. Call (800) 639-3317 for more information or visit www.concordtrailways.com.

Greyhound

Greyhound also makes stops in Maine, connecting coastal communities to to Portsmouth and Boston. Its route arcs through the inland cities of Lewiston and Bangor before heading back down to the coast in Bar Harbor, so it's not the

> **i** Local bus services in Maine have "Free Fare Fridays" during the Holidays. Ride for free in Bath, Biddeford, Mount Desert, Portland, and many other communities. Find out more at GoMaine.org.

most convenient for coastal travelers. But it's the cheapest way to go between Boston and Portland at $19.75. Find out the complete schedule by calling (800) 231-2222 or by visiting www .greyhound.com.

BY BOAT

Casco Bay Lines

Maine was first "discovered" by boat, and a good many people still get around that way. In the Greater Portland area, Casco Bay Lines is the lifeline for six islands with year-round populations: Peaks, Long, Cliff, Chebeague, Little Diamond, and Great Diamond. Founded in the 1920s, the company is the oldest continuously run ferry service in the country, and it's now owned and operated by the very people it serves. More than 800,000 passengers a year drive down to Commercial Street on the Portland waterfront and file aboard the Casco Bay Lines' distinctive black-and-yellow ferries. The vessels run daily year-round, setting off as early as 5 a.m. and continuing operations until almost midnight. Summer, with its fair seas, is the ferry's busiest time. Round-trip fares range from $7.75 to Peaks to $11.50 for passage to Cliff Island. Cars can be ferried as well, for $34 to $120 depending upon what island they're bound to. For more information call (207) 774-7871 or visit www.cascobaylines.com.

Chebeague Ferry

Great Chebeague Island, a part of the town of Cumberland, has its own ferry service, which leaves from Cousins Island, a small isle linked to the town of Yarmouth by bridge. Vans and buses ferry passengers from the Chebeague Transportation Company parking lot on Route 1 down to the tiny dock on Cousins Island for the 15-minute trip out to the island. The ferry makes a dozen trips daily in summer, fewer in the off-season, and round-trip passage is $13. For more information call (207) 846-3700 or visit Web site www .chebeaguetrans.com.

State Ferry Service

It seems only fitting that the Department of Transportation in a seafaring state like Maine would have its own ferry service. The Maine State Ferry Service (www.state.me.us/mdot/ opt/ferry/ maine-ferry-service.php) sails to six islands off the Midcoast and the Down East coast, moving both passengers and cargo.

To Islesboro, from Lincolnville

The *Margaret Chase Smith* makes the 3-mile crossing to the long, pretty isle of Islesboro, seven times a day in summer, beginning at 7:30 a.m. and ending at 4:30 p.m. (It makes five runs daily in winter.) The boat leaves from a ferry terminal at Lincolnville Beach, right on Route 1. Call (207) 789-5611 for more information. The rate is $8.50 for a round-trip.

To Vinalhaven, North Haven, and Matinicus, from Rockland

State ferries leave the big Maine State Ferry Service Terminal on Route 1 in Rockland on a daily basis bound for Vinalhaven (six trips) and North Haven (three trips) but visit remote Matinicus only every great once in a while, even in summer. Call (207) 596-2202 for more information. Rates are $16.00 round-trip for Vinalhaven and North Haven and $33.00 for Matinicus.

To Swans Island and Frenchboro, from Bass Harbor

The *Captain Henry Lee* sets off for the 40-minute jaunt to Swans Island five times daily in summer and scales back in winter. It makes two trips to Frenchboro. The ferry leaves from the small town of Bass Harbor on the back side of Mount Desert Island. Call (207) 244-3254 for specifics. Round-trip costs $16.00.

Monhegan Ahoy

The beautiful "artists' isle" of Monhegan, an idyllic outpost 12 miles out to sea, is served by boats that depart from three communities.

From Boothbay Harbor

The *Balmy Days II* visits Monhegan daily in summer, pushing off at 9:30 a.m. and returning at 4:15 p.m. Round-trip fare is $32. Call Balmy Days Cruises for more information at (207) 633-2284 or (800) 298-2284 or visit www.balmydayscruises.com.

From New Harbor

The 60-foot *Hardy Boat III* makes two daily summer runs out to Monhegan, leaving the dock in New Harbor at 9 a.m. and picking up passengers on Monhegan at 3:15 p.m. Round-trip fare is $30. Call (207) 677-2026 or (800) 278-3346 for details or visit www.hardyboat.com.

From Port Clyde

Sailing from the mainland point closest to Monhegan, the *Laura B.* and the *Elizabeth Ann* are among the most popular ways to get to the island. The Monhegan–Thomaston boat line offers the hour-long trip three times daily in summertime—7 a.m., 10:30 a.m., and 3 p.m.—but less frequently in the off-season. Reservations are necessary. Round-trip fare is $32. Call (207) 372-8848 for details or visit www.monheganboat.com.

To Isle au Haut

Relatively few visitors to Acadia National Park are aware that the island of Isle au Haut is part of the park. The 5,800-acre isle is indeed—and it's well worth seeing. The Isle au Haut mailboat takes passengers and freight across isle-strewn Deer Island Thorofare on a daily basis in summer. The boat leaves the dock in Stonington Harbor five times each day in high summer—and runs a shortened schedule in the winter and shoulder seasons. Round-trip fare for the 45-minute passage is $34. Call the Isle au Haut Boat Company for more information at (207) 367-6516 or visit www.isleauhaut.com.

The Speedy Cat

Bar Harbor's Cat ferry claims to be the fastest car ferry in all of North America. It's a bold statement, but if the Cat isn't the swiftest boat, it must be close. The 300-foot catamaran hits speeds of 50 mph or more and makes its daily run between Mount Desert Island and Yarmouth, Nova Scotia, in less than three hours. (The trip would take you some 600 miles and a day's drive if you were to do it on land.) And, high speeds aside, the ride is fun. Onboard are more than 120 slot machines, a duty-free shop, a movie lounge, and decks for surveying the passing seas. When the long-running cruise ship the Scotia Prince quit making the trip from Portland to Yarmouth, the Cat expanded down into Portland, adding trips out of Maine's largest port on the weekends. The ferry leaves Bar Harbor most days at 8 a.m. between the end of May and October. One-way passage for an adult in summer is $69 from Bar Harbor and $99 from Portland. With car it' $115. Call (877) 359-3760 or visit www.cat-ferry.com for more information.

HISTORY

Many people who know the state of Maine well say it makes the most sense from the water. Driving around on U.S. Route 1, you wonder sometimes why this village grew up there or why that community became a population center while the one over there didn't. Hop into a boat, and it all becomes clear. The region's European settlers first arrived on ships, of course, and they migrated north and east on the water, building their homes not far from the shore and its resources. Everything developed from there, spreading inland. History and the coast are inextricably linked.

EARLIEST INHABITANTS

The first aboriginal people on the coast of Maine—and we're talking prehistory here, thousands of years B.C.—that historians and paleontologists know much about at all were called the Red Paint People because they buried their dead in graves of rich red ocher. (Similar burial traditions have been found in Newfoundland, and some historians think the peoples in Maine and northern Canada may be related.) This unusual culture seemed to arrive out of nowhere, but archaeologists have found points, bone, and stone tools that shed a little light on the lifestyle of these nomadic tribespeople.

In 1892 an archaeologist named C. C. Willoughby began to put the pieces together, but it wasn't until 1912 that another professor, Warren Moorehead, began to study them in detail. (This period of Archaic history is now called the Moorehead Phase.) Burial grounds filled with the signature crushed red hematite have been discovered along East Penobscot Bay, at points Down East, and all the way up to the Saint John River Valley at the top of Maine, which suggested that the Red Paint People migrated with the seasons and were capable of building seaworthy vessels. All of their dead were interred on or near rivers or the coast, except for two small sites. The tools found at these places were of a finer quality than those that later Indian peoples used, and many were types of stone of unknown origin.

Despite investigations by Harvard's Peabody Museum and other archaeological outfits, there has never been unearthed traces of a village or habitation of the Red Paint People, only the ocher-filled burial grounds. (Early Maine settlers considered it a bad omen to dig up a red grave.) And, around 1800 B.C., their highly evolved civilization seems to have disappeared without a trace.

The coast was just as important to the Native Americans who followed them. Mainers today like to joke about who qualifies as a native and who's "from away," but there is nobody more native than a member of the Maliseet, Micmac, Passamaquoddy, or Penobscot tribes, which date back centuries. These four bands were collectively called the Wabanaki, which means "people of the dawnland," a name given to them because they were from the most easterly part of North America, where the sun rises first.

Ethnologically, all of these Maine tribes are of Algonquin stock, a people whose nations are found across North America, and the Maine tribes coexisted relatively peacefully compared to the warring Native American nations elsewhere. They'd pay one another visits, intermarry, make treaties, and trade, and their history is confusing due to the sheer numbers of interwoven bands. Early English settlers referred to them by the name of the river or region where they lived—Saco, Androscoggin, Kennebec, Penobscot, and so on, and though there were some cultural differences, these tribal groups had a largely similar way of life. Woodland peoples, they hunted, fished, farmed, and moved about with the seasons. Spring found them planting crops of vegetables and fishing for salmon, herring, and other anadromous fish. Early summer meant trips to the coast in birchbark canoes for more fishing and lobstering—and, of course, to avoid the bugs. Autumn meant harvest and hunting, winter more search for game, which were easier to track and bag due to snow.

The era of European contact, with its strange illnesses, lies, and displacement, was rough on these peoples, and some estimates show the population gutted by disease, going from 35,000 or more in 1616 to about 5,000 a few years later.

Small populations of these tribal groups survive to the present day at three reservations. The Penobscots live on Indian Island in Old Town. The Passamaquoddies live Down East at Pleasant Point in Perry and at Indian Township in Princeton. Micmacs and Maliseets live up-country in Aroostook County. The Abbe Museum in Bar Harbor, the Hudson Museum in Orono, and other collections in Old Town, Perry, Augusta, Hinckley, and New Portland are great repositories of information on Native American culture in Maine, and there are gatherings like the Native American Festival at the College of the Atlantic in Bar Harbor where you can enjoy dancing, singing, boatbuilding, and basketmaking.

EUROPEAN ARRIVAL

Some people say the first Europeans to land in the New World actually did so in Maine. A Norse coin dating back to A.D. 1000 was found in 1957 in the small coastal village of Brooklin, predating Columbus by almost half a millennium. Whether or not the Vikings actually set foot on the shore of what is now Maine is still a matter of debate; many scholars think that the coin was traded farther away and brought to the site by the Native Americans who lived there. Historians are certain that Leif Ericson ventured across the Atlantic and attempted to set up a colony in a piece of land he "discovered" in North America and called Vinland.

The Center for Maine History

There's great irony to the fact that the home of the venerable Maine Historical Society is a decidedly postmodern building in Portland. Most of the state's historical societies—there's one in almost every town—use the oldest structure in town as their museum and headquarters, but not here. In the late 1990s, when these chroniclers of Maine's past were looking for a new home, they decided they wanted to stay next to the other properties they own in town—the Wadsworth-Longfellow House and the society's library building just behind it. So they moved into the old bank at 489 Congress Street right in front of them, opening the Maine History Gallery there. This is where you'll find generally exceptional exhibits about facets of Maine life and politics in the past and resources for research into history Down East. The library, too, is a good place to look into all things venerable, with 125,000 volumes, newspapers, and printed items, and it has a handy genealogy section as well. For more information call (207) 774-1822 or visit www.maine history.com.

But there are compelling theories placing Vinland in Labrador, Nova Scotia, and even Massachusetts and Rhode Island. No one is quite sure.

Five hundred years later the picture was a bit less murky, though still not entirely clear. A pair of British brothers, John and Sebastian Cabot, gained the permission of King Henry VII of England to sail to this New World of which they'd heard—it was recently "discovered" by

Christopher Columbus—to make claims in the name of the English crown. John Cabot crossed the Atlantic in 1497 with a crew of 18, making it to what is now North America, a point that most scholars agree is Cape Breton. He made the trip again a year later, this time landing somewhere much farther to the south. Was it as far down as what is now called the Maine coast? Historians are still unsure.

The first confirmed reports of European explorers in Maine took place a few decades later. Italian explorer Giovanni da Verrazzano cruised the Maine coast under the auspices of the French government in 1524. The English had claimed the land based on the sightings of the Cabots but didn't appear willing to settle there, and the French thought if they swept in and set up villages, they could grab squatter's rights. The services of Verrazzano were secured, and he sailed up the Gulf of Maine, keeping sight of the coast, and wrote a detailed account of his findings for the king of France before departing for Europe. He was impressed with the rugged landscape but wasn't so taken with its inhabitants.

"The people were entirely different from the others we had seen whom we had found kind and gentle," Verrazzano wrote. "These were so rude and barbarous that we were unable by any signs we could make to hold communication. . . . The country which has been discovered, and which was unknown to the ancients, is another world compared with that before known, being manifestly larger than our Europe. . . . In a short time, I hope, we shall have more certain knowledge of these things by the aid of Your Majesty."

Portuguese explorer Esteban Gomez sailed along the coast of Maine in 1525 searching for a way west to the Orient. He was sent on behalf of the Spanish government by King Charles V after word got back about Verrazzano's trip for the French. Gomez's travels took him up the Penobscot River, to present-day Bangor, and all along the coast, but the Spanish were none too interested in his discoveries and kept their focus on New World points south.

A handful of English explorers were similarly inspired by a Verrazzano, this time by the mention of a city called "Oranbega" made by Giovanni's brother, Girolamo, on the 1529 maps he drew of his brother's voyages. The mythology of a city of riches grew with each expedition to the New World and its name was changed to Norumbega, though no one actually set food on its gold-cobbled streets. English sailor David Ingram crossed the pond in the late 1550s and went looking for Norumbega, and added his own embellishments to the tale.

In 1602 winds blew the British captain Bartholomew Gosnold in to what is now southern Maine, and he ventured from there south as far as Martha's Vineyard, looking for a place to colonize, before heading back to England. He too met Native Americans and described them as being very familiar with European fishing customs—he even saw some sailing a Basque boat. (Fishing boats from England, Portugal, and the Basque and Biscay regions of Europe had been crossing on a regular basis to fill up with fish from the banks of Newfoundland, which is surely the source of the Native Americans' vessel.)

The fishing proved just as good in the Gulf of Maine. Gosnold wrote of the rich stocks of cod in the waters they fished. His crew dropped lines and soon found the fish "so pestered our ship . . . that we threw numbers of them overboard." His expedition was quickly followed by that of Captain Martin Pring, who explored sections of the coast in 1603, and by George Waymouth, who landed at a site on the St. George River near present Thomaston in 1605, capturing five Native Americans. His idea was to take them back to the British Isles, teach them English, and gain intelligence about this new land. His dastardly plan worked—the stories the captives told were inspiring, and soon boatloads of Britons were arriving on the shores of what is now Maine.

Among them was George Popham, who had talked King James into granting his family a charter for a new colony in "Virginia." The scouts they sent to look for land—one of whom was Martin Pring—thought there was a preferable site at the base of either the Kennebec or Sagadahoc rivers. So off went 120 colonists aboard a pair of ships, the *Mary and John* and the *Gift of God*, in 1607.

The Popham colony built a village, a bastion they called Fort Saint George, and storehouses, and began to barter with the indigenous peoples, but the winter that befell them was more than many were prepared to take, and 75 of the colonists left by December. The rest made it through to the fall of the following year, but the settlement was eventually disbanded.

The French and English continued their duel over the New World, and at about the same time the Popham Colony was being established, French explorer Samuel de Champlain was touring and mapping the coast of what is now Maine under the blue, white, and red stripes of the French flag. From 1604 to 1606, he sailed between Martha's Vineyard and the Bay of Fundy, charting and naming points and places as he went. Many Maine places got their names at this time. In 1604 Champlain and French Lieutenant General Sieur De Monts made an attempt to settle on the island of St. Croix in the St. Croix River, which is now way Down East. But winter proved harsh—"there are six months of winter in this country," he wrote—and his band also retreated.

Back and forth went the English and the French. Next up for the Brits was famed adventurer and explorer Captain John Smith, who had made a name for himself fighting wars in the Netherlands and Hungary, by helping to settle Jamestown, and by escaping the wrath of Chief Powhatan thanks to the intervention of the chief's merciful daughter Pocahontas. In 1613 he was sent by the English crown to once again look into colonization of this cold northern region, and he was given the title Admiral of New England, for whatever that was worth. He spent the next several years journeying along the Maine coast, mapping what he saw, and ultimately throwing in his lot with Sir Ferdinando Gorges, who was a mucky-muck among the Pilgrims of the Plymouth Company.

As a firsthand witness to the success of the Plymouth colony on Cape Cod, Gorges was sure that the coast of Maine could and should be settled. In 1622 Pilgrim governors jointly gave Gorges and Captain George Mason, another pro-ponent of settlement, the land between the Merrimac and Sagadahoc Rivers, or the chunk of terrain from northern Massachusetts and New Hampshire all the way up to Bath, and they called the land the Province of Maine, the first official use of the word Maine. The origins of the name of the state of Maine are still unknown. Some say it's derived from the word mainland. Others think it refers to a province in France.

Small settlements were beginning to multiply all along the coast. Monhegan Island, York, and New Harbor became fishing outposts, and some reports count as many as 84 families living along the Saint George and Sheepscot Rivers by 1630. Grants and deeds were multiplying, and by 1639, it became clear that some form of official governance was needed. That year the region was incorporated as the Province and County of Maine. The king of England turned back to Sir Ferdinando Gorges, dubbed him lord of the area, and the Province and County of Maine grew and grew. The first city was incorporated at York in 1641, and villages were being established along the length of the coast.

All sorts of internal squabbles arose over the next several years, and Sir Ferdinando Gorges died in 1647, leaving something of a power vacuum. In 1652 the Commonwealth of Massachusetts essentially annexed the Province of Maine—it became formal in 1677—and the commonwealth would hold onto the territory until 1820, much to the chagrin of Mainers.

FRENCH AND INDIAN WARS

Just as they were warring on continental Europe, the French and English continued to fight over the New World, including the Province of Maine. By the middle of the 1600s, as communities were being settled along the length of the coast, the state of Maine as we now know it was divided roughly in half by the Penobscot River, with the English controlling the west and the French the east. It was a natural split, as the English held most of the rest of the territory to the southeast—offshoots of the Plymouth and Jamestown colonies—and the French occupied the land

Close-up

A Maine Coast Time Line

circa 3000–1800 B.C.: Mysterious society of Red Paint People, early Native Americans that historians don't know much about, live along Maine coast. Red Paint People bury their dead along the coast in graves of rich red ocher.

A.D. 80–350: Oyster Shell People, Native Americans known for their huge shell middens, roam Maine coast.

A.D. 1000: Norse explorers discover "Vinland." Some historians say that the Viking land discovered by Leif Ericson was in Maine.

1524: Italian explorer Giovanni da Verrazzano explores the Maine coast on behalf of the king of France.

1525: Esteban Gomez sails the coast of Maine for Spain, "discovering" the Penobscot River.

1569: An Englishman passes through Maine and tantalizes other explorers with tales of a mythical city of gold, Norumbega, on the Penobscot River.

1602: Captain Bartholemew Gosnold visits Maine for the British government, returning with a load of woods cargo.

1603: The coast between the Piscataqua and the Penobscot is surveyed by Martin Pring.

1604: French Lieutenant General Sieur de Monts establishes a colony near present-day Calais. Samuel de Champlain maps many of the islands and much of the coast of Maine.

1605: Captain George Waymouth lands at Monhegan in the Archangel and explores up the St. George River. Five Native Americans are captured by Waymouth and his crew and taken back to England for show-and-tell.

1607: The Popham Colony is established by George Popham at present-day Phippsburg.

1614: Captain John Smith explores Maine and maps the region from Cape Cod to Nova Scotia, calling it New England.

1617: A party led by Captain Richard Vines winters at Saco to prove the Maine climate is palatable by Europeans.

1620: A permanent settlement is set up on Monhegan Island.

1622: The word *Maine* is officially used for the first time to describe the land between the Merrimac and Sagadahoc Rivers.

1629: Plymouth Colonists able to pay bulk of debts incurred on their *Mayflower* passage by selling furs collected in the Kennebec area.

1632: The English cede the area known as Acadia to the French.

1635: A shipyard—the first in the New World—is established on Richmond Island.

1636: King Charles I of England appoints Sir Fernando Gorges lord of New England. Gorges sends nephew William to govern the colonies and later calls the area New Somersetshire.

1639: Region is incorporated as the Province and County of Maine.

1641: York is chartered as the first English city in the New World.

1673–1745: Dutch, English, and French fight over Maine territory.

1675: Settlements at Casco and Scarborough are destroyed by Indian attacks during King Philip's War.

1677: Maine officially becomes part of Massachusetts, having been purchased by the commonwealth from the Gorges heirs for about $6,000. Three years later Maine gets its first "president," Thomas Danforth.

1713: The Treaty of Utrecht helps define the political boundary lines of the modern state of Maine.

1719: First schoolhouse built in Berwick

1740: Population of Maine is about 12,000.

1770: Rebel fervor grips Mainers as John Adams visits York.

1775: Residents of Maine join the rebel cause. Benedict Arnold leads troops through Maine for a disastrous raid on Quebec. The city of Portland (then known as Falmouth) is burned by the British. The first naval battle of the American Revolution takes place as Mainers capture the British ship Margaretta off Machias.

1779: Colonial navy suffers its worst defeat in Castine, getting pummeled by British.

1785: First newspaper founded in Maine, at Falmouth (now Portland).

1787: Maine adopts a constitution and becomes a representative district, with 93 towns and plantations.

1788: Slavery is abolished in Maine.

1791: George Washington orders construction of Portland Head Light in Cape Elizabeth.

1800: Population of Maine is 151,719.

1802: Bowdoin College opens in Brunswick.

1807: Poet Henry Wadsworth Longfellow is born in Portland.

1812: The War of 1812 slows shipping along Maine coast and leads to smuggling, the heyday of "rum-running" Down East.

1814: The British occupy the coast from the Penobscot River to the St. Croix until 1815.

1820: Maine becomes a state, admitted to the Union as part of the Missouri Compromise. William King is elected the state's first governor. A state legislature is set up in Portland.

1832: The state capital moves from Portland to Augusta.

1840: Quarrying for granite begins on Vinalhaven Island.

1849: Author Sarah Orne Jewett is born in South Berwick.

1851: Maine enacts first Prohibition laws in nation.

1860: Mainer Hannibal Hamlin elected vice president of the United States on ticket with Abraham Lincoln.

1861: Civil War breaks out. Maine will send about 73,000 men.

1862: Maine State College of Agriculture and Industrial Arts established at Orono (now the University of Maine).

1865: Famed Maine general Joshua Chamberlain is commander of the Union troops during the surrender of the Confederates at Appomattox.

1866: Portland struck by its second great fire, losing more than 1,800 buildings. Aid is rushed in from all over the country.

1870: Maine begins to blossom as a vacation destination with influx of "summercators."

1879: A freak snowstorm hits Portland on July 4.

1884: Bath Iron Works is established. Winslow Homer moves to Prout's Neck.

1892: Edna St. Vincent Millay is born in Rockland. Archaeologist C. C. Willoughby discovers early evidence of Red Paint People.

continued

1900: Population of Maine is 694,466.

1912: Professor Warren Moorehead begins a detailed study of the prehistoric Red Paint People.

1917: As the nation enters World War I, the first navy-built submarine is launched in Kittery at Portsmouth Naval Shipyard.

1919: Lafayette National Park opens on Mount Desert Island (it will be renamed Acadia).

1920: Maine women are the first to exercise right to vote.

1931: Former Governor Percival Baxter makes his first gift to the state, forever wild Mount Katahdin, the basis of what would become Baxter State Park.

1932: Portland-to-Boston steamer service is curtailed.

1935: The Quoddy Tidal Project, a quixotic New Deal attempt to harness tidal power way Down East, is launched.

1941: Nazi spies are captured on the Maine coast.

1946: Rural electrification begins.

1947: Maine Turnpike is built from Kittery to Portland. Forest fires tear through Mount Desert Island, destroying 1,000 homes and more than 17,000 acres at Acadia.

1950: Hurricanes savage the coast, doing $2 million worth of damage. Passenger rail comes to a slow halt on the Maine coast.

1962: Mainer Rachel Carson's book *Silent Spring*, an ecological wake-up call, is published, becoming an inspiration to the burgeoning environmental movement.

1970: Maine's sesquicentennial population is just shy of one million.

1972: Maine Yankee nuclear power plant opens in Wiscasset.

1975: The last river drive, a logging tradition, occurs in Maine.

1976: Maine's Native American tribes file legal claims to more than 60 percent of the state.

1979: Mainer Edmund Muskie becomes President Jimmy Carter's Secretary of State.

1980: Jimmy Carter signs the Indian Land Claims agreement, settling disputes with the Native Americans.

1984: Freeport marathon runner Joan Benoit wins a gold medal at the first women's marathon at the Summer Olympics in Los Angeles.

1994: Angus King, a resident of Brunswick, becomes only the second elected Independent governor in U.S. history.

1997: Maine Yankee nuclear plant closes.

1998: A severe ice storm cripples Maine in January.

2001: Passenger rail service between Portland and Boston resumes.

2003: Governor John Baldacci introduces Dirigo Health, a ground-breaking state-run health care program with the goal of providing all Maine residents with access to health care by 2009—so far it's yet to make good.

2005: The cruise ship *Scotia Prince* discontinues its Portland-to-Yarmouth, Nova Scotia run.

called Acadia, what is now the Down East coast and Canadian Maritimes. The French had a distinctly better relationship with the Native Americans at this point, having lived among them and gained their trust as traders and trappers, and as war spread from Europe to North America, they enlisted the aid of their Native American friends. This alliance was bad news for the English.

Over the course of about a hundred years, 1675–1760, the two nations had at each other in the Province of Maine, and it was a bloody, restless time for the settlers attempting to carve out a home on the Maine coast. A series of wars broke out beginning in 1675 with King Philip's War (1675–1678), which started in the vicinity of Plymouth, Massachusetts, and spread to Maine after a bunch of English idiots in Saco killed the child of an influential Saco chief. These sailors wanted to test the veracity of the old legend that a Native American baby could swim at birth, so they placed a Saco baby in a canoe and then overturned the canoe. Of course the baby drowned. The baby's father, Squando, leader of the Sacos, eked out his revenge quickly. War spread from Saco to Scarborough to South Berwick to York and beyond.

The conflict and bloodshed would hardly let up over the next century, with turmoil starting anew only a few years after a peace was brokered. King William's War (1688–1699) picked up not long after King Philip's, and then came Queen Anne's War (1703–1713), Dummer's War (1721–1726), King George's War (1744–1748), and finally the war that defined them all, the French and Indian War (1754–1760). As a consequence of the 1713 Treaty of Utrecht, which settled Queen Anne's War, the French lost control of their Acadia lands, an event that helped define the political boundary lines of the modern state of Maine.

i The Maine state government has an excellent online history of the Pine Tree State at www.maine.gov/portal/facts_history/history.html that includes time lines, narratives, and a host of links.

REVOLUTIONARY MAINE

The tranquil years that followed the French and Indian Wars resulted in a boom in settlement along the Maine coast. By 1740 the state's population was about 12,000. The census of 1764 reflected a doubling of that, and it doubled again by the time of the American Revolution. These Mainers were as bothered as anyone else by the arrogance of the British toward the colonies, and they showed solidarity with their Boston neighbors when the port of Boston was closed by act of Parliament, sending relief south.

Troops would soon follow. A company of 60 or more men marched from York to Massachusetts as soon as word came about the Battle of Lexington, and several more from the Portland area followed a day or so later. The war under way, Maine paid the price for rebellion when Portland (then called Falmouth) was bombarded in 1775 and much of its infrastructure destroyed. But Mainers would play important roles in the fight for independence, winning, for example, the first naval battle of the Revolution when Machias patriots captured the British warship *Margaretta*.

One of the most famous Maine incidents during the war occurred in 1775 when Colonel Benedict Arnold made a march through the wilderness of Maine to attack the British in Quebec City. The bold and self-possessed Arnold, who had yet to turn traitor, sailed to the mouth of the Kennebec River south of Bath with 1,100 troops and began an arduous journey upstream. The trip was undertaken in the autumn, and the men were beset with fatigue and sickness, almost starved, and got lost on several occasions. The force that arrived at Quebec was less than half of what started the expedition, and the bedraggled troops were handily routed. Another pummeling by the British occurred in 1779, when the colonial navy suffered its worst defeat of the Revolution at Castine.

Hundreds of Mainers served and died in the contest. Those who made it came home to a place now officially known as the District of Maine in the state of Massachusetts. Things were booming along the coast, with towns and cities incorporating left and right and many soldiers and sailors taking advantage of land deals offered by the Massachusetts government—a dollar an acre, including riverfront properties. A 1786 lottery dispensed with more than a million acres Down East, all the way up to the new border of the District on the St. Croix River. A constitution adopted in 1787 made Maine a representative district, with 93 towns and plantations. Slavery was abolished the following year. By the turn of the 19th century, the population of Maine stood at 151,719.

NEW NATION, NEW STATE

Because of its easternmost location, the District of Maine was put in an interesting position when the United States declared war on Britain in 1812. The years prior had seen a boom in smuggling Down East, especially around Eastport, as Mainers tried to cope with the slowing economy caused by President Jefferson's 1807 Embargo Act. One merchant estimated he was losing as much as $5,000 a month due to this prohibition on trade with foreign nations. Jefferson was attempting to keep sailors safe from the French and English, who were harassing ships at sea, but it was severely hurting the Maine economy, which was built around shipping.

Tensions between the United States and England led to declaration of war, and Maine was right in the middle of things—literally. It sat between the English cities of Quebec and Halifax and was in the midst of a shipbuilding boom, churning out vessels that could be used as warships. The English knew this, of course, and swept in, occupying the coast from Passamaquoddy Bay all the way down to Belfast. They stayed there until 1815, after the war had ended, and Mainers could again set about settling and developing their district.

It wouldn't be a district for long. Ever since the nation was founded, Mainers were on a quest for statehood. As far as time and distance went, it only made sense to have a separate government north of the Piscataqua. New Hampshire, to use a Maineism, was a "gawmy" wedge right in

between the district and the Commonwealth of Massachusetts, and Boston, in those days of limited communication and slow travel, seemed so far away. Mainers had to travel for court cases, for trade disputes, and for all sorts of lesser concerns, and many people in the district felt underrepresented politically, with a lot of places having no voice in the legislature. Plus, some Down East felt that the Bay State had been of little help when Maine was under such duress during the recently concluded War of 1812.

So Mainers rallied for statehood. A group representing almost all of the 236 incorporated towns gathered for a constitutional convention at the First Parish Church in Portland to discuss the many facets of state government. First, there was the name of the new state. What would they call it? Some voted for Columbus, others for the Commonwealth of Maine. Many thought that was too fancy-sounding and advocated plain old Maine. The name stuck. They debated the size of the legislature, whether or not to have a lieutenant governor, as Massachusetts had, what qualifications residents would need to meet to be eligible to vote, whether religion should be acknowledged in the state constitution. Finally these framers had a document, and they sent it out to be voted on by the general population on December 16, 1819—10,000 voted yea and only 797 nay.

Next the state had to win admission to the Union. It received approval—but at a price. Maine would become the 23rd state as part of the Missouri Compromise, which used the Pine Tree State as a balance to the slave-trading state of Missouri. It was a bitter victory for many Down East, as Maine had long been staunchly abolitionist. But on March 15, 1820, papers were signed at the Jameson Tavern in Freeport, making the old district official. The man who had pushed hardest for statehood, William King, would be elected the first governor in April, and the seat of government would be Portland (though it would change to more centrally located Augusta in 1832). The population of the new state was 228,705 at about that time (1821), and within 20 years it more than doubled again to more than 500,000.

ℹ️ The rich history of Maine goes on display every summer at a variety of historic homes, historical societies, and museums along the length of the coast. You'll find them listed in the Attractions chapter, under History.

THE CIVIL WAR

The peace and prosperity that pervaded the Down East coast would see some waves with the advent of the Civil War. The author of *Uncle Tom's Cabin*, Harriet Beecher Stowe, was living in the Brunswick area while her husband was working as a professor at his alma mater, Bowdoin College, when she was inspired to write the hugely influential antislavery text. This tale of the south, which would sell upward of three million copies in its day and caused President Lincoln to call her "the little lady who started the big war," was written from her home at 63 Federal Street.

The war resonated loudly in Maine, and Mainers rallied to the call for volunteers put out by President Lincoln. The state sent some 72,945 residents to the conflict—more than any other place in the North, per capita—in 32 infantries, three cavalry regiments, seven companies of sharpshooters, one heavy artillery, seven field artillery batteries, seven coast artillery companies, and six companies to fortify coastal points. Thirty-one Union generals hailed from the Great State of Maine, and Ulysses S. Grant, who would navigate the Union to victory, was made a colonel by one of the famous Washburn brothers of Livermore. The state of Maine also contributed warships and, by some accounts, 5 percent of all the gunpowder used by the Union.

Perhaps no one was more important to the Union cause than Bowdoin professor Joshua L. Chamberlain, however. At least that's how things are remembered these days, after the generously mustachioed brigadier general has been immortalized in several well-known books and a couple of major feature films, *Gettysburg* (1993) and *Gods and Generals* (2003). Chamberlain led the Twentieth Maine Regiment at Gettysburg, where he was assigned to the far left flank of the Union line on the exposed hill of Little Round Top. The Confederates had been making gains in the weeks prior and, if things went their way, could sweep past the federal army and make a bold push north against weakened forces. Gettysburg had to be held, and this small hill was strategically imperative. Despite overwhelming odds, Chamberlain and the men of the Twentieth Maine did just that, at one point charging at a Confederate force of superior numbers with only fixed bayonets and surprise on their side. One-third of the Mainers died, but the hill held, and with it the Union. Chamberlain was later awarded the Congressional Medal of Honor and actually received the surrender of Robert E. Lee at the end of the war.

The Southern colonel who faced the young Bowdoin man that day later wrote: "There were never harder fighters than the Twentieth Maine men and their gallant colonel. His skill and persistency and the great bravery of his men saved Little Round Top and the Army of the Potomac from defeat. Great events sometimes turn on comparatively small affairs."

RECONSTRUCTION AND THE TURN OF THE 20TH CENTURY

The years after the Civil War were not the best of times in Maine. Portland lost more than 1,800 buildings in a fire that engulfed the city in 1866. Having seen greener grass elsewhere, many Maine war veterans trended westward, planting roots in places they'd visited during the war that seemed to have soil more amenable to farming than the rocks they were used to Down East. ("You can't keep the boys on the farm after they've seen Paree" was a popular quote at the time.) This migration so alarmed state officials that they went out and started actively recruiting settlers.

The state's traditional industries would go into a gradual decline, too. People weren't traveling in wooden ships as much with the advent of steel boats, nobody seemed to want granite after cement was invented, and mills elsewhere presented stiff competition to those turning out textiles in Maine. But the Bath Iron Works was established in 1884 and became successful. Papermaking was one of the few manufacturing industries that was on the rise at the turn of the 20th century, and by 1909 it would place Maine third in the nation, behind Massachusetts and New York, in production. By 1914 papermaking was bringing in more than $40 million a year and employing almost 100,000 people.

The other industry that was growing steadily in the late 1800s was tourism. Many of Maine's great resorts began to prosper in the 1870s, with grand hotels flourishing in places like York, Old Orchard, Kennebunkport, and Bar Harbor. Wealthy summercators were moving to enclaves in Northeast Harbor, Prouts Neck, and Islesboro for July and August and bringing their wallets with them. And it wasn't just the wealthy who were flocking north by east to escape the heat of the cities—the middle-class travel trade was important to Maine as well, and the beaches in southern Maine were soon awash with vacationers. Trains, steamboats, and soon automobiles were depositing people from all over on the coast for a week or two at a stretch. The establishment of Acadia National Park in 1919 helped draw people farther Down East. By 1929 the state was bringing in some $30 million in annual revenue from tourists.

20TH-CENTURY MAINE

By 1900 the state of Maine had about 700,000 residents, most of them living in rural areas. The state managed to send 35,000-plus troops to Europe to fight World War I, and it launched the first navy-built submarine in Kittery at the Portsmouth Naval Shipyard. Hundreds of boats were constructed for World War II, too, with 75 submarines alone at Kittery and 236 Liberty ships in South Portland. Almost 100,000 troops would participate in the Second World War, and bases along the coast were integral to the war effort—Portland did a spell as the naval operating base of the Atlantic Fleet, and Brunswick Naval Station helped patrol the skies in search of German U-boats. A pair of Nazi spies were headline news

in 1941, going ashore at Hancock Point after being dropped off by a submarine. They would later be arrested by the FBI in New York City.

Between the wars Mainers made history in 1920 by being the first place women voted in the nation after winning the suffrage battle. Maine also became a hot spot for smuggling during the Prohibition era. Teetotalism had had advocates Down East for ages, dating back to Neal Dow, sometimes called the father of Prohibition. A mayor of Portland, he managed to get a law passed in the Maine legislature banning the sauce in 1851. When the rest of the nation enacted Prohibition laws in 1919, though, Mainers were quick to defy them, beginning the rum-running trade Down East. Some say that today's lobster boat races can be traced back to those days when lobstermen would speed over into Canada to procure some hooch and transport it back to Maine under the cover of darkness. The throttle on these vessels was often open as they tried to avoid and evade the authorities.

After the Civil War tourism continued to explode as city slickers from Boston, New York, Philadelphia, Washington, and the rest of the Northeast flocked north to escape the heat. They established summer colonies from York to Hancock Point and moved up for July and August, a tradition that continues to this day. Some would even head deep into the North Woods to climb Mount Katahdin, which Percival Baxter gave to the people of Maine in 1932. These visitors "from away" were among the first to bring automobiles to Maine. The opening of the Maine Turnpike in 1947 accelerated both the tourism industry and the pace of change in Maine. Automobiles would become the preferred way to get here as passenger rail slowly ground to a halt beginning in the 1950s.

After the Second World War, rural electrification projects began another great change, bringing power to outlying areas. By the 1960s and 1970s, a great influx of "back to the landers" began in a lot of these quiet small towns, introducing the bohemian to the backcountry. In 1962 summer resident Rachel Carson published the landmark book *Silent Spring*, helping to galvanize these newcomers—and Mainers everywhere—into an environmental movement that would become among the strongest in the nation. It helped to bring an end to the logging drives, which polluted rivers, and fought the development of Maine Yankee, a nuclear power plant that was built in 1972 only to be dismantled less than 30 years later.

The 1970s and 1980s brought with them a lot of suburban growth—especially in southern Maine and Greater Portland—and that helped launch retail booms at the Maine Mall in South Portland, in Portland's Old Port, and in outlet towns like Kittery and Freeport. More and more summer vacationers, too, were moving up permanently, building homes all along the coast. This development has prompted many Mainers to worry about the small-town life that has so long been tradition here.

The 20th century continued the political traditions begun after the Civil War in Maine. Despite its relatively small population, the Pine Tree State has had a large impact on the nation's politics. Maine has produced scads of top-level politicos since the late 1800s, when Mainers were represented in Washington by a vice president, a Secretary of State, a Speaker of the House, and a Senate majority leader. That tradition continued into the 1950s, when Margaret Chase Smith was elected to fill the House seat left vacant by her late husband, going on to become the nation's first female senator, delivering her famous "Declaration of Conscience" speech, which helped derail McCarthyism. About the same time, Democrat Edmund Muskie was elected governor back in Maine, breaking the Republican stranglehold on state politics, and he'd go on to a distinguished

i Anyone interested in Maine history will want to check out www.vintage maine.images.com. A project of the Maine Historical Society, it's a gold mine of venerable Down East photos, prints of which can be purchased.

career, serving as President Jimmy Carter's Secretary of State after years in the Senate. George Mitchell and William Cohen, a Democrat and a Republican, respectively, both rose to prominence in the 1980s and 1990s, when Mitchell served as Senate majority leader and Cohen as Secretary of Defense during the Clinton administration. These days, Maine is known for its two dynamic senators, Olympia Snowe and Susan Collins, both Republicans.

THE 21ST CENTURY

Through the years, tourism has remained a constant. Today visitors to the state and the jobs they spin off account for $5.4 billion. Though still more dependant on natural resources than some places, Maine has seen the same economic cycles as the rest of the nation. Manufacturing has dwindled, with even the mighty paper industry gasping in the past several decades, and high-tech has moved in with the emergence of telemarketing. Maine has one of the best infrastructures for communications in the nation, with a network of fiber-optic cable that is second to none at 80,000 miles long. Health care has been another growing sector. Retail and service industries, especially as they relate to the massive influx of summer visitors, remain important as well.

ACCOMMODATIONS

Maine has been a tourist getaway now for more than a century, so it has its fair share of places to stay. In fact, there's a remarkable array of lodging choices available to visitors, depending upon where you want to be and when you want to visit. You can pitch a tent on a cliff top way Down East, enjoying completely unspoiled vistas all to yourself, or stay in a luxurious suite at a South Coast beach town resort, with hundreds of other guests. There are inexpensive motels with never-ending sea views in the Boothbay area, cool cottages in Machias, farm bed-and-breakfasts in Jefferson, grand old hotels on Monhegan Island, and urban high-rise(ish) hotels in Portland. Take your pick.

A few things to keep in mind when considering accommodations: Hotels are generally limited to the cities and resort towns, and there are only so many true resorts in Maine and fewer overnight spas. Cottages, motels, inns, and bed-and-breakfasts can be found along the length of the coast. Cottages are the way to go if you want an extended stay and don't mind doing your own cooking and cleaning. There are hundreds up and down the coast. Check in the phone book or with a Realtor in the area you want to be in.

Likewise, there are seemingly zillions and zillions of B&Bs in Maine now—500 or more at last count—and Mainers like to joke that after visiting the state in the summertime, every other tourist wants to move to the coast and open his or her own place. Bed-and-breakfasts can be great for new visitors, though, because they tend to be run by personable hosts who are very familiar with their area and can be your personal guide. Of course, some of these eager innkeepers can be overbearing, too.

You can find a searchable database of places to stay at the Maine Innkeepers Association (304 Route 1, Freeport; 207-865-6100; www.maineinns.com). It's a handy resource.

That covers the *where*.

The *when* is a bit easier these days than it used to be. Maine tourists used to leave as soon as the leaves fell, and consequently so did all the innkeepers, closing up their shops until spring returned. More places are open year-round now, but there are still many that close for at least some part of the winter, so it's best to call ahead and check. The slowdown of the tourist season can be a boon to visitors, though—rates at many fine inns and hotels can be slashed dramatically in the fall and winter, making a stay at a swanky spot affordable for the average traveler.

Wherever you decide to stay, and whenever you decide to go, make a reservation ahead of time so you won't be disappointed.

Price Code

Except where noted, prices represent the average rate or range for a double-occupancy room in the high season. Most inns, bed-and-breakfasts, motels, and resorts offer a range of pricing options based on the size of the room, the view, and the amenities. Prices do not include taxes, parking, phone usage, room service, or any other added-on costs. Most hostelries also offer bargain and package rates in the off-season.

$.....................	$90 or less
$$	$91 to $150
$$$	$151 to $199
$$$$	$200 or more

SOUTH COAST

Kittery and Surrounding Area

PORTSMOUTH HARBOR
INN AND SPA $$–$$$$
6 Water St., Kittery
(207) 438-4040
www.innatportsmouth.com

As you might surmise from its name, this distinctive brick inn is a great launching pad for exploration of nearby Portsmouth (you can hoof it from here), as well as a fine place to rest between trips to the outlets. Of course it's a very pleasant place to simply be, to sit on the porch, look at the garden, or indulge in any number of treatments (facials, massage, body work) in the spa on the premises. The inn's owners have individually decorated its five guest rooms, which have private bathrooms, air-conditioning, cable TV, and Wi-Fi, and they've thoughtfully added things like beach chairs and bikes. The inn is open all year.

The Yorks

DOCKSIDE GUEST QUARTERS $$–$$$$
Harris Island, York Harbor
(207) 363-2868 or (888) 860-7428
www.docksidegq.com

This complex—a main house and a series of condo cottages—sits on seven seaside acres on York Harbor and began as a marina back in

i The chambers of commerce in resort communities like Ogunquit, Kennebunkport, and Boothbay Harbor got so used to visitors to the area coming in exasperated after an unsuccessful search for a room in high summer that they began to keep lists of beds available for any given evening. Now many chambers up the coast provide this service. If you don't have a reservation, the local chamber is often a good place to find out what's available. Many chambers of commerce—like the one in Wells—keep track of longer-term rental properties, too.

1953. So many visiting skippers would ask about a room that the owners, the Lusty family, decided to renovate the derelict 1895 house on the property. With its wraparound porch, sweeping lawn, and chairs on the shore, the main house is now a white clapboard classic. The Lookout, Crow's Nest, Quarterdeck, and Captain's Quarters cottages are clustered along the shore, making good use of sliding glass doors and banks of windows. You can choose from a variety of floor plans— suites with kitchenettes, studios, and individual rooms are available—but everything comes with a private deck, water view, and air-conditioning. Also on the property is the Dockside Restaurant, a well-liked eatery where you can fill up on seafood.

STAGE NECK INN $$$–$$$$
8 Stage Neck Rd., York Harbor
(207) 363-3850 or (800) 340-1130
www.stageneck.com

If wraparound panoramas of the open Atlantic, an indoor pool, your own private beach, and exceptional dining are the sorts of things you're looking for during your Maine stay, the Stage Neck Inn is for you. A sprawling resort complex, the 58-room inn is a self-contained vacation, with two good restaurants, a fitness center, a full-service spa, an outdoor pool, a Jacuzzi, tennis courts—just about everything you need for a getaway. Harbor Beach, which has no public parking and is all but inaccessible to the public, is right next door, and the famous York Cliff Path is, too. York Harbor's tiny downtown is a stroll away.

SUNRISE MOTEL $$–$$$
Long Beach Ave., York Harbor
(207) 363-4542 or (800) 242-0750
www.sunrisemotel.net

When you stay at a place like this boxy, three-story motor inn, you're not looking for the high-end fineries, just a spot to lay your head between visits to the beach, which is right across the street. And if you go in with that in mind, the place is fine. It has nice balconies overlooking the crashing surf and simple rooms with bright carpeting equipped with air-conditioning, microwaves, and clean, private baths. You probably won't even remember the inn, but you will remember the week you spent at the beach.

YORK HARBOR INN $$–$$$$
Route 1A, York Harbor
(800) 343-3869
www.yorkharborinn.com

The new hotels and inns that have been popping up along the coast in recent years could learn a thing or two from this old place. Everything is done with taste and attention to detail, from the 300-year-old common area to the 54 guest rooms to the dining room. The inn feels old—and when your lobby dates back to the 17th century, that helps—and its rooms are outfitted with antiques and reproductions to give you that New England country inn vibe. But all the conveniences modern travelers want are mixed right in, from private baths and Jacuzzis to phones, Internet access, and air-conditioning, to ensure that you're comfortable. The inn is divided into several distinct sections—the Main Inn, the Yorkshire Building, Harbor Hill, and Harbor Cliffs Bed and Breakfast, and the new 1730 Harbor Crest Inn—offering varying degrees of luxury. Many of the rooms have decks with views out to the harbor; some have fireplaces. The main dining room is generally excellent and has received high marks from the likes of *Food & Wine* magazine, serving a lot of local seafood, creatively prepared. There's a pub here, the Ship's Cellar Pub, with drinks and less expensive fare as well. The inn is right across from a neat park, and the Harbor Beach is a skip away, too. The inn has periodic Internet specials to fill vacancies at the last minute, and they can include some great deals.

ANCHORAGE INN $$$–$$$$
265 Long Beach Ave., York Beach
(207) 363-5112
www.anchorageinn.com

Put the word motor in front of inn and you get a better idea what this sprawling gray complex is like. It's more motel than inn and has 200 rooms, many with water views, three swimming pools, and all the modern conveniences. The location of the Anchorage on Long Beach Avenue puts you right across the street from Long Sands Beach, which means you're right in the middle of the York Beach hullabaloo, like it or not. There's a fitness center on-site, the rooms are nice if not posh, and the new pool in the atrium is a cool, hourglass-shaped indoor wonder. Some rooms have whirlpools, and all have private baths, color TVs, and air-conditioning. With its grassy lawn and gray shingles, the Anchorage is a step up from most of the other motels that line the beach here, but not a gigantic step up. (It's one of the rare places open year-round, however, and also has a cool catch phrase—Why Resort to Anything Less.) Rates vary widely depending upon room and season.

UNION BLUFF HOTEL $$$–$$$$
8 Beach St., York Beach
(207) 363-1333 or (800) 833-0271
www.unionbluff.com

This big, white hotel dates back to 1868 and imparts a little class to the honky-tonk atmosphere of York Beach, towering over rocks not far from the sands—at least from the outside. All white clapboards, balconies, and turrets, it's reminiscent of the grand hotels of yore. The rooms are not as nice as all that—they tend toward the modern motel end of things—but they're comfortable enough, and the views out across the water are superb. There are more than 60 rooms, with a variety of amenities. Some have fireplaces, others whirlpools, but all have private bath, cable TV, and air-conditioning. Family-style eats are available at the Beach Street Grill, and the hotel has access to local golf courses in season. It's not a bad place to stay at all, but it's not the cheapest.

Ogunquit and Wells

BEACHMERE INN $–$$$$
Beachmere Rd., Ogunquit
(207) 646-2021 or (800) 336-3983
www.beachmereinn.com

Another one of those old seaside Victorians, complete with turrets, the Beachmere was a private home that just kept expanding, and it's

Maine Farm Vacation B and B Association

Farm vacations came into vogue in the 1990s, and Maine has close to 20 agricultural bed-and-breakfasts now, with half on or near the coast. The idea behind farm B&Bs is this: You spend your vacation at a working farm, enjoying country living, helping out with the chores if you feel like it, and getting back to the land. You learn something, enjoy the "real Maine," meet some interesting Mainers, and help preserve open space while you're at it. "Our primary product is peace and quiet," says the association—and who doesn't want some of that? It's a great hands-on experience, especially for kids. For details visit www.maine farmvacation.com.

which sprawls across a bold, 70-acre headland on the way in to Ogunquit. Things look a little different here today than they did when Elsie Jane Weare opened a hotel on the site in 1872 and charged guests $6 for a week of rest, relaxation, swimming, fine dining, and hikes around Bald Cliff. (Costs a bit more, too.) Today on the site of the original hotel is a full-service spa, where you can have interesting things done to you with flora and fruit, like rose body wraps and blueberry facials. You can work out in the fitness mezzanine over the 75-foot indoor pool, maybe play tennis in the pine grove, then head outside for a swim in the outdoor pool. All of the gazillion guest rooms feature bay windows and decks with absolutely stunning views of the open sea, as well as private baths, modem lines, air-conditioning, coffeemakers, and all the conveniences. Dining remains a hallmark, much as it was when Elsie Weare was doing the cooking. The menu is thoroughly New English, with lots of seafood, and everything presented with a special twist. As nice as the Cliff House is, though, you'll pay for it—rates are high.

now a multilevel, multiporched wonder. The main building is just one of the many options at the inn, which has several cottages, off-site houses, and a motel unit. But the big old manor is the grandest, lording over expansive lawns and a rocky shore, and it has its own little beaches and access to the oceanfront walking path called the Marginal Way. The rooms are pleasant and several have fireplaces or kitchenettes in addition to balconies that look out over the Atlantic. All have private baths. They have Wi-Fi and cable TV as well, but you're going to want to watch the beach instead. Many rooms are large enough to accommodate Mom, Dad, the kids, and maybe an extraneous grandparent, aunt, or uncle.

CLIFF HOUSE $$$–$$$$
Shore Rd., Ogunquit
(207) 361-1000
www.cliffhousemaine.com
Talk about your compounds—Maine resorts don't get any more "resorty" than the Cliff House,

GRAND HOTEL $$$–$$$$
276 Shore Rd., Ogunquit
(207) 646-1231 or (800) 806-1231
www.thegrandhotel.com
You have to be somewhat confident to call yourself the Grand Hotel, and this place certainly makes a statement (with a lot of gilding thrown in). Right in the thick of things in Ogunquit, between Perkins Cove and downtown, the Grand has 28 well-appointed suites from which to choose, all of them with a living room, private deck, full bath, and bedroom, and each with a fridge, VCR, cable TV, Wi-Fi, and air-conditioning. The third-floor penthouse suite comes with a fireplace and grand-size deck, and its indoor heated pool and hot tub are fairly attractive. The underground parking garage is a good idea in a place like Ogunquit.

JUNIPER HILL INN $$-$$$
196 Main St., Ogunquit
(207) 646-4501 or (800) 646-4544
www.ogunquit.com/juniperhill

Not to be confused with the Pine Hill Inn, this Main Street hostelry is more motel than inn, but it does a good job and is within walking distance of downtown and the beach. Five whole acres of space and comfortable rooms with fridges and cable TV, a fitness center, indoor and outdoor pools, newspapers and coffee, and golf privileges at the Cape Neddick Country Club, a semiprivate club, are just some of the amenities. The Juniper is the recipient of a AAA Three Diamond rating, which suggests it's better than your average motel. And it is.

MARGINAL WAY HOUSE $-$$$$
Wharf Lane, Ogunquit
(207) 646-8801
www.marginalwayhouse.com

Can't have an inn in southern Maine without adding "motelly" units, and that's the story at this big gambrel-roofed colonial, which has been welcoming guests since the 1920s. If you have a location like this one—right in the village and a short stroll from the beach, with the water ever present—you might as well take advantage of it. There are now lodging options in five buildings here at the end of an anonymous lane. The main house has 12 rooms and three suites, each with private bath, cable TV, Wi-Fi, and air-conditioning (except for rooms 4 and 6). Many of the rooms have views and/or private balconies. The Wharf House setup is somewhat similar with five rooms and a common living area, and the Dockside Motel has six more rooms, even closer to the drink. Seven efficiency apartments are available (at $1,095 to $1,795 per week) for longer stays. Open from mid-April through late October.

THE MORNING DOVE $-$$$
13 Bourne Lane, Ogunquit
(207) 646-3891
www.themorningdove.com

The gardens are very appealing at this big white Victorian farmhouse, which feels quiet and sedate but is within walking distance to Perkins Cove. The full breakfast is served on the porch. There are six rooms, with king- or queen-size beds topped with handmade quilts, Wi-Fi is standard, and Rachel Ray smiled on the place on *Everyday* a couple years back. Minimum stays are sometimes required in high summer.

RIVERSIDE MOTEL $-$$$
50 Riverside Lane, Ogunquit
(207) 646-2741
www.riversidemotel.com

From the road, this long, low-slung carriage house–looking motel is pretty unassuming, like any other motor inn on the South Coast. But this baby backs right up to Perkins Cove, where much of the Ogunquit action goes down. You can walk from your room to the foot drawbridge the cove is famous for and enjoy the restaurants and shops without having to worry about parking, which is an absolute nightmare in these parts. There are 41 basic rooms in total, each with cable TV, Wi-Fi, and a small fridge, and many have balconies with the million-dollar view. Breakfast, included in the price of the room, is offered in the lobby. An adjacent cottage built in 1874 has four additional rooms appropriate for families or groups.

SPARHAWK OCEANFRONT RESORT $$-$$$$
85 Shore Rd., Ogunquit
(207) 646-5562
http://thesparhawk.com

The Marginal Way, Ogunquit's hugely popular oceanfront walking path, starts right outside this Shore Road favorite. That and the gardens alone are worth visiting for. But there is much more to like. The Sparhawk has 87 guest rooms spread across four buildings, with suites and cottages among them, so it's comfortable for a longish stay, and it sits on six acres overlooking the booming surf. The grounds are expansive and pleasant to wander; you'll find tennis and shuffleboard courts and a heated pool for dipping. Everything in town is within walking distance—from the beach and the shops to Perkins Cove. You can even get a guest membership to the local golf course. The rooms are varied; some are motelish, some are more innlike, so you're certain to find what you're looking for. The Sparhawk has been welcoming guests in some incarnation for more than a century, and you'll understand why if you choose to stay here. There's a one-week minimum stay required in high summer, but you can get good deals in the shoulder seasons when it's more pleasant to be in Ogunquit anyway.

STUDIO EAST MOTEL $-$$$
Main St., Ogunquit
(207) 6466-7297
www.studioeastmotel.com

Clean rooms, good rates, and a great location are the appeal of this motel right on Main Street. You can walk downtown, to the beach, to restaurants, and forget about parking your car, which can be a nightmare in Ogunquit. (Hop on the trolley if you need to travel any distance.) The rooms are basic motel rooms, maybe a step up from average, and you can even get suites. All units feature private bath, cable TV, climate control, and a fridge; some come with kitchenettes. The motel is open from April through mid-December.

YARDARM VILLAGE INN $-$$
406 Shore Rd., Ogunquit
(207) 646-7006 or (888) YARDARM
www.yardarmvillageinn.com

The first thing you'll likely notice at this white-clapboard B&B is the big old porch. Every New England inn should have one, and this one is a beauty. The inn doesn't have a water view, but it's within an easy stroll of all the shops and restaurants of Perkins Cove, and it's far enough away to be quiet. So the veranda makes for good sitting, maybe with a glass of wine and some cheese and crackers, both of which the innkeepers sell in a little shop on the first floor. The six rooms and four suites are comfortable if not exceptional, and they're clean and outfitted with quilts. All of the units have a private bath, air-conditioning, refrigerator, and Wi-Fi, in addition to the ubiquitous cable TV. Perfect as a launching pad for Perkins Cove explorations, the inn also has its own sailboat and offers charters to guests, a nice surprise.

BEACH FARM INN $-$$
97 Eldridge Rd., Wells
(207) 646-8493
www.beachfarminn.com

Wells is known for its salt marshes, and this pretty, 19th-century farmstead used to be a saltwater farm. A sunny breakfast porch, a plum-colored dining room, antique furnishings, and an inviting pool are among the many amenities. There are eight guest rooms, several of which have a shared bath, and they are decorated with thoughtful details like damask curtains, satin moiré bedcovers, and hand-stitched pillows. The third floor is cooled with air-conditioning. Rates are extremely reasonable for a place this nice. Two cottages are also available for weekly rental.

BELLE OF MAINE VACATION VILLAGE $-$$
1139 Post Rd., Wells
(207) 646-2668 or (800) 943-5222

Seven new cottages were added to this little "village," but you'll want one of the funky older ones with pine paneling on the walls and varnished cabinets over the sink. Reminiscent of the old Maine and a whole lot of fun, these places are almost like going to camp! The cottages, with their clapboard sides, red roofs, and porches, cluster around an inground pool, with the marshes of the Rachel Carson National Wildlife Refuge and the ocean in the distance. They come in a variety of configurations, all heated and air conditioned—you can choose a cottage with one or two bedrooms, and they all come with a kitchenette. Gas grills are also available. (There are motel units as well.) And the trolley stops out front to trundle you off to the beach.

i There is a bed-and-breakfast garden tour every June in the Kennebunks, which can be a great way to get a tour of many of the area's B&Bs in one fell swoop— so you can pick the one you want to stay at next year. Check with the local chamber of commerce at 207-967-0857 or click over to www.kennebunkkennebunkportchamber .com to find out this year's date and time.

The Kennebunks

THE BEACH HOUSE INN $$$$
211 Beach Ave., Kennebunkport
(207) 967-3850
www.beachhseinn.com

Another luxury country inn owned by the talents behind the White Barn (they seem to be taking over), the Beach House gives them the beach site they never had. Kennebunk Beach is just across the way, and this place has the feel of an old beach cottage—if it were owned by your loaded grandfather. Supremely tasteful, with white-clapboards and a pretty porch, and its Pottery Barn-esque décor, the inn spares no comforts. Rooms came in a variety of sizes—"traditional" to suite—and some include whirlpools and magnificent views. The US Hotels group doesn't do anything poorly, so you know you're in good hands.

THE BREAKWATER INN
AND SPA $$$-$$$$
127 Ocean Ave., Kennebunkport
(207) 967-5333
www.THEbreakwaterinn.com

Another in the mighty empire of the local US Hotels Group (the outfit behind the White Barn, the Beach House Inn, and the Yachtsman), the Breakwater is the inn of the future in Maine. It's been in business for more than a century and a half, with the historic feel and seaside locale that visitors come to Maine for—check out that pebble beach. But it adds to that every comfort of a modern luxury inn. Accommodations run from the Inn rooms—with their sea tones and views—to the more contemporary Spa rooms to the waterside cottages. You won't be disappointed in any of them.

LAKE BROOK BED AND BREAKFAST $-$$
57 Western Ave., Kennebunk
(207) 967-4069
www.lakebrookbb.com

This four-room inn has what you call curb appeal. The grayish farmhouse dating back to the turn of the 20th century is set beside a saltwater marsh on a quiet road in Kennebunk, with overflowing gardens and a wraparound porch. The rooms are comfortable, with country furnishings and local art; there are three rooms of standard size and one suite with a kitchenette. One of the area's best restaurants, On the Marsh, is across the street. Though it feels like the country, the shops and restaurants are a quick stroll away.

WALDO EMERSON INN $$
108 Summer St., Kennebunk
(207) 985-4250 or (877) 521-8776
www.waldoemersoninn.com

Don't go thinking this big old colonial is where Ralph Waldo Emerson came up with his transcendental ideas—this house, Kennebunk's oldest, was built by his great-uncle, who made his fortune in the local shipbuilding trade. (Of course, little Ralphie was a visitor in summers.) Subsequently owned by other shipbuilders (they liked it because the Kennebunk River is out back), it went up in 1753, when Kennebunk was a thriving shipbuilding port. The inn's history is still written in the architecture and details—there are heavy hand-hewn beams overhead as you enter, there's the big working fireplace from the 1770s, which is still used to take the chill off at breakfast, and there are wide pine planks on the floors of some guest rooms. The rooms are cozy in a decidedly old-fashioned way, but they do have private baths, and there is a living area for guests with books, cable TV, and games. Most rooms don't have TV..

THE COTTAGES AT CABOT COVE $-$$$$
7 South Maine St., Kennebunkport
(207) 967-5424, (877) 524-2004
www.cabotcovecottages.com

No, this little inlet isn't from the TV show *Murder, She Wrote*. The cottage campus hard by the shore of Chick's Cove did take its name from the show, but don't hold that against it. The 16 cottages here range from tasteful and traditional to great fun in a family-good-times-at-grandma's-cottage-by-the-shore sort of way.. The April 2006 issue of *Cottage Living* magazine proclaimed them "the cutest cottages ever," and one has to presume the magazine knows cottages. The grounds are fantastic with everything Mom, Dad, and the kids need for a week on the water—rowboats, canoes, badminton, croquet, horseshoes, a jungle gym, and a grill for cooking out. But you can also walk to Dock Square without too much difficulty.

CAPE ARUNDEL INN $$$$
208 Ocean Ave., Kennebunkport
(207) 967-2125
www.capearundelinn.com

You can't really talk about the Cape Arundel Inn without mentioning the fact that it stares out at Walker Point, the home of the Bush family. All but two of the inn's rooms have a view of the presidential compound jutting out into the open Atlantic, and the wraparound porch takes it all in, too. Built as a summer cottage in 1895, the inn is a shingle-style showplace, with its own turret, and it's been run since 1997 by Jack Nahil, the innkeeper who made a world-class facility out of the White Barn Inn, so you know it will be comfortable. The dining room is one of the area's best, and the rooms are right up there. Seven are in the main house itself, and they all have sitting areas. On the side of the building is Rockbound, a "motelly" spot built in the 1950s, where there are six large rooms with handcrafted furnishings, and there is also the Carriage House suite, on the second level of the carriage house, which has its own private deck. The main house rooms don't have TVs, but the others do; all have direct-dial phones and Wi-Fi, and all have private baths. The gardens are beautiful, and the white Adirondacks on the lawn are inviting.

CAPTAIN JEFFERDS INN $$$-$$$$
5 Pearl St., Kennebunkport
(207) 967-2311 or (800) 839-6844
www.captainjefferdsinn.com

We should all get wedding presents like this. This absolutely beautiful Federal was built in 1804 and given to Captain William Jefferds and his bride, Mary, by her father in 1805. It was converted into an inn in 1982 and has been lovingly restored by its current owners. There are 15 rooms, several of which—the Santa Fe, the Assisi, and the Chatham—outclass most everything else around. Many places claim to be decorated with antiques

and reproductions, but the Captain Jefferds Inn truly is and puts them to fine, extremely tasteful use, placing four-posters just so on hardwood floors beneath high ceilings and before original fireplaces. Several rooms have claw-foot tubs or tile showers or even, in one case, a whiskey barrel whirlpool. Breakfasts draw raves. Highly recommended.

COLONY HOTEL $$-$$$$
140 Ocean Ave., Kennebunkport
(207) 967-3331 or (800) 552-2363
www.thecolonyhotel.com

Enjoy the coast grand hotel style. On 11 acres at the place where the Kennebunk River meets the sea, the 1914 Colony Hotel harks back to Maine's golden age of tourism, when the wealthy would flock north to escape the heat of the cities and set up for weeks in simple yet classic old hotels. Yet it's got all the amenities of a modern resort—a heated outdoor saltwater pool, private beach, acclaimed dining room, poolside lunches, afternoon tea, beautiful gardens, a putting green, badminton, shuffleboard, croquet, bike rentals, and even movies in summer. You can even bring the dog. There are 124 rooms of varying degrees of luxury (none are really posh, though). They range from those in the Garden House, adjacent to Maine hotel, which are standard affairs with TV, private bath, and king, queen, or two queen beds up to the Ocean Grand Balcony level, which is a king-size room with a spectacular sea view and a shared balcony.

1802 HOUSE BED AND
BREAKFAST $$-$$$$
15 Locke St., Kennebunkport
(207) 967-5632 or (800) 932-5632
www.1802inn.com

You could say that this classic 1802 colonial is away from all the action in Kennebunkport, but in this case that would be a very good thing. Rather than be in the midst of the madness that is Dock Square in summer, this graceful clapboard place feels more like a country inn, sequestered away in a residential neighborhood by the 15th fairway of the Cape Arundel Golf Course. The five guest rooms and single three-room suite here are all different, but each has a queen-size bed (most are four-posters), several have whirlpools, a couple have gas fireplaces, and some even have heated tile flooring. The Sebago suite has a private deck. Check out the big old beams in the house proper. The inn is open year-round.

GREEN HERON INN $$-$$$$
126 Ocean Ave., Kennebunkport
(207) 967-3315
www.greenheroninn.com

One of the most pleasant things about a stay at the Green Heron Inn is that you get to wake up to breakfast here. It's arguably the best in town. The 10 rooms in the inn are plenty cozy, though, not particularly fancy but with all the comforts you may want—from air-conditioning and private bath to TV. If you're vacationing with your pet, you get a special room with its own entrance. Families like the little, two-bedroom cottage on the cove, which sleeps five and has a kitchenette and a tiny porch. The Green Heron is ideally located for exploring town because you can walk to both the beach and Dock Square. Open all year.

KENNEBUNKPORT INN $$$-$$$$
1 Dock Sq., Kennebunkport
(207) 967-2621 or (800) 248-2621
www.kennebunkportinn.com

An imposing 1890s mansion in the heart of Dock Square, this sprawling old hotel has four different sections: the main house, the 1930s-era Riverhouse, the cottage-style Wharfside, and the 1980s Federal-style addition. Each of the 49 rooms offers something different, but all have private baths and are decorated with period antiques. (If you're into history, you'll appreciate the hallway downstairs where there are neat old photos of the inn and Kennebunkport.) All of the rooms, regardless of where they are, also have air-conditioning, phones, TVs, and Wi-Fi, and many have gas fireplaces and/or river views. From May through September you can take a dip in the pool and look out at the river; year-round you can dine in the Port Tavern and Grille, a steakhouse with a piano and bar.

LODGE AT TURBAT'S CREEK $-$$$
7 Turbat's Creek Rd., Kennebunkport
(207) 967-8700 or (877) 594-5634
www.turbatscreek.com

A motel that's just around a quiet corner from Dock Square, this 26-room hostelry has some surprisingly nice touches for what's essentially a motor lodge. One example is the large, heated pool, another is the complimentary use of bicycles, which will get you quickly into town or to the beach without the hassle of using your car. Each room has a little deck, air-conditioning, cable TV, and Wi-Fi, and it is furnished with either one king-size or two double beds. Certain rooms are available to pet owners, with advance notice.

KING'S PORT INN $$$-$$$$
18 Western Ave., Kennebunk
(207) 967-4810 or (800) 286-5757
www.kingsportinn.com

The King's Port gives fans of the Lodge at Turbat's Creek a more centrally located option. Owned by the same folks, this 34-room "country inn" is a skip to Dock Square, and it has an array of lodging options, from their Premium Queen rooms, with two queen beds, to their Presidential Suite, a three-room stunner with a cherry four poster, a marble Jacuzzi, and a full kitchen as complete as in an average suburban house.

MAINE STAY INN AND COTTAGES $$$-$$$$
34 Maine St., Kennebunkport
(207) 967-2117 or (800) 950-2117
www.mainestayinn.com

The sparkling 1860 Melville Walker House, all porches and white clapboards, is the very picture of what an in-town New England bed-and-breakfast should look like. On the National Register of Historic Places, the graceful home is in a residential area filled with fine old homes, but it's close enough to walk to Dock Square. There are six guest rooms inside, 11 suites tucked discreetly around to the side of the inn, and the owners recently opened the Artist's Studio, another cottage. The rooms inside are very nice with details like Waverly wallpaper and French doors, and the occasional Jacuzzi, and they're furnished with antiques. But the suites are knockouts with fireplaces, stuffed chairs, kitchenettes, and even whirlpools in some. They're the ultimate in privacy—you can go over to the main inn for breakfast or have it delivered.

OLD FORT INN $$$–$$$$
Old Fort Rd., Kennebunkport
(207) 967-5353 or (800) 828-3678
www.oldfortinn.com

This 16-room inn on a quiet residential side street presents guests with an interesting scenario—it is far enough from the bustle to be serene and peaceful, sitting on 15 acres, yet it's within walking distance of several good places to eat and even Dock Square, if you feel like strolling a bit. Very tasteful, very discreet, the former carriage house has all the comforts people have come to expect in a fine bed-and-breakfast—four-poster beds, whirlpool baths, heated pool, tennis courts, great morning eats—but it's decorated with fine Victorian furnishings and has a relaxed feel.

RHUMB LINE MOTOR LODGE $$–$$$
Ocean Ave., Kennebunkport
(207) 967-5457 or (800) 337-4862
www.rhumblinemaine.com

Less than a mile from the Bush compound at Walker Point in a residential area, this sprawling motel "resort" has surprises around every corner. How about a poolside restaurant? A Swedish massage or a facial? An outdoor lobster bake on the weekend? All at a motel? Four acres of woods surround the place, and the first thing motorists driving by notice is the stone building out front (that's where the trolley stops to whisk you into town or to the beach). The rooms are motel rooms, with air-conditioning, private decks and porches, cable TV, Wi-Fi, and fridges, and they come with two queen-size or one king-size bed. But it's in the amenities that this place shines—there are indoor and outdoor pools, indoor and outdoor tubs and spas, a sauna, and a well-outfitted fitness center. There are various packages and specials available, making things even more affordable than the standard rates. And it's open all year.

THE TIDES INN $$$–$$$$
Goose Rocks Beach, Kennebunkport
(207) 967-3757
www.tidesinnbythesea.com

The location of this Victorian charmer is ideally suited for beachgoers—Goose Rocks Beach is right across the street. Designed by famous shingle-style architect John Calvin Stevens, the inn used to be known as the New Belvidere, and it hosted such eminent guests as Teddy Roosevelt and Sir Arthur Conan Doyle back in the day. (It's said that original owner Emma Foss, who died many decades ago, still looks after things.) Gracious today, the inn has nice porches with fine views and 22 bedrooms, each individually decorated. These rooms are on the small side, and they don't have phones or TVs or other distractions (those are available in the lobby), but several do have absolutely stunning panoramas out their windows. Adjacent to the inn is Tides Too, a condo complex with two-bedroom suites and more modern amenities. Also on the premises is the Belvidere Club, which is popular with the locals ("inn-toxicating," they say).

WHITE BARN INN $$$$
37 Beach Ave., Kennebunkport
(207) 967-2321
www.whitebarninn.com

Lauded far and wide for excellence, the White Barn sets the standard in southern Maine— and, when it comes right down to it, the entire state. A member of Relais & Chateaux, that club for über inns and hotels, the White Barn has a list of accolades from major publications that could fill a book. If you can think of something you might like in an inn, this place has already thought of it, anticipating

> **i** The monks at St. Anthony's Franciscan Monastery (207-967-2011, www.franciscanguesthouse.com), a fine Tudor manse, enjoy prime real estate right on the Kennebunk River, and they take in guests. It's an inexpensive way to stay in Kennebunkport and a one-of-a-kind experience, especially if you go to mass.

the every need of guests. There are 25 rooms in all, and several are actually smallish, but they are very comfortable. Every one is set with fresh flowers and fruit, plush terry robes, and CD systems. Many rooms have extra touches like fireplaces, and some have rain- or steam-style showers in their bathrooms with granite floors. Jacuzzis are options. Every night your covers are turned down, you can get laundry done the same day, and you may order in for breakfast if you like. If you can rouse yourself, you can get a massage poolside, and if you're really ambitious, you can get active with complimentary canoes and bikes. You can even get lunch by the pool or packed up for a picnic on the go. And the dining room is hands-down the best around (see Restaurants chapter). New cottages have been added down the road a bit, and they are every inch as nice as the inn itself, but they sit on the waterfront, which the inn doesn't. (Ironic, isn't it, that the nicest inn in Maine is not on the water?) You can still enjoy all of the amenities of the inn as well, including the full breakfast. Of course, you'll pay dearly for all this, but it's worth it.

YACHTSMAN LODGE AND MARINA $$$$
Ocean Ave., Kennebunkport
(207) 967-2511 or (800) 992-2487
www.yachtsmanlodge.com

All 30 rooms at this riverside hostelry have French doors that allow guests to step out onto private patios overlooking the Kennebunk River and all its boats. The talents behind some of Kennebunkport's best places—the White Barn Inn and Grissini Italian Bistro—are also behind the Yachtsman, and each room has been designed to evoke the interior of a yacht, using mahogany moldings. (If you have an actual yacht, you can slide right up to a mooring in the marina outside your room; if you don't, you can rent a canoe.) The patios alone are worth the room fee, but these quarters are eminently comfortable, with much higher ceilings than you'd ever find in a yacht. Each room has private bath, cable TV, phone, and the use of a bike—or even a canoe— which is again sensible for a town like Kenne bunkport. Dining packages taking advantage of the owner's fine restaurants are also available.

Ocean Park and Old Orchard Beach

BILLOWHOUSE $-$$
2 Temple Ave., Ocean Park
(207) 934-2333 or (888) 767-7776
www.billowhouse.com

A rambling 1881 Victorian mansion on the beach—with a turret and all—this old place serves as a nice base for exploring Ocean Park, a seaside community established the same year as the inn as a Free Will Baptist summer colony. There are still interdenominational services, but these days the beach fun seems to have gained ground, pushing aside the Chautauqua-type lectures a bit. But it's still much tamer than Old Orchard, which many people find refreshing, and you can enjoy movies, talks, and concerts, or simply walk around and check out all the little cottages. There are a variety of types of accommodations at the Billowhouse, from bed-and-breakfast rooms to suites to efficiency apartments, and they are well looked after. The beach is close enough that you can track sand into the house. And the rates—and your hosts—are great.

NAUTILUS BY THE SEA $-$$
2 Colby Ave., Ocean Park
(207) 934-2021 or (800) 981-7018
www.nautilusbythesea.com

Another Victorian fronting the 7 miles of Ocean Park beach, the 1890 Nautilus has 12 rooms. Most have views of the sea, which is just out the window. The amenities vary from room to room—some have shared baths, some full-size or queen-size beds, some king-size beds, some patios, some TVs, some fridges. All are clean and comfortable and the rates are eminently reasonable.

THE ATLANTIC BIRCHES INN $-$$
20 Portland Ave., Old Orchard Beach
(207) 934-5295 or (888) 934-5295
www.atlanticbirches.com

This attractive Victorian inn, built in 1903, seems a bit above the fray in Old Orchard, more tasteful and refined than most of the area's hostelries. A five-minute walk from the beach and just around the corner from shops and eateries, the Atlantic Birches has five guest rooms, a heated inground pool, and a very nice wraparound porch shaded by those birch trees. An adjacent cottage has five more rooms, two with kitchen facilities. All of the rooms are chintz and printsy but each has unique decor, private baths, and names like the Old Orchard House, the Velvet, the Fisk, and the Abbot, taken from the grand hotels of the resort's turn-of-the-20th-century golden age, when this inn was built. You can select among canopied and four-poster beds, king-, queen-, and twin-size, and several rooms are well outfitted for families. A nice escape from the hurly burlesque this town is known for.

OCEAN WALK HOTEL $$–$$$$
197 East Grand Ave., Old Orchard Beach
(207) 934-1013 or (800) 992-3779
www.oceanwalkhotel.com
A big modern motel complex at the north end of Old Orchard Beach, this place presents lodgers with rooms in a variety of configurations. You can get a tiny studio with a double Murphy bed all the way up to an oceanfront suite with a full kitchen and sliding glass doors out onto a deck overlooking the water. The rooms are bright and open and fairly straightforward. The place has recently gone green, so you can feel good about that hot shower—the water's heated by the sun. Open April through October.

OLD ORCHARD BEACH INN $$–$$$$
6 Portland Ave., Old Orchard Beach
(207) 934-5834 or (877) 700-6624
www.oldorchardbeachinn.com
This old inn is a recreation of the Ye Old Staples Inn, which was supposedly the first hotel in Maine. Built in the 1730s, it began taking in guests in the 1830s when it was one of four buildings in town. Expanded several times over the centuries, it's now an 18-room inn, with a lot of history still in its walls. There's a big porch out front. Some of the rooms have nice beams and old floors, others antique beds and quilts. Each room has the modern conveniences, though—air-conditioning, TV, phone, Wi-Fi, and private bath. The third-floor

suite has a full kitchen. As Old Orchard goes, this is a relatively nice, tasteful place, and it's within walking distance of the pier.

GREATER PORTLAND

Prouts Neck

BLACK POINT INN $$$$
510 Black Point Rd., Prouts Neck
(207) 883-2500 or (800) 258-0003
www.blackpointinn.com
At the Black Point Inn they like to say that the inn will remain as you remembered it, meaning it isn't going to change much from year to year. And here, at the point where Winslow Homer found his inspiration, that's a very good thing. Tradition is everything at this history-steeped shingle-style inn—it even has its own crest. Built in 1878, the Black Point was originally called the Southgate, and it still has many antiques that date back to its early days. The inn has so many amenities it can be difficult to keep track of them all. Foremost is probably service, so you can easily get help sorting out all the options. There are 25 rooms in total, and they are spacious and sweet, with ocean or bay views, Gardens seem to flow every which way, and there are nice walking paths that meander here and there. Two beaches welcome swimmers, as does the outdoor heated pool. The exclusive enclave of Prouts Neck surrounds the property, and it's the sort of place where they'll have your car towed if you even attempt to slow down. A stay at the Black Point allows you to go anywhere you like, from Homer's studio to the Cliff Walk, a private seaside walking path. You can also use the Prouts Neck golf course. You'll find few rivals in the Portland area, and that isn't likely to change for a long time.

Scarborough

HIGGINS BEACH INN $$
34 Ocean Ave., Scarborough
(207) 883-6684 or (800) 836-2322
www.higginsbeachinn.com
Built as a summer place back in 1897, this three-story "colonial revival" institution began life as an

eight-room home. The enterprising man who originally owned it, Edward Higgins, quickly realized people would pay to visit the nearby beach, and he put a 25-room addition on and turned it into an inn. Guests have been coming here ever since, looking to escape the annoyances of everyday life by spending time on the beautiful strand just a short walk from the inn's porch. There are 24 rooms, 14 of which have private baths, and they are simple and basic and just right in a visiting-Grandma's sort of way. Well looked after by Bob Westburg and Diane Garofalo, they are tidy and pleasant without being at all fancy. Likewise, the eats served up in the dining room are straightforward family favorites, with a hint of Sicily, but they're good enough to earn four stars from the *Portland Press Herald.* Comfortable and homey is the word, and the reasonable rates make the inn a great deal.

Cape Elizabeth

INN BY THE SEA   **$$$–$$$$**
40 Bowery Beach Rd., Cape Elizabeth
(207) 799-3134 or (800) 888-4287
www.innbythesea.com
From the road this modern complex has a shingle-style air to it that harks back to the halcyon days of Maine summers past, but inside it's a thoroughly contemporary facility—newly made over in a large, multi-million-dollar way—with 57 one- and two-bedroom suites that overlook the smashing sea. A variety of choices are available—from decor to layout to view—with balconies, sunken tubs, Chippendale cherry furnishings, full kitchens, fireplaces, and all sorts of other posh amenities. With an excellent dining room, tennis and shuffleboard courts, an outdoor pool, a full-service spa, bicycles, and walking paths to popular Crescent Beach, this is the sort of inn where you could happily set up for weeks. The inn also has an exclusive arrangement that allows for use of the private Purpoodock Golf Course a couple miles down the road. The inn can be very busy in summer, and recent kudos from *Travel + Leisure,* which called it one of the top 100 hotels in the

United States and the *Maine Sunday Telegram,* which gave it top marks as "Best Maine Inn," will only make it more so. Reserve early.

Portland

CLARION HOTEL   **$$$**
1230 Congress St., Portland
(207) 774-5611 or (877) 424-6423
www.clarionhotel.com/hotel-portland-maine-ME061
This big corporate box replaced the DoubleTree a few years back, and the best thing about it might be that it is right next to the Portland Transportation Center, the bus and rail hub of the Forest City. Otherwise it's another mid-level chain of a place. The rooms are exactly what you'd expect, but you do get free local calls and Wi-Fi, and you can bring your dog.

EASTLAND PARK HOTEL   **$$–$$$$**
157 High St., Portland
(207) 775-5411 or (888) 671-8008
www.eastlandparkhotel.com
There isn't really any park at the Eastland Park Hotel. You won't find any green space for blocks, anyway. You'll know you're in Maine if you spend a night there, though, because the seagulls tend to scream at each other at the top of their lungs on the roofs of nearby buildings, echoing off all the brick and glass. The hotel here has been active since the Eastland went up in 1927, but it has changed ownership several times. That was the year Governor Ralph Brewster symbolically chucked the keys of the place into Portland Harbor to demonstrate that the Eastland will always be there and open, and, for the most part, it has been. All sorts of faded photographs tell the story of the place in its lobby and hallways, and they're fun to peruse. All told there are 202 rooms in the old hotel, and they come in varying degrees of poshness. At the standard level, they're not really posh at all—comfortable, simple, and with a host of amenities including Wi-Fi, cable TV, voice mail, and 24-hour room service—but their glory days seem a bit behind them. (Some rooms have

dents, stains, peeling paint, and loose bathroom fixtures.) The longer your elevator ride, the nicer your room, though, and the better your view. The luxury suites at the concierge level pamper you with plush bathrobes and evening cocktails. Be sure to make it all the way to the Top of the East, a popular rooftop lounge. It has amazing views of the city, Casco Bay, and the White Mountains in the distance.

HOLIDAY INN BY THE BAY $$-$$$
88 Spring St., Portland
(207) 775-2311 or (800) 345-5050
www.innbythebay.com
As downtown hotels go, this place has about as much charm as the Civic Center across the street—it's 11 stories tall, blocky, and completely devoid of character. But that's on the outside. Once you get into a room and look out the window, your impression will change, and that's where you're going to spend your time anyway. This place must have the best views of any Holiday Inn, overlooking a Casco Bay panorama that is something to see (and the White Mountains on the other side of the building). It's a prospect that few lodging establishments in town can come close to. And although the 239 rooms and two suites themselves are not beautiful, they're comfortable enough, and the amenities here are fairly extensive—air-conditioning, dataports, cable TV, Wi-Fi, an indoor pool, saunas, fitness center, and did we mention the views? The hotel is also well located for exploring the city—it's an easy walk downtown and an easy walk to the Old Port and the waterfront.

Chain, Chain, Chain

Looking for the chain hotels? Most of the less expensive places are in suburban South Portland. That's where you'll find the **Howard Johnson South Portland** (675 Main Street, 207-775-5343; hojo.com) the **Days Inn** (461 Maine Mall Road; 207-772-3450; www.daysinn.com), the **Wyndham Portland Airport Hotel** (207-775-6161; www.wyndham.com), **Holiday Inn Express** (303 Sable Oaks Drive, 877-863-4780; www.hiexpress .com), **Best Western Merry Manor** (700 Main Street, 207-774-6151; www .bestwesternmaine.com), the **Rodeway Inn** (738 Main Street, 207-774-5891; www.rodewayinn.com), **Sable Oaks Suites** (303 Sable Oaks Drive, 207-775-3900; www.sableoakssuites .com), **Courtyard South Portland** (100 Southborough Drive, 207-253-5005; www.marriott.com), and the **Maine Motel** (606 Main Street, 207-774-8285; www.mainemotelinn.com).

INN AT PARK SPRING $$-$$$
135 Spring St., Portland
(207) 774-1059 or (800) 437-8511
www.innatparkspring.com
The Portland Peninsula is a very walkable place—just 3 miles across—and this 1835 town house is well situated to explore it all. The historic West End, the Portland Museum of Art, and Congress Street are all handy, and even the Old Port is only 10 minutes away. The six-room inn has an urban charm that belies its small size, and while it behaves a lot like a bed-and-breakfast—it has nice touches like personal service, fireplaces, sitting chairs, reading lamps, fresh flowers, and a smashing breakfast—it also has the private baths, privacy, and efficiency of a small hotel. One example: You get your own key to the front door.

INN AT ST. JOHN $-$$$
939 Congress St., Portland
(207) 773-6481 or (800) 636-9127
www.innatstjohn.com
This 39-room hotel has been one of the better bargains in Portland for the past decade. Built in 1897, it's among the oldest hostelries in the Forest City, and it sits down near the bus sta-

tion on Congress Street. The place isn't much to look at from outside—and the usual bus station transients in the neighborhood can make you nervous, especially at night—and its inexpensive price might make you think you're getting into something sketchy, which is what makes it such a surprise to find the rooms themselves eminently comfortable and tasteful even, in a European sort of way. They're furnished with antiques and period reproductions and are complemented by the usual amenities—air-conditioning, cable TV, Wi-Fi, coffee, and breakfast—but you may have to share a bathroom. Downtown Portland is several blocks up the road, but with rooms as cheap as they are here, you can afford a cab.

POMEGRANATE INN $$$-$$$$
49 Neal St., Portland
(207) 772-1006 or (800) 356-0408
www.pomegranateinn.com
Housed in an 1884 Italianate mansion, this eight-room B&B shines. Another hostelry in the West End, it is proximate to everything downtown—and from there it's a short walk to everywhere else. The decor is colorful and fun, with you've-got-to-see-it-to-believe-it wall painting and fresh flowers beside the bed. Several rooms have gas fireplaces, all have private baths, and personality and charm are included. No children under age 16.

PORTLAND HARBOR HOTEL $$$-$$$$
468 Fore St., Portland
(207) 775-9090 or (888) 798-9090
www.portlandharborhotel.com
Right smack-dab in the middle of the Old Port, the Portland Harbor Hotel has an enviable location, and for the most part it makes good use of it. Relatively luxurious by Portland's standards, the hotel's rooms overlook Casco Bay, the city's streets, or its own garden; they come as deluxe single units or two-room suites; and they have amenities aplenty—concierge service, Wi-Fi, nightly turndown, granite bathrooms with their own sound systems and European-style showers, plush robes, two TVs in some rooms, and hot tubs. The lobby has a nice fireplace, and the courtyard area is a pleasant spot to sit and eat or read. The dining room, Eve's, is well regarded; its chef was Maine Restaurant Association chef of the year in 2006. The place has a corporate feel to it, but the setting and amenities are hard to argue with and it's the only four-diamond hotel in town.

PORTLAND REGENCY HOTEL $$$-$$$$
20 Milk St., Portland
(207) 774-4200 or (800) 727-3436
www.theregency.com
Once the default downtown hotel in Portland, the Regency now has a lot of competition. (Though it will probably always have its partisans for its location and many amenities.) Housed in an 1895 armory right in the Old Port, 2 blocks from the waterfront, the hotel has 95 rooms. After serving for more than half a century as a place of munitions (trouble was brewing with Cuba when it was built) and municipal uses, it opened in 1987 as a hotel to complement the newly revitalized Old Port. It pretty much functions as an urban hotel should, with every convenience you could want (except windows in some rooms). There is a dining room that serves all three meals, as well as a fully equipped gym and spa, and valet service. Local phone calls are free, newspapers complimentary, and every room has air-conditioning and a minibar. Shuttles are available to whisk you across the city, so there are no parking hassles, and service is generally pretty good.

FREEPORT

BEST WESTERN FREEPORT INN $$
Route 1, Freeport
(207) 865-3106 or (800) 99VALUE
www.freeportinn.com
This place always looks so appealing to travelers motoring up I–95, sitting on a hill overlooking the tidal Cousins River. And it is, with 25 acres to wander, a nice pool, a great little on-site cafe, and rental canoes to explore the river and salt marsh. More motel than inn, it's now a Best Western property and features 80 rooms, which have been spruced up lately, and they're plenty

comfortable, with private baths, cable TV, air-conditioning, phones, Wi-Fi—some even have water views. Just across the river is the Topside Building, which is quiet and offers even better views and easy access to the Muddy Rudder, a popular local eatery. Pets are allowed in many rooms, and there's a kids' play area outside, which makes the place a nice choice for families. The on-site Freeport Cafe has its own following, serving breakfast all day, and the shops of Freeport are moments away up Route 1. Open all year.

HARRASEEKET INN $$$$
162 Main St., Freeport
(207) 865-9377 or (800) 342-6423
www.harraseeketinn.com

CondeNast Traveler named this old downtown beauty to its Top 700 places to stay in the world, and anyone who likes shopping will certainly agree. It's but 2 blocks to L.L. Bean and the center of outletville (you could even carry heavy shopping bags that far). Actually, anyone who likes classic comforts and appreciates good taste and country inns will feel comfortable in this Federal-style hostelry. There are 84 rooms in all—as well as nine town houses designed for longer stays—and they are nicely appointed with details like actual antiques and canopy beds, cable TV, and Wi-Fi, as well as fireplaces and Jacuzzis and wet bars in some rooms. Other amenities include an attractive pool and two nice dining rooms—the elegant formal room with its white linens and Windsor chairs, where you can get one of the best brunches in the state on Sundays, and the Broad Arrow Tavern, a more casual place decked out like a North Woods lodge, complete with snowshoes and an overhead canoe. The place even hosts guest speakers. It is run by the Gray family, and they do a bang-up job.

KENDALL TAVERN BED & BREAKFAST $$-$$$
213 Main St., Freeport
(207) 865-1338 or (800) 341-9572
www.kendalltavern.com

A pretty yellow farmhouse with a fine porch, restored barn, and acreage to wander, this 200-year-old place is within walking distance of downtown Freeport but feels more like a country inn. There are seven rooms inside, each tastefully done with warm colors, sitting chairs, quilts, and, in some cases, four-poster beds. Fireplaces warm the parlors, where you can set up with a book or simply relax on the porch.

MAINE IDYLL MOTOR COURT $
1411 Route 1, Freeport
(207) 865-4201
www.maineidyll.com

Visible from I-95, this complex of 20 white cottages is very evocative, harking back to the motor courts of the 1950s. Very cute little clapboard-sided camps with wood-paneled interiors, they are set in a grove of trees, providing shade and atmosphere. They can accommodate couples or families and, despite their antique look, they have modern baths, color TV, and kitchenettes. Outside are play sets, picnic tables, and some trails through the woods. Pets are welcome. Rates are truly amazing for a place with such character just a few miles north of downtown. Open May to October.

MIDCOAST

Brunswick and Surrounding Area

BRUNSWICK BED AND BREAKFAST $$-$$$
165 Park Row, Brunswick
(207) 729-4914 or (800) 299-4914
www.brunswickbnb.com

The town green in Brunswick has always been one of the community's best attributes, wide open and lined with graceful historic homes. This picket-fence beauty is one of them. It's got a nice location, within walking distance of Maine Street and everything downtown and Bowdoin College in the other direction. There are 15 guest rooms from which to choose, and they all have little extras like terry robes in the private baths, desks with wireless Internet access, and quilts atop the beds. The suites are private and make for nice longer stays. The porch out front is what every porch should look like, and the fresh flowers at breakfast are a nice touch. The innkeepers have added a new wine bar, the Cygnet Lounge, which could be a plus or a minus, depending on your preferences. Whatever they're doing, they're doing it right—they won Midcoast Maine's best bed and breakfast award from Market Surveys America in 2008.

THE PARKWOOD INN $$-$$$$
Route 24, Cooks Corner, Brunswick
(207) 725-5251 or (800) 349-7181
www.parkwoodinn.com
This big white modern box of a place likes to bill itself as Brunswick's Crown Jewel, which is a bit of a stretch, but it's got 68 perfectly acceptable guest rooms. These rooms are a step up from your average motel quarters and have Jacuzzis and fireplaces in some cases, as well as large TVs with cable, fridges, Wi-Fi, and complimentary morning copies of *USA Today*. The suites have a bit more space to them, divided up in some cases, and have microwaves. There's also an indoor heated pool and fitness center for your use.

THE CAPTAIN'S WATCH $$-$$$
Bed and Breakfast and Sail Charter
926 Cundy's Harbor Rd., Harpswell
(207) 725-0979
On the New Meadows River, Cundy's Harbor is a classic fishing village, right in the middle of the Midcoast but away from all the bustle. From the harbor you can see this stunning old Greek Revival home, up a rise with its cupola towering over nearby homes. The cupola is only one of the fine features of the place (two guest rooms have access), which dates back to 1862. Another nice one is the *Symbion*, the house sloop, available to take you out on the water. The rooms have private baths and are in keeping with the rest of the house with their antiques and quilts, and all have water views. Breakfast can be enjoyed in the formal dining room or on a tray outside. The Captain's Watch is a fine old place in a spectacular setting.

LITTLE ISLAND MOTEL $$
44 Little Island Rd., Orrs Island
(207) 833-2392
www.littleislandmotel.com
On its own two-acre peninsula, this small motel has nine rooms and a fantastic setting. Each unit has a TV and is comfortably outfitted with pine paneling and plaid bedspreads. Guests can make use of bikes and the motel's boats and private dock for splashing around offshore. There's even a little beach. Rates include the buffet-style breakfast.

THE LOG CABIN: AN ISLAND INN $$-$$$$
Bailey Island
(207) 833-5546
www.logcabin-maine.com
Part of the fun here is simply selecting a room—you can check out pictures on the Web. The variety among the nine guest quarters at this rustic retreat is cool, going from fairly modern-feeling spaces with big bay windows overlooking Casco Bay to funky retro rooms like the Wiseman where you can lie on the bed and look up at the knotty pine rafters. You could be comfortable and content in any one of them, and the amenities here are plentiful—bay vistas are common, and all have private baths, TVs, phones, and decks. Some have woodstoves, some Jacuzzis, and four have either a full kitchen or a kitchenette. An outdoor pool with views of the bay is available for dipping. Breakfast is included and is served in the dining room from 8 to 9:30 a.m. from a set menu—juice, coffee, tea, fresh fruit, pastries, and an egg dish or French toast or pancakes. Dinner, which is not included, happens between 6 and 7 p.m.; it's a surf-and-turf affair with a full bar.

Other Accommodations in the Brunswick Area

A nice 19th-century Federal-style B&B, the **Black Lantern** (57 Elm Street, Topsham; 207-725-4165 or 888-306-4165; www.blacklanternbandb.com) gets you up close to Topsham's pretty, historic district. The **Middle Bay Farm Bed and Breakfast** (287 Pennellville Road, Brunswick; 207-373-

1375; www.middlebayfarm.com) dates to the 1830s and has four guest rooms and a cottage with six more rooms on the bay. The **Driftwood Inn and Cottages,** are old-style cottages, simple and shingled, with exceptional views (Bailey Island; 207-833-5461; www.thedriftwoodinnmaine.com). The **Harpswell Inn** (108 Lookout Point Road, Harpswell; 207-833-5509 or 800–843-5509; www.harpswellinn.com) is a three-story inn dating to 1761 with 12 guest rooms and suites.

Bath and Surrounding Area

BENJAMIN F. PACKARD
HOUSE BED AND BREAKFAST $–$$
45 Pearl St., Bath
(207) 443-6004 or (866) 361-6004
www.mainecoast.com/packardhouse

A sea captain's home on a quiet side street, the Packard House is a Georgian mansion built in 1790. The Kennebec River is only a block away. The inn has three large rooms and one suite available, and each has a private bath. The Garden Suite has a sitting room and a pullout queen-size bed for more sleeping space. No children under age 10. Rates include a full breakfast. There's a two-night minimum stay required in season. Open year-round.

FAIRHAVEN INN $–$$
188 North Bath Rd., Bath
(207) 443-4391 or (888) 443-4391
www.mainecoast.com/fairhaveninn

Unlike most of the other bed-and-breakfasts in Bath, the Fairhaven is not downtown. Rather it's about a half mile out in the Kennebec riverside North Bath area. This location is great for visitors who prefer quietude and a bit of acreage in their hostelry. The Fairhaven sits on 16 acres of meadows and woods, with views of the river, and it's a rambling old farmhouse with weathering shingles. Inside are eight guest rooms, most of which have private baths, and a couple of common rooms perfect for lounging. Golfers will find the Bath Country Club nearby and the grounds are pleasant to wander.

GREY HAVENS $$–$$$
Seguinland Rd., Georgetown
(207) 371-2616 or (800) 431-2316
www.greyhavens.com

This is the place you picture in your mind's eye when you think of a Maine vacation. A shingle-style castle with turrets on either end, it was built in 1904 by the man who gave the people of Maine the land for Reid State Park, which is just up the road. The vistas from its wraparound porch are overwhelming, staring out across Sheepscot Bay. The owners of the place have left the old inn as untouched as possible, while making it comfortable for the guests of today, and it is a rustic beauty, from the rockers on the porch to the fieldstone fireplace to the simple, whitewashed wood-paneled rooms. All of the 18 rooms have a private bath (which wasn't the case when this place opened with 26 rooms and two baths). Four of them are in turrets with 180-degree views that are just stunning, and the lobby and sitting area downstairs hark back to simpler times. Not where you want to come if you like your vacations to be all TVs and bustle, Grey Havens is an escape from all of the annoyances of modern life, a restful spot to relax and refresh. Read a book in an Adirondack chair on the lawn, play a board game, paddle the canoe out to a nature preserve for a walk, or head on down to the beach. The inn is open from May through October. No children under age 12.

THE INN AT BATH $$–$$$
969 Washington St., Bath
(207) 443-4294 or (800) 423-0964
www.innatbath.com

Bath's Washington Street is a graceful old avenue, and it's thanks to houses like this 1810 Greek Revival beauty. The City of Ships is filled with fine sea captains' homes, and the area surrounding the inn is rich with them. The inn itself has eight rooms and a suite, each individually decorated and some—like the yellow Sail Loft, with its four-poster, and the Lavender Room, with its canopied full-size bed—that feel more historic than others. All have private baths, cable TV, Wi-Fi, and air-conditioning. Some have fireplaces, Jacuzzis, writing desks, and outdoor entrances. There are various specials and packages to choose from.

ROCK GARDENS INN AND COTTAGES $$$-$$$$
Sebasco Estates
(207) 389-1339
www.rockgardensinn.com
On its own peninsula, the Rock Gardens complex has 10 cottages with living rooms, fireplaces, private baths, and porches—just about everything you need to enjoy a spell on the shore. Decorating is kept simple and comfortable like Grandma's cottage. The main inn has an airy dining room, a living room with a fireplace, and a TV room, and on the grounds are a heated swimming pool and access to golf and tennis. A clambake on the water's edge is a Rock Gardens tradition.

SEBASCO HARBOR RESORT $$$$
Route 217, Sebasco Estates
(207) 389-1161 or (800) 225-3819
www.sebasco.com
With its own tour boat, golf course, kayak and sailing lessons, fishing, evening theater—indeed, its own village—Sebasco is a full-service resort unlike most others in Maine. There are umpteen rooms here on the 550-acre compound, and they are divided into three types. There are 37 rooms in the Main Lodge, which, with its rocking chairs and screened-in porch, has an old-fashioned feel. Views here are of the village, the golf course, and Wat Tuh Lake (no lie). The four-story lighthouse, an unofficial sentinel built as a beacon for boaters by the resort's original owner, has 10 more rooms, most with a grand prospect out over Casco Bay (those who don't get a view with their room can take a peek out the cupola-like observation room at the top of the building). Then there are the 22 cottages, scattered here and there, many with kitchenettes and fireplaces and with as many as 10 bedrooms available, and the deluxe new Harbor Village Suites. Some cottages are sequestered away for privacy. There are packages available to take advantage of the three dining rooms.

SQUIRE TARBOX $$-$$$
1181 Main Rd., Westport
(207) 882-7693 or (800) 818-0626
www.squiretarboxinn.com
Many inns and B&Bs like to use the word farm in their name to convey a bucolic image, but this Federal-style farmhouse, built in 1763, is the real deal, with dairy goats, laying hens, and other barnyard animals on a peaceful setting on Westport Island between Woolwich and Wiscasset. The 11 guest rooms are country comfortable, with their fireplaces, antique beds, and braided rugs, and the grounds are very nice to stroll, with paths that lead down to a bend in a saltwater river. Mountain bikes and a rowboat are available for adventuring, and the dining room is first-rate. The shops and restaurants of Wiscasset, Boothbay Harbor, Bath, and Damariscotta are all easy drives away. Open from April through December.

Wiscasset and Surrounding Area
MARSTON HOUSE $$
Main St. at Middle St., Wiscasset
(207) 882-6010
www.marstonhouse.com
Mainers like to joke that every other person who visits the coast wants to return and open a bed-and-breakfast—and the rest want to open antiques shops. At the Marston House, the proprietors apparently couldn't decide between the two, so they've done both. In the front of their Main Street building is an antiques shop, specializing in smalls, folk art, painted furniture, and textiles. Upstairs are two very fine guest rooms with fireplaces, queen-size beds, private baths, and private entrances. Sunlit and airy, they're as tasteful as the goods in the store. Breakfast can be served in room if you like. Rates are quite reasonable—extremely reasonable, really, for such a nice place. Open from early May through October.

SNOW SQUALL $$-$$$
Route 1 and Bradford Rd., Wiscasset
(207) 882-6892
www.snowsquallinn.com
The theme of clipper ships carries through this

1850s-era inn—the *Snow Squall* was a famous clipper, and each of the seven guest rooms is named after other vessels. All of the rooms have private baths and phones. Two have working fireplaces, all but one are air-conditioned, and a few have private decks. They're all well appointed, featuring a king- or queen-size bed, and the suites have accommodations fit for families. Enjoy a spell in a rocker on the porch or in one of the cushy chairs in front of the fire in the living room. Rates include a full breakfast.

SHEEPSCOT HARBOUR VILLAGE AND RESORT $-$$$$
306 Eddy Rd., Edgecomb
(207) 882-6343 or (800) 437-5503
www.sheepscotriverinn.com

This plumb location on the edge of the Sheepscot just across the river from Wiscasset has seen all kinds of inns and restaurants come and go. This is the latest version and it's big and impressive, with a 13-room inn, a fleet of cottages, and a raft of condo-type hotel suites. Rooms in the inn have nice views out over their balconies, and they are equipped with all the modern amenities from air-conditioning to Wi-Fi to cable. Closer to the water's edge are the cottages, which are freshly shingled 1920s-era structures that have been rehabbed and would be comfortable for a week or more. Longer than that and you probably want a condo-style townhouse, which has a full kitchen and a living room overlooking the Sheepscot.

Boothbay Harbor and Surrounding Area

BOOTHBAY HARBOR INN $$-$$$
31 Atlantic Ave., Boothbay Harbor
(207) 633-6302 or (800) 533-6302
www.boothbayharborinn.com

A sprawling white inn right on the water, this full-service hotel dominates the quiet side. There are 60 rooms inside the blocky place, each with air-conditioning, color TV, and private bath. Most also have a balcony or patio that hangs right out over the water. The interior decorator should be

run out of town, but you can't beat the views from the private decks, some of which take in the harbor, some the whole waterfront. There are several levels of rooms—most are motel standard—and packages from which to choose. Windows on the Harbor Restaurant provides just that and serves up traditional New England fare with a small submenu of Caribbean cuisine, a nice treat.

HARBORAGE INN $-$$$
75 Townsend Ave., Boothbay Harbor
(207) 633-4640 or (800) 565-3742
www.harborageinn.com

Boothbay Harbor seems to have a corner on the B&B market. Every block there's another one. This 1869 colonial has been a guest house since the 1920s, making it one of the oldest inns in the harbor, if not the oldest. The water is right off the backyard, and the wraparound porch—just what you want—takes it all in. The rooms are decorated a la Laura Ashley, whose floral designs are either to your taste or not, and all of them have private baths. They also have their own discrete entrances from the porch, which is welcome if you value quiet and privacy. Some are one-room affairs, others suites. Try the Blueberry Bay Suite, which has wood paneling and wraparound windows that frame the bay. The harborfront hot tub is a hoot. New in 2007 were seven larger suites, each with a waterview.

SPRUCE POINT INN $$$-$$$$
Atlantic Ave., Boothbay Harbor
(207) 633-4152 or (800) 553-0289
www.sprucepointinn.com

Smart Money magazine named the Spruce Point Inn in Boothbay Harbor as one of the 12 best getaways—not in Maine, not in New England, but in the entire country. And, as gamblers know, you always have to follow the smart money. If budget is not a concern, this is the place to stay in the Boothbay area, perhaps even in the entire Midcoast. The gardens alone are incredible. The inn sits on its own 57-acre peninsula, and it's more of a resort than an inn, with the main building, condos, and little shingle-style cottages—each with various levels of luxuri-ousness—to choose from. This place began life as a 19th-century hunting and fishing lodge and expanded and added on until it reached its current 104-unit status. Every room has a private bath, private deck, fridge, and cable TV, and many also have a fireplace, whirlpool, and kitchenette. On the grounds there are almost too many amenities to list, from the expected pools (saltwater and heated freshwater), tennis courts, and fitness center to the neat touches like hammocks, a kids' program and play area, massage therapy, and a private pier. You can dine fancifully at the inn's award-winning for-mal dining room ("smart casual dress") or enjoy more relaxed fare at Bogie's Hide-away. Service, anywhere you go on the premises, is great, a Spruce Point hallmark. The inn is open from late May through mid-October. Get your reservations early because it tends to fill up fast.

LINEKIN BAY BED AND BREAKFAST $$
East Boothbay
(207) 633-9900 or (800) 596-7420
www.linekinbaybb.com

Former Lewiston cop Larry Brown and his wife, Marti Booth, are the gracious hosts of this fine old inn. The couple have painstakingly restored an 1878 white clapboard gem into a fine four-room B&B right on Linekin Bay in the quiet village of East Boothbay. They left the old floors but made sure each of their four rooms had a water view, private bath, fireplace, plush chairs, Wi-Fi and nice touches like stenciling and clawfoot tubs. Good muffins, too! One of the Boothbay area's excel-lent preserves is within easy walking distance across the street, and your hosts can steer you toward all of the famed resorts sites.

SHIP AHOY MOTEL $
Route 238, Southport
(207) 633-5222
www.shipahoymotel.com

A room on the waterfront in the Boothbay area with a private seaside deck for only $79? That's the story at this motel complex a few miles outside of Boothbay Harbor. The rooms may be typical motel fare, but they all have color TV, private bath, air-conditioning, access to the nice freshwater inground pool, and better still, a direct line to a quiet section of Southport waterfront where there is a dock from which you can fish or launch boats. Unbelievable, really. The Ship Ahoy campus has four motel options on it now, each with varying degrees of comfort, none of which costs more than $79, and some of which can be had for $49—and that's in high season. And the setting is truly spectacular.

NEWAGEN INN $$–$$$$
Route 27, Cape Newagen
(207) 633-5242 or (800) 654-5242
www.newagenseasideinn.com

Truly a breath of fresh air in the Boothbay area, the Newagen is like the grand hotels of yore—they call it "understated elegance," and it is all that: unpretentious, unfancy, but timeless and classic. This is the sort of place that the wealthy rusticators of Maine's golden age might have come to in the summer for a month or two. Set on a 20-acre, spruce-covered property at the tip of Southport Island, the inn has magnificent views of sea all around. Park yourself in one of the whitewashed Adirondack chairs overlooking the briny sea, and you may never want to leave. There are 30 guest rooms in all, with varying degrees of luxuriousness, as well as the option of staying in a cottage, which can be rented by the week. The amenities are so many that you could indeed stay for weeks and not even have to leave the property. They include a heated outdoor pool, an oceanside hot tub, tennis, boating, biking, nature trails, candlepin bowling, billiards and Ping-Pong, croquet and horseshoes, volleyball and badminton, a library of books, and those Adirondack chairs set before a sparkling Atlantic panorama. The dining room is very pleasant, with banks of windows lining the wall, and serves a broad range of well-prepared surf and turf. This is the stuff of a truly memorable vacation.

New Harbor and Pemaquid Point

BRADLEY INN $$$-$$$$
3063 Bristol Rd., New Harbor
(207) 677-2105 or (800) 942-5560
www.bradleyinn.com

An absolutely beautiful inn on Pemaquid Point, this rambling, 16-room, turn-of-the-20th-century hostelry has fine views and a variety of lodging options. Choose from among rooms in the main inn, with four-poster beds, period furnishings, views, and private baths; in the Carriage House Suite, which occupies an old barn; or in the Garden Cottage, with its fieldstone fireplace and screened-in porch. The dining room here is about as good as it gets in Maine, and the rooms are very well appointed.

HOTEL PEMAQUID $-$$$
3098 Bristol Rd., Pemaquid Point
(207) 677-2312
www.hotelpemaquid.com

This funky old place—all towers, veranda, and dormers—welcomed its first guests in 1888, and it's been keeping guest registers ever since (read them and it will be obvious people like the inn). Anyone with a strong arm can practically throw a stone at Pemaquid Light from the inn, even though the inn doesn't have water views of its own. No matter, it's a really fun venerable sort of place where you can just feel the happy ghosts of summers past. Neat decor—fieldstones and stained glass—and the rooms are comfortable, with private baths, and with cable TV in some cases. Accommodations range from cottages to suites to simple quarters with twin beds.

Newcastle

FLYING CLOUD BED AND
BREAKFAST $$-$$$
45 River Rd., Newcastle
(207) 563-2484
www.theflyingcloud.com

Once the home of sea captain George Washington Tukey, who set a world speed record in 1851 in his clipper, the *Flying Cloud*, this pretty white clapboard Greek Revival sits across the street from the Damariscotta River. The five guest rooms are named for the ports visited by Captain Tukey in his ship, and four of them have views out across the water (the other looks over the garden). All have private baths, and they are each tastefully appointed, with details like a claw-foot tub here, gas fireplace there, a four-poster bed, and pumpkin pine floors. The porch out front is delightful, and the screened-in breakfast area is a treat as well. Rates include the great breakfast.

NEWCASTLE INN $$$-$$$$
River Rd., Newcastle
(207) 563-5685
www.newcastleinn.com

With 15 rooms and suites, the Newcastle Inn sits right on the Damariscotta River with nice views back at the village of Damariscotta. The guest rooms are each uniquely decorated, many with antiques, lace curtains, canopied beds, and unusual touches, like the Victorian couch in the Seguin Island Room. Some have fireplaces, and all have private baths. Choose from options like Jacuzzis, private entrances, and queen- or king-size beds. Rates include breakfast.

Waldoboro

BLUE SKYE FARM $$
1708 Friendship Rd., Waldoboro
(207) 832-0300
www.blueskyefarm.com

One of the many architectural delights of the Friendship Road in Waldoboro, Blue Skye Farm is a distinctive Federal-style home built in 1775 and surrounded by acres of meadows. It is brimming with old details, from stenciling most likely done by the famed Moses Eaton to perfectly preserved rooms with aged fireplaces and quilts. Jan and Peter Davidson run the five-bedroom inn, and they have restored the historic charmer in loving fashion, saving the beams, the creaky floors, and period furniture (check out the four-posters), but tastefully blending in thoroughly modern comforts like private baths in four of six rooms. One-hundred acres are out the back door.

Tenants Harbor

EAST WIND INN $$–$$$$
Tenants Harbor
(207) 372-6320 or (800) 241-8439
www.eastwindinn.com

The porch at the East Wind alone is worth the price of a room. It's a fine wraparound veranda overlooking Tenants Harbor. You could happily spend days just taking it all in. The majority of the 22 rooms inside have private baths (all but six), and they are simply furnished but country inn comfortable with water views. Rates include full breakfast. The inn also has apartments and suites.

Port Clyde

OCEAN HOUSE $–$$
Port Clyde Rd., Port Clyde
(207) 372-6691 or (800) 269-6691
www.oceanhousehotel.com

It doesn't get much more charming than this venerable 1830s-era hotel. Port Clyde, of course, is one of the principal jumping-off points for trips out to Monhegan, and people often stay in one of the 10 rooms here in order to easily catch the early boat. The rooms are comfortably old-fashioned, with their lace curtains and mirror-topped dressers, and many have views out onto the water.

Monhegan Island

ISLAND INN $$$$
Monhegan Island
(207) 596-0371
www.islandinnmonhegan.com

An impressive shingle-style castle of a place, this gray beauty dates back to 1816, or at least part of it does. It sits on a rise lording over Monhegan Harbor and Manana Island, and it has two types of accommodations inside. There are 34 rooms and suites, some of which share baths, and the sunlit-rooms have nice painted floors, cushy wicker chairs, and down comforters for those cool September evenings. The inn's dining room is arguably the island's best, and its wraparound porches and Adirondack chairs are fine places to while away a day.

MONHEGAN HOUSE $–$$
Monhegan Island
(207) 594-7983
www.monheganhouse.com

Monhegan has a handful of places to overnight, and they all have different things to recommend them. The Monhegan House is just plain classic, the oldest continuously operated place on the island, dating back to the 1870s and with 28 rooms on its four floors. Everything about the boxy old inn is comfortable, from the long porch out front, topped with rockers, to the spare, quiet, breezy rooms. The floors creak underfoot, the bedspreads are the white nubby ones your grandmother used to use, and there are big leather chairs near the fieldstone fireplace in the lobby for lounging. Some people are bothered by the fact that bathrooms are shared—all of the showers and toilets are grouped together on the second floor—but it is very clean and almost has a summer camp vibe, making it a fun adventure. Right near the center of the village, the porch has traditionally been a center of activity on the island, so spend any time on it and you'll quickly feel tuned in to local goings-on. Rates include breakfast. Open from mid-May to mid-October.

TRAILING YEW $$
Lobster Cove Rd., Monhegan Island
(207) 596-6194
www.trailingyew.com

If you had an eccentric grandmother with an island cottage, it might feel a bit like the nifty Trailing Yew. The simplest and least formal of all of the island's lodging options, the place is actually a compound of four weathered cottages clustered around a hilly courtyard. There are 35 rooms to choose from, and electricity is scarce—just turn on the kerosene lamp. Baths are shared, and only some have electricity. Dining here is an experience, with meals served family style so that you're literally rubbing elbows with strangers. But everyone is having such a good time, it's a pleasure. Not fancy, this place, but fun. Don't forget your flashlight.

Spruce Head

CRAIGNAIR INN $–$$

Clark Island Rd., Spruce Head
(207) 594-7644 or (800) 320-9997
www.craignair.com

In the 1920s, Clark Island was a bustling place with stonecutters carving granite out of the earth to be used in the Brooklyn Battery tunnel and the Library of Congress. This inn dates back to 1928, when it was built to house these quarry workers, and it became an inn in the 1940s. There are 28 guest rooms, some of which have private baths and most of which have jaw-dropping views of the island and the sea. People love to walk Clark Island, and there are trails all through it to explore. Check out the old quarries or hike to the far side where there are nice views out to the islands of Two Bush Channel. Work up an appetite and take yourself to the dining room—you won't be disappointed. Open year-round.

Vinalhaven

TIDEWATER MOTEL $$

12 Main St., Carvers Harbor, Vinalhaven
(207) 863-4618
www.tidewatermotel.com

You can certainly watch the tide if you stay at this thirtysomething Vinalhaven motel. Built in 1970 by the parents of current owner Phil Crossman, the place is just feet above the ocean. The rooms are nicer than a typical motel, and have decks that extend right out over the water, and if you leave your windows open, you can let the ocean's swells sway you to sleep. You'll be awakened by the activity that keeps the working harbor alive, and you'll be able to see most of the goings-on right from your room. Some rooms have kitchens, all have cable TV and a private bath. The Tidewater is open year-round, and the owners also offer a beautiful cottage right on Carver's Pond for a more private stay.

Rockland

BERRY MANOR INN $$$$

81 Talbot Ave., Rockland
(207) 596-7696 or (800) 774-5692
www.berrymanorinn.com

On a quiet residential side street, the Berry Manor Inn is one impressive place—it's one of the finest old homes in all of Rock City and arguably the place to stay. (It is also the only historic inn in the Midcoast to receive a Four-Diamond rating from AAA and was named one of the top 10 B&Bs and inns in the country by TripAdvisor in 2008.) Built in 1898 as a giant Victorian wedding gift, the inn is quite luxurious by local standards, with a dozen large rooms split between the original home and the adjacent carriage house. All but one of the guest chambers has its own fireplace, each has a private bath, and they are furnished and decorated in grand style with all sorts of fancy flourishes like sleigh beds, four-posters, and antique rockers. But not at the expense of comfort: Owners Cheryl Michaelsen and Mike LaPosta, exactly the kind of B&B hosts you want, made sure to incorporate such contemporary necessities as stuffed chairs and cozy robes. Downtown Rockland and its great restaurants are only a few blocks away—but you might not want to ever leave your room. Great reduced rates in the off-season.

LIMEROCK INN $$–$$$

96 Limerock St., Rockland
(207) 594-2257 or (800) 546-3762
www.limerockinn.com

In a residential neighborhood within walking distance of downtown, the Limerock is a lime-colored Queen Anne mansion with eight very comfortable guest rooms inside. Each has a private bath, some have whirlpools (or European soaking tubs), one has a fireplace. Guests are welcome to enjoy the formal parlor and the porch with its wicker chairs. Rates include a well-regarded breakfast. Be sure to visit the gardens.

NAVIGATOR MOTOR INN $-$$
520 Main St., Rockland
(207) 594-2131 or (800) 545-8026
www.navigatorinn.com

A Rockland mainstay for more than three decades, the Navigator is just across the street from the Maine State Ferry Terminal, It is more motel than inn, with 86 rooms and suites inside, as well as a bar that's a favorite watering hole among locals. Rooms are fairly standard motel fare, and many have a balcony and a fridge as well as cable TV and private bath.

OLD GRANITE INN $$-$$$
546 Main St., Rockland
(207) 594-9036 or (800) 386-9036
www.oldgraniteinn.com

This place is indeed old and made of granite, and it has been lending a bit of class to the north end of Rockland's Main Street since the mid-19th century. A Federal-style building, it's made of stone quarried a few towns over in St. George, and it sits right across from the ferry terminal. There are eight rooms, each with its own wallpaper pattern and private bath; some of those on the second floor have great views out to the bay. A little-known gem in Rock City.

Rockport

SAMOSET RESORT $$-$$$$
220 Warrenton St., Rockport
(207) 594-2511 or (800) 341-1650
www.samoset.com

The Samoset sprawls across 230 acres right on Rockland Harbor and features 178 guest rooms and suites. Each has a marble bath, big TV, Wi-Fi, coffeemaker, and balcony or terrace overlooking the sea or the Samoset's golf course. As of 2008, these chambers were undergoing a $3 million makeover, including new moldings, fixtures, lighting, window treatments, and down bedding, and the first three floors are done. A full-service place, the Samoset has a fitness center, two pools (one indoor, one outdoor), basketball and tennis courts, massage, a formal dining room, and a couple of less fancy options, the Breakwater Cafe

and the Clubhouse Grille. You can sleep in and get breakfast delivered to your door or have a candlelit dinner served on your terrace.

Camden

THE BELMONT $$-$$$
6 Belmont St., Camden
(207) 236-8053 or (800) 238-8053
www.thebelmontinn.com

A charming Edwardian inn on a quiet side street in Camden, this place has been providing lodging since the 1920s. Its six guest rooms are just perfect, with nice amenities like gas stoves, window seats, and views of Mount Battie. Try the Jo Spiller room with its big mahogany sleigh bed, loveseat, and Oriental rug. Rates include a full breakfast.

CAMDEN HARBOUR INN $$$-$$$$
83 Bayview St., Camden
(207) 236-4200 or (800) 236-4266
www.camdenharbourinn.com

Built in 1874, this big white inn commands one of the best views in town, set on a hill looking out across both the harbor and the mountains. There are 14 guest rooms, three suites, and a junior suite here on three floors, and they're very tastefully furnished. Many feature fireplaces, patios, or decks, and all have private baths, TVs, phones, and dataports. The porch is instantly relaxing and the views to the bay and the mountains are extraordinary. Natalie's, the inn's French dining room, is an area favorite.

HARTSTONE INN $$-$$$$
41 Elm St., Camden
(207) 236-4259 or (800) 788-4823
www.hartstoneinn.com

The dining room here draws raves, and the same attention to detail that makes it exceptional goes into the inn's 14 rooms. Each of the guest quarters in the 1835 Mansard-style showplace is air-conditioned and furnished with heirlooms and antiques. Claw-foot tubs, down comforters, fresh flowers, rich colors, woodstoves, and chocolate truffles all make it a step up from your average B&B. Located a half block from the Hartstone proper is the new Hideway, seven more rooms in a neighboring white clapboard home. Breakfast is good, and the afternoon cookies are nice. Spring for a package that includes dinner. Open year-round.

LORD CAMDEN INN $$$-$$$$
24 Main St., Camden
(207) 236-4325 or (800) 336-4325
www.lordcamdeninn.com

This downtown favorite is a unique place with four floors of rooms upstairs above Main Street storefronts. It manages to do a nice job, though, of making people comfortable in nontraditional rooms among the hurly-burly. All rooms have air-conditioning, private baths, phones, and Wi-Fi, and several have big balconies. Whichever one you choose, you can give yourself an instant upgrade by laying down a bit more scratch for the "in-room extras," which are gift baskets. (Wine and cheese, spa essentials, and champagne and chocolate are the themes for the $59–75 goodies.) You can't get any closer to downtown.

MAINE STAY $$-$$$
22 High St., Camden
(207) 236-9636
www.camdenmainestay.com

The Maine Stay has been the very definition of a bed-and-breakfast in Camden for years. The Greek Revival house is in relatively new hands now, but it remains a gem, the second oldest of all of the 66 homes in its National Register of Historic Places district. Built in 1802, the inn has eight bright and airy rooms, each with its own bath and decorating scheme. The Smith-Robson Room has an antique brass bed and was named in honor of the inn's previous owners, who became well known for their hospitality. The two acres of grounds, with their blooming gardens, are pleasant to wander, and it's an easy walk into town. You'd have a hard time finding a better B&B for miles.

NORUMBEGA INN $$$$
63 High St., Camden
(207) 236-4646
www.norumbegainn.com

Europeans traveled up the Penobscot River in the 16th century looking for the mythical city of Norumbega, a place of gold and luxury. Today travelers drive up Route 1 along Penobscot Bay to lay their heads at Norumbega, where they'll certainly pay a lot. The original owner of this big stone showplace traveled throughout Europe researching castle design, and he incorporated his favorite elements. There's no question that the 1886 inn is striking and beautiful, but its 12 rooms and suites are awfully expensive for what you get. Still, it's pleasant just to get inside this landmark to see the fancy design. Guest quarters have private baths, TVs, and phones, and they come furnished with antiques. A full breakfast is included in the price of the room.

WHITEHALL INN $$-$$$
52 High St., Camden
(207) 236-3391 or (800) 789-6565
www.whitehall-inn.com

The classic old Whitehall has gotten a lot of mileage out of the fact that Edna St. Vincent Millay got her start here, reading her famous poem "Renascence" to appreciative guests. That's all very nice, but there's plenty more to like about the inn, which dates back to 1834. Start with the porch, a graceful veranda topped by rockers. Then there is the dining room—an underappreciated treat—and the rooms, which are simple in the best, most relaxing way with wainscoting and wooden floors. No noise, no ringing phones, just peaceful and pleasant spaces with antiques, grandfather clocks, clawfoot tubs, and lace curtains that dance with the afternoon sea breeze. Some rooms have shared or "hall" baths. Make sure you get what you want. Tariffs—and they're tariffs here, not rates, mind you—are fairly reasonable.

Lincolnville

CEDARHOLM GARDEN BAY INN $$$$
Route 1, Lincolnville
(207) 236-3886 or (800) 5401-3886
www.cedarholm.com

There are a lot of cottage villages along the coast, and this is the cottage villager's cottage village. No pine-paneled roughing it here—these are fairly luxurious little affairs with whirlpools, tile showers, stone fireplaces, waterside desks, and wet bars. A romantic little byway takes you from Route 1 down to the shore, and the gardens on the 16-acre property are something to see—you could get lost in them. For privacy, views, and uniqueness, you can't beat these cute cottages, and they've won accolades from the national media again and again.

SPOUTER INN $$-$$$
Route 1, Lincolnville
(207) 789-5171 or (866) 787-5171
www.spouterinn.com

Built in 1892, this expansive inn has been lovingly restored. Across the street from Lincolnville Beach and Penobscot Bay, it has seven rooms, each of which provides a good look at the water. They're well appointed and spotless, with braided rugs and four posters and exposed beams, and each has a private bath. Some have fireplaces, and the Captain's Quarters has a Jacuzzi, too. Very pleasant, and all of the restaurants and shops of Lincolnville—and the Islesboro ferry—are handy by. Fantastic bargain for the quality and location.

Belfast and Surrounding Area

HARBOR VIEW HOUSE $$
213 High St., Belfast
(207) 338-3811 or (877) 393-3811
www.harborviewhouse.com

Formerly the site of one of Belfast's better galleries, this antique Federal sits high atop Primrose Hill with views out toward Belfast Bay. Renovated with utmost care, the inn has pumpkin pine floors, pretty fanlights, 10-foot ceilings, and six quiet guest rooms with fireplaces, private baths, and down comforters. Guests are welcome to use the back deck with its glorious prospect, and downtown Belfast is just down the hill.

THE WHITE HOUSE $$-$$$
1 Church St., Belfast
(207) 338-1901 or (888) 290-1901
www.mainebb.com

It would be understandable if this Greek Revival mansion were so named simply because it's white and undeniably imposing. But it's actually the James P. White House, and takes its title from the man who built it more than a century and a half ago. A Belfast landmark that everyone who passes by wonders at, it's just as impressive on the inside, with marble fireplaces and ornate molding, brocades and canopies. Rooms have private baths and phones. In a town of architectural distinction this place is distinct.

Other Belfast Accommodations

The **Belfast Harbor Inn** (91 Searsport Avenue; 207-338-2740 or 800–545-8576; www.belfastharborinn.com) is a modern motel on six oceanfront acres in East Belfast. The **Alden House** (63 Church Street; 207-338-2151 or 877-337-8151; www.thealdenhouse.com) is an 1840 brick mansion with seven B&B rooms not far from downtown.

Blue Hill and Castine

THE BARNCASTLE HOTEL $$$
125 South St., Blue Hill
(207) 374-2330
www.barn-castle.com

The name of this fantastic hostelry is really right on—a castle, with all that implies, and a barn, with the history and rural nature that conjures. Huge and truly impressive. Guest chambers like the Turret Room 3—with its arcing windows and tin ceilings and are just not found here. Very very nice.

CASTINE INN $$-$$$$
Main St., Castine
(207) 326-4365
www.castineinn.com

Gardens and water views are two of the attractions at this 1898 inn a block from the harbor.

There are 17 guest rooms inside the big old place, on the second and third floors. Each has a private bath and is simply furnished. Many have views of Penobscot Bay or the inn's own gardens. Pretty porches out front. And the dining room is one of the best in Castine. Breakfast is included in the price of the room. Open from May through October. No children under eight.

PENTAGOET INN $-$$$

26 Main St., Castine
(207) 326-8616 or (800) 845-1701
www.pentagoet.com

Castine's oldest summer hotel, built in 1894, the Pentagoet is a gracious place, with its turret, window box, and bunting. The 1894 Queen Anne–style mansion has 16 rooms inside, each with nicely aged furnishings, vintage lithographs, a big headboard, and a private bath. Dining here is good as well. Rates include breakfast and use of the inn's bikes to see what there is to see in this historic town.

Deer Isle–Stonington

PILGRIM'S INN $$-$$$

Main St., Deer Isle
(207) 348-6615 or (888) 778-7505
www.pilgrimsinn.com

A gambrel-roofed barn of a place centrally located in Deer Isle village, this 1793 inn is on the National Register. Rooms are comfortable and commodious, and they offer water views, private baths, and their own sitting areas. Each has a different decor scheme, but they typically have Oriental or braided rugs on hardwood floors and pretty, old antique beds, and Deer Isle granite, of course. The inn also has three two-bedroom cottages with kitchenettes and private decks. Open mid-May through mid-October. The inn's dining room, the Whale's Rib Tavern, is a favorite.

GOOSE COVE LODGE $$-$$$

Goose Cove Rd., Sunset
(207) 348-2508 or (800) 728-1963
www.thecockatoorestaurant.com/lodge.asp

How did we love Goose Cove Lodge? Let us count the ways. On Goose Cove near Stonington, the lodge sat on 22 stupendously beautiful acres of woods and waterfront, and it had a real natural bent. Guided nature walks, mountain biking, kayaking, stargazing parties, bird-watching, and more were an everyday part of life. The gray-shingled place changed hands recently and it remains to be seen if it will continue its wonderful ways.

BOYCE'S MOTEL $-$$

Main St., Stonington
(207) 367-2421 or (800) 224-2421
www.boycesmotel.com

Comfortable rooms with access to a deck overlooking Stonington Harbor are offered at this circa 1960s motel. Guest quarters are equipped with cable TV, fridges, phones, air-conditioning, and in-room coffee, and all have private baths. Some even have kitchenettes and private decks, and there are apartments available as well with fine views of one of Maine's most picturesque harbors. Everything in town is within walking distance. No matter where you stay, you can use the motel's sun-deck and stare at the harbor to your heart's content—and that alone is worth the price of admission. Rates are eminently reasonable.

INN ON THE HARBOR $-$$$

Main St., Stonington
(207) 367-2420 or (800) 942-2420
www.innontheharbor.com

The name says it all at this attractive downtown hostelry—it's on the harbor to such a degree that the water actually passes under some rooms. Long known as the Captain's Quarters, the inn was purchased and revamped in the 1990s, and it's now a very pleasant place to stay on Deer Isle Thorofare. More of a compound than anything else, the place is made of a few buildings from the 1880s—a mansard-roofed classic with a few adjacent storefronts—joined by walkways and decks. There are 13 rooms in all, 10 of which face the waterfront, with its working boats and all its islands, and many have private entrances. Named after vessels in the state's windjammer fleet (the

Mary Day, for example, which has overstuffed chairs, a king-size bed, and a large bath), these quarters are comfortable and homey without a lot of froufrou, and there are a lot of thoughtful touches, from binoculars with which to watch the activities in the harbor to fresh flowers. A breakfast of fruit and muffins comes with the room fee.

ACADIA AREA

Bar Harbor and Surrounding Area

BALANCE ROCK INN $$-$$$$
21 Albert Meadow, Bar Harbor
(207) 288-2610 or (800) 753-0494
www.barharborvacations.com
Few hostelries survived the great fire of 1947, which swept through Bar Harbor, leveling everything in its path. This is why the Balance Rock Inn is such a pleasure. Built in 1903 by a Scottish rail baron, the century-old place continues the area's genteel tradition. You might even feel like a rusticator. An easy walk to town, the shingle-style manse has a country-estate feel, with pretty lawns, privacy, and quietude. The Shore Path, a spectacular seaside footpath, curls around the grounds. Frenchman Bay seems out every window. The rooms are comfortable and, although decorated with reproduction wallpaper and furnishings, they have the amenities of today with private baths, decks, whirlpools, and phones.

BAR HARBOR INN $$$-$$$$
Newport Dr., Bar Harbor .
(207) 288-3351 or (800) 248-3351
www.barharborinn.com
It would be hard for the Bar Harbor Inn to get much closer to the harbor without falling in. The eight-acre compound is right on Frenchman Bay, and many of its rooms have balconies with a real good look at it. Because the inn is so huge, with more than 150 units in three buildings, there are a wide variety of rooms to choose from. But all have, at the very least, air-conditioning, free HBO, and Wi-Fi. They're very comfortable without being posh. The other amenities are many, from

the spa treatments to the fitness room to the heated outdoor pool.

LEDGELAWN $$-$$$$
66 Mount Desert St., Bar Harbor
(207) 288-4596 or (800) 274-5334
www.ledgelawninn.com
One of Bar Harbor's last turn-of-the-20th-century summer cottages (the others burned), this red-shingled house has 23 rooms inside its main section and another 12 in an added carriage house. All rooms have private baths (some with whirlpools), some have saunas, and many have fireplaces. Open mid-May through October.

MIRA MONTE INN $$-$$$$
69 Mount Desert St., Bar Harbor
(207) 288-4263 or (800) 553-5109
www.miramonte.com
The 13 rooms at this 1864 estate may have a bit much froufrou, but the gardens are pretty amazing and have been featured on Home and Garden TV and in national magazines. Make sure you get out into them. Room rates on the high end of the range are for those chambers with whirlpools, fireplaces, and private decks. The breakfast, served from 8 to 10 a.m., seems unending.

THE TIDES $$$$
119 West St., Bar Harbor
(207) 288-4968
www.barharbortides.com
There are only three suites and one room in this 1887 Greek Revival home, but that allows for a lot of attention to detail. Every unit has a fantastic view of the bay, private bath, fireplace, and even a formal parlor. With tiled baths, damask sofas, and French sitting chairs, the Tides has many amenities for a small inn. With your back to the inn, looking out at Frenchman Bay across its acre and a half of lawn, it's easy to forget you're right downtown.

ULLIKANA BED AND BREAKFAST $$$-$$$$
16 The Field, Bar Harbor
(207) 288-9552
www.ullikana.com
Bed and Breakfast and Country Inns of New Eng-

land, a popular guidebook, calls this quiet inn "one of the secret treasures of Bar Harbor," and it's right. The 1885 Tudor provides guests with the best of two worlds. On the one hand, it is out of the way and a tad hard to find, giving it a quietude and serenity uncommon in the hurly-burly of Bar Harbor. On the other hand, it is only a few hundred yards from the point where Cottage and Main Streets meet—in other words, the epicenter of downtown. How can that be? The inn is buffered by the huge Field, a broad meadow not too far from Frenchman Bay that wraps around Ullikana, so the location is truly remarkable. Said to be the first cottage in town, elegant old place has nine guest rooms each of which is very comfortable with touches old and new. Several have fireplaces and/or private porches, all have private baths, and each has its own design theme. Six more rooms are available in the neighboring Yellow House. It's hard to find a better place to stay in Bar Harbor, which is saying a lot.

Other Accommodations in Bar Harbor

Bar Harbor Regency Hotel (123 Eden Street; 800–23-MOTEL; www.barharborregency.com) is a big corporate resort with its own marina. **Manor House Inn** (106 West Street; 207-288-3759 or 800–437-0088; www.barharbormanorhouse.com) is an 1887 manse within easy walking distance of Bar Island. The **Primrose** (73 Mount Desert Street; 207-288-4031; www.primroseinn.com) is a 13-room, Stick Style Victorian from 1878.

Northeast Harbor

ASTICOU INN $$$–$$$$
Route 3, Northeast Harbor
(207) 276-3344 or (800) 258-3373
www.asticou.com
Living is good at the Asticou, a turn-of-the-20th-century inn overlooking Great Harbor in tony Northeast. The views of Mount Desert's most famous features—ocean and mountains—are absolutely spectacular. The 48 rooms and suites spread across its main inn, cottages, and lodges-all have private baths, but they don't make too many concessions to the times. Most are

cozy and bright, with nice views and relatively straightforward furnishings that are comfortably old-fashioned. The adjacent cottages are ideal for families. Many rooms are booked long in advance by repeat visitors. Asticou is famous for its azalea gardens, so make it a point to wander through them. The inn also has clay tennis courts, a heated outdoor pool, and easy access to Acadia—trails head into the park from right across the street. Service is a hallmark, of course.

HARBOURSIDE INN $$–$$$$
Northeast Harbor
(207) 276-3272
www.harboursideinn.com
A short walk from downtown Northeast, this 1888 shingle-style cottage is set against a woody hillside and isn't really on the harbor, but you can see the harbor through the trees. There are 11 guest rooms and three suites spread across three floors here. Though the rooms retain a simple, venerable style, they have private baths and some have working fireplaces and even kitchenettes. Breakfast is taken on the bright and airy wood-paneled porch—all floor-to-ceiling windows and wicker—every day between 8:30 and 9:30 a.m.

Southwest Harbor

THE CLAREMONT HOTEL $$$–$$$$
Claremont Rd., Southwest Harbor
(207) 244-5036 or (800) 244-5036
www.theclaremonthotel.com
The rambling old Claremont offers accommodations in the grand hotel style of Maine summers past—not fancy, mind you, but classic, tasteful, simple. Amenities are plentiful for an old-fashioned place, and they tend toward the old-fashioned as well—clay tennis courts, croquet courts (this place is famous for its croquet tournaments), bikes, rowboats, library, concerts, lectures, and afternoon tea. A favorite are simply the Adirondack chairs lined up on the grounds with a fantastic Southwest Harbor panorama spread before them. The 24 rooms in the main hotel have recently been renovated and they are

comfortable but spare, and the Phillips House has six more, two with fireplaces. And then there are 14 cottages of varying styles and degrees of luxury, from split log to contemporary, all with fireplaces and living rooms. Dining is in the Boathouse in the summer. If you want to relax, this gracious old inn is the place. Open from late May to late October.

CLARK POINT INN $$–$$$
109 Clark Point Rd., Southwest Harbor
(207) 244-9828
www.clarkpointinn.com

Three stories of 1883 colonial charm are to be found at this old inn across from the town dock. The three rooms are all decorated to a theme—and have water views, private baths, queen-size beds, TV, Wi-Fi, and fineries like damask loveseats and quilted coverlets. There are also two third-floor suites with living rooms and fireplaces.

INN AT SOUTHWEST $$–$$$
371 Main St., Southwest Harbor
(207) 244-3835
www.innatsouthwest.com

An extraordinary 1884 Mansard-roof Victorian overlooking Southwest Harbor, this seven-room inn is pleasasntly appointed with nice touches like sleigh beds, four-posters, wrought iron beds, down comforters, sitting rooms, and gas stoves. Some have a bit of a water view, and all have private baths. Breakfasts are served on the wrap-around porch or patio in nice weather; they're highly regarded and might include cheesecake crepes, rhubarb crunch, or Belgian waffles with raspberries.

SEAWALL MOTEL AND RESTAURANT $–$$
Route 102A, Southwest Harbor
(207) 244-9250 or (800) 248-9250
www.seawallmotel.com

No doubt what the principal attraction is here—the famous seawall of Southwest Harbor, an expanse of rocky shore that seems to be holding back all of the Atlantic when the waves hit hard. It's right across the street from this motel com-plex, and the lagoon created by the wall is adjacent, with all its birdlife. Eagles, seals, muskrats, and a range of ducks and other shorebirds are commonly spotted, and Acadia wraps around the back of the motel. Rooms are simple motel units, no frills but clean and with phones and Wi-Fi. The room rate includes the continental breakfast. You can hop on the Island Explorer shuttle right here and enjoy everything on the island without having to worry about driving and traffic. Open year-round. Rates are reasonable in summer and a real bargain in the off-season—which could even be the end of June.

DOWN EAST

Hancock

CROCKER HOUSE $$–$$$
967 Point Rd., Hancock Point
(207) 422-6806
www.crockerhouse.com

Built in 1884 as part of one of the great hotels that catered to vacationers at the turn of the 20th century, the inn has been thoughtfully restored over the years, and it's quite comfortable in a country sort of way, with quilts, and antiques, twig wreaths, and private baths. There are 11 guest rooms in its three stories, each of which has been newly redone, and common areas for hanging out. Dinner here is an event (not included in room rate), with the public flocking in, but Sunday brunch is the real treat. Don't miss it.

LE DOMAINE $$$$
Hancock
(207) 422-3395 or (800) 554-8498
www.ledomaine.com

It's still hard to fathom this place—so good yet seemingly so far from everything. The dining room at Le Domaine has people driving in from miles around, but the three rooms and three suites are worth the trip beyond Ellsworth as well. They, too, bear the hallmarks of innkeeper Nicole Purslow's French upbringing (she grew up here, but her mother was from France). The three guest rooms and two suites have a Provencal touch to them with select furnishings and fabrics, and they have all the niceties, down to the heated towel racks, flower arrangements, and plush robes. Rates include breakfast. You'd be remiss if you didn't spring for dinner as well.

Winter Harbor

MAIN STAY COTTAGES　　$-$$
66 Sargent St., Winter Harbor
(207) 963-2601

On the way down to the Schoodic section of Acadia, these five cottages each offer guests a different experience. The 150-year-old Boathouse, for example, is one of the original structures in Winter Harbor, a small, weathered gray building on pilings right over the water. It offers views of Mark Island Light from the deck and a queen bed, kitchenette, and gas fireplace to keep you cozy inside. Ledgelawn Cottage is a more contemporary option, about 20 feet from the water, with one bedroom, a living room/kitchenette, and water views. For the best experience, though, reserve the Molasses Pond Cottage, which is down the road in Eastbrook, right on the water with its own private beach. It features two small bedrooms, a kitchenette, and endless entertainment in the Down East woods.

Addison

PLEASANT BAY BED AND BREAKFAST　　$
386 West Side Rd., Addison
(207) 483-4490
www.pleasantbay.com

A working llama farm, this three-room, one-suite inn is a real charmer, overlooking the very pleasant Pleasant River in the tiny village of Addison. Owned by Leon and Joan Yeaton, the home sits on 110 acres of waterfront, and there are nice trails that skirt the bay. The rooms are nicely laid out with views and with hope chests, quilts, and rocking chairs, and the suite has a kitchenette. The porch is set before some nice vistas of the tidal river, and there's a fireplace inside to take the chill out of the late summer air. The Yeatons are quite familiar with the area and can give you good tips on exploring, from Moosehorn National Wildlife

Refuge to Campobello, and they welcome you to even help out with the llamas if you like. And the river is right there, just waiting for your canoe or kayak. Homey is the word—but so is value.

Machiasport

MICMAC FARM　　$
Route 92, Machiasport
(207) 255-3008
www.micmacfarm.com

Micmac Farm was better known as a restaurant than as a place to stay, but that may change once people spend a night in one of the three guest cabins behind the farm. Set in a forest overlooking the Machias River, these camps are straightforward affairs, with board and batten siding, pine-paneled interiors, two double beds, and a kitchenette. Sliding glass doors allow you to step out onto the back deck to enjoy the views of the river, and there are paths through the grass down to the water. The accommodations are inexpensive, allowing you to set up here for a long time.

Eastport and Surrounding Area

HOME PORT INN　　$-$$
45 Main St., Lubec
(207) 733-2077 or (800) 457-2077

One of the bright spots on Lubec's down-at-the-heels Main Street, this 1880s bed-and-breakfast has seven rooms, each with a private bath. Several overlook Cobscook Bay and Eastport across the way. Some have four-posters and antiques, others handpainted tiles and sitting chairs. Very pleasant, and the dining room here is recommended as well.

KILBY HOUSE INN　　$
122 Water St., Eastport
(207) 853-0989 or (800) 853-4557
www.kilbyhouseinn.com

A nicely restored Queen Anne, the Kilby House has five pleasant bedrooms inside. Each has its own unique style and is furnished with antiques and heirlooms, some of which are from the Kilby family who originally lived here. Some have water views, and downtown Eastport is within walking distance. Breakfast is "full," all right, and the place is an amazing value for what you get—you could set up for a week in Room 4 for the price you'd pay for a single night's stay in a comparable chamber in parts south.

MOTEL EAST $–$$
23A Water St., Eastport
(207) 853-4747

Sitting just up the road from the downtown, Motel East has the blue expanse of Passamaquoddy Bay as its backyard, and it makes good use of it with broad picture windows in each of its straight-forward rooms. Motel fare, but with an inspired vista, Wi-Fi, and easy access to all that Eastport has to offer.

CAMPING

There's nothing quite like sleeping under the stars when you're in Maine. The state is, of course, famous for its fresh air, natural beauty, and piney woods, and sleeping in a tent allows you to get away from the hustle and bustle and enjoy the "real Maine" at its most real. Literally hundreds and hundreds of campgrounds are spread across the state—from the truly primitive to the RV park—and there are just too many to list here. What follows are the best of the private camping areas. You'll find the state parks listed in the Green Space chapter.

The Maine Campground Owners Association annually publishes a 100-page directory—the Maine Camping Guide—and it's a very useful resource for finding and comparing new campgrounds. Get your copy at a chamber of commerce, state visitor center, or by calling (207) 782-5874. Or visit the Web site www.camp maine.com.

South Coast

RECOMPENCE SHORES FREEPORT
(207) 865-9307
www.freeportcamping.com

If you run into a problem with your gear while

ℹ The state of Maine has a very useful Web site for making campground reservations. You can find all the information you need on camping in the state parks—from maps, rules, and fees to general visiting information—at www.campwithme .com.

tenting at this seaside park, you can just zip up the road to L.L. Bean. These 100 tent sites astride Casco Bay are only a few minutes from the giant outfitter, down a quiet peninsula near Wolfe's Neck State Park. Run by Wolfe's Neck Farm, an agricultural operation known for its beef and environmental consciousness, the campground is one of the best in southern Maine and certainly the best in Greater Freeport. A network of trails makes for good hiking, too.

Midcoast

HERMIT ISLAND PHIPPSBURG
(207) 443-2101
www.hermitisland.com

Hermit Island is a Maine classic, one of those places where you have to work to get a site, because so many people begin planning their trip for the next year before they've even gone home. Right on Small Point Harbor in Phippsburg, the campground is an oceanfront resort of sorts and it offers some of the best oceanfront camping in the state. It's been there for decades. A total of 275 sites occupy the 255-acre island; they're spaced for privacy and set up to accommodate tents, small pop-up trailers, and pickup campers but not RVs. Many are just steps from the ocean, others are in spruce or birch groves, and some face the camping area's harbor. All are a pretty easy walk to white-sand swimming beaches. Amenities here include a camp grocery (yes, fresh lobster), boat rentals and launching sites, pay phones, drinking water, and warm showers. The campground is quite the village in midsummer, with teens doing their mating dance, families having reunions, and anglers spinning their reels, but it is big enough that you can get away from it all if you want. The most obvious appeal of Hermit Island is for beach lovers—the island's own or Popham, just a few miles down the road—but kayakers, sailors, and hikers enjoy stays here, too. Look into reservations sooner than later.

LOBSTER BUOY CAMPSITES
280 Waterman Beach Rd., South Thomaston
(207) 594-7456

Forty sites are spread across a spectacular shorefront here, and the place is known for its quietude. Explore the beach, bask in views of offshore islands, or launch a kayak and go for a paddle—the options are all there. A small store sells basics and homemade donuts in the mornings, and there is a simple shower facility—bring your quarters.

MEDOMAK FAMILY CAMP
178 Liberty Rd., Washington
(207) 845-6001
www.medomakcamp.com

Don't you wish you could still go to summer camp, maybe bring the whole family this time? At this fine camp in the inland town of Washington (30 minutes from Rockland), hard by the shore of Washington Pond, you can. The motto here is "relive the best summer of your life," and it certainly gets you started with many of the hallmarks you remember from your summer camp days. There are the cabins, the meals in the lodge, swimming in the lake, arts, crafts, canoeing, fishing, games, new friends—everything you'd find at a traditional summer camp, but you don't have to be 12 to enjoy it. (Oh, and there's lobster dinner once a week.) You might be too old to sneak over to the girls' camp, though. Sessions run for a week at a time from the end of June through mid-August. Call or check the Web for this year's dates.

Acadia Area

MOUNT DESERT CAMPGROUND
516 Sound Dr., Somesville
(207) 244-3710
www.mountdesertcampground.com

Sitting right at the end of Some Sound, the only fjord for miles, suffice it to say, this quiet campground has a rather ideal location. And it has built up a loyal clientele with its policies of serenity and for limiting the size of hulking RVs. Tenters particularly are drawn to the spot, though motor homes of 20 feet or less are welcome, too, but it isn't any sort of wilderness. Electric hookups, showers, and a store known for its muffins and ice cream are all available. Many of the campground's sites are right on the sound, and boat launching ramps make it easy to jump in, an attractive feature for kayakers.

Down East

OCEAN WOOD BIRCH HARBOR
(207) 963-7194

Owner Michael Brunton hasn't done much advertising for this extraordinary seaside camping area, mostly because he wants to keep it a quiet, special place. And quiet and special it is. Run primarily as a nature preserve, the 70-site campground wraps around a peninsula that pokes into the cold Atlantic Down East, and there is plenty of space between sites, making it serene and cozy. Brunton doesn't allow radios or partying, and there are a bunch of sites that are walk-in only, which further removes you from the noise. Many bivouacs are right smack on the shore, and there's a large seawall of a beach for enjoying by those on an inland spot. Perhaps best of all, the sights of the Schoodic Peninsula are less than 5 miles away. It's truly a remarkable campground. So don't tell anyone about it; just call for reservations.

RESTAURANTS

Yes, we have lobster. Everyone knows that, and probably two-thirds of the state's visitors indulge in a little red crustacean when they're vacationing on the Maine coast. The Pine Tree State also boasts a lot of other homegrown delicacies, though, from blueberries to potatoes, and it's home to a wide variety of restaurants, from the eclectic to the ethnic to the family style. Some cosmopolitan types from away, in fact, are surprised by both the quantity and quality of fine restaurants that can be found here. You won't go hungry traveling up Route 1, that's for sure.

The best places to go looking for a great meal are Greater Portland and the resort communities. In the late 1990s, Portlanders claimed that they had more restaurants to choose from—per capita—than any other city outside of San Francisco. Whether or not that is the case, it might as well be, and it seems that since then things have just gotten better with more and more eateries opening up. The state's largest city is a foodie's paradise, with a dizzying array of great places, from the hip and of the moment to the tried and true.

The resort communities tend to be a little more straightforward—more seafood, less inventive, fewer ethnic options—but that's not always the case. There's great Thai food to be had in Belfast, and Kennebunkport's Hurricane is nothing if not creative. The same is true in Bar Harbor at George's.

Maine chefs have access to great raw ingredients—in the form of locally grown produce and the freshest of seafood—and the best of them put it to excellent use. Look around, and you won't be disappointed.

Price Code

Except where noted, prices represent the cost of a single adult dinner entree, not including tax or tip, and are intended to convey a general idea of how expensive the restaurant may be. Total cost will vary depending on type and quantity of additional food and beverages ordered, such as appetizers, desserts, coffee, or wine. Lunches are usually cheaper than dinners. The prices at many seafood restaurants fluctuate greatly due to changes in the market.

$.................$9.99 or less
$$ .... $10.00 to $15.99
$$$ .... $16.00 to $24.99
$$$$ .... $25.00 or more

SOUTH COAST

Kittery and Surrounding Area

BOB'S CLAM HUT $$
315 Route 1, Kittery
(207) 439-4233
www.bobsclamhut.com
Founded in 1956 by Bob Kraft, Bob's Clam Hut has been steaming clams for generations of southern Mainers. The tasty little bivalves are the staple here and are served every which way, but people come for a host of other seafood treats, from scallops to shrimp to oysters to calamari. If it's edible and from the sea, you'll find it here at prices that are easy to take. Used to be Bob's was just a hut, now it's a sit-down eatery as well. Good stuff.

CHAUNCEY CREEK LOBSTER PIER $–$$$
16 Chauncey Creek Rd., Kittery Point
(207) 439-1030
www.chaunceycreek.com

The creek and the pier make a beautiful backdrop for shore dinners at this classic Maine lobster house. You can select a "bug" from the tank, sit back and enjoy the views of the saltwater river while it boils, and then make a mess. They may call it lobster in the rough, but it's not too hard to take. Steamers are excellent as well, and you can even get raw oysters if that's your thing. Open May through September from 11 a.m. to 7 p.m.

Other Dining Options in Kittery

Cap'n Simeon's Galley (Route 103, Pepperrell Cove; 207-439-3655; www.capnsimeons.com) and Warren's Lobster House (1 Water Street; 207-439-1630; www.lobsterhouse.com) are both very popular for seafood.

The Yorks

CAPE NEDDICK HARBORSIDE RESTAURANT $$$
Shore Rd., Cape Neddick
(207) 363-5471
www.capeneddick.com

Like the best of the state's lobster pounds, Cape Neddick has a deck where you can sit and watch the action in the harbor as you tear apart your crustacean. The dining area inside is open and bright from big windows that shine over the simple wooden tables, and there's a bar where the locals like to gather. Fare is a tad broader than you might expect from a pound, with the lobsters, of course, but also with small-plate items like smoked Maine shrimp ravioli, scallops wrapped in apple-smoked bacon, and fried calamari. Seafood is obviously the draw, but there are grilled options, too, in the form of steak and chicken. You can't beat the view.

CLAY HILL FARM $$$
220 Clay Hill Rd., Cape Neddick
(207) 361-2272
www.clayhillfarm.com

Leave time for wandering the grounds when you visit Clay Hill Farm. The restaurant sits on 30 acres, and it is the only restaurant in the country (so it says) to be certified by the National Wildlife Association as wildlife habitat. Chef Melissa Ettinger calls her cuisine "New American" or "American Fusion," both of which seem about right. Entrees might include roast half duckling, chicken piccata, grilled lamb chops, and Haddock Maison, which comes topped with a lobster soufflé. The restaurant has received the Distinguished Restaurants of America Award of Excellence nine times and is always winning local most-romantic polls, so you want to bring your appetite and maybe your sweetie. Open year-round.

FLO'S STEAMED DOGS $
Route 1, York
www.floshotdogs.com

Expect to wait in line at Flo's, which has been pulling in the crowds since it opened in 1947. Open only from 11 a.m. to 3 p.m., the York institution has six stools that fill up fast and a secret hot sauce that keeps people coming back. Hot dogs, chips, soda, and milk—that's all Flo wrote. Closed Wednesday.

FRANKIE AND JOHNNY'S NATURAL FOODS $$
1594 Route 1, Cape Neddick
(207) 363-1909
www.frankie-johnnys.com

An unassuming place on Route 1, this dinner spot quickly gets creative when you step inside. The menu is known for its Whole-food fare, and everything is made from scratch with fresh ingredients, from the signature crustolis—which are French bread rounds topped with goodies like a pizza—to the smoked lobster salads to the blackened pork Demonico. You can get as wacky as you like here, in terms of the cuisine, or keep it fairly traditional (baked chicken), and you'll always go home happy. There's a bit of a Mediterranean flavor to Frankie and Johnny's, and the candlelight is a nice touch. Oh, and bring cash—plastic is not "natural," and they don't accept it here.

YORK HARBOR INN $$$–$$$$
Route 1A, York Harbor
(800) 343-3869
www.yorkharborinn.com

One of the best inns in the Yorks serves one of the finest meals around as well. *Food & Wine* magazine gave the dining room here the nod, and locals have always liked its creative uses of local seafood. Lobster lovers will want to try the Yorkshire Lobster Supreme (lobster stuffed with scallops and shrimp with thermidor-style sauce), the lobster-stuffed breast of chicken, or the ravioli and lobsters. Others might like the roast rack of lamb, the filet mignon, or the vegetable melange. Service is generally very good. Open nightly for dinner from 5:30 to 10 p.m. and from 9:30 a.m. to 2:30 p.m. for Sunday brunch. Reservations are always wise.

Ogunquit

ARROWS RESTAURANT $$$$
Berwick Rd., Ogunquit
(207) 361-1100
www.arrowsrestaurant.com

The accolades that this 18th-century farmhouse has garnered are fairly astounding. How about one of the top 50 restaurants in America? That's what *Gourmet* magazine said in its October 2006 issue. Or one of the 10 most romantic restaurants in the country? That's *Bon Appetit* speaking. Or "hands down the best dining in the area"? That would be the influential Zagat Survey. The place is indeed very, very good. (It also happens to have a savvy press person.) And the goodness starts in the garden. Arrows is now famous for its produce, which it grows right on-site (guests are welcome to wander the grounds). The menu tends to favor whatever's in season, and every element on the plate is integral. Main courses—and there are usually only about a half dozen choices—might include grilled veal rib chop and crispy Arborio rice; Alaskan wild king salmon wrapped in papillote with spring leeks and black truffles; or Maine lobster and sautéed jumbo Maine sea scallops with a ginger noodle pillow, spring vegetables, and a rhubarb, pinot blanc, and Sichuan peppercorn sauce. There's a tasting menu as well. Be sure not to wear jeans or shorts or jean shorts or you won't be seated—guests are encouraged to dress up. Reservations are a good idea. Open at 6 p.m. for dinner Wednesday through Sunday in June and September, Tuesday through Sunday in July and August. Hours are reduced in the off season.

BARNACLE BILLY'S $–$$$$
Perkins Cove, Ogunquit
(207) 646-5575 or (800) 866-5575
www.barnbilly.com

You wouldn't expect a place with a name like Barnacle Billy's to have valet parking, but that's become the necessity in the Perkins Cove of today, where you can circle for hours—days, it seems—before finding a spot to ditch the car. Famous for its seafood dinners, Barnacle Billy's has been at it for ages, serving up tons of lobster to eager diners. You can get it boiled, on a roll, in a salad, in a sauté, in a stew, by the pound, you name it. Other seafood standbys—from tuna salad to steamed clams to crab rolls—are also available, but you can find some turf options as well, including a great barbecued chicken. This is all at the original Barnacle Billy's—as opposed to Barnacle Billy's Etc., which is a fancier seafood place right next door. The original is a better deal for much the same fare.

VILLAGE FOOD MARKET $–$$
230 Main St., Ogunquit
(207) 646-2122 or (877) 646-2122
www.villagefoodmarket.com

If you're in town for a while, don't feel like waiting in line at a restaurant, or just want a nice dinner in, get thee to this downtown market, which has a great selection of prepared meals. Soups, salads, grilled meats, fish—take your pick. Grab a bottle of wine, a blueberry pie, and some scones for breakfast, and you're ready to go. Their Pick Three deal—an entrée, and two sides, for $7.95—is a real deal.

Other Dining Options in Ogunquit

98 Provence (262 Shore Road; 207-646-9898; www.98provence.com) is a good bet for rustic French foods. **McPerkins Cove** (Shore Road; 207-646-6263; www.mcperkinscove.com) is the new venture by the team behind Arrows, so you know it's good. **The Cliff House** (Bald Hill Cliff; 207-361-1000), the famed resort and spa, has an upscale dining room with fancy views and great food. The breakfasts at **Egg and I** (501 Main Street; 207-646-8777; www.eggandibreakfast.com) have been voted the best in southern Maine, which is a stretch, but they're very good. The northern Italian fare at **Roberto's** (200 Shore Road; 207-646-8130; www.robertos.com) packs them in. **Raspberri's,** the dining room at the Gorges Grant Hotel (449 Main Street; 207-646-7003), is another good breakfast option, known for its waffles.

Wells

MAINE DINER $-$$
2265 Post Rd., Wells
(207) 646-4441
www.mainediner.com
Over 5 million served here. Why? Because this old institution knows how to do diner fare right. "Like grandma used to make," is the motto and the food served up by the Henrys is just such comfort food. Try the homemade baked beans, or the codfish cakes, or the macaroni and cheese and see if you can do so without smiling.

JOSHUA'S RESTAURANT $$$-$$$$
1637 Post Rd., Wells
(207) 646-3355
www.joshuas.biz
Having your own organic vegetable garden seems to be a recipe for success among Maine restaurants. It's the practice at two longtime favorites, Arrows in Ogunquit and Chase's in Belfast, and it's also the plan at the new Joshua's Restaurant in Wells. Chef/owner Joshua Mather grew up in a beautiful 1774 house on an organic farm 6 miles from his new dining room, and his dad provides the vegetables for his restaurant.

The chef's plan is not to do too much to what his dad, and his other suppliers, bring to him, and his menu is fairly simple—pork tenderloin, duck, haddock, rack of lamb, filet mignon—but expertly crafted, and with some unusual combinations. The chicken is stuffed with prosciutto, the lobster comes as a pie, the haddock is carmelized. The young chef's attention to detail has the place already thriving. The *Boston Globe* calls Joshua's "fabulous," and *Travel + Leisure* recommends that people "keep an eye on this guy." We'd have to agree.

The Kennebunks

THE CLAM SHACK $-$$
Lower Village Bridge, Kennebunk
(207) 967-3321
www.theclamshack.net
A writer once joked that the state should pass a constitutional amendment to keep this bridge-side take-out stand open year-round, and many locals sigh a sad sigh when it closes in the fall. Clams are obviously the appeal here, and they are very good, with a homemade tartar sauce, but the place turns out a mean lobster roll as well. At least that's what Martha Stewart thought. And *Coastal Living* magazine. And *Travel + Leisure,* which called it the best in Maine in its August 2006 issue. Oh, and the Food Network. Plus Epicurious.com, which called the place one of the top 10 seafood shacks in the nation. Pick up a Maine Lobster Roll Kit, which contains freshly picked lobster meat, traditional rolls, the shack's own mayo, and the recipe, all packed into a tiny lobster trap. Open May through September.

HURRICANE RESTAURANT $$$$
Dock Sq., Kennebunkport
(207) 967-9111
www.hurricanerestaurant.com
A Maine original, the Hurricane in Ogunquit may have closed, but its sibling in Dock Square is going great guns and remains as good as ever, turning out plate after plate of superbly crafted surf and turf. Try one of the small entrees—the crispy crab cakes ($15), the skewered chicken

i A lot of people are unaware that the breakfast at the Green Heron Inn (126 Ocean Avenue, Kennebunkport; 207-967-3315) is open to the public—it is, and it's arguably the best in town.

satay ($9), or the baked Vermont brie ($18). Or step up to a larger plate like the fettucine Alfredo ($16), the yellowfin tuna burger ($12), or the pièce de résistance—baked stuffed Maine lobster with scallops, shrimp, and crabmeat stuffing ($45). The place is always busy, but you'll be glad you put up with the hassles. Be sure to make a reservation.

ALISSON'S RESTAURANT $$–$$$
11 Dock Sq., Kennebunkport
(207) 967-4841
www.alissons.com

Arlo Guthrie should write a song about this Dock Square stalwart. (Its name was actually inspired by his classic "Alice's Restaurant.") The place has been an anchor in the square for more than three decades, and everybody loves it. The atmosphere is very comfortable and casual—with the ball game going on the TV over the bar—but it's the food that brings people back. The chowder has been voted southern Maine's best, the fried clams have their own partisans, and the menu is fairly long with seafood, steak, chicken, and sandwich options (try the prime rib sandwich). Especially good for lunch. Open daily, year-round, for lunch from 11:30 a.m. to 5 p.m. and for dinner from 5 to 9 p.m., with the hours cut back a bit in the off-season.

CAPE ARUNDEL INN $$$$
Ocean Ave., Kennebunkport
(207) 967-2125

People flock to Kennebunkport to get a look at the Bush compound on Walker Point, and the summer home of the presidents forms much of the view of this fine dining room. (George the First occasionally even sups here, so you can get a real close look.) The food, however, should be the real attraction. After establishing the White Barn Inn as the place to stay and eat in Maine, Jack Nahil sold the famous hostelry and turned his attention to this new project. The cuisine is thus exceptional, with seafood and continental favorites done with ingenious twists, like crab cakes with a ginger sesame rémoulade, for example, or lobster stew with truffle oil drizzle. Quite aside from the views of crashing surf and Secret Servicemen out the windows, the dining room is very comfortable, with its candles and white linens, and the service is exceedingly professional. Open Monday through Saturday for dinner from mid-April through December.

GRISSINI ITALIAN BISTRO $$–$$$$
27 Western Ave., Kennebunkport
(207) 967-2211
www.restaurantgrissini.com

"Quintessential Tuscan cooking with a New England accent" is how this fantastic bistro describes its fare, and that about sums it up. Featuring some of the talents who have made the White Barn Inn world famous, the kitchen here turns out absolutely delicious northern Italian cuisine using fresh local fish and just the right spices. Try the wood-grilled pork with chunky apple sauce, the pan-seared cod, or the polenta lasagna. Guaranteed you won't forget Grissini if you eat here. It has a nice downstairs bar, big fireplace, and patio. Just great. Open nightly for dinner from 5:30 to 9 p.m. On Saturday they open at 5 p.m.

ON THE MARSH $$$–$$$$
46 Western Ave., Kennebunkport
(207) 967-2299
www.onthemarsh.com

The Salt Marsh Tavern used to be one of the finer restaurants in this resort community, and when Denise Rubin purchased it in 2000, she only made it better. Much better. Retrofitted into an old farm and barn, the eatery was completely redone, and it is sparkling, from the twinkling lights outside to the candles inside. The menu likewise was reborn, and it is a comfortable mix of classics done with artful twists. The filet mignon has a wild mushroom ragout, for example, and the pork tenderloin comes with roasted shallots.

Not only immensely flavorful, dishes here are a treat for the eyes as well as the palate. Those in for a real spectacle can be seated in the kitchen, where they can watch the chefs at work. Another intriguing note: If you really like the unique antique sculpture on the wall near your table, you can buy it—the dining rooms are filled with art, furnishings, and collectibles that are for sale. Neat idea.

STRIPERS $$$–$$$$
127 Ocean Ave., Kennebunkport
(207) 967-5333
www.thebreakwaterinn.com

The executive chef here is Jonathan Cartright, better known as the man behind arguably the best dining room in Maine, the White Barn Inn, so you can expect quality at this eatery tucked into the Breakwater Inn. Simple, flavorful, seafood is the specialty. Oysters are hallmark, so you'll want those, but you might also try the lobster-and-little-neck stew or even the beef duo. The windows look out on the very seas this stuff came from, a feature that the White Barn never had, and the accolades are unending for the fishy fare.

WHITE BARN INN $$$$
37 Beach Ave., Kennebunkport
(207) 967-2321
www.whitebarninn.com

You could spend almost an hour reading all the accolades written about the White Barn. *Food & Wine* magazine calls it one of the top 50 hotel restaurants in the nation, *Conde-Nast Traveler* puts it atop its "gold" list, *New England Traveler* calls it a "most notable gem," the *Maine Sunday Telegram* deemed it "perfect" and "otherworldly," and the kudos go on and on, literally dozens worth. Suffice it to say the place is good, and in a way that outclasses just about everywhere else in Maine. Its dining room is five-diamond good, the only recipient of AAA's highest honor in the whole state.

Actually built into a pair of 19th-century, timber-framed barns—heavy beams, rafters, hayloft, and all—the inn's dining room is both rustic and fancy, with candlelit, white-linen–covered tables, cushy chairs, ample flowers, and picture windows overlooking gardens. The country feel puts you completely at ease and ready to savor four courses of prix-fixe excellence. Chef Jonathan Cartwright's menu changes weekly but always draws inspiration from the seasons, Maine seafood, and European traditions. Beef, veal, lamb, and fowl are generally options, and house specialties include delicacies like lobster spring rolls, forest-mushroom soup, saffron-scented Maine shrimp, and seared Quebec foie gras. Everything is presented as a form of art, and service is as good as it gets in Maine. The desserts are astonishing, like the vanilla goat cheese timbale and raisin compote. You'll be back. Open Monday through Thursday from 6 to 9:30 p.m. and Friday through Sunday from 5:30 to 9:30 p.m. Jackets required.

LUCAS ON 9 $$–$$$
62 Mills Rd., Cape Porpoise
(207) 967-0039
www.lucasonnine.com

The team behind the ever-popular Fisherman's Catch in Wells, the Lane family, has purchased and renamed the old Lobster Pot in Cape Porpoise, one of the few real villages left in southern Maine, so the people who show up here will probably be expecting seafood. And that's largely what they'll get, in the form of baked stuffed flounder with Newburg sauce, and spicy tuna with kiwi. But you can also get baby back ribs, chicken, and other meats. The menu is actually quite long and well-rounded, with both swimmers and walkers. You could happily fill up on a couple of smaller plates or go home with a doggie bag by ordering an entree. Worth a stop.

Other Dining Options in the Kennebunks

Nunan's Lobster Hut (207-967-4362) packs in the seafood fans. Along with being the best big hotel in town, the **Colony** (Ocean Avenue, Kennebunkport; 207-967-3331) also sets one of the best tables, heavy on the seafood. **Bartley's Dockside** (By the Bridge, Kennebunkport; 207-

967-5050; www.bartleysining.com) is the place to turn for blueberry pie. And **Federal Jack's Restaurant and Brew Pub** (8 Western Avenue, Kennebunk; 207-967-4322; www.federaljacks. com) is where you'll find great beer brewed on the premises and good pub food.

Saco

RAPID RAY'S $
179 Main St., Saco
(207) 282-1847
www.rapidrays.biz

Everything about Rapid Ray's feels classic, from the diner exterior to the simple menu of burgers, dogs, lobster rolls, onion rings, and similar fare. The place has been at it for more than four decades and is still going strong. You walk in, make your selections from the list near the ordering window, get your chili dog or clam cake burger with fries in a little box, and eat it at the thin, wraparound counters. Best of all, most items on the menu will set you back only a few bucks—even the seafood. The lobster roll is great, and it costs half of what you'd pay just up the road in Kennebunk.

GREATER PORTLAND

Scarborough

CLAMBAKE SEAFOOD RESTAURANT $$–$$$
Route 9, Scarborough
(207) 883-4871
www.clambakerestaurant.com

Not far from Pine Point Beach, this seafood joint has both a cafeteria-style sit-down dining room and take-out, which is nice because you can grab a pint of fried clams and head to the beach. There is seating for 700 here, which all but eliminates any waiting, and many tables have nice views of Scarborough Marsh. Always busy in midsummer, the Clambake is a favorite among Greater Portland seafood fans, and it's popular with tourists as well. The menu is deep with seafood, but you can get grilled chicken if you must. Start with some chowder and follow it up with a twin

lobster dinner. All dinners are served with choice of potato, Caesar salad, coleslaw, and bread. You won't go home hungry; the place prides itself on serving size.

Cape Elizabeth

SEA GLASS $$$–$$$$
Inn by the Sea
40 Bowery Beach Rd., Cape Elizabeth
(207) 767-0888
www.innbythesea.com

When this seaside inn went through its multimillion dollar makeover recently, it updated its dining room as well. The old Audubon Room at this seaside inn had a reputation as one of the best places to eat in Maine, so you have to assume the new Sea Glass will be good. Like that eatery this one specializes in well-done surf and turf, using mostly local ingredients, but it will take a light and fresh approach, allowing the food to speak for itself. Look for dishes like the macadamia-crusted northern halibut ($25), the grilled lobster ($26), and the Gulf of Maine seafood paella ($25).

THE GOOD TABLE $
527 Ocean House Rd. (Route 77)
Cape Elizabeth
(207) 799-4663
www.thegoodtablerestaurant.com

A devastating 2002 electrical fire didn't stop this local favorite—it rebuilt in no time, bringing Greater Portland residents the "honest food and honest prices" they want. The family-style fare is a mix of hearty comfort foods with Greek overtones here and there (spanakopita, gyros). The turkey dinner is pretty much perfection, the lobster roll is fine, the desserts are tempting, and the cinnamon buns swoonworthy. Sunday brunch here fills up fast. Open Tuesday through Friday from 11 a.m. to 9 p.m., Saturday 8 a.m. to 9 p.m., and Sunday 8 a.m. to 3 p.m. Closed Monday.

LOBSTER SHACK $$
225 Two Lights Rd., Cape Elizabeth
(207) 799-1677
www.lobstershack-twolights.com

You don't have to be a fan of seafood to enjoy a visit to the Lobster Shack, just below the twin towers that give the Two Lights area of Cape Elizabeth its name. The view of the open Atlantic from the picnic tables outside the small eatery is simply jaw-dropping, and it alone is worth the trip. It certainly helps if you enjoy fried clams, haddock, shrimp, lobsters, or scallops, though. (No fear, landlubbers—fried chicken, hot dogs, and hamburgers are also "specialties.") See why *Gourmet* and Bobby Flay paid the place visits.

South Portland

JOE'S BOATHOUSE $$$
Spring Point Marina, South Portland
(207) 741-2780
www.joesboathouse.com
The many masts and sparkling waters of Spring Point Marina are out every window at this South Portland favorite. And a patio gives you an even better look out onto Casco Bay. Some say the views here are among the best of any Greater Portland restaurant, and the fare holds its own. Lunch and dinner are popular with the boating crowd, and people make the drive over from Portland to sit at one of the 45 seats here and enjoy them. The Sunday brunch, though, is the real treat, with Port Harbor pancakes, Peaks Island French toast, and corned beef hash and eggs.

RICETTA'S BRICK OVEN PIZZERIA $$
29 Western Ave., South Portland
(207) 775-7400
www.ricettas.com
If you can't get a table at Ricetta's, you can always take out. This beloved pizzeria in a South Portland strip mall has become so popular that it's often difficult to even get in the door, and people become resigned to getting their pies to go. Diners consistently vote the thin-crust, gourmet pizzas here the best in the Portland area, and they are eminently customizable. A nice way to experiment is to visit during the lunchtime buffet, so you can sample several varieties. Various other entrees—from pasta to soups to calzone—are on the menu, but you likely won't even notice. Ricetta's has expanded into Falmouth and now Kennebunk, and its satellite restaurants are hard to get into, too.

Other Dining Options in South Portland

Imperial China (220 Maine Mall Road; 207-774-4292), located in the uninspired confines of the Mallside Plaza, is often called the best Chinese place in Maine. Much-better-than-average pub fare and great beer are available at **Sebago Brewing Company** (150 Philbrook Avenue; 207-879-2537 and 164 Middle Street; www.sebago brewing.com). **Mr. Bagel** (locations across the city; www.misterbagel.com) has great—you guessed it, bagels—including a lobster bagel. More bagels, really fine bagels, can be had at **158 Pickett Street Cafe** (158 Benjamin Pickett Street; 207-799-0668). **Beale Street Barbeque** (725 Broadway; 207-767-0130; www.mainebbq .com) is exceptional for barbecue and blues.

Portland

BACK BAY GRILL $$$–$$$$
65 Portland St., Portland
(207) 772-8833
www.backbaygrill.com
It isn't all that uncommon for Portland visitors to enjoy a restaurant on one vacation only to return a year later and find it long gone. There's been a lot of turnover in the city, but here is one eatery that has managed to survive and thrive since the late 1980s. And this despite its unlikely location on a side street in a neighborhood that is if not sketchy then at least far from trendy. The food—inventive takes on tried-and-true American favorites—simply keeps people coming back. Try the filet mignon with Roquefort, the lamb with potato gnocchi, or the Scottish salmon. The seafood is fresh, the produce organically grown, the wine list strong. Restaurateur Larry Matthews puts a premium on comfort and service and he's been lauded by little outfits like, oh, the James Beard Foundation.

BECKY'S $

Hobsons Wharf, 390 Commercial St.
Portland
(207) 773-7070
www.beckys.com

Everyone seems to love Becky's, from the fishermen who catch the seafood for the diner's famous chowders, to *Gourmet* and *Esquire* magazines, to lawyers in suits and ties, to those tourists lucky enough to find the place. Well-prepared diner fare—heavy on the seafood—is what you can expect here, at very reasonable prices. Try the fried haddock with fries and slaw or the clam cakes and slaw. You can even get a hot dog. The ambience and staff are just right, and, for all the accolades, the place is still real. Look for the red awning on Commercial Street.

BIBO'S MADD APPLE CAFE $$$

23 Forest Ave., Portland
(207) 774-9698
www.bibosportland.com

When the Portland Performing Arts Center's calendar is in full swing, so is Bibo's. It's a favorite among the theatergoing set. The colorful place sports an eclectic menu from a world of flavors—it has Asian, Italian, and French influences—served up with flair in a brightly painted dining room a few steps from Congress Street. Everything begins with bread, which is served with olive oil and dukka, a nut blend. Entrees include salmon with sesame vinaigrette and pork tenderloin with avocado and lime. The wine list has many fans.

CAIOLA'S $$-$$$

58 Pine St., Portland
(207) 772-1110
www.caiolas.com

Besides simply providing the city with great food, Portland's two culinary institutions, Street and Company and Fore Street, have done the city—the state even—a great service by spinning off so many other great restaurants. Alums of the two titans have been opening up new restaurants all over the place. This comfy West End eatery is a case in point. Chef Abby Harmon

worked for years as the top chef at Street and Company before opening her own place, and she continues the high standards set there. Here she's set up a European-style bistro featuring simple peasant foods done exactly well. The menu changes daily and might include anything from a Caesar salad with fried oysters to a bacon-cheeseburger to paella to bouillabaisse, all served on handcrafted wood tables in warm little spaces divided by walls with rustic murals.

DIMILLO'S FLOATING
RESTAURANT $$-$$$

Long Wharf, Portland
(207) 772-2216
www.dimillos.com

A tourist staple on the Portland waterfront, DiMillo's is a restaurant retrofitted into an old car ferry. It's big enough at 260 feet to avoid the swells when the seas get to rocking, but it still provides a great window onto the harbor, and out-of-towners eat it up. Grab a table outside on one of the decks if you can. As you might expect, seafood takes up much of the menu that comes out of the galley, but steaks, poultry, the occasional Italian dish, and other landlubber fare are also available. The cuisine isn't going to win any awards, but the views make it a worthwhile lunch or dinner option.

DUCKFAT $

43 Middle St., Portland
(207) 774-8080

Seems you can't be a restaurateur in Portland without having at least two restaurants to your name. This "sandwich shop" is the second venture by Rob Evans of Hugo's fame and like that bistro it's been gaining accolades. The *New York Times, Boston Magazine, Food & Wine, Travel + Leisure,* they've all been and love the place. The name comes from the Belgian fries, which are cooked in duckfat and they are the signature dish here. Mostly what we're talking are lunch foods—homemade meatloaf, corned beef tongue Rueben, spicy Italian sandwich—that are exquisitely done and flavorful. They'd put your average burger joint to shame and they'll set you back about the same amount of scratch—most items are $8 or less. Wow, we'd be singing its praises, too, if it were polite to talk with mouth full.

FEDERAL SPICE $
225 Federal St., Portland
(207) 774-6404

Federal Spice has a lot of the angles covered. The small joint across the street from the post office serves up healthy fare with unique tastes, it's inexpensive, and it's hip to boot. All that has made it a go-to place, a default lunch spot for many Portlanders. The eatery serves a world of flavors in the form of wraps, and they're the best in the state. Try the curry chicken and Asian slaw, the smoked turkey and green onion quesadilla, or the Chinese mako shark. You get delicious chips with your wrap as well, and you can eat inside or cafe style on the sidewalk. You won't be disappointed. (Just avoid the upstairs on hot days in summer—it's suffocatingly hot.) Open for lunch and dinner.

FORE STREET $$$
288 Fore St., Portland
(207) 775-2717
www.forest.biz

After a decade, this place is still setting the standard for Portland. Since it was founded in 1996, chef Sam Hayward's Old Port enterprise has been packing people in with its grilled peasant food. Walk in and you can smell the delicious seared aroma of the grill, and you can watch food roasting on the soapstone hearth from your table. Seafood is a staple, but there are plenty of tasty meat dishes as well, from the turn-spit roasted pork to the marinated hanger steak. People swear by the roasted mussels. Hayward is painstakingly good—the eminent James Beard Foundation named him Best Chef in the Northeast in 2004—and his people scour the fish markets and farmstands for the freshest and best organic ingredients. This has won the place a devoted following. Some would say that the only place that might be better in Portland is Street and Company, which is part of Hayward's empire, along with Standard Baking Company and Two Fat Cats Bakery.

If you know you're going to be around awhile and you enjoy a bargain, the Portland Dine-Around Club (207-775-4711; www.dineportland.com) is a great deal. Annual membership is $29.95, and it gets you discounted meals and more, usually a two-for-one entree arrangement at more than 230 eateries in Portland and beyond. Eat out a couple of times and it pays for itself very quickly.

THE FRONT ROOM $-$$
73 Congress St., Portland
(207) 773-3366
www.thefrontroomrestaurant.com

Portland's Munjoy Hill, traditionally a down-at-the-heels sort of neighborhood, has been enjoying a bit of a renaissance lately, and places like this comfortable eatery are among the reasons why. An old Victorian apartment building on the Eastern Prom is the setting for a restaurant that chef/owner Harding Lee Smith hopes will become a community gathering place. All three meals are offered daily, and the menu is described as "New American comfort food," which means the kinds of macaroni and cheese, burger, BLT, grilled meatloaf, and lamb pot roast that won't scare off the natives. But you also get the occasional twist—such as corned hake, cedar-planked salmon, or Casco Bay scallops in mustard sauce. It's a fine combination, and the dining room is a place you can return to several times a week.

GILBERT'S CHOWDER HOUSE $$
92 Commercial St., Portland
(207) 871-5636

Right on the waterfront, Gilbert's is about as salty an eatery as you'll find in Portland, and it serves up a raft of good seafood dishes in addition to its famous chowders. Clam, corn, seafood, and super seafood, these chowders come the best way—in bowls made of fresh bread. Not the least bit pretentious, fishermen and lawyers sit at adjacent tables, hungrily digging into clam cakes, lobster stew, fried haddock, and scallops. The lobsters and fish are literally just off the boat, sometimes even that morning, and Ed Gilbert has attributed the success of the venture to this freshness. Great word of mouth doesn't hurt, either.

THE GRILL ROOM AND BAR $$–$$$$
84 Exchange St., Portland
(207) 774-BEEF

Part of chef Harding Lee Smith's overnight empire, this is the burger and pizza joint of the future. Which is to say the burger comes with tomato tapenade and the pizzas might be BBQ duck. The menu is long and, just as he does at his Front Room Restaurant, Smith mixes it up, giving you plenty of inexpensive options, from the $8 potato pizza to the $13 chicken, but including some high-end entrees as well, like the $42 grilled ribeye. And it's all good.

HUGO'S $$$$
88 Middle St., Portland
(207) 774-8538
www.hugos.net

Dana Street has been very complimentary of Rob Evans, chef at this longtime restaurant on Franklin Arterial. No small thing, considering that Street runs two of Portland's best and most popular eateries, Fore Street and Street and Company. Evans bought the restaurant from founder Johnny Robinson several years back, and he's truly put his stamp on the bistro. He was the chef at the old Hugo's, before leaving to study at cooking schools, and when he returned to buy out Robinson, he really got things going, combining French and Italian accents with the culinary traditions of New England in a way that is amazingly original. Try the Vermont quail breast, the Casco Bay cod, or the Maine gray sole. Delightful.

LOCAL 188 $$–$$$
685 Congress St., Portland
(207) 761-7909
www.local188.com

Guidebooks don't know where to put this Portland hipster hangout. By day it's an art gallery. By night it's one of the city's more interesting restaurants. The young and happening like to

visit regularly because the staff is made up of artists, writers, and musicians worth knowing. Other cool kids are always there, and foodies and fans of good wine are right behind them, hankering for the tapas cooked up Jay Villani. The food is as good as anything else being served in the city, and Villani and his staff have expanded the once tapas-only menu to include larger entrees. Staples include paellas, pastas with romesco sauce, and creatively prepared meat dishes. The price-portion ratio allows for sampling several dishes and sharing, the service is great, and there is always something interesting to look at, from cutting-edge art to cutting-edge people.

NORM'S BAR AND GRILL $$
617 Congress St., Portland
(207) 828-9944

Eager diners will occasionally walk into Norm's on the east side of Congress Street only to find that they're in the wrong place. They've walked into Norm's Downtown Lounge, which is not to be confused with Norm's Bar and Grill. That Portland favorite—formerly in this location—has moved across the street. Seems this Norm fellow is taking over the city. Now there are three outlets for his talents. (Norm's East End Grill, a barbecue hot spot, is over on Middle Street.) The Bar and Grill still has the red walls and the checkerboard floors, the booths of burgundy pleather (faux leather), the bar with the ball game on, about a dozen tables, and, thankfully, the menu filled with grilled items, urban eclectic pub food, not-really tapas, and good beers and wines. Try the baked meat pie, the fried sea scallops, or the barbecued chicken tacos.

PEPPERCLUB $$
78 Middle St., Portland
(207) 772-0531
www.pepperclubrestaurant.com

When you've had your fill of lobster rolls and fried clams, head over to this beloved eatery, just a few blocks from the Old Port across the Franklin Arterial. Readers of the local alternative weekly have tabbed the restaurant as the place with the best food for under $10 in years past, but prices have gone up a bit. The fare is still indisputably good, though. It's a smorgasbord of cosmopolitan, nouvelle flavors inspired by eats from all over the globe, and you order off a chalkboard covered with colors. You might find on any given night Moroccan chicken, sesame vegetable spring rolls, curried organic beef pie, or lamb in phyllo with Greek salad. Everything comes recommended, and the knowledgeable staff will help you sort things out.

PORTLAND FLATBREAD CO. $-$$
72 Commerical St., Portland
(207) 772-8777
www.flatbreadcompany.com

This isn't your grandfather's pizza place. This Commercial Street pizza house serves up all-natural pizzas baked in "primitive," wood-fired clay ovens, using flatbreads of organic wheat. Part of a small chain, the eatery has a nice spot on the Portland waterfront, and there are views of the harbor visible from its wooden booths. One of these pies is large enough to feed two people. Choose from the nitrate-free pepperoni; the Casco Bay community flatbread, which comes with caramelized onions, organic mushrooms, cheeses, and herbs (exactly like the Amesbury community flatbread, in Amesbury, Massachusetts); or the vegan, which has caramelized onions, kalamata olives, garlic oil, and herbs. Portlanders seem to be into this joint, and there can be a wait.

RI RA $$$
72 Commercial St., Portland
(207) 761-4446
www.rira.com

Always a hopping joint, this Irish place enjoys good word of mouth for its brews, bands, bonhomie, and Emerald Isle–inspired fare. Yet somehow it doesn't seem quite so special—the hometown pub spirit is diminished—when you find out it's part of a chain with pubs in Providence, Burlington, and as far south as North Carolina. You might begin with some tasty Irish potato leek soup, which comes with brown bread and Guinness butter, then move onto the Linguine Galway, which combines shrimp, mus-

sels, tomatoes and white wine with spices on a bed of linguine; Dublin Fisherman's Stew, which combines lobster, mussels, and fresh fish in a light seafood broth with garlic, spinach, and fennel (yes, that's Maine lobster). Fun stuff, though a franchise, and at least here on the Portland waterfront on a foggy day, you could imagine you were in County Cork.

THE ROMA CAFE $$$
769 Congress St., Portland
(207) 773-9873
www.theromacafe.com

With its chandeliers, heavy drapes, and white linens, this Congress Street favorite has a decidedly old-school feel, and it is, in a classic sort of way. The Roma has been feeding Portlanders since 1924 with fine Italian-accented continental fare. It's the sort of restaurant where you take that special someone on that special occasion, when a little romance is required. (Roma puts the roma in romance—it's been voted Portland's most romantic restaurant several years running.) The 1887 Rhines mansion serves as the setting, the service is known for being impeccable, and the fare is prepared with supreme care. You won't soon forget the Roma seafood lasagna, the chicken and Maine shrimp fettuccine, or the roast pork tenderloin.

SCRATCH BAKING CO.
416 Preble St., Portland
(207) 799-0668
www.scratchbakingco.com

Bob Johnson, Allison Reid, and Sonja Swanberg opened One Fifty Ate Willard Square, a place where people in their Portland neighborhood could grab a bagel or a cookie (try the chocolate chip hooray), and it didn't take long for them to outgrow the place or the name. They've expanded and changed their name but the whimsical spirit and delicious homemade breads and bagels and brownies and blondies and biscotti and bearclaws, and blueberry bran muffinettes haven't changed. Which is good for Portland.

SILLY'S $

40 Washington Ave., Portland
(207) 772-0360
www.sillys.com

Silly's enjoyed its 15 minutes of fame a few years back when famed pranksters the Jerky Boyz called the little restaurant up to ask them what was going on there that was so silly. Portlanders already know the answer. The funky eatery has become known for a "silly" array of items—the place's burgers are called the city's best by some. Others hail the jerk chicken, the pizza, and the milk shakes. It's also famous for vegetarian options. The atmosphere is kooky, the staff fun, and everything is inexpensive. As the slogan goes: EAT AT SILLY'S.

STREET AND COMPANY $$$–$$$$

33 Wharf St., Portland
(207) 775-0887
www.streetandcompany.net

Along with Fore Street, this place has been setting the standard in Portland since 1989, and it's surprisingly informal. The specialty is grilled seafood, and nobody does it better. Entrees come right out of the kitchen and onto your table, often in the skillet they were cooked in. Specialties include lobster diavolo and scallops in Pernod and cream, but everything is excellent. Space has always been a concern—the restaurant is so popular, there's often a wait. Expanded seating and outdoor dining have been added, but it's still best to make a reservation.

WALTER'S CAFE $$$

15 Exchange St., Portland
(207) 871-9258
www.walterscafe.com

Since 1989 Walter's has been showing the world what can be done with pasta and seafood, and the restaurant, right smack in the heart of the Old Port, has developed a loyal following in the process. (Apparently Springsteen is a fan.) Very pleasant, with its windows onto the street, exposed brick, tin ceilings, and cozy tables, the cafe melds a wide variety of culinary cultures on its menu—from the Caribbean to the Mediterranean. Dinner might start with the crackling calamari, a Walter's specialty, and move on to shrimp and lobster skillet pie, another longtime favorite here. Or it might include the pan-seared salmon with pineapple crab salsa or angel lobster, which mixes the Maine ingredient with scallions, mushrooms, and a marsala cream and tops it off with Parmesan. Dress may be casual but the fare isn't. Reservations are a good idea, as the place is popular.

Other Dining Options in Portland

The **Old Port Sea Grill and Raw Bar** (93 Commercial Street; 207-879-6100; www.theoldport seagrill.com) is the sort of yupscale place where you can down uncooked oysters while watching TV and having a drink. At **Standard Baking Co.** (75 Commercial Street; 207-773-2112) you can pick up a loaf of what must be Maine's best bread along with a host of desserts. Stop by **Harbor Fish Market** (9 Custom House Wharf; 207-775-0251 or 800–370–1790; www.harborfish .com) to buy lobster and fish fresh off the boats; it's the kind of salt-steeped place where people walk around in rubber boots. **Granny's Burritos** (420 Fore Street; 207-761-0751) serves up the best burrito in New England and is a great, inexpensive lunch or dinner option. **Cinque Terre** (36 Wharf Street; 207-347-6154; www.cinqueterre maine.com) receives raves for its traditional Italian fare. **Hi Bombay** (1 Pleasant Street; 207-772-8767; www.hibombay.com) makes some of the best Indian curries in town—try the Friday lunch buffet. **Sala Thai** (1363 Washington Avenue; 207-797-0871) is your best bet for Thai food. **Miyake** (129 Spring Street; 207-871-9170) and **Yosaku** (1 Danforth Street; 207-780-0880) are generally regarded as the places to go for Japanese and sushi. The **Cafe at Pat's** (484 Stevens Avenue; 207-874-0706; http://cafeatpats.com) continues to garner raves for its European comfort food. **Borealis Breads Bakery and Bistro** (182 Ocean Avenue; 207-541-9600) takes some of the best-known breads in Maine and builds meals around them. **Bresca** (111 Middle Street; 207-772-1004) is a tiny *it* place for Basque fare.

Falmouth

O' NATURALS $$
240 Route 1, Falmouth
(207) 781-8889
www.onaturals.com

Don't be surprised to see this fast-food joint taking over the country. Founded by some of the folks behind popular Stonyfield Yogurt, the eatery provides a healthy alternative to the greasy, processed McGrub at your chain burger joints. The menu is built around soups, sandwiches, salads, noodle dishes, and, yes, burgers made with organic and local produce, free-range meats, and no preservatives, additives, or "multiple-syllable stuff that you find in processed foods." How's it taste, though? Great. Try the miso noodles, the curried chicken, the spicy peanut salad, the chap chae Korean noodles, or the hoisin portobello sandwiches on flatbread—all delicious and prepared on demand for you in woks and grills by an eager young staff. Amazingly, it comes out just about as quickly as it does at the Golden Arches across the street. The ambience is nice—like a comfortable cosmopolitan coffee bar, with its art deco lights and exposed industrial piping. Opened in the late 1990s, the place has already expanded three times—it now has restaurants in Portland's Old Port and in Asheville, North Carolina, and Wichita, Kansas—and with food this good and an idea this sensible, it's sure to grow again soon.

Chebeague Island

CHEBEAGUE ISLAND INN $$$
61 South Rd., Chebeague Island
(207) 846-5155
www.chebeagueislandinn.com

Floating in Casco Bay just to the south of Yarmouth, Chebeague Island is a treat to visit. It's the largest of the bay's isles at 5 miles long and 3 miles wide, and it's great fun to walk, bicycle, and explore. And, now, to eat. The Island Inn has relatively new owners, and they've transformed their dining room into a showplace—white tablecloths, fieldstone fireplace, and all. The menu's not going to surprise anyone, featuring the expected upscale surf and turf—well, maybe the tapas you wouldn't expect—but it's very nicely done. And the whole package—the boat ride, the romantic old inn, the fine fare—makes for a memorable outing.

Yarmouth

ROYAL RIVER GRILLHOUSE $$-$$$
106 Lafayette St., Yarmouth
(207) 846-1226
www.royalrivergrillhouse.com

The restaurateur behind this local favorite learned his trade from Sam Hayward, the chef at the extraordinarily popular Fore Street in Portland. Which is a good thing, when you consider that he's running a grill where seafood is prominent on the menu. This place is quite popular, getting people talking about dishes like wood-grilled yellowfin tuna, sautéed Prince Edward Island mussels, fresh Maine crab cakes, and warm spinach and Maine shrimp salad. The menu changes nightly. Everything is presented in a nice dining room overlooking the Royal River, and there are tables on the deck in summer. Open daily from 11:30 a.m. to 9 p.m. Reservations are a good idea.

STONES CAFE AND BAKERY $
424 Walnut Hill Rd., North Yarmouth
(207) 829-4640
http://stonescafeandbakery.com

Just inland from Cumberland in North Yarmouth, this is a breakfast and lunch favorite. People here swear by the monster hash and eggs and the vegetable benedict in the morning and the veggie wraps and king burgers in the afternoon. Everything is from scratch and won't cost you a lot of scratch, either. On your way out, grab a scone.

THAI GARDEN $
491 Route 1, Freeport
(207) 865-6005

Pop in here for your pad Thai. This strip-mall joint has all your Thai favorites and everyone loves the place.

South Freeport

HARRASEEKET LUNCH AND LOBSTER $-$$
Main St., South Freeport
(207) 865-4888
You'll never believe you're still in Freeport as you stare out at this working waterfront on Casco Bay. Fresh lobster, well prepared, is on the docket at the lunch half of this equation, and it can attract crowds (which might remind you you're in Freeport). The other half—Harraseeket Lunch—is where you'll find all sorts of fried seafoods, sandwiches, chowders, and desserts. Try the fried clams, and follow it up with a whoopie pie. See why the Food Network stopped by.

MIDCOAST

Brunswick and Surrounding Area

COOKS LOBSTER HOUSE $$$
Off Route 24, Bailey Island
(207) 833-2818
www.cookslobster.com
When an ad agency went looking for an authentic Maine lobster pound for the Visa "It's everywhere you want to be" campaign, it settled on Cooks. Not hard to understand why. In business since 1955, it's everything a lobster pound wants to be: a neat old dining room of varnished pine booths with a wraparound panorama of the green-blue waters of Casco Bay. Obviously the lobster is the main attraction here, and you can get it baked, stuffed, stewed, Newburged, or plain-old boiled. A raft of other choices are there for the picking as well, from oysters to clams to fried fish. Cooks does lobster right, and they'll even ship some home for you by overnight air if you just can't get enough.

FRONTIER CAFE $-$$
14 Maine St., Brunswick
(207) 725-5222
It's really nice to see people putting Maine's old mills to good use. This place impresses with its high ceilings, neat old wood floors, picnic tables, and especially its high-end soups and sandwiches. Locals love the market plates, which bring a nice selection of meats, vegetables, cheeses, and breads on a platter and lets you do with it what you will.

GREAT IMPASTA $$
42 Maine St., Brunswick
(207) 729-5858
www.thegreatimpasta.com
Though some might be tempted to call it the *Good* Impasta, this place certainly has staying power—it's been a local favorite for ages. The specialty here is pasta—obviously—with a mix of seafood, veal, chicken, and veggies on top. Try the Pollo Spinaci, which is chicken sautéed with fresh spinach, or the manicotti, the primavera Alfredo, or Melanzana Parmigiano, which is sliced baked eggplant stuffed with smoked mozzarella.

RICHARD'S RESTAURANT $$-$$$
115 Maine St., Brunswick
(207) 729-9673
www.richardsgermanamericancuisine.com
Richard's is a find, if only because you can indulge in a little bratwurst, Wiener schnitzel, or Rhein-ischer sauerbraten (Rhineland-style marinated roast beef) right there in downtown Brunswick. This Maine Street classic is a house divided—on the one hand, you can get good old New English favorites like shrimp and scallops, steak, and sautéed chicken breast, and on the other hand, you can enjoy genuine Deutsch delicacies. German beer is also on tap. Open Monday through Saturday from 11 a.m. to 2 p.m. for lunch and 5 to 9 p.m. for dinner (Friday and Saturday till 9:30 p.m.). Closed Sunday.

SCARLET BEGONIAS $-$$
212B Maine St., Brunswick
(207) 721-0403
www.scarletbegoniasmaine.com
This small eatery has all the hallmarks of your neighborhood pizzeria, from the college kids behind the counter to the regulars picking up their to-go pies, but it's much more than that. Typical, Scarlet Begonias is not. Start with the flowers on every table, the local artworks on the walls, the words of high praise from the naval

air squadron down the street. Then move to the menu, from which you can order a pizza, yes, but it might be topped with broccoli or hot cherry peppers or even corn. Try the Simon Says, which adds sausage, chicken, peppers, mushrooms, and corn to your average pepperoni. Or try pasta, like the Scarlet Harlot, a classic putanesca with garlic, olives, and fresh herbs over penne. Sandwiches and salads abound, and they too are a step up from the usual. How about the terrapin tuna sandwich, for example, which has cheddar, tomato, and Bermuda onion in addition to the fish, on pizza bread? The choices go on and on.

SHERE PUNJAB $-$$
46 Maine St., Brunswick
(207) 373-0422
www.sherepunjabme.com

It's amazing that this Indian eatery at the end of Maine Street is not more popular. If people knew better the quality of the curries, chutneys, and especially the samosas served here, they'd be lining up and fighting over the handful of tables inside. But the small restaurant is rarely full, and you often have the place to yourself. You can usually get one of the tables set up in the window, which is a nice spot to take in all the colorful goings-on out on the street while you wait to feast on nan, dal, and chicken vindaloo. Service is good, food is great, and the menu is deep and long with rice, seafood, chicken, lamb, and vegetarian "delights," so everyone should be able to find something. Prices are probably the catch; they're a little more expensive than other area Indian dining rooms. But they often have specials, and they have a more affordable lunch menu, too.

SWEET LEAVES TEAHOUSE $
22 Pleasant St., Brunswick
(207) 725-1326
www.sweetleaves.com

A white clapboard tea room near the post office on the way into town, this nifty little cafe serves more than simply tea (although you can get that in a couple dozen varieties). There's also a fair-size menu of salads, soups (try the "kitchen sink"

chowder), and sandwiches on panini, as well as beer and wine, and the emphasis is on local and fresh. For dessert you'll want to try the home-made ice cream. Definitely worth a lunch stop—for under $10 you can eat very well here.

WILD OATS BAKERY AND CAFE $
149 Maine St., Brunswick
(207) 725-6287
www.wildoatsbakery.com

What a great place this is. First you have to arrange to meet someone here, because this is one of the town's community gathering places. Second, order up a sandwich, a bowl of soup, or some salad and take it to the tables outside, if it's nice, or to the overstuffed chairs in the Tontine Mall, if it's not. The baked goods section—date bars, pecan bars, strawberry snickerdoodles, plus a zillion other cookies and brownies—is amazing. The salad sandwiches—curried chicken, tuna, egg—are fantastic, and every day brings with it a new type of bread. A half sandwich will fill most anybody's belly.

Other Dining Options in the Brunswick Area

Great German food can be found at the **Old Munich Biergarten** (6 First Street, Topsham; 207-729-1688). **Fat Boy Drive-In** (Old Route 1, Brunswick; 207-729-9431) has to be one of the last restaurants around with carhops, and its burgers, fries, and prices are great. **Bangkok Garden Restaurant** (14 Maine Street, Fort Andross, Brunswick; 207-725-9708 www.bangkokgarden-restaurant.com) is a fine place to turn for pad Thai. Great seafood abounds in the area, especially down in the Harpswells. Try the **Dolphin Marina** (Basin Point Road, South Harpswell; 207-833-6000 www.dolphinmarinaandrestaurant.com) or **Block and Tackle** (Cundy's Harbor Road, Harpswell; 207-725-5690) for an indoor, sit-down meal, and **Estes Lobster House** (Route 123, South Harpswell; 207-833-6341) and **Holbrooks Wharf Lobster** (994 Cundy's Harbor Road, Harpswell; 207-725-0708) for waterside lobster in the rough.

Bath and Surrounding Area

BEALE STREET BARBECUE $$
215 Water St., Bath
(207) 442-9514
www.mainebbq.com

The staff at this exceptional barbecue joint wear T-shirts that read "It's a long way to Memphis," which is where the real Beale Street is. But, like that avenue, famed for its food and its blues, BSB serves up good eatin' and music, and Mid-coast residents are thankful for it. The menu is deep with barbecue choices, from pulled chicken sandwiches served on corn bread to jambalaya to the grilled fish of the day. The coleslaw is great, the baked beans even better, and the fries have a spice all their own. The portions satisfy even the hungriest iron workers.

THE CABIN $$
552 Washington St., Bath
(207) 443-6224

Serving arguably the best pizza in Bath, the Cabin is an institution, a gathering place of lots of locals and hungry shipbuilders—the restaurant sits across the street from the massive yards of Bath Iron Works. The dimly lit joint has been packing them in for more than three decades, and it is always busy. Its wooden booths are filled shortly after they're emptied, and take-out is ever popular. There's a nice outdoor courtyard as well. The pizza is great, with a tangy sauce that has just the right combination of spices and a crust that is baked to perfection. If you're in the area and have a hankering for pizza and beer, this is the spot. It's an especially nice option if you're in town and it's late—the Cabin stays open until 11 p.m. Thursday through Saturday and until 10 p.m. during the rest of the week. Open year-round.

FIVE ISLANDS LOBSTER CO. $$
1447 Five Islands Rd., Georgetown
(207) 371-2990
www.fiveislandslobster.com

Food with a view is what you'll find at this Mid-coast staple. A long wharf extends out into the island-studded drink south of Bath, and there are tables atop it at which to enjoy a traditional lobster dinner. Local fishermen help run the place—they're usually hard at work on the other side of the wharf—so you know the bugs have just arrived, but there are plenty of other options, too. You'll find excellent fried clams, made from a secret family recipe, as well as mussels, shrimp—you name it, as far as seafood goes—and locally famous onion rings.

ROBINHOOD FREE MEETINGHOUSE $$$$
Robinhood Rd., Georgetown
(207) 371-2188
www.robinhood-meetinghouse.com

Chef Michael Gagne made quite a name for himself at the old Osprey Restaurant on the Georgetown peninsula in the early 1990s, and when he opened this beautiful eatery in the spring of 1996, a lot of people followed him. He's built a larger clientele since, making the Robinhood Free Meetinghouse into one of the state's finest dining rooms. That's no small feat, as this is a tiny village far from the usual corridors of tourist traffic. Gagne's menu is a diverse and worldy affair, with as many as 40 different dishes on any given evening. You might try the Szechuan rib eye, the grilled duck breast with shiitake soy broth, or the haddock Oscar with Maine crabmeat. And he manages to pull it off admirably. The setting is as pretty as they come, too. Built in 1855, the restaurant's home is one of the state's distinctive old meetinghouses, a post-and-beam structure that's all white clapboards on the outside, 16-foot ceilings and 10-foot windows on the inside. As fine as dining comes in Maine and well worth the drive. Reservations are a good idea.

SOLO BISTRO $$$$
128 Front St., Bath
(207) 443-3373
www.solobistro.com

Modern food, contemporary taste. That's how this hip joint in downtown Bath bills itself, and by the standards of Victorian downtown Bath—Mid-coast Maine, even—it rises to the occasion. The cuisine, as you might guess, is on the nouvelle end of the spectrum. It features New American stuff like grilled hanger steak with carmelized onions and a $21 french-fry main course, with carmelized shallot gravy and seasonal vegetables. Everything is done very well and the wine list is obviously a specialty. People seem to be digging the place and it's bringing a cachet to the City of Ships.

SQUIRE TARBOX INN $$$$
1181 Main Rd. (Route 144),
Westport Island
(207) 882-7693 or (800) 818-0626
www.squiretarboxinn.com

A lot of people like to spend a few minutes with the goats when having dinner here, and they are a charming bunch. Meals are served in a 1763 saltwater farm, which is run as a dairy of the goat variety these days, and many of the nice touches during dinner are goat derived. The cheeses are delicious, and the warm buns, made with whey (a cheese by-product), have become a signature dish. Entrees might be rosemary roasted rack of lamb with garden mint sauce, filet mignon, sauteed giant shrimp, or Maine sea scallops. Reservations required. If you can't get enough, you can stay in a room at the inn.

Other Dining Options in the Bath Area

The **Kennebec Tavern and Marina** (119 Commercial Street, Bath; 207-442-9636; www .kennebectavern.com) serves fairly good surf and turf right at the side of the river. **Maryellenz Cafe** (15 Vine Street, Bath; 207-442-0960) is enjoying good word of mouth for its Italian fare. Lunch fare is a treat at **Star Light Cafe** (15 Lambard Street, Bath; 207-443-3005), and the lunch pail crowd—read, Bath Iron Works workers—lines up at the **Sandwich Shop** (45 Vine Street, Bath; 207-442-7858).

Wiscasset
LEGARAGE $–$$$
Water St., Wiscasset
(207) 882-5409
www.legaragerestaurant.com

When they built the garage here in the 1920s, they gave it a remarkable view of the Sheepscot River. Now it's a restaurant, which puts the panorama to good use—walls of glass on the porch frame the scene nicely. LeGarage is known for its lamb and its finnan haddie (which Mainers line up for), but it has plenty of seafood and vegetarian options as well. Try the lobster pie. Sit on the porch. Open for lunch and dinner and for Sunday brunch.

RED'S EATS $$
Water and Main St., Wiscasset
(207) 882-6128

This tiny red shack on Route 1 is legendary for its lobster rolls—they've been voted the best in Maine many times over and been featured in innumerable magazines and newspaper articles from coast to coast. And deservedly so. These hot-dog-roll delicacies aren't exactly cheap, but they're worth every penny. More than one whole lobster supposedly goes into just one roll, and you can choose the amount of mayo or butter you want to add. Other options include plain ol' dogs, fried shrimp, and fried clams. Classic. Just be prepared to wait. Lines are so long on Main Street it looks like a parade.

SARAH'S CAFE $$
Route 1, Wiscasset
(207) 882-7504
www.sarahscafe.com

Many Maine restaurants have trouble staying open in the off-season, when the hordes of tourists leave and take their wallets with them. This has never been a problem for Sarah's Cafe. Yes, things do slow down considerably after school goes back into session, but Sarah's has built up such a loyal local clientele that her cafe on the Sheepscot never seems to suffer. In fact, Sarah's has been expanding ever since she first went into business in Boothbay in 1982.

Her business has constantly expanded, and the menu has, too, incorporating Mexican-via-Maine favorites (haddock burritos, chili boats, etc.), along with seafood courtesy of Sarah's fisherman brother, and her now-famous soups. Area residents will come one night for her beloved pizza and be back again that same week for soup—with trips to the bread bar—or a Whaleboat, her own version of a calzone. She's been serving breakfast for a few years now as well. The atmosphere is extremely comfortable, with wooden booths, tables topped with nautical charts of the area, and seating on a deck overlooking the Sheepscot. All told, it's one of the more memorable dining experiences you'll have in the Midcoast.

THE SEA BASKET $$
Route 1, Wiscasset
(207) 882-6581
www.seabasket.com

Residents of Greater Wiscasset all but cry when this local institution closes its doors in December with another season behind it. Some people from the area have been known to take more than one meal here a day, and others make sure to slide into one of the orange, Formica-topped booths at least once a week. You'll get an inkling of how good the place is as you wait for your order to come up—several framed articles on the wall from the likes of the *New York Times* attest to the Basket's greatness. The name of the eatery pretty much says it all—the majority of people order platters of fried haddock, clams, shrimp, or scallops that come with fries and coleslaw. It's simple but delectable, and the restaurant's method of frying, using soybean oil and a high-tech convection system, cuts down on absorbed fats and is cholesterol-free, so it isn't even as sinful as it tastes. Other recommended options include the clam chowder, the lobster roll, and the lobster stew. (Landlubbers have a few choices as well.) Think of the Sea Basket as a fishy diner and you have the right idea, both of the type of food and the atmosphere.

Other Dining Options in the Wiscasset Area

Treats (80 Main Street, Wiscasset; 207-882-6192; www.treatsofmaine.com) is a great gourmet market at which you can provision for a fine meal.

Mark Antony's Italian Cuisine (65 Gardiner Road, Wiscasset; 207-882-9888; www.markantonysitaliancuisine.com) is a local favorite for its, um, Italian cuisine.

Boothbay Harbor and Surrounding Area

BAKER'S WAY $
89 Townsend Ave., Boothbay Harbor
(207) 633-1119

A big yellow building with ample parking out front, this place looks for all the world like your average bakery—and then you see the little sign that says VIETNAMESE FOODS. Step inside and you'll find all the doughnuts, bagels, pastries, and croissants of a traditional bakery, but you'll also discover a menu that is long and deep and filled with traditional Vietnamese dishes like yellow curry (excellent), stir-fried beef, stuffed rice pancakes, and stir-fried lobster. If the TV inside bothers you, step out back into a little garden where there is seating cafe style ringed by greenery. A visit here has a Tourist in Wonderland feel to it—so incongruous is the idea of a great Vietnamese restaurant hidden in a Boothbay bakery—but you'll be glad you went in.

BET'S FISH FRY $-$$
Town Sq. (off Route 27),
Boothbay Harbor

This is the kind of place you want to find on your vacation—a take-out lobster shack at the side of the town green, owned by a real character, and serving delicious inexpensive lunches. The haddock sandwiches turned out by Bet Lauriat look like the cartoon eats that Shaggy from Scooby-Doo digs into—a real tower of goodness. Another option is the fish and chips. Bet's been at it since the early 1990s, delicately frying away, to the delight of locals and the tourists lucky enough to stop here and dine at one of the funky, cafe-style tables out front. The sign on the side of the place always says jokingly FREE BEER TOMORROW, and may it ever be so.

ANDREW'S HARBORSIDE
RESTAURANT $$–$$$
12 Bridge St., Boothbay Harbor
(207) 633-4074
www.andrewsharborside.com

If you were to conjure up a seafood restaurant in a Maine resort town in your mind's eye, it would probably look a lot like this eatery just above the harbor. But it'd be better than you think. Known around town for its breakfasts, the place turns to seafood for lunch and dinner, serving up dishes like Cajun salmon, lobster in a puff pastry with lavender butter, and pepper-crusted yellow tuna with a wild mushroom risotto.

KALER'S CRAB AND LOBSTER HOUSE $$
48 Commercial St., Boothbay Harbor
(207) 633-5839
www.kalers.com

You could come here just for the views—just about every table looks out at the harbor. With its weathering shingles and varnished pine walls and gingham-checked tablecloths, this place has the tourist lobster house look nailed, and the eats fit, too. Seafood served baked, fried, stewed, grilled, and sautéed makes up most of the menu, but you can get steak and chicken as well. People have been known to wax enthusiastic about the fried clams. Kids like the touch tank. Open daily at 11:30 a.m.

BOOTHBAY LOBSTER WHARF $$–$$$
97 Atlantic Ave., Boothbay Harbor
(207) 633-4900 or (800) 996-1740
www.boothbaylobsterwharf.com

USA Today singled out this eatery, run by area lobstermen, as one of the best places to find a "New England Lobster Roll," and whether the editors of "the nation's newspaper" know much about seafood, they're right in this instance. Among the reasons are the ample amount of meat the cook here crams into a bun. Their lobster bake on a platter—boiled bug, a couple ears of corn—is great, and it's nice to know you're directly supporting area fishermen and not some middleman. It also doesn't hurt that the tables look out on the quiet side of the harbor.

LOBSTERMAN'S WHARF $$
Route 96, East Boothbay Harbor
(207) 633-3443
www.lobstermanswharf.com

This is the place where the locals get their seafood, so you know it must be good. The tourists tend to stick to downtown Boothbay Harbor, but area residents know they'll find consistently good lobster dinners on this rambling wharf right on the water. Picnic tables overlook the harbor, with all its activity, and they're topped with traditional shore platters, complete with crustaceans and corn, with lobster rolls overflowing with meat, with clam chowder, and with bowls full of steamers, all done with a bit more flair than your average lobster pound. Regulars have been coming here for decades—always a good sign.

ROBINSON'S WHARF $$
20 Hendricks Hill Rd., Southport
(207) 633-3830

Watch lobsters being hauled on Townsend Gut, a stretch of saltwater that gets busy with lobster boats, while you wait to haul your own. Lobster is served any number of ways, and those immune to the charms of red crustaceans can dig into burgers and fries. The fish chowder has its fans, and people like the crabmeat roll as well. New management is getting raves.

Other Dining Options in the Boothbay Harbor Area

Don't forget the fine dining available at the area inns—the **Newagen** and **Spruce Point** (see Accommodations chapter)—they're among the best meals you'll find in town. The **Ocean Point Inn Restaurant** (191 Shore Road, East Boothbay; 207-633-4200; www.oceanpointinn.com) is popular for its Black Angus steaks. **McNab's Tea Room** (Back River Road, Boothbay; 207-633-7222; www.mcnabstea.com) is a British tearoom and fun for it. Despite its name, **Dunton's Doghouse** (40 Sea Street, Boothbay Harbor; 207-633-2403) is known for its seafood. If you can't get enough lobster, try the **Lobster Dock** (49 Atlantic Avenue, Boothbay Harbor; 207-633-7120; www.thelobsterdock.com).

Damariscotta and Surrounding Area

THE BREAKFAST PLACE $
95 Main St., Damariscotta
(207) 563-5434

Homey is the word at this corner shop in downtown Damariscotta. The coffee cups are kept on a neat hutch that seems taken from your grandmother's, the waitress may well call you "dear," and every table has a rooster lamp atop it. So the place is very comfortable, and the fare is good, solid, morning comfort food. If you want something more adventurous than bacon and eggs or pancakes, you can try the McRoss, the house special. It's a French toast sandwich with egg and bacon or sausage. Or order up the broccoli and cheese omelet or the corned beef hash with a single poached egg. The bread is homemade, the coffee has a kick, and the service is just right. Open daily from 7 a.m. to 1 p.m.

DAMARISCOTTA RIVER GRILL $$$
155 Main St., Damariscotta
(207) 563-2992
www.damariscottarivergrill.com

Chef Rick Hirsch likes to say that the secret to his cuisine is simplicity, and, whatever it is, it's working. Tourists, locals, regional magazines, and *Wine Spectator* all eat the place up, so to speak. Surf and turf, with flavorful fusion twists, made from simple and local ingredients is the order of the day. If you like your chicken "voluptuous and moist" or your steak "sustaining and earthy" you'll like it, too. The talents here are behind the dining room at the Anchor Inn in Round Pond, too.

KING EIDER'S PUB $$
2 Elm St., Damariscotta
(207) 563-6008
www.kingeiderspub.com

This Damariscotta watering hole has a cool cartoon logo, good beer, and a nice selection of pub foods—its burgers are a favorite. The ball game will be on above the bar downstairs, the waitresses will be friendly, and the desserts are not to be missed. Slide into one of the comfortable wooden booths, and order a bowl of the seafood chowder or maybe some local oysters, and you won't be disappointed.

NEWCASTLE PUBLICK HOUSE $$–$$$
52 Main St., Newcastle
(207) 563-3434
www.newcastlepublickhouse.com

The Newcastle Square Building lords over the corner on which it sits in Newcastle, a historic four-story brick eminence with two chimneys, and it's always screamed "nice restaurant." So locals have scratched their heads why it hasn't been put to use in any long-term, successful way. This venture has promise, an informal pub with better than pub fare—grilled steaks and seafood, local oysters, some unexpected optiions like karubi pork ribs and smoked duck salad—and a selection of Maine microbrews. The place aims for the neighborhood pub—board games to play, a Mug Club, live entertainment some nights—and it makes for a pleasant bonhomie.

BRADLEY INN $$$–$$$$
3063 Bristol Rd., New Harbor
(207) 677-2105 or (800) 942-5560
www.bradleyinn.com

A real find, this turn-of-the-20th-century inn serves up some fantastic Pemaquid oysters (the Damariscotta region is famous for the little bivalves). Seafood is prominent on the menu, from salmon to halibut. Try the tasting menu to sample several different flavors and see if you agree with some that the inn's dining room is among the best in the state. Open year-round.

Other Dining Options in the Damariscotta Area

Right downtown the **Salt Bay Cafe** (Main Street, Damariscotta; 207-563-3302) fills up at lunchtime. A big-time lobster fishing area, the Pemaquid Peninsula has no shortage of lobster pounds. Try **Shaw's Wharf** (Route 32, New Harbor; 207-677-2200), **Muscongus Bay Lobster** (Round Pond; 207-529-5528; www.mainefreshlobster.com), **Round Pond Lobster Co-op** (Round Pond; 207-529-5725), or **Pemaquid Fisherman's Co-op**

Harbor View Restaurant (Pemaquid; 207-677-2801; www.pemaquidlobsterco-op.com).

Waldoboro

BOREALIS BREADS $
Route 1, Waldoboro
(800) 541-9114
www.borealisbreads.com

Bodacious, baby. In 1993 Borealis launched under the name Bodacious Breads before discovering that a company of the same name already existed in California. So owner Jim Amaral changed the name to its current, northerly moniker. But the bodacious spirit still animates the bright yellow headquarters kitty-corner across Route 1 from Moody's. Fifteen varieties of freshly baked breads are made here—pick up a loaf of the salty rosemary or the French peasant—and they all have their fans. The real secret, though, is that you can get one of the best inexpensive sandwiches you're ever going to find at lunchtime here. "The Van Gogh of Dough" is the Borealis slogan, and you gotta think old Vincent would be stopping by for lunch if he were vacationing in the Mid-coast. There's another retail store in Wells, and Borealis is sold in stores across the state.

MOODY'S DINER $–$$
Route 1, Waldoboro
(207) 832-7785
www.moodysdiner.com

The sign above the door says simply EAT and under it MOODY'S DINER in bright neon, and people seem to take the message to heart, swinging in off Route 1 as if they have no choice. Moody's is the single-most famous restaurant in the state, the L.L. Bean of diner cuisine, and a visit is all but obligatory. Rare are the moments when its parking lot is empty. The Moody family has been feeding generations of Mainers—and their hungry guests—since they opened for business on the old Atlantic Highway in 1927. Back then the road was longer and the ham-and-egg sandwich cost 20 cents. Over the years the humble diner has gained wide acclaim for its fare, especially for its pies and muffins—*Gourmet* magazine asked for

the recipe for the walnut pie, *Saveur* named the Moody's whoopie pie a 1999 "food find," and the Culinary Hall of Fame gave the blueberry muffins top honors. Plenty of locals eat at Moody's on a weekly (or even daily) basis, and the eats are dependably good. You'll find all the usual diner suspects—burgers, fries, shakes, turkey sandwiches, tuna melts, but with several Maine twists, like chowders and corned beef hash. You may have to wait a few minutes, though. Pick up a T-shirt that says "I'm a Moody Person" on your way out the door.

KRAUT HAUS RESTAURANT
3856 Washington Rd.
207-832-5569
www.morsessauerkraut.com

Morse's has been selling its famous sauerkraut on a back road since 1918, and people go out of their way to make the pilgrimage. A few years back, the couple that runs the place opened the Kraut Haus Restaurant, which takes their kraut and incorporates it into a vary of German entrees, from sausage sandwiches to sauerbraten. For what you get it's not expensive, and the experience is neat, and, according to an overheard diner who was born in Berlin, authentic, to boot. In front of the eatery is a gourmet foods store where you can buy sauerkraut, horseradish, pickles, and a variety of European delicacies.

Monhegan Island

There are a surprising number of dining options for such a tiny isle. For fine food you might want to start at the **Island Inn** (207-596-0371), a huge, shingle-style castle of a place with windows overlooking Monhegan Thorofare. The fare here tends toward well-prepared American favorites, heavy on the seafood—a traditional lobster spread, prime rib, and roast duck, that sort of thing ($15–$30). The **Monhegan House** (207-594-7983) is another choice for seafood and steaks, and guests like it for its breakfast omelets as well ($15–$25). Dinner at the **Trailing Yew** (207-596-0440) isn't about the food—not that it isn't good—but for the fun. Meals here are on a weekly schedule—

Monday is roast beef, Saturday, of course, is hot dogs and beans—and they're taken family style, so you get to know your fellow islanders. The **Novely,** behind the Monhegan House (207-594-7983) has wraps and salads, dinner-to-go items, and famous whoopie pies.

Thomaston and Surrounding Area

BILLY'S TAVERN $$
1 Star St., Thomaston
(207) 354-1177

This place may be inspired by the public houses of Ireland, but there's no pretension here, just good drinks, neighborhood charm, and pub food that isn't really pub food. There's an oyster bar, for example. Have a cheesesteak or a bacon burger, play a game of Jenga or foosball, and enjoy yourself.

SILVER LANE BISTRO $$–$$$
1 Silver Lane, Warren
(207) 273-6464
www.silverlanebistro.com

You can hardly drive around the Midcoast without hearing an ad for this up-and-comer on the radio. Built around old barn on a side road off Route 1, the small place serves a globe-trotting mix of surf and turf. One day you might want the shrimp scampi, the next the Asian trout, the beef tenderloin with chimichurri sauce, or the duck a l'orange. With its exposed beams and warm wood grain, the dining room is cozy and the desserts worth sticking around for. The place is open for dinner Thursday through Monday. Reservations are a good idea.

THOMASTON CAFE AND BAKERY $$$
154 Main St., Thomaston
(207) 354-8589
www.thomastoncafe.com

Herbert Peters, owner-chef of this downtown favorite, got a nod from *Gourmet* magazine for his fish cakes, so you may want to order those. Everything in this small cafe is good, however, and made from scratch. Ingredients tend toward organic, and the fish is not long off the boat. The menu is small but inventive, with a lot of traditional favorites done with flair, like lobster ravioli with fresh oyster sauce or Frenched lamb chops. The fish chowder comes highly recommended as well, and the soups are always a good selection. Quiche, pasta, and sandwich options change on a regularly basis. The seating area is casual, comfortable, and bright, and lunch is fairly inexpensive for food of this quality. Recommended.

WATERMAN'S BEACH LOBSTER $$–$$$
343 Waterman's Beach Rd.
South Thomaston
(207) 596-7819

The actual eatery here might not be large, but its reputation certainly is. And the salty panorama is pretty huge, too. Waterman's is in a section of South Thomaston that's off the radar of your average tourist, not that travelers are exactly beating a path to South Thomaston anyway. But to get there you have to swing off the main thoroughfare in these parts, Route 73, onto Spruce Head Road, turn again onto Waterman Beach Road, and then make your way down a fire road. When you do, though, you find yourself staring out at island-dotted Mussel Ridge Channel and are happier for it. Then you get a taste of the lobster and understand what the fuss is about. It's prepared a variety of ways—grilled, on a roll, in a pie—and they're all worth the calories. Waterman's won a James Beard Award, that culinary stamp of greatness, which is not granted to lobster shacks every day. *Travel + Leisure* called it one of the state's "10 Best Lobster Shacks."

Other Dining Options in the Thomaston Area

The **Dip Net** (Port Clyde; 207-372-6307; www .dipnetrestaurant.com) has a loyal following for its soups, salads, seafood, and frankly, its seats, overlooking the harbor. For seafood consider **Miller's Lobster Company** (Off Route 73, Spruce Head; 207-594-7406; www.millerslobster.com) or **Cod End** (Tenants Harbor; 207-372-6782; www .codend.com).

Rockland

AMALFI $$-$$$

421 Main St., Rockland
(207) 596-0012
www.amalfionthewater.com

Amalfi always had the food and now it's got the view to go with it, having moved into the old MBNA compound just feet from the waterfront. The house specialties include paella, tapas, and seafood dishes, especially oysters, and on any given night there might be a dozen or more entrees to select from in addition to the tapas, salads, soups, and appetizers like Moroccan meatballs and manicotti. From the steamed mussels to the pan-seared Atlantic salmon to the braised shank of lamb, the grilled strip steak to the scallops St. Jacques, everything is uniformly good. The wine list draws praise for its quality and affordability, too. The bread that comes out first goes quickly, and the desserts that cap the meal—the crème brûlée is a favorite—have gained themselves quite a following. All told, a very fine dining experience. Reservations are a good idea.

BROWN BAG $

606 Main St., Rockland
(207) 596-6372
www.thebrownbagrockland.com

A lunch spot *par excellence,* the Brown Bag used to be so popular that locals would avoid it in summer. You simply couldn't get a parking spot, never mind a table in the restaurant's pretty brick confines. Things seem a little better these days, but it isn't because the food has gotten worse. The fare is still the same: great, made-from-scratch sandwiches, soups, and specials, fresh comfort food of the finest kind. Roast turkey—cut right off the bird—has always been a particular specialty, and you can get it a number of ways: in sandwiches, in pie, in soups, and in wraps. Seafood is big as well. Everything comes with chips and a pickle. Don't forget to stop in the bakery on your way out.

CAFE MIRANDA $$-$$$

15 Oak St., Rockland
(207) 594-2034
www.cafemiranda.com

The pink flamingos stuck in the window boxes out front should give you the idea that Cafe Miranda is a kooky place, and it is, but in a very good way. The building used to be a men's club—the Owls Fraternal and Benevolent Club—but you'd never guess it now. The waitstaff is cool to a person, the ambience is fun—you'll feel part of the hip crowd because of all the interesting artsy types who eat here regularly—and there are endless neat touches, like the whimsical salt and pepper shakers on each table, the over-the-top Elvis-themed bathroom, and the colorful slang names for the items on the menu. These entrees, of course, are the real reason for seeking the place out. There's a genuine danger of filling up on the focaccia before you even get to them, though—the salty flatbread here ranks among the best ever—but you gotta resist it in order to enjoy the saucy, wood-grilled dishes that owner-cook Kerry Altiero serves up. The menu is extensive and covers both sides of a legal-size sheet of paper with small, handwritten entries. (It changes often.) The fare is an eclectic, inventive, international mélange, heavy on the seafood and with a slight Italian slant. From the dozens of appetizers you might try the roasted leek pâté or the oyster mushrooms or the fish tostada. Entrees could be panfried haddock and kimchi, barbecued brisket, chili pork posole, seafood in green sauce, or veal scaloppine. And each comes highly recommended. Many good restaurants have popped up in Rockland since Cafe Miranda first lit its neon sign in 1993, but there are few that are more fun. Loincloths and tool belts are discouraged.

PRIMO $$$$

Route 73, Rockland
(207) 596-0700
www.primorestaurant.com

When Primo opened in April 2000, the buzz was so hot—thanks to reviews in such high-profile magazines as *Esquire, Gourmet, Town & Country, O, Food & Wine,* and *Wine Spectator*—that you almost had to know somebody who knew somebody or be willing to wait a long time to get a table. It's a little better than that now, but you're still going to want a reservation. What's all the excitement about? Call it pedigree. The principal players at the restaurant, Melissa Kelly and Price Kushner, came from the Old Chatham Sheepherding Company, an upstate New York dining room that is frequently considered one of the nation's best, and executive chef Kelly had won the James Beard Foundation's American Express Best Chef for the Northeast award as well as a nod as an upcoming chef from *Food & Wine*. Luckily for Midcoast Mainers, she wanted to open her own place on the coast of Maine, where she's been visiting for years. Primo, retrofitted into an old Victorian house south of Rockland, is the result. The food has Italian and French overtones, and Kelly uses as much farm-fresh produce and newly landed seafood as she can get. Try the pan-roasted Port Clyde halibut, the "wood-grilled, grass-fed New York strip steak braised local beef," or the grilled organic chicken breast. Pizzas make for a relatively affordable lunch. Open year-round for dinner Thursday through Monday at 5:30 p.m.

ROCKLAND CAFE $
441 Main St., Rockland
(207) 596-7556
www.rocklandcafe.com

This downtown Down East diner has a devoted following—many people eat at the Rockland Cafe several times a week. The family-style menu is filled with seafood options. A lobster roll and fries is a favorite, or you might want to try the homemade fish chowder. From hot pastrami sandwiches to burgers to tuna melts, all the usual suspects can be found here. The specials board is always leaned against the entrance so it can be read from the street. Open year-round daily from 6 a.m. to 9:30 p.m. (closes at 8 p.m. in winter).

WASSES HOT DOGS $
2 North Main St., Rockland
(207) 594-7472
www.midcoastmaine.net/wasseshotdogs/

Wasses Hot Dogs are legendary in Knox and Waldo Counties. This take-out–only outfit has one of those McDonald's-inspired TWO MILLION SOLD signs, and it's not hard to believe when you see the lines of eager people at the counter on the average workday and figure that most people buy more than one dog. (You can easily do so for under $7.) You can smell the grilling onions even before you park your car. There are now four Wasses stands—one in Thomaston and the other in Belfast, in addition to the two in Rockland—and the locales aren't particularly inspired. You'll usually find the little shacks in parking lots. But the hot dogs are as good as they come, grilled in peanut oil, topped with onions, and served on a warm roll. There are a handful of choices—your basic dog, bacon dogs, cheese dogs, chili dogs, and kraut dogs, and combinations of the aforementioned. Keith Wass was studying psychology when he opened the first stand in 1972, and he apparently understands the human psyche—at least where weiners are concerned.

Rockport

MARKET BASKET $
Routes 1 and 90, Rockport
(207) 236-4371

The Market Basket has had a full parking lot seems like forever. Ostensibly a specialty foods store—known for its gourmet groceries and good selection of wine—the cheerful green barn of a building at the corner of U.S. Route 1 and Route 90 becomes a lunch counter at midday and serves up a host of inventive and delicious ready-made dinners in the late afternoon. Diners can choose from a variety of cellophane-wrapped sandwiches in the coolers off to one side or custom-order one on homemade bread or baguette with choices of meats and toppings. There are always a couple of soup options—often tasty and exotic, like African chicken stew or Shaker chicken—as well as a variety of creative salads and deli counter specials. Made from roast turkey, stuffing, and cranberry sauce, the Thanxgiving Sandwich is recommended, as are the Indian chicken salad and the Caesar salad with chicken. There's usually a wait involved with a visit here, but it's always worth it.

PRISM GLASS CAFE $$
297 Commercial St., Rockport
(207) 230–0061
www.prismglassgallery.com

When this purple place opened on Route 1, people at first didn't know what to make of it. Was it a gallery? Or a cafe? Turns out Prism Glass Cafe is actually both, combining "high-design glass art" with high-design food art. The *Boston Globe* has called it a "one-of-a-kind experience," and it's that, too. The fare injects traditional New England foods—read seafood and steak—with Italian tastes, so you might find swordfish puttanesca one day and Tuscan meatballs marinara on another. Lobster is well represented, but meat-and-potatoes people should have no fear. The entrees are quite artful themselves, and the glass is fascinating to look at, making a meal here as much a visual as a gustatory treat. The combination of glass gallery and cafe is unique, but it works.

ROCKPORT CORNER SHOP $
Main and Central St.s, Rockport
(207) 236-8361

This is the sort of cool diner you wish you had in your hometown, the kind where they still sling hash, friends meet over a real burger and fries, and the coleslaw's good. Open only for breakfast and lunch, the place serves up some good eggs and French toast, and lunchtime brings BLTs, grilled cheese, tuna melts, and a wide variety of diner favorites. Good milk shakes, good service, good times. Good people-watching, too, when the Maine Media Workshops are in session across the street.

Camden

BOYNTON MCKAY FOOD COMPANY $
38 Main St., Camden
(207) 236-2465
www.boynton-mckay.com

When Boynton McKay pharmacy filled its last prescription not too long ago after more than a century in downtown Camden, local residents were worried that the distinctive 1890s drugstore would become another T-shirt shop or other tour-ist magnet of some sort. So they were pleased to learn that the building would be saved by a group of business owners, its interior preserved and turned into a cafe serving excellent meals year-round. The place still has its cool tin ceilings, soaring glass cases full of pharmaceutical oddments, and an old counter, where you can get a coffee or a delicious dessert, and six booths have been added on the opposite wall. (There are a couple of bars with stools, too.) Up above, clocks tell the time around the world, but it's always Coffee Time in Camden. You place your order with the cooks at the back of the shop, choosing from an eclectic menu that might include chicken chimichangas, wraps, fajitas, gazpacho, stir fries, Thai chicken on skewers, and a wide variety of sandwiches and salads. Boynton McKay is very popular with the morning crowd—exceptional coffees, you see—and breakfast items are available all day long. The prices combined with the creativity of the cuisine make this arguably Camden's best lunch bet. Again, expect a wait for a booth (in summer), and say hello to Jim and Tim. Open for breakfast and lunch.

CAMDEN BAGEL CAFE $
Mechanic St., Camden
(207) 236-2661

For breakfast on the go, pop into the old Brewster Mill, find the Camden Bagel Cafe, and grab a freshly baked bagels. You'll find an array to choose from—from salt to onion to pumpernickel—and tofutti to slather on top. There are several booths and tables if you feel like lingering, coolers to get your OJ, and a slew of coffees. You may end up standing in line for a few minutes, but you'll feel a part of the local crowd and might even learn something about the community. The bulletin boards inside are among the better in town and you can quickly see what's going on.

CAMDEN DELI $
37 Main St., Camden
(207) 236-8343
www.camdendeli.com

Half the reason to eat at the Camden Deli is the view of the falls where the Megunticook River meets Camden Harbor. The water goes right under the restaurant and tumbles spectacularly down a bank on the other side. Windows in the dining area overlook it all—and the panorama of the harbor itself isn't too shabby, either. The other reason to visit is simply the extensive list of sandwiches—more than 40—and soups, which are fairly traditional but always good.

EPHEMERE CAFE $$-$$$$
51 Bayview St., Camden
(207) 236-4451

A word of mouth favorite around town for a sophisticated night out, this place draws raves for its seafood (try the mussels) and carmelized sea scallops and it's a wine bar as well, so get yourself a glass of vino. The owner is a character and brings a European flair to Camden.

FRANCINE BISTRO $$-$$$
55 Chestnut St., Camden
(207) 230-0083
www.francinebistro.com

Chef/owner Brian Hill has quite the résumé, having cooked at Olives in Boston and in L.A., Hawaii, and New York, and he puts everything he's learned into good use at this cafe up the road from the post office. He also grew up on an organic farm, though, and so he brings to his menu both a sophistication and an understanding of fresh food, plundering the local farmer's market for produce and getting his meats at area farms. Perhaps this explains why he's less seafood-oriented than most of his Midcoast neighbors. You might find braised pork chops with turnip fondue or seared duck breast with a plum sauce, but you can find salmon as well. Dinner here is cozy (dig the pillows), hip (Hill used to be a rock star, among other things), and something of an event.

FRENCH AND BRAWN $
Main St., Camden
(207) 236-3361
www.frenchandbrawn.com

Every town ought to have a grocery like French and Brawn. The store manages to cram a little bit of everything into a relatively small space

in downtown Camden, complete with a meat counter, produce section, and small bakery. It's the sort of neighborhood market where the staff knows all the customers, you're always bumping into friends and acquaintances, good local gossip goes around, and there's even an old-fashioned credit system if you're sticking around a while. Besides carrying your average grocery store items, the place has a good selection of gourmet items, as well as premade sandwiches, salads, soups, and even sushi at the back, which you can pick up to go and eat in one of the many parks in town. Makes for a nice picnic option.

HARTSTONE INN $$$$
41 Elm St., Camden
(207) 236-4259 or (800) 788-4823
www.hartstoneinn.com

Wow. Would that every Maine B&B could wine and dine like this Camden sleeper. Like any other inn in town from the street, the Hartstone becomes a world apart when you sit down for a meal cooked up by chef Michael Salmon. Once the head of a staff of 200 cooks turning out meals for hundreds of diners, Salmon now concentrates on pleasing the appetites that can be seated in the dining room of the old Victorian inn. Call it more refined. His influences range from the Caribbean to Europe to Asia, and his menu changes based on what's fresh on any given day. Dishes might include Ducktrap smoked salmon and Maine crabmeat terrine with capers, roasted duckling cannelloni with caramelized onions and a port wine reduction sauce, Chinese five-spice quail, or lobster and asparagus quiche. Desserts are just as appetizing. The inn was lovingly restored and is elegant in a French Country and crystal sort of way, and the service is impeccable. Reservations are essential as word is getting out about the place.

NATALIE'S $$$$
83 Bayview St., Camden
(207) 236-7008
www.camdenharbourinn.com/natalies

Once located at the Knox Mill downtown, Natalie's merged with the Camden Harbour Inn, becoming the house dining room. With its scarlet tablecloths and fringed red lights, it has a nice ambiance. The French-country fare has been praised loud and long. Try the lobster and truffle mac and cheese or the Maine crab ravioli. Or, if everything looks good, spring for the five-course tasting menu. (Chef Lawrence Klang won the 2008 Maine Lobster Chef of the Year, so you may want to go this latter route.)

THE WATERFRONT $$
Bayview St., Camden
(207) 236-3747
www.waterfrontcamden.com

The name says it all here. The Waterfront has cafe-style dining under umbrellas right at the side of Camden Harbor, where you can watch the megayachts parade ostentatiously in and wish for a moment that you could be a reef. The fare is among the more dependable in town, trending toward the seafood. Dinner might be a sesame seed–seared salmon or blackened haddock with cilantro marinated cukes; lunch could be an herbed salmon burger or a grilled panini sandwich. There's plenty of seating inside the cedar-shingled building, but it's really nicest out on the deck on a sunny day. The Waterfront doesn't take reservations and can fill quickly, so keep that in mind when making your plans.

Other Dining Options in Camden

Cappy's Chowderhouse (Main Street; 207-236-2254; www.cappyschowder.com) is a family favorite for a cup of chowder with a slice of anadama bread. People love the pizza at the **Elm Street Grill** (115 Elm Street; 207-236-7722) and at **Paolina's Way** (10 Bayview Landing; 207-230-0555; www.paolinasway.com).

Lincolnville and Lincolnville Beach

YOUNGTOWN INN $$$
Route 52, Lincolnville
(207) 763-4290 or (800) 291-8438
www.youngtowninn.com

The Youngtown Inn is the very picture of a New England country inn, a three-story, white-clapboard, 1810 colonial that used to be part of

a dairy farm, but the delectable dishes it presents in its white-linen dining room are straight from France. Owner-chef Manuel Mercier hails from Paris, where he learned to cook, and his menu combines fresh Maine ingredients with French culinary traditions. When your waiter brings out your entree—say, the Faisan Perigourdine (grilled farm-raised pheasant breast with foie gras and brandy), the Loup de Mer au Safran (marinated striped sea bass with saffron broth), or the Filet d'Autruche au Poivre (grilled ostrich with black pepper and brandy), you'll wonder why it was so easy to get a table. The service is first-rate, the dining room is beautifully done, and the wine list is highly recommended. The inn has six rooms upstairs should you decide you need to eat here more than once, and it's only 4 miles from Camden on a spectacular stretch of road pinched between the cliffs of Mount Megunticook and the lake of the same name.

THE LOBSTER POUND $$
Route 1, Lincolnville Beach
(207) 789-5550
www.lobsterpoundmaine.com

The staff at this Midcoast landmark probably spends a lot of time cleaning sand out of the entryway—it's literally steps from the beach. Crowds throng here for its reliably good seafood, especially the shore dinner. The surprise is that you can also get a good turkey dinner or a well-done steak. Exceedingly comfortable, the restaurant can seat large groups and has tables on a patio overlooking the water. Service is friendly and relatively efficient. The parking lot fills quickly, and reservations are highly recommended during the blush of summer.

Other Dining Options in Lincolnville Beach

Chez Michel (Route 1; 207-789-5600) is a favorite for its French food. **Whale's Tooth Pub** (Route 1; 207-789-5200; www.whalestoothpub.com) is a great seaside pub with better-than-average pub fare and a nice fireplace for sitting by with your French onion soup.

Northport

DOS AMIGOS $–$$

Route 1, Northport
(207) 338-5775

You can always tell when this pink Mexican restaurant just south of Belfast opens for the season—the parking lot overflows with loyal regulars who just couldn't wait for the place to get hopping once again. You'll find dependably good Mexican fare in this cozy place—the nachos are grande and the margaritas not small. Try the fried ice cream. Open mid-March through the end of November.

Belfast

BAY WRAP $

20 Beaver St., Belfast
(207) 338-9757
www.baywrap.com

Belfast has its own healthy and delicious alternative to fast food in Bay Wrap, a flatbread wonderland retrofitted into an old pharmacy on a side street in the Penobscot Bay city. The original sandwich material, flatbreads have been a staple of on-the-run foods for centuries, and Bay Wrap uses them to good effect, loading them up with a variety of flavors. Anyone could find something on the eatery's globe-trotting menu. If you're hungry for barbecue, order up the Ayuh, It's BahBQ, which combines chicken or steak with barbecue sauce, jasmine rice, roasted zucchini, and Asian slaw. Perhaps you're feeling Japanese? Try the Samurai Salmon, a mix of grilled salmon, nori, sprouts, cukes, avocado, scallions, and jasmine rice with a wasabi vinagrette. The choices go on and on, and there are soups and salads and bowls of noodles as well. Eat in or take out. All this for just a bit more than a trip to McDonald's.

CHASE'S DAILY $$

96 Main St., Belfast
(207) 338-0555

Tables can be hard to come by at this vegetarian hot spot in downtown Belfast. Waldo County residents—and plenty of people from farther afield—are wild about the creative fare served here. Though everyone just calls it Chase's, the proper name is Chase's Daily, and that's how frequently many people seem to visit. Breakfast is arguably the best in Belfast, lunch is usually packed, and dinner is now served on Fridays and Saturdays in the summer. Veggies come from the family farm in Monroe, and they make their way into an array of innovative and eclectic dishes. Soft tacos; curried fried rice with fresh vegetables, herbs, nuts, and tofu; sandwiches like the fresh tomato, mozzarella, and basil on a baguette; and specialty salads like the all-tomato salad, which features four types of the red fruit with basil and oil, are all regularly featured. There are daily soups and daily pastas and daily breads. The decor is very comfortable with tin ceilings above, wide boards below, and brick everywhere, and you'll rub elbows—sometimes literally, as the tables are close together—with the Greater Belfast "hipoisie." You'll often find produce being sold farm style at the back; get there by noon if you want fresh breads to go or inexpensive bouquets of cut flowers.

DARBY'S $$

155 High St., Belfast
(207) 338-2339
www.darbysrestaurant.com

This old eatery used to be the default restaurant in Belfast. There weren't many dinner options back before the arrival of Chase's and Thai Bhurapar, and Darby's was always dependable. If you wanted pad Thai, you went to Darby's. If you wanted a Cajun chicken sandwich, you went to Darby's. If you wanted a drink after the movies … you get the idea. Food has been served at this

i Clams don't have to cost a lot of clams these days, especially if you dig them yourself. The state allows you to pick up to two pecks for personal use, as long as you dig in areas that aren't restricted. Equipment is widely available, and you'll get the hang of digging right quick. It's backbreaking work, but you'll feel like a Mainer—and your dinner will taste better somehow.

locale since the Civil War—check the beautiful tin ceilings—and the kitchen here continues to turn out good, unusual fare. In fact, the travel Web site Visiting New England gave the award for "most eclectic restaurant" to Darby's, praising the fact that it mixes Thai, Mexican, and good old Maine cuisines with aplomb. Try the crab cakes or the fish and chips.

DOCKSIDE RESTAURANT $
Main St., Belfast
(207) 338-6889

A favorite of locals and the travelers who wander down Main Street to the waterfront, the Dockside is your typical Maine family-style, seafood-place diner but with the focus on the fish and crustaceans. Wooden booths, vinyl seating, big portions, friendly staff—it's all very comfortable and familiar. The lobster stew is a crowd-pleaser and, even though it's an appetizer, it's almost a meal in itself, stuffed as it is with meat. You can get a traditional turkey dinner if you like, but it's the seafood that you'll remember.

Other Dining Options in the Belfast Area

Three Tides (2 Pinchy Lane, Belfast; 207-338-1707; www.3tides.com) is the best place around for bar food and bar fun. Young's Lobster Pound (Mitchell Avenue, East Belfast; 207-338-1160) is a lobster-in-the-rough classic. And the Belfast Co-op (123 High Street, Belfast; 207-338-2532), a grocery-store–size cooperative that caters to the organic and proud crowd, has great lunches in its cafe, and is a good Belfast microcosm. Bell the Cat (Reny's Plaza, Route 3, Belfast; 207-338-2084) was once a downtown cafe—now it's the eatery in Mr. Paperback bookstore, and it's a great sandwich place.

Searsport

RHUMB LINE RESTAURANT $$$–$$$$
200 East Main St. (Route 1), Searsport
(207) 548-2600
www.therhumblinerestaurant.com

Finally, fancy-pants dining comes to Searsport.

Waldo County foodies, especially those north of Belfast, have been rejoicing about this place, a fine restaurant on the left as you head out of town. The chef-owners of the Rhumb Line, Charles and Diana Evans, formerly ran an eatery on Martha's Vineyard, and they bring their talents to this pretty old farmhouse. Their menu is creative American fare, making good use of produce from the inn's own garden, which might include entrees like spicy seared medallions of pork tenderloin, grilled rack of lamb, or curried Contessa shrimp. Desserts are knockouts. Reservations are a must in summer.

Bucksport

MACLEOD'S RESTAURANT $$
Main St., Bucksport
(207) 469-3963

There are simply not a lot of dining options in Bucksport—this is the tried-and-true place. Family comfort foods, heavy on the seafood, are what make up the long menu. Choose from among MacLeod's own baked meat loaf, the baked scallop strudel, or the grilled lemon chicken. Everyone in town goes here, sometimes several days a week. Open for lunch and dinner, year-round.

Blue Hill and Surrounding Area

ARBORVINE $$$
Main St., Tenney Hill, Blue Hill
(207) 374-2119
www.arborvine.com

Named for the vine that arcs around the front door of its 1823 Cape, the Arborvine has been offering fine dining to residents of the Blue Hill area since 2000. The house has been lovingly restored, with the beams and floorboards and fireplaces left in place, which lend the dining rooms a quiet elegance, and the landscaping is classic as well. The menu is traditional New English fare, heavy on the meats, which might be anything from noisettes of lamb chasseur, tenderloin steak with three peppercorns, or fresh fish in season. Make sure to allow space down below for the desserts, like the crème caramel.

BROOKLIN INN $$$
Route 175, Brooklin
(207) 359-2777
www.brooklininn.com

If you're into wine you're going to want to stop at this Victorian inn. *Wine Spectator* has called the line up of vino here "one of the most outstanding wine lists in the world." Order a bottle and sit down for a menu that changes daily but might include peeky-toe crab cakes, coq au vin (naturally), sesame seared scallops, and finnan haddie with lobster. The produce tends to be organic and in season, the seafood fresh, and the poultry free-range and local. Served in a nice dining room with well-worn floors, Oriental rug, sashed windows, and French doors, it all amounts to an exceptional dining experience.

MORNING MOON CAFE $
Route 175, Brooklin
(207) 359-2373

A local breakfast and lunch favorite, this cafe sits right in Brooklin village proper. The pizza here is quite good—actually everything's pretty good, from the soups and salads to the sandwiches. To-go options are available.

RUSTICATOR RESTAURANT AT
OAKLAND HOUSE $$–$$$
435 Herrick's Rd., Brooksville
(207) 359-8521 or (800) 359-RELAX
www.oaklandhouse.com

This classic old inn—a mansard-roofed Maine beauty—has been serving dinner for a half century, and it sets a beautiful table, with candles, Blue Onion china, and flowers. Traditional fare with contemporary twists peppers the menu and comes in five courses. The chef here used to be at Jonathan's, the much beloved eatery in Blue Hill. Try the prime rib, the Arctic char with tomato and pesto, or the wild salmon. On Thursdays in summer the inn serves a lobster bake on the beach. Very nice.

WESCOTT FORGE
66 Main St., Blue Hill
(207) 374-9909

The new go-to place in Blue Hill, Wescott Forge is a big red clapboard on Main with a nice fireplace and it actually served as a forge back in the day. What you'll find inside now is a menu of worldly flavors, heavy on the seafood, and a fine wine list. This is the first word out of anyone's mouth locally when you ask for a dinner recommendation, and it's full of inspired twists like the salads that come in bowls of cucumber and the goat cheese salad, with its fried rice wrapping. Weeknights they serve bistro style, and weekends they offer fine dining. Yummy.

Other Dining Options in the Blue Hill Area

Set at the reversing falls, **Bagaduce Lunch** (19 Bridge Road, North Brooksville; 207-326-4729) dishes up take-out seafood you can carry to a picnic table overlooking the water. **First Light Books** (58 Main Street, Blue Hill; 207-374-5422) has a great bakery—same staff as the old Pain de Famille—where you can get all sorts of carryout items, from soups to salads. The **Birdwatcher Store Cafe** (37 Water Street, Blue Hill; 207-374-3740) is an unusual lunch spot that's for the birds.

Castine

BAH'S BAKEHOUSE $$
Water St., Castine
(207) 326-9510
www.bahsworld.com

Bah's is the sort of place you hope to find in every town you visit, that comfortable eatery with great food, delightful personnel who remember you, entertaining locals, and prices that allow you to return several times during your stay. Baked goods are the staple here, but people often start their day at Bah's with coffee, return at lunch for one of the area's best sandwiches, and maybe pick up some wine on the way home. Open daily 7 a.m. to 2 p.m. in summer; during off-season hours are reduced. Really remarkable baked goods.

CASTINE INN $$$-$$$$
Main St., Castine
(207) 326-4365
www.castineinn.com

Chef Tom Gutow has been praised all over for his culinary talents. He was the Maine Governor's Lobster Chef of the Year in 1998, the Castine Inn was chosen as one of the nation's 50 best by Food & Wine magazine, and countless magazines have weighed in with their approval. What's the fuss? Again, creative use of fresh local ingredients and, yes, a way with seafood. Try the Penobscot Bay mackerel with green peppercorn pickled onions, the loin of lamb with pickled fiddleheads, and farm-raised striped sea bass. He even offers cooking classes if you want to understand the source of the magic. The 1898 inn with wrap-around porch serves as a perfect backdrop. Open for dinner, May through October.

DENNETT'S WHARF $
15 Sea St., Castine
(207) 326-9045
www.dennettswharf.com

On pylons over Castine Harbor, the seating area at Dennett's Wharf puts you right out on the water, almost like dining on a boat. It's a great place to watch the action on East Penobscot Bay, especially in high summer, when the windjammers are running. The fare is made up primarily of stuff that's recently been pulled from that very same drink—oysters are a specialty, as are steamers. Try the boiled Stonington lobster, the roasted chicken, or the grilled barbecued salmon brochettes. If you feel like you've eaten too much, rent one of Dennett's bikes or kayaks and work it off. Open daily from 11 a.m. to midnight, from May through Columbus Day.

STELLA'S $$
26 Water St., Castine
(207) 326-9710
www.bahsworld.com

Run by the same Bah as Bah's Bakehouse, which is upstairs, Stella's is a treat, featuring a nice light menu of entrees that show the proprietor's New Orleans heritage, like her famous fish cakes, as well as salads and soups that transcend. All set to cool jazz that is so good it will make you think you're in the Big Easy. Unexpected and wonderful.

Other Dining Options in Castine

The **Manor Inn** (76 Battle Avenue; 207-326-4861; www.manor-inn.com) and the **Pentagoet** (Main Street; 207-326-8616; www.pentagoet.com) both open their dining rooms to nonguests and have nice, high-end menus.

Deer Isle and Surrounding Area

GOOSE COVE LODGE $$-$$$$
Route 15A, Sunset
(207) 348-2508
www.goosecovelodge.com

The setting at this nifty inn is positively magical, overlooking the cove of the same name (you're going to want to get a gander at this Goose), which is an inlet on East Penobscot Bay. Isles and islands, spruce forests, and shimmering sea everywhere you look, and you have to travel some off-the-beaten-track byways to get there. There's dining on the deck or in the dining room known as the Point, with wood grain all around. Surf and turf with occasional Mediterranean influences comprises the menu. Try the porterhouse steak, the Mediterranean seafood stew (lobster, clam, mussels, shrimp, scallops and fish in an orange fennel broth), or grilled Italian sausage served over penne pasta. (See if you can weasel your way into an invitation to stay at the stargazing parties that often occur here in summer.) No kids' menu. Full bar. Open from mid-June through mid-October. Reservations advisable.

FISHERMAN'S FRIEND RESTAURANT $$-$$$
5 Atlantic Ave., Stonington
(207) 367-2442
www.fishermansfriendrestaurant.com

This place surely must be a friend to fishermen. It serves so much seafood, it must keep half the local fleet in business. If you like your lobster you'll find 30 reasons to be happy here. The chowders and seafood stews are fan favorites, but you'll also find a turkey dinner with home-made stuffing that's no slouch, either. Portions are hearty enough for a day at sea, prices very fair, and the service very friendly. Definitely save room for the pies or you'll regret it. The views from their new location, right on Stonington's fantastically picturesque Atlantic Avenue, are as good as the food.

MARITIME CAFE $$$
27 Main St., Stonington
(207) 367-2600
Doesn't get much more maritimey than an old Main Street building overlooking Stonington Harbor. And this little cafe, with big windows out the back, makes good use of it. The entrée menu at lunch consists of lazyman's Stonington lobster and Stonington lobster with mussels and corn, but there is an array of sandwiches available, many of them also of the seafood variety, naturally. Dinner brings a handful of other choices—crab cakes, roasted halibut, and a couple of meat items—all of which are tempting.

Other Dining Options in the Deer Isle Area

Harbor Cafe (Main Street, Stonington; 207-367-5099) is where the locals turn for breakfast. **Lily's Cafe** (Route 15, Stonington; 207-367-5936) is great for lunch. The **Cockatoo Portuguese Restaurant** (Goose Cove Road, Deer Isle; 207-348-2300; www.thecockatoorestaurant.com) is the new restaurant at the new Goose Cove Lodge Resort, and it's surely your only place to find bife ha Portuguesa Down East.

Ellsworth
THE BANGKOK RESTAURANT $-$$
321 High St., Ellsworth
(207) 667-1324
This place is a real find—some of the best Thai food on the coast served in a small restaurant attached to a motor lodge. Who'd guess? On the hill as you head out of town, Bangkok serves up traditional fare, from great pad Thai to delectable drunken noodles. Prices are reasonable, to boot.

CLEONICE MEDITERRANEAN BISTRO $$$$
112 Main St., Ellsworth
(207) 664-7554
www.cleonice.com
Now, this is the stuff. The tastes of southern Italy and Spain in a pretty, old downtown landmark in a small Maine town. Cleonice pairs good Maine ingredients—of the land and sea—with the spices and tastes of Europe in a delectable way, offering what it says are the only tapas served north of Portland. The menu is deep and long, with a half-dozen specials per night complementing just as many seasonal entrees and at least a dozen tapas. Try the lamb and pumpkin tagine Marrakesh or the "symphony of seafood," or make a meal of two or three tapas for a feast of flavors. It all adds up to a very welcome addition to the Ellsworth scene. Foodies Down East must be doing backflips.

THE MEX $
191 Main St., Ellsworth
(207) 667-4494
www.themexrestaurant.com
Mexican fare done well has kept this place hopping since 1980. Atmosphere is fun—nice stuccoed walls, cozy rooms, wooden booths, and beaded curtains—the service is good, and the menu both has some wit to it and is well rounded. Try the chile relleno, the chimichanga, or the enchilada salad. Margaritas, frozen daiquiris, and Mexican beer are readily available. Open daily for lunch and dinner.

RIVERSIDE CAFE $
151 Main St., Ellsworth
(207) 667-7220
A longtime favorite in Ellsworth with the breakfast and lunch crowds, Riverside Cafe is truly a pleasant cafe. The chowder is very good, the omelets are recommended (try the State Street, with spinach, Swiss cheese, mushrooms, and onion), and there are plenty of sandwich, burger, and even vegetarian options. Breakfast is served all day—and people seem to like that—and the Sunday brunch is a local event. Open all year, seven days a week, from 6 a.m. to 3 p.m.

UNION RIVER LOBSTER POT $$
8 South St., Ellsworth
(207) 667-5077
www.lobsterpot.com

Tucked away on the river behind Rooster Brothers, this seafood staple serves up a mean lobster dinner, complete with drawn butter, french fries, coleslaw, and homemade biscuits. That's just the beginning. From clam chowder, lobster stew, and steamers to fried scallops, clams, shrimp, and fish—all the usual suspects are here, served cafe style along the river. Open from mid-June through September.

Other Restaurants in the Ellsworth Area

Crazy Dave's Pit BBQ (Route 3, Ellsworth; 207-479-9393; www.crazydavesbbq.com) has great pulled pork, chicken, ribs, and sausage.

Trenton

TRENTON BRIDGE LOBSTER POUND $$
1237 Bar Harbor Rd., Trenton
(207) 667-2977
www.trentonbridgelobster.com

Hard to resist to anyone driving by on Route 3 en route to Acadia, this restaurant places its cookers right outside by the road—and you just know what's inside: fresh lobster. They've been at it since 1956, making this pound one of the oldest in the state, so you know they must be doing something right.

ACADIA AREA

Bar Harbor and Surrounding Area

BEN AND BILL'S CHOCOLATE EMPORIUM $
66 Main St., Bar Harbor
(207) 288-3281 or (800) 806-3281
www.benandbills.com

Lobster ice cream may be the confection that turns heads at this Bar Harbor staple, but there is so much more to like here than that acquired taste. From truffles to brittles to fudges to suckers, the place is colorful as a cartoon and smells like heaven. You can watch the machines at work at the back while you try to decide between home-

made ice cream or a piece of thick fudge. Ben and Bill's retains the ambience of an old-fashioned candy store, but it's very much a part of the Bar Harbor of the present, serving up ice cream and goodies to crowds and open until midnight in summer.

CAFE THIS WAY $$$
14½ Mount Desert St., Bar Harbor
(207) 288-4483
www.cafethisway.com

Everything about this place is imaginative and whimsical, from the burgundy walls to the shelves full of books to the eclectic menu. Sit by the fireplace and order up the Bibimbap, a Korean vegetable stir-fry, or the lemon vodka lobster and be prepared to be delighted when your entree arrives. Or come for breakfast and sit on the deck and try Kit's burrito or the Harney, which is This Way's own corned beef hash. You'll remember which way it is to This Way, and you'll surely be back for more.

HAVANA $$$–$$$$
318 Main St., Bar Harbor
(207) 288-CUBA
www.havanamaine.com

Who ever would have thought that Cuba would be such a big draw in Bar Harbor, past home of capitalist barons and now filled every summer with middle-class tourists? You can hardly get a seat in this Main Street eatery, with its ruby-red walls and hip wicker chairs. If you do get in, you can enjoy island drinks at the newly expanded bar or outside in the rock garden while you wait for your "innovative American cuisine with Latin flair"—which could mean crab cakes with roasted corn and cilantro cream or lobster in a quesadilla with charred jalapeño and corn salsa or sole roulades. The menu changes frequently. Open daily from 5 to "9-ish."

MACHE BISTRO $$$
135 Cottage St., Bar Harbor
(207) 288-0447
www.machebistro.com

An intimate space on the main drag, Mache is a true bistro, comfortable and cozy and a place where you feel compelled to linger. The chef here once worked at Portland's famed Fore Street, and his menu is highly regarded for its inventiveness and use of fresh local products. There's a French country influence. Try the seared foie gras, the polenta cakes, or the waterzooi, a fish and shell-fish stew. The wine list is impressive as well.

MAGGIE'S RESTAURANT $$–$$$$
6 Summer St., Bar Harbor
(207) 288-9007
www.maggiesbarharbor.com

Maggie O'Neil knows her way around seafood, having shucked scallops on a commercial drag-ger back in the mid-1970s and worked in the fish marketing business. She personally selects the fish that she now serves at her Bar Harbor restaurant, and she also grows many of her vegetables. Even the beef and poultry are local. So things tend to be good and fresh at Maggie's. The menu changes weekly and is heavy on the seafood, but the chefs here do artful vegetarian dishes with all that produce. Try the Maine crab cakes with mustard-caper remoulade, the lobster crepes, the crab enchiladas, or the seafood Provençale.

POOR BOY'S GOURMET $$–$$$
300 Main St., Bar Harbor
(207) 288-4148
www.poorboysgourmet.com

You'll find this place by the gardens out front, which bloom colorfully and all but obscure the porch. Your best bet here is the early-bird extrav-aganza, an all-you-can-eat pasta smorgasbord with 10 or so options, from baked stuffed farfalle to linguine with clam sauce to linguine with pesto. Sample all you like, but be sure to leave room for the famous cheesecakes. The a la carte menu is extensive, with lobster 10 different ways as well as steak, chicken, and vegetarian choices. Open seven days a week.

READING ROOM RESTAURANT $$$$
Bar Harbor Inn
Newport Dr., Bar Harbor
(207) 288-3351 or (800) 248-3351

Once was, you had to be some sort of magnate or nabob to dine at the Reading Room—during the golden age of Bar Harbor it was a gentlemen's club of the rich and famous. Today you don't even need to wear a jacket (dress is informal). The views of Frenchman Bay from the big bay windows, though, are still extraordinary. Fare is fairly traditional New English—boiled lobster and lobster pie are specialties, and seafood domi-nates the menu, with charbroiled swordfish and Frenchman Bay bouillabaisse being another pair of options. Terra firma is represented by selec-tions like the Dijon roasted rack of lamb and the citrus grilled breast of chicken. Sunday brunch is a good time to visit, as is lunch any day, when you can enjoy the Reading Room's menu at the Ter-race Grille, an outdoor cafe overlooking the bay.

ROSALIE'S PIZZA $$
46 Cottage St., Bar Harbor
(207) 288-5666

This is the place for pizza on Mount Desert Island, and it's one of the best pizza joints in all of Maine, frankly. Unless you get here early, you'll have to stand in line with the locals and tourists for a table. Enjoy the 1950s kitsch while you do. The homemade pies come in four sizes, and the sauce and spices are exactly how you want them. Worth the wait—or call in an order and picnic by the water. Beer and wine are served.

RUPUNUNI $$
119 Main St., Bar Harbor
(207) 288-2886
www.rupununi.com

This place right downtown is always spirited. The name is from Guyana, but the cuisine doesn't really show any one strong influence other than Maine seafood. There are hints of the Mediterra-nean in the Porcelli's veal piccata and the lobster fettucine and a little bit of the South in the bour-bon pork chops and Louisiana gumbo. A raw bar appeals to oyster lovers; others like the burgers, from beef to veggie, ostrich to buffalo. A fun spot, and there is often live entertainment happening.

BURNING TREE $$$
69 Otter Creek Dr., Otter Creek
(207) 288-9331

The specialties at this excellent eatery are gourmet seafood and vegetarian fare, and people routinely make the 5-mile journey out of Bar Harbor to get a table here. An open and airy place, it tries to utilize seafood newly arrived from the boats and produce from its own gardens. The menu is witty and fun. Try the blueberry lavender soup, which comes chilled, or the squash blossoms stuffed with goat cheese. Entrees might include sautéed halibut in a Parmesan crust or salmon grilled over sweet corn bread pudding. Yum. Reservations are a good idea.

Other Dining Options in Bar Harbor

Michelle's (194 Main Street; 207-288-0038) at the Ivy Manor Inn is an elegant pairing of French and New English. **Lompoc Cafe and Brewpub** (36 Rodick Street; 207-288-9392) is Bar Harbor's oldest brewpub and has a beer garden with boccie. **Jordan's Restaurant** (80 Cottage Street; 207-288-3586) is the place to get breakfast.

Northeast Harbor
DOCKSIDER RESTAURANT $
14 Sea St., Northeast Harbor
(207) 276-3965

People rave about the lobster served at this straightforward place not far from the marina, whether it be the traditional boiled version or the lobster roll. Locals and visitors line up for it. The chowders have their fans, too, as do the crab cakes, and there are plenty of salads and burgers for those who prefer not to eat seafood.

REDBIRD PROVISIONS RESTAURANT $$$
11 Sea St., Northeast Harbor
(207) 276-3006
www.redbirdprovisions.com

Housed in one of the town's fancy old cottages, Redbird features the cooking talents of Chef Jesse Perrin, who did his understudy work in Boston at places like the famed Blue Ginger. Look for dishes like "Spruced Up" Breton pork loin and organic Scottish salmon, as well as items that show Italian influences. With a nice porch and outdoor garden area, rattan chairs, and ample flowers, Redbird is a treat.

TAN TURTLE TAVERN $$
151 Main St., Northeast Harbor
(207) 276-9898

A long, long menu of is the order here—some diners have likened it to a catalog—and seafood is prominent. Yeah, you'll find steak and pasta, but what you'll want is the ale-battered jumbo shrimp or the crunchy fish sandwich or the lobster roll. And of course, it being a tavern, you can expect to find some tasty regional microbrews on tap.

Other Dining Options in Northeast Harbor

Don't forget the inns. The **Asticou** (Route 3; 207-276-3344; www.asticou.com) has an elegant dining room. For more picnic fare try the **Pine Tree Market** (Main Street; 207-276-3335), an excellent little grocery.

Southwest Harbor and Surrounding Area
BEAL'S LOBSTER PIER $$
182 Clark Point Rd., Southwest Harbor
(207) 244-3202
www.bealslobster.com

Right next to the local Coast Guard base, this lobster pound has an incredible view, overlooking Southwest Harbor and the mountains of Acadia. Beals have been working the waterfront here for generations, and the seafood at their restaurant is newly landed. Chowders, clams, and lobsters a variety of ways are the specialties, and they're done right. If you fall in love, you can ship whatever you want home via next-day air.

FIDDLER'S GREEN RESTAURANT $$$
411 Main St., Southwest Harbor
(207) 244-9416
www.fiddlersgreenrestaurant.com

Like the best of Maine's restaurants, this place

makes fine use of fresh local fish and seasonal ingredients. The chef here makes everything possible on the premises, smoking the fish, stuffing the ravioli, baking the breads. The menu changes frequently, and guests in the eatery's three dining rooms can choose from a half dozen specials in addition to the nightly fare, which might be smoked rainbow trout, seared and roasted duck breast with pomegranate glaze, or grilled and marinated rib-eye steak. Extensive wine list.

LITTLE NOTCH PIZZERIA   **$$**
340 Main St., Southwest Harbor
(207) 244-3357
The name of this place suggests a small alpine eatery sandwiched between tall peaks. But it actually comes from the notch in the side of Acadia's Western Mountain, which cafe owner Arthur Jacobs grew up looking at. The Seal Cove native left Mount Desert for cooking school and returned to open this great lunch spot smack in downtown Southwest Harbor. The gourmet pizzas, sandwiches, salads, and soups attract a whole host of regulars, and the smartly decorated cafe, with its picture windows looking out on the street and wrought-iron chairs, has enough curb appeal to attract passersby. Pizzas are topped with an array of original flavors, like turkey sausage, prosciutto, hot chili peppers, and artichoke hearts. The sandwiches are just as creative—sweet Italian sausage with Parmesan, say, or roasted broccoli, onions, and cheddar—and they come on delectable focaccia.

RED SKY RESTAURANT   **$$$–$$$$**
14 Clark Point Rd., Southwest Harbor
(207) 244-0476
www.redskyrestaurant.com
With its tile floor, central fireplace, wood-panel ceiling, and white table cloths, Red Sky is a welcoming place, and that was the intent of owners Elizabeth and James Lindquist. Delicious without being stuffy. The fare is as fresh and local as they can get it and it might be a roasted chicken from Sunset Acre Farms or lobster shucked and sautéed, all served with veggies from a trio of area farms. The breads are baked daily, the meats cut

by hand, and the desserts from scratch and worthy of genuflection. Even the ice teas are brewed by the glass.

Other Dining Options in the Southwest Harbor Area

Beech Hill Farm (Beech Hill Road, Somesville; 207-244-5204) is a fine source for organic produce, locally made breads, meats, and gourmet items. **Sawyer's Market** (344 Main Street, Southwest Harbor; 207-244-3315) is an upscale market with a gourmet deli. For lobster try **Thurston's Lobster Pound** (Steamboat Wharf Road, Bernard; 207-244-7600; www.thurstonslobster.com).

DOWN EAST

Hancock and Hancock Point

CROCKER HOUSE   **$$$–$$$$**
967 Point Rd., Hancock Point
(207) 422-6806
www.crockerhouse.com
One of the best places to stay Down East is also one of the best places to dine. A country inn in exclusive Hancock Point, the Crocker House serves up a fairly traditional menu that is exceedingly well done. Try the house special—Crocker House scallops, which are served with a lemon wine sauce—the broiled swordfish, or the shrimp scampi. Veggies come straight from the garden, desserts are homemade and fresh. Fine food is hard to find the farther you go down the coast—but this place holds its own with just about anyone. Open daily from mid-April through October and weekends in the off-season.

LE DOMAINE   **$$$$**
Route 1, Hancock
(207) 422-3395 or (800) 554-8498
www.ledomaine.com
Less than 10 miles from Ellsworth, this inn feels a world away, and part of that is due to Nicole Purslow's exquisite French country cuisine. The place is warm and welcoming with its Provençal fabrics and fireplace, and when you sit down, you'll not believe the dishes that come out of the kitchen.

Traditionally French, the entrees make use of fresh ingredients, and they might be Coquilles St. Jacques Saute Provençale, which are Maine sea scallops pan-seared; Filet Mignon Bordelaise, which is steak in a rich bordelaise sauce; and Le Charlotte d'Agneau aux Aubergines, a braised lamb dish. The desserts are fantastic, especially the house's special bread pudding Le Domaine, and there are 5,000 French wines in the wine cellar.

Other Dining Options in the Hancock Point Area

For lobsters in the rough, you can't beat the **Tidal Falls Lobster Pound** (Off Route 1, Hancock; 207-422-6457). **Ruth and Wimpy's Kitchen** (Route 1, Hancock; 207-422-3723; www.ruthandwimpys.com) serves lobster 100 ways as well as great specialty sandwiches.

Jonesboro and Milbridge

44 DEGREES NORTH $-$$
17 Main St., Milbridge
(207) 546-4440
www.44-degrees-north.com
Just the sort of place Milbridge needed, this restaurant and pub offers a nice alternative to seafood joint after seafood joint. Yes, you can still get lobster and seafood lasagna but you can also get a teriyaki steak or penna alla Arrabiata or any of a dozen burgers, and it'll be worth your time. Comfortable overstuffed booths, and a full bar in the pub.

THE WHITE HOUSE $
Route 1, Jonesboro
(207) 434-2792
Like Moody's Diner down the coast, this Down East restaurant has achieved legendary status (though mostly to residents of Washington County). And again, like Moody's, a lot of the esteem in which people hold the place is due to the pies it serves. People swear by them. The parking lot here is filled most of the time with diners interested in the pies, the seafood platters, the fish chowder, and the breakfast, which begins

at 5 a.m. Try the homemade molasses doughnut, the corned beef hash, or the waffles. Just about everyone has a different favorite, from the eggs to the pancakes, so it must be good. Sit down at the counter or one of the tables, and you can say you've had breakfast, lunch, or dinner at the White House.

Machias

BLUE BIRD RANCH $-$$
78 Main St., Machias
(207) 255-3351
With its bright blue metal roof and Coca-Cola sign, you'd guess this Main Street eatery was a Down East family-style favorite and you'd be right. Not much about this place is unexpected—seafood, steaks, salas, a bar—but it will pleasantly fill you up.

HELEN'S RESTAURANT $-$$
28 E. Main St., Machias
(207) 255-8423
This family favorite has become legendary Down East for its pies—try the blueberry. The fare is best described as "Maine seafood dinery" and consists of a lot of fried fish, stews (excellent), and the usual assortment of burgers and dogs. But what you really want is a piece of pie. Open from 6 a.m. to 8:30 p.m. daily year-round.

RIVERSIDE INN $$
Route 1, East Machias
(207) 255-4134
www.riversideinn-maine.com
Machias is not brimming with creative eateries, which makes the dining room at the Riverside Inn a treat. Here you'll find entrees like red tuna wontons, pistachio-crusted pork medallions, lobster and scallops in Champagne sauce—you know, the kind of stuff you're not supposed to find outside of cities and resorts and certainly not in remote fishing villages. Your table overlooks the Machias River, so you can enjoy views while you take your meal. Nice.

WHOLE LIFE NATURAL MARKET $

4 Colonial Way, Machias

(207) 255-8855

www.wholelifemarket.com

This funky co-op is exactly the sort of thing a small Down East college town needs. You've got your natural and gourmet products, your supplements, your bulk items, and a neat little counter where you can pick up a garden burger, garden salad, or tofu, hummus, or vegetarian wrap. Very nice in a seafood-and-potatoes town like Machias.

Lubec

HOME PORT INN $$–$$$

45 Main St., Lubec

(207) 733-2077 or (800) 457-2077

www.homeportinn.com

Lubec isn't exactly bursting at the seams with fine restaurants, and this place is the best of them. The dining room is in a pretty old 1880s inn, tastefully done, and the menu is slanted toward seafood. You might start with some cold smoked salmon, move on to Down East scampi, flounder, or steak au poivre, and finish up with some blueberry shortcake. Reservations are advisable. Open from 5 to 8 nightly.

Eastport and Surrounding Area

WACO DINER $

Water St., Eastport

(207) 853-4046

Don't let the locals intimidate you away from this legendary diner dive on the waterfront (they like to turn and give newcomers a menacing stare). It actually isn't even dark and smoky anymore, thanks to a new expansion that has made way for a deck over the water and a face-lift to the exterior (due to its status as an extra in *Murder in Small Town X*, perhaps?). WaCo stands for Washington County, and this place has been a fixture since the 1920s. Breakfasts are great, and there are all your favorite diner foods from the roast turkey dinner to good burgers. And, of course, plenty of seafood. Open year-round.

Other Dining Options in the Eastport Area

Eastport Chowder House (167 Water Street, Eastport; 207-853-2345; www.eastportchowder house.com) has great, yep, chowders.

Robbinston

KATIE'S ON THE COVE (AKA KATIE'S CHOCOLATES) $

Route 1, Robbinston

(207) 454-8446

www.katieschocolates.com

Who knew there even were chocolate recipes from "Down East candy makers of the past"? Lea and Joseph Sullivan have been using those old-fashioned notions to make some of the best chocolates you'll ever find. They're hand formed and hand dipped and so popular they get mailed out around the globe. It's hard to find better fudge, truffles, and bark anywhere.

Calais

BERNARDINI'S $–$$

89 Main St., Calais

(207) 454-2237

www.bernardinis.com

One of very few reasons to go to Calais to eat, Bernardini's is a fairly straightforward Italian place with all the expected pastas and marinaras. But Marilyn Bernardini is a gifted enough chef to win the Maine Restaurant Association's Restaurateur of the Year of award in 1999. Try one of her soups or even the lobser rolls, which were pleasant surprises. The place is comfortable, with checkerboard walls and glass-topped tables, but not fancy. Open year-round from 11 a.m. to 8 p.m. Monday through Saturday; closed Sunday.

Other Dining Options in Calais

Chandler House (20 Chandler Street; 207-454-7922) serves very well-prepared seafood. Sandwich Man (206 North Street; 207-454-2460) has reliably good subs.

FARMERS' MARKETS

Farmers' markets are still a big deal in Maine—from roadside stands to small shops to once-a-week parking lot gatherings, they're the source of produce for a lot of Mainers. The food is fresh, and the farmers are often fun characters. They give you an excuse to venture out into the countryside, and by spending your money at the source, you help preserve both sustainable agriculture and open space.

Oftentimes, the veggies are even less expensive at farm stands than they are at the grocery store, and they're a lot less work than doing it yourself. (Some residents of Knox and Lincoln Counties don't even bother to plant gardens anymore because they know the produce is better at the legendary Beth's Farm Market in Warren.) Many farmers are organically certified, and many markets carry much more than greens and corn. Some have meats, ciders, honeys, jams, yarns, and cut flowers. If you're in Maine for any length of time and have access to cooking facilities, farmers' markets are the way to go for good, cheap meals. Find a list of all of the state's farmers' markets at www.get realmaine.com/buy/farmers_markets .html.

ICE CREAM

Lobster ice cream? It seemed inevitable that someone would come up with the idea of combining the favorite dinner of Mainers with one of their favorite desserts. (Ben and Bill's Chocolate Emporium in Bar Harbor has the crustaceanary cream, if you're interested.) Ice cream is indeed one of the preferred snacks in Maine, second maybe to whoopie pies in the estimation of the state's residents, and it's available all along the coast at various stands and shacks. You can get a wealth of flavors, soft serve and hard packed varieties, edible cones, and toppings galore. But there are a handful of places that make ice cream that transcends, crafting dairy art out of a few ingredients. Those are listed here.

South Coast
BIG DADDY'S ICE CREAM
Route 1, Wells
(207) 646-5454
A favorite for decades, Big Daddy's can have lines well after 9 p.m., thanks to excellent homemade dairy goodness. Some 30 flavors are available, from the usual—vanilla and chocolate—to more exotic treats like ginger and coconut and strawberry cheesecake. Summer in Wells wouldn't be the same without it.

BROWN'S OLD FASHIONED ICE CREAM
232 Nubble Rd., York Beach
(207) 363-1277
You'd figure that Ben Cohen, of Ben and Jerry's fame, might know a thing or two about ice cream, so when he goes nominating an ice-cream stand as one of the 10 best in the nation, it must mean something. He did just that for this low-slung brown ice creamery near the Nubble Light, calling it "the quintessential summer ice cream stand" in the pages of *USA Today*. Not bad for the neighborhood favorite that has been scooping out cones since 1967. Try the Maine Survivor flavor. To be fair, Ben goes on to say that the ice cream here is good, but the view is the real treat. Still, the cold stuff holds its own.

THE GOLDENROD
York Beach
(207) 363-2621
www.thegoldenrod.com
Best known for its saltwater kisses, the century-old York Beach favorite also makes 135 flavors of homemade ice cream dished up at an old-fashioned marble soda fountain, as it should be.

SHAIN'S OF MAINE
1491 Main St., Sanford
(207) 324-1449 or (800) 324-0560
www.shainsofmaine.com
Besides being one of the best and brightest wholesalers of ice cream in Maine, Shain's has supplied the Portland Sea Dogs baseball team with their delicious "dog biscuits." And Shain's has a retail operation in Sanford where you can tour the factory and sample the more than 100 flavors the company turns out. Delightful.

Greater Portland
BEAL'S FAMOUS OLD-FASHIONED ICE CREAM
161 Pine Point Rd., Scarborough
(207) 883-1160
www.bealsicecream.com
Beal's ice-cream stands look like any other small roadside take-out—but when the staff person opens the window and hands you a homemade "Swiss" cone filled with rich, creamy, cold, and sweet vanilla, you know you've found something special. Beals serves up 150 homemade flavors at six locations all across greater Portland.

Midcoast
DOWNEAST ICE CREAM
Pier One, Boothbay Harbor
(207) 633-3016
Ice cream with a view is the focus here (of course, you can get seven frozen yogurt, sherbet, and sugar-free cones, too).

WANNAWAF
At the Footbridge
Under the Harborside Restaurant
Boothbay Harbor
(207) 837-1274
This take-out stand would be better served listed under a waffle heading, but since there isn't one of those, it goes here. Since the late 1980s this spot has been the site of an ice-cream stand, and for the past few it's been home to Wannawaf, which combines ice cream with hot Belgian waffles. Try the Maine Squeeze, which adds blueberry ice cream, blueberries, blueberry syrup, and whipped cream to a waffle, or the Classic, which is a waffle with vanilla ice cream, strawberries, and whipped cream. Decadent.

ROUND TOP ICE CREAM
Business Route 1, Damariscotta
(207) 563-5307
Round Top not only sells its 52 flavors in stores across the Midcoast, it sells them in an ever-expanding gambrel-roofed stand on the way out of Damariscotta. Round Top has been in business since 1924, and the crowds still come.

DORMAN'S DAIRY DREAM
Route 1, Thomaston
(207) 594-4195
Sure, the name has a preciousness to it, but this roadside ice-cream stand is the real deal, having been a hugely popular institution for more than half a century. Kendrick Dorman started serving homemade ice cream out of a little white building on the Rockland–Thomaston town line, back before Route 1 was even Route 1. His brother, William, was doing the same thing down the road, making cones from ice cut on northern Maine lakes. Sugar shortages during the Second World War forced the pair to combine their efforts, and their enterprise as it stands today was born. Family members still run the shop, dishing out 22 flavors of homemade goodness, and crowds line up for it, particularly the pistachio. Good to see it survive all the development occurring in the neighborhood.

SHOPPING

A fellow by the name of Leon Leonwood Bean put Maine on the retail map back in 1912, and credit-card–toting visitors have been pounding their way along the coast ever since in search of good values. In terms of shopping, Maine is really about three things: bargains, antiques, and fine arts and crafts. The outlets that have sprouted up around the store that L.L. Bean founded in Freeport and those located down in Kittery are among the best in the nation. And the state also has some native job lot favorites like Marden's and Renys, discount department store chains where trucks pull in from all over carrying everything under the sun at sometimes ridiculously low prices. Some people have an almost devotional attachment to these places and visit daily, and houseguests always want to get to one of them during their stay.

Because Mainers have long been pack rats and the state has its share of historic homes, and simply because there's tourist demand, Maine has quite the antiques culture—it's no surprise that one of the biggest and best national periodicals on the subject got its start here—*Maine Antique Digest*—and that some of the region's largest antiques shows happen here. Auctions, a great place to find older items at affordable prices, are a Maine tradition, too—some people go just for entertainment. Antiques lovers will find a lot to love just by staying on U.S. Route 1, and they'll want to be certain to hit Wells, Wiscasset, the Damariscotta area, and Searsport, all of which have developed reputations as repositories of the good and old.

And craftspeople, aware of the "Made in Maine" mystique, have turned the Pine Tree State into a nice place to hunt for more high-end items as well. Visit Camden, for example, if you're looking for fine jewelry, as there is an unusually high concentration of gold- and silversmiths in that Penobscot Bay town and its neighbors. Deer Isle is a good place to go if you're looking for ceramics, thanks to the Haystack School of Arts and Crafts, and Greater Portland has finely made furnishings.

There are a few towns, such as Kittery and Freeport; a few districts, like Portland's Old Port and downtown Bar Harbor; and even a few legendary stores, like the Big Chicken Barn in Ellsworth, that are absolutely can't-miss with shoppers. But there are many lesser-known gems scattered along the coast in unexpected places, which makes shopping in Maine always an adventure.

Most shops are open from 9 a.m. to 5 p.m. Monday through Saturday and closed Sunday, except the big chain stores and the Maine Mall, which tend to be open from 9 a.m. to 9 p.m. Monday through Saturday and 9 a.m. to 5 p.m. Sunday. Good luck.

SOUTH COAST

Kittery

Anyone entering Maine gets a look at the back of Kittery's famous outlets, sitting there next to Interstate 95 enticingly flashing sale signs. And the handful that can be seen from the road are just the beginning. Kittery's outlet row is home to more than 120 stores and sprawls for more than a mile in strip malls along Route 1—the local business association calls it "America's Maine Street for Shopping"—but you don't want to walk on this Main Street. You'll need wheels. (And you should proceed with caution everywhere you go, because people here are tourists who don't know the place and spend more time looking up at store names than they do paying attention to where they're driving.)

You'll find all of the big-name brands along this miracle mile—Banana Republic, Ralph Lauren, J. Crew, Old Navy, Tommy Hilfiger, Reebok, Calvin Klein, Gap, Timberland, Eddie Bauer, Brooks Brothers, Coldwater Creek, Bass, Geoffrey Beene, Brookstone, Skechers, Crate and Barrel, and on and on. Some amazing deals await in town—if you can remain patient enough to navigate the crowds.

The stores collaborate a lot to keep the registers ringing. Most keep the same hours: 9 a.m. to 8 p.m. Monday through Saturday and 10 a.m. to 6 p.m. on Sunday in summer. You can buy gift certificates good all over town, and there are special sale periods that most outlets participate in. These include mid-June around Father's Day, mid-August for back-to-school shopping, Labor Day, and Columbus Day. You can find out the exact dates, see a list of stores, find maps, and discover all sorts of interesting poop at www.thekitteryoutlets.com. Or call (888) KIT–TERY for more information.

KITTERY TRADING POST
301 Route 1, Kittery
(888) 587-6246
www.kitterytradingpost.com
Kittery Trading Post plays a role in Kittery similar to the one L.L. Bean plays in Freeport—the outfitter is a bit of real, old Maine made good, a one-room shack turned into a 90,000-square-foot outdoor empire that more than holds its own against all the chains from away. Where L.L. Bean has gone soft, selling more clothes and "lifestyle" goods than tents and packs, Kittery Trading Post has remained true to the sporting goods it began with when it was founded in 1938. Blood sports remain a staple—hunting and fishing rule much of the store, which claims the largest selection of top-quality firearms on the East Coast. But you'll also find acres of camping gear, canoes, kayaks, bikes, backpacks, boots, and apparel. Open Mon-

i Anyone interested in antiques would be wise to grab a copy of the *Maine Antique Dealer's Directory,* which lists many of the state's biggest and best shops and is available for $2 at many stores and chambers of commerce. Or you can order a copy by calling (207) 872-5849.

day through Saturday from 9 a.m. to 9 p.m. and Sunday 10 a.m. to 6 p.m.

The Yorks
BELL FARM ANTIQUES
244 Route 1 South, York
(207) 363-8181
www.bellfarmantiques.com
With its red picket fence, curving walkway, and red, cupola-topped shop, Bell Farm is an inviting place. The sign above the porch simply reads ANTIQUES, and you'll find plenty of them. Rex and Judy Lambert run a group shop with two whole floors of Victorian and country furniture, rugs, quilts, art, silver, stoneware, dinnerware, and early glass. Flow blue china, a Maine favorite, is here, too.

STONEWALL KITCHEN
Stonewall Lane, York
(207) 351-2712 or (800) 207-5267
Once sold in a farmers' market stall, Stonewall Kitchen's delicious specialty foods—jams, jellies, mustards, chutneys, relishes—can now be found all across Maine, and there are company stores in Portland and Camden. But it all began right here in York. The business's headquarters is right next to the York Chamber of Commerce, and it is perpendicular to the road you hop onto when you take the York exit, so you can't miss it. A big, colonial-looking complex of buildings with nice courtyards and gardens, Stonewall has an outlet where you can shop, ask questions, and taste products. The company sells an array of cookbooks, as well as some housewares, in addition to its now-famous condiments. There's also a viewing area next door, where you can watch employees in aprons and hats working

machines and conveyors, filling, capping, labeling, and packing the bottles. Stonewall has even expanded into home and garden products. Quite the little empire.

WOODS TO GOODS: MAINE PRISON PRODUCT OUTLET
891 Route 1, York
(207) 363-6001 or (888) 966-3724
www.woodstogoods.com
The Maine State Prison store on Route 1 in Thomaston has become well known as a place to buy kitschy prison-made items, and this small York emporium is much the same but farther off the radar of your average tourist. Inside you'll find all sorts of wares made in the wood shop by inmates—imprisoned from Maine to Oregon—from furniture to lamps to boat models and ship wheels. You'll find jewelry, kitchenware, toys, birdhouses, and even egg separators.

GRAVESTONE ARTWEAR
250 York St., Lower Level, York Village
(800) 564-4310
www.gravestoneartwear.com
Gravestone rubbing is an age-old New England tradition, and Cassandra and Paulette Chernack have taken rubbing to the next level by screenprinting old burial-ground art onto note cards, stamps, soaps, window decals, coffin boxes, and a whole line of clothing. The mother-and-daughter team have combed the cemeteries of New England in search of cool designs, and they have found them aplenty. They've taken these artistic engravings and transferred them to velvet scoopneck tops, dresses, cloaks, pouches, and scarves, but it's their T-shirts that are the most fun, with artful displays both somber and humorous ("Time Cuts Down All, Both Great and Small" and "Happy Valley Cemetery Pit Crew," for example). They have shirts inspired by Shakespeare, H. P. Lovecraft, and Ichabod Crane of Sleepy Hollow fame, and many have cool border designs on them. Most are available only in black. Ingenious stuff, and very good-looking to boot.

KNIGHT'S QUILT SHOP
1901 Route 1, Cape Neddick
(207) 361-2500
www.mainequiltshop.com
Quilters in southern Maine make frequent pilgrimages to Michelle Knight's Route 1 Cape in search of all their stitchery necessities. With more than 4,000 bolts, she has the area's largest inventory of quilt fabrics, from the simple to the designer. And of course she carries all the supplies that one would need to do the job, including batting, stencils, pattern books, thread, and other notions. The service can't be beat.

Ogunquit
OGUNQUIT WOODEN TOY
19 Chestnut Rd., Ogunquit
(207) 646-3718
www.ogunquitwoodentoy.com
Could there be a more appropriate name for a wooden toy builder than William John Woods? Or a better street than Chestnut for him to locate his studio? That's where you'll find Woods and his Ogunquit Wooden Toy, which features all manner of playthings crafted from maple and walnut and cherry. There are cars and helicopters, tractors and boats, all curvaceous and colorful. (Woods incorporates plantation-grown redheart, purple-heart, and cocobolo for contrast.) Each toy is finished with walnut oil and buffed with beeswax to give it a soft feel. In this day of plastic everything, these wooden toys are a delightful throwback any kid could love.

i "Made in Maine" mean anything to you? If you're like a lot of people, those three words have become synonymous with excellence and quality. The state has a mystique and a reputation for a reason—traditions of craftsmanship, hard work, and high standards. You can find lists of a variety of made-in-Maine items—and find out where to buy them—at www.mainemade.com.

SWAMP JOHN'S
Perkins Cove, Ogunquit
(207) 646-9414
www.swampjohns.com

Fine art, blown glass, and jewelry are the stuff here, and much of it is impressive. Graceful glass roses, wrought-iron candleholders and statuary, beach glass jewelry, a blue heron desk light of granite and steel—the place is filled with goods by artisans who make use of natural resources in whimsical and arty ways.

Wells

THE ARRINGTONS
1908 Post Rd., Route 1, Wells
(207) 646-4124

If you're looking for a first edition of some obscure World War II epic, you'll probably find it at this bookstore. The Arringtons has long been the go-to place for military titles. They stock everything else—more than 3,000 general titles are here, too—but it's in war books that the place really shines, especially for those interested in the American Revolution, the Civil War, the World Wars, and particular unit histories. Practically across the street from Hardings, it makes for a good twofer.

DOUGLAS N. HARDING RARE BOOKS
2152 Post Rd., Route 1, Wells
(207) 646-8785
www.hardingsbooks.com

Legendary in Maine's antique book circles, Hardings has an enormous inventory—as many as 100,000 books at any given time—as well as maps and prints, and if they don't stock the title you're looking for, they can probably get it for you. A family-owned operation in business since 1960, Harding's has particularly strong selections of Maine, New England, maritime, and Americana titles. You could spend hours, days even, perusing the shelves—and many people do. A great rainy-day option.

R. JORGENSEN ANTIQUES
502 Post Rd., Route 1, Wells
(207) 646-9444
www.rjorgensen.com

One of the better antiques shops in a town known for them, Jorgensens is a sprawling operation, stuffing two whole buildings with 18th- and 19th-century furnishings and accessories, both American and European. And you'd hardly know it driving by, because the place is mostly obscured by hedges. Make the turn into the driveway and you'll be glad you did.

MACDOUGALL-GIONET ANTIQUES
2104 Post Rd., Route 1, Wells
(207) 646-3531
www.macdougall-gionet.com

An old red barn serves as the home of close to 70 dealers at this South Coast staple, which specializes in antique furniture, fine, formal, and country, as well as smalls and folk art. Just don't show up on Monday when the place is closed.

MARDEN'S
1247 Main St., Sanford
(207) 324-1239
www.mardenssurplus.com

Mickey Marden was definitely on to something when he opened his first store in Fairfield in the 1960s. He bought job lots, stuff from bankruptcy courts, flood and fire sales, factory overruns—anything that needed to go soon and cheap—and built the largest surplus and salvage empire in Maine. Now the store that bears his name, Marden's, has a dozen stores and more than 850 employees. And more than that, Marden's has become like a religion to bargain-conscious Mainers. Many people stop by almost daily to see what has arrived on the Marden's trucks, and they never know what they might find. One day it may be the contents of a Radio Shack store, the next Armani suits, the next a software bonanza. There are also stores on the coast in Sanford, Biddeford, Portland, Ellsworth, and Calais, as well as a whole fleet inland, and they all stock everything from books to electronics to clothes to furniture in their many departments. Every week brings something new, so it's always an adventure.

The Kennebunks

CATWEAR
8 Spring St., Kennebunkport
(207) 967-5060
www.catwear.com

Not the clothier for kitties that its name implies, Catwear is a warm, fuzzy company that makes women's clothing out of fleece. These are cardigans and vests and pullovers that have more in common with couture than with fleece jackets as we've known them. Nice stuff, and nice people, too.

KENNEBUNK BOOK PORT
45 Portland Rd., Kennebunkport
(207) 467-3300
www.kbookport.com

The shelves full of new books are only part of the charm at this second-floor shop in the heart of "K'port." The owners are the kind of genial, knowledgeable proprietors every good bookstore should have—and they've tucked a zillion thoughtfully selected titles into their new Route 1 space. You're sure to find that perfect vacation book here, as well as signed books, a fine selection of Maine titles, and some children's classics. And remember, "Friends don't let friends buy books at chainstores."

LOVELL DESIGNS
17 Ocean Ave., Kennebunkport
(207) 967-8534
www.lovelldesigns.com

Ken Cantro's jewelry is handcrafted in pewter, sterling, and gold plate, and it picks up themes from both Maine and the natural world. Truly classic stuff that transcends age and style—it's liked by everyone, from Goth kids to grandmothers. There are Lovell stores in Freeport, Portland, Portsmouth, and then this place, one of the better spots to spend your dollars in Dock Square.

MARLOW'S
64 Main St., Kennebunk
(207) 985-2931
www.marlows-maine.com

This nifty department store is sort of a case study in how to grow a small retail store into a local institution. The company began in the early 1980s as a 500-square-foot shop in an old mill, where you could buy stationery. Every few years the place would add products—usually whole departments at a time. In 1994 Marlow's moved and quadrupled its size, and it doubled it again with another move in 1999. What does all this mean to you? Well, it means that you can now find home furnishings, garden items, bath and body products, toys, jewelry, gourmet foods, candles, and, yes, stationery at the 5,000-square foot little retailer that could.

OLD HOUSE PARTS
One Trackside Dr., Kennebunk
(207) 985-1999
www.oldhouseparts.com

Any fan of *This Old House* will want to wander around here. Now located off Route 35 (Summer Street), about a half mile from its old location, this is one of the state's best architectural salvage operations, and you'll have your choice of old doors, windows, stained glass, doorknobs, balustrades, moldings, and all sorts of architectural oddments from the 18th to the early 20th centuries. While of most interest to people owning houses that predate World War II, the goods here can add a bit of character to any home. Prices can be a bit steep, though.

TOM'S OF MAINE NATURAL LIVING STORE
52 Main St., Kennebunk
(207) 985-5-6331
www.toms-of-maine.com

The story goes that when American troops invaded Manuel Noriega's home in Panama in 1989, they found some Tom's of Maine toothpaste among the notorious general's toiletries. If he likes Tom's earth-friendly line of products, he'd go crazy at the company's factory store in an old mill in downtown Kennebunk. Toothpastes, soaps, herbal goods, tote bags, and more by Tom's and select others are all available at greatly reduced prices. Ask about the tour of Tom's factory across town. (Legendary in Maine for its eco-friendly, socially conscious business practices, Tom's broke a few hearts in 2006 when it became part of the Colgate-Palmolive empire.)

WALLINGFORD FARM
21 York St., Kennebunk
(207) 985-2112
www.wallingfordfarm.com
Anyone with a home, garden, or taste for Maine delicacies will find something to like about this neat store housed in a sprawling 19th-century barn on Route 1. The place is a country store in the truest sense, stocked practically to the exposed rafters with farm-related goods, from local produce to Maine-made foods, flowers to garden tools, handmade soaps to books on landscaping. The goal of owner Charles Godfrey has been to supply area residents with reasonably priced specialty items they can't get at supermarkets, and he's done a great job at it. Worth a detour.

Saco
STONE SOUP ARTISANS
228 Main St., Saco
(207) 283-4715
www.stonesoupartisans.com
Not to be confused with the Portland restaurant of the same name, Stone Soup is a co-op gallery sponsored by the Society of Southern Maine Crafstmen. More than 30 artisans—including potters, jewelers, and glass and fabric artists—consign their work to be sold here, and they staff the place as well. New material goes through a juried selection process so you know there's quality involved.

GREATER PORTLAND
Scarborough
CABELA'S
100 Cabela's Blvd., Scarborough
(207) 883-7400
www.cabelas.com
Word on the street had it that L.L. Bean was nervous about the arrival of this outfitting giant in Maine in the spring of 2008. And well it should be. Cabela's caters to all those outdoorsmen and -women who wouldn't be caught dead in L.L. Bean's lifestyle wear. Bean has let its hunting and fishing and camping market share slip in favor of ladies clothing and housewares. Cabela's, the Nebraska-based retailer, is glad to pick up the disaffected Bean customers, selling all manner of goods for the outdoors, from fudge to footwear, in this gargantuan new 130,000-square-foot depot. There's even an indoor archery range, a 10,000-gallon aquarium, a horse corral, and parking for semis.

South Portland
MAINE MALL
364 Maine Mall Rd., South Portland
(207) 774-0303
www.mainemall.com
Mainers have a love-hate relationship with "the Mall." They love the ease, convenience, and selection that more than 140 stores in one place afford, but they hate the traffic, congestion, and tackiness that go along with it. The state's largest shopping center, the Maine Mall is anchored by Sears, Macy's, Best Buy, and JCPenney, and inside are the kinds of stores you expect to find in a major mall: Gap, Victoria's Secret, Olympia Sports, Eddie Bauer, Abercrombie, and Brookstone. In recent years, this one-level mall has turned a bit yupscale with the addition of Pottery Barn and Williams Sonoma. Several other retail plazas have sprung up all around the mall, as well as chain eateries like Olive Garden, Macaroni Grill, and Pizzeria Uno, and movie theaters. There's a big

Borders bookstore in the parking lot. The food court is open Monday through Saturday 9:30 a.m. to 9 p.m., Sunday from 11 a.m. to 6 p.m.

Portland

AMARYLLIS CLOTHING CO.

41 Exchange St., Portland
(207) 772-4439
www.amaryllisclothing.com

Maine designers Jill McGowan, Kendra Haskell, and Cindy Hanley contribute their creative works to this, Portland's best women's clothing store. Inspired and often whimsical contemporary fashions, formal wear, jewelry, and accessories are offered for sale.

BOOKS ETC.

38 Exchange St., Portland
(207) 774-0626
www.mainebooksetc.com

Arguably downtown Portland's best store for new books, Books Etc. has been a popular destination on Exchange Street, thanks to a good selection of contemporary fiction, Maine books, and pop culture titles. They now have a store in Falmouth, too.

BROWNE TRADING COMPANY

262 Commercial St. #3, Portland
(207) 775-3118 or (800) 944-7848
www.brownetrading.com

The Browne family has been in the seafood biz for generations, specializing in caviar, and fancy chefs all across the country currently turn to Browne's for fresh seafood. And you can, too. The company has its retail store just steps from the docks the fish come in on, and you can find everything from Casco cod and monkfish to Jonah crabs and scallops. (Lobster, too, of course.) And that's just the local stuff. Browne also offers sole from France, tai snapper from New Zealand, and arctic char from Iceland. Then there are the innumerable caviars the place stakes its reputation on. . . . Anyone with a jones for seafood will want to make the pilgrimage.

BULL MOOSE MUSIC

151 Middle St., Portland
(207) 780–6424
www.bullmoose.com

Maine's native record-store chain, Bull Moose was born in the early 1990s by a Bowdoin student in Brunswick, but this is the best-stocked of the company's nine stores. Not as good as it once was, Bull Moose remains the place to turn in downtown Portland for CDs by underground and independent artists. You can find Top 40 stuff, too, and the prices are guaranteed to beat your mega-chain stores. The pierced and tattooed employees will order whatever they don't have on hand.

CARLSON-TURNER BOOKS

241 Congress St., Portland
(207) 773-4200
www.carlsonturnerbooks.com

At the Munjoy Hill end of the Forest City's old retail corridor, Carlson-Turner has arguably the biggest selection of used books in town—more than 40,000 titles—with specialties in antiquarian, Maine, Civil War, and "unusual and eccentric" books. Great fun to peruse.

CASCO BAY WOOL WORKS

10 Moulton St., Portland
(207) 879-9665
www.cascobaywoolworks.com

An Old Port staple for more than a decade, Casco Bay Wool Works has become known for its fine wool capes and shawls, but it also turns out fishermen's sweaters of Shetland wool, refined women's sweaters, blankets and throws, all of which make perfect sense for Maine winters—or even a late summer boat ride.

CUNNINGHAM BOOKS

188 State St., Portland
(207) 775-2246

Cunningham's is a favorite in the city's Longfellow Square area, with some 50,000 titles to explore on its shelves, all thoughtfully organized by shopkeeper Nancy Grayson.

DECORUM

231 Commercial St., Portland
(207) 775-3346
www.decorumonesource.com
The Forest City's best bets for architectural salvage are two shops on opposite ends of the peninsula—Decorum and Portland Architectural Salvage. You'll have a hard time maintaining a sense of decorum if you visit Decorum, on Commercial Street, so excited will you be. It's a great place to look for bathroom fixtures, lighting, and details like knobs, switches, and drawer pulls. It specializes in specialty hardware, and the selection is amazing. Very inventive, fun, and inspiring stuff.

PORTLAND ARCHITECTURAL SALVAGE

131 Preble St., Portland
(207) 780–0634
www.portlandsalvage.com
Newly located on Preble Street, Portland Architectural Salvage is your best bet for larger pieces, old built-ins, doors, windows, posts, and cabinets—more than 12,000 square feet of the stuff on four floors. They'll even track items down for you, with their personal shopper service. Both this and Decorum are enticing places for the old-home owner.

FERDINAND

243 Congress St., Portland
(207) 761-2151
www.ferdinandhomestore.com
What if your friend the hipster ever got it together enough to open a housewares store? It might result in something like Ferdinand, a fun and funky downtown shop where the goods are handmade ("fashioned by Ferdinand") and/or vintage ("found by Ferdinand"). Great for thoughtful gifts—who wouldn't want a hand-sewn potholder—it's also the sort of place where you can get yourself an extra cool T-shirt, monster patch, or arty bobbie pin.

FETCH

195 Commercial St., Portland
(207) 773-5450

It'd be hard to find a store in Portland that's more fun than Fetch—especially if you have four legs. A spirited supply store for cats, dogs, and their people, it brims with wit and whimsy. Dog packs, travel bowls, feed bags, tents, sleeping bags, sunscreen, bug spray, laser play toys, place mats, sock toys—these sorts of goods fill a pretty old building on Commercial Street. Not a superstore like PetCo, this is a mom and pop with spunk. They regularly host events—Wednesday is Pug Night, for instance—and they seem as enthusiastic about pet toys as a pug puppy.

FOLIA

50 Exchange St., Portland
(207) 761-4432
www.foliajewelry.com
Folia (which used to be called Fibula) has long been a favorite place among shoppers looking for inventive, creative, one-of-a-kind jewelry. A group of local jewelers is behind the place.

GREEN DESIGN FURNITURE

267 Commercial St., Portland
(207) 775-4234 or (866) 756-4730
www.greendesigns.com
You're going to be wanting to take some of this stuff home with you. Douglas Green's black cherry furniture is fantastic—updating and contemporizing Shaker and Mission–inspired designs. His new pieces have clean and curvaceous lines, and they are all very functional. Open Monday through Saturday from 10 a.m. to 6 p.m.

LEROUX KITCHEN

161 Commercial St., Portland
(207) 553-7665
www.lerouxkitchen.com
Formerly known as the Whip and Spoon, this kitchenware store makes amateur chefs gaga. From creative colanders to crazy cookbooks, brilliant bread machines to bagel cutters, anything and everything a cook could want can be found here. The store also has specialty foods and one of the city's best wine selections. The owners host cooking classes at the rear of the place.

MAINE POTTERS MARKET
376 Fore St., Portland
(207) 774-1633
www.mainepottersmarket.com
Several pottery co-ops exist in Maine, and this is the largest and arguably the best, representing the work of 13 craftspeople from across the state. Founded in 1978, the shop is right in the heart of the Old Port, and the works within are unique and functional—"art you can handle."

MEXICALI BLUES
9 Moulton St., Portland
(207) 772-4080
www.mexicaliblues.com
Maine seems to have a particular fondness for jam bands and the neohippie phenomenon—Phish has played some of its largest gigs here, and shows by Strangefolk and Moe are always well attended—and that support has kept this Old Port emporium busy since 1987. All the requisite tie-dye, batik, flowing dresses, drums, incense, patchouli, beads, jewelry, and wall hangings can be found inside. The shop's owners cruise the globe—from Bali to Baja—to track down unique items, and they have their own lines as well. This is a convenient, one-stop shop for the whole happy hippie family. There are other stores in Freeport and Newcastle.

ROGUES GALLERY
41 Wharf St., Portland
(207) 773-4900
www.roguesgallery.com
Where do Brad Pitt and Bono get their T-shirts? In Portland, apparently. That's where you'll find Rogues Gallery, a hipster boutique and home to Alex Carleton, who's done design work for L.L. Bean, Abercrombie & Fitch, among others. Carleton moved back to Maine and founded Rogues Gallery in the Old Port. The tees are most famous and they're made from recycled shirts, dyed, and printed with "subversive" designs. But you'll also find everything from suits to sweaters to footwear. If you want to dress like Brad Pitt you better have a similar bank account, though, because T-shirts here retail for close to $100.

Yarmouth

F. O. BAILEY ANTIQUARIANS
11 Yarmouth Crossing, Yarmouth
(207) 781-8001
www.fobailey.com
Long the name in Portland antiques—it claims to be Maine's oldest business, founded in 1819—F. O. Bailey specializes in fine furniture, rugs, and art, and the place hosts auctions regularly as well. Now off peninsula in Yarmouth.

DELORME MAP STORE
2 DeLorme Dr., Yarmouth
(43 48.491N, 70 09.844'W)
(800) 642-0970
www.delorme.com
Stop at the DeLorme Map Store in Yarmouth on your way north—you can't miss it, it's the place with the three-story, glowing globe—and you won't get lost during your Maine travels. Famous in the state for its indispensable *Maine Atlas and Gazetteer*, DeLorme sells that book of maps and so many others in the store at its headquarters. You can buy maps for every state, travel guides, globes, world maps, GPS accessories, software, and more. Plus you can check out Eartha, reportedly the world's largest rotating globe.

MAINE COTTAGE FURNITURE
Lower Falls Landing
106 Lafayette St., Yarmouth
(207) 846-3699
www.mainecottage.com
You know that feeling of relaxation and contentment you get when you hit the cottage by the shore for a week's vacation? Somehow Maine Cottage Furniture has managed to distill that and paint it onto their line of colorful, whimsical home furnishings. From beds to desks, dining tables to wicker, the company's "spirited furniture" is fun and stylish and reminiscent of lazy days on the coast. You might not feel as good when you see the prices, though.

Freeport

While Kittery is a place where the automobile rules, Freeport is much more walkable and retains the appeal of a Maine village. The presence of one of the more desirable anchor stores any one could ever want—a little outfitter called L.L. Bean—attracted dozens of major retailers to downtown Freeport, creating one of the nation's biggest outlet bazaars—more than 200 stores clustered in a handful of blocks. Step along its sidewalks, and you'll pass a who's who of American retailing, heavy on the clothes—Polo, J. Crew, Brooks Brothers, Patagonia, Anne Klein, Cole Haan, Maidenform, Jockey, Jones New York, Burberry, Coach, Samonsite, and too many more to count. There are plenty of crafts, gifts, and housewares packed onto the town's side streets, but it's apparel where Freeport truly shines. Contact the Freeport Merchant Association (207-865-1212; www.freeportusa.com) for a list of stores, events, and dining and lodging options.

A handful of Maine stores have been able to carve out their own niches in town. Some of the more notable ones follow.

ABACUS AMERICAN CRAFTS
36 Main St., Freeport
(207) 865-6620 or (800) 206-2166
www.abacusgallery.com

Mainers love Abacus, a functional arts store in a few locations along the cost (they can also be found in Kennebunkport, Portland, and Boothbay Harbor). As much an art gallery as a store, it has been purveying kooky, fun, and often beautiful furnishings, jewelry, pottery, and blown glass since 1971 and has been voted one of the top 10 retailers in the country by *Niche* magazine.

CUDDLEDOWN
475 Route 1, Freeport
(888) 235-3696
www.cuddledown.com

Begun in the early 1980s as a home business making down comforters, Cuddledown has grown and grown into one of the nation's leading makers of bedding. Their outlet store in Free-port stocks all the exquisite goose feather puffs they've become famous for as well as sleepwear, rugs, pillows, sheets, mattress pads, and all sorts of other housewares, and there's another outlet in Kittery.

L.L. BEAN
95 Main St., Freeport
(800) 559-0747
www.llbean.com

By now just about everyone knows about L.L. Bean and its customer-friendly policies—the store's open 24 hours a day, 365 days a year, and everything you buy inside is unconditionally guaranteed. While the store has turned more toward lifestyle goods—apparel, housewares, etc.—you'll still find plenty to like in the outdoors sections on the first floor and there are whole stores devoted to hunting and fishing and biking, boating, and skiing.

L.L. BEAN FACTORY STORE
Main St., Freeport
(207) 552-7772

Locals remember when Bean sold its seconds and discontinued items out of the warehouse down the road, but it proved so popular the original factory store is now up on Main. The deal on the imperfect items found here is the same as it is on the perfect ones on Bow Street—everything's satisfactory or your money back—which is why it's a good idea to start at the Factory Store first before heading to the main store. If you do find what you're looking for here, which is a good possibility, you'll pay up to 60 percent less than what you might just a few blocks away. Open seven days a week from 8 a.m. to 10 p.m.

THOS. MOSER CABINETMAKERS
149 Main St., Freeport
(207) 865-4519 or (800) 708-9041
www.thosmoser.com

Don't be confused by the name. Thos. Moser makes a lot more than cabinets. Since 1973 the fine wood craftsman—along with his sons—has turned out beautiful hardwood furnishings inspired by Shaker, Pennsylvania Dutch, and Queen Anne designs. In the beautifully restored 19th-century home that serves as the company's only Maine showroom (others are in places like New York, LA, DC, and Seoul, Korea), you'll find two floors full of tables, chairs, beds, and desks, each an heirloom in the making.

MIDCOAST

Brunswick

BRUNSWICK BOOKLAND
Cooks Corner Shopping Center, Brunswick
(207) 725-2313
www.booklandcafe.com
The once mighty Bookland chain fell to competition from book megastores and bad accounting years ago, going from 13 shops down to this one and filing for bankruptcy in 2000. This is one of two left, managing to stay afloat with a great selection of magazines, discounted best sellers, lots of remainders, several racks of used books, and a cafe that encourages lingering.

CABOT MILL ANTIQUES
14 Maine St., Brunswick
(207) 725-2855
www.cabotiques.com
Fort Andross, an imposing old mill building on the Androscoggin, is the nicest antique at this 15,000-square foot showroom. But there are plenty of furnishings and collectibles to like, too. More than 140 displays are here to peruse, filled with china, Oriental rugs, decorative items, porcelain, bottles, Victorian furniture, and more. There are flea markets at Fort Andross on summer weekends. Open seven days a week from 10 a.m. to 5 p.m.

GULF OF MAINE BOOKS
134 Maine St., Brunswick
(207) 729-5083
One would think that as a college town, Brunswick would have some truly great bookstores. The community disappoints a bit, but Gulf of Maine is the standard-bearer downtown, with

a diverse selection heavy on the environmental and countercultural titles. Owner Gary Lawless is a legend in his own right—he's a poet with a regional reputation and is the publisher behind Blackberry Books, among other things—and the place is definitely worth a visit, especially if you're into poetry or literature with a conscience.

F. W. HORCH SUSTAINABLE GOODS AND SUPPLIES
56 Maine St., Brunswick
(207) 729-4050
www.fwhorch.net
What a cool place this is. A sort of green department store where you'll find everything from solar space heaters to building supplies to cookware, cleaning supplies, and even gifts, like hemp tote bags, F.W. Horch is the sort of store where you can feel good parting with your cash. "Practically, saving the planet," they say, and if everybody shopped here instead of the big boxes we'd be on our way.

Other Shopping in Brunswick

For more music stop in the original **Bull Moose Music** (151 Maine Street; 207-725-1289), though this isn't the site where it was born. **Indrani's** (149 Maine Street; 207-729-6448) has had a corner of the Tontine Mall for a lot longer than most other places make it, and it specializes in African imports, women's clothing and jewelry. **Huston Company** (11 Pleasant Street; 207-967-2360) has fine custom furniture made in Kennbunkport. Gift shoppers will want to poke their heads in **Seaside Mercantile** (47 Maine Street; 207-373-0340; www.seasidemercantile.com), which has all kinds of neat pottery and dinnerware.

Bath and Surrounding Area

BATH GOODWILL
Bath Shopping Center
Route 1, Bath
(207) 443-4668
www.goodwillnne.org
A certain internationally known outfitter based a few towns over sends this thrift store its seconds

Bath Antiques

Downtown Bath is both an antique itself—it dates back to the 1890s—and is brimming with antiques shops. Among the best of them are **Pollyanna Antiques** (182 Front Street; 207-443-4909), which is a good place to turn for vintage clothing and old tools. **Brick Store Antiques** (143 Front Street; 207-443-2790) is known for country and formal goods. **Cobblestone and Company** (176 Front Street; 207-443-4064) for antiques, art, and accents. And for books, try the **Open Door Bookstore** (178 Front Street; 207-443-8689), which specializes in rare and out of print titles. Also try Route 1 in Woolwich on the other side of the bridge.

and blemished items, and you can often score some great finds on the racks and racks of clothing here. Just a hint. Proceeds benefit people with disabilities.

HALCYON YARN
12 School St., Bath
(207) 442-7909
www.halcyonyarn.com
More than 100 varieties of yarn and a host of wools, merinos, felts, kits, books, videos, and classes make Halcyon Yarn a haven for knitters, spinners, and fabric artists of all sorts.

BATH CYCLE AND SKI
Route 1, Woolwich
(207) 442-7002
www.bikeman.com
An excellent full-service bike and ski shop with a gondola out front, this place has been around for ages. You'll find mountain and road bikes; kids' bikes; downhill, cross-country, and telemark skis; snowboards; snowshoes; and a great staff inside.

MONTSWEAG FLEA MARKET
Route 1 and Mountain Rd., Woolwich
(207) 443-2809
www.montsweagfleamarket.com
In 1976 Norma Scopino lost her bookkeeping job, and she set up a little bazaar on her front lawn to take advantage of tourist traffic. That yard sale has grown into one of the state's biggest—and certainly most widely known—flea markets. More than 100 tables are now part of the action, some of them semipermanent, like the tool area, and they are topped with everything from CDs and books to antiques and old toys. On Wednesdays the focus becomes antiques and collectibles, but on weekends it's a free-for-all. Always fun to explore.

Wiscasset and Surrounding Area
EDGECOMB POTTERS
727 Boothbay Rd., Edgecomb
(207) 882-9493
www.edgecombpotters.com
Specializing in porcelain and known for their glazes, Edgecomb Potters have been at it since 1977, when Richard and Chris Hilton opened shop in an old schoolhouse. Today they have more than 30 employees and three galleries—here in Edgecomb, and ones in the Old Port and Freeport—each filled with artfully crafted shell bowls, ikebanas, vases, glass works, and even jewelry. And they always seem to be expanding their base (recently adding a 25,000-square-foot storage building).

MARGONELLI FINE FURNITURE
780 River Rd., Edgecomb
(207) 633-3326
David Margonelli's showroom is all but obscured by the foliage on River Road, but you're going to want to turn into the drive and have a look. The contemporary furniture here is exquisite—handmade and known for clean lines, elegant

curves, and a classic simplicity—and it's often constructed with Margonelli's Flexure system, which allows for curving pieces to be interchanged for different looks and flexible uses.

SHEEPSCOT RIVER POTTERY
Route 1, Davis Island, Edgecomb
(207) 882-9410
www.sheepscot.com

When looking for wedding presents and Christmas gifts, this is one of the places to turn. While lovingly glazed pottery with Maine themes is the staple, on everything from vases to tiles and sinks, you'll also find rugs, artwork, and other gifts at this showroom on the banks of the Sheepscot. Another store is in Damariscotta.

Boothbay Harbor

MCKOWN SQUARE QUILTS
14 Boothbay House Hill Rd.,
Boothbay Harbor
(207) 633-2007

Seven rooms in this old farmhouse are brimming with handcrafted quilts, clothing, and boutiquey gifts. Peruse purses and scarves and custom-order a quilt from the 1,000 fabrics in stock.

MUNG BEAN
37 Townsend Ave., Boothbay Harbor
(207) 633-5512

In the same spot since 1977, this gift shop is a tourist favorite, and inside you'll find all manner of crafts and souvenirs. You can find the balsam pillows and the handpainted slate welcome signs you might expect in a Maine resort town gift store, but you'll also come across some items that are a step up from that, like Anne Kilham's always tasteful cards, cool wooden toys, and some nice jewelry. So it's worth a peek on a rainy day.

PALABRA SHOP
53 Commercial St., Boothbay Harbor
(207) 633-4225

The Palabra has been going strong in Boothbay for decades, and it claims the "World's Largest Collection of Moses Bottles," which were created

Wiscasset Antiques

The old town of Wiscasset, on the Sheepscot River, has long been known for its antiques shops, and there are many—about 20 at last count. Find out more at www.shopwiscasset antiques.com, but here are a few you shouldn't miss. **Marston House** (101 Main Street; 207-882-6010; www.mar stonhouse.com) specializes in 18th- and 19th-century painted furniture as well as textiles, rugs, toys, and French pottery. **Lilac Cottage** (Route 1; 207-882-7059; www.lilaccottage antiques.com) has a lot of American and English furniture and decorative items. American country painted furniture, hooked rugs, quilts, and folk art are among the specialties at **Stauble and Chambers Antiques** (Pleasant and Main Streets; 207-882-6341; www.staublechambersantiques.com). **Snyder Wilson Antiques** (72 Main Street; 207-882-4255; www.snyder wilsonantiques.com) carries American pieces and folk art.

for the grand opening of the Poland Spring Hotel in 1876. Ten rooms here are filled with primitives, nautical items, Shaker boxes, fine art glass and china, and estate jewelry. Just don't bump into anything.

RIVER'S END FARM
409 Wiscasset Rd., Boothbay
(207) 633-4044
www.riversendfarm.com

Hankering for a free-range chicken sandwich? Or a fine Maine wine? Perhaps a taste of emu? This cool specialty store is your friend. Inside its barnlike confines you'll find all kinds of exotic meats, organic vegetables, jams and preserves, condiments, wines, beers, and more, the vast majority of which is grown or made within a 100-mile radius.

SALT RIVER GALLERY
Route 27, Boothbay
(207) 633-0770 or (877) 725-8748
www.saltrivergallery.com

Another one of those nifty co-op stores that's owned and run by a group of artists, Salt River brims with handmade home furnishings, the sorts of lamps and benches that elevate simple household items to the level of art. Each of the nine artisans has a specialty and seems to excel at it; simply finding so many talented individuals in one spot makes this a rewarding stop.

Other Shopping in Boothbay Harbor

Don't forget **Sherman's** (5 Commercial Street; 207-633-7262), the great old Maine bookstore. **Westwind Design Gallery** (36 Sea Street; 207-633-3787) has a large collection of art, antiques, Oriental rugs, and decorative items. **A Silver Lining** (17 Townsend Avenue; 207-633-4103) is a shop run by metalsmiths with a large selection of original jewelry.

Damariscotta Area

MAINE COAST BOOK SHOP
158 Main St., Damariscotta
(207) 563-3207
www.mainecoastbookshop.com

One of those local-business-makes-good success stories, this Damariscotta bookseller was so popular, it moved out of its small old store into a former supermarket, which it has filled with a great selection of children's books and Maine titles. You can find the best sellers, of course, but you can also pick up signed Down East titles. The staff is what makes the place great.

PINE TREE YARNS
74 Main St., Damariscotta
(207) 563-8909
www.pinetreeyarns.com

Maine has all kinds of yarn makers, but there are a few whose fibers and colors seem to transcend. Elaine Eskesen's company, Pine Tree Yarns, which operates out of the historic Nathaniel Austin House, is one of them. Eskesen has wool that she dyes herself, as well as yarns and natural fibers from around the state. At Pine Tree Yarns you can pick up a colorful skein to knit your mom a sweater—or buy her the sweater instead. There are kits for dyeing, books, hats, mittens, gloves, and scarves, as well as all sorts of knitting knick-knacks and accessories. You'll be "yarning" before you know it.

RENY'S
33 Main St., Damariscotta
(207) 563-5757
www.renys.com

Mainers have quite the love affair with Reny's. These small neighborhood department stores are brimming with an amazing variety of goods—from jeans to DVD players to vitamins—and they inevitably have things cheaper than anywhere else if they have them. Usually a great deal cheaper, thanks to the chain's pipeline of brand-name suppliers, who send them their seconds and refurbished items. Just about every neighborhood has one now, it seems. Reny's are spread across the state in Bath, Belfast, Bridgton, Camden, Damariscotta, Dexter, Ellsworth, Farmington, Gardiner, Madison, Pittsfield, Saco, and Wells. This store is the flagship, though. Actually it's two stores that sit on opposite sides of Main Street, one for clothes, the other with everything else. You'll inevitably leave with something. It's that good.

SCOTTISH LION WROUGHT IRON
587 Bristol Rd., Bristol
(207) 563-5788
www.scottishwroughtiron.com

This smithy features the work of Andrew Leck, who forges all manner of household items, from the expected—fireplace tools and towel bars—to the unique—shelf stands for plates and bowls, birdbaths, beam racks, and lamps. His Christmas stocking hooks are nicely formed and keep you from having to make holes in your mantle. Beautiful stuff.

WEATHERBIRD
72 Courtyard St., Damariscotta
(207) 563-8993
A sort of yupscale country store, Weatherbird has an inventory that's difficult to classify. A small grocery and specialty food store greets you as you walk in off the street; it's filled with wine, teas, and gourmet foods of all varieties. A small nook filled with neat toys then leads you to a section of nice, creative women's clothes. Tucked here and there are housewares, rugs, mobiles, and soaps.

Other Shopping in the Damariscotta Area

The **Puffin's Nest** (36–40 Main Street, Damariscotta; 207-563-1815) is where you can grab novelty gifts and souvenirs (balsam pillows, lobster bibs) for your friends back home; **Two Fish** (Main Street, Damariscotta; 207-563-2220) has nice women's apparel and jewelry. Try **Salt Bay Art Supply** (Main Street, 458 Main Street, Damariscotta; 207-563-8377) and **Brush and Easel** (Main Street, Newcastle; 207-563-3559) for art supplies.

Waldoboro

WELL-TEMPERED KITCHEN
122 Atlantic Hwy. (Route 1), Waldoboro
(207) 563-5762
www.welltemperedkitchen.com
An old barn here is filled with a stupendous array of kitchenwares for the gourmet cook—not necessarily what you'd expect to find on the outskirts of Waldoboro. Cookbooks, pots, pans, cutlery, tableware, and unique cooking gadgets are all here. Quite a surprise, and it's even better than it sounds.

WOODEN SCREEN DOOR COMPANY
3542 Route 1, Waldoboro
(207) 832-0519
www.woodenscreendoor.com
Nothing says summer in Maine like the thwack of a screen door slamming shut. Somehow only

a good one made of wood will provide that resounding sound, which will take you back to Grandmother's house and summer camps past. This small outfit has about a dozen designs to choose from, and it will customize to your specs. A variety of themes are available, and they evoke the Maine coast, from canoes to fish, from schooners to blue herons, and the doors are built of weather-resistant Honduran mahogany. They run from $450 up to about $1,000.

South Thomaston

ART OF THE SEA
Route 73, South Thomaston
(207) 594-9396
www.artofthesea.com
Owner Joan Woodhull has joked that her museumlike gallery of nautical art makes up two-thirds of beautiful downtown South Thomaston, and she's right. Also known as the Old Post Office Gallery, the shop is about the biggest thing going in this hamlet on the fantastically picturesque Weskeag River, encompassing 10 rooms on two huge floors of the building. Scores of paintings by some of the biggest names in the world of maritime art are on the walls—names like John Stobart, William Bishop, Michael Karas, and Marlene Evans—fetching thousands of dollars, and they're complemented by photographs by Mainers like Peter Ralston and Benjamin Mendlowitz. Ship models, books, prints, lamps, scrimshaw, instruments, and various other nautical items fill cases and floor space. It's a remarkable collection that would seem more appropriate in a resort community than in a small, salty hamlet. You don't even have to have salt in your blood to appreciate it, and it's a great excuse to see this neat Maine fishing village.

Rockland

ARCHIPELAGO
386 Main St., Rockland
(207) 596-0701
www.thearchipelago.net
What an appropriate name for the gift store of the Island Institute. The shop looks more like a

gallery and brims with arts and crafts from the Maine islands (more than 100 artisans). Check out the granite vases from Island Granite Works ($25).

BLACK PARROT
328 Main St., Rockland
(207) 594-9161
This staple on Main is primarily known for its tasteful women's clothes, but it also carries an assortment of accessories and housewares and even products for the home and office. If you want a high-end duster or a nice hand cream or a whippa (Maine-speak for "great") journal, you'll find it here. The shoes are funky and unique, and there is always a lot of neat knitwear.

FOUR TWELVE
412 Main St., Rockland
(207) 596-2412
www.shopfourtwelve.com
Rockland's resident fashion designer Beth Bowley—we're talking Parsons School of Design attending, former Perry Ellis–staffing, *Elle* and *InStyle* featuring type stuff—opened this women's clothing boutique in 2007. The shop is stocked with fashion-forward dresses, bags, and jewelry the likes of which you wouldn't expect to find in a fishing town.

GRASSHOPPER SHOP
400 Main St., Rockland
(207) 596-6156
One store in a small chain, the Grasshopper Shop has nice enough women's clothes to keep the ladies from having to drive to Portland for their blouses, skirts, and shoes. It also carries jewelry and accessories, some unique toys, several lines of housewares, and a really good selection of cards. Check the other shops in Searsport, Ellsworth, and Bangor, too. Open all year.

PLANET TOYS
318 Main St., Rockland
(207) 596-5976
As much an experience as a store, Planet Toys

is an offshoot of the Planet World Marketplace, a gift store in Camden (which has great toys itself). It's the kind of overwhelming toy store you expect to find in cities, not small Maine communities. It sells everything under the sun, from plastic Playmobil sets to homemade wooden whirligigs. The store has a great kids' books section, hosts all sorts of special events, and can amuse even the oldest kids.

ROCK CITY BOOKS AND COFFEE
328 Main St., Rockland
(207) 594-4123
www.rockcitycoffee.com
Rockland's hip bookstore and coffee shop is the place to find good used books in Rock City, and what a pleasant destination it is. Open and airy, with big windows overlooking Main Street and a series of clocks telling you what time it is around the world, comfortable chairs for sitting, and an Internet connection, it makes searching for books and beans a whole lot of fun. The titles are all thoughtfully chosen and are a really good deal for relatively new titles in good condition and there's always new stuff coming in. Bean buffs will find a fine selection of coffees, cappuccinos, lattes, and espressos—including the local Rock City brand—and there are yummy sandwiches and salads. The staff—book manager, Geri Coughlin especially—is great and there are occasional shows by jazz and folk artists.

Other Shopping in Rockland

Caravans (415 Main Street; 207-594-0293) has a really nice selection of worldly women's wear and jewelry. **Huston Tuttle** (365 Main Street; 207-594-5441) has all the art supplies you'll ever need. **Trillium Soaps** (68 Crescent Street; 207-594-5003) has handmade soaps that you can smell from the street. **Handle It!** (403 Main Street; 207-594-5333) is the place to turn to for, well, handles and decorative hardware.

Rockport

MAINE SPORT OUTFITTERS

Route 1, Rockport

(207) 236-7120

www.mainesport.com

A gigantic outfitter, this Midcoast staple recently finished another expansion and now has 30,000 square feet of space. It fills it with a good selection of outdoor products, from tents to packs to canoes, but the place has a reputation for being expensive (and you don't get the unconditional guarantee here that you do at L.L. Bean).

MICHAEL GOOD DESIGNS

Rockport

(207) 236-9619

www.michaelgood.com

Anticlastic raising—this guy is synonymous with it. If you want anticlastic raised jewelry, you want Michael Good's designs. What is it? It's a jewelry-making process taken from hammered sheet metal, and it's characterized by twisted and flattened pieces. Good has made a big mark in the field. See his Spirit Sun pendant; it's truly beautiful.

STATE OF MAINE CHEESE COMPANY

461 Commercial St., Rockport

(207) 236-8895 or (800) 762-8895

www.cheese-me.com

There's a lot more going on at this Route 1 store between Rockland and Camden than simply cheese making. The company expanded a while back and opened a 9,500-square-foot space where they both make their Katahdin cheddar, Saint Croix black pepper, Casco Bay garlic jack, and variety of other flavors—you can watch the production from windows in the store—and where they sell a slew of Made in Maine items. You can load up on cheeses, condiments, jellies, coffees, mustards, pickles, honeys, even chocolates, bringing home the tastiest souvenirs you ever did buy, or fashion a gift basket for friends and family back home.

SWEET SENSATIONS

309 Commercial St. (Route 1), Rockport

(207) 230–0955

www.mainesweets.com

This is the pastry store of all pastry stores in the Midcoast. Great cakes and pies—by the slice!—cookies, macaroons, brownies, and sweets of all sorts fill a nice old Cape on Route 1. Certified pastry chef Steven Watts also does wedding cakes and custom orders.

Other Shopping in Rockport

Timothy Whelan Photographic Books and Prints (25 Main Street; 207-236-4795) is a tiny place with a big collection of photographic titles.

Camden

ABCD BOOKS

23 Bayview St., Camden

(207) 236-3903 or (888) 236-3903

www.abcdbooks.com

The go-to place for book collectors in Camden, this classic shop has an extensive collection of used and rare books—good Maine section, too—and is a pleasure to browse. You can spend a day here contentedly. Open year-round.

JOSEPHINE

39 Mechanic St., Camden

(207) 236-2123

www.ejosephine.com

Not every store in Maine has personal shoppers—you'd be hard-pressed to find them anywhere—but this boutique in the old Knox Mill is not every other store. The staff here is available to help you make stylish choices from the simply chic women's wear—lines like Theory, Michael Stars, Vince, Joes, and Citizens of Humanity—or from the accessories and unique furnishings. Inspired by the empress of France, the shop is filled with everything from earrings to linens and it promises "to save seasoned shoppers a trip to Boston or New York." It's certainly a start, and should you find yourself overwhelmed by all the "elements of style," you can arrange for help.

Close-up

Camden Jewelers

The resort town of Camden must have more jewelers—genuine gold- and silversmiths—than it does barbers, and not every community can say that. Since the 1980s more and more fine jewelry makers have settled in the Camden–Rockport area, and many of them have a national or even international reputation. Looking for wedding rings or a one-of-a-kind anniversary gift? This is the place to come. Here are a few ideas.

Camden Jewelry Co.
4 Bayview Street, Camden
(207) 236-8124
www.camdenjewelry.com
Ensconced on Bayview Street for ages now, this goldsmith's shop has cases filled with goodies, like their trademark gimmal rings, interlocking hoops of contrasting metals, or their Munsteiner tourmaline necklaces, which break into smaller, wearable pieces (one can be worn as a pendant or a brooch).

Etienne Fine Jewelry
14 Sea Street, Camden
(207) 236-9696 or (800) 426-4367
www.etienne.com
Known for his work with diamonds, Etienne Perret comes from Swiss stock, and he incorporates a lot of European sensibilities into his designs. His pieces are sold from coast to coast. He has won two Diamonds of Distinction awards and his designs are now selling in the millions. Check out the starlight bands, which are gold rings with a constellation of diamonds.

Thomas Michael Designers
7 Bayview Landing, Camden
(207) 236-2708
www.thomasmichaels.com
You've most likely seen this guy's stuff in fashion magazines. His store on Bayview Landing requires you to be buzzed in. Known for jewelry, Michael and his wife, Nora, craft contemporary rings and fine items like titanium cuff bracelets and elevate them to art levels.

ONCE A TREE
46 Bayview St., Camden
(207) 236-3995 or (800) 236-0440
www.onceatree.net

If it's made of wood, you'll find it here, as this shop's slogan goes, "from grandfather clocks to alphabet blocks." Bowls and canes and kitchen utensils and cutting boards and fanciful fish—it's all in this attractive shop on the waterfront. Open year-round.

SAGE MARKET
40 Washington St., Camden
(207) 230-0800
www.sage-market.com

You just knew this great gourmet market, squeezed into an old storefront on Main Street in Rockland, was going to get too big for its britches, and now it has closed its Rockland location and consolidated itself into a bigger space in downtown Camden. Everyone loves its artisan breads and cheeses, its selection of spices, and its handcrafted chocolates. From pan de higo almendrado fig and almond cake to Edmond Fallot comichons, you can find it here. It's a foodie's fantasy.

UNIQUE ONE
2 Bayview St., Camden
(207) 236-8717 or (888) 691-8358
www.mainesweaters.com
Original sweaters handmade by native knitters are the appeal of this longtime Bayview Street favorite. Yarns come from Maine sheep farms (and there's a selection here of yarn as well), and the sweaters are beautiful and one-of-a-kind. They can run you as much as $110, but they'll wear for ages—and look good doing so. Some cutesy moose designs, yes, but a lot of classics like the snowflake pullover. If you see something you like but they're out of your size, you can order one and have it shipped. They also carry patterns, needles, books, and other knitting-related items.

Other Shopping in the Camden Area

For lingerie try **Theo B. Camisole** (24 Bayview Street; 207-236-0072). **Heavenly Threads** (57 Elm Street; 207-236-3203) resells clothing, and in a tony town like Camden you can make some real finds. **Wild Rufus** (22 Main Street; 207-236-2263) is actually rather tame, but it's your best bet for CDs for miles around. Out in the hills of Hope, you'll find **metalworker Benjamin Leavitt** (446 Camden Road, Hope; 207-763-4645; www.benjaminleavitt.com) who crafts beautiful furnishings out of wrought steel.

Lincolnville
MONROE SALTWORKS
Route 1, Lincolnville Beach
(207) 338-3460
Begun in the tiny town of Monroe, inland from Belfast, this pottery emporium has grown exponentially, and it now ships its cool, grainy, salt-glazed wares across the country (there are stores in Copley Place, Boston, and Arlington, Massa-

chusetts, as well as here and in Ellsworth). You can get seconds here on their plates, bowls, serving platters, and mugs, which makes things affordable. Check out the crow line.

Belfast and Surrounding Area
BELFAST CO-OP STORE
123 High St., Belfast
(207) 338-2532
www.belfastcoop.com
Not every small Maine town can support a grocery-store–size co-op filled with organic produce, natural meats, enviromental magazines, green health and beauty products, organic snacks and chips, and on and on, but Belfast isn't every Maine town. The Co-op is a meeting place—it has a nice little cafe—and an important grocery to many who live in Waldo County. It's been at it for three decades now. You may fall in love with a product, though, only to have it never available again. That happens here.

BRAMBLES
Main St., Belfast
(207) 338-3448
You don't have to have a garden to appreciate this Main Street favorite. While the store specializes in upscale garden goods—tools, ornaments, statuary, planters, herb markers, and on and on—it also carries fanciful housewares and gifts, note cards, soap, and ribbon. It's a can't-fail place to buy Mother's Day presents or housewarming items for your friend with the new cottage.

CHERISHED HOME
Route 1, Belfast
(207) 338-4111
www.thecherishedhome.com
If you're like 30 million other people, you remember the 1981 wedding of Luke and Laura on ABC's *General Hospital*. The "it" couple's nuptials drew the largest daytime audience in history. People still ooh and ah at Laura, but today they do so in East Belfast, Maine. That's where actress Genie Francis and her husband, Jonathan Frakes (known to Trekkies everywhere as Commander

Riker of *Star Trek: The Next Generation*), run this fancy housewares store on busy Route 1. Inside you'll find furnishings of all sorts—new and antique, rugs and end tables and linens and table settings and even robes—anything that might "make a house into a home." And you might find Laura herself; Francis not only runs the place, which is set up in an 1890 home overlooking the harbor, but has poured herself into it, having long been interested in interior design.

COYOTE MOON
54 Main St., Belfast
(207) 338-5659

Coyote Moon is something of a reflection of Waldo County. It has all the funkiness and whimsy you might expect of a boutique catering to ex-hippies and back-to-the-landers and then some, with dresses from India, crazy cool mobiles hanging from the ceiling, neat turquoise jewelry, and gifts and accessories. And it has somehow managed to thrive for more than a decade while other stores on Main Street boarded up or changed hands long ago.

THE GREEN STORE
71 Main St., Belfast
(207) 338-4045
www.greenstore.com

This place bills itself as the general store for the 21st century, and we can only hope that people will be as forward-thinking as the Green Store. From health and beauty products to rugs to clothing to solar technology, the store has environmentally sustainable goods galore. Check out the horse tire swing, the Audubon birdcalls, the natural cotton baby slings, and the rack of environmental magazines.

LIBERTY TOOL
Main St., Liberty
(207) 589-4771
www.myspace/libertytool.com

This is the sort of funky old place where you can get happily lost for hours. Four stories of second-time-around tools fill this creaky old building on Main Street, as well as a mixture of antiques, junk, and books. It's always fun to peruse the electric hand tools, axes, drill bits, and dusty shelves here, and few people leave without buying something.

Other Shopping in Belfast

Perry's Nut House (Route 1; 207-338-1630; www.perrysnuthouse.com), the once legendary, strange gift store, is not quite the same anymore. **The Good Table** (68 Main Street; 207-338-4880; www.goodtable.net) carries an astonishing array of kitchenwares. **Colburn Shoe Store** (79 Main Street; 207-338-1934) claims to be the nation's oldest shoe shop. The **Fertile Mind Bookshop** (105 Main Street; 207-338-2498; www.fertile mindbooks.com) is an independent bookseller with not a lot of books. **Mr. Paperback Music and Cafe** (Reny's Plaza; 207-338-2735) has a mediocre selection of books but a surprisingly good selection of music.

Searsport
PENOBSCOT BOOKS
Route 1, Searsport
(207) 548-6490

Art books are the specialty at this lemon-yellow bookshop a mile shy of Searsport, and there are several rooms filled with them, from obscure titles about the Middle Ages to more recent tomes about current painters. There are so many books—40,000 at last count—that owners Howard and Kate La Rue have made floor maps to guide you through. You'll also find good sections on religion, poetry, cartography, and Maine subjects, all personally selected by your hosts.

Bucksport
BOOK STACKS
71 Main St., Bucksport
(207) 469-8992
www.bookstacksmaine.com

Bucksport isn't exactly a bookish town, but it certainly has a great bookstore in this place. Proprietor Andy Lacher does a bang-up job, with a good selection of new titles, a nicely juried selection of used books, and a pleasant atmosphere.

Castine

COMPASS ROSE BOOKSTORE AND CAFE
3 Main St., Castine
(207) 326-9366
www.compassrosebooks.com
At this longtime favorite they take bookselling seriously. You can get great recommendations, peruse well-selected shelves (especially the Maine and maritime titles), linger over a cup of tea and a cookie at the cafe, and order whatever you can't find. You'll quickly see why the place has a loyal following.

LEILA DAY ANTIQUES
53 Main St., Castine
(207) 326-8786
www.leiladayantiques.com
Leila Day has been at it here since 1978, and she has a nice selection of antique furniture, both formal and country. You'll find nautical accessories, folk art, and fine art as well, all housed in the pretty old Parson Mason House on Main. Open daily in summer, by appointment in the off-season.

M & E GUMMEL CHAIRWORKS
600 The Shore Rd., Castine
(207) 326-8122
www.gummelchairworks.com
How do you make a historically accurate chair? You use historically accurate tools. That's one of the secrets at this fine furniture maker in Castine, a place that knows a thing or two about history. Known for their Windsor chairs, the father-and-son team here turns out fanbacks, spindle backs, bow backs, and continuous-arm chairs as well as dining tables and wooden bowls, and they do it all by hand, at benches, using hand planes, spokeshaves, and drawknives. The results are exquisite, colonially correct furnishings that would look appropriate in any old house. Prices range from about $550 to $2,000. The shop is in a neat old barn. Call for hours.

Harborside

ARCHITECTURAL ANTIQUITIES
Harborside
(207) 326-4938
www.archantiquities.com
At it since the 1980s, this fun shop seeks out all the distinctive architectural salvage it can find, cleans it up, organizes it, and fills its showroom with mantles and columns, stained glass and lighting, hardware and fixtures. Victorian-era items are a specialty. If you don't see the perfect piece for your old home, ask, and they'll keep an eye out for you. Great stuff.

Blue Hill

BLUE HILL ANTIQUES
8 Water St., Blue Hill
(207) 374-8825
www.bluehillantiques.com
When that pretty old estate in Brooklin goes under this is who they call. Hutches, chairs, sideboards, art, lighting, you'll find it all here, whether it dates back to 1790 or 1970. The owners spend time cruising the back roads of France looking for antiques and you'll come across those as well.

BLUE HILL COMMUNITY MARKET AND CAFE
4 Ellsworth Rd., Blue Hill
(207) 374-2165
www.bluehill.coop
The name of this old enterprise is about the best descriptor you'll find. Like co-ops everywhere, it's about the people and the place as much as the food. They have plenty of organic, locally produced, specialty, and bulk items (more than 500 of the latter), but you'll also find a lot of bonhomie to go with your beets, and botanical herbs, blueberry teas, and backwoods beauty aids.

NORTH COUNTRY TEXTILES
Main St., Blue Hill
(207) 374-2715
www.northcountrytextiles.com
This Main Street staple has all sorts of gifts—candles, wooden utensils, wind-bells—but it is

the textiles that got the place started that are the real attraction. The throws, rugs, baby blankets, and shawls are extraordinary. The folks here have been at their looms since 1976, making most everything themselves but carrying some items made by other area talents. Open all year.

Other Shopping in the Blue Hill Area

Peninsula Weavers (Route 172, Blue Hill; 207-374-2760) turns out beautiful woven items, like rugs and scarves. **Blue Hill Books** (Pleasant Street, Blue Hill; 207-374-5632) is your source for reading material. **Andean Downeast** (27 Water Street, Blue Hill; 207-374-2313) your one-stop shop for alpaca sweaters, pottery, and South-western jewelry. **Bella Colore** (27 Water Street, Blue Hill; 207-374-5343) has all kinds of supplies for beaders and crafters. **Bianco Provisions** (21 Barnacle Lane, Brooklin, 207-359-4999; www .biancoprovisions.com) is a specialty foods store with the kinds of meats and cheeses that you normally only find in the city.

Little Deer Isle

HARBOR FARM
Route 15, Little Deer Isle
(207) 348-7737 or (800) 342-8003
www.harborfarm.com
The selection of housewares, pottery, blown glass, and especially handmade tiles here is truly impressive—you'd think you were in Portland. It's especially nice to visit at Christmastime (they sell some of the best wreaths around).

Ellsworth

BIG CHICKEN BARN
Bucksport Rd. (Route 1), Ellsworth
(207) 667-7308
www.bigchickenbarn.com
On the way to Acadia, the Big Chicken Barn is just that, a large and long former chicken barn, and it's brimming with books and antiques of all sorts—we're talking 21,600 square feet of stuff. Dozens of dealers show their wares in the downstairs, divided into booths. The upstairs is practically groaning under the weight of thousands upon

thousands of books and magazines. You could return each day of your weeklong vacation and not make it through everything here. And people do. Great for rainy days—great for any day.

ACADIA AREA

Bar Harbor

ALONE MOOSE FINE CRAFTS
78 West St., Bar Harbor
(207) 288-4229
www.finemainecrafts.com
The name may be cutesy, but the wares certainly are not. Proprietors Sherry and Ivan Rasmussen put the work of prospective artisans through an application process much like a juried competition, so not much second-rate stuff shows up on their shelves. You will find an array of fine arts and crafts—sculpture, pottery, photography, furniture, and jewelry.

BARK HARBOR
150 Main St., Bar Harbor
(207) 288-0404
www.barkharbor.com
Be sure to visit this kooky shop when you bring Fido to Acadia. From gourmet treats to "paw-tery" dog bowls, you'll discover a lot of neat stuff for man's best friend here. Leashes, collars, doggie towels, and breed-specific T-shirts for you—it's all here.

MYSTERY COVE BOOK SHOP
Crooked Rd. at Dewey St., Hulls Cove
(207) 288-4665
www.dpbooks.com
You have to do some serious sleuthing to find this gem of a mystery book store, but any fan of noir thrillers and whodunits will want to track down owner Steve Powell and check out his collection of close to 10,000 rare and hard-to-find titles. Together with his partner, William Dunn, who runs a shop in Connecticut, Powell has access to 20,000 more books, so if there is an obscure gumshoe you're into, you'll likely be able to find the tome here. And if you can't, Powell will surely know

how to get it. Bar Harbor itself has a history with the mystery—they've been written in town since before the turn of the 20th century and continue to this day with the works of Janwillem van de Wetering. Powell deals in mysterious cinematic materials as well. Worth the detective work.

GET CLOCKED
119 Main St., Bar Harbor
(207) 288-1149
www.getclocked.com
This must be where Father Time shops. Every imaginable timekeeping device is stocked here, from cuckoos to fancy marble clocks. You'll never be late again. Open daily from 9 a.m. to 9 p.m. (check your watch).

SHERMAN'S BOOKS AND STATIONERY
56 Main St., Bar Harbor
(207) 288-3161
www.shermans.com
There are not many Bar Harbor businesses that can claim to have been founded in 1886, but that's exactly the case at this favorite, which has rescued generations of vacationers from rainy days. Bill Sherman opened up that year, printing the local paper and selling books. They don't print papers and more but have plenty of books; there's a good Maine section and a fine lineup of maps and trail guides. You'll also find gifts and stationery and a smattering of toys, but it's the books that make Sherman's. A visit to Bar Harbor just wouldn't be the same without this old place, and there are now stores in Freeport, Boothbay Harbor, Camden, and nearby Northeast Harbor as well.

Other Shopping in Bar Harbor

Willis' Rock Shop (69-73 Main Street; 207-288-4935) is the best place to turn for rocks and beach stone bracelets. **Window Panes** (166 Main Street; 207-288-9550) has a great selection of housewares. The **Alternative Market** (16 Mount Desert Street; 207-288-8225) is your gourmet grocery and hipster hangout. And if you're into Maine's state stone, tourmaline, get over to **Jack's Jewelry** (23&27 Main Street; www.jacksjewelry.com).

Uncle Henry's

While not a store per se, *Uncle Henry's* is something every Maine shopper should be familiar with. The Augusta-based weekly swap-it-or-sell-it guide is a genuine phenomenon in the state. The digest-size book of classifieds has transcended ordinary usefulness and become something of a bible for thousands of Mainers, and it's undoubtedly the most-read periodical Down East. Everything one can imagine has been sold in its 400-or-so pages, from snakes to fire trucks, houses to guitars, and people read it carefully cover to cover. It comes out on Thursdays, and the good stuff inside is often gone by the weekend. Still, there are some truly great deals to be had in its newsprint pages, and even if you're not in the market for something, it's an entertaining read simply for the craziness of some of the ads. You can find out more by logging on to www.unclehenrys.com or by picking up a copy at the local convenience store.

DOWN EAST

Gouldsboro

BARTLETT MAINE ESTATE WINERY
Off Route 1, Gouldsboro
(207) 546-2408
www.bartlettwinery.com
Maine's most famous winery, this is where to turn for local favorites like blueberry wine. Specializing in fruits other than grapes, the owners have won many national and even international awards for their vino.

Perry

45TH PARALLEL
Route 1, Perry
(207) 853-9500
www.fortyfifthparallel.com

Housed in an old elementary school, this home furnishing store calls itself the answer to the question "Where in the world did you find that?" And it's apt, both because you'll be very surprised to find a shop this fun and funky in Perry, Maine, and because proprietors Philip and Britani have filled their shop with cool and creative oddments from all around the globe: "exotic" antiques, nautical items, architectural pieces, souvenirs, and unique decorative accessories—neat stained glass, candleholders, funky lamps, artful clocks. It's an intriguing mix of stuff, and you'll hardly believe you're still Down East. Open daily from May through October and weekends in November and December.

Eastport

THE EASTPORT GALLERY
74 Water St., Eastport
(207) 853-2965
www.eastportgallery.com

Few Eastport shops have a lot of staying power, but this downtown gallery has been around a while. The 30 area artists represented here are affiliated with the great local Eastport Art Center, and this gallery is where you can buy their work. You'll find painting, sculpture, and photography. There's a gift shop as well. Open seven days a week from June through September.

RAYE'S MUSTARD MILL
Route 190, Eastport
(207) 853-4451 or (800) 853-1903
www.rayesmustard.com

Eastport's most famous attraction, Raye's has been grinding out mustards for more than a century. Their mustards come in more than a dozen flavors, and you can get a gift pack at their Pantry Store. Try the smooth Down East Schooner or the Hot and Spicy. You can also get coffee and a tour of the factory here, and it's a fascinating slice of Maine history. Open daily from 9 a.m. to 5 p.m. in season.

Other Shopping in the Eastport Area

Wood on Water (75 Water Street, 207-853-9633; woodonwater.com) has custom wood-burned, handpainted giftware. **Lewis Flower and Gift Shop** (31 Water Street, 207-853-4466) has, yes, flowers and gifts, but also the area's famous Passamaquoddy basksets.

ATTRACTIONS

Whether you like your culture of the high variety or the pop, you'll find what you're looking for on the coast of Maine. Thanks to its age, the state is home to a vast number of historic house museums—often the headquarters of the local historical society. We have two truly exceptional art museums, the Portland Museum of Art and the Farnsworth Art Museum, and any number of eclectic collections, from vintage autos to butterflies. We also have a couple of sports franchises in Portland with legions of fans. And there's plenty more to discover. Just turn the pages and read on.

Price Code

Except where noted, prices represent cost per person for admission, not including tax. In cases where donation is listed, there is no mandatory admission fee, but a donation is appreciated and recommended to support upkeep of the facility.

$.....................$5.99 or less
$$ ....$6.00 to $12.99
$$$ .... $13.00 to $19.99
$$$$ ....$20.00 or more

MUSEUMS

South Coast

OGUNQUIT MUSEUM OF
AMERICAN ART $
543 Shore Rd., Ogunquit
(207) 646-4909
www.ogunquitmuseum.org
It stands to figure that Ogunquit would have a good art museum, as it earned a national reputation as an art colony a long time ago. But it's still surprising that such a tiny town would have such a fine museum. Dedicated to 20th-century American art, the collection here includes more than 1,300 works by such talents as Marsden Hartley, Edward Hopper, and Walter Kuhn, and many other internationally famous artists. Built in the early 1950s due to the hard efforts of Ogunquit painter and scenester Henry Strater, it opened in 1953 and grew impressively thanks to a lot of

donations by big-name artists. Floor-to-ceiling windows frame ocean views like living paintings, and they are as beautiful as anything on the walls. The museum hosts rotating exhibits and has lectures and workshops in the summer. Open from 10:30 a.m. to 5 p.m. Monday through Saturday and 2 to 5 p.m. Sunday from July through October. Free for children 11 and under.

WELLS AUTO MUSEUM $
Route 1, Wells
(207) 646-9064
More than 80 classic cars are on display here, including a Stanley Steamer, a Stutz Bearcat, and a 1908 Baker Electric Car once owned by John D. Rockefeller. (Check out the 1940 Bombardier snowmobile.) And strangely the museum isn't just about wheels—there is collection of nickelodeons and toys as well. Of course, the cars are why you come to this warehouse on Route 1, and you can even get a ride in a vintage car. The museum is open from 10 a.m. to 5 p.m. daily from Memorial Day through Columbus Day.

BRICK STORE MUSEUM
117 Main St., Kennebunk
(207) 985-4802
www.brickstoremuseum.org
Four pretty old commercial buildings—basically one block in downtown Kennebunk—serve as the headquarters for this local institution. The collections here are a mixed bunch, showcasing the

Maine Archives and Museums is a consortium of museums, historic homes, historical societies—all manner of venerable institutions, really—and it has a handy Web site. Visit www.mainemuseums .org and you can find everything from museum locations and hours to interesting historic tidbits, like the fact that two Civil War engagements happened Down East.

history of the Kennebunks. The museum dates back to 1936, and it's known for its decorative arts but also for maritime artifacts, and even exhibits about the Bush family, who have summered for ages in Kennebunkport. Some spaces look like rooms in an old home, others more like museum galleries. Nice quilts and shipbuilding tools. The Brick Store hosts rotating exhibitions, educational programs, and walking tours. Open year-round Tuesday through Friday from 10 a.m. to 4:30 p.m. and Saturday from 10 a.m. to 1 p.m. Donation.

SEASHORE TROLLEY MUSEUM $–$$
195 Log Cabin Rd., Kennebunkport
(207) 967-2800
www.trolleymuseum.org
Trolleys have been a part of summer in the South Coast for ages, and this fine museum explores every aspect of them. This is the oldest and larg- est electric railway museum in the world, dating back to the 1930s, and it includes more than 225 vehicles. Favorites are the snow sweepers, like the 1920 Russell Car and snow sweeper with its big bristle brushes, and the ones from Maine, like the 12-seat, red, open-air car from Biddeford-Saco. Rides along a 4-mile loop happen regularly from 10 a.m. to 4:15 p.m., and they are noisy good fun. If you're really into this sort of thing, consider the Be a Motorman program. Pony up $50 and you can drive one of these babies. The museum is open from 10 a.m. to 5 p.m. daily in summer and on weekends only in May and September. At 7:30 p.m. every Wednesday and Thursday in July and August, the museum conducts sunset and ice- cream trolley rides that are popular with families.

SACO MUSEUM $
371 Main St., Saco
(207) 283-3861
www.sacomuseum.org
A distinctive brick building downtown, this colo- nial revival place looks like a library from the street, but it's actually a little-known gem of a museum. (The building was designed by noted architect John Calvin Stevens in 1926 to house Maine's third-oldest museum, which dates back to 1866.) Five period rooms serve as the backdrop for a fine collection of early American furnishings, artworks, and artifacts. Some of the more notable pieces are the 850-foot-long *Panorama of Pil- grim's Progress*, one of few surviving 19th-century panoramas, and paintings by John Brewster Jr., Charles H. Granger, and Gideon Bradbury, as well as a daguerreotype camera that was the first of its kind in the country and a re-created colonial revival kitchen. The museum frequently hosts lectures, workshops, classes, and walking tours. Open Tuesday, Wednesday, Friday, and Saturday from noon to 4 p.m. and Thursday from noon to 8 p.m. year-round and weekends in summer.

Greater Portland
PORTLAND HARBOR MUSEUM $
Fort Rd., South Portland
(207) 799-6337
www.portlandharbormuseum.org
Once known as the Spring Point Museum, this neat little repository of Casco Bay history is housed in a building that once served as Fort Preble's Ord- nance Machine Shop. The grounds, part of the Southern Maine Community College campus and right next to the Spring Point Ledge Light (see Lighthouses chapter) and the Spring Point Walk- way, are alone reason to visit. But the museum, founded in 1985 to conserve the bow of the Snow Squall, the only surviving remnant from the glory days of American clipper ships, has a nifty collec- tion of nautical items. Among them are more than 500 glass plate negatives that tell the compelling story of the harbor, and there are still more photos that depict the building of the South Portland Lib- erty ships that helped turn the tide in World War

II. The small museum regularly hosts changing exhibits that explore the history of the great bay out its doors. Open daily from 10 a.m. to 4:30 p.m. from Memorial Day through mid-October, and on a limited basis in the off-season.

MUSEUM OF AFRICAN CULTURE $
13 Brown St., Portland
(207) 871-7188
www.africantribalartmuseum.com
That you can wander among tribal masks from Nigeria, sacred carvings from Ghana, and bronze statuary from Benin in Portland, Maine, is pretty astounding. But it's the result of Oscar Mokeme and Arthur Aleshire's dream to preserve tribal artworks. The small museum—it has more than 500 artifacts but is feeling pinched for space—is the only place in New England to see sub-Saharan tribal art. It was founded in 1998 and has a variety of educational programs like Discover Africa, which it takes into communities to help shed light on a region of the world with which many Mainers are unfamiliar. The museum is open Tuesday through Friday from 10:30 a.m.to 4 p.m. and Saturday from 12 to 4 p.m.; closed Monday.

PORTLAND MUSEUM OF ART $$
7 Congress St., Portland
(207) 775-6148
www.portlandmuseum.org
The Portland Museum of Art is a major anchor in the Forest City's Arts District, and it has become a huge draw since it was established more than a century ago. Housed in an impressive, award-winning I. M. Pei–designed building at the upper end of Congress Street, the museum has a fine collection of American and European art and regularly welcomes major traveling exhibitions. Maine is well represented in the American collection, especially in the Elizabeth Noyce collection, which was given to the museum by the late Intel heiress and includes works by Andrew and N. C. Wyeth, George Bellows, Mary Cassatt, Frederick Childe Hassam, and Fitz Hugh Lane, among others. The European collection includes works by such greats as Edgar Degas, Claude Monet, Henri Toulouse-Lautrec, and Pablo Picasso.

The newer LDM Sweat Memorial Galleries are home to the museum's collection of paintings by Winslow Homer, who lived for many years just a few miles down the coast at Prouts Neck. And the PMA also has a decorative arts showcase on the lowest floor that includes more than 2,000 pieces of glass and artistic housewares.

Educational opportunities abound at the PMA, and there are frequent talks and workshops. The cafe here has a decent reputation as well, and you can get an array of good titles, including several related to Maine, at the gift shop. The museum is open Tuesday through Sunday from 10 a.m. to 5 p.m.; it's open until 9 p.m. on Friday and is free to visit after 5 p.m. that day.

PORTLAND OBSERVATORY $
138 Congress St., Portland
(207) 774-5561
In the early 1800s scouts used to climb this 86-foot tower atop Munjoy Hill to look for ships coming into Portland Harbor. They'd then use coded flags to alert merchants about arrivals so warehouses could prepare wharves and line up stevedores. (They didn't have cell phones, remember.) The vista from atop the octagonal red structure was extraordinary—and it still is today. On a clear day you can see miles out to sea and as far as the White Mountains of New Hampshire, and tourists and schoolkids love to climb it to do just that. The observatory is the only remaining marine signal tower in the nation, and children find it particularly entertaining. But there are few people who don't enjoy the view. Open Memorial Day to Columbus Day from 10 a.m. to 5 p.m. daily.

SALT GALLERY FOR DOCUMENTARY FIELD STUDIES
561 Congress St., Portland
(207) 761-0660
www.salt.edu
Dedicated to field journalism—photography is the specialty—Salt has a fine gallery at its new home in the heart of the Arts District, where you can see work by students and faculty of the Salt Institute. Often black-and-white but occasionally

in color, these shows explore places and themes with genuine intimacy and gritty reality. Shows change about four to six times a year. The gallery is open from 9 a.m. to 4:30 p.m. Monday through Friday year-round; closed weekends. Free.

Midcoast
BOWDOIN COLLEGE MUSEUM OF ART
Walker Art Building
Bowdoin College, Brunswick
(207) 725-3275
www.bowdoin.edu/art-museum
One of the great surprises here is the world-class collection of classical items, including pieces from ancient Greece, Rome, and Asia. But you'll also find a worthy assemblage of American and European paintings, sculpture, drawings, and photographs. The beautiful old Charles McKim–designed building is newly renovated with more exhibit space than ever. Open Tuesday through Saturday from 10 a.m.to 5 p.m. and Sunday from 1 to 5 p.m. year-round. Donation.

PEARY-MACMILLAN ARCTIC MUSEUM $
Bowdoin College, Brunswick
(207) 725-3416
Admiral Robert Peary was the first man to reach the North Pole. That's what you'll learn at this collection—whether or not it was actually the case—controversy still rages about whether Peary made it. The place is is stuffed with diaries, letters, and photographs of the trip he took with his assistant, Donald MacMillan. In these days of Gore-Tex, it's interesting to look at some of the gear they used, and the museum has displays on the peoples and environments they found up there. Inquire about Peary's summer home on Eagle Island. Open Tuesday through Saturday from 10 a.m. to 5 p.m. and Sunday from 2 to 5 p.m. year-round.

MAINE MARITIME MUSEUM $$
43 Washington St., Bath
(207) 443-1316
www.mainemaritimemuseum.org
The City of Ships is where you'll find the state's

largest nautical museum, right on the Kennebec River and just downriver from the massive shipyard of the Bath Iron Works. People around here know boats, and you can tell by strolling through this excellent collection. Just about anything you ever wanted to know about ships is here in this incredible complex of buildings. There's the big brick Maritime History building, which brims with paintings, models, pieces of boats, documents, and other artifacts—reportedly more than a million pieces—and has permanent displays on fishing, canning, and, of course, shipbuilding. If you can't get enough about this last, simply step outside and venture over to the famous Percy and Small Shipyard, the nation's only remaining yard devoted exclusively to wooden vessels. Walk on over to the Maine Watercraft Exhibit, and you can see a variety of small vessels straight out of the state's history, from rowing boats to canoes to bateaux. And if you feel like actually getting out on the water, you can do that, too. The museum sponsors excursions all summer long, which leave right from its own pier. You could easily spend a few days here. Open from 9:30 a.m. to 5 p.m. daily.

MORRIS FARM
156 Gardiner Rd. (Route 27), Wiscasset
(207) 882-4080
www.morrisfarm.org
In 1994 it looked like Wiscasset was going to lose a bit more of its precious open space. A 60-acre local farm was up for sale and could have well become condominiums or another convenience store. But a group of concerned citizens built a nonprofit corporation, purchased the land, and thus Morris Farm was born. Today it's a working farm and educational center set up to celebrate an agricultural way of life that's becoming endangered in Maine (and everywhere else, for that matter). Children come for summer camp; there's a great farm store with Morris Farm's own organic milk, free-range eggs, broilers, and turkey at Thanksgiving; garden tours are hosted; educational seminars are scheduled; and the public is welcome to stroll the grounds with its barns, meadows, woods, and waterfall from dawn to dusk. You'll want to move back to the land. Free.

MUSICAL WONDER HOUSE $$–$$$$

18 High St., Wiscasset
(207) 882-7163
www.musicalwonderhouse.com

A strange and fascinating collection of music boxes, player pianos, mechanical musical instruments, and melodious oddments make up this museum on a quiet Wiscasset side street. Austrian-born Danilo Konvalinka assembled the collection, and it fills an 1825 sea captain's home. Check out the musical candy dishes in the Green Room or the shadow box with sailing ships and windmill in the Red Room. Guided tours are offered, and they're the best way to get a handle on it all. You can get the abbreviated standard tour, which lasts 35 minutes; the standard tour, 1 hour, 15 minutes; or the be-all and end-all, the Grand House Presentation, which lasts for an exhausting 3 hours. Open Monday through Saturday from 10 a.m. to 5 p.m. and Sunday from noon to 5 p.m. from Memorial Day through October 15.

WISCASSET, WATERVILLE, AND FARMINGTON RAILWAY MUSEUM $

97 Cross Rd., Alna
(207) 882-4193
www.wwfry.org

This is another museum devoted to the unique Maine 2-foot railroad, a diminutive cousin to the railroads across the nation. In their heyday, these rails, 2 feet wide as the name suggests, traversed 200 miles of track in Maine, running dozens of trains, hauling thousands of passengers and tons of freight. The museum here is a nonprofit dedicated to restoring the operation of these trains in the Sheepscot Valley, and it's done a fine job since opening in a small way in 1989. There's a small museum on site that tells the story of the trains and actually takes you out for rides on Saturdays and Sundays. The trains run every 45 minutes from Sheepscot station, from Memorial Day to Columbus Day, beginning at 10 a.m. and ending at 4:45 p.m. It's a neat jaunt through the woodlands along the Sheepscot and a bargain at $6.

BOOTHBAY RAILWAY VILLAGE $$

Route 27, Boothbay Harbor
(207) 633-4727
www.railwayvillage.org

This museum re-creates an old Maine village, down to the narrow-gauge working train that runs through and around it. See the Kidstuff chapter for a more detailed description.

FARNSWORTH ART MUSEUM $$

356 Main St., Rockland
(207) 596-6457
www.farnsworthmuseum.org

These are renaissance days for the Farnsworth, and we're not talking Florentine painting. No, one of the best collections of Maine art has a nicely redone home that's enjoyed considerable expansion and refinement since the 1990s. And it's never been more popular. Established in 1948, the museum was once hard for some tourists to find, sequestered away on a side street in downtown Rockland. But the museum built a Main Street gift shop and entrance in the 1990s, which has doubled the number of visitors and touched off a downtown revitalization that has breathed a lot of life into the city on Penobscot Bay.

The Farnsworth's campus now includes five buildings, among them the Wyeth Center in Maine, which houses the works of the dynastic First Family of American Art. In a pretty, restored church across the street from the main Farnsworth building, the Wyeth Center is where you'll find paintings by patriarch N. C. Wyeth, the famed illustrator, and Jamie Wyeth, his grandson. (Most of the museum's collection of egg tempera paintings and drawings by son Andrew Wyeth are in the Farnsworth proper.) Entrance is free with the purchase of a ticket to the museum.

The Farnsworth had interesting beginnings. When reclusive Rockland resident Lucy Farnsworth died, she left behind $1.5 million for the establishment of a museum and library and the preservation of her family home. But she had never shown any interest in the worlds of arts or letters, so the 1935 gift was a complete surprise. Boston Museum of Fine Arts advisor and Farnsworth agent Robert Bellows roamed far and wide in search of good buys in the 1940s and came back with loads, from the likes of Andrew Wyeth, Winslow Homer, Maurice Prendergast, and Eastman Johnson. Over the years the collection evolved, becoming ever more Maine-centric and featuring significant pieces by many of the greats to live and work here, from George Bellows, Rockwell Kent, and Robert Indiana to Neil Welliver and Alex Katz. The best of these works can be found in the exceptional permanent exhibition "Maine in America," which showcases the considerable impact the state has had on the art world for the past two centuries. Also on continuing display are many pieces by local favorite Louise Nevelson, who emigrated to Rockland and lived in town for years before going on to world fame as a sculptor. All told there are more than 6,000 works in the museum's collection. The Farnsworth owns the old Farnsworth homestead, as well as the Olson House, which served as the backdrop for one of the most famous American paintings of all time, *Christina's World*. The site of many Wyeth paintings, the Olson House is open to tours.

You can always tell when people have been to the Farnsworth—they usually end up wearing the colorful little admission sticker all around town. The little round Day-Glo badge is proof that they've visited one of the nation's best regional museums and arguably the best collection of Maine art in the state. Open daily from 10 a.m. to 5 p.m. from Memorial Day through Columbus Day, and Tuesday through Sunday from 10 a.m. to 5 p.m. during the remainder of the year.

PROJECT PUFFIN VISITOR CENTER
311 Main St., Rockland
(207) 596-5566
www.maineaudubon.org/explore/centers/
projectpuffin.shtml
The puffin is one of the more beguiling characters on the coast of Maine, and the story of the birds is an epic one. The colorful feathers of the small sea parrots were valuable commodities in the 19th century—ladies liked them in their hats—and the birds were hunted to the point of extinction Down East. Though puffins once inhabited six

islands along the coast, there was only one pair left nesting at Matinicus Rock by 1902. Around the turn of the century, public outrage about the decline of sea bird populations led to the passage of legislation protecting our feathered friends. By the early 1970s there were two small puffin colonies left in Maine, the one on Matinicus Rock and another on Machias Seal Island. But the bird hadn't returned to the other islands it once called home. Project Puffin was begun by the National Audubon Society in 1973 to help puffins take back their neighborhoods. The society transplanted young puffins from Newfoundland to Eastern Egg Rock in Muscongus Bay, hoping they'd take root. And they did. In 1981 four pairs nested on the rocky isle. By 2006 there were 80 pairs. You can learn the whole tale at this new Project Puffin Visitor Center on Main Street in downtown Rockland, where there are interpretive maps, murals, displays, photographs, and even video cameras you can operate yourself. It's open daily from 10 a.m. to 5 p.m. and Wednesday until 7 p.m. from May through October.

OWLS HEAD TRANSPORTATION MUSEUM $$
Route 73, Owls Head
(207) 594-4418
www.ohtm.org
There's hardly a weekend between May and October when something isn't going on at this Rockland-area institution. From vintage car meets to air shows, the museum's calendar is chock-full of events, and they're almost more interesting than the goings-on inside the big building. The museum has more than 100 vehicles on display—planes, cars, bikes, motorcycles, and carriages—all of them intriguing in one way or another. From one of the earliest bicycles, the colorfully named 1868 Velocipede Boneshaker, a brutal, suspensionless ride in those days of rutty roads, to the 1953 Whizzer Sportman, a protomotorcycle, from the carriagelike 1885 Benz automobile to the Model T–based 1926 Ford Snowmobile, the collection is fascinating. Car, airplane, and motorcycle buffs travel from around the globe to visit, but there

is plenty to enjoy if your world doesn't revolve around engines. Plenty of educational opportunities are offered here as well as well as guest lectures and workshops. And don't miss the air show. Open daily from 10 a.m. to 5 p.m.

PENOBSCOT MARINE MUSEUM $-$$
5 Church St., Searsport
(207) 548-2529
www.penobscotmarinemuseum.org
Long ago, Searsport, Maine, used to boast more sea captains than any other community in the country. Several of their homes—and many of the treasures they brought back from around the globe—are on display at the Penobscot Marine Museum. The maritime museum occupies a campus right in the center of town, which includes an even dozen buildings. Inside are all manner of nautical art and artifacts, chronicling the rich seafaring history of Maine and particularly of Penobscot Bay and the Down East coast. Paintings, models, vessels—the collection numbers more than 10,000 pieces. And the very buildings they are housed in are themselves antiques, furnished much the same way they were when 19th-century salts called them home. The museum hosts a slate of changing exhibits as well as workshops and programs. Not long ago it built a Main Street gift shop, which is pleasant to visit and actually helps you find the place. Open Monday through Saturday from 10 a.m. to 5 p.m. and Sunday from noon to 5 p.m. from Memorial Day through mid-October.

DEER ISLE GRANITE MUSEUM $
Stonington
(207) 367-6331
Stonington takes its very name from the bedrock of granite on which it sits, and the community was the site of quite the quarrying industry in the late 19th century. Stone slabs from this picturesque village made their way into some American landmarks, from the George Washington Bridge to Rockefeller Center to the Smithsonian, and you can learn all about it at this small

museum. An 8-by-15-foot working model depicts what Stonington and nearby Crotch Island, where stonecutting continues to this day, looked like in the golden age of granite. Open in July and August. Call for hours.

STANWOOD HOMESTEAD MUSEUM $
High St. (Route 3), Ellsworth
(207) 667-8460
www.birdsacre.com
Former home of noted ornithologist, photographer, and author Cordelia Stanwood, the museum features an impressive collection of mounted bird specimens and eggs, too. Real live birds flock to the wooded nature trails on the 160 acres outside. It's an incredible bit of green on the notoriously overdeveloped strip-mall stretch east of downtown Ellsworth. The grounds are open year-round during daylight hours and the museum is open daily from June through September from 10 a.m. to 4 p.m.

Acadia Area

ABBE MUSEUM $$
26 Mount Desert St., Bar Harbor
(207) 288-3519
www.abbemuseum.org
The Abbe Museum was always much bigger than its 2,000-square-foot confines at Sieur de Monts Spring in Acadia National Park. The collection, representing 10,000 years of Native American life Down East, numbered some 50,000 pieces assembled over the museum's 75-year history, and it just didn't fit in such a small space. People used to visit and go away yearning for more than the single exhibit the museum was able to host. Not anymore. In 1997 the museum bought the old YMCA building in downtown Bar Harbor and set about transforming it into a first-class exhibition space. Designed by Schwartz/Silver Architects of Boston, the 17,000-square-foot museum opened in 2001, and has proved to be just what the Abbe needed. There is now room for multiple exhibitions at a time, and the museum can show a lot of the collection that was packed away

in storage, items like Micmac quill boxes and woven sweetgrass baskets, Penobscot pottery, and a 3,000-year-old flute made from the bone of a swan. It also allows the museum to host a full schedule of educational programs—and remain open year-round. The old octagonal building at Sieur de Mont will still be used, too. Open daily from 10 a.m. to 6 p.m. Hours are reduced during the winter months, so call ahead.

GEORGE B. DORR NATURAL HISTORY MUSEUM $
College of the Atlantic
105 Eden St., Bar Harbor
(207) 288-5015
www.coamuseum.org
A fine collection of flora and fauna indigenous to the Acadia area is on display in a relatively new home on the campus of the College of the Atlantic. Kids like the indoor tide pools. Even if whalebones, stuffed puffins, and student-designed nature dioramas are not your thing, the museum is a good excuse to pay a visit to COA, always ranked highly among the most beautiful college campuses in the country. Open Monday through Saturday from 10 a.m. to 5 p.m. from mid-June through Labor Day.

SEAL COVE AUTO MUSEUM $
Pretty Marsh Rd., Mount Desert Island
(207) 244-9242
www.sealcoveautomuseum.org
Definitely worth a look-see if it's open when you visit, this eccentric museum boasts more than 100 old autos and more than 30 antique motorcycles in a collection known around the world. Some of these beauties date back to the turn of the 20th century. Check out the 1911 Thomas Flyer or the 1907 Chadwick. They're in pristine condition, all shiny and gleaming, and some evoke Chitty Chitty Bang Bang. Others are of relatively recent vintage (1973 Toyota Land Rover, 1974 Volkswagon Bug). Open from 10 a.m. to 5 p.m. from June through mid-September.

HISTORIC HOMES AND SITES

South Coast

KITTERY HISTORICAL AND NAVAL MUSEUM $
200 Rogers Rd., Kittery
(207) 439-3080
This cool maritime history museum has a lot in the works. It's close to its fund-raising goal to erect a new wing, which it will use to house a rebuilt garrison that stood on a hill overlooking Brave Boat Harbor in the 1720s. But there's plenty to like here now. The small collection, which grew out of a bicentennial project in 1976, features all sorts of nautical items, from ship models and replicas (including the USS *Ranger*, made famous by John Paul Jones) to a permanent shipbuilding display, as well as intriguing objects like the light from Boon Island, site of a disastrous shipwreck that led to cannibalism. Anyone interested in Kittery or nautical history will find enough to while away an hour or two. Open Tuesday through Saturday from 10 a.m. to 4 p.m. from June through late October.

HAMILTON HOUSE $$
40 Vaughns Lane, South Berwick
(207) 384-2454
www.historicnewengland.com
Maine doesn't have a lot of mansions, but this is one of them, a distinctive three-story Georgian on the sleepy Salmon Falls River. Built in the 1780s, the home was purchased in 1898 by a mother-daughter pair, and they restored it beautifully, furnishing it with antiques and country items in keeping with the house's history. The grounds are just as lovely as the home, beautifully landscaped and featuring formal gardens. The property is now owned by the Society for the Preservation of New England Antiquities, and tours of the place are offered on the hour between 11 a.m. and 4 p.m. daily in summer. There's also a concert series on the gracious lawns. Open Wednesday through Sunday from June through mid-October; the grounds are open from dawn to dusk.

SARAH ORNE JEWETT HOUSE $
5 Portland St., South Berwick
(207) 384-2454
www.historicnewengland.com
Former home of celebrated 19th-century author Sarah Orne Jewett (she of the environmental classic *The Country of the Pointed Firs*), this old place—circa 1774—looks much the same as it might have when Jewett lived here. It is a pretty Georgian with period furnishings collected by Jewett and her sister. The pair were friendly with the family that owned the Hamilton House nearby, and Jewett helped make sure that home was preserved. This is also a Society for the Preservation of New England Antiquities property, and it's open Friday through Sunday from 11 a.m. to 5 p.m. from June 1 through October 15. Tours are given on the hour between 11 a.m. and 4 p.m.

OLD YORK HISTORICAL SOCIETY $–$$
207 York St., York Village
(207) 363-4974
www.oldyork.org
It seems fitting that one of the state's most historic communities should have one of the best historical societies. A very active bunch, the Old Yorkers keep seven venerable properties hopping throughout the summer. They provide guided tours—in costume—and living history demonstrations, and they set up self-guided walks of their antique buildings. Mixed right into downtown York Village, these buildings include the society's headquarters at Jefferds Tavern, a watering hole on the route between Portland and Portsmouth that dates back to 1750. (It's painted an unfortunate brown color.) Then there's the Old Gaol, which, built in 1719, is considered one of the oldest British public buildings in the country. Better than that, it's a fascinating look at the treatment of prisoners in the colonial area—you wouldn't have wanted to be one. It's a favorite among visitors, as is the Old Schoolhouse, a one-room school from 1754. Other stops to check out are the John Hancock Warehouse, where you can see displays depicting York's maritime heritage, and the Wilcox House, a 1742 picket-fenced beauty with more

displays of York history inside. These buildings are open every day but Sunday from 10 a.m. to 5 p.m. from June through Columbus Day. Also plan to hit the Museum Store, which has the same hours. Children 6 and under free.

SAYWARD-WHEELER HOUSE $
9 Barrell Lane Extension, York Harbor
(207) 384-2454
www.historicnewengland.com
Another property maintained by the Society for the Preservation of New England Antiquities, this 1718 gem has its original furnishings—and a nice view of the York River. It was once the home of a Loyalist who served in the Massachusetts legislature, and it was opened to tours as far back as the 1860s to show how people used to live in the colonial era. Open from 11 a.m. to 5 p.m. on the first Saturday of the month from June 1 through October 15. Tours are offered on the hour between 11 a.m. and 4 p.m.

HISTORIC MEETINGHOUSE MUSEUM $
Buzzell Rd., Wells
(207) 646-4775
The town of Wells's original meeting place serves as the home of the historical society's collection of nautical and local memorabilia and a trove of genealogical information about area families. Open Tuesday and Wednesday from 10 a.m. to 4 p.m. and Saturday by appointment from mid-May through mid-October.

RICHARD A. NOTT MEMORIAL HOUSE $
8 Maine St., Kennebunkport
(207) 967-2751
www.kporthistory.org
A Greek Revival mansion decorated with original furnishings, the Nott house is known locally as White Columns for the distinctive Doric columns that wrap around. Built in 1853, it's an example of the prosperity that shipbuilding brought to this community on the Kennebunk River. Be sure to hit the gift shop in the carriage house. Open Wednesday through Friday from 10 a.m. to 4 p.m. and Saturday from 10 a.m. to 1 p.m. from mid-June through mid-October.

Greater Portland

NEAL DOW MANSION

714 Congress St., Portland

(207) 773-7773

www.mewctu.org

Neal Dow was the mover and shaker who made Maine the first state to outlaw alcohol, and his 1829 mansion has been the home of the upstanding teetotalers of the Maine Women's Christian Temperance Union for years. Dow came of age when Portland was a port in the rum trade from the West Indies and drunkenness and disorder were not uncommon. Dow was bothered by that, and he crusaded to get booze banned. He was also an ardent abolitionist who commanded a regiment of volunteers and rose to the rank of brigadier general in the Civil War. Whether or not you agree with his politics, he was an interesting fellow, and his house is fun to explore. Open Monday through Friday from 11 a.m. to 4 p.m. Free.

TATE HOUSE $

Westbrook St., Portland

(207) 774-6177

www.tatehouse.org

This Georgian was built in 1755 by the colonial mast agent for the British navy. Restored at the turn of this century, the home has historic landscaping and an 18th-century herb garden among its attractions. Now owned by the National Society of the Colonial Dames of America, it is the only pre-Revolutionary home that is open to the public in Greater Portland. The furnishings are something to see—check out the cool fireplace in the kitchen with its crane and cast iron pots. Open June 15 through mid-October, Tuesday through Saturday from 10 a.m. to 4 p.m., and the first Sunday of every month from 1 to 4 p.m.

VICTORIA MANSION $-$$

109 Danforth St., Portland

(207) 772-4841

www.victoriamansion.org

How did an ornate—overwrought, even—New Orleans–inspired Italian villa end up in Yankeeville? Also known as the Morse-Libby House, this Victorian showplace was built in the 1850s by Ruggles Morse, a Mainer who made his fortune running New Orleans hotels and pumped a good deal of his money into his Maine summer home. Morse hired almost 100 highly skilled craftsmen to work on this brownstone to make it a place his wife would want to be, and the result is an extraordinary, head-spinning treasure trove of Victoriana complete with intricate wall painting, soaring staircases, elaborate stained glass, angels and gilding everywhere, and even a Turkish smoking room. The house included such contemporary comforts as central heating, hot and cold water, and a call system for servants, which were unusual for the day. Today 90 percent of the furnishings and details are still intact, making this into one of the finest examples in the nation of how the ultra-affluent lived prior to the Civil War. Gaudy is the word. Perhaps the best time to visit is during the city's Victorian holiday celebration at Christmastime, when the mansion is richly decorated for the yuletide. The museum is open from 10 a.m. to 4 p.m. Monday through Saturday and 1 to 5 p.m. Sunday from May through October and again for the holidays. Tours of the mansion are 45 minutes long and are given at quarter past and quarter 'til the hour. Holiday hours vary, so call ahead. Children 6 and under free.

WADSWORTH-LONGFELLOW
HOUSE $-$$

Congress St., Portland

(207) 772-1822

www.mainehistory.org

Part of the Center for Maine History complex right downtown, this 1786 colonial set back from the street right in the heart of Portland was the boyhood home of famed poet Henry Wadsworth Longfellow. Opened as Maine's first historic house museum in 1901, it underwent considerable renovation in 2002 and is now in grand form. Many of the original furnishings used by little Henry and his family are still intact, and the shaded gardens out back are a nice sanctuary of quiet from the hubbub of Congress Street. Tours of the house, which will fill you in on this fascinating family and the ways of life in 19th-century Portland, are offered on the hour. Open Tuesday to Saturday from 10 a.m. to 4 p.m. p.m. from May through October, and sporadically during the holidays. The Center for Maine History is right next door.

THE FIFTH MAINE REGIMENT
COMMUNITY CENTER $
Peaks Island
(207) 766-3330
www.fifthmainemuseum.org
You don't have to be a Civil War buff to enjoy a visit to this old hall, but it certainly helps. Built in 1888 as a meeting place for veterans of the Fifth Maine, the small museum brims with memorabilia from the Civil War. Exhibits rotate in and out, there's a gift shop, and programs are hosted during the summer months. Many people get married here, too. Open from noon to 4 p.m. from July through September and on a limited basis in the off-season.

Midcoast

JOSHUA CHAMBERLAIN MUSEUM
226 Maine St., Brunswick
(207) 729-6606
If you wonder what it might have been like to stand in Joshua Chamberlain's boots during his star turn at Gettysburg, you can see for yourself at his former residence, across the street from Bowdoin College in Brunswick. The very boots he wore at Bull Run are right there (of course, you can't actually try them on), along with original furnishings and other war memorabilia. Interesting stuff, and a fine tribute to one of the state's proudest sons. Open Tuesday through Saturday from 9 a.m. to 4:15 p.m. from late May to October.

PEJEPSCOT MUSEUM/SKOLFIELD WHITTIER
HOUSE
161 Park Row, Brunswick
(207) 729-6606
The history of Brunswick is the big draw at this

local landmark. On the one side you can see how Midcoast residents might have lived in the Victorian age—there are original furnishings, down to the spice rack—and on the other you can see the story of the larger community told through exhibits and 19th-century memorabilia. The museum is open Tuesday through Friday from 9 a.m. to 5 p.m. (Thursdays to 8 p.m.) and Saturday from 9 a.m. to 4 p.m. The house is open to tours Tuesday through Saturday from the end of May through October at 10 and 11:30 a.m. and 1 and 2:30 p.m. Free.

CASTLE TUCKER AND THE
NICKELS-SORTWELL HOUSE $
Wiscasset
(207) 882-7169
www.historicnewengland.com
Here is another pair of buildings kept up by the Society for the Preservation of New England Antiquities. Castle Tucker was built in 1807 and remodeled shortly before the Civil War, and many of the furnishings of the bright yellow showplace are original. Also dating to 1807, the Nickels-Sortwell House is a Federal mansion of unique architectural details and a lot of antique furnishings—just one look at the place and you'll understand quickly how well some of the more prosperous sea captains lived. Castle Tucker is open Wednesday through Sunday from 11 a.m. to 5 p.m., and Nickels-Sortwell Friday through Sunday from June 1 through October 15. Tours are given on the hour between 11 a.m. and 4 p.m.

THE 1811 LINCOLN COUNTY MUSEUM
AND OLD JAIL $
Federal St., Wiscasset
(207) 882-6817
www.lincolncountyhistory.org
In a residential area packed with old homes is this old penitentiary—the state prison until the one in Thomaston was built—and woe be to anyone who got stuck in here. The jail dates back to 1809–1811 and was in use until the 1950s. In its history it has been home to your usual thieves

and murderers, but it was also used to imprison French sailors, back when privateering was happening off the coast, as well as British POWs. The interior consists largely of big, cold granite blocks with barred windows and iron doors, and there is still some neat graffiti—ships, names, dates, and poetry—scratched on the walls. Open from 10 a.m. to 4 p.m. Tuesday through Saturday in July and August and Sundays from noon to 4 p.m. with varying hours in the off-season.

FORT EDGECOMB STATE
HISTORIC SITE $
66 Fort Rd., Edgecomb
(207) 882-7777
An octagonal blockhouse built in 1809 to protect Wiscasset Harbor, Fort Edgecomb is the best-preserved fort of the period in the nation, and its grassy slopes overlook the Sheepscot River. The old bastion is a fairly simple affair made of blocky wood, and you can run through it in no time, reading the interpretive panels and peering out through the musket holes. But the grounds offer some of the best picnicking you're going to find in the area. Try not to look at the power plant offshore, and concentrate on the scenic coves instead. You may see circling osprey or bobbing seals. The fort is just a skip from Route 1, so you can wait out Wiscasset's infamous traffic if you like. Open daily from Memorial through Labor Day.

CHAPMAN-HALL HOUSE $
Main St., Damariscotta
A fine old cape, this Damariscotta institution has been sitting at the top of Main Street since the 1750s, making it one of the state's most venerable buildings. It was built by Nathaniel Chapman, who was part of the family that settled the area, and inside you'll find period furnishings and historical memorabilia of the area. Many examples remain of the way the place was constructed, and there are famous herb beds and 18th-century roses outside. Hours of operation vary from year to year.

COLONIAL PEMAQUID STATE
HISTORIC SITE $
Pemaquid
(207) 677-2423
One of Maine's oldest settlements was here at the end of the Pemaquid Peninsula, where the English arrived in the 1620s. Over the years a village took shape that once included many houses and 1692 Fort William Henry. The remains of this compound are being excavated by archaeologists today in one of the longest-running digs in the state, and visitors are welcome and typically fascinated. Several cellar holes scattered about show exactly how the compound was laid out, and they've yielded a lot of finds to archaeologists. Little interpretive pedestals sit next to them, and they tell the story of the village, which grew when a pair or merchants from Bristol, England, acquired patent rights to the area and began recruiting settlers. It's estimated that by 1665 there were 30 homes by the water here, but this was on the outskirts of British territory then, and Pemaquid residents were beset with raids by the French and Indians—hence Fort William Henry. Though it was a big and impressive bastion for those days, with walls close to 40 feet high, 20 cannons, and 60 soldiers, the fort was overrun by the French and Indians only four years after it went up, and the Brits decided not to rebuild. (The current fort is a replica of a section of the original.)

Visitors today can learn about all this early history by stepping into the museum and visitor center and perusing the more than 75,000 artifacts that have been unearthed here. From tools, hardware, and pipe fragments to fine china and ceramics from across Europe, these items—and the other displays nearby—paint a compelling picture of life in the early days of Maine settlement. There are so many various elements here—the fort, sea vistas, the museum, the excavations—that everyone finds something of interest. The museum is open daily from 9 a.m. to 5 p.m. from Memorial Day through August.

OLD GERMAN CHURCH $
Route 32, Waldoboro
(207) 832-5100

The story behind this landmark house of worship is as compelling as the unique box pews found inside. German immigrants migrated to Waldoboro in 1740 with the idea that they would be moving to a thriving city. Instead they "found nothing but wilderness." (Seems town father Samuel Waldo may have exaggerated a bit when he did his recruiting.) The Germans decided to stay and make the best of things and built a village here, erecting this pretty old church in 1772 on the Medomak River. (They hauled it across the ice to its current site in 1794.) It's one of the oldest houses of worship in the state and has several remarkable meetinghouse features, like the hanging pulpit. Open daily from 1 to 3 p.m. in July and August.

MONTPELIER GENERAL $–$$
Knox Mansion High St., Thomaston
(207) 354-8062
www.generalknoxmuseum.org

This grand white mansion lords over Route 1 as it heads north after Thomaston. (Unfortunately so does the Dragon Cement plant behind it.) Though it looks straight out of the colonial era, it is a reconstruction of the former estate of Henry Knox, George Washington's secretary of war—the original was torn down to make room for the Thomaston railroad station. But the Daughters of the American Revolution thought that Knox deserved a tribute and worked tirelessly to have this exact replica built in the 1930s. The inside has been designed to replicate even the minutest of details, and the house is filled with antiques and some furnishings rescued from the original. The museum and gift shop are open from 10 a.m. to 4 p.m. Tuesday through Saturday from late May through late September and opened occasionally afterward for special occasions. Tours are given on the hour and half-hour from 10 a.m. to 3 p.m.

FARNSWORTH HOMESTEAD $$
Rockland
(207) 596-6457
www.farnsworthmuseum.org

When Lucy Farnsworth left her fortune for the establishment of a museum, she also specified that a portion of the monies be used for upkeep of her family home. This Greek Revival building, adjoining the Farnsworth Art Museum, is the result. Many original furnishings remain, depicting the life of a Victorian businessman and his family in the Penobscot Bay area. Open daily from 11 a.m. to 4 p.m. from Memorial Day through Columbus Day. Admission includes the Farnsworth Art Museum.

OLD CONWAY HOMESTEAD AND MARY MEEKER CRAMER MUSEUM $
Route 1, Camden
(207) 236-2257
www.crmuseum.org

A restored 19th-century farm serves as the centerpiece for this historical society headquarters. The Old Conway Homestead is furnished as it might have been when it was home to the old Conways, and the surrounding buildings are filled with antique carriages, tools, sleighs, a blacksmith shop, and a maple sugar house, where displays of sugaring occur each spring. The Cramer Museum is a contemporary building that serves as a repository of local history, from photographs to apparel to guns and swords. Open Tuesday through Friday from 11 a.m. to 3 p.m. in July and August.

FORT KNOX STATE HISTORIC SITE $
711 Fort Knox Rd., Prospect
(207) 469-7719 (in summer)

Not to be confused with the U.S. Treasury and mint, this Fort Knox was named for Henry Knox, George Washington's secretary of war, and it's Maine's largest fort. Built of granite and an imposing presence looming large over the Penobscot River across from Bucksport, the roughly pentagonal bastion was begun in 1844, when tensions were great over the Maine–Canada border. It never took a bullet, either—but it was capable of raining shot down on the river from 69 cannons. This place is fascinating to explore, especially the underground bunkers (bring a flashlight). And the grounds are impressive, with a fair prospect. Nice picnicking as well. This is the state's most visited historic site—renovated a few years back by an excellent friends group—and it's a must if you're in the area. Open May 1 through October 31 daily from 9 a.m. to sunset.

PENOBSCOT NARROWS OBSERVATORY
711 Fort Knox Rd., Prospect
(207) 469-7719 (in summer)
At 420 feet up in this magnificent new tower, the views of Bucksport, the Penobscot River, and beyond are pretty dizzying. The facility sits atop one of the stanchions of the new Penobscot Narrows Bridge, and it's the highest public-bridge observatory in the world. Right next to Fort Knox, making for a perfect two-fer. Open daily from May 1 to October 31 from 9 a.m. to 5 p.m. and later in high summer.

FORT GEORGE
Battle Avenue, Castine
Not much is left of this fort built in 1779, but it saw its share of action back in the day. The British erected it, lost it to the upstart Americans, gained it back, and lost it again. This was the last post surrendered by the defeated redcoats at the close of the Revolutionary War, but they took it again a few decades later during the War of 1812. Legend has it that you can hear the sounds of a ghost drummer boy if you visit during August. It's mostly grassy hills and picnicking facilities here now, but placards tell the site's rather amazing story. Free.

JOHN PERKINS HOUSE $
Court St., Castine
(207) 326-9247
www.wilsonmuseum.org
The town of Castine is a treasure trove of American architecture, and this is the only pre-Revolutionary building left in town, a white clapboard

classic, built in 1763. It has all the details of an early American home, from hand-split, feather-end clapboards on the outside to the beautiful timber framing on the inside. The furniture is accurate to the period. Open daily from 2 to 5 p.m. from Memorial Day through September.

WILSON MUSEUM
Perkins St., Castine
(207) 326-9247
www.wilsonmuseum.org
All of Castine feels like a museum, so historic and well-preserved is the old village. The former home of John Howard Wilson is an actual museum, though it's as eccentric as Wilson must have been. The anthropologist first came to town in 1891 and over the years amassed a unique collection of everything from Native American artifacts to ship models to antique tools to rocks to seashells to firearms. It's an amazing assortment of unusual items and spreads across two floors. Open daily from 2 to 5 p.m. from Memorial Day through September.

HOLT HOUSE $
3 Water St., Blue Hill
(207) 326-8250
www.bluehillhistory.org
An 1815 Federal-style home, the Holt House was one of the early homes built at the head of Blue Hill Bay. Home of the Blue Hill Historical Society, it has become known for its period stenciling and is furnished with antiques reflecting the town's history. Note the four chimneys, eight fireplaces, and wide plank flooring. Call for hours.

JONATHAN FISHER HOUSE $
Route 15, Blue Hill
(207) 374-2459
www.jonathanfisherhouse.org
Jonathan Fisher was quite the renaissance man. His motto was "Let every hour be filled to the brim," and he did his best to achieve it, working as a preacher, carpenter, artist, scientist, surveyor, teacher, and writer. The Calvinist parson was given 300 acres, a barn, $200 annually, and help in building his home when he moved here in the

late 18th century, according to a local history. He built his house in 1796 and added to it in 1814, and the addition is what is left standing today. It's an interesting testament to an interesting fellow, with its built-in Fisher-made grandfather clock in one corner and paintings here and there. It was renovated using the parson's own detailed notes. Open Thursday through Saturday from 1 to 4 p.m. from July through mid-September.

DANIEL MERRILL HOUSE
Sedgwick
(207) 359-4447
Built in 1795, this straightforward two-story (plus) home was named after the Reverend Daniel Merrill, the first clergyman to serve the area. The townspeople had it constructed for the minister as part of his compensation package; today it serves as the local historical society and is open for tours. Open on Sunday in July and August from 2 to 4 p.m. Free.

COLONEL BLACK MANSION $-$$
Route 172, Ellsworth
(207) 667-8671
www.woodlawnmuseum.com
As nice an example of Georgian architecture as you're going to find in Maine, the Black Mansion was named for Colonel John Black, and it went up in the early 19th century. Sometimes called Woodlawn, sometimes the Black House, it is filled with original furnishings and has been open as a museum since 1930. Be sure to check out the amazing spiral staircase as you wander through. Also leave time to wander the grounds, which are known for their gardens and incorporate more than 2 miles of woodland trails. Tours are offered on the hour. Open Tuesday through Saturday from 10 a.m. to 5 p.m. and Sunday from 1 to 4 p.m. from May through October.

THE TELEPHONE MUSEUM $
166 Winkumpaugh Rd., Ellsworth
(207) 667-9491
www.thetelephonemuseum.org
Inside this big barn on a back road, you'll discover a world of communication technology. Begin-

ning with Alexander Graham Bell's telephone patent in 1876, it follows the currents through hand cranks and switching systems, through operators to automated systems up to the digital age. It will make you think about that cell phone in your pocket in a new light. Open Thursday through Sunday from 1 to 4 p.m. in July, August, and September.

Acadia Area
MOUNT DESERT HISTORICAL SOCIETY
MUSEUMS $
(207) 276-9323
www.mdihistory.org
Few communities in Maine have a history as rich as the one on Mount Desert, which was discovered by painters in the mid-nineteenth century and became one of the most fashionable resorts in the country. So the local historical society has a lot to work with and for the most part they do a good job (street addresses in this day of GPS would help). They have four museums and gardens to visit. The **Old School House** (373 Sound Drive, Mount Desert) was built in 1892 for the children of the village of Sound, and recreates the educational experience of kids at that time. The **Farm Stand** at the Old School House (same address) has artifacts related to transportation and farming in the old days of the island. In the picturesque village of Somesville is the **Somesville Historical Museum and Gardens** (Main Street and Oak Hill Road, Somesville), which hosts rotating exhibits chronicling the history of the area—from its world-renowned summercators and their mansion "cottages" to the great fire that ate up much of the island in 1947. Adjacent are gardens featuring plants from the 19th and early 20th century bloom. And of course there's the

i The Bar Harbor Historical Society has a lot to work with, as the history of Mount Desert Island is rich. Its home at 33 Ledgelawn Avenue (207-288-0000) brims with early photographs, paintings, exhibits on landscape architect Beatrix Farrand and architect Fred Savage, and even a milk bottle collection from former island dairies.

Close-up

Portland Sports—the Sea Dogs and Pirates

The term *sport* has a different meaning in Maine than it does elsewhere. (Here it refers to people who hunt and fish.) Besides, fans of professional sports don't have a lot to cheer about here—there are only a handful of professional teams in Maine. But two of them are in Portland—the Double-A Portland Sea Dogs baseball team and the American Hockey League's Portland Pirates.

The **Sea Dogs** are a farm club for the Boston Red Sox, and they play at the nifty 6,500-seat Hadlock Field, right off Interstate 295. City residents have really gotten behind the team over the course of a decade, and the Sea Dogs do a good job of marketing themselves with promos—re-creating the Field of Dreams cornfield, for example—special events, and inexpensive seats. The stands consequently fill up quickly, especially when the Dogs are winning, as in 2006, when they won their first Eastern League championship. General admission seats are only $7 for adults and $4 for kids (reserved seating is just a buck or two more), which makes going to a Dogs game a lot more affordable than going to a Sox game. Call (207) 879-9500 or (800) 936-3647 for tickets or visit www.portlandseadogs.com.

The **Portland Pirates** do their skating at the Cumberland County Civic Center, a big ugly box on Free Street. They're the farm team for the Buffalo Sabres of the NHL, and they've also been in town since the early 1990s, taking up where the beloved Maine Mariners left off. They took home the Calder Cup in the 1993–1994 season, and had a banner year in 2005–2006, when they won the Atlantic Division and set 11 franchise records. They average about 4,400 fans a game (Civic Center capacity is 6,733, so it's pretty easy to get tickets). Tickets range from $9 to $20 for adults. Call (207) 775-3458 to get yours or visit www.portlandpirates.com.

Selectman's Building and Bridge (Main Street and Oak Hill Road, Somesville), which was the town office until 1911, and has a neat cobblers display inside with antique tools and handcrafted items like shoes and reins. The arcing white span out front might be the most photographed site on an island of photographed sites. Exhibits rotate in and out. Open Tuesday through Saturday from 10 a.m. to 4 p.m. from July through mid-September. Children free.

Down East

RUGGLES HOUSE $
Columbia Falls
(207) 483-4637
www.ruggleshouse.org
Welcome to Plantation 13. That's what this part of Maine was called when Thomas Ruggles moved here in the early 19th century. His home, an 1820

Federal showplace known for its suspended, or "flying," staircase and its carved paneling, is testament to the riches he made as a timber baron. Neat antiques, like a tall old spinning wheel, are spread throughout. Open Monday through Saturday from 9:30 a.m. to 4:30 p.m. and Sunday from 11 a.m.to 4:30 p.m. from June 1 through October 15.

BURNHAM TAVERN $
Route 192, Machias
(207) 255-6930
www.burnhamtavern.com
When rebels were looking for a place to plot their attacks on the British during the Revolutionary War, they settled down for a pint at this tavern, built in 1770. It's the oldest building Down East and is still furnished much the way it was during its heyday in the 1770s. After the war's fateful first

naval battle, the injured were treated here. Open Monday through Friday from 9:30 a.m. to 4 p.m. from mid-June through late September.

SPORTS

Greater Portland

BEECH RIDGE MOTOR SPEEDWAY
70 Holmes Rd., Scarborough
(207) 885-0111
www.beechridge.com
This ⅓-mile oval is a well-known short-track facility and home to stock car races several times monthly. Events run from April through mid-September and might be truck rallies or NASCAR races. Check the Web or give a call to find out the schedule. Admission fees vary with the race.

SCARBOROUGH DOWNS
90 Payne Rd., Scarborough
(207) 883-4331
www.scarboroughdowns.com
Here is another racetrack in the southern Maine town of Scarborough, but this one is of the harness variety. For more than half a century the half-mile track has been hosting horse and chariot races, and it's one of the few things that can be bet upon in Maine. Races run from late March through late December and are usually held on Wednesday, Friday, and Saturday in the summer. Good luck. Admission fees vary with the race.

Midcoast

WISCASSET RACEWAY
West Alna Rd., Wiscasset
(207) 882-4271
www.wiscassetraceway.info

An antidote to the slow-going Route 1 traffic this town has become famous for, the Wiscasset Raceway—the biggest and fastest asphalt oval in the state—holds events on most weekends from May through mid-October. These might be anything from monster truck rallies to the Friday night racing series. It's noisy and fast and everything you want regional stock car racing to be. Tickets range from $10 to $20, depending on the races.

GREAT MAINE LUMBERJACK SHOW
Route 1, Trenton
(207) 667-0067
www.mainelumberjack.com
Timber Tina, the vibrant woman behind this Acadia-area attraction, has won logging titles from Australia to South Africa. A world champion lumberjill (as opposed to lumberjack), she can chop, saw, and roll logs with the best of them, and she's been featured in *National Geographic* and *Sports Illustrated*, on ESPN, and even on MTV. Summers she can be found here on the way to Acadia, hosting nightly exhibitions of logging sports. The events are the kinds of activities that were—and are to a certain extent—prevalent in Maine's North Woods. And they make for some rousing entertainment. At a show you can watch as contemporary woodsmen and women—mostly students who compete in collegiate lumber meets—throw axes, roll logs, and climb 65-foot poles, among other things. And you'll also get a good dose of Maine lumbering history, which is fascinating stuff. Shows are nightly at 7 p.m.

LIGHTHOUSES

Maine's lighthouses were built to be beacons for sailors, keeping them safe from the state's serrated shoreline, but they might as well have been put up to attract tourists. The state's sentinels seem to have a gravitational pull on visitors, drawing them in with their blinking beams. There are dozens upon dozens of them—more than 60—and these stoic icons of the sea are ever-popular among people from away.

The lighthouse has been an evocative symbol of the Maine coast ever since the tall towers started going up in the 18th century, and they now adorn everything from the state quarter to T-shirts to key rings to car commercials. Their endlessly tracking lights and lowing horns have kept generations of mariners safe, allowing the Maine coast to be a thing of beauty rather than something to be feared. Which might explain why many Mainers have a soft spot for them, too, creating preservation organizations and friends groups whenever a light seems to be in need of help.

Maine's lights are certainly nice places to visit, if only because they sit on some of the finest acreage in the state—on rocky promontories, headlands, islands, and other scenic settings. Lighthouses are perfect for picknicking, and they offer up just the right amount of history for the average visitor. Stir in a little fog and you have instant romance.

Most are fairly accessible, serving as the centerpieces of many a state park or owned by local trusts that allow visitors. Some have attendant museums, others nearby trails, and some are even free to visit. What follows are the most notable of Maine's lighthouses. Look for others offshore on your drive up the coast or click over to www.visitmaine.com and look up lighthouses in the search box.

SOUTH COAST

CAPE NEDDICK LIGHT
Nubble Rd., York
(207) 363-1040
Built in 1879, this 41-foot, cast-iron tower is formally known as Cape Neddick Light, but it's popularly called the Nubble, the name given to the point it sits on by fishermen long ago. The great irony of the Nubble is that while it's one of the state's best-known lights—and one of the most photographed in the world—it sits on a small isle offshore and is all but inaccessible to the public. Originally red, the tower was painted its white color in 1902 and was automated in 1987. The town of York owns the property and maintains

the Sohier Park Welcome Center on the mainland within full view of the light. The center has restrooms and lighthouse memorabilia, but you might have to wrestle for a parking space in high summer. The center is open from Memorial Day through Columbus Day from 9 a.m. to 7 p.m.

BOON ISLAND LIGHT
Off York
Six miles out to sea, this 133-foot gray tower is no tourist favorite. But it sits on an island with an interesting history. All but submerged in storms, the isle is considered one of the most dangerous pieces of rock on the state's coast, which is why the light was originally built during the War of 1812. In 1710 Boon Island was the site of one of

the most grisly episodes in Maine history, during which a group of British sailors got marooned on the island after the wreck of their ship, the Nottingham, and ended up resorting to cannibalism in order to survive. The story is recounted in Kenneth Roberts's famous book *Boon Island*. And the light here is the subject of a poem by the daughter of a lightkeeper, Celia Thaxter, one of the more beloved of Maine's writers. It can be seen from a few mainland points on Cape Neddick.

GOAT ISLAND LIGHT
Pier Rd., Cape Porpoise
Somehow the hamlet of Cape Porpoise in Kennebunkport has managed to remain a little fishing village even as the southern Maine coast booms with development all around it. Goat Island Light, a 25-foot tower built in 1833, is a pretty landmark offshore. Inaccessible to visitors, it's still photogenic.

GREATER PORTLAND

PORTLAND BREAKWATER LIGHT
Bug Light Park, South Portland
Called Bug Light affectionately by its neighbors, this short tower stands guard over the west side of Portland Harbor. It was built in 1855, and though it's inactive today, it was restored in 1990 and is on the National Register of Historic Places. The surrounding park is popular with walkers and Frisbee throwers and has a fine view of the harbor and the city of Portland.

i The Lighthouse Depot (Route 1 in Wells and One Park Drive in Rockland) is a must for lighthouse fans, featuring books, maps, gifts, and ornaments. If you need more information or memorabilia, this is the place. The owners also publish the monthly *Lighthouse Digest,* have a thick catalog, and run an excellent Web site, www.lighthousedepot.com. Call (800) 758-1444 for details.

SPRING POINT LEDGE LIGHT
Southern Maine Community College
Broadway, South Portland
Not as well known as some of Maine's sentinels, the Spring Point Ledge Light should be more popular. The 54-foot tower looks like a spark plug set down in Portland Harbor. A 1,000-foot breakwater connects the 1897 beacon to the mainland and invites walkers. The view of the city of Portland and the harbor from the tip is fantastic. If that isn't enticement enough, the Spring Point Walkway, a very pleasant 3-mile greenway along Casco Bay, passes right nearby. The Portland Harbor Museum, a must-visit for people interested in maritime history (see Attractions chapter), is a short walk away, too. The museum (207-799-6337; www.portlandharbormuseum.org) occasionally offers tours of the light in summer.

PORTLAND HEAD LIGHT
Shore Rd., Cape Elizabeth
(207) 799-2661
www.portlandheadlight.com
When people picture a Maine lighthouse in their mind's eye, this is probably the one they conjure up. Like the Nubble, the Portland Head Light is one of the most painted and photographed lighthouses in the world and is among the most visited lighthouses in the country. It's also often called the oldest beacon on the Atlantic Coast, and whether or not that's true, it has to be close, built by order of George Washington in 1791.

The light itself is a 58-foot conical tower built of white fieldstone and rising above a restored keeper's house. Since the light was automated in 1989, this pretty building has been converted into an excellent little museum, telling the story of this sentinel, Portland Harbor, and the surrounding area. It's open from 10 a.m. to 4 p.m. daily from Memorial Day through Columbus Day and weekends only from mid-April to the Sunday before Memorial Day and between Columbus Day and Christmas. Admission is $2 for adults, $1 for children age seven or older, and free for youngsters age six or younger.

The grounds on which the light sits are truly magnificent, looking out over the open sea in one direction and back toward Portland Harbor in another. The surf rages here, and several ships have wrecked on the rocks below the light, even when the light was working. The worst was the *Annie C. Maguire*, which went aground on its way from Buenos Aires to Quebec in 1866. The crew of 15 was saved by the quick actions of Portland Head's fabled lightkeeper, Joseph Strout, but the ship was bashed into splinters.

People have been flocking here ever since poet Henry Wadsworth Longfellow used to walk over from his home in Portland to enjoy the views. Ninety-four-acre Fort Williams Park wraps around the headlight and is the place where Portlanders take their houseguests—to the tune of nearly a million people a year. It's particularly popular among picnickers and kite flyers and features a beach and tennis course in addition to sweeping lawns.

MIDCOAST

SEGUIN ISLAND LIGHT
Phippsburg
At 180 feet above the sea, the Seguin Island Light is a fairly dramatic lighthouse, and the view from its tower is exceptional, taking in Portland, Mount Washington, and Monhegan Island all at once. Relatively few people ever get to see it, though, because of the fact that Seguin Island is 2 miles from the end of the Kennebec River and is deserted for most of the year. Visitors are welcome to climb the 1795 lighthouse tower, and there's even a three-room museum on the island filled with lighthouse memorabilia.

PEMAQUID LIGHT
Route 130, Bristol
(207) 677-2494
When storms threaten to batter the Midcoast, many residents will make a trip down to this 32-foot fieldstone tower because the surf here is always impressive. Pemaquid is among the most popular lighthouses to visit in Maine, and with its ample parking, public grounds, and adjacent museum, it's very welcoming. Plus, it's one of the few that you can actually climb.

The light has one of the more romantic settings of any lighthouse in Maine, sitting at the end of the Pemaquid Peninsula south of Damariscotta and overlooking open sea. The tower went up in 1827, was replaced in 1835, and in 1934 became the first Maine beacon to be automated. In the former keeper's house is the Fishermen's Museum (207-677-2494), run by the town of Bristol. Open daily in summer from 10 a.m. to 5 p.m., it's a good excuse to get inside a keeper's house. The museum also houses a collection of artifacts that shed light on the fishing industry in Maine. Admission is free, but donations are greatly appreciated.

MONHEGAN LIGHT
Lighthouse Hill, Monhegan Island
(207) 596-7003
www.monheganmuseum.org
There are many reasons to plan a visit to Monhegan Island (see Area Overview chapter), 10 miles off the Midcoast, and one of them is this 47-foot tower. A dull gray granite, it isn't the most impressive of the state's beacons, but its location most certainly is. The light is set high atop a hill where the island meets the sky, and it lords over both Monhegan and Manana Island, its uninhabited sister isle across Monhegan Harbor. The place is so grand you could sit on the lawn here for the better part of a day and never get tired of it. If you visit only one lighthouse in Maine, make it this one.

The light was automated in the late 1950s, and the grounds and buildings surrounding the tower were sold to the local island association. Today there is a very fine museum in the keeper's house that documents the natural and cultural history of the island. It includes exhibits that explore the fishing industry and early island life, and it features works by some of the nation's most famous artists, many of whom—George Bellows, Rockwell Kent, Jamie Wyeth—came here to live and paint. In recent years some of the collection was moved to the renovated and climate-controlled assistant keeper's house, making the museum twice as impressive. It's open daily from 11:30 a.m. to 3:30 p.m. from July through September. Admission is free, but a donation is encouraged.

MARSHALL POINT LIGHT
Marshall Point Rd., Port Clyde
(207) 372-6450
www.marshallpoint.org

Marshall Point is another one of Maine's oft-photographed lighthouses, thanks to its distinctive footbridge. The white tower protects the south entrance to Port Clyde Harbor, and it was built in 1832 at a time when the small community was an important Maine port thanks to its granite quarries, shipbuilding yards, and canneries. Today the town owns the light, and its grounds are open to walkers and picnickers. There's also a small museum on the premises that tells the story of this light and a few others in the area. It's open Sunday through Friday from 1 to 5 p.m. and Saturday 10 a.m. to 5 p.m. from Memorial Day through September. Admission is free, but a donations is appreciated.

ROCKLAND BREAKWATER LIGHT
Jameson Point, Rockland

The lighthouse here is not the primary attraction. An 18-foot-tall square tower, it sits on a fog signal house and is pleasant enough, but the real appeal is the breakwater itself, a granite cribwork that stretches for close to a mile into Rockland Harbor. Put in place to protect the harbor from crashing waves, the breakwater was built across the span of 18 years, a massive undertaking that took close to 700,000 tons of the area's famed granite. Walkers, anglers, photographers, hand-holding couples—everyone loves the result, as it affords a magnificent view of the city of Rockland, Penobscot Bay and its islands and tall schooners, and the Camden Hills in the distance. The light is open from 9 a.m. to 5 p.m. on weekends from Memorial Day to Columbus Day.

OWLS HEAD LIGHT
North Shore Rd., Owls Head

Owls Head Light serves as the centerpiece of Owls Head Light State Park, just south of Rockland. This little-known green space occupies a pretty headland overlooking Rockland Harbor and the open blue of Penobscot Bay. The prospect is fine, and there are nice picnicking facilities and a little pebble beach.

The light is a 20-foot, white-brick tower that was built to protect mariners heading into the harbor in 1825, when the lime trade brought many vessels to Rockland and Thomaston. One local history recounts how a spaniel here named Spot learned to pull a rope and ring the fog bell when he saw ships coming into view, saving the day on a few occasions.

Both the light and the keeper's house are closed to the public, but the grounds alone make this beacon worth visiting.

CURTIS ISLAND LIGHT
Curtis Island, Camden

Many things make Camden Harbor dramatic—the rounded green backs of the Camden Hills towering above, the pretty brick town below it, and Curtis Island at the harbor's entrance. A small, piney isle, Curtis is home to a 26-foot sentinel, built for $4,500 in 1896 on the order of President Andrew Jackson.

The island is reachable by kayak or dinghy, and it is now a public park owned by the town of Camden. Respectful visitors are always welcome. If you don't have a boat, the light is easily viewed from a variety of Camden points, including Bayview Street, the Public Landing, and the tops of Mount Battie and Mount Megunticook.

FORT POINT LIGHT
Fort Point Rd., Stockton Springs
(207) 567-3356

Many of the roads that take a right off coastal U.S. Route 1 and wend their way down peninsulas hold little-known treasures on them, and Fort Point State Park in Stockton Springs is one such place. The 154-acre state park features a mile of shoreline at the point where the Penobscot River floods into the ocean, a 200-foot pier for fishing, trails for exploring, the earthworks that remain from historic Fort Pownall, and Fort Point Light.

The 31-foot, square white tower was erected in 1836 (and rebuilt in 1857) by order of President Andrew Jackson to provide safe passage for boats bound for Bangor, at that time a major timber port. Besides the keeper's house and other outbuildings, the complex here includes a cool 1890 bell tower in the shape of an obelisk that's on the National Register of Historic Places. The park is open from Memorial Day through Labor Day.

DICE'S HEAD LIGHT
Battle Ave., Castine
Castine positively looks historic, with its white clapboard homes, tidy streets, brick downtown, and all-American campus, and Dice's Head Light certainly doesn't detract. The old town sits at the end of an ax-head–shaped peninsula, dangling into East Penobscot Bay, and the lighthouse itself occupies a headland at the top cutting corner of that ax, with panoramic views all around. It was built in 1828 to help guide ships to the opening of the Penobscot River, not far away, and the stone tower was once wrapped with a wooden frame. The site is owned by the town and is no longer operational, but a neat set of stairs leads

i Any lighthouse lover would be foolish to pass by the new Maine Lighthouse Museum at the Maine Discovery Center in Rockland. The collection here used to be housed up the road at the Penobscot Bay city's popular Shore Village Museum, and it includes the largest assemblage of lighthouse lenses in the world and an important collection of lighthouse memorabilia and Coast Guard artifacts as well. It's located in the same building as the Lighthouse Depot at One Park Drive and is open daily (except Sunday in winter), so it's twice as good for buffs. Admission is $5. Call (207) 594-3301 or visit www.mainelighthousemuseum.com for details.

down to the rocks on the shore below where there is a small working beacon built to replace Dice's Head.

ACADIA AREA

BASS HARBOR HEAD LIGHT
Lighthouse Rd., Bass Harbor
Bass Harbor resides on the "quiet side" of Mount Desert Island, the end of the island opposite Bar Harbor and Acadia National Park and thus much less visited. Still, many people make their way over to this small village each summer, and Bass Harbor Head Light is one of the reasons why. Though privately owned, the lighthouse is among the most accessible lights in Maine, and it certainly adorns its share of calendars.

Erected in 1858 to mark the eastern flank of Blue Hill Bay, the white brick tower is set on a small cliff and hidden from mainland viewers by a stand of spruce. The adjacent keeper's house has traditionally been home to the commander of the Coast Guard station in Southwest Harbor and thus is closed to the public. But there are paths through the forest here and walkways that take you down to the shore where viewing of the light is most impressive. And just up the road are two of Acadia's best secrets, the Ship Harbor and Wonderland trails, shore paths that take you to beautiful prospects.

MOUNT DESERT ROCK
Open Atlantic
Far from the radar of most visitors to the Acadia area, Mount Desert Rock is still a fascinating place. Eighteen miles southwest of the island, the rock is just that—a small, wave-battered ledge amid the constant swells of the Atlantic. The light is a 58-foot, gray granite tower, and it is routinely thrashed by storms. Back when keepers lived here, they attempted to plant vegetable gardens, and each one was washed away by late fall.

Early lights here burned on whale oil. Today the rock is a research station for the Bar Harbor–based College of the Atlantic and its Allied Whale program, which has been monitoring and cataloging whale populations for decades and now has the largest collection of photo-identified humpback and finback whales in the world.

DOWN EAST

WEST QUODDY LIGHT
West Quoddy Head Rd., Lubec
(207) 733-0911 (in season)
(207) 941-4014 (winter)
West Quoddy Light has a lot of unique distinctions: It sits on the easternmost point of land in the United States, it presides over the most dynamic tides in the nation, and it's Maine's only red-and-white-striped tower. The pretty light station was built in 1808 on the order of Thomas Jefferson and is the focal point of Quoddy Head State Park, one of the more breathtaking of the parks in the state's system. The views that stretch before it are absolutely astonishing.

The light itself is positioned near some of the tallest cliffs in Maine and overlooks all the world,

it seems. On the horizon, across the Grand Manan Channel, is Grand Manan Island, a tall, arcing isle in New Brunswick, Canada. Whales frequently swim through the channel and can be spotted from the lighthouse grounds often enough in summertime that people like to sit here and look for them. The tides below swing as much as 24 feet in and out.

The light was built in 1808 and rebuilt 50 years later, and its beacon still shines through its original Fresnel lens. The lightkeeper used to have to ring a fog bell by hand to warn approaching vessels; later a steam-powered foghorn was put in place. The light was automated in 1988 and became part of Quoddy Head State Park.

Because the property is state owned, you can get right up and have a close look. Then you'll want to wander the 4.5 miles of trails here, which skirt 100-foot cliffs, splinter off to amazing overlooks, wend through cool bogs, and more. Very worthwhile. Quoddy Head State Park is open from May 15 through October 15.

BEACHES

For a state famous for its rocky coast, Maine has its share of wide, sandy beaches. The rocks don't really begin to rule until after Portland; the South Coast is a place of fine strands, great swimming, and a genuine beach culture. People flock to Ogunquit and Old Orchard and Goose Rocks and Scarborough beaches like seagulls to the snack bin, and whole communities have been built to cater to these sun worshippers. At the other end of the spectrum are the beaches east of Ellsworth, which tend to be rockier, quieter—and colder, if that's at all possible. From quiet neighborhood beaches to big amusement park–style strands, you can find whatever you're looking for in Maine.

SOUTH COAST

Kittery

FORT FOSTER PARK
Pocohontas Rd., Kittery
(207) 439-2182
This old bastion on Gerrish Island was put in place to protect the entrance to Portsmouth Harbor in 1872 and was in use through World War II, when an antisubmarine net was stretched from here to Fort Stark across the way in New Hampshire. There are enough ruins of fortifications scattered across this 90-acre park to amuse history buffs, but you don't have to worry about U-boats much anymore. The island has a few swimming areas as well as places for windsurfing and scuba diving. When you're done splashing, you can eat at the picnic tables, play in the grass, or enjoy the playground. It's a nice family destination because there are shallow stretches and gentle waves. Nice views as well of Whaleback Light. The park is open from 10 a.m. to 8 p.m. from Memorial Day through Labor Day. Admission is $10 per car.

SEAPOINT AND CRESCENT BEACHES
Seapoint Rd., Kittery
These two beaches lie on either side of Seapoint, a small peninsula in the state's southernmost town between Gerrish Island and Brave Boat Harbor. The pair are adjacent to a marshy area known for its wealth of birdlife, so it isn't uncommon to see binocular-toting birdwatchers as well as cooler–toting beachgoers. Both beaches are in the 600-yard range, small by southern Maine standards. Facilities are limited, parking is scarce, and you have to look out for yourself—no lifeguards. Kids have been known to party here, to the consternation of area residents, so you might want to head out by dinnertime.

The Yorks

HARBOR BEACH
York Harbor
(207) 363-4422
Harbor Beach is truly a stunner, but good luck finding parking. There isn't any at the parking area nearby (it's all reserved), so your best bet is to try to leave your car up on the street in one of the spots across from the York Harbor Inn and right next to Hartley Mason Park. They go very quickly, however, on a fine August day.

The beach is a little cul-de-sac with gentle surf backed up to rocks and the Stage Neck Inn's massive resort. You can set up your towel, enjoy the swells and the pebbly sands, and then go climb along the cool Cliff Path, if you want. Porta-potties are here, and lifeguards will look after you from the end of June through Labor Day.

LONG SANDS BEACH
Route 1A, York Harbor to York Beach
Not many of Maine's beaches have a designated

surfing area, but there's the sign at Long Sands in York, imploring dudes to hang ten. And they actually gather here when the waves are rolling. Of course, everyone, it seems, comes to this southern Maine favorite on a hot summer afternoon. The beach here stretches for about 1.5 miles, paralleling U.S. Route 1A as it travels between York Harbor and York Beach. When the tide's out, it exposes about a half mile of sand, and the slope is very gradual, making it a good place to take children. The beach is the heart of a summer colony, and motels line the road for much of its length. Across the street from all of these is metered parking, which goes fast. Lifeguards stand on duty in July and August, and there are both bathhouses and restrooms.

SHORT SANDS BEACH
Route 1A, York Beach
On the other side of Cape Neddick from Long Sands Beach, Short Sands is just that, a petite crescent compared to its lengthy sibling. The sands are so short here, in fact, that the beach completely disappears when the tide is high. So make sure you check the tide charts before you pay a visit. Like Long Sands, Short Sands has metered parking off Route 1A, bathhouses, restrooms, and lifeguards in high summer. All of the amusements of York Beach—the stores, the amazing Goldenrod candy store, York's Wild Kingdom, the playground, the arcades, the basketball courts—are within easy walking distance, so families tend to like the beach here.

Ogunquit
OGUNQUIT BEACH
Ogunquit
The natives called Ogunquit a "beautiful place by the sea," and 3.5-mile-long Ogunquit Beach—all fine white sands and clear surf—is a large part of what makes this community attractive. Residents made a real effort to preserve the sanctity of the strand, pleading with the state legislature to cede the area between the beach and the river to the town, and they did a good job—most of the commercial activity in town is kept at bay, but

there are a couple of snack shacks handy when you get hungry. You can easily walk into town if you've forgotten sunscreen or your smokes.

The beach is unbelievably popular in summer, so forget about parking anywhere nearby—best to take the trolley in; it makes trips to both ends of the beach three or four times an hour. The beach is divided into a variety of sections. There's Footbridge Beach, the large section known as plain old Ogunquit Beach, and Moody Beach up by Wells. The Ogunquit River slides in behind the beach, separating it from the main, and kids often like to splash in the warmer, protected basin the river creates.

Ogunquit is a very gay-friendly town, so don't be surprised to see his-and-his and hers-and-hers couples. A cool sand-castle–building contest is held here every summer, so you can try your hand at that château you've always wanted. You're in good hands when you do your swimming here, too—the lifeguards of Ogunquit Beach have placed high in the state's lifeguard contests for years running. There is parking for a fee, if you can find a spot, and there are changing areas as well.

Wells
The community of Wells is one long beach, basically, from the town line near Ogunquit to the border with Kennebunk. There are several small, lesser-known beaches, which are worth seeking out, as well as Wells Beach proper, a lengthy beauty on a long, narrow peninsula separated from the mainland by the Webhannet River. Wells Beach is by far the most popular. The sands sit across the road from a line of cottages—this is a big summer resort community—which spill bathers out onto the strand all day long.

CRESCENT SURF BEACH
Wells
The tides put the squeeze on these sands, eliminating most of the beach when the water is high. The facilities are fairly limited—no lifeguards, no picnic areas, no ice-cream stands—so if you want to make a day of it, you should bring your

own lunch and be prepared to watch the kids. Portapotties are it as far as relief is concerned. Everyone enjoys the tide pools here, which can be rife with life and can entertain for hours, and the bird-watching is good as well, because of more National Wildlife Refuge marshes. Parking is available at the Gold Ribbon Drive lot, accessible from Webhannet Drive.

DRAKES ISLAND AND LAUDHOLM BEACHES
Wells

This pair sit adjacent to one another, and combined they sprawl for about 1,000 yards. Drakes is the second largest of Wells's beaches, behind Wells Beach proper, and it's framed by dunes, sea grass, and seawalls, sitting at the end of Drakes Island Road near another little cottage village. There are far fewer distractions near the sands here than there are at Wells Beach, with its summer homes and boardwalk, but the ice-cream truck appears occasionally in summer. Everybody loves the ice-cream guy.

Erosion has been a concern here, and the Army Corps of Engineers has pumped dredged sand onto the beach to offset the gradual removal by natural forces. It's still beautiful, though, and naturalists dig the eastern end of the beach, because it's adjacent to more Rachel Carson National Wildlife Refuge lands. Fishermen take to the stone jetties. There is some public parking just before you get to the beach, which will cost you, and there are restrooms and lifeguards.

You can walk to Laudholm Beach or drive down to the Wells Reserve/Rachel Carson Wildlife Refuge. Enjoy the sands or hop onto the network of trails that thread through the reserve. Laudholm is a truly beautiful beach because it's been protected as part of the reserve. The area is home to rare least terns and piping plovers, which run about in packs and streak down to the water, comically touching their toes in and racing away.

WELLS BEACH
Wells

Besides simply being one of the finer stretches of sand and surf on the coast—4,000 feet of fun

and sun—Wells Beach offers some interesting bird-watching, thanks to the Webhannet Marsh, where there are often waders, shorebirds, and migrating waterfowl of all sorts. But it also has many of the hallmarks of resort beaches, those conveniences and superficial delights that seem to grow up wherever there is a natural wonder—an arcade, playground, take-out stands, and restrooms. Lifeguards patrol all summer long. Parking is limited, so you might consider paying to put your car in a lot.

Kennebunk and Kennebunkport

The sands just continue to roll from the Wells town line all the way through the famed Kennebunks. There are a slew of small beaches along the way. Parking is by permit only at many of these spots, and you can get a pass at the chamber of commerce, the town hall, the police station, or, depending where you're staying, area motels and inns.

CLEAVES COVE BEACH
Off Ocean Ave., Kennebunkport

A small strand off Ocean Avenue, Cleaves Cove has no parking, no lifeguards, no restrooms, just a very private little arc of sand.

COLONY BEACH
Off Ocean Ave., Kennebunkport

Right across the street from the grand Colony Hotel, this vest-pocket beach sits at the mouth of the Kennebunk River. All of 150 feet, it is best reached by foot or bike, because there is very limited parking. No lifeguards, either.

GOOSE ROCKS BEACH
Kings Hwy., Kennebunkport

The Goose Rocks are a little archipelago of tiny isles in Goosefair Bay, and you can see them from this picturesque beach. Backed up to the larger village of Goose Rocks, the sands stretch for 3,600 yards here and have a reputation for being soft and friendly to the feet. As southern Maine beaches go, Goose Rocks is relatively unspoiled, quiet, and scenic, with both dunes and tide pools. Endangered birds nest here, and at one end is another marsh with good bird-watching. The sandy slope is gradual, so it's good for kids and hesitant swimmers. Parking is by permit only—$15 per day, $25 per week, and $50 for the season—and the permits only allow you to park; they don't guarantee you a spot.

KENNEBUNK BEACH

All told, the sands of Kennebunk Beach are among the longest in Maine, and they're divided into three sections. Parking is by permit only—again $15 per day, $25 per week—so taking the trolley is a good idea.

Mother's Beach: A short section of Kennebunk Beach on the west end of Beach Avenue, off Routes 9 and 35 near Lords Point, Mother's is within walking distance of the Lower Village if you feel like stretching the gams a bit. (Might be a half mile.) Parking is limited, so it might be easiest to take the trolley. Though it's only 750 feet or so, Mother's Beach has many of the amenities of the super strands, including a playground, public restrooms, and lifeguards.

Middle Beach: The central section of Kennebunk Beach, between Mother's and Gooch's, Middle Beach is a 1,200-foot rocky strand with black stones. (Some locals call it Rocks Beach.) This is where you want to go if your idea of going to the beach includes Rollerblades—a sidewalk runs along the top. No lifeguards here.

Gooch's Beach: The largest stretch of greater Kennebunk Beach at 3,346 feet, Gooch's Beach is well within view of many of the condos and hotels of Kennebunk, which makes it not as pretty as some of Maine's beaches. The fine, fine sand almost makes up for it, though, and attracts big crowds. This is the most popular stretch of Kennebunk Beach, and it can be swarming with sunbathers, surfers, picnickers, and castle builders on a hot summer day. You can watch the pleasure boats cruise down on the Kennebunk River, which empties into the Atlantic nearby. Lifeguards are on duty in high summer.

Biddeford and Saco

BIDDEFORD POOL BEACH
Off State Route 208, Biddeford

Biddeford Pool was created by the movement of barrier beaches, with sand and sediment sifting in from the nearby Saco River. It seemed like prime real estate for summer home development when cottages began to go in, but since then hurricanes and tidal swings have made the ground shift under some properties, and city officials wonder whether it made sense to build here in the first place. Still, these sands make for a pretty beach. Lifeguards patrol the beach, and there are restrooms. Parking is by permit only, and the stickers can be picked up at Biddeford City Hall ($10 for 1 day; $25 for 3 consecutive days; $40 for the week).

FORTUNE'S ROCKS BEACH
Fortune's Rocks Rd., Biddeford
(207) 284-9307

This 3,740-foot gem curves up and away from Kennebunkport toward the summer colony of Biddeford Pool. It's open to the full force of the Atlantic, facing the sea unprotected. The sands are long, and there are lifeguards and restrooms. Parking for the season is by permit only ($10 for 1 day; $25 for 3 consecutive days; $40 for the week).

FERRY BEACH STATE PARK
Bay View Rd., Saco
(207) 283-0067

Maine's state parks sit on some prime real estate, and this preserve named for the old ferry across the nearby Saco River is perhaps the best example. Its 1,700 yards of white-sand waterfront and 117 acres of property sit in booming southern Maine, where houses are going for millions these days. The views out to sea are fantastic, the sands warm. There are a bunch of trails through unique woodlands (where you'll find tupelo trees, which are rare this far north), and there's even a freshwater pond for fishing. And it's all yours to use. There are restrooms, changing rooms, and picnic areas. The rangers even provide guided nature tours. Open from Memorial Day through Columbus Day.

Close-up

Old Orchard Beach

What can one say about Old Orchard Beach? It's the beach of beaches in Maine—if you like big beach culture, you'll like Old Orchard. The 7 miles of sand here are more a phenomenon than anything else, backed up to a pier with arcades and greasy fried foods, to an amusement park with screaming rides, and to a village of pizza joints and souvenir shops with cheap T-shirts and plastic stuff from China. People stroll around in scanty Speedos and sometimes less, and there can be tens of thousands on a hot day, making the beach into the biggest "city" in Maine. Volleyballs get smacked around all day, and bands play at night. Motels sprawl for miles behind the waterfront, and some inns can be found on side streets. The big strand is consistently voted best beach in the state by readers of the local newspaper. Old Orchard is the closest thing Maine has to a Coney Island, a Jersey Shore, or an Ocean City, and there are free concerts, fireworks, and all sorts of scheduled amusements on a weekly basis. Bring change for the parking meters, patience, your swimsuit, perhaps a French dictionary (the beach has long been a favorite of the French Canadians), and be prepared for some serious people-watching. Lifeguards will be watching you. You can change up at the bathhouse on West Grand Avenue. For more information, contact the local chamber of commerce at (207) 934-2500.

GREATER PORTLAND

Scarborough

FERRY BEACH AND WESTERN BEACH
Off Route 207, Scarborough

A Prouts Neck neighborhood beach, Ferry Beach here is not to be confused with Ferry Beach State Park in Saco. This one is much smaller and much more difficult to get onto, as there is very limited parking. Still, between Ferry Beach and neighboring Western Beach, there are 1,700 yards of sand to be enjoyed.

Ferry faces the outlet of the Scarborough River and the summer colony of Pine Point; Western looks out at Pine Point. You won't think you're on a deserted isle here—despite some good bird-watching, the vistas tend toward the heavily developed. No lifeguards. Limited facilities.

GRAND BEACH (PINE POINT BEACH)
East Grand Ave., Scarborough

This is the spot where the beaches of York County meld into the beaches of Greater Portland (it connects to the end of Old Orchard), and it is indeed a grand beach, 2,500 yards of fine white sands. Good swimming, nice views of the tony cottages

of Prouts Neck, and there's a rocky breakwater where people like to fish. There's a snack bar, changing area, and some parking.

HIGGINS BEACH
Off Spurwink Rd. (Route 77), Scarborough

The beach used primarily by the summercators who have cottages in the small village of Higgins Beach, this strand is about 900 yards long and has nice dunes and tide pools. Parking is not available anywhere unless you stay in one of the cool inns nearby. Residents of Higgins Beach have been concerned with all the traffic the area sees and have had erosion concerns as well, but it's a very pleasant strand if you can find a place to put your car. Surf is good for riding.

SCARBOROUGH BEACH STATE PARK
Route 207, Scarborough
(207) 883-2416

Prouts Neck has been a very exclusive enclave for more than a century, the province of the wealthy and a place where no one would dare to park without permission. Scarborough Beach is the great equalizer, one of the best beaches in Maine, 2,060 yards of fine sands just a short walk up the road from Prouts Neck. The great barrier beach protects the outlet of Scarborough River and the wild estuarine oasis of Scarborough Marsh. You can park and enjoy the sands and facilities here—there are changing rooms and lifeguards—and walk down Black Point Road to see the summer colony or do some beach hopping and take your towel to Ferry Beach. You'll still need to arrive early if you want a parking spot, and while it's technically a state park, it's run by the town, so you can't use your state park pass here.

Cape Elizabeth
CRESCENT BEACH STATE PARK
Route 77, Cape Elizabeth
(207) 799-5871
There are several popular Maine beaches called Crescent Beach, but this is probably the best, a 1,560-yard expanse of fine sand not too far from Portland. As such, it's always busy in summer. Because it's a state park, there are plenty of amenities—a playground, a picnic area, a snack bar, a group site, nature trails, and a bathhouse with cold showers—which makes it a good option for families. The water is maybe even a tad warmer here than at other beaches, which is a welcome benefit. There's even a boat launch, but it requires a permit from the Cape Elizabeth Public Safety Office (on Route 77). The park is technically open from Memorial Day through Columbus Day, but the state welcomes skiers and hikers in the winter and even folks just out for a walk in the off-season.

South Portland
WILLARD BEACH
Willow St., South Portland
(207) 767-7651
In one of the city of South Portland's residential neighborhoods, Willard is maintained by the local parks and recreation department. It's a nice sand beach with a good look at Spring Point Lighthouse, a few Casco Bay forts, several islands, and scads of pleasure and working boats—including massive oil tankers on their way to the tanks on the Fore River. A concession area, outdoor showers, and a playground make it popular with kids;

lifeguards please the parents. Because it's a city beach, you may wonder about the cleanliness of the water, but it's tested twice weekly.

Portland
EAST END BEACH
Eastern Promenade, Portland
This small beach is the city's only public strand, and it's located—you guessed it—on the eastern edge of the Portland Peninsula underneath the Eastern Prom. On the rocky side, it affords a spectacular gander at the myriad delights of Casco Bay—forts, islands, lighthouses, and boats galore. Trails connect with the fine network laid out by Portland Trails, and there is a boat launching area for getting out onto the bay. Changing areas and restrooms are available.

Yarmouth
SANDY POINT BEACH
Cousins Island, Yarmouth
Not too many people know about this short stretch of sand on Casco Bay's Cousins Island, part of the town of Yarmouth and attached by a bridge. Right below where the bridge meets the isle, there's a beach good enough for dipping. A small parking area is available here, as is a boat launch. Not much, but it gets increasingly more difficult to find beaches from here to Popham Beach State Park.

Freeport
WINSLOW MEMORIAL PARK
Staples Point Rd., Freeport
(207) 865-4198
What a find this 90-acre park is. Owned by the town of Freeport, it has stupendous views of the Harraseeket River and Casco Bay and its islands, and there's a small tidal beach that makes for good swimming. (Get here two hours before or after high tide.) The facilities include picnic areas large enough for groups, a nature trail, a boat launch site, and a playground. Good stuff and only minutes from all the shopping downtown. You can even set up camp in one of the 100 sites here if you bring your tent. Admission is $2 per person. Open Memorial Day weekend through Columbus Day.

MIDCOAST

Brunswick

THOMAS POINT BEACH
Thomas Point Rd., Brunswick
(207) 725-6009
www.thomaspointbeach.com
A small, privately run beach on Thomas Bay, an inlet of the New Meadows River, this 290-yard strand is a beachgoer's paradise, if only because it's one of the rare Midcoast beaches open to the public. The water is tidal, so make sure you check the charts before packing the car. The facilities are pretty lavish as beaches go, with hot showers, picnic areas, lawns to explore, playgrounds, fireplaces to cook at, an arcade, a snack bar, and lifeguards. It's a great choice for functions or family get-togethers, and there are special events here all summer long, like the Thomas Point Bluegrass Festival. Open from 9 a.m. until sunset daily. Admission is $3.50 for adults, $2 for kids age 12 or younger.

Freshwater Alternatives in Brunswick

Brunswick's parks and rec department runs the ominously named **Coffin Pond** (River Road; 207-725-6656), an artificially created basin very popular in the summer. Also busy is **White's Beach** (Durham Road; 207-729-0415), a 9-foot-deep pond that's part of a campground but open to the public. Small fees are charged at both places.

Georgetown

REID STATE PARK
375 Seguinland Rd., Georgetown
(207) 371-2303
All of Maine's beaches front some famously frigid water, but Reid State Park has a reputation for being the coldest. The inviting, bodysurfable breakers here offer bathers swimming that often results in an all-over ice-cream headache sort of feeling. Mainers, of course, call this invigorating. People from away consider it just shy of arctic and spend most of their time at this mile-and-a-half beach just testing the water with their toes,

as if they can't believe it. The saving grace of the place for these people, and for kids, is the lagoon, a strip of sand that is protected from the freezing water by a sandbar and fronts a small pool that is noticeably warmer.

Along with Popham, about 4 miles away by boat, Reid serves up the big one-two punch of Midcoast beaches—there are a few sandy strands east of here, but they're much, much smaller. Consequently the pair are extraordinarily popular. The bathhouses are crawling with people, and you usually have to wait for a while at the snack bar. Bring your own hot dogs and burgers for the grills in the picnic area if you don't want to wait. You'd better arrive early if you want a parking spot. Open year-round. A small fee is charged.

Phippsburg

HEAD BEACH
Small Point Rd., Phippsburg
On the same peninsula as Popham Beach, Head is a sand beach of 360 yards that's a bit of a local secret. Parking is the problem here, but you can pay a small fee and leave your car after the gate on the peninsula and walk over. Hand Beach is a nice strand facing the beautiful eastern edge of Casco Bay.

POPHAM BEACH STATE PARK
10 Perkins Farm Lane, Phippsburg
(207) 389-1335
Sitting on an elbow-shaped peninsula between the Kennebec and Morse Rivers, Popham Beach is a wonderland of sand and surf. The grainy expanse sprawls for 3 miles, by far the longest beach in the Midcoast, and it's got a little of everything—ledges, tide pools, offshore islands, nearby lighthouses, great shell collecting, picnicking facilities, and on and on. People even ride the fast current of Morse River like a waterslide (Popham's well known for its riptides and strong underwater pulls, so be careful if attempting these sorts of activities). And beachgoers will often walk across the sands to Fox Island when the tide's right. Schedule a full day here or you'll be disappointed.

Whenever the sun makes an appearance during the warm-weather months, from the time the park opens in mid-April until it closes in October, there will be people at Popham—lots of them. The beach is the most popular strand north of Portland and south of Acadia, which means the parking lot is almost always full—cars line the approach road for miles on a hot summer weekend. But the beach is so long, it can absorb the thousands who show up, and you can almost always find an uncrowded spot to sit.

Pemaquid Peninsula

PEMAQUID BEACH PARK
Route 130, Bristol
(207) 677-2754
www.bristolparks.org/beach.htm
Facing Johns Bay to the south, Pemaquid is a nice sandy strand of about 600 yards not too far from popular Pemaquid Lighthouse. It's really your only chance for a day at a saltwater beach between Reid and Popham and the Penobscot Bay area. Backed up to sea grasses and woods and looking out at Johns Island, the beach is thus understandably popular in summertime with locals and tourists. People truly care about the swimming area, too. Local groups check water quality weekly and have started dune protection programs. There is a snack bar, as well as coldwater showers, toilets, and picnic tables.

Freshwater Alternatives in the Pemaquid Peninsula Area

Damariscotta Lake State Park (Route 32, Jefferson; 207-549-7600) is a popular choice for lake swimmers, with its sand beach, picnic area, and lifeguards, several miles inland from Damariscotta in the pretty old town of Jefferson. **Biscay Pond** (Biscay Road, Damariscotta) is another local favorite.

i   If you plan on visiting Popham Beach, call the tide and parking hotline at (207) 389-9125 or visit www.pophambeach .com to find out tide, weather, and sunset information. The site is updated every 15 minutes.

Owls Head and Rockland Area

BIRCH POINT STATE PARK
Ballyhac Rd., Owls Head
(207) 941-4014
One of the state's newest parks, this 220-yard arc of sand and stones is known locally as Lucia Beach, and it has long been a place to go for a quick dip in the Rockland area. The state officially protected 5.5 acres here with funds from the Land for Maine's Future program in 1999. They put up a big brown sign at the entrance, improved access a bit, put in a couple of pit toilets, and otherwise didn't change much. It's still free, there are still great views out across Mussel Ridge Channel, and the water is still absolutely frigid. For privacy, locals like to crawl into their own crannies in the rocks that flank the beach. You can usually find parking somewhere down here.

CRESCENT BEACH
Owls Head
About 1,100 yards of rare Midcoast sand beach can be found here south of Rockland, staring at Sheep Island. Just below a summer community, these great grains can be very popular in summer, and parking is notoriously hard to come by.

Freshwater Alternatives in the Rockland and Camden Areas

North of Owls Head, **Johnson Memorial Park on Chickawaukee Lake** (Route 17, Rockland) fills up fast with swimmers. Not the prettiest place, but it'll cool you off. **Shirttail Point** (Route 105) in Camden is a good place for kids to splash around in the sandy Megunticook River. An even better spot in Camden is **Barrett's Cove** (Route 52), under Maiden's Cliff on a cove of Lake Megunticook.

Lincolnville

LINCOLNVILLE BEACH
Route 1, Lincolnville
This beach must be one of Maine's easiest to find, sitting right off U.S. Route 1 within full view of everyone charging north to Acadia. Across the street are the handful of gift shops and restaurants of the village known as Lincolnville Beach;

down the sand a bit is the large pier where the state's ferry to Islesboro docks. The beach is relatively short—850 yards—and skinny. Some people find it a little awkward to be frolicking in front of all the drivers passing by and the diners at the Lobster Pound restaurant, which is right next to the sands, and with the local residents going to the post office across the street. If you can get used to that and can deal with parking hassles and crowds, you'll enjoy this little beach. You can take in the nice views of Penobscot Bay, you can watch the ferry run to and from Islesboro 3 miles offshore, and when you get hungry you can wander across to the Beach Store. Free parking if you can find a spot, and there are portapotties.

DUCKTRAP BEACH
Off Route 1, Lincolnville Beach

Locals try to keep this point where the Ducktrap River pours into Penobscot Bay a secret (you didn't hear about it here). Turn onto the Fire Road just before the bridge after Lincolnville Beach. Not the best place to lay down a towel—it's very rocky—but it's always pleasant to swim here. It's relatively private, set back from Route 1 down a dirt road. It's got a nice view of the Ducktrap Bridge, and you can swim on either side of a little peninsula—or ride the current between the two basins. Fun stuff, and free.

Searsport

SANDY POINT BEACH
Searsport

Despite the fact that this 1,370-yard beach is less than half a mile off Route 1, few tourists find this strand tucked away in the quiet old colony in Sandy Point between Searsport and Bucksport. The sands here sit just above the point where the Penobscot River meets Penobscot Bay. Fine swimming and nice views of Verona Island. Parking is fairly limited, though, as are the facilities.

ACADIA AREA

LAMOINE BEACH
Route 184, Lamoine
(207) 667-4778

Some people feel that the real appeal of Lamoine Beach isn't the beach at all but the jaw-dropping views of the mountains of Acadia National Park that you can see while standing on its sands. Mount Desert Island is just across Eastern Bay, and the 2,740 yards of fine beach give you an ideal prospect. But it's hard to argue with this much sand beach in a part of the state where you're not supposed to find any. The facilities are limited—picnic tables and a boat ramp—but you can find more (showers, bigger play areas, larger picnicking spots) up the way a bit at Lamoine State Park.

SAND BEACH
Acadia National Park
Loop Rd., Bar Harbor

Not the most original name, but the sand here is literally it for miles around, so at least it's apt. There are 290 yards of the precious stuff here, and it is extremely popular. There are not really many other places to get into Acadia's famous seas. The water is positively bone-chilling, but the views of Great Head, a bold headland, on one end of the beach and of the Beehive, a cliff face, on the other are fantastic. Parking goes very quickly, so be sure to arrive early. You'll have to pay the park entrance fee to get in. It's always fun to scale Great Head and look back down, and there are some cool marshes in the area to check out as well. You might recognize the beach from photographs and from movies like 1999's *The Cider House Rules,* in which Tobey Maguire and Charlize Theron frolic here.

Freshwater Alternatives in the Acadia Area

Echo Lake (Route 102 near Somesville) is by far the most popular place to swim on the island outside of Sand Beach. Lifeguards will look after you. **Lake Wood** (Park Road, Mount Desert) is known as a nudie spot.

DOWN EAST

SANDY RIVER BEACH
Off Route 187, Jonesport
Though the parking can be difficult, the sands rocky, and the water icy, this 500-yard natural wonder—sands Down East?—is always busy because it's all there is. Nice views of Roque Island and the neat tidal river.

ROQUE BLUFFS STATE PARK
145 Schoppee Point Rd., Roque Bluffs
(207) 255-3475
This Down East park is unusual in several ways. First, it's a fairly large sand and pebble beach at 910 yards. Second, there is a big freshwater basin right behind it, so you can swim in the sea and then wash off the salt in the 60-acre pond. And finally, as Maine state parks go, it sees few visitors for the beauty of the spot. The park covers a total of 274 acres, and there's plenty of space for picnicking, with tables and grills. There's a bathhouse for changing and a playground for the kids. All the amenities you could ever want in a Maine beach are here, and then some, without all the commercial distractions and superficialities of those found in southern Maine.

ON THE OCEAN

Many people say that a Maine vacation isn't quite complete unless you've gotten out onto the ocean, felt the sea spray on your face, smelled the rich brine, and seen the state from the deck of a boat. And plenty of options for seagoing await, whether they be climbing aboard a classic schooner for a six-day sail, heading out on a half-day nature cruise in search of whales and puffins, dropping a line from a deep-sea fishing boat, sliding into a kayak and exploring coves, or donning a wet suit and diving under for an hour.

The best places to start your search for offshore adventure are resort communities like Kennebunkport, Boothbay Harbor, Camden, and Bar Harbor or the state's largest city, Portland, where there is an infrastructure for tourism. These towns are where excursion boats are most concentrated and most easily found, but even tiny Cutler and Jonesport have their boat rides. If you're interested in kayaking, your options multiply, as that graceful sport has exploded in Maine since the 1980s, and it's hard to find a town without a sea kayak outfitter.

While heading out on a windjammer cruise will set you back some serious change—some boats are more than $100 a day—there are plenty of ways of getting afloat that won't sink your bank account. An afternoon kayak tour can be as little as $25, and there are sunset cruises and half-day sails that are eminently reasonable.

Many vessels offer more than one type of trip, maybe whale watching one day and deep-sea fishing the next. They're listed in this chapter by their primary specialty. We tried to include excursion boats with regular schedules rather than charter vessels.

WINDJAMMER CRUISES

Berthed in Rockland

The timbers of the tall old ship creak and sway with the waves. The sails luff and flap overhead. The sea sparkles in the sun, while dolphins do loop-the-loops off the bow. You can almost imagine the year is 1854. Welcome aboard a Maine schooner. More than a dozen of these historic vessels offer tours of the Down East coast, some putting together weeklong packages where you sleep in a small berth, help out on deck if you wish, eat the fleet's famous food, and enjoy spectacular sunsets and star shows as you travel to quiet coves and gunkholes along the coast. Each vessel is unique and has its own story to tell, but several boats are genuine antiques and are National Historic Landmarks. The captains and crews, too, come from all sorts of backgrounds, but they all tend to be charismatic, outgoing, and

some of the more interesting people you'll meet. Most provide a raft of options, from half-day to three-day to week-long cruises, and rates tend to be in the same ballpark for all of them, about $550 for a three-day cruise, up to $900 for a week. Some welcome children, others don't. Many of these boats are represented by the Maine Windjammer Association (P.O. Box 1144, Blue Hill 04614; 800-807-9463; www.sailmainecoast.com), which is a great resource for one-stop shopping.

AMERICAN EAGLE
North End Shipyard, Rockland
(207) 594-8007 or (800) 648-4544
www.schooneramericaneagle.com
The 92-foot *American Eagle* was launched in 1930 and was the last fishing schooner in the famous Gloucester fleet. It made its final fishing trip in 1983, was completely rehauled in 1986, and is now a Historic Landmark. Captain John Foss

offers primarily three-, four-, and six-day cruises, but in 2008 he hosted an epic 11-day exploration of the Gulf of Maine and the Bay of Fundy.

HERITAGE

North End Shipyard, Rockland
(207) 594-8007 or (800) 648-4544
www.schoonerheritage.com
Built right in Rockland's North End Shipyard in 1983, the *Heritage* was designed along the lines of the coasters of the 19th century. It accommodates 30 people, and Captains Doug and Linda Lee have been gracious hosts for as many years. These days they offer four- and six-day excursions.

ISAAC H. EVANS

North End Shipyard, Rockland
(877) 238-1325 www.midcoast.com/~evans
The *Isaac H. Evans* was built in Mauricetown, New Jersey, in 1886 and spent years in the oystering trade on Delaware Bay. Rebuilt in 1973 to carry passengers, it's now a Historic Landmark. Captain Brenda Thomas offers three-, four-, and six-day cruises.

J&E RIGGIN

136 Holmes St., Rockland
(207) 594-1875 or (800) 869-0604
www.mainewindjammer.com
The *J&E Riggin* is another old oystering vessel, built in Dorchester, New Jersey, in 1927. It is 90 feet long on deck, was granted Historic Landmark status in 1991, and is captained by Jon Finger and Anne Mahle. They provide three- to six-day jaunts and spice things up with sailing concerts and kids' cruises.

NATHANIEL BOWDITCH

P.O. Box 459, Warren 04864
(207) 273-4062 or (800) 288-4098
www.windjammervacation.com
Another speedy schooner, the *Nathaniel Bowditch* was built in East Boothbay in 1922 to be a racing vessel. It hauled its 82-foot frame to special-class honors in the Bermuda Race of 1923 and served in the Coast Guard during World War II before

being rebuilt for windjamming in the 1970s. Captain Owen and Cathie Dorr welcome passengers aboard for two-, three-, four-, and six-day sails.

STEPHEN TABER

P.O. Box 1050, Rockland
(207) 236-3520 or (800) 999-7352
www.stephentaber.com
Built in 1871, the *Stephen Taber* is the oldest continuously operating sailing vessel in the United States, and it's another National Landmark. At 68 feet, it accommodates 22 passengers, and it has become famous for its food, with its own cookbook, *The Taste of the Taber,* and was recently featured in the PBS show *Culinary Travels with Dave Eckert.*

SUMMERTIME

115A South Main St., Rockland
(800) 562-8290
www.schoonersummertime.com
The only pinkie schooner in the Maine fleet, the *Summertime* was locally built in 1986 on designs that replicate the classic New England pink. Popular as mackerel fishing vessels, pinks have been in use in the Gulf of Maine since the 1700s and got their name because of their uplifted, or "pinked," stern. The 53-foot *Summertime* does a lot of day sails during the summer and heads for multiday excursions, including 10- and 11-day cruises, as well. The ship accommodates seven people.

VICTORY CHIMES

P.O. Box 1401, Rockland 04841
(207) 594-0755 or (800) 745-5651
www.victorychimes.com
Built in Delaware in 1900 as a work vessel, the *Victory Chimes* is the largest American passenger sailing vessel at 132 feet. It's the only original three-masted schooner on the East Coast, is now a National Historic Landmark, and it is the schooner pictured on the Maine quarter. ("Tails Never Fails"). Captains Kip Files and Paul DeGaeta will even let you barter for your trip, especially if you have World War II collectibles or a spare MG lying around.

ℹ️ Bring a sweater. It's always a lot cooler on the water than you expect, even in August.

Berthed in Camden

ANGELIQUE

P.O. Box 736, Camden 04843
(207) 785-6036 or (800) 282-9989
www.sailangelique.com

The *Angelique* was built specifically to work the windjammer trade, launched in 1980. Ketch-rigged, with beautiful maroon sails, it is 95 feet long and was modeled after English fishing schooners of the 19th century. Captain Mike and Lynne McHenry offer primarily three- and four-day trips, though they sail for as many as 11.

GRACE BAILEY

Maine Windjammer Cruises
P.O. Box 617, Camden 04843
(207) 236-2938 or (800) 736-7981
www.mainewindjammercruises.com

The flagship of the Maine Windjammer Cruise fleet, the *Grace Bailey* got its start hauling timber and granite to the West Indies. A 123-foot coaster, it was built in 1882. Captain Ray and Ann Williamson offer weekend and five-day cruises.

LEWIS R. FRENCH

P.O. Box 992, Camden 04843
(207) 236-2463 or (800) 469-4635
www.schoonerfrench.com

The *Lewis R. French* was bestowed National Historic Landmark status in 1992, and it was about time, since it was launched in 1871 in Christmas Cove and is the oldest schooner in the Maine windjammer fleet. The ship is 64 feet long and previously served as a working vessel, hauling lumber, bricks, granite, lime, and Christmas trees—all those classic Maine exports. Captain Garth Wells runs three-, four-, six-, and 11-day getaways.

MARY DAY

P.O. Box 798, Camden 04843
(207) 785-5670 or (800) 992-2218
www.schoonermaryday.com

The schooner *Mary Day* was built in the 1960s with the aim of being a comfortable passenger vessel—and it succeeds. Ninety feet long, it was the first pure sailing schooner built in Maine since the 1930s, and it's known as a very fast vessel, perennially winning the Great Schooner Race. Captains Barry King and Jen Martin are first-rate hosts, and they offer lighthouse cruises, naturalist trips, foliage tours, and even a folk-music outing, in addition to their usual three-, four-, and six-day sails.

MERCANTILE

Maine Windjammer Cruises
P.O. Box 617, Camden 04843
(207) 236-2938 or (800) 736-7981
www.mainewindjammercruises.com

This was the ship that started it all in 1942, back when legendary captain Frank Swift started taking people out on cruising vacations and thus founded the Maine windjammer trade. The 115-foot *Mercantile* dates back to 1916 and served its prepassenger life as a cargo ship, toting barrel staves, salt fish, and firewood. Today it offers three- and four-day cruises.

MISTRESS

Maine Windjammer Cruises
P.O. Box 617, Camden 04843
(207) 236-2938 or (800) 736-7981
www.mainewindjammercruises.com

The *Mistress* is the specialty boat in the Maine Windjammer Cruises fleet, built on the lines of a coasting schooner but laid out like a yacht below-decks, allowing for more room and privacy for passengers. It's 60 feet long, accommodates just six passengers, and can be chartered.

Berthed in Rockport

TIMBERWIND

P.O. Box 247, Rockport 04856
(207) 236-0801 or (800) 759-9250
www.schoonertimberwind.com

The *Timberwind* was constructed in 1931, served as the harbor pilot boat in Portland Harbor for 38 years, and has berths for 20 passengers. Owners

Robert and Dawn Tassi are especially eager to have you aboard, and, unlike many of the other windjammers, welcome families with children age five or older for their three-, four-, and six-day cruises.

BOAT RIDES AND DAY SAILS

Almost inexhaustible options await those looking for boat rides and day sails on the Maine coast—you could head out on all 14 days of your two-week vacation and do something different every day. From types of vessels—old lobster boats, car ferries, and yachts—to the kinds of trips available, variety is the word. Ship out for a breakfast cruise, go lobstering, sail to lighthouses, watch for seals, cruise to museums, explore islands, enjoy the sunset—there's plenty to do and see.

South Coast

FINESTKIND SCENIC CRUISES
Barnacle Billy's Dock, Perkins Cove, Ogunquit
(207) 646-5227
www.finestkindcruises.com
Finestkind is a Down East term for "the best," and this company certainly ranks very highly, having been cruising the coast since 1956. The Finestkind vessels—there are now three—make 14 trips daily out of Perkins Cove, offering breakfast outings ($19), trips to the Nubble Lighthouse ($20), cocktail cruises ($13), and genuine lobstering jaunts ($13), where you can see what it's like to pull a trap.

BELLATRIX
Nonantum Resort
Ocean Ave., Kennebunkport
(207) 590–1125
www.sailingtrips.com
"Captain Jim" and his 37-foot yacht Bellatrix are based on the Kennebunk River behind the Nonantum Resort, and they do two or three sails daily depending upon weather and the tides. The three-hour tours are $50, and they're limited to six people, so calling ahead is a good idea, especially in high summer. These pleasant runs are a good way to get a gander at the Bush com-

pound on Walker Point without having to worry about crowds.

ELEANOR
Arundel Wharf, Ocean Ave.
P.O. Box 572, Kennebunkport 04046
(207) 967-8809
One of the prettier day sailers you're going to find, the schooner Eleanor is a modern vessel, launched in 1999 and built by its captain, Rich Woodman. The 55-footer has the gaff rigging and the traditional lines of a classic Herreschoff windjammer and yet boasts all the comforts and security of a contemporary cruiser. Eleanor leaves Arundel Wharf one to three times daily for two-hour trips (it can be chartered, too). Passage is $40 per person, and reservations can be made by calling ahead or by stopping by the Schooner Shack on the wharf.

Greater Portland

BAYVIEW CRUISES
184 Commercial St., Portland
(207) 761-0496
Seal cruises, harbor lunch cruises, lighthouse cruises, sunset cruises, even "attitude adjustment" cruises—BayView Cruises of Portland offers them all on a daily basis, June through September. The tours vary in length from an hour to two hours, but they all take you out onto the waters of Casco Bay, giving you a look at Portland Harbor and all its boats, forts, and nearby islands. You can also charter the 117-foot sightseeing vessel if you need more time than that and want to

When Portland area residents have houseguests in town who are interested in going for a boat ride, they know just where to send them—the Casco Bay Lines mail boat run, which services the populated Calendar Islands. It's a three-hour trip around the bay for the fee of $13.50. There's no better deal on the coast. Contact Casco Bay Lines, Commercial Street, Portland; (207) 774-7871; www.cascobaylines.com.

bring along 89 friends. Look into the lobster bake option, which can be added to any of these trips at a moment's notice.

EAGLE ISLAND TOURS
Long Wharf
Commercial St., Portland
(207) 774-6498
www.eagleislandtours.com
Eagle Island Tours provides passengers with the usual one-and-a-half-hour tour of Portland Harbor and Casco Bay—seals, lighthouses, etc.—which is all good fun, but the really cool thing they do is a trip out to Eagle Island, former home of Admiral Robert Peary, supposedly the first person to reach the North Pole. There's a nifty museum on the island documenting the explorer's feats. The Eagle Island cruise ($29) departs Long Wharf at 10 a.m. on Tuesday, Thursday, Friday, Saturday, and Sunday from June 28 through August 31.

DOWNEAST DUCK ADVENTURES
177 Commercial St., Portland
(207) 774-DUCK
www.downeastducktours.com
It's a boat! It's a bus! It's a Downeast Duck! So goes the marketing behind Maine's only amphibious tours. And they're amusing stuff. The open-air blue Ducks take you on a quick-and-quacky tour of Portland's history before driving right into the harbor for a jaunt around the city's working waterfront. The "Duckaneer" trips run $24, and, as Portland is inextricably tied to Casco Bay, they're arguably the best way to get a quick-and-dirty—and entertaining—feel for the city.

ATLANTIC SEAL CRUISES
25 Main St., South Freeport
(207) 865-6112
Most visitors to Freeport are unaware the famous outlet town even has a waterfront, let alone a cruise company offering seal and osprey watches, foliage cruises, lobstering trips, and excursions to Eagle Island to see the former home and museum of Admiral Robert Peary, the first man to the North Pole. But there's Captain Tom Ring,

owner of Atlantic Seal Bed and Breakfast, shoving off from the Freeport Town Wharf on a daily basis in summer (late May through October).

Midcoast
SEA ESCAPE CHARTERS
P.O. Box 7, Bailey Island 04003
(207) 833-5531
www.seaescapecottages.com
Captain Les McNelly will take you out on a two-hour tour of Casco Bay and the Bailey Island area whenever you're ready. He does sunset and seal-watch cruises as well as trips to Eagle Island, on an on-demand basis. And he also takes people out after mackerel, striped bass, and bluefish aboard his *Sea Escape Too*. If you can't get enough, you can hole up for the night at one of McNelly's cottages—they're fantastic—and go out again the next day. Two-hour tours are $80 per person for two people, $50 each for four.

YANKEE
Hermit Island, Small Point
(207) 443-2101
Hermit Island is one of the best oceanfront camping areas in Maine, and every afternoon and evening the campground's 50-foot boat, *Yankee,* makes a nature or sunset cruise on which noncampers are welcome. While the trips are fun, one look at Hermit Island and you'll be making a reservation for next year.

BALMY DAYS CRUISES
Pier 8, Commercial St., Boothbay Harbor
(207) 633-2284 or (800) 298-2284
www.balmydayscruises.com
Balmy Days has a veritable cruising empire in Boothbay Harbor, one of the best outfits on the coast. A family business run through the years by Captains Bob and Bill Campbell, Balmy Days has four vessels and as many options, taking passengers aboard for trips to Monhegan Island, day sails, harbor tours, and mackerel fishing. Rates vary with the nature of the trip but are reasonable.

CAP'N FISH'S CRUISES
Pier 1, Wharf St., Boothbay Harbor
(207) 633-3244
www.mainewhales.com
Cap'n Fish is the other biggie on the scene in Boothbay Harbor, offering all manner of boat rides. The schedule is exhaustive, and some of its highlights include seal watches, Kennebec River journeys, Damariscove Island tours, a Pemaquid Lighthouse cruise, and a few mix-and-match options. Call or see the Web site for the complete lineup.

HARDY BOAT CRUISES
Shaws Fish and Lobster Wharf,
Route 32, New Harbor
(207) 677-2026 or (800) 278-3346
www.hardyboat.com
One of the companies that provide service to enchanted Monhegan Island, Hardy Boat also offers any number of trips on a daily basis aboard its 60-foot excursion vessel, *Hardy III*. Among the highlights is the one-hour lighthouse cruise, a sunset ride that departs New Harbor at 7:30 p.m. daily in summer and heads to Pemaquid Light to watch it and a handful of other beacons blink on with the coming darkness. Reservations are recommended for the $12 trip. Another good one is the fall foliage cruise past the islands of Muscongus Bay, a 90-minute ride where you can see the glows of red and orange against a backdrop of dark sea and black spruce. Spectacular. That cruise goes out daily through September (better viewing is the latter half of the season), and on Wednesdays and weekends after that. The trip is $16 for adults, $11 for children.

APPLEDORE
Bayview Landing, Camden
(207) 236-8353
www.appledore2.com
The last schooner custom-built by the well-known Harvey Gamage shipyard in South Bristol using age-old shipbuilding methods, the 86-foot *Appledore* was launched in 1978. It works both Key West and Camden now, offering two-hour tours of Penobscot Bay four times daily in spring,

summer, and fall, including a sunset cruise. You can help raise the sails and even take a turn at the wheel if you like, all while taking in vistas of islands, mountains, birds, and seals.

BETSELMA
Bayview Landing, Camden
(207) 236-4446
www.betselma.com
The 30-foot *Betselma* was once a working lobster boat and now takes passengers where the hauling used to be done. Captained by Les Bex, it leaves the public landing in the Camden harbor on one-, two-, and three-hour cruises around Penobscot Bay and its islands, with the captain narrating away. He has 35 years of experience and will fill you in on the lobster industry, the three lighthouses you pass, the seabirds and seals you see, and local history. Rates are $10 an hour per adult, half price for kids.

OLAD
Bayview Landing, Camden
(207) 236-2323
www.maineschooners.com
The schooner *Olad* sails from Camden Harbor five times daily, beginning at 9:45 a.m., but the trip you shouldn't miss is the one that pushes off at 5 p.m. every day from mid-June through mid-August for a two-hour sail about Penobscot Bay. The sun falling behind the round, green heads of the Camden Hills is a sublime sight. So is the *Olad*, for that matter. The graceful 57-foot, two-masted schooner is a classic wooden windjammer, and it once whisked Walter Cronkite about. Passage is $29 per person.

SURPRISE
Bayview Landing, Camden
(207) 236-4687
www.camdenmainesailing.com
The oldest of Camden's day-sailing windjammers, the schooner *Surprise* was built in 1918 to be a racing yacht, and it was granted Historic Landmark status in 1991. A 57-foot beauty, *Surprise* putters out of Camden's photogenic harbor for two-hour sails four times daily from July 1 through mid-September (three times daily after

that through October 15) before hauling sails and running with the wind. Rates are $30 per person, and smoking is not allowed.

SCHOONER *HERON*
Rockport Harbor, Rockport
(207) 236-8605 or (800) 599-8605
www.woodenboatco.com
Not to be confused with *Wooden Boat* magazine, Wooden Boat Co. is a boatbuilding outfit in Rockport. They constructed the beautiful 65-foot schooner *Heron*, launching it in 2003. They offer a variety of cruises on a daily basis on the graceful vessel, including a lobster lunch ($65), a lighthouse-and-wildlife sail ($38), and a sunset hors d'oeuvres cruise ($50); the latter is a fine cap to a day spent on the Midcoast.

ISLE AU HAUT COMPANY
Sea Breeze Ave., Stonington
(207) 367-5193 or 367-6516
www.isleauhaut.com
The *Miss Lizzie* navigates Deer Island Thorofare on a daily basis as the ferry and mail boat to the island of Isle au Haut, so it knows these island-dotted waters better than most—which is what makes a sightseeing cruise aboard the local institution a pleasure. That and the captain's narration about marine life, the many islands, Mark Island Lighthouse, and the history of granite quarrying in the area. The boat leaves Stonington Dock daily at 9 a.m. and 2 p.m.

OLD QUARRY OCEAN ADVENTURES
130 Settlement Rd., Stonington
(207) 367-8977
www.oldquarry.com
Half- and whole-day trips aboard the 38-foot lobster boat *Nigh Duck* are Captain Bill Baker's specialty. With more than a quarter-century on the water, he's a wealth of information about the seabirds, sights, and history of the Stonington area. You can even try your hand at sailing if you like. Morning cruises sail from 9 a.m. to noon, and afternoon trips are from 1 to 4 p.m. The rates are $40. He also offers whale-watching jaunts and whole-day trips.

Acadia Area
BAR HARBOR WHALE WATCH CO.
1 West St., Bar Harbor
(207) 288-9800 or (888) 533-WALE
www.whalesrus.com
A multifaceted excursion boat company with a whole fleet of vessels, Bar Harbor Whale Watch does two-hour lighthouse and nature tours of Frenchman Bay. These trips take you to the seal haul-outs and tall beacons off Mount Desert, with naturalists narrating all the while. They head out at 10 a.m. and 1:15 p.m., 3:30 p.m., and 6 p.m. daily from July 1 through the end of August and two or three times a day in the off-season. Call for the full schedule.

DOWNEAST WINDJAMMER CRUISES
Bar Harbor Inn Pier, Bar Harbor
(207) 288-4585 or 288-2373
www.downeastwindjammer.com
At 151 feet, with four masts and nine deep-red sails taking in 4,800 square feet of wind, the *Margaret Todd* is an impressive vessel. It's the only four-master to cruise New England waters in a half century, and perhaps more than any other of Maine's schooners, it seems to be sailing right out of history when it comes in off the harbor—which is quite ironic, because it was launched in 1998. Named for Captain Steve Pagels's grandmother, the ship sets sail twice daily, plying the waters of Frenchman Bay. Eagles, seals, porpoises, and even whales might be spotted, and the ship passes before a lot of the "cottages" that made Bar Harbor famous. Plus it gives you a prospect of Mount Desert and Acadia, mountains soaring high above, that every visitor should see. Tickets are $32 per person. Captain Pagels also offers trips across the bay to the other Acadia—the Schoodic Peninsula in Winter Harbor—narrated by national park rangers. Inquire about the schedule or see the Web site.

RACHEL B. JACKSON
Beal's Lobster Pier, Southwest Harbor
(207) 288-2216
www.downeastsail.com

Built to resemble an 1890s schooner, the *Rachel B. Jackson* has quite an interesting history. It has circumnavigated the globe, been the state of Maine's representative in the Tall Ships 2000 race, served as a whale research vessel for the National Geographic Society, and been used to train student sailors as a Sail Training Association ship. The salient point to you, though, is that this 67-foot beauty takes passengers out on cruises around Frenchman Bay daily in summer at 10 a.m., 1 p.m., and 6:30 p.m. You might see porpoises, ospreys, eagles, and seals, and even if you don't, you'll enjoy breathtaking vistas of Acadia, Bar Harbor, the bay, and its islands. Passage is $30 per person.

SEA PRINCESS
Municipal Pier, Sea St., Northeast Harbor
(207) 276-5352
www.barharborcruises.com
Somes Sound is the only true fjord—a place where mountains plunge directly into the sea on both sides—on the eastern seaboard, and perhaps the best way to get a look at this magnificent natural spectacle is aboard the 75-foot *Sea Princess*. The boat makes a 90-minute circuit from the town dock in Northeast Harbor well up into the sound on a daily basis. Sights include Acadia, Norumbega, and Saint Sauveur Mountains, tumbling Man-O-War Brook, the working waterfront of Southwest Harbor, Bear Island Lighthouse, Hall Quarry, and all of the wildlife that lives in this valley of sea. The boat also makes daily trips to the beautiful Cranberry Isles, one of which is narrated by a ranger from Acadia, and a sunset cruise as well.

ISLAND CRUISES
Little Island Marine,
Shore Rd., Bass Harbor
(207) 244-5785
www.bassharborcruises.com
The Strauss family runs the Bass Harbor outfit, Island Cruises, motoring from the hamlet of Bass Harbor to Frenchboro Island for a walk and lunch and simply out nature watching through Blue Hill Bay. Their boat, the *R. L. Gott*, a 41-foot vessel

named for a family friend, putts out past Bass Harbor Light and across the way to Frenchboro, pausing long enough on this small island of about 50 year-rounders for lunch at the local eatery and a guided tour of the village. Reservations are necessary for the three-and-a-half-hour trip. Passage is $27.

Down East
CAPTAIN LAURA FISH
Kelley Point Rd., Jonesport
(207) 801-1957
www.cruisedowneast.com/cruise-maine.php
The personable Captain Laura Fish takes as many as six passengers out on the 23-foot *Aaron Thomas* on a daily basis in summer from Jonesport harbor. Her three-hour tour takes in many of the sights in Moosabec Reach, from Great Wass Island, where there's a Nature Conservancy preserve noted for its wildflowers, to the colorfully named Mistake Island. Reservations are necessary.

SYLVINA W. BEAL
Downtown Eastport
(207) 853-2500
www.eastportwindjammers.com
For years, the classic schooner *Sylvina W. Beal* sailed out of Boothbay Harbor, but it has ventured Down East and now calls the city of Eastport home. Built in East Boothbay in 1911, the 84-foot vessel is a knockabout schooner, which means it doesn't have a bowsprit, and it served years as a fishing boat. Movie buffs might recognize the *Sylvina W. Beal* from its roles in *Amistad* (1997) and *The Age of Innocence* (1993). These days the schooner takes passengers out on two daily cruises: a whale-watching trip (1:30 p.m.) and a sunset sail (7 p.m.) under the experienced hand of Captain Butch Harris. This is the prettiest way to see whales on the coast. Rates are $27 to $37 per person.

WHALE AND PUFFIN WATCHING

Maine is prime whale-watching country, especially in spring and fall, when the gentle giants migrate

Close-up

Sailing Schools

Ahoy! Some people assert that the Maine coast is among the best sailing grounds in the world, if not the best. And there are any number of places along it where you can learn to sail, acquiring the skills to safely get out among it all. These range from free outfits like CFAIR in Rockland, which is done as a community service, to adventure schools like Outward Bound, also in Rockland, where you learn to sail as part of a deeper exploration of yourself. Some programs operate by the day, others overnight. Here are a few examples.

School of Ocean Sailing
www.maine.sailingschool.com
This is a 10-day course that takes you from Portland to Yarmouth, Nova Scotia, and back, all the while providing you with an in-depth course in seamanship.

Sail Maine
58 Fore Street, Portland
(207) 650–7878
www.sailmaine.org
A nonprofit, Sail Maine is devoted to support sailing at the grassroots, community level, and to that end it offers basic classes to both adults and children.

Sawyer's Sailing School
Harpswell
(207) 783-6882
http://2009sail.homestead.com/untitled1.html
Captain Bob offers basic ASA-certified courses in coastal cruising and keelboat sailing out of the Brunswick area.

CFAIR Sailing School
SBI Marine, Rockland
(207) 594-2891
The initials stand for Citizens for an Improved Rockland, and this extraordinary group of volunteers believes that sailing is a fine way to do just that. It's a pay-it-forward operation—someone once taught these folks to sail, so all that they ask is for you to try, to be on time, and to pass on what you learned to someone else. Classes take place on evenings and weekends and are intended for those ages 12 and up.

Outward Bound
Rockland
(866) 467-7651
www.outwardboundwilderness.org
The nation's leading outdoor adventure program has several sail-training–based exercises each year, where you'll gain a basic understanding of seamanship—and your own self.

north and south. Humpbacks and finbacks are the most commonly spotted, but minkes and rare right whales also swim the Gulf of Maine. Whale-watching companies are so certain of spotting these leviathans that most offer some sort of guarantee (usually a voucher good for another trip). Sightings can be very up close, as whales swim up to the boat for a bit of mammal bonding, but more typically you get to see their fins and flukes as they come up for air. There's something truly transcendental about the experience.

South Coast
DEBORAH ANN
Perkins Cove, Ogunquit
(207) 361-9501
www.deborahannwhalewatch.com
Built in 1994, the 40-foot *Deborah Ann* is one of the smaller boats in the whale-watching fleet, and because it's based in Ogunquit, it's closer than many other outfits to the prime whaling

grounds of Jeffrey's Ledge, so you get an intimate experience. Reservations are a good idea for the four-and-a-half-hour trips, which leave at 8 a.m. and 1:30 p.m. Rates are $50 for adults, $45 for seniors, $35 for children.

INDIAN WHALE WATCH
Camp Ellis Pier, Camp Ellis
(207) 985-5993
Indian departs the Landing Restaurant at 10 a.m. from July through September, and also offers sunset trips in July and August. Expect to see dolphins, sharks, and seals, as well as the whales you're after, Ishmael. Fare for adults is $30 and fare for children 12 and under is $20.

FIRST CHANCE WHALE WATCH
4 Western Ave, Lower Village, Kennebunk
(207) 967-5507
www.firstchancewhalewatch.com
Like the other vessels in the southern Maine whale-watch fleet, First Chance travels to Jeffrey's Ledge for its whale hunt. The very comfortable 80-foot *Nick's Chance* makes the journey on a daily basis at 9 a.m. and again at 3 p.m. in July and August. In late May and from September through mid-October, the boat sails only on weekends. Passage is $48 for adults, $28 for children.

Portland
ODYSSEY WHALE WATCH
170 Commercial St., Portland
(207) 775-0727
www.odysseywhalewatch.com
The *Ahabs of the Odyssey* heads out of Portland Harbor every day in search of white whales—or any whales. They have a close to a 100 percent track record and they also regularly spy white-sided dolphins, basking sharks, ocean sunfish, the occasional sea turtle, and countless birds. She sails at 10 a.m. returning at about 3 p.m. Adults are $45, juniors and seniors are $40, and children under 12 are $35.

Midcoast
BOOTHBAY WHALE WATCH
Pier 6, P.O. Box 547, Boothbay Harbor 04538
(207) 633-3500 or (888) WHALE–ME
www.whaleme.com
Every Boothbay Whale Watch tour begins with a narrated trip through the harbor itself, during which the naturalist on the 100-foot *Harbor Princess* discusses the homes, lighthouses, islands, and wildlife seen on the way out to the whales' feeding grounds. Then it's all hands on deck— or rather, all eyes on the water—as the search begins for finbacks and humpbacks. The boat sails twice daily from July through Labor Day at 9:30 a.m. and 1:30 p.m., and it goes out once daily at 11:30 a.m. during the off-season.

CAP'N FISH'S CRUISES
Pier 1, Wharf St., Boothbay Harbor
(207) 633-3244, (207) 633-2626
(800) 636-3244
www.mainewhales.com
Whale-watching expeditions are a daily occurrence at Cap'n Fish's in Boothbay Harbor. The Boothbay legend claims to have the fastest vessels around, which gets you out to the whales quicker and allows for longer sightings when you're out there. This outfit also makes trips to National Audubon Society's puffin colony on Eastern Egg Rock. Call for the complete schedule.

HARDY BOAT CRUISES
Shaws Fish and Lobster Wharf,
Route 32, New Harbor
(207) 677-2026 or (800) 278-3346
www.hardyboat.com
Best known as a ferry to Monhegan Island, the folks at Hardy Boat also make daily runs to Eastern Egg Rock to see the crazy puffins there, and they have a trip that goes to Monhegan first and then to the puffins, combining two Maine favorites. Puffin watches leave New Harbor at 5:30 p.m. and last an hour or so every day from mid-June through late August, and on Wednesday, Saturday, and Sunday from mid-May through mid-June. Fare is $22 for adults, $14 for kids.

Acadia Area

BAR HARBOR WHALE WATCH CO.
1 West St., Bar Harbor
(207) 288-2386 or (888) WHALES
www.barharborwhales.com
Bar Harbor Whale Watch Co. sends an armada of vessels out in search of whales on a daily basis in summer, with tours leaving at 8:30 and 9 a.m. on a whale and puffin cruise; and at 1 p.m., 2:30 p.m., and 4:30 p.m. for whales. The last run is a three-and-a-half-hour sunset cruise that makes for beautiful viewing. Check the Web site or call for details.

Down East

NORTON OF JONESPORT
118 Main St., Jonesport
(207) 497-2560
www.machiassealisland.com
Puffins may be charismatic critters, with their cute sea-parrot faces, but they had nothing on Captain Barna B. Norton of Jonesport. A character, a genuine old-time Maine boat captain, and a legend Down East, the late Norton took single-handedly took on the Canadian government, fighting for rights to access Machias Seal Island, one of the few Maine isles with a breeding puffin colony. Marlin Perkins of Wild Kingdom, famed birdwatcher Roger Tory Peterson, *National Geographic,* and just about every worthy magazine and newspaper in the land all have ventured offshore with Norton. His daughter Holly now runs the show, making the 80-minute crossing to Machias Seal Island daily at about 7 a.m. from Memorial Day through the end of August. You'll have a few hours on the island to take pictures. Reservations are recommended, and Holly asks that you also call the night before you expect to make the trip to establish the exact time she's heading out. The cost is $100 per person.

BOLD COAST CHARTER COMPANY
P.O. Box 364, Cutler 04626
(207) 259-4484
www.boldcoast.com
The hamlet of Cutler is one of the finest Maine communities you're ever going to find, a few

houses and some fishing boats sitting on the Little River way Down East. One of these boats belongs to Captain Andrew Patterson, who offers cruises out to see the puffins of Machias Seal Island, the largest colony of the cute bird on the coast of Maine. Patterson makes the trip to the island on the *Barbara Frost,* a lobster boat, on a daily basis from May through August. He shoves off at 7 or 8 a.m. for the five-hour round-trip, and reservations are recommended. (Call the night before to find out what time the trip will commence.) The cost is $80 per person.

HARRIS WHALE WATCHING AND FISHING
Downtown Eastport
(207) 853-2500
www.eastportwindjammers.com
There are so many reasons to recommend a whale-watching trip out of Eastport. First, the city is handy to the Bay of Fundy, an oceanic region known for its large whale population. Second, you have to cruise past the Old Sow, a legendary whirlpool, on your way out to the whaling grounds. And finally, you're most likely going to be aboard the *Sylvina Beal,* a graceful windjammer. Most whale-watching vessels are boring new motorized craft, but Captain Butch Harris's ride is a pretty knockabout schooner. The trip is three hours, and the sightings often include puffins, seals, dolphins, ospreys, and eagles as well. The ship sails at 1:30 and 7 p.m., and passage is $37 for adults, $20 for kids age 12 or younger.

SCUBA TOURS

With its dark waters and cold temperatures, the Maine coast hasn't developed the sort of reputation that the Caribbean has when it comes to scuba diving. There are no azure vistas of coral reefs, no garishly colored fishies or bathwater-warm lagoons. You have to be a hardy type to enjoy diving here, but if you are, there is plenty to see, from seals and porpoises, lobsters and skates, to shipwrecks and seawalls. You just have to know where to look. Several dive outfitters know just that and will take you out on an undersea excursion. Here are a few ideas.

SEAFARI CHARTERS
7 Island Ave., Kittery
(207) 439-5068
www.seafaricharters.com

The *Seafari* may be a 44-foot sportfishing boat, and it may do mostly fishing charters these days, but it was custom-built as a dive platform for scuba diving. It's available for charters to such fantastic diving locales as Boon Island, site of a grisly stranded-island tale; Nubble Light; the Isles of Shoals; and Fort Foster. Call or visit the Web site for a rate schedule.

DIVERS LOCKER
460 Old North Berwick Rd., Lyman
(207) 985-3161

Diver Mike Bridges, owner of the Divers Locker in Lyman, will give certified divers a guided tour of the wreck of the steamer *Wandby*, which went aground off Kennebunkport in 1921—among other great Maine dives. And you can rent gear from him if you don't want to tote yours along.

SEA VENTURES CHARTERS
Saint George
(207) 685-4693
www.divefishmaine.com

Divers will find a lot to like about Sea Ventures Charters, based in Saint George. The small outfit provides all types of certification courses—from beginner to advanced stuff like nitrox and ice diving—and they do several cool charters as well. The most notable perhaps are the shark dives offered in August, when Maine waters are busy with 12-foot blue sharks (they sometimes even see big and scary makos). Divers are sent down in a cage, the waters are chummed, and they get an up-close-and-personal visit with these menacing predators. It can be spine-tingling, and it's available to anyone with basic certification, because the cage, while in 500-foot-deep waters, is only 10 feet below the surface. The company also regularly dives off Monhegan Island, a treat because of the unusually rich sea life and great underwater terrain, as well as to the *Scottish Pride,* a 44-foot fishing boat wrecked in 115 feet of water. Deep-sea fishing is another option from

these guys. Prices vary per trip and are based on six people participating; they can be $660 for an open-water dive to $1,140 for shark dives. Call or visit the Web site for full details.

DOWNEAST DIVING
1267 Route 1, Perry
(207) 263-8251
www.downeastdiving.com

Some say that the best diving in the state is along the Down East coast—and that's just where you'll find Dennis Dorsy's scuba outfit. Downeast Diving will take you out for simple shore dives or more technical stuff like ice and night and wreck diving. They even do a shark trip (and yes, there are sharks in Maine). If you don't know how to dive, they can help you with that, too. Check the Web site for details.

FISHING

Thanks to years of overfishing, the fisheries in Maine might not be what they once were—early English explorers described cod practically jumping into the boat—but they're still healthy enough to support an afternoon of deep-sea angling. Boats the length of the coast will take you out for mackerel, bluefish, stripers, cod, cusk, haddock, and more, for reasonable sums. Here are few places to start.

BUNNY CLARK
P.O. Box 837, Ogunquit 03907
(207) 646-2214
www.bunnyclark.com

The term bottom feeder is usually considered derogatory, but not when it comes to fishing the Maine coast. The bottom is where the cod, pollock, halibut, haddock, hake, cusk, redfish, monkfish, and wolffish can be found, and Captain Tim Towers of the legendary *Bunny Clark* knows how to find them. Not only can you catch an award-winning fish aboard the 40-foot fiberglass boat—it's seen a lot of record-breaking fish—but the captain and crew will even filet your catch for you to take home. The Bunny Clark is built for fishing, with seats and rods on deck, and its captain is one of the more experienced of the Maine deep-sea fleet. All gear is provided. Half-day, full-day, and "marathon," or 12-hour, trips are available daily from April 1 through November 9 for $45, $75, and $155, respectively.

UGLY ANNE
Perkins Cove, Ogunquit
(207) 646-7202
www.uglyanne.com

There's nothing unattractive about the Ugly Anne, a 44-foot red-and-white wooden vessel that takes anglers out of Perkins Cove to plumb the depths for cod, pollock, halibut, hake, haddock, cusk, and wolffish. It offers two half-day trips daily from mid-June through Labor Day, with the morning boat departing the docks at 8 a.m. and the afternoon boat leaving at 1:15 p.m. Daylong outings occur in the offseason. The half-day trips are $45 to $50 per person.

CAPTAIN SATCH DEEPSEA FISHING
Town Dock, Wells Harbor
(207) 324-9655
www.wellsharbor.com

Captain Satch McMahon and his sons Whit and Dennis welcome guests aboard a pair of vessels on a daily basis in summer: the Gath IV, a classic 34-foot lobster boat that does inshore runs for striped bass, and the India Marie, a 32-foot Cape Islander that heads offshore for cod. The most popular excursions are their four-hour ($70) and 6-hour ($85) inshore fishing expeditions, using light lines for stripers, mackerel, and bluefish, but they also do two-hour introductory outings as well as 10-hour marathons in the course of their season, which runs from the end of April through the end of October.

SEA ESCAPE CHARTERS
P.O. Box 7, Bailey Island 04003
(207) 833-5531
www.seaescapecottages.com

Mackerel, striped bass, and bluefish are what Captain Les McNelly is after when he takes anglers out on the Sea Escape Too. (See the earlier Boat Rides and Day Sails section of this chapter for details on his operation.)

BALMY DAYS CRUISES
Pier 8, Commercial St., Boothbay Harbor
(207) 633-2284 or (800) 298-2284
www.balmydayscruises.com

Mackerel fishing from the back of the Miss Boothbay, a converted lobster boat, is just one of Balmy Days Cruises's many offerings (see Boat Rides and Day Sails section earlier in this chapter). Two-hour angling adventures are offered four times daily from Pier 8 in Boothbay Harbor. The experienced captains know where to drop anchor, the scenery is fine, and all tackle is provided. The trips are $22 for adults, $16 for kids age 11 or younger.

BINGO DEEPSEA FISHING
100 Commercial St., Boothbay Harbor
(207) 633-3775

From the pier behind the Tugboat Restaurant in Boothbay Harbor, the 52-foot Bingo chugs 60 miles out to sea before anchoring in 300-foot water and dropping 10-ounce diamond jigs in search of good old staples like cod, pollock, haddock, and cusk. The fishing is usually very good, and being this far out, you often see whales and porpoises as an added bonus. If you get lucky, the crew will dice up your dinner for you on the 90-minute trip back into port. The boat goes out daily, and reservations are a good idea. The daylong trip is $125.

JANNA MARIE
Bar Harbor Inn Pier, Bar Harbor
(207) 288-4585
www.downeastwindjammer.com

Part of Captain Steve Pagels's armada, the 56-foot Janna Marie sets out on four-hour trips in search of cod, cusk, pollock, mackerel, cunner, sculpin, black sea bass, and redfish at 8 a.m. and 1 p.m. daily in summer. Trips are limited to 35 anglers, and all bait and tackle is provided. Passage is $39.50 per person.

HARRIS WHALE WATCHING AND FISHING
Downtown Eastport
(207) 853-2500
www.eastportwindjammers.com

Captain Butch Harris has quite the excursion boat

empire in Eastport, and his 35-passenger *Quoddy Dam* is the deep-sea representative. Eastport is ideal for deepwater fishing because, as the second-deepest natural seaport in North America, it sits only minutes from 300-foot waters rather than the hours required by most Maine boats—which means longer fishing for you. Bald eagles, porpoises, seals, and whales may be your companions. Four-hour trips leave daily at 8 a.m., and gear is provided. The fee is $25 per person.

LOBSTERING

Maine lobstermen have been called the cowboys of the sea, rugged independent types who ride the waves, spending all day outdoors and risking rough conditions so that they can have their freedom. Tourists tend to buy into this image, seeing the romance of life on the glorious coast of Maine—out at sea all day, breathing the salty air, enjoying the sunshine and the views. And lobster fishing is all that, but it's also difficult, backbreaking work with uncertain results; you never know what's going to be in your traps when you haul them up—they might well be empty—and you have that expensive boat and all the gear to pay for. Still, most lobstermen will fish until they can't anymore. Several current and former lobster-men take passengers out on their boats in summer, showing them the ins and outs of hauling traps, from bait to catch. Don't plan your trip for a Sunday, though, because it's against Maine law to lobster on Sunday (gives the fishery a breather). Here are a few ideas.

FINESTKIND SCENIC CRUISES
Barnacle Billy's Dock,
Perkins Cove, Ogunquit
(207) 646-5227
www.finestkindcruises.com
Providers of the best known of Maine's lobstering trips, perhaps because they're in bustling Ogunquit, Finestkind Scenic Cruises offers hour-long jaunts six times daily from July 1 through Labor Day—9:20, 10:30, and 11:30 a.m. and 1, 2,

and 3 p.m.—and four times daily in the shoulder seasons. Fee is $13 for adults and $8 for kids, who tend to get a big kick out of the whole thing.

FIRST CHANCE
4 Western Ave.,
Lower Village, Kennebunk
(207) 967-5507
www.firstchancewhalewatch.com
Kylie Chance's lobster cruise has quite the pedigree, having been written up in *USA Today* and featured on the *Today Show*. The tour takes passengers down the Kennebunk River, past the Bush family compound on Walker Point, and out to the open Atlantic, stopping to haul traps. As the captain and crew bait and haul traps, you'll learn about the lifecycle of lobsters, their habits, loves, and hates, as well as the fishing industry and its importance to Maine. Added bonuses are trips to Bumpkin Island to see seabird colonies and fat seals, and a bit of lore about Kennebunk port to boot. All for $20. The hour-and-a-half runs ship out at 10 a.m. and noon, 2 p.m., and 4 p.m. daily from Memorial Day through Columbus Day.

LUCKY CATCH
170 Commercial St., Portland
(207) 761-0941
www.luckycatch.com
They don't come out of the water red. That's one of the many things you'll learn on a cruise with the *Lucky Catch*, a 37-foot lobster boat that works out of Portland Harbor, carrying passengers in summer and lobstering in the winter. The appeal of these 90-minute tours is that they trace a variety of scenic routes while stopping to pull and reset 10 or so traps. The 10:30 a.m. and 2 p.m. tours head over to Portland Head Light, the 12:15 p.m. and 3:45 p.m. go to ledges known for their seal populations, and in July and August there's an additional run to White Head. The trips are $22 for adults, $14 for kids, and perhaps best of all, if you call ahead, you can buy a "mess of bugs" (lobsters) for your dinner.

ATLANTIC SEAL CRUISES
25 Main St., South Freeport
(207) 865-6112
Captain Tom Ring hauls a trap on his narrated tour of Casco Bay, just one of the many offerings of Freeport-based Atlantic Seal Cruises (see the section Boat Rides and Day Sails earlier in this chapter). Tours are offered on a daily basis in summer (late May through October).

LIVELY LADY TOO
Bayview Landing, Camden
(207) 236-6672
www.livelyladytoo.com
A former biology teacher, Captain Alan Philbrick knows his way about the marine environment, and he offers passengers aboard his lobster boat, the *Lively Lady Too,* a lively question-and-answer session while checking traps on the magnificent waters of Penobscot Bay. Binoculars and cameras are recommended on this trip, as seals, eagles, ospreys, sea ducks, and other seabirds are often spotted. Three trips are done daily in summer at 10:30 a.m., 1 p.m., and 3 p.m.

OLD QUARRY OCEAN ADVENTURES
130 Settlement Rd., Stonington
(207) 367-8977
www.oldquarry.com
Lobstering aboard the *Nigh Duck* is just one of the zillions of trips and tours offered by Old Quarry. Help haul traps if you like—or just sit back and watch, learn, and enjoy the spectacular scenery off Stonington. The boat heads out at 9 a.m. sharp and returns at about noon on Monday, Tuesday, Thursday, Friday, and Saturday. Adults are $40, children age 11 or younger $24.

LULU LOBSTER BOAT RIDE
Golden Anchor Pier, Bar Harbor
(207) 963-2341 or (866) 235-2341
www.lululobsterboat.com
Lobster boxing? Captain John Nicolai will explain what that is if you step aboard *Lulu,* his traditional lobster boat based in Bar Harbor, for a cruise out into Frenchman Bay. He'll explain all sorts of neat facts about everyone's favorite crustaceans—that they smell with their leg hairs, for example—while hauling and baiting traps. The trips clock in at close to two hours, they're very informative, and they're the only lobstering cruises out of Bar Harbor. From June 14 to August 19 they depart daily at 10 a.m. and 1 p.m., 3:30 p.m., and 6 p.m., and while they are still offered on Sundays, no actual traps are hauled. Fare is $30 for adults, $27 for seniors, $17 for kids age 11 or younger.

SEA KAYAKING

It's surprising that the sea kayaking explosion in Maine took until the 1980s to happen, because the long, skinny vessels are perfect for navigating the myriad coves, inlets, salt marshes, and island-studded bays Down East. But boom it did, and now kayak outfitters are ubiquitous, almost as common as lobster shacks on the state's shoreline. You can buy boats, rent boats, and, if you're new to the sport, learn how to paddle properly at locales from Kittery to Calais. And a host of guide services take guests out on tours. The state requires that kayak guides be licensed, and thus all of your hosts will be genuine Registered Maine Guides, who have to pass tough written and oral exams to earn their red-and-green badges. The tours they offer might be two-hour get-to-know-me harbor paddles for beginners, half-day expeditions, or overnight voyages. There are few better ways to experience the Maine coast than being right down in it.

South Coast
HARBOR ADVENTURES
P.O. Box 345, York Harbor 03911
(207) 363-8466
Based in York Harbor, Harbor Adventures explores the coast from New Hampshire to the Kennebunks. This outfitter regularly schedules two-hour turns around York Harbor ($45), half-day tours ($60), and lobster luncheons up Chauncey Creek ($60), and sunset tours ($45). The company also does four-hour introductory courses ($70) that focus on types of boats, strokes, safety, and rescue.

EXCURSIONS COASTAL MAINE OUTFITTING COMPANY
Route 1, Cape Neddick
(207) 363-0181
www.excursionsinmaine.com

"Wanna get paddled?" That's the slogan of Coastal Maine Outfitting Company in York, and to that end it offers half-day paddles along area gunkholes, leaving at 8:30 a.m. and 1:30 p.m. and launching wherever conditions are best. These trips are $60 for adults and $50 for kids 13 and under.

WORLD WITHIN SEA KAYAKING
746 Ocean Ave., Wells
(207) 646-0455
www.worldwithin.com

With the great Rachel Carson National Wildlife Refuge marshes in its backyard, World Within has a prime playground. The most popular outing here is the Ogunquit River Plantation tour, which is designed for novice kayakers and doesn't venture out onto the open ocean, but the company also does sunrise, sunset, and full-moon trips. The plantation tour is $70 per person.

GONE WITH THE WIND
Yates St., Biddeford
(207) 283-8446
www.gwtonline.com

Frankly, you'll give a damn about Gone with the Wind's kayak tours, especially if you are at all hesitant about kayaking, intrigued by the sport but maybe a little nervous. The guides here take clients out in small groups, they use "umiaks," very stable open-topped kayaks, and they paddle in the protected waters of Biddeford Pool in Saco, which are usually placid. Favorite routes include trips to Wood Island Light, a beacon built in the early 1800s, and to Beach Island, where there is a colony of charismatic seals.

Greater Portland

MAINE ISLAND KAYAK COMPANY
70 Luther St., Peaks Island
(207) 766-2373
www.maineislandkayak.com

Tom Bergh is the kind of guy you want to go to sea with. He's been a guide for most of his life (mountaineering, backcountry skiing, river running, and hiking), and since 1986 he's been ensconced on Casco Bay's Peaks Island, where he runs Maine Island Kayak Company, aka MIKCO, among the biggest and best outfitters in the state. His slate at MIKCO is amazingly full: Bergh and his guides offer all manner of sea kayak trips, from half-day introductory paddles to full-on expeditions to points east. Amazing stuff. MIKCO also has its own Ocean School, where you can learn all things kayak.

L.L. BEAN OUTDOOR DISCOVERY SCHOOLS
3 Bow St., Freeport
(888) 552-3261
www.llbean.com/outdoorsOnline

Who better to take you out sea kayaking than L.L. Bean, which practically invented the outdoors? As part of its Outdoor Discovery program, Bean provides half-, one-, and two-day kayak schools, as well as three-day trips on Casco Bay, where you'll paddle in tandem kayaks by day, learning your way around the sport, and spend evenings at the company's Casco Bay Island Base Camp ($475). Call or visit the outfitter's excellent Web site for all of the options.

Midcoast

SEASPRAY KAYAKING
New Meadows River, Brunswick
(888) 349-SPRAY
www.seaspraykayaking.com

Growing like a rogue wave, Seaspray now has centers at four Midcoast locations, including its original base on the stunning New Meadows. It has a raft of kayaking options, among them bed-and-breakfast tours, moonlight paddles, and introductory splashabouts. But their coolest trip might be the one they do in search of the Midcoast's famed stripers, or striped bass. That's right, fishing from a kayak. You cast and catch right from the cockpit, and all tackle and techniques are provided. These tours are $85 per person, which includes a half-day kayak rental. See the Web site for details.

H2OUTFITTERS
P.O. Box 72, Orrs Island 04066
(207) 833-5257 or (800) 205-2925
www.h2outfitters.com
One of the oldest and best outfits on the kayak scene, H2Outfitters has its "galactic headquarters" on Orrs Island south of Brunswick (with satellite outposts in New Jersey, Pennsylvania, and North and South Carolina). H2O provides anything and everything you could want in the way of sea kayak instruction as well as multiday voyages along the coast. One of the more unique offerings is the Bed and Breakfast Trip, during which you stay at the some of the Acadia area's most fun inns—and paddle a variety of coves, bays, and islands around the park over the course of three days. This package costs $1,595 per person, based on double occupancy, and occurs several times during the summer. Call or visit the Web site for the complete list of adventures.

FROZEN PADDLER
271 Old Bath Rd., Wiscasset
(207) 882-9066
www.frozenpaddler.com
A spirited explorer who's out in all kinds of weather, Kurt Geib specializes in custom fitting tours to clients. He'll take people on half-day tours on the Sheepscot River, full-day paddles around Midcoast islands, or anywhere else you'd like to explore. He'll tote along some food, too, and he'll bring "other types of toys to play with." Two-hour tours, which he recommends for families, are $35, four hours are $75, and daylong outings are $95. As he says, "We have some ideas, but yours might be better. Let us see what we can come up with." Geib's a neat character. He might even quote some Zappa for you.

TIDAL TRANSIT
18 Granary Way, Boothbay Harbor
(207) 633-7140
www.kayakboothbay.com
Tidal Transit's been at it since the late 1980s, and it has a handful of fine offerings. Based in Boothbay Harbor, the outfitter's guides paddle out to Burnt Island Lighthouse, where they stop for a stroll ($35); they venture into prime marine mammal and bird territory in search of seals, herons, ospreys, and eagles on the Wildlife Tour ($40); and they paddle against a backdrop of lovely reds and yellows at the dimming of the day on the Sunset Tour ($35). Most of these paddles are in the two-hour range, and all gear is included. Reservations are required, so call ahead.

MAINE KAYAK
113 Huddle Rd., New Harbor
(866) 624-6352
www.mainekayak.com
Alvah Maloney has built himself quite the kayak empire, offering saltwater based trips from his Pemaquid Peninsula home—which gives great access to both John's and Muscongus Bays—and whitewater stuff up north. Muscongus especially is one of the nicest places to paddle in Maine (if not the world) and Maloney puts it to good use. He has half-day, full-day, and overnight trips that end the day either on an island or at an inn. Explore the options at his site.

BREAKWATER KAYAK
8 Mill St., Rockland
(207) 596-6895 or (877) 559-8800
www.breakwaterkayak.com
Founded by Mark DiGirolamo, Breakwater Kayak specializes in natural history tours, using Penobscot and Muscongus Bays as their campus. When he's not guiding, DiGirolamo spends his time working on birding projects for the Maine Department of Inland Fisheries and Wildlife or teaching in the local schools, so he knows of what he speaks when he takes you out for his daylong natural history tour. Birds are an obvious interest, and you can expect to spot ospreys, eagles, and warblers, as well as seals, and the trip always includes an exploration of the intertidal zone. The natural history tour pushes off at 9 a.m., returns at 4 p.m., and costs $110 per person. Breakwater Kayak also takes paddlers out to the mile-long breakwater for which it's named, to Owls Head Light, and around busy Camden Harbor. Camping excursions are another possibility.

Close-up

Maine Island Trail

Often referred to as the Appalachian Trail of the sea, the Maine Island Trail was founded in 1987, a 350-mile ocean corridor from Portland to Machias. More than 80 islands lie along the route, and, by arrangement with state and local officials and with private citizens, they can be used as overnight stops, allowing boaters to hop from one to the next almost the length of the Maine coast. The trail is principally used by sea kayakers, who make voyages both long and short along it, paddling by day, camping out by night like so many Robinson Crusoes, and enjoying a quasi-wild go of it. There's nothing quite like waking up amid the peaceful pines of a small, uninhabited island and basking in the serenity of the shore.

The Maine Island Trail Association (MITA), a nonprofit conservation organization, governs the use of the trail and publishes the only guide that lets you know which islands are open to the public. The outfit was founded to try to mitigate the overuse and abuse of islands by boaters, and it has imposed some guidelines to prevent such occurrences, from restricting the use of certain spots during seabird nesting seasons to encouraging low-impact camping. It's a worthy cause, and in recent years, despite the best efforts of MITA, there's been ever-growing concern that paddlers and boaters are loving the islands to death.

For more information contact the Maine Island Trail Association at (207) 761-8225 or visit www.mita.org. Membership, which gets you a copy of the trail guide, is $45 a year.

MAINE SPORT OUTFITTERS
Route 1, Rockport
(207) 236-8797 or (800) 722-0826
www.mainesport.com

On any given day in summer, the parking lot at Maine Sport is chock-full, and many of these cars belong to people out kayaking somewhere. Maine Sport has been guiding since 1976 and is single-handedly responsible for introducing thousands of people to the wonderful world of paddling. This outfitter has a calendar full of options. Some of the more popular outings include the Camden Harbor tour, a paddle around the protected haven known for its mountain views, lighthouse, windjammers, mega-yachts, and summer homes ($35); and the Harbor to Harbor Tour, which takes you from Rockport Harbor, once home of Andre the Seal, on up to Camden Harbor, stopping at Curtis Island for a picnic lunch ($75). Multiday trips, like the two-day island cottage trip to Muscongus Bay ($295), are another possibility, and there is no end to the instruction available. Visit Maine Sport online or in person for all the details.

DUCKTRAP SEA KAYAK TOURS
Route 1, Lincolnville
(207) 236-8608

The guides at this oldie but goody push off from Ducktrap Beach for tours out into the wilds of Penobscot Bay. They'll follow the coast to Belfast, work back Camden way, or head out into the deep water toward the long green island of Islesboro. Dolphins, seals, and loons are common paddling companions. Families with young children are often taken to the more placid waters of Megunticook Lake. Reservations are required and rates vary. Call for details.

WATER WALKER KAYAK TOURS
Route 52, Belfast
(207) 338-6424
www.touringkayaks.com

Registered Maine Guide Ray Wirth likes to give paddlers a lot of choices, and he has quite the menu to select from on his Web site. Two- or three-hour trips might include paddles around Belfast or Rockport or Blue Hill Harbor, Sears

Island, or Camden's Lake Megunticook. Half-day trips might be outings to Moose or Fort Points; to Flat, Ram, Seal, or Warren Islands; or to Camden or Owls Head. Full-day outings could be excursions to Islesboro, Great Spruce, Butter, or the Muscle Ridge Islands, or an exploration of Muscongus Bay. It's all up to the client, and Wirth is an accommodating and accomplished host. Rates depend on the number of people in the group—the more people the cheaper the individual cost.

CASTINE KAYAK ADVENTURES
Dennett's Wharf, Castine
(207) 866-3506
www.castinekayak.com
Castine Kayak Adventures are worth seeking out if only because they bring you to Castine, one of Maine's prettiest towns. Of course, these trips are quite something in and of themselves. Castine Kayak's overnights are particularly appealing, and they have three itineraries to choose from and are willing to customize, too. You might try the one- or two-night Exploration of Bagaduce Estuary, an inner waterway known for its reversing currents, islands, and seal haul-outs (this trip even features paddles to several restaurants), or the more ambitious 3-mile Paddle to Warren Island, a crossing of Penobscot Bay to the state park on Warren Island. The coolest offering, though, has to be the Bioluminescent night paddle ($55), which gets you up close and personal to the constellations of glowing critters in the Maine waters on some evenings.

OLD QUARRY OCEAN ADVENTURES
130 Settlement Rd., Stonington
(207) 367-8977
www.oldquarry.com
The 60-island archipelago off Stonington is the seascape worked by the guides of Old Quarry. An outdoor institution on Deer Isle, Old Quarry has a campground, provides sail and motorboat charters, rents bikes, and even does camping trips. The outfitter also offers full-day ($105) and half-day ($55) outings in single and tandem kayaks from June through September.

Acadia Area
COASTAL KAYAKING TOURS
48 Cottage St., Bar Harbor
(207) 288-9605 or (800) 526-8615
www.acadiafun.com
You can't walk down a street in Bar Harbor without bumping into someone toting a kayak paddle these days. Coastal Kayaking is one of the companies responsible for the proliferation of the sport, and the folks here take kayakers out like clockwork to paddle the pristine waters around Acadia National Park. Their half-day tour ($48) is popular, covering about 5 miles of coastline and featuring narration about the natural and geological history of Mount Desert Island, but you might also consider the two-hour harbor tour ($38), the 10-mile full-day tour ($69), or even the solo tour, which is a personalized outing geared toward improving paddling skills ($72). There are many other options as well. Call or see the Web site to find out more.

NATIONAL PARK SEA KAYAK TOURS
39 Cottage St., Bar Harbor
(800) 347-0940
www.acadiakayak.com
The name says it all with National Park Sea Kayak—though not officially affiliated with Acadia National Park, the outfitter uses the waters off the park as its playground. Depending upon the weather conditions and tides, the company's half-day or sunset tours might explore 5 or 6 miles of Frenchman, Western, Eastern, and Blue Hill Bays or Somes Sound. Departure times for the four-hour tours are at 8, 9, and 10:30 a.m. and 1, 2:30, and 4 p.m. The outfitter has a sunset paddle in the evening, too, and occasionally offers multiday expeditions. This is one of the oldest outfitters on Mount Desert, and it has gotten sea kayaking down to a science.

MAINE STATE SEA KAYAK GUIDE SERVICE
254 Maine St., Southwest Harbor
(207) 244-9500 or (877) 481-9500
www.mainestatekayak.com
A couple of major magazines (*National Geographic*

Adventure and *Travel + Leisure*) have given this outfit the nod in the past, and its good reputation might be due to 20-plus years of experience. Its specialty is introducing new paddlers to this graceful game, and its guides use the waters off Southwest Harbor to that end, regularly paddling five or six different routes, depending upon weather, tides, and clients. Half-day trips, giving you four hours of kayaking and instruction—a good taste—are $48 per person. They're available from mid-May through mid-October.

Down East

MOOSELOOK GUIDE SERVICE
Route 186, Gouldsboro
(207) 963-7223
www.mooselookguideservice.com
Though its name makes it sound more like an up-country outfit, Mooselook is actually based in the pretty coastal town of Gouldsboro, and while the guides here do offer canoe trips down the Narraguagus River, they do most of their work in the Schoodic area. The big blue expanse of Arcadia National Park, with its spruce-topped isles, pink granite ledges, seals, dolphins, and seabirds, is the setting for their half-day trips, which are open to novices as well as experienced paddlers. Individual or tandem kayaks can be used. Mooselook also offers some unique kayak-camping options, from the Honeymoon Special—during which a guide will paddle you out to a quiet island, make you dinner, and then leave you to your own delights, returning to make you breakfast—and a two-day, two-night trip for those interested in more time in the cockpit. Mooselook works every day in summer. Call for a reservation.

GREEN SPACE

The Maine coast may be largely developed these days, but thankfully, a lot of shoreline has been preserved over the centuries. From Kittery to Quoddy, there are miles and miles of forest to explore, many mountains to hike, routes to bike, gardens to enjoy, and unique nature preserves to visit. Outdoor adventurers will find no end of things to do and will have to come back again and again before they begin to see half of what the state has to offer.

Some of the finest stretches of green space on the coast are managed by the federal government or by the state, either as parks or public lands. There are 19 coastal state parks, and they provide visitors with truly great hiking (see Camden Hills or Quoddy Head in this chapter), exceptional swimming and sunbathing (see earlier Beaches chapter), and fine picnicking on the shore. The U.S. Fish and Wildlife Service has a handful of reserves along the waterfront, including the Rachel Carson, Petit Manan, and Moosehorn National Wildlife Refuges.

Other great recreation areas are overseen by conservation outfits. Maine Audubon has several properties, as does the Nature Conservancy. Even small local groups like the Damariscotta River Association, the Boothbay Region Land Trust, and the Georges River Land Trust have made their marks on the state, saving spectacular parcels of land from becoming condo communities or making arrangements with landowners to allow public use. All of this effort has resulted in an array of nature preserves and gardens.

You'll surely run out of time before you run out of places to explore.

ISLES OF SHOALS

Nine miles off the coasts of Maine and New Hampshire lie these nine islands, the site of early fishing activity in the 1600s and later divided up between the two states (Maine got five, New Hampshire four). Among the more romanticized islands off the Pine Tree State, they're remote, largely unchanged, and hard to get to, but Star and Appledore Islands once had grand hotels on them, were colonized by Unitarians, and allow limited visitation. Appledore was home to famed poet Celia Thaxter, who built beautiful gardens and entertained the literati, and people make the pilgrimage out to see her blooming beds. The **Isles of Shoals Steamship Company** (315 Market Street, Portsmouth; 603-431-5500 or 800-441-4620; www.islesofshoals.com) cruises to the islands all summer long.

With the price of gas volatile as ever, the East Coast Greenway will surely take on a new urgency. The trail will eventually link Maine to Florida, connecting bike paths and walkways and providing walkers, joggers, and cyclists with a "super-highway" of sorts, free of automobiles. Maine already has several sections in place. Find out more at www.exploremaine.org/bike/greenway.html.

PARKS, PATHWAYS, AND PRESERVES

South Coast

VAUGHN WOODS STATE PARK
28 Oldsfields Rd., South Berwick
(207) 490-4079
Famed writer Sarah Orne Jewett grew up not too

far from these woods, and one has to wonder how often the nature-loving author wandered the 250 acres here along the Salmon Falls River. If she were here today, she'd find much hasn't changed—at least at this small spot. The old-growth stands of pine and hemlock are still standing tall, and there are still nice looks at the Salmon Falls River. Handy to the Yorks, Ogunquit, Kittery, and points in New Hampshire, Vaughn Woods is, just as its name suggests, a woodland preserve, and it's rarely crowded, used more by locals than tourists. The spot makes a nice diversion or picnic setting when visiting the historic sites in the Berwicks—like Jewett's home.

CLIFF WALK
York Harbor
The equal of Ogunquit's famous Marginal Way or Bar Harbor's well-known Shore Path, the Cliff Walk is an extraordinary footpath that walks the fine line between the distinctive old summer homes of York Harbor and the crashing surf. It's never become as widely talked about as other paths because it has frequently been closed to the public. The walkway, you see, goes right through the backyards of some of the nicest homes in York, ducking under banks of bay windows, passing flower beds, and skirting rows of shrubs, and on occasions in the past, public use has been curtailed due to complaints over vandalism or property rights. But the Cliff Walk is once again open, and it's something to see. You can make the jaunt in less than an hour round-trip, beginning at Harbor Beach and walking to the pebble shore at which the path ends. The panoramas of open sea and smashing surf are as good as you'll see anywhere, and you can scramble along the rocks, peer into tidal pools, and have a very up-close look at some fine homes. About 50 feet above the serrated shoreline in some places and broadside to the open sea, the path threads through bird-filled bushes and little groves of trees, and much of the going is paved or gravel. It's open from 5 a.m. to 6 p.m. No dogs allowed, and don't even think about dropping that candy wrapper—there's a $1,000 fine for littering.

MOUNT AGAMENTICUS
Off Mountain Rd., York
(207) 363-1102
www.agamenticus.org
This 572-foot peak is more of an uppity hill than any sort of self-respecting mountain, but however you look at it, Agamenticus is by far the tallest thing around. As such it makes for a great playground for residents of the South Coast. In summer hikers enjoy the trails up its sides; in autumn, leaf peepers enjoy the prospect from its summit; and in winter it attracts sledders, skiers, and snowboarders galore. The town of York owns the property now, and there's a tangle of antennas at the top, but it's still plenty fun to scramble up.

STEEDMAN WOODS
Old Mill Rd., York Village
Reached by the famous Wiggly Bridge, a suspension span that is indeed wiggly, this 16-acre preserve is owned by the excellent Old York Historical Society, and it's a beauty. Spread across a peninsula between the saltwater Barrells Mill Pond on one side and the York River on the other, the preserve was given to the town's historians by the man it's named after, Charles Richard Steedman, with the proviso that it be kept "forever wild." (He borrowed a page from beloved Maine governor Percival Baxter.) A little plaque on site explains that the area was "the focal point of much of York's history for the first 300 years," and you can understand why early settlers were drawn to the spot. It's very beautiful, and a few trails run around its circumference, allowing for some fine water views and connecting with paths into York Harbor and York Village. You could walk the whole peninsula in a half hour or so, but it's also a nice place to sit and read a book or take a picnic.

MARGINAL WAY
Ogunquit
The best way to get between Perkins Cove and downtown Ogunquit in summer is this mile-long walkway. Forget about driving. Even this path can get elbow to elbow, but it's a lot easier to

take the traffic here than it is out on the street, thanks to fresh sea air and unparalleled vistas of the open ocean. When the going here is quiet, it's positively magical. Try it early in the morning, late at night, or in the off-season. You can get on the path behind the Sparhawk Resort downtown and at Perkins Cove. Along the way you'll see crashing breakers, rocks for scrambling, and tide pools. There are benches where you can pause to catch your breath.

RACHEL CARSON NATIONAL WILDLIFE REFUGE

321 Port Rd., Wells
(207) 646-9226
http://rachelcarson.fws.gov

Rachel Carson is often credited with helping to bring environmental consciousness to the average American with the publication of her landmark book *Silent Spring*. Less known is the fact that Carson spent many years working for the U.S. Fish and Wildlife Service. That same organization honored her years ago by naming its sprawling southern Maine reserve after the author, who did a lot of her work in Maine. Ten parcels on about 5,000 acres of coastline comprise the reserve, spread across towns from Kittery to Cape Elizabeth. (It hopes to be 9,125 acres when current land acquisition projects are completed.) Most are fairly small, purchased to help protect estuarine ecosystems important to migrating birds. A few of these preserves have trail networks and make for good visits. You can pick up a trail guide at the reserve headquarters and get started right here on a mile-long walk through the salt marsh.

WELLS NATIONAL ESTUARINE RESEARCH RESERVE

342 Laudholm Farm Rd., Wells
(207) 646-1555
www.wellsreserve.org

One of the last remaining saltwater farms in southern Maine, Laudholm Farm was saved by local residents years ago, and it now serves as the centerpiece for this 2,250-acre research sanctuary. Seven miles of trails wander through a wide diversity of ecosystems—from forest to sea

dunes to beach to meadow to marsh, and they're open for the public to use every day from 7 a.m. to sunset. Birdwatchers especially love the place, which is habitat to an array of seabirds. Trail maps can be picked up at the entry kiosk or at the visitor center, which is located in the old farm and has exhibits and informational displays. They'll show you where to find the scenic overlooks and how to get to the beach. The informative visitor center is open Monday through Friday from 10 a.m. to 4 p.m. in the off-season and on weekends also from May through October.

WATERBORO BARRENS

Buff Brook Rd., Waterboro
(207) 729-5181

Close to 2,500 acres of pitch pine barrens and scrub oak blanket this unique preserve in the inland town of Waterboro. Just 20 minutes from the coast—Waterboro is next door to York County seat Alfred—the barrens are among the best examples of pitch pine vegetation in the world, and they're owned and managed by the Nature Conservancy. Three trails loop through the scruffy ecosystem, which was caused by poor soils and glacial outwash. Rare and endangered species are concentrated here—an array of turtles, moths, and butterflies, especially near Round and Little Teeny Poverty Ponds—but you'll also see deer, grouse, and, if you're lucky, maybe even a moose. You'll also likely have the trails to yourself as the preserve is one of the least-visited of the Nature Conservancy's properties. It's open year-round, sunup to sunset, and is free.

KENNEBUNK PLAINS

Route 99, Kennebunk
(207) 729-5181

The Nature Conservancy and Maine Department of Inland Fisheries and Wildlife protect 2,000-some subtly beautiful acres, and the conservation outfit tends to be particular about the properties it preserves, so you know it must be special. And it is. Besides being the largest sand plain grassland in New England, it is habitat for a variety of birds that are rarish to endangered in Maine and elsewhere—grasshopper sparrows, horned larks, upland sandpipers, and vesper sparrows. These feathered friends intrigue birders, of course. Anyone who visits in autumn will be impressed by the vast plains of purple that occur when another rare species, the northern blazing star, puts on its September show—acres upon acres of vibrant hues. This used to be commercial blueberrying land, too, so you know a few tasty berries will be around if you time your visit right (that'd be August).

BUTLER AND MARSHALL PRESERVES
Off the Old Port Rd., Kennebunkport
(207) 985-8734
These two green Kennebunk Land Trust reserves frame the lower Kennebunk River. Forested gems, they're reachable by boat or by land. You can paddle a canoe downriver from town or take the Old Port Road 1.7 miles from Kennebunkport to the woods road on the right, which is marked with a KENNEBUNK LAND TRUST sign. Park there and walk in. A nice loop trail will link you to Picnic Rock, a popular spot for just what its name implies (and swimming) in the Butler Preserve, which is covered in red and white pine back from the river. The much larger 181-acre Marshall Preserve is accessed from the River Road in Arundel.

EAST POINT SANCTUARY
Lester B. Orcutt Blvd., Biddeford Pool
(207) 781-2330
www.maineaudubon.org
At the very tip of Biddeford Pool, jutting out into the Atlantic, this Audubon Sanctuary is a must-visit among Maine birders. The 30-acre property is a mixture of open meadow and low shrubs on the shore, and a trail takes you along the waterfront. Commonly spotted birds include gannets, red-throated loons, sea ducks, alcids, and terns. People also often see harbor seals. Open sunrise to sunset, year-round.

SACO HEATH
Buxton Rd., Saco
(207) 729-5181
One of the biggest bogs in Maine—and the southernmost raised peat bog in North America—this 1,000-acre wetland has a lot to recommend it. First, it's simply a bit of open space in a part of the state where that is increasingly difficult to find. Second, it's home to a bunch of rare and endangered species. This is the only place where Atlantic cedar is known to grow in a domed heath, and it's home to the Hessel's hairstreak, an uncommon butterfly, a bunch of cool shrubs and carnivorous plants, and even moose, which are usually found much farther north in Maine. Finally, a mile-long boardwalk makes it all accessible in a way that it never used to be, and the Nature Conservancy, which owns the property, provides maps for a self-guided tour that is worth doing. Autumn is a particularly good time to visit, thanks to glowing expanses of mountain holly and highbush blueberries.

Greater Portland

SCARBOROUGH MARSH
Route 9, Scarborough
(207) 883-5100
The largest salt marsh in Maine lies in one of the most booming towns in the state, the Portland suburb of Scarborough, a place where shopping centers and subdivisions grow like Topsy. So the 3,000-acre estuary is something of a wild oasis. A half dozen small rivers converge in the marsh, making it rich habitat for birds and wildlife, especially during the spring and fall migrations. The Maine Audubon Society manages the site and maintains trails and a nature center where you can rent canoes and kayaks ($15 per hour for nonmembers). Paddling is really the best way to see the marsh, and it truly rewards anyone who launches a boat. Naturalists lead 90-minute tours daily at 10 a.m., which is a great introduction to the estuary, and the center hosts a whole slate of cool programs, like moonlit paddles and early-morning bird tours. The marsh is open to the public from dawn to dusk, year-round.

SCARBOROUGH RIVER WILDLIFE SANCTUARY
Route 9, Scarborough
When you start off down the trail here, just up Route 9 from the wide green expanse of Scarbor-

ough Marsh, all you can hear is cars going by and orders being called out at Ken's Place, a seafood joint, across the street: "One-thirty-nine, please, one-thirty-nine." After a few minutes of walking, though, the traffic noise fades to a quiet hiss—like a waterfall in the distance—and it's eventually replaced by wind in the grass, birdcalls, and the singing of the trees. Then things get very pleasant. The town-owned 56-acre nature preserve is threaded with 1.5 miles of trails—grass, gravel, and dirt—none of which seems particularly well used. The nicest part of a hike through the area, though, is the front seat it gives you on Scarborough Marsh, the state's largest estuary and a truly stunning little bit of sea. Green ocean grasses, swirling rivers of salt water, and the open ocean beyond it fill your field of vision, and you actually have to look around a bit to find signs of civilization. You're sure to see a variety of birds, and perhaps something exotic. Open all year, sunrise to sunset.

TWO LIGHTS STATE PARK
66 Two Lights Rd., Cape Elizabeth
(207) 799-5871

You can look awfully hard for the pair of lighthouses that lent Two Lights State Park its name, but you won't find them in the 41-acre preserve. The first twin lighthouses built on the Maine coast, going up in 1828, they're down a nearby road and are inaccessible. What people will find on this rocky headland are sweeping vistas of Casco Bay, the ruins of a World War II fort, picnic tables, and some trails along the shore. The park is very popular among picnickers, Frisbee tossers, Portland houseguests, and hand-holding

---

i If you're up for a bit of outdoor recreation but can't convince others in your party to come along or are alone, look up the Maine Outdoor Adventure Club in Portland. A big outing club, MOAC sponsors trips several times a week and welcomes newcomers. Call the activity hotline at (207) 775-MOAC or visit www.moac.org for a list of upcoming events.

---

couples, and it's just a skip from Crescent Beach State Park. Hard to beat its prospect of the bay and the open Atlantic.

FORT WILLIAMS
Park Shore Rd., Cape Elizabeth
(207) 799-2868

If you have houseguests and you live in Greater Portland, chances are you'll all end up here at some point. Surrounding Portland Head Light in Cape Elizabeth, town-owned Fort Williams Park is the go-to place for visitors to the area (the place sees nearly a million visitors a year). Ninety-four acres of fun are what we're talking about, a Frisbee thrower's dream. Expansive lawns, some of the best ocean views in Greater Portland, a small waterfront, neat ruins of forts, perfect picnicking facilities, tennis courts, and ball fields—the park has a lot to like. And more than a million people a year take advantage of it.

Commissioned in 1894, Fort Williams was integral to keeping Portland Harbor safe in the Second World War, but it was deemed unnecessary in the wake of the conflict and was decommissioned in 1963. The town purchased it shortly thereafter. What's left of the actual fortifications are interesting to explore. Hardly a day goes by, year-round, that someone isn't having fun at Fort Williams.

CAPE ELIZABETH TRAILS
Cape Elizabeth Land Trust,
330 Ocean House Rd., Cape Elizabeth
(207) 767-6054
www.capelandtrust.org

Who knew Portland's affluent neighbor had so many nice hiking paths? Like a much smaller sibling of Portland Trails, the Cape Elizabeth Land Trust has preserved several parcels of land and opened them to walkers. The best of these might be the Robinson Woods Trail, which meanders for 3 miles in a bosk just to the west of the Shore Road. Some of the woods in question are more than 300 years old, and they connect to shorefront on Pond Cove. Other highlights might be the Cross Hill and Dyer-Hutchinson Farm trails, which intersect and provide miles of walking through forest, marsh, and meadow.

SPRING POINT SHOREWAY
Southern Maine Community College
Broadway, South Portland

Some of the best looks you'll get at Portland Harbor and Casco Bay can be found along this 3-mile seaside path on the campus of Southern Maine Community College. The trail connects some of the finest things South Portland has to offer. It begins at the Spring Point Ledge Light on one end and ends at Willard Beach on the other, going through the Spring Point Arboretum and connecting to the South Portland Greenway, from which point you can go just about anywhere. You'll get a self-guided tour of what's left of Fort Preble, see more forts and islands in the bay, and have a great prospect on the Portland skyline. Tourists don't generally find the walkway, but they probably should.

BACK COVE TRAIL
Portland

Not exactly a park, Back Cove Trail is a 3.5-mile, multi-use path that rings the city's Back Cove. Used by hundreds daily for walking, jogging, and biking, it is paved and it offers a great look back at the skyline of the city. Thanks to the good works of Portland Trails (see Close-up), it also connects to other great trail networks. Park in the Forest Avenue Hannaford parking lot.

BAXTER WOODS
Forest Ave., Portland

A 30-acre sanctuary between Forest and Stevens Avenues, Baxter Woods was donated to the city by former governor Percival Baxter—the same man who gave the state its wilderness treasure Baxter State Park. This place is no Katahdin, but its short trails are pleasantly shaded by some white oak and hemlock, which are good examples of the Forest City's early forest. A nice place to walk yourself and your dog.

DEERING OAKS
Park and Forest Ave.s, Portland
(207) 874-8793

Portland's nickname is the Forest City, and the 51 acres of Deering Oaks Park make the name at least a little bit fitting. The city's best-known park, Deering is a classic, and there are more than 1,000 trees on its grounds, including stands of red and white oaks, and three giants—a pin oak, a Siberian elm, and a yellowwood—on the state's list of big trees. A swath of green space between the highway and downtown, the park wouldn't be confused with a real forest, composed mostly of wide open lawns. With its grassy spaces, ponds, fountains, and recreation areas, it's the picture of a city park and has been voted best place to recreate many times by the readers of local papers.

And people recreate here en masse. Quite aside from the usual park entertainments of strolling, dog walking, and Frisbee tossing, there are a host of things to do. Eleven tennis courts, several basketball courts, and a ball field beckon to athletes; paddleboats and ducks attract children; there are rose gardens and a Saturday farmers' market to appeal to adults; and there are regularly scheduled events, from weekly concerts to the Deering Oaks Family Festival, that take place here every summer.

EASTERN AND WESTERN PROMENADES
Portland

Flanking the Portland Peninsula are two long grassy open spaces—the proms. Both loft up over the city's waterfront, the Eastern Prom offering exceptional views of Casco Bay and its islands and forts and the Western Prom overlooking the Fore River and beyond it the White Mountains. The pair are pleasant to walk, and there are some fine trails along the Eastern Promenade as well as access to Fort Allen Park, another nice place to mosey and relax.

The Western Prom, the street that fronts the green, is rightly famous for its Victorian architecture.

i Get halfway around the 1.5-mile trail that circumnavigates Mackworth Island, and you'll hardly believe you're just outside of Portland. Reached by a causeway off U.S. Route 1, the Falmouth island is a fantastic place to hike and enjoy Casco Bay.

Close-up

Portland Trails

Portland Trails at 305 Commercial Street is the best friend a Portland outdoorsperson ever had. A dynamic conservation outfit dedicated to creating greenways in the state's largest urban area, Portland Trails is responsible for many of the best places to walk in the Forest City. The group was founded in 1991, and it picked up where turn-of-the-20th-century urban planners left off. Former mayor James Phinney Baxter had hired the Olmsted brothers, the famed landscape architects, to come up with drawings connecting several of the city's parks with walkways. The project never was finished. Portland Trails is doing the work now.

And what a job they've done. In only a decade they've accomplished 14 miles of greenways, helping to establish a network of 23 trails in town. Ever-popular Back Cove is now linked to a trail along the Eastern Promenade, you can even cross a footbridge over into Falmouth, and they've helped create the trails on the 60-acre Presumpscot Preserve. The Portland map is all green and squiggly with their handiwork. The organization's goal is to create a 50-mile network of trails that allows people to walk clear across the city—and beyond. You can find maps, trail descriptions, plans for the future, and more on the group's Web site, www.trails .org, or call (207) 775-2411.

FORE RIVER SANCTUARY
Congress St., Portland

A beautiful spot where the Fore River begins to get marshy, this 85-acre preserve is owned by the Maine Audubon Society (207-781-2330), and it's popular with walkers and birds. Three and a half miles of walking trails meander along an estuary where hawks and warblers and seabirds can often be seen. Another treat is Jewell Falls, an actual waterfall within the city limits, which is something to see. Park at the Maine Orthopaedic Center, where Portland Trails has carved out access.

GILSLAND FARM
20 Gilsland Farm Rd., Falmouth
(207) 781-2330

It's somewhat surprising to find such a peaceful sanctuary in the town just to the north of the state's largest city, but then these 65 acres are the headquarters of Maine Audubon Society, so it makes a certain amount of sense. Still, 2.5 miles of trails wandering through woods and meadows and along the banks of marshes isn't what you expect scant minutes from downtown Portland. The beauty of the former cow farm is the diversity

of habitats—visitors can tromp through fields, explore woods, skirt a pond, and stand on the edge of a salt marsh on the three primary trails. Also on-site is the Gilsland Farm Environmental Center, where the society maintains three classrooms, and the Nature Store, where you can pick up those great Audubon field guides. The property is open from dawn to dusk, seven days a week, year-round. The center is open Monday through Saturday from 9 a.m. to 5 p.m. and Sunday from 1 to 4 p.m. year-round. Free.

MILL CREEK PRESERVE
Route 88, Falmouth
(207) 729-5181

Along with the neighboring preserve owned by the town of Falmouth, the Nature Conservancy's Mill Creek property protects some 50 acres of marsh on Casco Bay. There are trails on the town side, which make for great hiking through the woods and down to the water. Popular with great blue herons and snowy egrets, the preserve is enjoyed by those people savvy enough to find it. Take State Route 88 past the Falmouth Pumping Station and park in the next parking lot.

PINELAND PUBLIC RESERVED LAND
Gray Depot Rd., Gray
(207) 778-8231
Greater Portland kids were once creeped out by Pineland, which used to be a mental institution in the town of New Gloucester. Combined with the novels of Stephen King, some of which took place not far away in Durham, you had the grist for some pre-adolescent nightmares. The center closed years ago, and the state subsequently turned the 600 surrounding acres into a reserve for outdoor recreation. Thank goodness it did. Three miles of trails explore the old farm pasture and forest along the Royal River here, a refuge for deer, fox, hare, grouse, and a wide variety of other birds, and it's become something of a haven for walkers and hikers, too. A very pleasant place to walk, and not all that scary, either.

BRADBURY MOUNTAIN STATE PARK
528 Hallowell Rd., Pownal
(207) 688-4712
Bradbury Mountain isn't much of a mountain. At 462 feet, it's really a tall hill, and you can practically run up to its summit. But the little peak here, set between Lewiston and Portland and a skip from Freeport, has a truly great panorama at its top. Look in one direction and you can take in the distant seas of Casco Bay, turn in another and enjoy a look at the White Mountains of New Hampshire. For the amount of effort you expend getting to the top—the trail is less than a half mile—the vistas are incredible. The park in which the mountain sits is a 610-acre gem, one of Maine's original state parks, founded in 1939. Open all year, 9 a.m. to sunset.

MAST LANDING SANCTUARY
Upper Mast Landing Rd., Freeport
(207) 781-2330
www.maineaudubon.org
An Audubon sanctuary, this 140-acre refuge is popular with walkers and nature lovers. There are 3.5 miles of trails that thread through open fields, apple orchards, hemlock forest, and alder lowlands, and Mill Stream pours over an old dam and mill site. The preserve was so named because the Royal Navy used to use it as a source for its ship masts. Today you'll find few mast agents but a lot of songbirds and, if you visit in summer, a lot of schoolkids who go to a day camp here. Open sunrise to sunset.

WOLFE'S NECK WOODS STATE PARK
425 Wolfe's Neck Rd., Freeport
(207) 865-4465
One of the best-kept secrets in Freeport, Wolfe's Neck Woods is a marked departure from the retail madness of Bow and Main Streets downtown, and relatively few of the town's visitors ever find it. A forested preserve of 230 acres overlooking Casco Bay, the park is a fine mix of woods and water, with tide pools and salt marsh and estuaries. Five miles of trails—try the Casco Bay or Small Bog Trails—explore the beautiful meeting of sea and shore, along both the bay and the Harraseeket River, and interpretive signposts at various points clue you in on what you're seeing. Nearby Googins, Eagle, and Cousins Islands can be spotted, and there is an active osprey colony on Googins that's fun to scope out. Bird-watchers often search for seabirds here, and it's popular among families and picnickers.

Midcoast
ANDROSCOGGIN RIVER BICYCLE PATH
Water St. to Cooks Corner, Brunswick
When this 2.5-mile paved walkway was opened in 1998, town officials had no idea that it would be so successful. Right along the Androscoggin River, the path enjoyed heavy use from the outset and became a national model for other community paths. People use it to commute to and from work, to walk or jog, to sit on the benches and scan the skies for eagles, or even to, yes, bicycle. Fourteen feet wide, it's perfect for that. You can hop on at Water Street or Grover Lane.

BOOTHBAY REGION LAND TRUST PRESERVES
Boothbay Area
(207) 633-4818
www.bbrlt.org
It can be hard to find just a moment of quietude in Boothbay Harbor in summer, when the community is swarming with people. There are a handful of nature preserves, though, where you can enjoy a bit of peace among the madness. Twelve refuges are available on the mainland—there are a couple offshore as well—and they protect some 1,700 acres of prime real estate. Each has its own character, and all are within 10 miles of the busy harbor. The Ovens Mouth Preserve is the biggest at 150 acres, spread across three peninsulas where the Cross River meets the Back River, and you can look out at tidal coves and salt marshes from its network of trails. The Linekin Preserve is also on a river, the Damariscotta, and is home to 2.5 miles of trails. There's a small beach on the Sheepscot River at the Porter Preserve. The Kitzi Colby Wildlife Preserve, once the site of both saltworks and ice-works, is now a great birding area, thanks to its marsh habitat. You can pick up a map with information about all the preserves at the chamber or call the land trust and they'll hook you up.

HAMILTON SANCTUARY
Fosters Point Rd., West Bath
(207) 781-2330
www.maineaudubon.org
These 74 acres were given to Maine Audubon by local resident Millicent Hamilton. A 1.5-mile system of trails explores the peninsula on which the sanctuary sits, surrounded by the New Meadows River. These paths will take you across meadows, through a pine forest, past a former ice pond, and out to the river, known for its populations of ospreys, blue herons, snowy egrets, and horseshoe crabs. Open all year from sunrise to sunset.

JOSEPHINE NEWMAN SANCTUARY
Route 127, Woolwich
(207) 781-2330
www.maineaudubon.org
Twenty interpretive signs lead you along 2 miles of trails through this 119-acre preserve, pointing out all of the natural features you pass, from glacial erratics to reversing falls. A mature mixed forest covers much of the property, but you'll also find a beaver pond, brooks, a cattail marsh, and the tidal shore of Robinhood Cove. A booklet called "Forest, Fields, and Estuaries" will inform your self-guided hike if you pick up a copy ahead of time. Contact Maine Audubon. Open year-round, from sunrise to sunset.

ROBERT P. TRISTRAM COFFIN WILDFLOWER SANCTUARY
Route 128, Woolwich
Known by hardly a soul, this 180-acre preserve owned by the New England Wildflower Society is a wonderland filled with 200 species of flowers, grasses, trees, and shrubs. The sanctuary was named in honor of the Brunswick-born poet, who won a Pulitzer for his 1936 book *Strange Holiness*. Quite aside from the pretty flowers, the preserve features some nice walking in cobbled coves and hemlock stands.

DAMARISCOTTA LAKE STATE PARK
8 State Park Rd., Jefferson
(207) 549-7600
(207) 941-4014 (off season)
Sand beaches come in many shapes and sizes in Maine. This fine little strand isn't a salty one on the coast in Damariscotta; rather, it's on the very long lake of the same name. Drive Route 213 inland to the neat village of Jefferson, and you'll find the big brown state park sign marking the entrance. The park itself is tiny—only 17 acres—but it's very popular, especially with families. The swimming is good in the cul-de-sac of a lake, lifeguards are on duty to look after bathers, there are picnic tables and grills set up for après-dip dogs and burgers, and a field and playground provide a place for the kids to romp. Good, basic summer fun.

DAMARISCOTTA RIVER ASSOCIATION
109–110 Belvedere Rd., Damariscotta
(207) 563-1393
www.draclt.org
Founded in 1973, this little conservation orga-

nization has done a fantastic job helping to preserve the finest parcels of open space in the Damariscotta area, and it now manages more than 2,900 acres and 22 miles of shoreline. Many people have heard of the Damariscotta Shell Middens, big heaps of oyster shells discarded centuries ago by natives on holiday, but few have visited them. Step along on the Salt Bay Heritage Trail, and soon you'll find yourself staring up at them. Even if you have no interest in archaeology, the trail, which begins across from the Lincoln County Publishing Building, a skip from the Damariscotta exit off Route 1, is a beautiful 3-mile walk that skirts photogenic Great Salt Bay. On the other side of the bay is the Salt Bay Farm Heritage Center, a pretty old farm on Belvedere Road that serves as the River Association's headquarters, and there are miles of trails through the surrounding 100 acres of hills and meadows and down to the river behind it. It's open from dawn to dusk. Finally, off of old Route 1, just up the road from Hannaford, is the Whaleback Park, another great walk through eight acres of wide-open fields and down by the water.

DODGE POINT PUBLIC RESERVED LAND
River Rd., Newcastle
(207) 778-8231

The state acquired these 521 acres on the Damariscotta River in 1989, and people have been flocking to Dodge Point ever since. Why? The Damariscotta is a very scenic, wide saltwater river, and this piece of property has more than a mile of frontage. A few trails and an old woods road go here and there on lands that used to be an old tree farm, and they make good use of the river and its pocket beaches. Plans are to connect it with a new River Link trail to the nearby Sheepscot River, creating a long natural corridor extending all the way to Boothbay. Open from dawn to dusk.

RACHEL CARSON SALT POND AND
LA VERNA PRESERVES
Route 32 New Harbor, Bristol
(207) 677-2423

These two Nature Conservancy properties protect 189 acres along Muscongus Bay. The Carson pre-

serve is where the famed environmental author did some of the research for her book *The Edge of the Sea*. Tides leave much of the quarter-acre pond exposed, making for some of the best tide-pool hopping in the state. Seaweed here is slick, of course, and it's best to leave those who live in the area (the shells, mussels, crabs, periwinkles, starfish, sea urchins, and other creatures) in their native habitat. La Verna lies about 2 miles north, 119 acres along the bay. Woods, marshes, a tamarack swamp, and old cellar holes are what you'll find here, as well as some nice saltwater vistas when you reach the shore. A trail bisects the parcel.

CAMDEN HILLS STATE PARK
Route 1, Camden
(207) 236-3109
(207) 236-0849 (off season)

Mount Battie and Mount Megunticook provide the dramatic green backdrop for the town of Camden, and they also serve as the tall centerpieces of Camden Hills State Park, a green playground on Penobscot Bay. Both are fairly easy climbs, topping out at 1,380 feet, and the views from their summits seem never to end—downtown Camden, all white steeples and brick, is tiny down below, and the blue waters of Penobscot Bay wash to the horizon, interrupted by the black-green of several islands. A road scales Mount Battie, so you don't even have to sweat to take in the prospect, but it's preferable to walk through the forest.

Some visitors are surprised to learn that there are 30 miles of trails within the park—it's deceptively large, stretching inland behind the mountains for a few miles into neighboring Lincolnville. One of the best climbs is little-known Bald Rock Mountain, a 1,100-footer reached via Youngtown Road in Lincolnville (you'll see the parking lot). And surprisingly few people discover the fine picnic area right across the street from the main section of park. A mix of woods, grass, and looping roads, it slopes down toward the bay, providing some good ganders.

The 107 campsites at Camden Hills accommodate RVs as well as tents, and they're always busy. Open from May 15 through October 15.

COASTAL MOUNTAINS LAND TRUST
101 Mount Battie St., Camden
(207) 236-7091
www.coastalmountains.org
This fantastic Midcoast conservation outfit has been fighting the good fight since 1987, when it placed an easement on Beech Hill, site of a neat old stone tea house and 360-degree views of mountains and sea. Since then they've protected almost 7,000 acres from Rockport to Prospect, in 56 preserves. Quite aside from their significance in saving open space and wildlife habitat, these places make for great day hikes. You can scale Bald Mountain or Mount Percival, walk a spectacular saltwater headland in Rockport at Harkness, stroll along Lake Megunticook's Fernald Neck, hike the scenic Ducktrap River in Lincolnville, and trek miles along the Passagassawakeag Greenway in Belfast. And of course, take a picnic to the top of Beech Hill. The trust's Web site has all the details.

LANE'S ISLAND PRESERVE
Vinalhaven
(207) 729-5181
Forty-five acres of wide-open windswept moors, surrounded by rocks and beach, are what you'll find at this astonishingly beautiful isle off Vinalhaven. Because it was used for sheep pasture for ages, it's got an almost British Isles quality to it, grand and sweeping and romantic. All sorts of birdies favor the spot—including ospreys, great blue herons, spotted and least sandpipers, merlins, kestrels, and marsh hawks. Rough trails crisscross the entire island, and you can peek at the small cemetery, where generations of Lanes have been buried. Whether you just want a walk—it's 15 minutes or so from the ferry landing on Vinalhaven—to bird-watch, or to spend some time on the edge of the sea, it's a small paradise.

GEORGES HIGHLAND PATH
Route 17, Rockport
(207) 594-5166
www.grlt.org
A few years ago Rockland-based Georges River Land Trust began to make deals with landowners to allow public access to many of the Camden Hills. Up until that point, most of these picturesque peaks—and there are dozens trundling inland from the coast—were off limits to hikers. Not anymore. Dedicated to preserving the rural heritage of the St. George River Valley, along which many of these peaks lie, the ambitious conservation organization has opened more than 30 miles of trail along some of the finest acreage in the Midcoast. Ultimately the group hopes to establish a trail that runs the length of the St. George watershed, from Frye Mountain in Montville to the coast at Thomaston, and it's making good progress.

None of the hills of the Highland Path are particularly high—Camden's Ragged Mountain is probably the tallest at 1,300 feet—but because they lord over the coast, the river, lakes, and bucolic countryside, they provide some astonishingly good views. Trails now climb Bald Peak and Ragged Mountain in Camden, as well as Pleasant and Spruce Mountains in Rockport and Warren, and they are all exceedingly pleasant hikes. Some are more rugged than others. The Georges River Land Trust has also been quietly building preserves all over the Camden-Rockport-Lincolnville area. Pick up a map at the trailhead and parking area on State Route 17 in Rockport on Mirror Lake.

TANGLEWOOD 4-H CAMP
1 Tanglewood Rd., Lincolnville
(207) 789-5868
On the pretty, salmon-laden Ducktrap River, Tanglewood is busy with campers all summer long. In winter, though, the 830-acre woodland is a cross-country skier's dream—a free-to-use, virtually groomed, well-marked, and very beautiful 10-mile system of woods trails. So many skiers use it that you never have to break trail yourself, yet it's never so busy you feel overwhelmed. It's just perfect.

WARREN ISLAND STATE PARK
P.O. Box 105, Lincolnville 4849
(207) 941-4014
The state describes an overnight at its 70-acre Warren Island park as "Robinson Crusoe-esque," and if Crusoe had a nice log lean-to to retire to at night,

docks and moorings for his getaway boat, and fresh drinking water, then it might be something like it. One of the best of the campgrounds in the state park system, Warren Island is a fantastic retreat for a serene stay on a wild isle, and because you need your own boat to get there, it's quieter than most parks. Ten campsites and two Adirondack-style shelters provide the accommodations, and the sea and spruce island is wide open for exploration. The much larger isle of Islesboro is only a quarter mile away, and camping here allows you to get over there for a look-see without shelling out large dollars for one of Islesboro's fancy inns. (Camping is $19 a night.) You can easily reach Warren Island via canoe or kayak from Islesboro, so one idea is to take the ferry over to the big island and make the easy paddle from there. It's so simple, you won't need Man Friday.

FRYE MOUNTAIN STATE GAME MANAGEMENT AREA
Route 137, Montville

This 5,111-acre game preserve is better known to snowmobilers than hikers, but it shouldn't be. Astride the Knox-Montville town line in rural Waldo County, it is only 20 minutes away from Belfast but feels a world apart from the racket of Route 1. The area was once home to a farming community, which followed better times elsewhere, and it has sort of a ghost town vibe, especially when you stumble on old cemeteries and cellar holes. What most people come for, though, are the vistas from atop Frye Mountain, a small peak that offers a commanding look at the surrounding hills and valleys. A fire tower sits at the summit, and it lofts you up good and high to take in the scene. The setting is great for a picnic, and it's a pretty easy climb, too, because drivable old tote roads take you very close to the top.

MOOSE POINT STATE PARK
310 West Main St., Searsport
(207) 548-2882
(207) 941-4014, off-season

Believe it or not, moose are occasionally spotted along Route 1 in the vicinity of Moose Point. Not often, but sometimes. This small park on the coast

between Belfast and Searsport isn't exactly known for its large population of bullwinkles—they tend to habitate much farther north—but they've been seen in the area enough times for the DOT to install moose crossing signs. (Maybe those are just there to inspire people to stop at the park?)

What people really come to this 183-acre parcel for—those savvy enough to find it, anyway—is its Penobscot Bay panorama. The views are drop-dead gorgeous from the grassy lawns that comprise much of the park, and they're even better from the short hiking trail that meanders through a pine grove along the bay's edge. The facilities are limited to a few picnic tables and outhouses, but the fields are big enough for a group to gather on, or to host a ball game.

LAKE ST. GEORGE STATE PARK
Route 3, Liberty
(207) 589-4255

Another great swimming lake not too far inland from the coast, Lake St. George can get busy on a warm day. The water here is on the coolish side compared to other lakes, since it's spring fed, but that doesn't stop people from splishing and splashing under the watchful eyes of lifeguards. The 360-acre park is about halfway between Belfast and Augusta, 19 miles from the Penobscot Bay city, and it's well worth the trip out.

The grounds were once a pretty farm, and the old homestead and some barns are used by the rangers. There are 38 campsites—many of them right on the shore of the 1,017-acre lake—with hot showers, and flush toilets to boot. The sites can fill up quickly with locals, who like to swim and fish and use the boat launch and play areas here. The only drawback to camping is the proximity of Route 3, the primary thoroughfare between Belfast and the capital, and cars and big trucks whiz by at all hours. The park's open from May 15 through September.

SWAN LAKE STATE PARK
100 West Park Lane, Swanville
(207) 525-4404
(207) 941-4014 (off-season)

Swanville is not Maine's prettiest town, and Swan

Lake is not the state's most attractive lake, but somehow Swan Lake State Park manages to transcend its surroundings. It's a fine little park—and little it is at just 67 acres. Located 6 miles north of Belfast at the north end of Swan Lake, it is far enough away from the overdeveloped sections of waterfront and the depressing hovels on the roads on either side of the lake.

The focus here is on swimming and picnicking, and there are changing areas and lifeguards for the former and grills and tables for the latter. The bathing area is a sandy horseshoe backed up to a section of woods. Groups will also find a large shelter for gatherings as well as facilities for volleyball and other family-reunion–type games. The park's open from Memorial Day through Labor Day, 9 a.m. to sunset.

HOLBROOK ISLAND SANCTUARY
172 Indian Bar Rd., Harborside
(207) 326-4012
Cape Rosier could hardly be more beautiful, sticking out into the island-studded expanse of Penobscot Bay—and then you find Holbrook Island Sanctuary. The state owns just over 1,000 acres in Brooksville, looking out at the island the preserve's named after, and it's a fine meeting place of sea and shore. The sanctuary itself protects an array of ecosystems, from woods to marsh to meadows, and all the wildlife that live in such places. And the views of the bay are never ending. There are facilities for launching canoes and kayaks, trails for hiking, perfect picnic grounds, and all the makings of a great afternoon.

CROCKETT COVE WOODS PRESERVE
Off Whitman Rd., Stonington
(207) 729-5181
This sanctuary covers 100 acres of lush woods—fog forest, as Mainers call it—and four trails wind through it past a wide variety of lichens and mosses. The area is covered with spruce and fir and is rich with birdlife. You'll find tree beard lichen draping many trees and tamarack and cedar in the wet areas toward the middle of the preserve. The Nature Conservancy owns the

property, and a brochure describing what you'll see is available at the trailhead. Open from sunup to sundown.

LAMOINE STATE PARK
23 State Park Rd., Ellsworth
(207) 667-4778
(207) 941-4014 (off-season)
People clamor to get into the campgrounds of Acadia National Park and the private camping areas in Bar Harbor, going a little crazy to pack themselves in, while Lamoine State Park, about a half hour away under the same mountains and on the same sea, often has empty spaces in the evening. The savvy few who make it to these 55 acres in Lamoine have it good.

This is the sort of campground you won't find near the state's only national park. First off, it has fantastic views of the park's peaks, out across the glistening waters of Frenchman Bay, something you can't see when you're right underneath them at Seawall or Blackwoods. Lamoine is not usually overcrowded, there's a pebble beach, and, perhaps best of all, it's quiet and even has a sense of privacy, which are rare in Bar Harbor in summer. So the park definitely rewards those who seek it out.

Open from mid-May through mid-October.

Acadia Area
INDIAN POINT–BLAGDEN PRESERVE
Off Indian Point Rd., Bar Harbor
(207) 729-5181
Another Nature Conservancy property, this 110-acre parcel protects stands of trees that escaped the great fire of 1947, and it includes 1,000 feet of frontage on Western Bay. There is a seal haul-out just off the northwestern corner of the preserve, and you can watch them from the shore (be respectful). Paths thread through the sanctuary. Open from sunup to 6 p.m. year-round.

Down East
DONNELL POND PUBLIC RESERVE
T10 SD, between Franklin and Cherryfield
(207) 827-1818

Donnell Pond has a reputation as being a party zone, a place where kids—and many adults, too—go to drink, boat, and camp. And it is that. But this wild swath of public reserve land 12 miles east of Ellsworth covers more than 15,000 acres, and much of it is woods, so there's plenty to enjoy away from the yahoos on the lake. In fact, the state owns frontage on Tunk and Spring River Lakes as well, and most of Schoodic, Black, and Caribou Mountains. The landscape here feels almost like the North Woods, rugged, piney, largely undeveloped. Not to be confused with the Acadia property of the same name, Schoodic offers enviable vistas of the mountains of Acadia and is accessed by old logging roads and a trail. Those grown-over tote roads wander here or there, making for easy hiking, and a network of trails climbs Black Mountain, which is a little over 1,000 feet. Primitive campsites are available on all of the bodies of water.

MAINE COASTAL ISLANDS NATIONAL WILDLIFE REFUGE
P.O. Box 279, Milbridge 04658
(207) 546-2124
www.fws.gov/northeast/mainecoastal/
This sprawling "refuge" is actually a series of preserves, as it contains more than 49 islands as well as three mainland pieces. Intended as wildlife habitat first—and in this case that largely means birds—the refuge formerly known as Petit Manan has some nice hiking trails on its lands, especially at Petit Manan Point in Steuben. The best of these paths might be the Holingsworth Trail, a 1.5-mile loop through woods, across meadows, and down to cobbled beaches, with interpretive signs that fill you in on what it is you're looking at. The signs won't tell you what animals you'll see, but a wide variety of critters might be about as well. The preserve is open from sunup to sundown.

GREAT HEATH PUBLIC RESERVED LAND
Columbia
(207) 827-1818
The Great Heath is one of the many wonders of Maine's natural world—it's the largest raised bog in the state at 6,000-some acres and seems like

remotest Africa at points. Scruffy, flat, desolate, it occupies a huge chunk of land along the Pleasant River in Hancock County and is unlike anything else around. The state owns most of the territory here, but there are no facilities to speak of, and it's primarily of interest to canoeists, birdwatchers, and, well, heath lovers. Myriad birds, bears, moose, and beavers, who'll splash at your canoe with their tails, are frequently found here, and its flat water is easy and fun to paddle. Bring a map, though, or you'll never find the place. It's located on unmarked dirt roads in blueberrying country and requires a bit of cartography to locate. But it's worth it for sheer uniqueness and excellent canoeing.

GREAT WASS ISLAND
Route 187, Beals
(207) 729-5181
Yet another Nature Conservancy property, Great Wass is the largest island in an archipelago at Beals, south of Jonesport, and it's known for a couple of things: birds and wildflowers. There are some 104 species of the former, including spruce grouse, boreal chickadees, barred owls, and blackpolls, warblers that nest in the peat lands and coniferous forest. As for flowers, there are many varieties, which turn the island into a riot of color in spring and early summer. All told the preserve sprawls for about 1,600 acres, and there are a couple of popular trails that cover about 5 miles of fairly rugged terrain. The hiking can get a bit squishy after a rain.

ROCKY LAKE PUBLIC RESERVED LAND
Route 191, T18 ED BPP
(207) 827-1818
The East Machias River has long been a favorite canoeing and fishing spot among Down East outdoorsfolk, and some years back, the state obligingly purchased 11,000 acres around the river and its neighboring lakes, ponds, and streams. It's another public reserve prize, a big wildland full of prime canoeing, camping, fishing, and exploring opportunities. You'll hardly guess that you're just 10 miles from Route 1 and downtown Machias—it feels a world away. Facili-

ties are limited to a handful of boat launches and some primitive campsites.

CUTLER COAST PUBLIC RESERVED LAND
Route 191, Cutler
(207) 827-1818
Though it's a much quieter place than the rest of Maine, the Bold Coast of Washington County is still fairly well settled along the shore. Large tracts of undeveloped land are increasingly rare. But there is one stretch of wild woods that traces cliffs for close to 5 miles that was preserved by the state and turned into a public land. The parcel is one of the largest undeveloped expanses remaining on the East Coast.

You'll find it hard to believe that the Cutler Coast Unit isn't crawling with people when you stand atop one of its high cliffs overlooking Grand Manan Channel with the picture-perfect isles of the Canadian Maritimes floating offshore. A loop trail cuts across the roughly rectangular, 12,000-acre parcel and then follows the shore for more than 4 miles, hugging the cliffs, climbing through forests of spruce and fir, meandering through meadows, and passing all sorts of secret pocket beaches that you'll vow to return to. At the far end of the unit are three primitive campsites on headlands overlooking the sea. The views are truly spectacular.

SHACKFORD HEAD STATE PARK
Route 190, Eastport
(207) 941-4014
Shackford Head is a state park just like Reid or Popham or Sebago Lake, but you'd never know it. In fact, you'd probably never find it, unless you got directions from a kindly Washington County resident. A 90-acre green spot on Moose Island at the far right-hand corner of Maine, the tall headland lifts you up to fantastic views over Eastport after a simple 1-mile walk. But hardly anyone outside of Eastport knows it's there. The park is tucked away behind the "Boat School" (aka Washington County Technical College) on the edges of the attractive old burgh in a neighborhood where you wouldn't think to go looking for natural wonders. There it is, though, a woodsy nub

with a fantastic prospect, overlooking Cobscook Bay, Lubec, and Campobello. There isn't much to the place beyond the hill, the woods, and the trails up the mountain and along the shore, but that's all you need. The hike up the headland is easy, and the vista will knock you out—you can see right out into the salmon pens for which this part of Maine is famous. The trail to the shore is a little more challenging—you have to time it right with the tides—but is equally rewarding. Nice autumn fare, and you'll most likely have it all to yourself.

MOOSEHORN NATIONAL WILDLIFE REFUGE
R.R. 1, Box 202, Baring 04694
(207) 454-7161
http://moosehorn.fws.gov
Someone once likened a visit to this U.S. Fish and Wildlife property to going on a Down East safari. The 24,000 acres here are prime country for moose, bear, coyote, and all manner of birdlife, from impressive eagles to twittering woodcocks to cute and charismatic gray jays. The preserve is the easternmost national refuge on the Atlantic Flyway, and more than 220 species of birds have been identified on its grounds. Moosehorn is divided into two sections, or units. The largest part is a 17,000-plus-acre stretch of dense woods near Calais. The other is a 7,200-acre parcel on Cobscook Bay. Both make for fine exploring. More than 50 miles of roads and trails crisscross through these refuges, and maps are available at the preserve's headquarters on the Charlotte Road in Baring. Most of the reserve can be accessed by automobile, unfortunately, but there are wilderness sections. For easy hiking try the 1.25-mile Habitat Trail, which is an interpretive walk through woods that starts near the headquarters. When venturing into the backcountry, be sure to bring a map, compass, and plenty of food, water, and clothing. The refuge is open daily, year-round, from dawn to dusk.

COBSCOOK BAY STATE PARK
R.R. 1, Box 127, Dennysville
(207) 726-4412
That people cram themselves into camping areas

at Acadia and Sebago Lake is hard to understand when you visit this spacious Down East gem. Word is getting out about the myriad delights of Cobscook Bay State Park, especially among kayakers, but it is still far less traveled than parks in the Midcoast and in York and Cumberland Counties. You can still get a reservation on a whim for the 106 sites here, even in the summer, which is unheard of in points south, and for a good site, no less.

Just about all the sites at Cobscook are good. The park sprawls for 888 acres across a peninsula on the shore of the bay, and the camping area is ringed by the brine. Many sites are a skip from the water—so close, in fact, that campers arriving late at night have awoken to find salt water lapping at their tents. (The tides swing 24 feet here.) There's plenty of space at each site, and a nice buffer of spruce forest between them—Cobscook's famous for its privacy. Tenters have their pick in one area, RVs in another, and walk-in sites allow for real quietude. Kayakers like to push off right from their bivouacs, but there are proper boat launching sites. Swimming is not allowed, thanks to the undertows caused by the huge tidal rotation.

Hot showers, a wealth of birdlife in the park and next door at Moosehorn National Wildlife Refuge (200 species have been spotted in these parts), meadows of wildflowers, digging for clams, and a great launching pad for explorations of Eastport, Lubec, Machias, the rest of Washington County, and Canada, too—what more could anyone want in a park? Open from mid-May through mid-October.

QUODDY HEAD STATE PARK
Box 1490, Lubec
(207) 733-0911
(207) 941-4014 (off-season)
West Quoddy Head Light is the biggest attraction at this, the nation's most easterly state park, but nature lovers know that the real treats here are the soaring cliffs and jutting headlands overlooking the Bay of Fundy and Grand Manan Island.

Grand is the word. The lighthouse located just outside the park's grounds is nice and all, in a tall, red-and-white-striped kind of way, but the shoreline that it protects is nothing short of astonishing. Rising above the highest tides in the country, these cliffs approach 100 feet tall, lording over waters often frequented by spouting whales.

A trail wanders along the cliffs for close to 2 miles, occasionally letting out onto rocky ledges that are great for tide pooling or simply watching the crashing surf and the seabirds. The going is of moderate difficulty, climbing and falling through a dense, pleasantly scented pine forest, and benches are set at the outset of the walk and at a few places here and there along it. A little over a half mile from the outset is Gulliver's Hole, a frothy sea pocket that's worth checking out. All told, there are 4.5 miles of trails, including a boardwalk that leads inland to a mossy bog, where there are signs identifying this heath and that fern. Fun to peruse, it's a National Natural Landmark.

Near the light, there are picnic tables where you can enjoy a fine spread before a world-class backdrop. But you want to get out on that trail—the nice thing is, relatively few people make it more than a few hundred feet down it, so you'll have it all to yourself. The park is officially open from May 15 through October 15 but allows snowshoers and nature walkers in the winter, too.

PUBLIC GARDENS AND LANDSCAPE ART

Gardeners in Maine take to planting flowers like sunbathers take to the beach because they know their time is short. The results are show gardens up and down the coast. There are so many noteworthy garden and landscape sites in the state that the Maine Department of Agriculture decided to put together a map and tour of horticultural hot spots. Get your copy by calling (800) 782-6497. Here are several landmark landscapes sure to appeal to green thumbs—and anyone else who appreciates beauty. Admission is free unless otherwise stated.

South Coast

HAMILTON HOUSE
Vaughan's Lane, South Berwick
(207) 384-2454

One of the state's best-known historic homes, this 1785 manse has a colonial revival garden that reportedly dates back to 1898. It was renovated in the late 1990s and is something to see. Walking trails thread through 35 acres of attractive grounds here (not all garden, of course), and they overlook the pretty Salmon Falls River. Admission is $8 and includes house and grounds.

HARTLEY MASON ESTATE
112 Main St., Kennebunk
(207) 985-2173

This children's garden—including a touch-and-sniff section as well as flowers and herbs—was designed by the Seacoast Garden Club, and it has won some awards. Whimsy is the word.

ST. ANTHONY'S SHRINE AND FRANCISCAN MONASTERY
Beach Ave., Kennebunk
(207) 967-2011

What a nice place to be a monk. The grounds here were designed by the Olmsted brothers, famous landscape architects of the early 20th century who did a lot of work in Maine, and it's become known for its rhododendrons. A walking path explores the 25 acres here, and includes a boardwalk and a pavilion on the Kennebunk River.

Greater Portland

SPRING POINT ARBORETUM
Southern Maine Community College
South Portland
(207) 767-7670

It's hard to concentrate on the trees at this one-acre arboretum thanks to the magnificent views of Casco Bay that sit just beyond them. Planted by the city of South Portland in 1981, the tree garden features 70 species of trees, shrubs, vines, and groundcovers, and little interpretive signs tell you what you're looking at. The Spring Point

Walkway connects, making for a surprisingly fine afternoon.

EVERGREEN CEMETERY
672 Stevens Ave., Portland
(207) 874-8300

A National Register of Historic Places green space in Portland, this 300-acre park was laid out in 1854, and it's very popular with strollers and joggers. Quite aside from being a nice place to take the dog, it is pleasantly landscaped.

LONGFELLOW ARBORETUM
Payson Park
Ocean Ave., Portland

If you're curious what trees don't grow in Maine, visit this three-acre park in the Forest City—it was planted in 1976 and includes species not native to the state. The Longfellow Garden Club established the green with the help of the City of Portland.

WADSWORTH–LONGFELLOW HOUSE GARDENS
489 Congress St., Portland
(207) 774-1822

While the gardens here at the boyhood home of the great American poet Henry Wadsworth Longfellow (you remember him from English class, right?) are pleasant, the opportunity to find a moment's quiet and sit in the middle of downtown Portland is almost as fine. This green space went in in the 1920s, and the city continued to grow up around it.

HARRINGTON HOUSE
45 Main St., Freeport
(207) 865-3170
www.freeporthistoricalsociety.org

This circa 1830 Federal is the home of the local historical society's gift shop, which is particularly well done. But so are the gardens of antique roses and perennials to be found outside it.

PETTENGILL FARM GARDENS
45 Main St., Freeport
(207) 865-3170

Historic wild roses, lilacs, old-fashioned perennials, and cedars are among the draws at this 1810 saltbox in the state's famous outlet village. Antique apple orchards, woods, and salt marshes sit on the 140 acres here, which border the Harraseeket River and are run by the local historical society.

TIDEBROOK CONSERVATION TRUST
38 Bartol Island Rd., Freeport
(207) 869-1012
www.freeportconservationtrust.org
A 45-acre conservation easement has allowed the gardens here to grow undisturbed, and the old orchards bloom with wildflowers, native and ornamental flowering shrubs, and the plantings of a more formal garden.

Midcoast
HEATHER GARDEN AT WALKER ART BUILDING
Bowdoin College, Brunswick
(207) 725-3000
This museum should be visited more often than it is, and the same might be said of the heath and heather gardens that sit outside it.

LIBRARY PARK
Summer St., Bath
(207) 443-5143
A William Zorach sculpture might have been the most talked-about element of this five-acre park—it was the source of controversy in the 1960s—but the Victorian landscaping, pond, and fountain are certainly worthy of note, too. It's a nice place to sit or stroll.

NICKELS-SORTWELL HOUSE
Route 1, Wiscasset
(207) 882-7169
If Wiscasset is the "Prettiest Village in Maine" (which is debatable), it is pretty old houses like this one that are the reason why. The 1807 house museum sits on a plot that was landscaped in 1926 by noted architect Charles Eliott II and it's a National Historic Landmark.

COASTAL MAINE BOTANICAL GARDENS
Off Barter's Island Rd., Boothbay Harbor
(207) 633-4333
www.mainegardens.org
A lovely work in progress, these gardens have been under construction since the 1990s, and they continue to grow and grow, more than doubling there acreage. Some 300 native species have been planted, and there is a library and visitor center where you can find out about the long-term plans for the gardens. A mile of tidal shorefront doesn't hurt.

CHRISTINA'S GARDEN AT THE OLSON HOUSE
Hathorn Point Rd., Cushing
(207) 354-0102
Andrew Wyeth spent more time painting this house and its denizens than he did the small annual garden on the premises kept by Christina Olson. Nonetheless, the Farnsworth Museum, which now owns this famous property, has recreated the beds here from historical research.

VESPER HILL CHILDREN'S CHAPEL
Chapel Rd. (off Calderwood Lane), Rockport
(207) 236-0603
You have to practically wrestle to get a wedding scheduled for this nondenominational chapel nestled in the woods on Beauchamp Point, so popular is the site. The gardens that surround the rustic meeting place, which overlooks the sea, are part of the reason why.

CAMDEN PUBLIC LIBRARY
Route 1, Camden
(207) 236-3440
One of the state's more distinctive libraries, perched on a hill underneath Mount Battie and above the harbor, the library has a beautiful spread out front. Some call it the finest institutional garden in the state, and it is pretty all season long. The amphitheater designed by Fletcher Steele in 1929 is another reason to visit (as is the park across the street, which was laid out at the same time by the Olmsted brothers).

MERRYSPRING HORTICULTURAL NATURE PARK
Conway Rd., Camden
(207) 236-2239
www.merryspring.org
Truly an oasis of serenity amid the madness of summertime Camden, Merryspring can't be more than a mile from Route 1. But you'd never know it, stepping onto the preserve's 60-some acres. Lush woodlands, singing birds, trails overlooking the Camden Hills, gardens, interactive nature-trail displays, the place has a little of everything. The fairly complex network of trails takes walkers through an array of environments—marshes, shrubs, an arboretum, exposed ledges—and the Merryspring gardens are a treat for any green thumb. Hostas, perennials, roses, and heathers compete for the eye's attention. Step into the Ross Center, a visitor facility and library, to find out about all of the organization's classes, workshops, and programs. Or simply explore and be amazed that the whirl of Camden feels so far away.

Acadia Area
COLLEGE OF THE ATLANTIC
Eden St., Bar Harbor
(207) 288-5015
What would Eden be without gardens? (That's the paradisiacal name by which Bar Harbor used to be called.) The library grounds at this progressive learning institution include terraces that were designed by noted landscape architect Beatrix Farrand, a legend in these parts.

JORDAN POND HOUSE FLOWER GARDENS
Park Loop Rd., Bar Harbor
(207) 288-3338
People typically flock to the Jordan Pond House for its tea and popovers, but they should make sure to check out the perennial beds filled with dahlias, monkshood, delphiniums, and scads of other colorful flora.

ASTICOU AZALEA GARDEN
Route 198, Northeast Harbor
(207) 276-3727
www.gardenpreserve.org
The azaleas are the real draw here, obviously, but their springtime bloom is only one of the many reasons to visit. Others include the rhododendrons, the laurels, and the Oriental touches. Architect Charles Savage designed the gardens here, and he used many plants rescued from Beatrix Farrand's famed Reef Point estate.

JAPANESE GARDEN AT YOURCENAR
South Shore Rd., Northeast Harbor
(207) 276-3940
Better known for her books, Marguerite Yourcenar kept a garden at her Northeast Harbor home that is full of wild flowers, fruit trees, and walking paths. Yourcenar is one of the few women elected to the prestigious Academie Française, and her house-museum is open by appointment.

THUYA GARDEN
Route 3, Northeast Harbor
(207) 276-3727
www.gardenpreserve.org
Another garden designed by famous landscape architect Charles Savage and inspired by Beatrix Farrand, the semiformal, English-style perennial garden here is a true stunner, set against a backdrop of woods on a hill in Northeast Harbor.

Down East
COTTAGE GARDEN
North Lubec Rd., Lubec
(207) 733-2902
Two acres of old-fashioned roses, delphiniums, and other flowers sit at this public garden against the backdrop of beautiful Cobscook Bay. Orchards are all around.

BIKING

Despite its narrow, winding roads, Maine is a favorite among the two-wheel set because of its country byways and ocean vistas. Road biking has long been popular, and mountain biking has been growing in recent years. Options for the road are fairly limitless—you can pedal from one end of the coast to the other if you like, as long as you stay off the Maine Turnpike (Route 1) and I–95—and many communities are making themselves more attractive to bicyclists by creating dedicated bike paths like those in Portland and Brunswick or simply adding bike lanes onto current roads. Mountain bike trails are a little bit harder to find, but they're there if you look for them. The great paperback book Mountain Bike Maine (Menasha Ridge Press) lists scads of places for fat-tire freaks to find some doubletrack.

The state has very active biking clubs and groups helping to make the East Coast Greenway—that bike and walking path from Florida to Maine—a reality Down East. And there is also a lot of work going on in the state to transform old, unused railroad tracks into bike and walking paths. Forward-thinking motel owners in places like Kennebunkport now offer bikes as ways to get around to avoid the congestion of cars, and you can find rentals up and down the coast. Resort communities are the best places to look—Kennebunkport, Ogunquit, Bar Harbor, Camden—but you'll find rentals even in tiny spots like Chebeague Island. In fact, island biking continues to grow because most islands are relatively flat, the views are grand, and traffic is minimal. Ferries will transport your bike. (And, for that matter, the Downeaster train now has provisions for bikes as well.)

It's a good time to be a cyclist on the coast. Just remember to wear your helmet—it's the law if you're age 15 or younger, and it's just plain smart if you're not.

Riders' Resources

The best friend Maine bicyclists have is the **Bicycle Coalition of Maine,** a two-wheelers advocacy group. Its Web site—www.bikemaine .org—is a great help to anyone inter ested in pedaling in the state. You'll find information on the outfit's political and educational work as well as a lot of links of interest to bikers, from races to group rides.

The **Maine Department of Transportation** also has some helpful bicycling information on its Web site, including a great list of pedaling routes, trip planning resources, and links to clubs and shops. You can find it at www.stateme.us/mdot. Just type the word *bike* in the search box.

CANOEING

Most people think of canoeing as an up-country activity, best done in the state's wild interior. That's where you'll find the Allagash and the Saint John, Maine's two famous canoeing corridors, as well as places like Northeast Carry, which was named for portaging canoes. But there are several good places to paddle along the coast. (You can rent canoes at sporting shops up and down Route 1.) Here are a few ideas (DeLorme's ubiquitous Maine Atlas and Gazetteer has several more).

Saco River

This lazy river washes down from Crawford Notch, New Hampshire, to the sea in Saco, putting in 84 miles in Maine, and it's one of the most popular places to paddle in the state (which makes it a party zone if you go at the wrong time). A lot of people get their first taste of canoe camping on the Saco, paddling by day and sleeping in the campgrounds that line the river at night. Most people put in at Fryeburg up on the border, but there are plenty of places to launch for shorter trips closer to the coast. Try the section from Salmon Falls down.

Royal River

Considering that you're paddling through the suburbs of Greater Portland, this 6-mile route has a nice, bucolic feel to it, and you don't see that many homes when you're in the middle of it. Put in on Route 9 in North Yarmouth and take out at West Elm Street in Yarmouth proper. Allow yourself a few hours for a leisurely go of it. Rent canoes in Portland.

Sheepscot River

A nice trip here could take you the better part of a day. Put in at North Whitefield and paddle to the dam at Head Tide, a 12-mile run that will take you through some Class I and II rapids. Portage at Whitefield, and travel to the incredibly scenic village of Head Tide, where you portage at the dam. From there you can paddle to Sheepscot Village and take out at the bridge. This is a nice route with a variety of environments, woods, hamlets, fields, and farms, and a mix of water types. You can rent canoes at the Wiscasset Trading Post (Route 1; 207-882-9645; www.wiscassettrading post.com), which is 15 minutes from the take-out in Sheepscot Village.

Pemaquid River

On the Pemaquid Peninsula this quiet river runs between Pemaquid Harbor and Pemaquid Pond, flowing through 22 miles of lakes and ponds. It's flat-water paddling, and there is a launching point at Bristol where you can hop on and head north to Biscay Pond or beyond. The going is easy, the riverside quiet and woodsy, and there are always frogs sunning and turtles swimming in water so clear you can see them 4 feet down. There are plenty of places to pull out and take a swim or spread out a blanket for a picnic.

St. George River

A very picturesque paddle through the rural countryside of Knox and Waldo Counties, this route begins in Searsmont at the bridge and flows to Appleton Village. Typically run in the spring, it requires high water because of the boniness of the river through here. Lots of beaver dams, bird nesting areas, and stretches of quiet water, but there can be some Class III rapids. Portage the old dam—or paddle it if you dare. Rent canoes at Maine Sport Outfitters (Route 1, Rockport; 207-236-8797), 20 minutes south of Appleton.

Machias River

This is one of the biggies in Maine and is usually run only by experienced paddlers or people with guides. The section from Third Machias Lake to Whitneyville will take you some 50 miles through wild country, with many stretches of Class III rapids. You need to do a lot of scouting and several portages, and there is primitive camping at the river's edge. Rent canoes—or hire a guide—at Mooselook Guide Service (Schoodic; 207-963-0995).

ACADIA

The single biggest attraction Down East and the state's only national park, Acadia is the reason more than two million people a year visit Maine. It has been called the crown jewel in the National Park system, and it's truly a stunner. Occupying much of Mount Desert Island and a few other nearby points, Acadia is a geologic marvel, an Atlantic wonderland of sea and surf and summits. The park sprawls for close to 50,000 acres, including miles of dramatic shoreline, the only genuine fjord in the Lower 48, several lakes, 26 peaks, 120 miles of trails, and innumerable ponds. As such, it's an outdoor lover's paradise, with exceptional hiking, biking, walking, swimming, climbing, and kayaking. And there's plenty to see from a car window, too.

Acadia dominates the Mount Desert Island map, spread on either side of the island, which is divided in two by the sea, split by scenic Somes Sound. The heaviest concentration of parklands—and the most popular sites—are on the east side, where the resort town of Bar Harbor is also located. This is where you'll find the Park Loop Road, and where Thunder Hole, Otter Cliffs, Great Head, Sand Beach, Jordan Pond, Blackwoods Camping Area, and Cadillac Mountain all reside. Across the sound—a glacially carved fjord—is what is known as the island's "quiet side," a place that sees far less tourism than does Bar Harbor but that can still get busy in the full blush of summer.

Bar Harbor is all about tourism, the very picture of a resort community (see Area Overview chapter). It has all the restaurants, shops, and B&Bs anyone could ever want, all attractively packaged into the tidy brick streets and venerable lanes of one of the oldest summer colonies in the country. Several painters of the Hudson River school made their way to the island in the mid-1800s, among them Thomas Cole and Frederic Church, and the paintings they made here attracted many early vacationers. By 1880, there were 30 hotels on the island, and, not long after that, the captains of American industry began to summer over, building huge mansions and calling them "cottages." Originally drawn here to escape the heat of New York and Philadelphia, the Carnegies and Rockefellers, Vanderbilts and Astors soon remade the island in their own image, creating an exclusive community of estates, parties, and all the luxurious trappings.

Thankfully, though, these wealthy folks from away also had the foresight to see that the mountains and sea that they loved needed to be preserved for future generations. One of them, textile heir and conservationist George Dorr, devoted more than 40 years to making that happen. Dorr worked on his affluent friends and neighbors until they relented, donating land piece by piece. John D. Rockefeller himself helped acquire nearly a third of the park's acreage, and Harvard president Charles Eliot was instrumental as well. The land was then turned over to the federal government, and in 1919 Acadia National Park opened to the public as the first national park in the East. (It was originally called Lafayette National Park; in 1929 the name was changed to Acadia, derived from the term the French used for these lands, L'Acadie.)

Acadia has been extraordinarily popular since. Unfortunately, most people who visit miss the good stuff. They content themselves with a drive along the two-lane Park Loop Road, the 20-mile byway that circuits the eastern half of Acadia, and then head into Bar Harbor. And while the Park Loop Road is truly spectacular—an Atlantic Coast highway of sorts, passing underneath mountains, alongside cliffs, and a skip from the surging sea—there is so much more to the park than that. To best enjoy Acadia, you have to leave the car behind and get out into it.

ℹ️ The name of the national park on Mount Desert Island is pronounced Uh-cay-dee-*A*, not *AR*-cay-dee-a. While Bar Harbor was once known as Eden, Acadia is not to be confused with Arcadia, the pastoral setting for the poetry of ancient Greece. Innumerable visitors get the name wrong. Don't be one of them.

SOURCES OF INFORMATION

HULLS COVE VISITOR CENTER
State Route 3, Hulls Cove
(207) 288-3338
www.nps.gov/acad
This is the primary information clearinghouse for Acadia National Park, and it sits very close to the best access point for the park's main thoroughfare, the Park Loop Road. Open from mid-April through October, the center brims with relief maps, natural history displays, and other guides to the goods on Acadia. You can pick up maps and postcards, watch a film about the park, and get answers to all your questions here.

ACADIA NATIONAL PARK HEADQUARTERS
Route 233, Bar Harbor
(207) 288-3338
This is the place to turn for information in the off-season, when the visitor center is closed but the park isn't.

ℹ️ Many Acadia visitors enjoy their vacation without ever picking up a copy of the park's newsletter, the *Beaver Log* (so named because of the abundance of the toothy rodents throughout the park). That's too bad for them, because it's filled with a wealth of handy info, from the schedule of ranger-led programs to tide calendars. Grab your copy at the park information center.

GETTING AROUND THE ISLAND

ISLAND BUSES
Islandwide
(207) 667-5796
www.exploreacadia.com
When the Island Explorer bus service was first proposed as a way to alleviate the traffic headaches that can tie up Acadia on a hot summer day, there were a lot of naysayers. People are too tied to their vehicles to want to climb aboard propane-fired buses, they argued. They were proved spectacularly wrong. The buses turned out to be a great success—they carted 352,000 park visitors around the island in 2007, or more than 4,400 a day in summer—linking hotels, restaurants, campgrounds, boats, and ferries to the national park. Eight routes crisscross the island, taking passengers to popular destinations like downtown Bar Harbor and Sand Beach and traveling as far as the Schoodic Peninsula. They run as often as every 15 minutes, they're on time and efficient, and they'll take you virtually everywhere you might want to go on Mount Desert. And best of all they're free, thanks to support from the National Park Service, the U.S. and Maine Departments of Transportation, local businesses, Friends of Acadia, and L.L. Bean (which donated a grant to allow the buses to run through Columbus Day). Quite aside from the environmental benefit the fleet provides—taking all those cars off the roads and using the less-polluting propane gas—they take all the headaches away from drivers. The buses start to roll as early as 6:45 a.m. downtown and continue to do so until 11 p.m. Pick up a copy of the schedule at a variety of spots downtown, call, or visit the Web site for full details.

PARK LOOP ROAD

The primary thoroughfare through Acadia National Park, the Park Loop Road makes a 20-mile circuit on the east side of Mount Desert Island. Not only the best way to see the sights if you only have a day or so, it's also how you'll get wherever you're going in the park, as it links most of the major points. There are a few spots to get on, but it becomes a one-way route after Sand Beach. Driving the loop is practically mandatory to Acadia visitors. Vehicle passes good for a week are $20, and you'll be stopped and asked to pay at the tollbooths on the Loop Road. Many people get on in Bar Harbor and drive south, passing underneath the cliffs of Champlain Mountain and skirting the shore below Sand Beach. The road continues past the booming Thunder Hole, Gorham Mountain, and Otter Cliffs, and it hugs the water past Otter and Western Points before heading back inland toward Jordan Pond and Cadillac Mountain. The views of relentless surf, pine and birch forests, pretty ponds, and green-backed peaks don't get much better than this. A handy map available at the park's visitor center will inform your drive and make a neat self-guided tour.

Cars are a constant all-day long on the Loop Road, and bicyclists enjoy it, too. The speed limit is 35 mph, and drivers often have a hard time maintaining that thanks to traffic, lollygaggers, and all of the comings and goings at the scenic pull-offs and parking areas. Pedestrians cross at a variety of points as well, and you might even bump into a film crew (they love to make car commercials here). Best to be patient and enjoy the views or to get up early or visit in the off-season to have time by yourself.

ACADIA NATIONAL PARK TOURS

One of the better ways to get a broad overview of Acadia and all it offers is to hop aboard the green-and-white buses run by Acadia National Park Tours (www.acadiatours.com). They host

i Acadia has an exceptional series of ranger-led programs designed to help visitors get the most out of their time in the park. These workshops and seminars run the gamut from hikes to boat rides, and they're hosted by knowledgeable park staff. A complete list of offerings is available in the park's newsletter, the *Beaver Log.*

two-and-a-half-hour trips through the park twice daily, at 10 a.m. and 2 p.m. The bus drivers are full of knowledge and trivia, and they'll fill you in on all the backstory, from the rusticators of yore to the fledgling falcons of today. These tours are billed as being ideal for "nature lovers, history buffs, and photographers," and they make either a good starting point for your trip or an informative rainy-day option. They're offered daily from May through October for $27.50 for adults, $15 for kids age 12 or younger. Call (207) 288-0300 or look for the buses across from Testa's Restaurant on Main Street.

OLI'S TROLLEYS
Cottage St.
P.O. Box 784, Bar Harbor 04609
(207) 288-9899

Another option for a motor coach–based excursion is Oli's Trolleys, which offers one-hour and two-and-a-half-hour tours of Bar Harbor and Acadia in its colorful, open-windowed, ersatz trolleys. Like the bus tours, these trips combine a bit of cultural history—stories of old Bar Harbor as you pass by the venerable "cottages"—with visits to the more popular scenic spots in the park itself. Reservations are recommended, and tickets (about $15 for the short tour and about $30 for the longer one) can be purchased at One Harbor Place (next to the Town Pier) an hour before the tours.

CARRIAGE ROADS

If the Park Loop Road will take you to most of the major points in the park, the 57 miles of carriage roads that John D. Rockefeller helped establish in 1913 will get you just about everywhere else. Sometimes referred to as "Mr. Rockefeller's Roads," for the 27 years the philanthropist put into their creation, these wide, gentle, crushed-rock byways wend and wander deep into the interior of the park, linking everything from Jordan Pond and the Bubbles to remote ponds. They pass by lakes, climb to scenic overlooks, and get you well up some of the park's peaks. Perfect for an afternoon amble, for mountain biking, and even horseback riding, these roads are laid out in a well-organized network, and maps are available at the park's information centers. A visit to Acadia wouldn't be complete without a stroll along one. Try the network near Jordan Pond; it's especially scenic, rising high above the little basin and looking out at the green bonbons of the Bubbles.

WILDWOOD STABLES
Park Loop Rd., Box 241, Seal Harbor
(207) 276-3622
www.acadia.net/wildwood

What more perfect way to appreciate the carriage roads of Acadia than by a horse-drawn carriage? Wildwood Stables, a privately run livery, is located on the Park Loop Road not far from Jordan Pond and offers a variety of outings in open-air carriages. You might want to try the Day Mountain Tour, a one-hour trip that takes you from forest to peak and back again; the two-hour Tea and Popover Carriage Ride, which explores the terrain around Jordan Pond, stopping at the teahouse there for its famed popovers; or the beautiful two-hour Sunset Tour in the evening. Reservations are a good idea. Find out more at the Web site.

HIKING

Acadia is a day hiker's dream, with more than two dozen peaks, plenty of shore paths, and 120 miles of hiking trails of varying degrees of difficulty. You can do everything from climbing vertical ladders on the sheer faces of cliffs, like those on the Beehive and the Precipice, to simply trekking through pretty boreal forests just steps from the sea. Cadillac Mountain is the tallest peak on the island—in fact, it's the tallest peak right on the eastern seaboard at 1,530 feet—and most of Acadia's mountains are in the 1,000-foot range, so we're not talking Everests here, more like ambitious hills. Eager hikers have been known to do two or three in a day, because the climbs can be fairly easy, the peaks are often close together, and the trails are interconnected. Just about all of the mountains offer stunning prospects from their summits, though, a patchwork of green forest and blue sea and often other peaks in the distance.

Cadillac Mountain

There are many ways up the island's tallest peak, including an automobile road, but the South Ridge Trail will make you feel like you earned it. One of the longest hikes on the island at 3.5 miles, it starts across from Blackwoods Campground and climbs steadily northward through mixed forest. At about a mile there are good lookouts to the east and southeast at Eagles Crag; much of the climbing is done on exposed granite ledges, and the views just keep getting better and better. You might be annoyed at the commotion you find at the top—cars, crowds, and a gift shop—after the peace you found on the way up, but the astounding views in all directions will more than make up for it.

Ship Harbor and Wonderland

Twin trails on the island's quiet side, Ship Harbor and Wonderland are both relatively short, easy walks, coming in at under 1.5 miles each. They both get their starts on Route 3 in Southwest Harbor and head through bosky woods to end at the water. Birders particularly love them, but they are fun for anyone who wants a peaceful nature walk or a few private minutes at the ocean's edge.

Great Head Trail

Great Head is the tall green peninsula that wraps protectively around the far side of Sand Beach. It rises 145 feet from sea level and is among the highest headlands on the East Coast. The trail here makes a circuit from Sand Beach that climbs steeply at first and then levels off when it reaches the top of the head, circling around the promontory and skirting cliffs. Views of the open ocean, the Beehive, and Schoodic Point are magnificent, and the going is fairly easy. The hike takes you 1.6 miles. Park at the Sand Beach parking area on the Loop Road.

Beech Cliffs

There are few hikes in Maine that rival Beech Cliffs when it comes to the views you're rewarded with for the effort you make. The half-mile trail takes you only a few minutes to walk and deposits you atop Beech Cliffs. The vistas here are terrific, overlooking Echo Lake. Other trails will connect you to the summit of Beech Mountain (839 feet) and nearby Canada Cliffs. This is a great hike for a picnic lunch, as these trails are much quieter than those on the other side of the island. Take State Route 102 through Somesville and turn onto Beech Hill Road.

Beehive Trail

The Beehive is a whole lot of fun for hikers not afraid of heights. It is a very steep climb, though, and you cross narrow ledges from which some people have fallen. So due caution and respect are in order. This was the first piece of Acadia purchased back when the park was being founded, and it's a cool, craggy cliff face that rises up on one side of Champlain Mountain. The ledges here have a sort of honeycomb look to them (hence the name), and they are exposed for almost the entire ascent. The trail switches back and forth along them, using iron ladders for climbing sheer cliff faces at points. It'll get your heart pumping and will afford you a great prospect of Sand Beach, Great Head, Otter Cliffs, Gorham Mountain, and the open sea from the top. Other trails leave from the summit. Park at the Sand Beach parking area.

Precipice Trail

This is the be-all and end-all trail for adventure seekers at Acadia, a vertical ascent up a cliff face on Champlain Mountain. After a half mile of walking, the trail goes straight up for 500 feet, using iron rungs that were hammered into the mountain granite. It's downright terrifying for those afraid of verticality and should not be attempted by anyone under 5 feet tall, who might have difficulty reaching the ladders. Not for the faint of heart, for sure, and a place where it is essential that you stick to the designated trail. The views from the top are breathtaking, though, and you'll have earned bragging rights. There's a parking area off the Park Loop not far from the base of the trail.

Penobscot and Sargent Mountains

This pair rank among the loftiest on Mount Desert Island—Sargent is second to Cadillac, Penobscot fifth tallest—and the ridge linking them rises above the tree line for much of the way, making for fine views. The trail leaves from near Jordan Pond (park in the parking area there) and climbs up over Penobscot before descending to Sargent Pond and heading back up over ledges to the top of Sargent Mountain. The views of Jordan Pond, the Bubbles, Cadillac Mountain, and the sea in the distance are truly special. The hike from the start to Sargent summit is about 2.5 miles.

The Bubbles

A pair of cute green hills with perfectly rounded tops, the Bubbles hunker at one end of Jordan Pond in a most photogenic way—in fact, these twins make one of the most frequently photographed images in Acadia. Neither North nor South Bubble is a particularly difficult climb, topping out at 872 and 766 feet, respectively. You can park right below them on the Park Loop Road and scale either one in no time. People frequently do both in an afternoon, and you might still have the energy to hook up with the Jordan Pond Shore Trail or the Eagle Lake Trail, too. You'll get nice peeks at Jordan Pond and Penobscot and Pemetic Mountains from the tops of the Bubbles.

Champlain Mountain

The easternmost mountain on Mount Desert Island, Champlain is best known as the home of the Precipice, but there is a really nice trail on the other side of this long, sprawling thousand-footer that begins on Route 3. The Beachcroft Trail is one of the more elaborately designed of Acadia's hiking paths, following a carefully built stone staircase up the face of Huguenot Head, switching back and forth as it climbs like something out of a fairy tale. Once you've climbed the steps, you're on a false summit, overlooking the Tarn and Dorr Mountain, and you have to go another half mile or so, down into a bosk, and then climb up steeply to reach the actual peak.

It's windswept and wide open and quite scenic. There is parking near the base of the trail at the Dorr parking lot.

Gorham Mountain

Gorham is one of the smaller of Acadia's peaks, but it is an exceedingly pleasant hike and provides good viewing of Sand Beach, Great Head, the Bee-hive, and the open sea. Some say it offers vistas unparalleled on the island. The trail begins in the Gorham Trail parking lot, just down the Loop Road from Sand Beach, and climbs for a ways through a pine woods before reaching ledges of exposed bedrock. There's the option of taking the Cadillac Caves Trail at .3 mile, which is a worthwhile loop that takes you through some boulder-strewn, above-ground caves before rejoining the trail. (This option requires a bit of scrambling.) Then it's up over more open terrain to the panoramas that wait up top. This is a relatively easy hike that will keep your camera snapping.

CAMPING

If you're planning on staying overnight in Acadia, you'd better bring your tent—the only accommodations in the park are at two campgrounds, Seawall and Blackwoods, and a few remote camp-sites on Isle au Haut. The fee is $20 per site, per night, which is about the best deal you'll find for a place to stay on MDI during the summer. Seawall is on the Southwest Harbor side of the island, not far from the artificially created seawall from which it takes its name. Despite the fact that it has more than 200 sites, the place fills up quickly in summer on a first-come, first-served basis. It's a good idea to show up before 8 a.m. if you want to lay your head here. The amenities are limited— just restrooms and dumping stations—but the campground makes a good jumping-off point for explorations of the quiet side of the island by bike, boat, or foot. Rangers lead entertaining nature programs at the amphitheater here on summer evenings.

Blackwoods is the more popular of the two Mount Desert Island camping areas, with 300-some sites and a reservation policy good between May 1 and October 31 (800-365-2267). Just up the road from Bar Harbor on Route 3, it is divided into a few loops, and the sites are pretty tightly packed together. But the shore is an easy walk across the road and through a bit of woods, and you have easy access to Bar Harbor and most of the park. It too has an amphitheater at which rangers hold nature talks in the evenings.

Most people who visit Acadia do so unaware that the park owns a large parcel on Isle au Haut, reached by way of a mail boat from Stonington, many miles up the coast from Bar Harbor. Like the rest of the park on Mount Desert, the Isle au Haut section is a stunning place of peaks, cliffs, and sea, but it has a decidedly wilder feel enhanced by dense woodlands and the fact that access is limited to only 48 people on any given day. Those lucky few who find it (something like 5,000 people a year) tend to keep going back, though, which makes getting a site at one of the five lean-tos at Duck Harbor Campground a bit of a challenge. The sites are available from May 15 through October 15 and can be reserved for five nights at a time maximum.

Call Acadia for a reservation form (207-288-3338) and return it to Acadia National Park, P.O. Box 177, Bar Harbor 04609 prior to April 1 to request a space. Be sure to list alternate dates. It may be tough to get in here, but it is very definitely worth the effort.

i Visit Acadia in the off-season—May or November, say—and you'll have the place to yourself. The vast majority of the park's visitors come during high summer and when the foliage turns. If you plan your vacation at any other time of the year, the park will be wide open to explore and free to use (in winter). There also will be good deals at those inns and motels that are open year-round in Bar Harbor.

SCHOODIC PENINSULA

Some of the best views to be found of Mount Desert Island are not even on the island. Seven miles away, as the boat rows, is Schoodic Point, a headland in Winter Harbor on which Acadia owns 2,000 acres. While three million people visit the Bar Harbor area every year, only a few thousand ever make their way down this rugged, remote point of land to enjoy the parcel of parkland at its tip. The drive to get here is more than an hour from Acadia, but it's very worthwhile, especially if the Mount Desert crowds are getting you down. In 2003 the Island Explorer bus service began offfering free rides on Schoodic in conjunction with the Bar Harbor–Winter Harbor ferry (which isn't free and costs $29.50 for adults, $19.50 for kids under 12).

Schoodic Point is much like the rest of Acadia, only a bit more raw. It has its own Park Loop Road, which passes through woods of pine and spruce and under hills before arriving at the shoreline, where the surf booms and the look back at the mountains of Acadia is jaw-dropping. Bring a picnic (watch out for the brazen seagulls—they'll take your chips), park in the big lot at the end of the road, and revel in the rocks and sea. If the tides are high or the seas are stormy, the crashing surf is particularly impressive.

To get to Schoodic, take Route 1 to Gouldsboro and hang a right onto Route 186 to Winter Harbor. Then follow signs for the park.

BIKING

Cyclists have been smitten with Acadia for a century, and a mountain bike just might be the most perfect mode of transportation for a visit. With the carriage roads, the Park Loop Road, and back roads on the island's quiet side, there are plenty of extraordinary avenues to pedal. Some crazies even like to ride down the auto road on Cadillac Mountain, a winding road with precipitous drop-offs. Rentals are available at a variety of locations in Bar Harbor, and fees tend to be about $22 to $36 a day for a bike, a lock, and a helmet. Try **Bar Harbor Bicycle Shop** (141 Cottage Street; 207-288-3886 www.barharborbike.com), **Acadia Outfitters** (110 Cottage Street; 207-288-8118), or **Acadia Bike** (48 Cottage Street; 800-526-8615; www.acadiabike.com).

NATURE TOURS

DOWN EAST NATURE TOURS
P.O. Box 521, Bar Harbor 04609
(207) 288-8128
www.downeastnaturetours.com
Michael Good has been a guide for years and has about 30 years of experience studying birds. He'll take you on a four-hour tour of Mount Desert's avian species—focusing on bald eagles, ospreys, peregrine falcons, shorebirds, and warblers—or set up photography or camping trips. Rates vary according to the trip.

FRIENDS OF ACADIA

We should all have friends as dedicated and devoted as Acadia does. Friends of Acadia (FOA) is a membership organization whose mission is to help preserve and protect the natural resources of the park. Love it though they might, three million visitors can be hard on a place—even one made out of granite. FOA puts together work parties to shore up trails, raises funds to help defend Acadia against external threats, lobbies on behalf of the park when political issues arise, and does so much more. And they appreciate all the help they can get, both fiscal and physical. They accept donations and collect $35 annual membership dues, and they organize regular work parties that help get things done that the cash-strapped federal government can't seem to afford.

For more information on Friends of Acadia, call (207) 288-3340 or (800) 625-0321 or visit the Web site www.friendsofacadia.org.

GOLF

Golfers in Maine tend to be a lot like gardeners. Because their season is cut short by snow and ice, they take to their hobby with a passion not found elsewhere. It's not uncommon to see Maine golfers hitting the links very early in the morning, playing through rain and flurries, and pushing the season as long as possible.

Their zeal is understandable. Who wouldn't want to spend their days on some of the finest acreage in the state? Maine courses sit on prime property, on headlands overlooking the sea, tucked under mountains, along rivers. There are more than 120 in all—many of them on the coast—and they range from neat neighborhood greens like those at the tiny Northport Golf Club to upscale country clubs like Cape Arundel Golf Club to some of the oldest and toughest holes in the nation, like those at Kebo Valley in Bar Harbor.

I've listed the Maine courses that are public or semiprivate and open to nonmembers. These courses tend to be very busy in summer, so it's not a bad idea to call ahead about tee times. Greens fees vary wildly, depending upon the course and the time of week you go; ask when you call ahead to reserve a tee time.

SOUTH COAST

LINKS AT OUTLOOK
Route 4, Berwick
(207) 384-4653
www.outlookgolf.com

Designed "in the Scottish tradition," the links here nonetheless feel thoroughly New English, built as they are on the grounds of an old Maine farm—there's still a big, beautiful red barn on the premises (see if you can hit the broad side of it). The 18-hole course was designed by *Golf World* magazine's Architect of the Year 1999, Brian Silva, and its bent grass greens and fairways are thoughtfully laid out on 140 acres of rising and falling meadows. Here and there these grasslands are punctuated by sand bunkers and rolling dunes. Its 6,500, par 71 yards are very open and photogenic, and they play nicely, too. The season here starts in May and runs through autumn, and there are attractive off-season rates ($40 for 18 holes on a weekday, say, in foliage season). The Links also offers Twilight All You Can Play

times after 4 p.m. during summer, where $45 will get you as many hours of golf as you want. Then wind down on the patio with something from the bar. Find the latest golf fashions in the pro shop, sign up for instruction, or plan your wedding on the course—it's a full-service place. Rentals, practice green, and a driving range with targets at 100, 150, and 200 yards all await.

HIGHLAND LINKS GOLF CLUB
301 Cider Hill Rd., York
(207) 351-2727

Just inland in the southern Maine community of York Village, this is about as close to the entrance of the Pine Tree State as a golf addict's going to get. The nine holes here were built in 1995, and they're arranged into a fairly short course of 5,599 yards. The setting is pleasant, and golfers will find just about all they need: a pro shop, snack bar, club and cart rentals, a driving range, a practice green, a practice bunker, and instruction to boot. Reserving tee times is a good idea during the high season.

More on Maine Golf

A great source for additional golf information is the Maine State Golf Association. It has a handy Web site—www.mesga.org—which lists member clubs, golf-related events and tournaments, and other helpful links, and provides details on its member discount card, a bargain for people who log a lot of time on the fairways. If you want to know who the point leaders in Maine are or find out the Web address of your favorite club, this site is a good place to start.

THE LEDGES GOLF CLUB
One Ledges Dr., York
(207) 351-9999
www.ledgesgolf.com

The Ledges was voted the best new public course in New England by *Golf Magazine* in 1999, and it's indeed an impressive place. Eighteen holes are laid out across a hilly landscape (views of the Piscataqua River between Maine and New Hampshire can be dramatic at points), and it's not uncommon to see a critter or two during your round. Water plays a role on a few holes—the par-three 8th, the par-three 11th, the par-four 15th, and the par-five 18th—and there are islands of forests all around the fairways. The porch on the clubhouse is a particularly pleasant feature, and the food is good in the dining room. The pro shop has got what you need, there's a driving range and a practice green and bunker, and you can rent whatever gear you don't want to bring. All very nice. Tee times are recommended.

CAPE ARUNDEL GOLF CLUB
19 River Rd., Kennebunkport
(207) 967-3494
www.capearundelgolfclub.com

Established in 1896, Cape Arundel is a semiprivate, 18-hole course that President Bush the elder is fond of playing (his grandfather was a past club president), so it's not surprising that it's a tad exclusive—no jeans or sweatshirts. It's a Scottish-links course, and water comes into play on 13 holes. Caddies are available upon request. The season runs from mid-April through mid-November, and tee times are necessary. Greens fees are $65.

WEBHANNET GOLF CLUB
26 Golf Club Dr., Kennebunk Beach
(207) 967-2061

Yet another 18-hole semiprivate club in the Kennebunks, Webhannet was built in 1901 and is a very busy place in summer. The club offers a public tee time only once every hour, so it's definitely a good idea to call at least a day in advance. Nine holes were added to the original nine back in 1925, and now it's a 6,049-yard, par 72 course with bent grass greens, bluegrass fairways, several water hazards, 31 sand bunkers, and a snack bar on the eighth tee. The fairways are pleasant and open, with woods at their edge. The facilities are well equipped, including a pro shop, practice greens and bunkers, and club and cart rental.

DUTCH ELM GOLF COURSE
5 Brimstone Rd., Arundel
(207) 282-9850
www.dutchelmgolf.com

Perhaps the most welcoming course in the Kennebunk area, Dutch Elm is in the inland town of Arundel. It is public, has rentals, and at $25 for 18 holes, its greens fees are considerably cheaper than those of the coastal courses. The facility features a pro shop, club and cart rentals, a snack bar for a goodie after the ninth hole, and putting greens. You can also reserve tee times a week in advance. The only things that aren't welcome are short shorts, groups larger than four, and metal spikes.

PINE HOLLOW PAR 3
1486 Main St., Sanford
(207) 324-5271

A good club for up-and-comers, Pine Hollow is a short, par 3 course, with the longest of its 18 holes a distant 80 yards. This is a great place to come and practice and hone your game. You'll also find a practice green, rental options, and instruction offered. Open from April through September.

SANFORD COUNTRY CLUB
Route 4, Sanford
(207) 324-5462
www.sanfordcountryclub.com

Built in 1924, Sanford County Club sits on Bauneg Beg Pond and began its life as the Bauneg Beg Pond Country Club. The nine original holes were laid out by Maine course architect Alex Chisholm, and nine new holes were added in 1997 by Marvin Armstrong, when the unwieldy name was changed. The result is a popular, par 72, 18-hole championship course with four sets of tees. The facilities include a driving range, tee mats, a practice bunker, rentals, instruction, and the all-important snack bar and lounge. The course is open from April through October. Tee times are necessary and can be made a couple of days ahead of time. Eighteen holes are $41, $48 on weekends.

BIDDEFORD-SACO COUNTRY CLUB
101 Old Orchard Rd., Saco
(207) 282-5883
http://bscc.ghinclub.com

Back in 1987 the Biddeford-Saco club added a back nine to the nine holes that were originally built here in 1922 on a design by Donald Ross. Golfers here tend to be of the hardy variety, playing from April into mid-November, and it's not usually too difficult to get tee times despite the fact that these par 71 links are considered to be among the best in southern Maine. Pay your greens fee and you're a member for the day and get access to all the amenities, which are impressive. They include a full pro shop, a driving range, a practice green and bunker, cart and club rental, instruction, a locker room, and a restaurant and lounge. Find out why *Golf Digest* ranked these bluegrass fairways among the best in Maine in 1996.

DUNEGRASS GOLF CLUB
200 Wild Dunes Way, Old Orchard Beach
(207) 934-4513 or (800) 521-1029
www.dunegrass.com

One of Maine's newest courses, Dunegrass opened in 1998, and it's very popular. The *Boston Globe* has called it a "must," and word of mouth tends to bear it out. The greens fees are pretty steep to play on this 300-acre course, though. The large clubhouse features both a restaurant and a pro shop, and you can even enjoy "play and stay" vacation packages that include time at a two-bedroom condo on Fairway 1.

GREATER PORTLAND

NONESUCH RIVER GOLF CLUB
304 Gorham Rd., Scarborough
(207) 883-0007
www.nonesuchgolf.com

Eighteen-hole Nonesuch has been lauded for preserving much of the wildlife habitat it was built amid in the woods along Scarborough's Nonesuch River. The club was designed as something of a sanctuary, and it carefully tried to keep the living space of moose, deer, wild turkeys, and foxes intact, which has made the par 70 course unique and fun to play. The fairways and greens are bent grass and were constructed in the late 1990s to USGA specifications with the average golfer in mind. General manager Daniel Hourihan has been quoted as saying that what the course offers "is everything that's good about golf." There's something to that—the place is very welcoming, from the greens to the 2,500-square-foot clubhouse. Tee times are required, can be reserved a week in advance, and can even be made on the course's Web site.

PLEASANT HILL GOLF CLUB
38 Chamberlain Rd., Scarborough
(207) 883-9340

A nine-hole course handy to much of Greater Portland, Pleasant Hill was built in the early 1960s. The holes here are a par 34 and stretch 2,400 yards. The course's big greens and shortish layout make it forgiving to novice golfers. There's a snack bar, and both clubs and carts are available to rent.

WILLOWDALE GOLF CLUB
52 Willowdale Rd., Scarborough
(207) 883-9351
www.willowdalegolf.com
Willowdale is sandwiched between the horses and huff of Scarborough Downs harness-racing track and the salt marsh and seabirds of pretty Scarborough Marsh. And in the case of the latter, Greater Portland's big, beautiful estuary, that's not a bad thing. The front nine holes are open, the back nine are hugged by trees, and water separates the two but only comes into play on two holes. Because of the marsh, the par 71 course is among the most attractive in the area. The club is big on tournaments, so, depending upon when you visit, you can try your hand. There are plenty of amenities, from the modern clubhouse to the practice greens, rentals, snack bar, and lounge, and if you don't find what you want in the pro shop, you can always skip over to the Maine Mall, which is just minutes down the road. Tee times are recommended on the weekends.

SABLE OAKS GOLF CLUB
505 Country Club Dr., South Portland
(207) 775-6257
www.sableoaks.com
A public course, Sable Oaks has a reputation for being challenging—both the 18 holes themselves and getting tee time. Calling ahead is required to get onto the well-loved, par 70 greens here (a week in advance would help your cause). *Golf Digest* called it Maine's eighth best public course in 1996; *Travel Golf Maine* magazine says it's "certainly the Portland area's premier daily fee layout," and people do indeed line up to play these tight fairways and fast greens. The course is hilly and woodsy, ably masking the fact that the Maine Mall and the Portland International Jetport are scant minutes up the road, and water comes into play on seven holes. The facilities are first-class, with a beautiful banquet room, a fully outfitted pro shop, a locker room, rentals, and more.

SOUTH PORTLAND MUNICIPAL GOLF COURSE
155 Wescott Rd., South Portland
(207) 775-0005
The short nine-hole course run by the city of South Portland is known for being a good place to learn golfing. It's only 2,285 yards long, so you don't have to be Tiger Woods to be successful, and there are few hazards to worry about, just hills and trees, and pleasant ones at that. Par is 33, and you can get going early in the morning if you like. Club and pulled cart rental are available, and you can munch on goodies from the snack bar. Tee times are not necessary.

RIVERSIDE MUNICIPAL GOLF COURSE
1158 Riverside St., Portland
(207) 797-3524
Owned by the city of Portland, Riverside is actually two courses in one—Riverside North, an 18-hole, par 72 course, and Riverside South, a 9-hole, par 35 course. First opened to play in 1935, the 18-hole half is the more challenging setting—it hosts the Greater Portland Open—and it's among the most popular of all the courses in southern Maine. (Be thinking tee times if you want to play on the weekend.) The hills roll across its 6,406 yards, and it borders the Presumpscot River on the back part of the course. From the locker rooms and showers to the restaurant and lounge, it's a very professional operation. The facility also has a full pro shop, a driving range, practice greens, and rentals—the whole nine yards. In the winter the course becomes a popular cross-country skiing and snowshoeing destination.

RIVERMEADOW GOLF CLUB
216 Lincoln St., Westbrook
(207) 854-1625
Established in 1958, Rivermeadow is a par 35, nine-hole course in the Greater Portland mill town of Westbrook. The river in question is the Presumpscot, which helped make Westbrook into the industrious little city it is by getting things started at the local paper mill. The course is pleasant and tree lined, with water coming into

play on three holes and sand and grass bunkers. You shouldn't have too much difficulty arranging a tee time, especially if you show up promptly at 7 a.m. The club is well outfitted, with a full pro shop, a practice green, a lounge and snacks, rentals, and instruction available.

TWIN FALLS GOLF CLUB
364 Spring St., Westbrook
(207) 854-5397

This is a tough one, thanks to woods and hills and small greens. Built in 1971 on the site of an old dairy farm in the Portland suburb of Westbrook, Twin Falls measures only 4,880 yards (par 33), but they are full of intriguing difficulties for the average golfer. The course is open from April through October, and there are club and car rentals and a snack bar. You won't find tee times necessary.

WESTERLY WINDS SPORTS PARK AND GOLF LEARNING CENTER
853 Cumberland St. (River Rd.), Westbrook
(207) 854-9463
www.westerlywinds.com

Yet another set of Westbrook links, this is the Johnny-come-lately on the scene, built in 1985. Two nine-hole courses compete for the attention of golfers here: the old nine-hole, par 27 pitch-and-putt Westerly Winds Course and the new nine-hole, par 35 championship Sunset Ridge Golf Links course. The former is just good fun, the latter a serious course with white birch stands and apple orchards to play through and around. If it proves too challenging, you might want to switch over to the 18-hole minigolf course or the driving range, or put down the clubs altogether and hit a few balls in the batting cage, or try your luck at shuffleboard or tennis, or take a swim in the pool. This is quite the full-service facility and should keep the whole family happy.

GORHAM COUNTRY CLUB
134 McLellan Rd., Gorham
(207) 839-3490
www.gorhamcountryclub.com

In the college town of Gorham—half of the University of Southern Maine is located here

(the other campus is in Portland)—this is a fun course of bluegrass fairways and bent grass greens spread across a bosky, rolling landscape. The 18 holes are par 71, and water comes into play on four of them. Built in 1961 and designed by James MacDonald Sr., the course has played host to the Maine Open, and it has all the facilities to accommodate such an event. From a well-outfitted pro shop to cart and club rentals to the restaurant and lounge to the locker room and showers, everything a duffer would need is here. Unless you want to show up at 6:30 a.m. when the course opens, you might want to call ahead for tee times—and wear a shirt there, Tarzan, they're required (along with shoes).

VAL HALLA GOLF AND RECREATION CENTER
60 Val Halla Rd., Cumberland
www.cumberlandmaine.com/valhalla.cfm
(207) 829-2225

You won't find any Norse gods at Val Halla, but if you can avoid the brook on the 18th hole and come in somewhere around the 72 par, you might feel like one. Built in 1965 and expanded to 18 holes in the 1980s, the course is owned by the town of Cumberland, a pleasant suburb north of Portland. There's a whole complex of entertainments here, from tennis courts to a driving range to the Viking Grill. The place opens at 7 each morning, and you could easily fill a whole day playing 18 holes, having lunch at the grill, and then pulling on the tennis shoes. The course itself is 6,568 yards, and because it was designed in two phases, it has a different feel on the back nine. The facilities are excellent and include a well-stocked pro shop, a practice green and bunker, club and cart rental, and instruction. You can wind down with a cold beverage on the big deck off the back of the clubhouse overlooking the course.

FREEPORT COUNTRY CLUB
2 Old County Rd., Freeport
(207) 865-0711
www.harrisgolfonline.com

Thanks to the fact that it's visible from Interstate

95 and less than 10 minutes from L.L. Bean, Freeport Country Club is a particularly active course. A nine-hole set of links established in the late 1960s, it's a 36 par and begins in flat fields just off the highway, ending in the woods beyond. Easily walkable, its short track makes it a good course for beginners. The facilities are set up much like you'd expect a place that sees a lot of guests to be, with a full pro shop, club and cart rentals, a practice green, and a bar at which you can grab a snack after your round. Tee times are recommended.

MIDCOAST

BRUNSWICK GOLF CLUB
165 River Rd., Brunswick
(207) 725-8224
www.brunswickgolfclub.com
Brunswick has two interesting clubs that reflect the community. This is one of them, established in 1901 for use by Bowdoin College students. Now everybody seems to be enjoying its 18 holes on an average weekend. The course is divided into two nine-hole loops, the first original, the second added in 1970, and it's usually busy, so calling ahead is almost mandatory. There are all the major amenities, from club rental to eats to instruction, but you'll have to dress properly to enjoy them (no Bowdoin T-shirts—or tees of any kind—tank tops or cutoffs, etc). Open from April through mid-November. Eighteen holes in midsummer will set you back $40.

MERE CREEK GOLF COURSE
9 Merriconeag Lane, Brunswick
(207) 721-9995
On the grounds of the local navy base, this course was for years called the Brunswick Naval Air Station Golf Club, but the Feds thought the name might be scaring away potential business. The nine holes here have been open to the public for years, but many people—especially visitors and newcomers to the area—aren't aware of it. It's a fine, open course, not too far from the runways of the navy's airport, and you get to rub shoulders with military personnel. From a full shop to a driving range to a snack bar and lounge, all the amenities are here. Club and car rentals are available. Tee times are a good idea on busy summer weekends. Because the BNAS is slated to close, it's a good idea to call ahead, anyway.

SHORE ACRES GOLF CLUB
Sebasco Harbor Resort, Phippsburg
(207) 389-9060
The 9-hole course at this oceanfront resort was rebuilt in 2001, and it's open to nonguests. The panoramas of Sebasco Harbor are phenomenal, and the course takes full advantage of them. Holes are set up such that rank amateurs and experienced duffers alike can choose tees that match their skill level. There's even a three-hole, regulation-size practice course for beginners. The facilities also include a pro shop, club and cart rentals, and a restaurant and lounge. The views alone are worth the drive down the Phippsburg Peninsula. Open from late April through early November.

BATH COUNTRY CLUB
387 Whiskeag Rd., Bath
(207) 442-8411
www.skipworkplaygolf.com
These 18 holes have been renovated and expanded into an impressive course, and you should set aside a whole afternoon to play them. It's a good idea to come early for lunch at the clubhouse restaurant. There's also a pro shop on-site, along with practice greens, club and cart rental, and a lounge for bragging after the game is done. Tee times are necessary on weekends. Open from early April through October.

BOOTHBAY COUNTRY CLUB
33 Country Club Rd., Boothbay
(207) 633-6085
www.harrisgolfonline.com
Designed in 1921 by Styles and Van Cleek, the Boothbay Country Club expanded to 18 holes in 2000. The course is a scenic, rolling, par 70 affair, and the log-cabin–style clubhouse atop the first tee reminds you you're in Maine. Open from mid-April through October. The facility includes a full

pro shop, a driving range, a practice green, and club and cart rental. Instruction is available.

WAWENOCK COUNTRY CLUB
Route 129, Walpole
(207) 563-3938
www.wawenockgolfclub.com
What would Damariscotta area duffers do without Wawenock? A lot of traveling, that's what. This is the only course for miles, and it is consequently very popular on weekends. Established in the 1920s, the nine holes here have a reputation for being fairly challenging. Par is 70 for these 6,037 yards, and the hilly, tree-lined terrain makes for plenty of tough shots. The clubhouse is located across Route 129 from the actual links and is a neat old Victorian structure. It's fairly well stocked with a pro shop, snack bar, locker room, and showers. You can rent clubs and carts, practice on the green or the practice bunker, or hit a few on the driving range. Tee times are a good idea on weekends in high summer and can be arranged as much as a week in advance.

ROCKLAND GOLF CLUB
606 Old County Rd., Rockland
(207) 594-9322
www.rocklandgolf.com
An 18-hole public course established in 1942, Rockland Golf Club is open from April through October and rarely sees a day when it isn't in use by somebody. There are some nice views of the surrounding Camden Hills, as well as of Penobscot Bay from the first hole, Lake Chickawaukie from the 15th, and even some neat old lime quarries. The club serves breakfast and lunch and has a full bar, and the pro shop is well outfitted. You can rent whatever you might need. Tee times are required and should be reserved a few days in advance. A note: Be careful when crossing Old County Road; drivers are supposed to slow down due to the dramatic S curve here, but they are always zipping through. (Some have been known to toot in an attempt to throw off your swing out on the Route 17 legs of the course, too.) Oh, and leave your spikes behind.

GOOSE RIVER GOLF CLUB
50 Park St., Rockport
(207) 236-8488
www.gooserivergolf.com
Many people are unaware that there is a golf course in the Camden-Rockport area, so tucked away is this gem. On a back road on the inland side of Rockport, not far from Bald and Ragged Mountains, it's listed in guidebooks with both Camden and Rockport addresses, so it's understandably difficult for the casual visitor to the area to find. But anyone with an interest in whacking a few should seek these greens out. The course is a bent grass, par 71 setup with water in play. Alternate tees make the 9-hole course almost like an 18-holer. Weekends can be busy, so tee times are necessary, and they can be reserved a week in advance. There are a snack bar and lounge on the premise for après-swing, a full pro shop, cart and club rentals, and a resident pro handy to give you tips. Open from mid-April through late October.

SAMOSET GOLF COURSE
The Samoset Resort
220 Warrenton St., Rockport
(207) 594-2511 or (800) 341-1650
www.samoset.com
One of the most popular courses along the coast, the Samoset has 18 holes on a stunning piece of coast overlooking both Rockland Harbor and the open ocean. These holes have been lauded up and down, called "a golfer's paradise" by *Golf Traveler,* hailed as "the seventh-most beautiful course in America" by *Golf Digest,* and ranked 26th in Golf Digest's listing of the country's 75 best resort courses. It's easy to understand, as 14 holes have superb views of the sea and seven actually border it. Part of the Samoset Resort, these links are available to nonguests, but the fees tend to be steep—$110 these days—and tee times are scheduled to favor guests. Still, it's worth making the effort for the views alone.

NORTHPORT GOLF CLUB
581 Bluff Rd., Northport
(207) 338-2270
Backed up against the cottage community of

Bayside, just south of Belfast, the Northport Golf Club is a pleasure. Established in 1916, the course has nine holes and a par 36. It is fairly wide open with midsize greens of fast bent grass. Alternate tees are available for an 18-hole outing. The clubhouse is a nice old Victorian building, in keeping with the cool Victorian cottages of Bayside, which you should check out on your way in or out. Open from mid-April through October.

SEARSPORT PINES GOLF COURSE
240 Mount Ephraim Rd., Searsport
(207) 548-2854
www.searsportpines.com
Built by a retiree on his family farm in 1999, this nine-hole, par 36 course is surprisingly enjoyable, and it was voted Waldo County's best in 2007. The terrain is hilly and the fairways lined with pines, but it's a fairly short course at 5,766 yards, so it's not a difficult walk. The views can be very pleasant (as is the gazebo snack bar). Water comes into play on many of the early holes and then again on the ninth, where there's a large pond that undoubtedly has a bottom full of balls. Cart and club rentals are available, and tee times are recommended on the weekends.

COUNTRY VIEW GOLF CLUB
Route 7, Brooks
(207) 722-3161
The name says it all. Inland along Route 7, 15 minutes from Belfast, Country View rides the backs of a series of rolling hills and offers some fantastic scenery of the Camden Hills and even the White Mountains on a superclear day. Be prepared to do some walking, as the terrain is hilly (cart rental is available). The club is family owned and friendly. Best of all, the nine holes here are not usually too busy. Open from mid-April through October.

BUCKSPORT GOLF CLUB
Route 46, Bucksport
(207) 469-7612
www.bucksportgolfclub.com
Bucksport bills itself as Maine's longest nine-hole course, and if it isn't, it must be close—hole 5 alone is a 502-yarder. The facility includes a pro

shop, a snack bar, a driving range, cart and club rental, and two chipping greens. Open from mid-April through September, you can tee off as early as 7 a.m., and tee times are not usually necessary.

ISLAND COUNTRY CLUB
442 Sunset Rd., Deer Isle
(207) 348-2379
www.islandcountryclub.net
There's a lot to like at this nine-hole course. The greens were well laid out when the place was built in 1928, the clubhouse has recently been expanded, and it has a pleasant, welcoming air. You might be tempted to show up at 6:30 a.m. and play until dark after a few rounds here. The club is open from late May through mid-October. The facilities include cart and club rental, a practice green, a snack bar, and tennis courts.

CASTINE GOLF CLUB
200 Battle Ave., Castine
(207) 326-8844
www.castinegolfclub.com
Sprawling across one of the prettiest villages in Maine, the Castine club was opened in 1897, its fairways sweeping down toward the water. English designer William Parker Jr. crafted the original nine-hole layout, some of which is still the same. Instruction is available, as are club and cart rentals. Open from May 15 through October 15. There are tennis courts on-site, too, and you should make it in town to have a look at Castine, if you make it this far.

WHITE BIRCHES GOLF CLUB
20 Thorsen Rd., Ellsworth
(207) 667-3621
www.whitebirchescountryclub.com
One of the more unusual courses in Maine, this par 33 18-holer is part of a motel complex right on U.S. Route 1, the main drag to Acadia National Park. One might expect minigolf here rather than 18 nice holes, but that's what lies out behind the White Birches motel. The first nine holes were built in 1983 and the second added in 2000, and the course has added a new twist to

its offerings—golf under the lights. You'll feel like you're back in high school, playing the big game before the home crowd. The greens fees are eminently reasonable, and the club is well outfitted with a pro shop, practice green and bunker, and club and cart rental. And you can book a night in the motel if 18 holes during the day and another round under the lights just aren't enough. Open from April through October.

BAR HARBOR GOLF COURSE
Routes 3 and 204, Trenton
(207) 667-7505
www.barharborgolfcourse.com
This old favorite is not actually in Bar Harbor—or even on Mount Desert Island, for that matter. Established in 1965, the club is actually in Trenton, a few miles short of the island but with truly fantastic views of the green mountains of Acadia. The 18-hole, par 71 course gently rolls on small hills and the Jordan River plays through; other bodies of water provide challenges on a few holes, and the ocean makes itself felt, too, in the form of periodic breezes. The club is fully outfitted with a pro shop, driving range, restaurant, lounge, rentals, and a practice green. It's open from mid-April through October.

ACADIA AREA

KEBO VALLEY GOLF CLUB
136 Eagle Lake Rd., Bar Harbor
(207) 288-3000
www.kebovalleyclub.com
Bar Harbor is perhaps better known for its minigolf, but Kebo Valley is magnificent, one of Maine's best courses. In fact, it has a national reputation as a classic course, the eighth oldest in the nation. Built in 1891, the 18 holes here sit before some astonishing mountains-meet-the-sea vistas, which make a day on the links almost as much of a sightseeing trip as a hike in nearby Acadia National Park. Local legend has it that President Howard Taft needed 27 tries to sink the 17th hole on this par 70 course. The facilities live up to the greens and fairways, with a pro shop, rentals, instruction, club storage, a practice green

and bunker, and a fine restaurant and lounge. They have a full-service caterer here, so, theoretically, you could get a tasty lunch delivered to you halfway through your round. Might be expensive, is all. The place is understandably popular, and tee times are necessary. Open daily from May through October.

NORTHEAST HARBOR GOLF CLUB
Sargent Dr., Northeast Harbor
(207) 276-5335
www.nehgc.com
Much like Kebo Valley, in that it feels old and classic, Northeast Harbor Golf Club was built in 1895 on the side of Somes Sound, the only genuine fjord in the Lower 48. Duffers enjoy 18 short, hilly, woodsy holes here, with views of beautiful Mount Desert frequent companions. The course has a full pro shop, a practice green, and club and cart rental. The driving range is for members only. Make sure to wear clothes that are appropriate—no cutoffs or halters. You can tee off as early as 7 a.m., and the course is open from Memorial Day through Labor Day.

CAUSEWAY GOLF CLUB
10 Fernald Point Rd., Southwest Harbor
(207) 244-3780
www.thecausewayclub.com
Built in 1920, this nine-hole course is considerably simpler than some others in the Mount Desert Island area. It has some nice water views, a couple of challenging holes, and a pro shop. Clubs and carts can be rented, and snacks can be had when you start to get hungry. Allow three hours to play 18 holes, and don't worry too much about tee times.

DOWN EAST

BLINK BONNIE GOLF CLUB
Route 185, Sorrento
(207) 422-3930
This little-known gem has been around since 1916, but you'd never know it. Most people remain unaware of the nine holes here (par 70), so tee times are not usually hard to come by.

The layout is open, and the nearby sea factors in on a couple of holes. Open from May through September.

GRINDSTONE NECK GOLF COURSE
106 Grindstone Ave., Winter Harbor
(207) 963-7760
www.grindstonegolf.com
There isn't much unpleasant about this grindstone. Duffers have been whacking them here since the 1890s, when the rusticators used to summer in the exclusive enclave of Winter Harbor. Pause for a moment before you tee off, and you'll see why they came—the scenery is extraordinary, looking out at the waves and islands of Frenchman Bay and the mountains of Acadia. Water is ever present. Par is 36 for 3,095 yards, and the course has a reputation as being fairly challenging, with tight bluegrass fairways. The fun begins each morning at sunrise, from early June through September, and tee times usually aren't necessary.

GREAT COVE GOLF COURSE
Roque Bluffs Rd., Jonesboro
(207) 434-7200
www.greatcovegolf.com
Ample ocean views make playing this nine-hole course a real treat. These holes were built in the 1970s, and they tend to be on the easier side of things. The amenities are not abundant—snack bar, driving range, practice green, and club and cart rental—but the setting here is the key and more than makes up for it. Tee times are not necessary, and you can play until dark on the one greens fee. Open from May through September.

SAINT CROIX COUNTRY CLUB
Route 1, Calais
(207) 454-8875
www.stcroixcc.com
You can practice your French while you play on these nine holes—the club is bilingual, thanks to the fact that it borders the Canadian province of New Brunswick. The layout is open, and the St. Croix River comes into play on one hole. Greens are of bent grass, the fairways are of bluegrass, and par is 68 for 5,470 yards. You can tee off as early as 7 a.m., and when you do, chances are you'll be one of the first people to smack a ball in the United States, as this course is the easternmost in the country and gets the first rays of sun every morning. The facilities include a pro shop, club and cart rental, and a snack bar and lounge. Open from late April through late October. Très agréable.

BARREN VIEW GOLF COURSE
1354 Route 1, Jonesboro
(207) 434-6531
www.barrenview.com
The views are anything but barren here. This nine-hole course opened in 2003 and it has panoramas aplenty; it's just that you're looking at, well, barrens—the blueberry barrens that the Down East coast is famous for. Par is 34, and you may find it easier than some to make. There are the usual amenities—clubhouse with cafe, pro shop, and rentals—and you can start playing as early as 7 a.m. Play all day for $35, or just the nine holes for $15.

KIDSTUFF

Maine continually ranks among the top states in the country to raise children—it was fourth best in a recent national Kids Count survey by the Annie E. Casey Foundation—and millions upon millions of people have rosy memories of childhood vacations spent on the Maine coast. Kids just love the place.

It's easy to understand why—there are endless things to do by simply stepping outside: Beaches and tide pools await explorers, trees are there to climb, hikable mountains are everywhere to be found, and swimming holes dot the landscape. The state also boasts a lot of entertainment for the smaller set, from the children's museums in Portland and Bangor, to the Maine State Game Farm in Gray, to petting zoos and amusement parks in various communities up and down the coast. Some conservation groups have great day programs for kids and families, and there are YMCAs along the length of the coast that are perfect for rainy days. Mom and Dad shouldn't have to work hard to find stuff to keep the kids busy.

This chapter features kidstuff by region and ends by listing miniature golf courses along the Maine coast.

Several of the places and activities listed in previous chapters are just perfect for youngsters, too. These places include lighthouses (see Lighthouses chapter), beaches (see Beaches chapter), forts (see Attractions chapter), and state parks (see Green Space chapter). Check them out for still further ideas.

i Visit the Maine Secretary of State's kids' Web page—www.maine.gov/sos/kids—and you'll find a list of things to do with children, along with a bunch of facts and info of interest to the younger set. The site is hosted by Mozzie Moose and Loretta Lobster.

Price Code

Except where noted, prices represent cost per person for admission, not including tax. In cases where donation is listed, there is no mandatory admission fee, but a donation is appreciated and recommended to support upkeep of the facility.

$..................	$5.99 or less
$$	$6.00 to $12.99
$$$	$13.00 to $19.99
$$$$	$20.00 or more

SOUTH COAST

THE GOLDENROD
York Beach
(207) 363-2621
www.thegoldenrod.com

More than a candy store, this old York Beach favorite is a veritable candy factory, and it's been at it for more than a century. Most famous for its taffy, the Goldenrod produces nine million Goldenrod Kisses a year—that's 65 tons of fun—using an 1896 recipe created by the shop's founder. (The secret science of saltwater taffy is reportedly understanding the weather.) There are 12 flavors—try the peanut butter or wintergreen—and you can watch it all being turned into sticky goodness right in the windows of the shop. The place also has a host of other treats, from fudge to barc to peanut brittle to candy corn, and there is still a penny candy counter where little suckies cost, yep, a penny apiece. Quite aside from being a sweet and aromatic stop, the Goldenrod has an anachronistic appeal, taking you back to summers long past with its old building, marble soda counter, and stone fireplace—classic stuff that will entertain moms and dads almost as much as the kids.

YORK'S WILD KINGDOM $$$
Route 1, York Beach
(207) 363-4911
www.yorkzoo.com

This York Beach institution is much more than a zoo. There are plenty of beasties about, sure—they number in the hundreds now, from llamas and lions to elephants and bears to camels and sloths to everyone's favorite, Rewa the Bengal tiger. But there are also go-karts, arcade games, Skeeball, haunted houses, minigolf, batting cages, bumper boats and paddleboats, rides upon rides, and all the snacks you could eat. (This place is just a short walk from York Beach.) A variety of scheduled shows—like elephant shows and Wildlife Theatre educational programs—and other events occur on a daily basis, so be sure to call ahead for times. The Wild Kingdom is a fullfledged amusement park, and if you're into that sort of thing, it's very amusing. Admission prices do not include go-kart or pony rides, which cost extra. In the high season—basically when school is out—the zoo is open daily from 10 a.m. to 5 p.m. and the park from noon to 9:30 p.m. Special rates for children.

AQUABOGGAN WATER PARK $$$–$$$$
980 Portland Rd., Saco
(207) 282-3112
www.aquaboggan.com

The state's biggest water park, Aquaboggan is an endless source of fun for kids. Besides the waterslides, tubular slides, and suislides (dual high-speed cannonball runs), the facility offers an Olympic-size swimming pool, a wave pool, bumper boats, minigolf, water wars, paddleboats, go-karts, an arcade, and the Aquasaucer, a half dome of bouncy fun. Little people can—and do—spend days here before they get bored. Many of the activities, though, require that par-

ticipants be over 4 feet tall. Rates vary, depending upon which rides and slides you want to try. Open daily from mid-June through Labor Day from 10 a.m. to 6 p.m.

FUNTOWN USA $$$$
774 Portland Rd. (Route 1), Saco
(207) 284-5139
www.funtownusa.com

Not far from Aquaboggan, this amusement park has been voted Maine's number one tourist attraction, which makes one wonder who's doing the voting (people under the age of 14?). There is no end to the activities. They include the state's largest and tallest roller coaster, the Excalibur Wooden Roller Coast; the Dragon's Descent, a free-fall ride that drops you from 220 feet; the Thunder Falls Log Flume ride; go-kart rides; the water park of Splashtown; a whole slate of games; and enough food to keep you and yours going all day. The park opens in mid-May and runs through mid-September, with hours that vary upon the day of the week (basically 10 a.m. to 10 p.m. in July and most of August). Rates vary, too, and are based on height rather than age.

PALACE PLAYLAND $$$$
1 Old Orchard St., Old Orchard Beach
(207) 934-2001
www.palaceplayland.com

Palace Playland is a big part of what makes Old Orchard Beach Old Orchard Beach—four acres big—it's the state's only beachfront amusement park. Two roller coasters, a log flume ride, a 70-foot-high gondola-style Ferris wheel, and two scary new rides—the Adrenalin Drop Zone, on which you fall 60 feet, and the Cascade Falls, which soars up 50 feet—are available for the high-thrills seekers. And there are a host of teacup-type rides for folks who are smaller or fainter of heart. You can also get your palm read, visit a fun house, and try your hand at a variety of games of chance. This is an old-fashioned seaside carnival on the order of Coney Island, and it has an obvious appeal to kids. Admission to Palace Playland is free, but ride tickets are a dollar; most rides require two to four tickets each.

Directory of Summer Camps

Maine has long been synonymous with summer camp for many people, and with good reason. There are about 100 camps in the state. Many of them are in the western mountain region, where there are woods and lakes galore, but plenty exist along the coast, too. The Maine Youth Camping Association has an extensive directory of camps, broken down by gender, and with all the pertinent information you need to decide where your daughter or son should go, from camp history to current activities and programs. The camps offered by environmental groups, religious organizations, and schools, as well as those geared toward sports or music, are all listed. It's a very handy resource. Your kids may not want to go to camp, of course, but they'll be glad they did when they get there—especially if you pick the right one. Get your copy of the directory by calling (207) 780–4628 or click over to the Web site www.mainecamps.org.

GREATER PORTLAND

HAVENS CANDIES
87 County Rd., Westbrook
(800) 639-6309
www.havenscandies.com
You don't need a golden ticket to tour this candy factory. Call ahead and make and appointment, fork over the $2.50, and you're in. Haven's makes some of the best chocolate in Maine and it's a wonder to behold their operation. Smells so good they might want to change the name to Heaven's.

CHILDREN'S MUSEUM OF MAINE $$
142 Free St., Portland
(207) 828-1234
www.childrensmuseumofme.org
The highlight at this excellent kids' museum—where the motto is "please do touch"—might be the Camera Obscura, a dark room with a lens to the outside world, where you can see an extraordinary, 360-degree panorama of Portland flash before you. This is absolutely fascinating Renaissance-era technology, and there are only two others like it in the nation. But there's a lot more to enjoy here, from the Our Town exhibit, a miniature community where kids participate like grown-ups, to the L.L. Bear Discovery Woods, to the space shuttle, car repair shop, and climbing wall. They're all very well done, and they'll keep the kids entertained for hours. The museum hosts birthday parties, special camps, and a variety of events throughout the year. It's open Tuesday through Saturday from 10 a.m. to 5 p.m. and Sunday from noon to 5 p.m. The first Friday of each month, it's free to visit from 5 to 8 p.m.

CHILDREN'S THEATRE OF MAINE $$
317 Marginal Way, Portland
(207) 878-2774
www.childrenstheatremaine.org
This nifty drama outfit—the oldest continuously operating kids' theater in the country—has kids squarely in mind. It produces shows that are geared for younger audiences and hosts the Maine Young Playwright's Contest—the winner gets his or her show staged. Visit the Web site to see the current offerings.

MAINE NARROW GAUGE RAILROAD
AND MUSEUM $-$$
58 Fore St., Portland
(207) 828-0814
www.mngrr.org
Kids love those trains, and this neat museum has working engines that will haul them along the city's working waterfront. Open-air cars allow you to take it all in. These trains are all narrow gauge—the 2-foot-wide tracks that were big in Maine before the advent of the automobile—

and the museum has a fine collection of old examples. It also has a full schedule of special transportation-oriented events. The trains run daily on the hour from 11 a.m. to 4 p.m. from mid-May through mid-October, and weekends for much of the rest of the year. The museum is open daily except for major holidays, from 10 a.m. to 4 p.m.

PORTLAND MUSEUM OF ART $$
7 Congress St., Portland
(207) 775-6148
www.portlandmuseum.org
The Portland Museum of Art has a variety of offerings designed to introduce kids to the world of art. Among the best are the Art-squad programs, which happen on Tuesdays. These hour-long workshops—from 4 to 5 p.m.—take kids ages 6 to 12 through the galleries of the museum and then back to the art studios, where they can make their own works of art. Another idea might be ARTREK, a five-day summer camp for kids ages 6 through 15, where they'll explore the museum and then come up with their own creations. These programs run from early July through August, and each week is geared toward a different age group. And there is always the designated Family Room at the McLellan house, where Mom and Dad and the kids can see interactive computer displays about 19th-century life, puzzles of the art on view at the museum, and a variety of games, like Go Fish using cards depicting artworks from the museum's collection.

PORTLAND OBSERVATORY $
138 Congress St., Portland
(207) 774-5561
www.portlandlandmarks.org
This tall signal tower has an interesting history (see Attractions chapter), but kids don't care about that. They just like climbing its 103 steps to the top of the 86-foot tower for a view that takes in all of Portland, Casco Bay, the White Mountains, and beyond. Open daily from May through October, 10 a.m. to 5 p.m. Children 6 and younger free.

PORTLAND PUBLIC LIBRARY KID'S PLACE
Munjoy Hill, Portland
(207) 1-772-4581
www.portlandlibrary.com/kidsplace/ kids place.htm
The Portland Public Library is an exceptional resource for readers of all ages, and the staffers here get kids interested early with a full slate of programs for children, from story hour to bingo to finger fun for babies to family movies at their very own Children's Library. Call or check the Web site for more details. Free.

PORTLAND SYMPHONY ORCHESTRA $-$$
477 Congress St., Portland
(207) 773-6128
www.portlandsymphony.com
The state's best orchestra frequently hosts Kinderkonzerts, which are designed to introduce kids ages 3 through 7 to live classical music and various families of instruments through interactive programs with symphony musicians. These fun events occur across the state. Check the Web site to see when and where the next one is.

SHOESTRING THEATER
155 Brackett St., Portland
(207) 774-1502
www.shoestringtheater.org
Famous for their parades at the Common Ground Fair and other venues across Maine, the Shoestring Theater is a colorful cast of larger-than-life puppets, stiltwalkers, dancing dragons, and vegetables. The brain behind the operation, Nance Parker, offers workshops in puppetry, stiltwalking, community theater, and carnival craziness to kids of all ages. Call for details.

SOUTHWORTH PLANETARIUM $$
96 Falmouth St., Portland
(207) 780–4249
www.usm.maine.edu/~planet/
Part of the University of Southern Maine, Southworth is one of two planetariums in Maine (the other's in Orono). Every Friday and Saturday the auditorium here becomes the site of astronomy shows at 7 p.m. and laser light shows at 8:30 p.m.

Saturdays also have matinees. The planetarium also regularly holds special programs exploring space themes.

TREEHOUSE TOYS
47 Exchange St., Portland
(207) 775-6133
www.treehousetoys.us
One of those good-for-you toy shops that both parents and kids love, Treehouse features games, puzzles, wooden toys, handmade items, and all kinds of playthings sure to inspire the imagination. A neat shop and the perfect stop for kids.

MAINE AUDUBON SOCIETY $
20 Gilsland Farm Rd., Falmouth
(207) 781-2330
www.maineaudubon.org
Education has always been at the core of the Maine Audubon Society's mission, and the old conservation organization has helped generations of Maine kids gain a greater appreciation for the outdoors. The society hosts a vast array of workshops, programs, and field trips that are oriented toward families and children. These activities are open to nonmembers, and they have names like Explore Fields and Forest and Explore the Pond. There are also programs filled with nature walks, outdoor games, and songs geared to preschoolers, as well as a raft of summer camps for young kids, teens, and family groups. Call the society and ask for the full schedule.

MAZE CRAZE
Plummer-Motz Elementary School
Route 9 and Lunt Rd., Falmouth
The playground to beat all playgrounds, this gigantic wooden maze of a place is great fun for kids to get lost in. (They're fine; don't worry.) Schools from all over bus their children here to explore the castlelike structure, swing on the swings, slide on the slides, and make like monkeys on the monkey bars. A play area for kids with disabilities is right here, too. Open dawn to dusk. Free.

MAINE WILDLIFE PARK $
Route 26, Gray
(207) 287-8000
www.maine.gov/ifw/education/wildlifepark/ index.htm
Formerly known as the Maine Game Farm and Visitors Center, this state-run animal rehabilitation center functions a lot like a zoo, and kids love it. Strolling around the farm, you can see bears, moose, eagles, lynx, wild turkeys, bobcats, and a host of other charismatic critters. Most of the inhabitants of the park are animals that have been injured or orphaned and are being rehabilitated to be released again into the wild, and while they're doing their physical therapy, they entertain the kids. The Maine Department of Inland Fisheries and Wildlife is in charge, and it has set up interactive displays that will teach you and yours about the various animals and their habitat—the Maine woods. You are welcome to stroll the trails of the 200-acre farm or even have a picnic. A fun outing for the whole family, it's worth the short drive inland.

DESERT OF MAINE $-$$
95 Desert Rd., Freeport
(207) 865-6962
www.desertofmaine.com
Camels, anyone? The Desert of Maine doesn't actually have any camels, but they'd feel comfortable in this 300-acre Freeport oddity. Ages of overgrazing and a sandy, arid substratum have turned this old farm into a veritable desert of giant dunes. There are guided safaris of the area on the half hour, but you're welcome to explore the walking trails through the desert on your own. On a hot summer day, you'd swear you were in the Sahara (except for all the pine trees that surround). There are a gift shop, picnic area, and convenience store here where you can learn more about this freakish oasis. Kids love the place, and parents usually find it unusual enough to be worthwhile. Open from early May through mid-October. Children 4 and under free.

Close-up

Why the Y?

Many Maine communities have excellent YMCAs these days, and they often have short-term or even daylong membership options that can be great for visiting families. The Boothbay Region Y, for example, has nice facilities, with its Olympic-size pool, fitness center, gym, racquetball courts, game room, and day camp at a private lake, and it offers a monthly membership that allows for use of everything for $42 for the whole family. This membership can be a vacation saver on a rainy day. The Y here also has day-care programs in the summer, if you happen to be staying for a while. Most other Ys along the coast have similar deals. On the coast, Ys can be found in the following places:

Sanford Springvale YMCA, Sanford; (207) 324-4942; www.sanfordymca.org

Northern York County YMCA, Biddeford; (207) 283-0100; www.nycymca.org

Cumberland County YMCA, Portland; (207) 874-1111; www.cumberlandcountyymca.org

Casco Bay Regional YMCA, Freeport; (207) 865-9600; www.cascobayymca.org

Bath Area Family YMCA, Bath; (207) 443-4112; www.bathymca.org

Central Lincoln County YMCA, Damariscotta; (207) 563-3477; www.clcymca.org

Boothbay Region YMCA, Boothbay Harbor; (207) 633-2855; www.boothbayregionymca.org

Penobscot Bay Area YMCA, Rockport; (207) 236-3375; www.penbayymca.net

Waldo County YMCA, Belfast; (207) 338-4598; www.waldocountyymca.org

Down East Family YMCA, Ellsworth; (207) 667-3086; www.defymca.org

Mount Desert Island YMCA, Bar Harbor; (207) 288-3511; www.mdiymca.org

WOLFE'S NECK FARM
184 Burnett Rd., Freeport
(207) 865-4469
www.wolfesneckfarm.org
Natural foods may be all the rage these days, but this environmentally conscious farm on Casco Bay has been raising beef cattle the all-natural way since the 1950s. In keeping with its philosophies (natural, organic, pesticide-free foods, family farms, knowing where food comes from, sustainability), the farm has an educational arm and offers an array of programs to kids. Favorite activities, according to farm staff, are bottle-feeding baby pigs, going on hayrides, canoeing on the bay, and helping sell produce. Workshops may be half-day, full-day, or weeklong, like the Farm School program, where kids in third through eighth grade work on the farm, learning sustainable principles, and helping grow gardens. April and May are special months, because that's when all the baby animals are born—as many

as 80 calves—and who doesn't like baby animals? Summer brings day camp activities; winter brings skiing and sledding. A visit to the farm is a rich experience and one that kids won't soon forget. You can visit the farm for free, but a fee is charged for activities and workshops. Call for current rates.

MIDCOAST

CHEWONKI FOUNDATION SUMMER CAMPS
485 Chewonki Neck Rd., Wiscasset
(207) 882-7323
www.chewonki.org
The Chewonki Foundation has been involved in environmental education since 1962, and it's got its business down to a science, teaching people of all ages about the outdoors at its 400-acre center in Wiscasset and on field trips to remote locations. The outfit has a variety of offerings for kids, too, including several summer camp

programs. These are fairly traditional summer camps for both boys and girls ages 8 through 15. Kids live in cabins and learn sailing, swimming, kayaking, canoeing, arts and crafts, and farm skills. There are three-and-a-half-week and seven-week sessions, and in August there are five-day adventure camps for children ages 10 through 13 that put them through challenges on ropes and in canoes and sea kayaks. Kids tend to have fun at all of these programs and walk away at the end with some new skills and, it is hoped, a new or renewed love or appreciation for the great outdoors.

MORRIS FARM
156 Gardiner Rd. (Route 27), Wiscasset
(207) 882-4080
www.morrisfarm.org
Here's another fantastic old farm in the Midcoast region where kids can learn about sustainable agriculture, pet a few cows, and sign up for workshops or courses. The 60-acre working farm has agriculture, community, and education as its basic tenets, and it's the last one that grabs the kids, even if they're having too much fun to know they're soaking up information. Since the late 1990s, when the farm was rescued from development by a group of concerned area citizens, it's made great progress. The site now features an operational dairy, a 68-tree organic orchard, a half acre of raspberries, another half-acre market garden, yet another children's garden, a small poultry operation, and an interpretive trail through 10 acres of woodlands. The farm's school programs are operated in keeping with the state's learning standards. There are workshops like the Afternoon at the Farm series, where kids can spend several hours after school on Monday, Wednesday, and Friday and do easy and fun chores, like feeding and milking cows, feeding rabbits, gathering eggs, making cheese or butter, or putting up canned items. And in summer there are day camps where kids learn all that and more, play games, do crafts, and even do some science projects. The opportunities are many, and there are plenty of one-day programs available. You're welcome to simply visit and have a look around, too.

BOOTHBAY RAILWAY VILLAGE $–$$
Route 27, Boothbay
(207) 633-4727
www.railwayvillage.org
Ten acres and 28 historic buildings provide the backdrop for train tours at the Boothbay Railway Village, an ersatz hamlet on the main route to Boothbay Harbor. The steam engine makes runs at least hourly (sometimes twice an hour) around a short, narrow-gauge rail through the village to the delight of passengers young and old. Many of the trains in the collection here date back to the heyday of train travel—the late 1800s—and there is a vintage vehicle exhibit, too, which includes all sorts of automobiles.

MAINE STATE AQUARIUM $
McKown Point Rd., West Boothbay
(207) 633-9559
www.maine.gov/dmr/rm/aquarium/
A petting zoo of sorts resembling the Maine coast, this small aquarium opened in 1993. Kids love to lean over the side of the 20-footl-ong touch tank and handle the invertebrates, feeling the sea urchin and getting squirted by a sea cucumber. And they like to peer into the 850-gallon tank filled with sharks and skates, even getting a chance to feel a shark's skin. Then there's Fritz the Lobster, who weighs close to 23 pounds. The aquarium is run alongside the Department of Marine Resources' fisheries research station, and there are occasional presentations about the state of the state's fisheries. Tours of the research facility are also available. Open daily from 10 a.m. to 5 p.m. from Memorial Day through September 4. Children 4 and under free.

DAMARISCOTTA MILLS ALEWIVES RUN
Off Route 215, Damariscotta Mills
This is a miracle of nature that's fascinating to see. Old-time Mainers used to talk about fish so thick you could walk across the river on their backs, and you'll believe them if you make it to see the spring run of alewives (tiny herring) up from Great Salt Bay to their spawning grounds in Damariscotta Lake. Every May and June—and you can always tell it's time when you see the

circling seagulls and ospreys—the alewives scale a concrete fish ladder, climbing from sea level up more than 40 feet to ponds that connect to the lake. They move en masse—hundreds of thousands have been counted—and it's an epic struggle. Some make it, some don't. If you think the Maine Turnpike is bad in August, get a load of this. They wriggle, they fight, their silver bodies twist and turn, and you can watch them go for much of their run. You'll feel like you've watched *Rocky* again when you see them splash into the pond at the end of the ladder. Kids are transfixed. Take the Mills Road out of Damariscotta; you'll see the cars and birds if it's happening. Free.

FAWCETT'S ANTIQUE TOY MUSEUM $
Route 1, Waldoboro
(207) 832-7398

Former art professor John Fawcett has filled a deceptively large colonial in Waldoboro to the brim with toys and toys and more toys. There are pictures, posters, and artifacts about toys, and actual toys themselves. Disneyana is a specialty—which is to be expected from a curator and artist whose work is in the book *The Art of Mickey Mouse*—but there are also whole sections devoted to the Lone Ranger. Also look for Peanuts, Looney Tunes, Superman, Popeye, Pogo, Rocky and Bullwinkle, Star Trek—they're all represented. If it was a toy, it's in here. Geared for adults, it's a treasure trove for kids, too. Open Memorial Day through Columbus Day Thursday through Monday from 10 a.m. to 4 p.m. Open weekends only from Columbus Day through Christmas from noon to 4 p.m.

THE FARNSWORTH ART MUSEUM $$$$
356 Main St., Rockland
(207) 594-6457
www.farnsworthmuseum.org

A favorite of grown-up visitors to Rockland, the Farnsworth hosts a few programs for kids, too. Most are art classes, in various disciplines, for various ages. An example might be Children's Class: Drawing and Painting II, a series of classes designed to bring out the budding Wyeth in kids, teaching youngsters ages 10 through 12 the ways

of the pencil and the brush. The museum also hosts afterschool programs for teens. Call or check the Web site for more information. (For more information on the museum's regular hours and its extensive collection, see the Attractions chapter.)

CAMDEN SNOW BOWL $
Hosmer Pond Rd., Camden
(207) 236-3438
www.camdensnowbowl.com

Every community should have a ski mountain like this one. The town-owned center sits on the side of 1,300-foot Ragged Mountain on the inland outskirts of Camden. There's plenty of skiing to be had here when the weather provides the fluffy stuff. Nine trails, most of them classified as intermediate, await schuss-boomers, so it's a good learning mountain. Better still, though, perhaps, for young kids is the tubing run at the base of the peak, which is a safe, fast, fun, and bouncy run. The Snow Bowl is also famous for its toboggan chute, a 400-foot trough that shoots the wooden sleds down the mountain at high speeds and out across Hosmer Pond. There is ice-skating on the pond as well. The well-run facility with its classic A-frame lodge is not about wearing the newest and tightest ski fashions or about zillion-dollar lift tickets, but about having an enjoyable day on the slopes with the rest of the community. In summer there is a rec program for kids between second and sixth grades that includes all sorts of sports, arts and crafts, hiking and canoeing, and day trips to beaches. There are also ball fields and tennis courts and concerts during the summer months.

SEACOAST FUN PARK $$–$$$$
Route 3, Trenton
(207) 667-3573
www.seacoastfunparks.com

One of those multifaceted amusement parks that inevitably seem to spring up near national parks, this small amusement complex 3 miles from Ellsworth has something for everyone: waterslides, minigolf, go-karts, a pool, a snack bar, an arcade, a trampoline, and even Maine's only tented paintball facility. Open daily from Memorial Day through Labor Day and weekends in the shoulder season.

DIVE-IN THEATER TOURS
Bar Harbor Inn Pier, Bar Harbor
(207) 288-3483
www.divered.com
Diver Ed is a clever fellow. From the puns of his
own name and business name to simply offering
the throngs of people who visit Acadia a chance
to see what's on the sea bottom—without even
getting wet—he's on to something. The Dive-In

Theater is Diver Ed's scuba tour, during which he
swims to the bottom with a camera and projects
video back to a large screen on the boat above
to the delight of passengers. They get to virtually
dive Frenchman Bay, seeing the rich array of sea
life in this fertile basin, and toward the end of the
two-hour jaunt, he scoops up a bagful of sea critters for the kids above to pet. Neat stuff. Diver Ed
also does dive charters on his boat the *Seal.*

MINIATURE GOLF

What kid doesn't love a round of miniature golf?
Especially if Dad lets him or her win. Here's where
you'll find some tiny links.

Wells Beach Resort
1000 Post Road, Route 1, Wells
(800) 640–CAMP
www.wellsbeach.com

Wonder Mountain Miniature Golf
U.S. Route 1, Moody
(207) 646-9655

Shakerland Golf
Route 202, East Waterboro
(207) 247-4653

Aquaboggan Water Park
980 Portland Road, Saco
(207) 282-3112

Cascade Miniature Golf
955 Route 1, Saco
(207) 282-3524

Funtown USA
774 Portland Road, Saco
(207) 284-5139

Schooner Miniature Golf
58 Ocean Park Road, Saco
(207) 284-6174

Pirate's Cove
70 First Street, Old Orchard Beach
(207) 934-5086

Adventure Falls Miniature Golf
510 Warren Avenue, Portland
(207) 878-5800

**Westerly Winds Sports Park &
Golf Learning Center**
853 Cumberland Street (River Road),
Westbrook
(207) 854-9463

Long Shot Golf Center
305 Bath Road, Brunswick
(207) 725-6377

Dolphin Mini Golf
510 Wiscasset Road, Boothbay
(207) 633-4828

Treasure Island Miniature Golf
125 Townsend Avenue, Boothbay Harbor
(207) 633-6669

Mini-Golf
773 Commercial Street, Rockport
(207) 594-5211

Finest Kind
Center District Crossroad
(halfway between Routes 15 & 15A), Deer Isle
(207) 348-7714

Pine Ridge Golf Center
R.R. 15, Sedgwick
(207) 359-6788

Vokes Mini-Strokes
Bar Harbor Road (Route 3), Ellsworth
(207) 667-9519

Whale-In-One Mini-Golf
Narrows Too Camping Resort
1150 Bar Harbor Road, Trenton
(207) 667-4300

Pirate's Cove
Bar Harbor
(207) 288-2133

ARTS AND ENTERTAINMENT

Artists of all sorts have drawn inspiration from the Maine coast. Painters were among the first tourists to discover its beauties, and some of the biggest names in American art have worked here. The state has an unusually high number of writers who have called it home as well. And for a rural state with few urban centers, there are a surprising number of world-class classical music festivals and schools.

When the affluent summercators moved north to places like Kennebunk and Bar Harbor for the season, you see, they didn't want to leave behind all the culture they'd grown accustomed to. So they brought it with them. Summer theater, summer concerts, summer dance—all have long traditions on the Maine coast. The resort communities seem almost as busy as Portland in the summer.

The state was once famous for its art colonies in Ogunquit, Monhegan, and Bar Harbor, and that heritage is carried on today as well. There are several galleries along the coast with art-works on their walls that can compete with the big guns in New York. You just have to look.

Unfortunately, the state still doesn't have much in the way of a live music scene—there's just no comparing Portland's nightlife to places like Boston, even on a per capita basis—but if you're lucky you might be in town when a good show is scheduled. We do have a large number of great downtown cinemas, though, where you can catch the arty films before they become national sensations, and plenty of soulless multiplexes as well.

Culture? We got culture.

The Maine Art Commission, a state-run, arts promotion organization, has a handy Web site—http://mainearts .maine.gov—with an events calendar, a news section, and an artist directory, which will help you find that gallery you remember visiting last time you came to Maine. It also publishes a bunch of useful guides, like the Maine Art Museum Trail, to various arts disciplines and organizations.

THEATER

South Coast

HACKMATACK PLAYHOUSE
538 Route 9, Berwick
(207) 698-1807
www.hackmatack.org
One of the nicest things about the Hackmatack

theater company is the neat old barn it performs in. Every summer for decades, the company here has presented a handful of musicals and comedies aimed at family audiences. Shows are held nightly at 8 p.m., Wednesday through Saturday, with matinees on Thursday at 2 p.m.

BOOTH THEATER
Beach St., Ogunquit
(207) 646-8142
www.boothproductions.com
Based in Worcester, Massachusetts, this theater troupe is in residence at the Betty Doon Motel in summer and stages old standbys one after another from July through September.

JOHN LANE'S OGUNQUIT PLAYHOUSE
U.S. Route 1, Ogunquit
(207) 646-5511
www.ogunquitplayhouse.org

The star power that this professional theater has seen since it opened in the 1930s is staggering. The playhouse is often referred to as "America's foremost summer theater," and "Broadway at the Beach," and it fits the bill. Shows run Monday through Friday at 8 p.m. and Saturday at 8:30 p.m. from late June through Labor Day. On Wednesdays and Thursdays there are matinees at 2:30 p.m.

ARUNDEL BARN PLAYHOUSE
53 Old Post Rd., Arundel
(207) 985-5552
www.arundelbarnplayhouse.com
This young company—formed in 1997—brings a mix of old and new productions to the restored Smith Sisters barn not far from the Kennebunks. In the same season, they'll do a New England premiere—like Roger Bean's *Route 66*—and follow it up with a weathered play like *Grease*. Call or visit the Web site for this year's schedule.

BIDDEFORD CITY THEATER
205 Main St., Biddeford
(207) 282-0849
www.citytheater.org
Murder mysteries, comics, big bands, *The Rocky Horror Picture Show*, Lazer Vaudeville—this is the rich mix you'll find at the City Theater, a great space in downtown Biddeford. It's enjoyed some revitalization since the early 1990s, after hosting such greats as Fred Astaire, Mae West, and W. C. Fields in earlier days. Active year-round.

Greater Portland
LYRIC MUSIC THEATER
176 Sawyer St., South Portland
(207) 799-1421
www.lyricmusictheater.com
This community troupe has been producing musicals since 1952. It stages four a year now at the Cedric Thomas Playhouse between September and May. Individual tickets are $20.

PORTLAND PLAYERS
420 Cottage Rd., South Portland
(207) 799-7337
www.portlandplayers.org
Arguably Maine's best community theater, the Portland Players actually work in South Portland, where they stage old standbys from September through June at the Thaxter Theater and typically do a good job of it. Tickets are in the $20 range.

PORTLAND STAGE COMPANY
25A Forest Ave., Portland
(207) 774-0465
www.portlandstage.com
Portland Stage is a professional troupe that presents performances from October through April at its own theater in an old Odd Fellows hall. From Shakespeare and *A Christmas Carol* to world premieres, it does a little of everything. Call or check the Web site for the current lineup.

Midcoast
MAINE STATE MUSIC THEATER
22 Elm St., Brunswick
(207) 725-8769
www.msmt.org
Broadway in Brunswick. That's the idea behind this Equity company, which performs in a beautifully renovated space just up the road from its old home on the campus of Bowdoin College. People turn out in great numbers for its summer season of old and new favorites. Local kids often get small parts. Summer shows are at 8 p.m. Tuesday through Saturday, with additional matinees on Tuesday, Thursday, Friday, and Sunday. Tickets are $36 to $52.

THE THEATER PROJECT
14 School St., Brunswick
(207) 729-8584
www.theaterproject.com
Founded in 1971, Theater Project produces innovative dramas and does a lot of work with kids. It has its own space in downtown Brunswick and works year-round.

CAMDEN CIVIC THEATRE
Camden Opera House
Main St., Camden
(207) 236-2281
www.camdencivictheatre.com
One of the state's best community drama programs, Camden Civic Theatre has been delighting area residents since the early 1970s. One of the nicest things about its productions is the venue—the restored Camden Opera House, on the second floor downtown, is a beauty. Tickets are $12 and $16.

BELFAST MASKERS RAILROAD THEATER
Front St., Belfast
(207) 338-9668
www.belfastmaskerstheater.com
A top-notch community theater, the Maskers have attracted some big-name stars to the stage in Belfast. Mostly, though, it's the work of dedicated Waldo County residents that lights up the stage at the Railroad Theater: classics and premieres, locally directed. Shows are on Saturdays. Tickets are $10 to $15. Call ahead for showtimes.

NATIONAL THEATRE WORKSHOP OF THE HANDICAPPED
96 Church St., Belfast
(207) 338-6894
www.ntwh.org
Belfast residents were excited when this school set up in town several years ago, and it produces several shows a year now. Look for local listings.

Acadia Area
DECK HOUSE RESTAURANT AND CABARET THEATER
11 Apple Lane, Southwest Harbor
(207) 244-5044
www.thedeckhouse.com
Show tunes in the round are on the menu at the Deck House, where the audience eats and the waitstaff doubles as the players. Music from Broadway is the usual fare, but dance, mime, puppetry, and barbershop harmonies have happened here in the past. Reservations are recommended.

ACADIA REPERTORY THEATRE
Route 102, Somesville
(207) 244-7260
www.acadiarep.com
More professional summer fare on the island. These guys have been at it for more than 30 years. A mix of comedies, dramas, mysteries, and children's shows make up their calendar, and the stage is at the neat old Masonic Hall in Somesville. Tickets are $22.

Down East
DOWNRIVER THEATER PRODUCTIONS
Liberty Hall, Machiasport
(207) 255-8940
This community theater puts on musicals every June through August. Call for current schedule.

STAGE EAST
Washington St., Eastport
(207) 853-4747
www.stageeast.org
When this community theater needed seats at its performance space, it went out and bought what it could afford—but the 100 new seats needed repair. So the community got involved, the local vocational school helped fix the hardware, a reupholsterer recovered them, and area residents bought them for $25 each, making it all possible. When they needed still more space, they bought the local Baptist church. This is what community theater is supposed to be about. They do several shows a year, from old standbys to new award winners.

PERFORMING ARTS CENTERS

South Coast
OGUNQUIT PERFORMING ARTS
Dunaway Center
School St., Ogunquit
(207) 646-6170
This local promoter presents a chamber music fest every June with name acts at the Barn Gallery and other venues, and it also sponsors film series, dance performances, and a variety of cultural events throughout the year.

RIVER TREE ARTS
35 Western Ave., Kennebunk
(207) 967-9120
www.rivertreearts.org
This local outfit sponsors contra dances, summer concerts, and all sorts of arts classes for adults and children. The tree has been 25 years and growing in Kennebunk and it recently set down roots in Biddeford as well.

Greater Portland

PCA GREAT PERFORMANCES
50 Monument Sq., Portland
(207) 842-0800
www.pcagreatperformances.org
Some of the best shows to have played Portland are those that are sponsored by this vibrant outfit. Each season—from fall to summer—PCA brings about 20 performers to the stage of Merrill Auditorium, from the hyperactive percussion of an ensemble like Stomp to the individual brilliance of an artist such as cellist Yo-Yo Ma. Drama, dance, and music are all represented, and the talents are always of the caliber that usually visit only much larger cities. Call or click over to the PCA Web site to find out this year's lineup.

THE ST. LAWRENCE ARTS CENTER
76 Congress St., Portland
(207) 775-5568
www.stlawrencearts.org
One of the city's more distinctive buildings, the St. Lawrence Church was in need of rescuing in the late 1990s, and a grassroots effort was undertaken to restore and preserve the 1897 stone Congregational church. The result is a really cool 110-seat, multifunctional venue for local arts and cultural organizations, including bands. Groups from around the state play the stage regularly, especially in summer.

Midcoast

THE CHOCOLATE CHURCH ARTS CENTER
798 Washington St., Bath
(207) 442-8455
www.chocolatechurch.com

This 1847 Gothic church is hard to miss, both because it's big and prominent, even from Route 1, and because it's painted a rich chocolate brown. And you wouldn't want to miss anything that goes on inside. A cultural bright spot in the City of Ships, the church is a multifaceted operation, presenting an array of concerts, lectures, and performances and hosting shows at its adjacent art gallery. Check the Web site for the latest information.

RIVERARTS
170 Main St., Damariscotta
(207) 563-1507
www.riverartsme.org
The community of Damariscotta was stunned in December of 2006 when it heard that the old institution, Round Top Center for the Arts, a cultural staple for 20 years, was going to close. Riverarts was born to fill the void it left behind, sponsoring art classes, shows, poetry readings, and other events on a year-round basis. See the Web site for the latest happenings.

LINCOLN ARTS FESTIVAL
Various locations, Boothbay Harbor
(207) 633-3913
www.lincolnartsfestival.org
Since 1980 this outfit—it's a cultural organization, not any kind of fair—has been sponsoring concerts and performances in the Boothbay area, from jazz to classical to pop, primarily by regional performers. Summer only. Call or check the Web site for this year's events.

GRAND AUDITORIUM
Main St., Ellsworth
(207) 667-9500
www.grandonline.org
Residents of towns within a 75-mile radius of this place ought to be singing their praises that it exists. From live music to theater to first-run and art films, this old space has it all. Check the excellent Web site or call for a list of upcoming events.

LIVE MUSIC—CLASSICAL AND OPERA

Portland

PORTLAND OPERA REPERTORY THEATRE (PORT)
P.O. Box 7733, Portland 04112
(207) 879-7678
www.portopera.org
Portland's resident opera company, established in 1995, PORT regularly brings big operatic productions to the stage of Merrill Auditorium. Call or check the Web site for the complete schedule.

PORTLAND STRING QUARTET
www.portlandstringquartet.org
Called "Maine treasures" by Colby College (the quartet members are artists in residence there), this combo performs frequently at venues across the state. Check the Web site for its schedule.

PORTLAND SYMPHONY ORCHESTRA
50 Monument Sq., Portland
(207) 773-6128
www.portlandsymphony.com
In 1997 Merrill Auditorium, the home of the Portland Symphony Orchestra, was completely refurbished, transformed from a tired old city hall auditorium into a world-class concert hall. Finally the PSO had a home worthy of the house band. The 80-member orchestra has been a popular draw in the city for decades. Particular crowd-pleasers are the PSO's annual summer pops and the December-long Magic of Christmas series.

Midcoast

KNEISEL HALL CHAMBER MUSIC FESTIVAL
Pleasant St., Blue Hill
(207) 374-2811
www.kneisel.org
Austrian violinist Franz Kneisel emigrated to the United States in 1885, joining the Boston Symphony Orchestra. He went on to work at the school that would become Juilliard, and he started summering in Maine. In 1902 he began bringing students to Blue Hill to study with him,

and thus this, one of the oldest chamber music festivals in the nation, was born. Students still come every summer to work on their chops, and they get to watch faculty and guests put on concerts from late June through mid-August—shows are on Fridays and Sunday afternoons—and present their own recitals on several occasions as well. You might not expect to find world-class string ensembles in Blue Hill, but here they are for everyone to enjoy. Tickets are $10 to $30.

BOWDOIN SUMMER MUSIC FESTIVAL
6300 College Station, Brunswick
(207) 373-1400
www.summermusic.org
What do you get when you bring 200 gifted students to a Maine college to be taught for months by some of the best known classical music teachers? A whole lot of great music at reasonable prices. There are several concert series each summer, and Midcoast residents turn out in droves. On Friday evenings there are performances by distinguished guest artists—of the world-renowned likes of Emanuel Ax, Julius Baker, and Eugenia Zukerman. Faculty members put on shows midweek, usually doing both contemporary and traditional works, and students perform at various times. Venues include Bowdoin buildings and the Brunswick High School. Tickets can be as much as $30 for big names, as little as $5 for stars to be.

BAY CHAMBER CONCERTS
Rockport Opera House
10 Summer St., Rockport
(207) 236-2823 or (888) 707-2770
www.baychamberconcerts.org
Best known for its summer chamber music concerts, this outfit established in 1961 also hosts jazz, folk, and world music shows by acts like the Paul Winter Consort, Judy Collins, and Inca Son. They do 30 shows a year, at 8 p.m. every Wednesday and Thursday in summer, and half the fun is just getting inside the beautiful old downtown opera house, which has been attractively renovated (and cooled with air-conditioning). Bay Chamber also has a radio broadcast series of its archived concerts. Ticket prices vary.

Acadia Area

BAR HARBOR MUSIC FESTIVAL
59 Cottage St., Bar Harbor
(207) 288-5744
www.barharbormusicfestival.com
Still more fine classical music can be found in Bar Harbor, where this annual festival has been hosting concerts since the early 1960s. But you'll also see Dixieland, opera, jazz, show tunes, and more contemporary fare as well. Concerts are at 8:15 p.m. at venues across town.

Down East

PIERRE MONTEUX SCHOOL FOR CONDUCTORS AND ORCHESTRA MUSICIANS
Hancock
(207) 422-3280
www.monteuxschool.org
Here is yet another opportunity for Mainers Down East to see top-flight classical music. (This part of the state must have more shows than Portland!) Like Kneisel, the Monteux School, in business since 1943, brings budding young classical talents to Maine for the summer, but often they are on the other side of the baton—conductors. Concerts are offered by students and faculty in June and July.

MACHIAS BAY CHAMBER CONCERTS
Centre St. Congregational Church
7 Centre St., Machias
(207) 255-4249
www.machiasbaychamberconcerts.com
Founded in 1970, this outfit could not ask for a more attractive venue for its excellent classical series, six concerts in July and early August. The church, with its soaring spires and riverside location, is a stunner, and the range of acts—from the Vermeer Quartet to the Los Angeles Guitar Quartet—is impressive as well.

LIVE MUSIC—NIGHTLIFE AND OTHER POPULAR MUSIC

South Coast

JONATHAN'S
92 Bourne Lane, Ogunquit
(207) 646-4777
www.jonathansrestaurant.com
How does Jonathan West manage to do it? He consistently books name acts of national repute for his small restaurant in Ogunquit, making it one of the best places to see a show north of Boston. Most are small combos, often folk or blues, but they could be anyone from protopunk troubadour Jonathan Richman to Arlo Guthrie to Cheryl Wheeler to Tom Rush. The current lineup is available on the Web.

Portland

ASYLUM
121 Center St., Portland
(207) 772-8274
www.portlandasylum.com
A new booking agent has this place busy with live music several nights a week now. This is the place to look for local, regional, and the occasional national hip-hop, metal, or jam band act. On Thursday there's an '80's Dance Night, and next door is a popular sports bar.

THE BIG EASY
55 Market St., Portland
(207) 775-2266
www.bigeasyportland.com
Thousands of miles from NO/LA, this Old Port oldie hosts shows by local acts and the occasional out-of-towner. Lots of hip hop and tribute bands. And hip hop tribute bands.

DOGFISH BAR AND GRILLE
128 Free St., Portland
(207) 772-5483
www.thedogfishbarandgrille.com
Just a few steps down from the Portland Museum of Art, Dogfish is both an eclectic restaurant and a bar where lesser-known local and national acts

play. The stage is tiny, the bar a fine watering hole, and the food is good enough that you should arrive early.

EMPIRE DINE AND DANCE
575 Congress St., Portland
(207) 879-8988
www.portlandempire.ning.com
Beer, burgers, and bands are what you need to know here. The food half of the equation is good, standard pub fare with a bit of a Mexican twist, and the music tends to be local.

GENO'S
625 Congress St., Portland
(207) 221-2382
Here is Portland's answer to CBGB, which is to say an age-old punk-rock dive with scuzzy decor, a lousy sound system, and a lineup of good, loud, fast young bands. A Maine classic.

THE SPACE GALLERY
538 Congress St., Portland
(207) 828-5600
www.space538.org
One part art gallery, two parts rock club, the Space Gallery took up where the late, great Skinny left off as Portland's best place to see the newest latest bands. Most of the acts that play here are from the indie and underground worlds, whether they be local combos like Seekonk or rural electric or national performers like Richard Buckner and Bob Mould. More cosmopolitan than many clubs of its ilk, Space serves alcohol, and you can peruse the gallery with its revolving shows of up-and-coming artists. And, somehow, it's just better lately. Call or check the Web site to see what's scheduled.

THE WHITE HEART
551 Congress St., Portland
(207) 828-1900
www.thewhiteheart.com
Another restaurant-cum-nightclub, the White Heart mixes a menu of soups and salads, steaks and spuds with live music by local acts, the occasional art and poetry shows, and deejay-

supported dance. All that and it's where the city's beautiful people hang out.

Other Portland-Area Venues

The **Cumberland County Civic Center** (207-775-3548; www.theciviccenter.com) might warrant a larger mention if it scheduled more shows. Primarily a hockey arena, "the Civic Center" hosts about seven or eight big rock acts a year, from Marilyn Manson to Cher. The **Old Port Tavern** (207-774-0444; www.oldporttavern.com) is Portland's best poolroom, and it provides entertainment seven nights a week. **The Station** (207-775-3466) hosts lots of heavy stuff and dance, too.

Midcoast
SEA DOG BREWING COMPANY
1 Main St., Great Mill Island, Topsham
(207) 725-0162
www.seadogbrewing.com
One of the surviving pubs owned by the Sea Dog Brewing Company, this cool bar is a good example of what can be done to save old mill buildings. It was retrofitted into the old Topsham Mill, and it's a beautiful space right on the Androscoggin River. Brews and views are good, and there's often music on Friday and Saturday at 9 p.m. Open daily from 11:30 a.m. to 1 a.m.

WALDO THEATRE
Main St., Waldoboro
(207) 832-6060
www.thewaldo.org
Music is but one of the offerings at this great downtown theater. Fiddle contests and folk singers and classical quartets have played here, but so have theater troupes, kids' programs, and films. Open year-round. Call or check the Web site for more information.

CAMDEN OPERA HOUSE
Main St., Camden
(207) 236-7963
www.camdenoperahouse.com
A surprising number of good shows pop up in

this beautiful, second-floor theater in downtown Camden. Singer-songwriter Iris Dement has performed here a couple of times, and even fairly big bands like Wilco have played this stage. Worth checking the Web site if you're in town.

Rockland Nightlife

A handful of venues in Rockland—mostly cafes and pubs—host live music. Try the **Time Out Pub** (275 Main Street; 207-593-9336), where you can see open mikes and often well-known blues acts. **Rock City Books and Coffee** (328 Main Street; 207-594-4123; www.rockcitycoffee.com) has hosted the occasional folk show. The beautifully restored **Strand Theater** (207-594-0070; www.rocklandstrand.com) has a variety of folk and classical shows scheduled when it isn't showing art films.

Acadia Area

CARMEN VERANDAH
119 Main St., Bar Harbor
(207) 288-2766
www.carmenverandah.com
This local cafe has a full slate of musical offerings in the summertime, usually local and regional performers in a wide range of styles. Check the Web site to see what's coming up.

LOMPOC CAFE
36 Rodick St., Bar Harbor
(207) 288-9392
www.lompoccafe.com
Another cafe with music in Bar Harbor, the Lompoc books bluegrass, jazz, rock, and blues for Friday and Saturday nights. Thursdays are for open mikes. Check the Web site for the lineup.

COMEDY

COMEDY CONNECTION
6 Custom House Wharf, Portland
(207) 774-5554
www.mainecomedy.com
This Old Port staple isn't where you want to turn for Down East "humah." But if you want to see good local stand-up—this place launched comic Bob Marley, who is now plying his trade in Hollywood—as well as some nationally known funny folks, this is the place to be. All shows are for guests age 18 or older. Tickets range from $6 to $16.

ART GALLERIES

South Coast

YORK ART ASSOCIATION GALLERY
Route 1A, York Harbor
(207) 363-4049
www.yorkartassociation.com
A nice space to see the work of area talents. Open Thursday through Sunday from 11 a.m. to 4 p.m. from May to October.

CUCKLE-BUTTON FARM GALLERY
Thompson Green, Ogunquit
(207) 646-1700
www.ogunquitgallery.com
Despite its cutesy-sounding name, this art showplace is the real deal. Just up the road from Perkins Cove, you'll find paintings by the likes of Charles Woodbury, John Neill, Ann Gallop, Henry Strater, and others who've made names for themselves in the once-famous art colony here.

THE BARN GALLERY
Shore Rd. and Bourne Lane, Ogunquit
(207) 646-8400
www.barngallery.org
Ogunquit is a Maine art hot spot, and this gallery is among the reasons why. The Ogunquit Arts Association got its start back in the 1920s, when the fishing village was enjoying its heyday as a nationally known art colony, and the group reinvented itself in the late 1990s and renamed its showplace the Barn Gallery. It remains a first-class exhibition space and one of the best places around to see works by area artists. The gallery regularly schedules classes, workshops, and educational programs.

MAST COVE GALLERIES
Mast Cove Lane and Maine St.
Kennebunkport
(207) 967-3453
www.mastcove.com
Mast Cove got its start in the early 1980s with a dozen artists, and it has since evolved into the biggest of the many galleries in the Kennebunks. In fact, it claims to be the largest privately owned group gallery in all of Maine now, representing more than 100 artists. From Robert Eric Moore to DeWitt Hardy, these galleries have a lot of good stuff inside.

Greater Portland

GREENHUT GALLERIES
146 Middle St., Portland
(207) 772-2693 or (888) 772-2693
www.greenhutgalleries.com
Peggy Greenhut Golden has an eye for talent, and she has some really fine works in the gallery she's run since 1977. The focus is contemporary art, and painters include regional talents like Mary Bourke, Leo Brooks, and Kathleen Galligan, whose work is showcased nicely in the bright, museum-like space. Open year-round, Monday through Saturday.

JUNE FITZPATRICK GALLERY
112 High St., Portland
(207) 772-1961
www.junefitzpatrickgallery.com
A good selection of contemporary works are hung here across from the Portland Museum of Art, and there's another space at 522 Congress Street, as well. Exhibits change monthly.

Midcoast

SPINDLEWORKS
7 Lincoln St., Brunswick
(207) 725-8820
www.spindleworks.org
Begun in the 1970s as a weaving program for people with disabilities, this creative arts organization now turns out fantastic paintings, draw-ings, sculpture, and poetry. And some of its artists even have New York representation these days. The Spindleworkers show their art at various galleries across the state—and right here at their own space. There are paintings, beautiful handwoven scarves and wall hangings, prints, and a variety of other cool items. Open Monday to Friday from 9 a.m. to 4 p.m.

WISCASSET BAY GALLERY
67 Main St., Wiscasset
(207) 882-7682
www.wiscassetbaygallery.com
Here is a fine gallery specializing in 19th- and 20th-century American and European paintings, especially those by painters from Monhegan Island and throughout Maine. The gallery also represents some contemporary artists from elsewhere in New England and displays rotating exhibits.

GLEASON GALLERY
31 Townsend Ave., Boothbay Harbor
(207) 633-6849
www.gleasonfineart.com
The Gleason Gallery isn't quite what you'd expect a resort town gallery to be. While many such places are filled with seascapes by second- and third-rate painters, the Gleason Gallery is full of works that might seem more appropriate on the walls of museums and can run into the tens of thousands of dollars. Housed in an 1807 brick town house right in the center of town, the gallery fills eight rooms with the handiwork of Maine and Northeast artists, particularly those associated with Boothbay and Monhegan. You might see lithographs by world-renowned Fairfield Porter; gouaches by Eleanor Parke Curtis, who painted in Boothbay in the 1920s; and watercolors by James Fitzgerald, among a handful of Monhegan painters. Depending upon when you visit, you could even pick up a Wyeth. Truly a cut above most of the rest of the state's galleries, and now with a second space at 545 Congress Street in Portland.

THE FIREHOUSE GALLERY

1 Bristol Rd., Damariscotta

(207) 563-7299

www.thefirehousegallery.com

This gallery makes for a nifty visit, housed as it is in a renovated mid-19th-century firehouse. Where there was once firefighting apparatus, there are now paintings by regional talents, crafts, folk arts, ceramics, and jewelry. The gallery has rotating exhibits.

HARBOR SQUARE GALLERY

374 Main St., Rockland

(207) 594-8700

www.harborsquaregallery.com

A neat former bank with three floors of fine art, Harbor Square represents a raft of artists. Inside you'll find everything from the colorful paintings of Sharon Larkin to the jewelry of goldsmith Thomas O'Donovan, and you may be mortified, like so many others have been, to see paintings and sculpture displayed right on the street. Fine art as sidewalk sale. "Won't it be stolen?" "What if it rains?" Good questions; you'll have to find out the answers when you visit.

BAYVIEW GALLERY

33 Bayview St., Camden

(207) 236-4534

www.bayviewgallery.com

If you buy a contemporary land- or seascape painting here, you can get it framed on the premises. Representing three dozen painters from Maine and away, the gallery also has made a name for itself as a custom framer. It has another location in Brunswick now (58 Maine Street).

ℹ️ Made famous by the likes of George Bellows, Edward Hopper, Robert Henri, and Rockwell Kent, Monhegan Island still has quite the artist culture, with more than 20 studios open to visits. Pick up a map and guide from the Monhegan Boat Line on your way out or click over to www .monhegan.com/artists.

Rockland Galleries

The renaissance of the Farnsworth Art Museum in the late 1990s helped spawn quite the gallery scene in downtown Rockland. Gallery owners used to be scared away by the grittiness of Main Street, but several have located here rather than Camden since the Farnsworth started its expansions. It was a wise move, which has resulted in a vibrant downtown arts scene. The **Caldbeck Gallery** (12 Elm Street; 207-594-5935; www.caldbeck .com) is the best of them, and it's been here the longest (since 1982). It represents such top-flight talents as William Thon, Lois Dodd, Sam Cady, and Abby Shahn.

More up-and-coming talents can be found at the **Gallery at 357 Main** (357 Main; 207-596-0084) and **Gallery 407** (407 Main; no phone). **The Art Space** (342 Main Street; 207-594-8784; www.artspacemaine .com) is home to two dozen fine local talents. Off the main drag on Winter Street you'll find the gallery of framer, teacher, and painter **Jonathan Frost** (21 Winter Street; 207-596-0800; www.jonathanfrostgallery .com), which represents the work of the eponymous artist as well as Rockland galleries usually have their openings on Wednesday night, and it's a nice excuse to grab something to eat downtown and wander the streets.

LEIGHTON GALLERY

24 Parker Point Rd., Blue Hill

(207) 374-5001

www.leightongallery.com

One of the longest-lived and, frankly, best Maine galleries, this Blue Hill institution was built into an old Maine barn. When she opened up in 1986, proprietor Judith Leighton purposefully set out to make her gallery as comfortable as can be, as opposed to the stiff and stuffy art showrooms you might find in more urban areas, and she left a lot of "barniness" intact when she designed her space. A few years later she built a sculpture-filled garden that alone is worth the trip, showcasing the works of Cabot Lyford, Melita Westerlund, and Elizabeth Ostrander, among others. The lineup and presentation here is first rate.

DEER ISLE ARTISTS ASSOCIATION
13 Dow Rd., Deer Isle
(207) 348-2330
www.deerisleartists.com
Deer Isle has become synonymous with crafts, thanks to the fact that the well-respected Haystack Mountain School of Crafts is located here. It seems everyone who attends the school decides to move to the island. That's an exaggeration, yes, but consider that there are 150 area artists represented at this co-op gallery where you can find fine art–quality ceramics, textiles, and more. Exhibits change every two weeks.

Acadia Area
ISLAND ARTISANS
99 Main St., Bar Harbor
(207) 288-4214
www.islandartisans.com
Also in Northeast Harbor, this crafts gallery represents more than 75 artisans working in Maine. They have a nice collection of fiber, jewelry, blown glass, stoneware, tiles, ceramics, and basketry. (Check out the sweetgrass baskets of Abigail Goodyear and the contemporary jewelry of Cherie Magnello.)

MOVIES

Great Downtown Movie Theaters

SMITTY'S CINEMA
1364 Main St., Sanford
(207) 490-6677 or the hotline (207) 490-0000
www.smittyscinema.com

Would you like some "Love Me Tenders" with your movie? Perhaps a "Chicken Little Sandwich?" Those are the sorts of offerings at Smitty's, where you can watch first-run films and enjoy a full meno of pub-type foods, micro beers, wines, even milkshakes while tucked into oversized seats. There's another theater in Biddeford, too.

LEAVITT THEATRE
40 Main St., Ogunquit
(207) 646-3123
One of the finer old downtown theaters in the state, the Leavitt has been an Ogunquit institution since 1923. First-run movies are screened nightly at 7 and 9 p.m. on a rotating schedule, unlike most cinemas. Check the listings carefully. Open May to October.

THE MOVIES AT THE MUSEUM
Congress Sq., Portland
(207) 772-9600
www.moviesonexchange.com
When you have the audacity to call yourself The Movies, you'd better be good. This grandaddy of independent cinema in Maine is that and more, and now, after 32 years as an Exchange Street staple it's joined forces with the Portland Museum of Art and moved downtown. The merger will allow the PMA to broaden its film fare and will give the Movies a better screen and a more comfortable auditorium. But the hip flix will still be there. You'll see the great flicks—daring foreign films, underground classics, American indies—here months before they end up on screens elsewhere. Will they be as avant garde? That remains to be seen. Museum admission is not required in the price of your ticket.

EVENINGSTAR CINEMA
Tontine Mall, Brunswick
(207) 729-5486
www.eveningstarcinema.com
Another one of those cool downtown theaters, Eveningstar has stayed in business longer than just about anyone else in the tiny Tontine Mall. And it provides a good alternative to the bland multiplex at Cooks Corner for all the college

students and arty types in Brunswick. Art films, indies, foreign pix, and all those great movies that come out every year that the suburban theaters can't seem to fit on their 10 screens are regularly shown here. Nice matinee programs for kids as well.

HARBOR THEATER
Meadow Mall, Route 27, Boothbay Harbor
(207) 633-0438
This tiny cinema used to be called Harbor Light Cinema, and it screens first-run films on a daily basis in summer. What's really neat is the pre-movie slide show, which features photographs of the Boothbay Region (local gardeners, for example, are invited to bring pictures of their flower beds—it's a hoot). Two shows nightly in summer—plus matinees on rainy days—and on weekends from October through May.

LINCOLN THEATER
2 Theater St., Damariscotta
(207) 563-3424
www.lcct.org
A state-of-the-art showplace when it was built in the 19th century, this aging gem now shows first-run movies, one a week, in summer.

THE STRAND THEATRE
345 Main St., Rockland
(207) 594-0070
www.rocklandstrand.com
Film fans have been enjoying movies at the Strand since 1923, and it's only gotten more fun. The beautifully restored cinema screens an art movie a week on those nights when it doesn't have a concert or a lecture or a stage performance. Local theaters don't come much finer.

COLONIAL THEATRE
High St., Belfast
(207) 338-1930
www.colonialtheater.com
That the Colonial is painted aquamarine and pink and has an elephant on the roof should tell you something about the three-screen cinema. It has a lot of spunk and is a ton of fun. A celebra-

---

Northeast Historic Film

The **Alamo Theater** on Main Street in Bucksport has always been among Maine's coolest downtown cinemas, and since 1986 it's been home to **Northeast Historic Film,** an organization dedicated to preserving the cinematic heritage of New England. Surprisingly there's a lot to save, and NHF has been doing a great job of it. Maine looms large in its archives, the setting, as it was, of the North Woods dramas that were so popular in the silent-film age. NHF has a fascinating series of videos available for purchase that cover a wide array of old Maine themes, from early rail history to fishing to logging to native life to Joshua Chamberlain, and they occasionally screen historic movies, in addition to the first-run fare that the place screens year round. An inspired outfit. For more information call (800) 639-1636 or visit oldfilm.org

---

tion of moviegoing, the landmark theater has art deco detailing all over the place, a dizzying carpet of electric colors, and even ticket takers in old-fashioned costumes when big movies open. Run by former Belfast mayor Michael Hurley and his wife, Therese Bagnardi, it somehow manages to snag blockbuster movies on their opening weekend, something most independent theaters can't seem to do, and screens arty pictures in the winter. Belfast filmgoers have enjoyed going to the movies here for generations, and it just keeps getting better.

CRITERION MOVIE THEATER
35 Cottage St., Bar Harbor
(207) 288-3441
www.criteriontheater.com
This is another one of those Maine downtown

cinemas that screens first-run flicks in repertory. Each week movies play for two-night runs, which allows the single-screen theater to show all sorts of offerings in the average week. Going to the movies here is worth it simply to get inside this art deco gem, circa 1932. Concerts and special events—plays, puppet festivals—happen here on occasion, too.

REEL PIZZA CINERAMA
11 Kennebec Place, Bar Harbor
(207) 288-3811
www.reelpizza.com
Whoever thought of pairing pizza and movies—good arty and independent movies, at that—is a minor genius and they added beer and wine. That's what's offered at this hip little spot, along with a healthy dose of community.

The movie listings at the *Portland Press Herald*'s Web site are very up to date and comprehensive, which is nice when you're looking for some cinematic alternatives. Click over to http://movies.mainetoday.com/theater.html to see what's playing along the coast.

MILBRIDGE THEATER
Main St., Milbridge
(207) 546-2038
It's a good thing that this old movie house is such a pleasure, because it's the only place to see first-run films for many miles around. (Nightlife is seriously scarce Down East.) But it's great—air-conditioned and with stereo surround sound. Shows are at 7:30 p.m.

ANNUAL EVENTS

You might expect Maine to have windjammer races and blueberry fairs. But conferences about the future of technology? And nationally regarded blues festivals? The calendar down east is not only full, it's full of surprises. Who would ever have guessed that there would be as many concerts of world-class classical music in Brunswick and Blue Hill and Hancock as there are in Portland? Or that famous thinkers and politicians from around the world would gather every year in Camden to discuss solutions to the world's problems? You never know what you'll find on the Maine coast if you look. What follows are some of the highlights.

JANUARY

ANNUAL MAINE LOBSTER DIP
Old Orchard Beach
(800) 365-9386

Northern states everywhere have their traditional first-of-the-year "polar bear challenges," those crazy occasions when seemingly normal people jump into the ocean on a freezing winter's day. This is the same sort of idea, Maine-style. You'll certainly emerge looking like a lobster (the cooked variety, anyway), with skin that's all red and hard from the cold. Sponsored by the Portland Rugby Club, the event takes place in front of the Brunswick Hotel in Old Orchard Beach. Usually about 300 hardy souls participate, running down into the water, diving in, screaming, and running back out as fast as they can. It's probably the only time you'll see Old Orchard Beach with so few people on it. And it's for a worthy cause—it benefits Maine's Special Olympics program. Find out more at the Old Orchard Beach Chamber of Commerce Web site at www.oldorchardbeachmaine .com or by calling (800) 365-9386.

FEBRUARY

CAMDEN CONFERENCE
P.O. Box 882, Camden 04843
(207) 236-1034
www.camdenconference.org

Unusual though it may sound for a town of 5,000 far away from any major metropolis to host an influential conference on foreign affairs, that's just what happens every February in Camden. The Camden Conference got its start in 1987, drawing on the experience of retirees from the CIA and the Foreign Service, and it has evolved over the years into a real draw. High-ranking mucky-mucks turn out every year for two days of seminars and discussions on such topics as: Islam, the global environment, the world's population, and issues related to the countries of Latin America as well as Russia, China, and Japan. The whole town gets involved—area restaurants serve food, art galleries have shows, there are book discussions and concerts, and schoolchildren do research, all on the year's theme. Definitely unique, undeniably informative, the program is worth exploring. Call or check the Web site for the current year's topic.

U.S. NATIONAL TOBOGGAN CHAMPIONSHIPS
Camden Snow Bowl
P.O. Box 1207, Camden 04843
(207) 236-3438
www.camdensnowbowl.com

Where can you see the Mount Washington Morons take on the Last of the Monhegans 2 at speeds of up to 45 mph? At the U.S. National Toboggan Championships, of course. This campy event has been a staple at the Camden Snow Bowl ski area since 1990. Participants don costumes, form two-, three-, and four-person teams, grease up their toboggans, and hit the 400-foot toboggan chute on the side of Ragged Mountain with all they have. With the short walls and wooden trough of a funky old bobsled course, the long, straight chute is covered with ice, sends sledders down at high speeds, and shoots them out across Hosmer Pond to the delight of the gathered spectators. Times are recorded, and the fastest toboggan wins (there are also prizes for best costume, team spirit, and so on). There isn't anything quite like it anywhere else, and everyone is welcome to enter. There is a fee to enter the contest but none to watch.

MARCH

MAINE MAPLE SUNDAY
Farms statewide
www.getrealmaine.com
Maine is second only to Vermont when it comes to maple sugar production in the United States, and on the last Sunday of March every year, the state sponsors an open-farm day during the annual harvest. The public is invited to sample the goods and see how the delicious amber delicacy is produced. More than two dozen farms along the coast participate. Sweet.

APRIL

FISHERMAN'S FESTIVAL
Boothbay Harbor Region Chamber of Commerce
Route 27, Boothbay Harbor
(207) 633-2353
www.boothbayharbor.com
Ever tried to race with a frozen cod in your hands? That's one of the many challenges facing game participants at this Boothbay Harbor fest. Boothbay Harbor may be better known now as a resort than as a fishing town, but it still has one of the largest fleets of any working harbor in the state, and since the early 1970s, the last weekend in April has celebrated them. There's the fish relay

race, lobster trap hauling contests, shucking, shelling, and filleting events, and lobster trap racing, during which people run across the tops of a string of floating lobster traps. Food, dancing, a Miss Shrimp Princess Pageant, lighthouse tours, church suppers, and more are all tradition. This is Boothbay at its best—before the huge influx of tourists and summer "complaints" arrive to clutter things up.

MAY

DOWN EAST SPRING BIRDING FESTIVAL
Eastport, Lubec, Calais
(207) 733-2201
www.downeastbirdfest.org
More than 400 species of birds visit Maine annually, and about 75 percent of those have had the good sense to visit the "real Maine," the Down East coast. The area sits along the Atlantic Flyway, that superhighway for migrating birds, and every May these summercators make their way back to the coast in big flocks. It's a sight to see, and folks in the Eastport, Calais, and Lubec areas put together quite a welcoming party in their communities.

JUNE

LA KERMESSE FESTIVAL
Downtown Biddeford
(207) 282-1567
www.lakermessefestival.com
Maine isn't exactly overflowing with festivals that celebrate ethnicity, but there are a few, and the biggest is La Kermesse (which in French means "the fair"), the largest French-Canadian party in the country. Maine has a rich Franco-American

i NASCAR's got nothing on Maine. Lobsterboat racing is a huge sport in summertime—rip-roaring contests in souped-up lobsterboats that take place along the length of the coast. Find out the schedule at the Web site www.lobsterboat racing.com and be prepared to get wet.

heritage, and this city of 21,000 is one of the cities where it is most strongly felt, never more so than during La Kermesse, which brings crowds of 50,000 to the city on the last weekend of June. If you're not of French descent, don't worry. You'll be adopted for the length of the event, and organizers have made an effort to broaden its appeal, multiculturally. It's Franco first and foremost, and you'll have an opportunity to try all those dishes you always wanted—from boudin to crepes to our favorite, poutine, which is French fries with gravy and cheese. Block parties, French singers and national acts, traditional dancing, and a parade are highlights, and there are the typical festival delights of a midway and fireworks. The 10K La Kermesse Road Race is popular too. Maybe it's all that poutine. The bulk of the activities take place at St. Louis Field downtown.

INDEPENDENCE POPS PORTLAND SYMPHONY ORCHESTRA
477 Congress St., Portland
(207) 773-6128
www.portlandsymphony.com

Every summer in the week leading up to the Fourth of July, the Portland Symphony Orchestra performs a five-date series of concerts at a handful of places along the coast. Popular, patriotic favorites are the order of the day, and the shows are followed by a fireworks display in the evening. Fans bring lawn chairs, blankets, picnics, and wine, and they enjoy fine summer evenings of Maine's best classical music in beautiful locales. Check the Web site or give a call for this year's dates and locations.

BOWDOIN SUMMER MUSIC FESTIVAL
Bowdoin College
6300 College Station, Brunswick
(207) 373-1400
www.summermusic.org

Bowdoin College is never quite deserted, the way some schools are in summer. In fact, the liberal arts college is abustle every June through July with the Bowdoin Summer Music Festival. Two hundred music students—high school through college and graduate level—move in for a six-

week residency on campus. Renowned teachers and classical artists show up to teach all these kids, and everyone gets a chance to play. The school holds performances several times per week, including student concerts, contemporary shows, and, on Friday evenings, faculty and guests the likes of Emanuel Ax, Lucy Shelton, and Eugenia Zukerman performing. Students learn by playing in front of audiences and watching top talents, but fans of chamber, orchestral, and even modern music may benefit the most. Most shows are inexpensive, and the artists can be world class. See the Web site for details.

WINDJAMMER DAYS
Boothbay Harbor Region Chamber of Commerce
Route 27, Boothbay Harbor
(207) 633-7448
www.boothbayharbor.com

Maine has an impressive fleet of windjammers, those classic old, tall-masted ships, and every June they rally in the resort community of Boothbay Harbor. Explore the local Coast Guard base, poke around area boatbuilding facilities, and enjoy parades, arts and craft fairs, kids' events, and even fireworks.

GREAT SCHOONER RACE
Maine Windjammer Association
(800) 807-WIND
www.sailmainecoast.com

People often refer to Penobscot Bay as one of the finest sailing grounds in the world, second only to the Mediterranean for its views and cruising conditions. And if salty panoramas are your thing, there's no better time to pay this Midcoast bay a visit than during the Great Schooner Race, when as many as 28 old windjammers vie for top honors in the competition that began in 1976. The sight of these pretty three-masters—most more than 100 feet long—straining in the breeze, huge sails taut, crashing through the chop, crews rushing about—harks back to the great age of sail in Maine and won't soon be forgotten. It's the largest annual gathering of tall ships in North America.

KNEISEL HALL CHAMBER MUSIC FESTIVAL
P.O. Box 648, Blue Hill 04614
(207) 374-2811
www.kneisel.org

World-class chamber music in Blue Hill, Maine? Sounds unlikely, but it's true, thanks to a trip Austrian violinist Frank Kneisel made to the area in the late 19th century. Kneisel was the chair of the Department of Strings at what is now called the Juilliard School and in 1902 began bringing his most gifted students to his summer retreat in Blue Hill every year. The tradition has continued—the Kneisel Hall Chamber Music Festival is now the oldest chamber music fest in the United States—and each summer, a group of talented young chamber musicians ventures north to live and learn on the shores of Blue Hill Bay. On Friday evenings and Sunday afternoons the school offers performances to the public, and they are some of the finest classical music concerts anyone's going to see anywhere in Maine.

JULY

FOURTH OF JULY CELEBRATIONS
Used to be the Fourth of July was the official beginning of summer and tourist season in Maine. That changed long ago, when people started pushing the shoulder seasons as far as possible, but Mainers still enjoy their Independence Day festivities. From Kittery to Calais, there are celebrations up and down the coast and they are especially big in Portland, Bath, Thomaston, Bar Harbor, and Eastport. Check local listings.

i Some time ago, community organizations discovered garden tours, and now they're one of the principal fundraising methods Down East and a high point of July and August in many communities. You can find out the complete schedule in the April issue of *Down East* magazine or at the Web site of *People, Places, and Plants* magazine—www.ppplants.com.

YARMOUTH CLAM FESTIVAL
Yarmouth Chamber of Commerce
162 Main St., Yarmouth
(207) 846-3984
www.clamfestival.com

How many clams does it cost to get into the Yarmouth Clam Festival? Not many. In fact, most of the entertainments at this three-day Greater Portland favorite are free. Not quite as huge as the Maine Lobster Festival, the clam festival has been packing people in since it was founded in the mid-1960s. Kids and teenagers are naturally drawn to the midway set up by Smokey's Greater Shows, with all the arcade games, rides, cotton candy, and questionable carnies you could want. Younger folks like the parade as well. Everyone enjoys the firefighters' muster, the Maine State Clam Shucking Contest, and the street dancing. Parents are fond of the art show on the library lawn, the "pink elephant" sale across from the First Parish Church, and the live music on stages across the village in the evening. Good times for everyone and loads and loads of clams, sold to benefit various sports teams and community organizations.

NORTH ATLANTIC BLUES FESTIVAL
Harbor Park, Rockland
(207) 596-6055
(207) 593-1189 (festival hotline)
www.northatlanticbluesfestival.com

The coast of Maine is not exactly the first place anyone would go looking for the blues. Perhaps they should. Started in 1994, this July staple has become one of the most prestigious blues fests on the East Coast, even winning a Keeping the Blues Alive award from the Blues Foundation, something that normally goes out to big-city events like the Chicago Blues Festival. Thirteen thousand people can't be wrong, though, and that's the size of the crowd that typically turns out to Harbor Park to listen to the work of some of the top names in the blues—singers and guitar slingers like Susan Tedeschi, Jimmie Vaughan, Eddie Kirkland, James Cotton, Koko Taylor, and Bo Diddley. The stage is set up right on the harbor, there's food, and you don't want to miss the Club

Crawl, which fills "Rock City" clubs with area talent during the two days of the festival. Some really good stuff can be found, like local legend Blind Albert and his blues band. Fun, fun, fun. Bring a blanket or a lawn chair, and arrive well before gates for optimum viewing.

OPEN FARM DAY
Statewide
(207) 287-3491
www.mainefoodandfarms.com

One of the consequences of all the growth, change, and development Maine has seen since the 1970s is the loss of a lot of family farms. This loss of farms is sad not only for the families involved but for communities, too, which lose good neighbors, access to fresh produce, and open space. The state of Maine has recognized this problem and begun to take steps to help the farms that are left, launching several agricultural campaigns. One of these is Open Farm Day, the last Sunday in July, when agrarian operations all across the state welcome the public in for tours, wagon rides, animal petting, berry picking, and walks around farm meadows. You can see how dairy cows are milked, tickle little lambies, learn about beekeeping, and get your picture taken with a llama. There's usually the opportunity to buy produce and crafts and sample fresh foods. You might not want to leave.

AUGUST

MAINE LOBSTER FESTIVAL
Harbor Park, Rockland
(207) 596-0376 or (800) LOB–CLAW
www.mainelobsterfestival.com

Plan far ahead if you want to attend the five-day Maine Lobster Festival in Rockland. It's almost impossible to get a room anywhere nearby due to the extraordinary popularity of this event. Since it was begun in the 1950s, the Lobster Fest has graduated from a fun family fair into a genuine phenomenon with a life of its own (we're talking lines of clothing, shuttle services, and kings and queens here). Tens of thousands of people descend upon the Penobscot Bay city in the last week of July and first week of August to feed at the World's Largest Lobster Cooker. In 2008, for example, more than 10 tons of lobster were devoured, along with untold amounts of clams, mussels, and fried shrimp. Food is the focus, but there's so much more to the festival. Highlights include the lobster crate race, open houses at the Coast Guard base, marine tank tent displays, merchant showcases, King Neptune and his parade, and the unforgettable Sea Goddess pageant. The music tends to be worthy, too, with recent headliners including Willie Nelson, the Dixie Chicks, Ricky Skaggs, and Dwight Yoakam. About the only people who don't like the Maine Lobster Festival are the activists from People for the Ethical Treatment of Animals, who stage protests every year. These protests are usually very clever, though, so even the angry people entertain. Summer in Maine wouldn't be quite the same without it.

WILD BLUEBERRY FESTIVAL
Centre St. Church, Machias
(207) 255-6665
www.machiasblueberry.com

Chances are, if you've ever munched on a blueberry, it came from Washington County, Maine. The most Down East county Down East, Washington produces 85 percent of the world's blueberry crop, and every year in mid-August the region salutes that fact with the Maine Wild Blueberry Festival in Machias. A weekend-long immersion in all things berry, the fruity fair is the highlight of summer in the small town of Machias, and most of the events revolve around its stunning Centre Street Congregational Church. The community promises "an old-fashioned country good time," and it delivers, with a children's parade, a fish fry, a locally produced musical, an arts and crafts show, a pancake breakfast, a road race, bands and music, and many, many a blueberry. These blue guests of honor show up at the breakfast, at the pie-eating and cooking contests, on a quilt, and even at the post office, in the form of a blueberry letter cancellation.

INTERNATIONAL HOMECOMING FESTIVAL
St. Croix Valley Chamber of Commerce
P.O. Box 368, Calais 04619
(207) 454-2308 or (888) 422-3112
www.visitcalais.com

So many family and friends would return to the Calais–St. Stephen area every year for the annual International Festival that organizers decided to rename it the International Homecoming Festival. "Two Countries, One Heart" is the fest's motto, and while that may sound a little precious, this celebration of life on the U.S.–Canada border is kind of fun and funky. Taking place over the course of two weeks, the event includes beauty pageants for girls and teens—where else can you win the Miss International crown?—golf tournaments, lots of bands, lumberjack and rock-skipping competitions, a "food fest," a street dance, various suppers, chocolate pudding wrestling, cow patty bingo (yes, real cow patties), a road race, volleyball tournament, and much more. (Did we mention the pudding wrestling?) Events are held at sites on both sides of the border.

COMMON GROUND COUNTRY FAIR
Unity

One of the most beloved of all of Maine's summer shindigs, the Common Ground Fair takes place on the third weekend of September every year. People mark that date on their calendars and keep it open at all costs, to be sure they can attend— for many, it's the highlight of the year.

What's there to love? The fair is a celebration of rural life, born in the late 1970s, a time when Waldo County had seen a large influx of countercultural types interested in moving "back to the land." They moved to the country, set up farms, and learned by doing, getting together in September to share ideas and the harvest. That's still what the fair is about today, but it has grown and grown and attracts 60,000 fairgoers every year, most of whom are no longer farmers.

Hosted by the Maine Organic Farmers and Gardeners Association, the fair has many goals but a core few stand out. First, it's organic through and through (all vendors sell organic foods—they don't even allow coffee to be sold on-site), it's all about sustainability, and it places a premium on community and sharing.

Held at MOFGA's own farm in Unity, the event features new activities every year, but much remains the same. There's always great food, with scores of booths selling everything from Indian curry to the old favorite, turkey dinners from the free-range Turkey Farm in New Sharon. Acres of tents are filled with the wares of Maine country craftsmen and women, many of whom elevate their work to the level of art—there are always remarkable jewelers, canoe builders, and sweater makers—as well as political action booths. There are also stages on which bands play and people dance. Speechifying happens on the Common, usually by progressive activists the likes of Jim Hightower; there's the ever popular Parade of Vegetables, which kids love, and there are several days' worth of agricultural workshops and demonstrations.

Big crowds gather to see border collies herd sheep, hear talks about small woodlot forestry, pat the animals in the barns, and file through the displays of award-winning fruits and vegetables. Perhaps best of all, people are constantly bumping into friends and family. The Common Ground Country Fair is like your average state fair run by tasteful ex-hippies—and that's definitely a good thing. If you leave the fair without feeling warm and fuzzy and wanting to simplify your life, you have issues. The fair is about a half hour drive from Belfast on Route 137, but it's well worth it, and people commonly drive from out of state to attend. For more information, call (207) 568-4142 or visit www.mofga.org.

SEPTEMBER

CAPRICCIO OGUNQUIT PERFORMING ARTS
(207) 646-6170

The tiny beach town of Ogunquit has been a haven of the arts since before the turn of the 20th century, and in the early days of September every year they take to the fore, with a weeklong celebration on the beach and in the village.

Events include live theater, ballet, poetry readings, a fashion show, an art show, and musical performances—last year by such names as Kaki King and Tom Rush. The largest spectacle just might be the Festival of Kites at the end of the week. This annual event fills the skies over Ogunquit Beach with color and movement—and sometimes awful tangles.

WINDJAMMER WEEKEND
Camden-Rockport-Lincolnville Chamber of Commerce, Camden
(207) 236-4404
www.windjammerweekend.com

Enjoy a sea chantey? Attracted to schooner bums? Then get thee to Camden over Labor Day weekend for Windjammer Weekend, the last of the season's grand parades of sail. The age of tall ships is roasted over the course of three days with songs and music, the telling of tall tales, a schooner bum talent show, nautical workshops, the ever-popular lobster crate races, and fireworks. With Camden's compact harbor abrim with graceful schooners, it's quite a spectacle.

EASTPORT SALMON FESTIVAL
Downtown Eastport
(207) 853-4644
www.eastportme.net

Fish helped build the city of Eastport, one of the most picturesque communities in all of Maine. In the 1880s the sardine canning industry was booming here, with 18 factories providing jobs for a population that was almost three times the 2,000 that it is today. The canneries went bust long ago, but fish—these days salmon in pens in the bay—remain very important to the local economy. And the city on Moose Island gives them a tip of the hat with its Salmon Festival every September on the first Sunday after Labor Day. The day typically includes a road race, boat rides, a walking tour, crafts displays, and barbecued salmon dinner, all before the beautiful edge of Passamaquoddy Bay. If you enjoy salmon, best get yourself Down East.

OCTOBER
POPTECH!
P.O. Box 1405, Camden
(207) 230-2425
www.poptech.org

What's Brian Eno doing in Camden, Maine? The eminent recording artist (Roxy Music, solo stuff) and producer (U2, Peter Gabriel, David Bowie, Paul Simon) was speaking at PopTech!, an annual conference that explores science and technology and the future of ideas. Every October this rather remarkable confab attracts some 500 visionaries from the worlds of technology, arts, design, education, business, government, and the sciences to the beautifully restored Camden Opera House. So Eno was in good company. If you're interested in where we're all headed—or just want to ogle celebrities—you'll find PopTech! a fascinating weekend.

YORK HARVESTFEST
Greater York Region Chamber of Commerce
1 Stonewall Lane, York Village
(207) 363-4422
www.gatewaytomaine.org

When York claims its celebration is old-fashioned, people should listen, this being one of the oldest towns in the nation. The community's annual Harvestfest is built around all sorts of traditional foods and entertainments—a Native American powwow, craft demonstrations, puppet shows, antique car displays, tours of historic sites, all complemented by an ox roast, chowders, cider, apple crisp, and good old Maine baked beans. Events get under way on the Village Green—just across from Olde York Village (see, it's so old they have to put an e on the end) and move to Ellis Park on Short Sands beach for the Hannah Jackson 5K race.

FALL FOLIAGE FAIR
Boothbay Chamber of Commerce
Route 27, Boothbay Harbor
(207) 633-2353
www.boothbayharbor.com

Autumn in Maine is as beautiful as it is in Vermont

and New Hampshire, perhaps even more so, because the state has the sea off which the colors can reflect. But, perhaps due to marketing, those states are the ones people associate with glowing foliage. Several Maine communities have put together festivals to pay homage to the season (and attract visitors), and one of the better ones is in Boothbay at the Railway Village Museum. More than 100 vendors typically show up to display Maine-made crafts, woodworking, art, and jewelry, and to sell locally canned and baked goods. Local bands play on stages, to the delight of adults, and the trains of the popular little museum chug around their track to entertain the kids. Plenty of chowders and cider are available, too. It's a good excuse to drive down to the Boothbays at a particularly beautiful time of year.

NOVEMBER

MAINE BREWERS' FESTIVAL
Downtown Portland
(207) 771-7571
www.mainebrew.com

Somehow Maine's version of Oktoberfest got bumped into November (which actually makes sense because the second-to-last month of the year, a dark time when the days are short, is now known as "Drink Maine Beer Month" Down East). The Oktoberfest is now called the Maine Brewers' Festival, a jolly and sudsy gathering of the many brewers that have put the state on the microbrew map since 1993. Anyone who enjoys a pint—or six—wouldn't want to miss it. For the price of entry, attendees are given 12 tickets, each worth a single four-ounce tasting. They also get a souvenir tasting glass to tote around to the more than 20 booths. Of course, you're welcome to buy more. The festivities typically get under way at 3 p.m. on a Saturday afternoon and last until after midnight. Besides the beer, there are booths by local restaurants and blues bands to take you into the evening. Don't even think about showing up if you're under 21, because the brewers enlist members of the Portland Rugby Club to do their bouncing. Portland has lots of taxis if you need a post-party lift.

TWELVE DAYS OF CHRISTMAS
Portland
(207) 772-6828
www.portlandmaine.com

The Twelve Days in question begin at the end of November and continue each Friday, Saturday, and Sunday through Christmas. Highlights include Santas arrival by ferry, the Window Walk, and the Portland Symphony Orchestra plays its annual Magic of Christmas concert series, a truly magical batch of shows. An array of other arts, cultural, and business organizations across town—from the Portland Museum of Art to the Portland Public Market to the Maine Historical Society—host events. Perhaps there will even be an enchanting dusting of snow on the pear tree.

DECEMBER

CHRISTMAS PRELUDE
Townwide, Kennebunkport
Kennebunkport Business Association
(207) 967-0857
www.christmasprelude.com

Often described as "quaint," Kennebunkport makes a particularly fine backdrop for a holiday celebration. And, boy, does this venerable village of historic homes, shops, and restaurants on the Atlantic throw one. Christmas Prelude, it's called, and after hosting it since the 1980s, the community pretty much has it down—the name is even copyrighted now. Dreamed up as a method of drawing tourists to a resort area that was all but boarded up in wintertime, Prelude revolves around shopping but somehow manages to transcend the commercial. The festivities get under way on the first Friday of December and usually begin with shopping, arts and crafts shows, open houses, and walking tours in the afternoon. This activity is followed by a chowder supper and then a tree lighting downtown in Dock Square, and then after that the action shifts to a bonfire for carols. Saturday is all consumed with pancake breakfast, Christmas fairs, free sleigh rides, open houses, lunches and teas, and later dinner and then caroling. One of the more unique elements is the traditional candlelit walk to the local Franciscan monastery for more caroling. Sunday is a quieter day of more craft fairs and the arrival of St. Nick by sea. And there's so much to do, events spill over into the following weekend. This is a rare opportunity to see beyond the resort facade and get a glimpse of Kennebunkport as a small Maine town, with a strong sense of community, and it's particularly welcome at Christmastime.

SPARKLE WEEKEND
Downtown Freeport
Freeport Merchants Association
23 Depot St., Freeport
(207) 865-1212 or (800) 865-1994
www.freeportusa.com
The town of Freeport doesn't really need any big events to entice shoppers during the holiday season. It already has a couple of the biggest draws any community could want at this time of year—L.L. Bean and several dozen factory outlets. The business organization put together the colorful Sparkle Weekend anyway, and, if you can deal with crowds and parking hassles, it's fun. The village gussies itself up with thousands of lights, sets up a talking Christmas tree, puts together a concert of traditional yuletide favorites—played by 50 tubas—enlists the help of Santa and some strolling carolers, organizes a Wine and Beer Garden, and holds what it claims is New England's only nighttime parade of lights. Whimsy is the word, and it all works. Plus it's free. And while you're in town, you can pick up something for everyone on your shopping list.

CHRISTMAS BY THE SEA
Downtown Camden
(207) 236-4404
www.camdenme.org
Where else in the world does Santa arrive by lobster boat? Well, he actually does so in many Maine towns, but few hold a Christmas candle to the extravaganza enjoyed during the first weekend of December in the picturesque Midcoast communities of Camden and Rockport. We're talking a holiday house tour, carolers strolling through historic neighborhoods, beachside bonfires, craft fairs and yuletide bazaars, carriage rides, old-fashioned baked bean suppers, a concert with the area's famous folksingers, and, yes, plenty of opportunities for shopping at the resort town's stores. The party gets under way on Friday afternoon and doesn't let up until Sunday evening. This is what the holidays should be all about.

DAY TRIPS

One of the great things about living on or visiting the Maine coast is its proximity to the state's famous interior, the woodsy wonderland of moose and mountains and lakes. Baxter State Park, one of the premier wilderness destinations in the East, is within a few hours drive of U.S. Route 1; Moosehead Lake, the largest freshwater body contained in one state east of the Mississippi and a wilderness playground, is about the same distance; and the Rangeley Lakes area, one of the oldest resorts in the state and a picturesque mountain town, is, too. The White Mountains, the tallest peaks in the northeast, are a skip from Portland, visible from various points in the city on a clear day. Of course, if you prefer more cosmopolitan entertainments, a pair of cool cities—Boston, Massachusetts, and Portsmouth, New Hampshire—are just a half hour and an hour away, respectively, from Kennebunk. Or you can head out the state's back door and cross the border into Canada to pay a visit to the Canadian Maritimes and Campobello.

On the Maine coast you can enjoy a day on the beach and head into the city for dinner with relative ease. Maybe shop in Freeport in the afternoon and hit a concert in Boston that night. Or you can spend the morning touring a quiet Atlantic cove in a kayak, and then shove off for a little après-supper canoeing on a remote river up-country later that evening. Many people like to visit the state's two premier parks—Acadia and Baxter—in a week or even a weekend, which is eminently doable (provided you make the necessary reservation at Baxter). The state of Maine has it all going on—really fun cities, picturesque fishing villages, romantic islands, sparkling sea vistas, majestic mountains, miles of spruce forest—and you have access to everything when you set up on the coast.

BAXTER STATE PARK

64 Balsam Dr., Millinocket
(207) 723-5140
www.baxterstateparkauthority.com

As wilderness parks go, it's hard to improve on the 200,000 acres of Maine wilderness that Governor Percival Baxter gave to the state back in the 1930s. A hiker's paradise, Baxter State Park was designed to be enjoyed on foot and has some 175 miles of trails. These woodsy walkways climb the state's highest peak, mile-high Mount Katahdin, the northern terminus of the Appalachian Trail, along with a score of other summits, and they wander out to moosey bogs, skirt photogenic lakes and ponds, and follow waterfalls for miles. Truly spectacular stuff.

When Baxter assembled this park two hours north of Bangor, beginning in the 1930s and ending in the 1960s (he left a trust to buy still more land, too), he did so with the provision that it would be managed for wildlife first and foremost, human use a distant second. "Forever wild" is how he put it, and over the years park management has lived up to that decree. No RVs or motorcycles are allowed in, and, unlike Acadia, this isn't a park where you drive around in your car gawking out the window. There is a tote road that traverses its edges, but its famous ribs are rough on cars. In order to see the real goods, you have to park, usually at one of 10 campgrounds, lace up your boots, and strike out into it the woods. And it's an infinitely rewarding place if you do.

Because of its outstanding beauty and wild nature, though, the park is busy these days, especially in the summer months. To camp anywhere you need a reservation, and if you want to find a parking place for a climb of Katahdin, you might want to consider getting there before 6 a.m. The "Mountain of the People of Maine" is the reason why most people make their way here north of Millinocket, and the staging points for all-day hikes up the imposing massif are usually very crowded. People will often arrive in the wee hours of the morning, get in line at the southern gate, and sleep in their cars to be sure they make it in before the parking areas close, which can be as early as 7 a.m. If you plan to hike Katahdin, a reservation for at least one night is advisable. Just by being there, campers get first dibs at the trails, the most major of which begin at Roaring Brook, Abol, and Katahdin Stream Campgrounds. People often find that after spending six hours or more hiking straight up, they don't feel much like driving when they get back down. There are oodles of other great climbs here as well, from the challenging ascent of Doubletop to the easygoing route up short but scenic Sentinel Mountain.

The majority of the campgrounds lie along the park's tote road and can be reached by automobile, but a few, like Russell Pond and Chimney Pond, are in the wild backcountry and require a backpack in. The most popular of the roadside areas are Roaring Brook, Katahdin Stream, and the cabin campgrounds of Daicey and Kidney Ponds. The camping is primitive, with just tents and small pop-up trailers allowed, and there are few amenities beyond a fire ring and picnic tables, though some sites do have lean-tos, open-faced Adirondack-style shelters, or even bunkhouses. Regardless of where you stay, you have to use common outhouses, carry out the trash you bring in, and tote your own water. Several lean-to sites are scattered here and there in remote areas for individual stopovers.

Your camping companions might be moose, black bear, deer, American martin, Canada jay, or any number of other beasties. Because the park is so wild, critters are wild about it. Moose are perhaps the biggest attraction for the average

visitor, because they're numerous, commonly spotted, and generally unbothered by respectful people—they willingly pose for pictures. Viewing is great at Sandy Stream Pond, just north of Roaring Brook Campground; at Abol, Tracy, and Stump Ponds near Abol and Katahdin Stream Campgrounds; and anywhere in the backcountry. Bears are a little more skittish.

Reservations for the most popular camping areas can be hard to come by, and Mainers have been known to sleep out in the frigid cold in January to be first in line when the reservation process begins for the year. It's a long drive to the park from the coast—about three and a half hours from the Midcoast and Down East regions—but is it ever worth it. People truly love this place, and it's easy to understand why.

MOOSEHEAD LAKE AREA

Look at a map of Maine, and sprawling Moosehead Lake does indeed resemble the profile of Bullwinkle's noggin. This is the state's largest freshwater body—its blue expanse covers 117 square miles of prime North Woods territory. A vast land of forest and rivers and, yes, moose, surrounds the big lake, whose nose points squarely at the small community of Greenville. The area has been a haven for outdoor lovers of all types since the 1880s, when "sports" from across the Northeast began to flock north in droves, spending a week or more in the woods and on the water hunting and fishing.

Those two pastimes still attract a lot of people to Moosehead, but many more come simply to see a bit of this rugged country, enjoy fresh air and wild views, and look for moose. So many of the awkward brown beasts can be seen wandering near the road and in the woods that the local chamber of commerce has come up with a monthlong celebration of all things moose called Moose-Mainea, and local outfitters have put together moose "safari" tours. MooseMainea features races by canoe, rowboat, and mountain bike, picture contests, and many moose safaris. Hiking, kayaking, white-water rafting, and sightseeing trips—out on the lake, aboard the old steamer

Katahdin (207-695-2716), or above the wilderness, with **Currier's Flying Service** (207-695-2778)—are other popular diversions. When snow flies this place is a snowmobiler's happy zone, with miles and miles of trails through the woods.

A tiny place with an up-country charm, Greenville (pop. 2,000) has enough treats to occupy an afternoon. There are a few cool shops to peruse downtown and the nifty hilltop **Indian Hill Trading Post** (800-675-4487), a woodsy outfitter with one of everything and a jaw-dropping look at the lake, and **Moosehead Traders** (207-695-3806), with moose antler furnishings. Some fun dining options await the traveler, too, from **Flatlanders** (207-695-3373), a diner where all the locals show up at one time or another, to the **Blair Hill Inn** (207-695-0224), an upscale place with a fancy chef. Accommodations run the gamut: There's the **Kineo View Motor Lodge** (207-695-4470), a 12-room motel with nice views of Mount Kineo in the middle of the lake; the **Greenville Inn** (207-695-2206 or 800-695-6000), a gracious Victorian hostelry with water views; and the **Birches** (207-534-7305 or 800-825-9453), a "wilderness resort" in nearby Rockwood with lakeside cabins, a great dining room, and a small excursion empire.

The woods around the lake are dotted with intriguing places. To the east is Kokadjo (pop. "not many"), a wee frontier hamlet on the edge of First Roach Pond where you'll find a trading post, some privately owned cabins, and **West Branch Pond Camps** (207-695-2561), a sporting camp of eight rustic cabins on West Branch Pond. To the north is Northeast Carry, an outpost at the spot between the West Branch of the Penobscot and Moosehead where canoes had to be portaged back in the glory days of Maine guides. A little general store is here that'll take you back a few years. And to the west is **Pittston Farm** (207-280-0000), a down-home restaurant on the site of an old logging farm that is legendary in the North Woods for its all-you-can-pile-on buffet.

A huge land owner, Plum Creek, has plans to do a massive development—thousands of homes, golf courses, a ski area, and more, which threatens the future of Moosehead, so see it before it gets spoiled.

For more information on the Moosehead Lake Region, contact the Moosehead Lake Region Chamber of Commerce at (207) 695-2702 or www.mooseheadlake.org.

RANGELEY LAKES REGION

It's hard not to like Rangeley. The town is undeniably appealing, high up in the western mountains of Maine and hard by Rangeley Lake. It's the most elevated community in the state at 2,000 feet and looks out over a landscape of lakes and mountains that trundle to the horizon. Woods cover every inch of ground that isn't water. The mighty Androscoggin River gets its start here, before tumbling south to enter the sea at Brunswick, and the area is famous for its fishing and its large population of moose.

With about 1,200 people, the town of Rangeley—which picturesquely wraps around Rangeley Lake, Mooselookmeguntic Lake, and innumerable small ponds—is the hub of the area, and it's a real cool combination of rugged outdoorsy and up-country gentility. Parks and preserves are everywhere, sportsmen and snowmobilers still flock to the community, and yet it has its own cultural appeal, with a movie theater, a few good restaurants, an offbeat museum, and the shows and concerts put on by Rangeley Friends of the Arts. A lot of affluent city folks have summer homes on the lake, and they don't want to give up their entertainments for the summer.

Downtown Rangeley is a few blocks of shops, eateries, and services on the northeast side of Rangeley Lake. It's the sort of place where you can see a floatplane land while strolling the sidewalk and gas up your snowmobile at a Main Street convenience store in winter. Good meals can be had at the **Rangeley Inn** (51 Main Street; 207-864-3341 or 800-666-3687), a classic up-country hostelry right downtown, or at **Loon Lodge** (Pickford Road; 207-864-5666), a turn-of-the-20th-century, three-room inn. The Rangeley Inn is also a pleasant place to stay—if you book a room in the inn itself and not in the adjacent motel.

Just up the road from Rangeley to the west is the village of Oquossoc on Mooselookmeguntic

Lake. Colonized by wealthy cottagers—there's an interior design firm in this tiny woods community—Oquossoc nonetheless is a pretty wild locale, and there's good hiking to be found on 2,400-foot Bald Mountain. The hairless summit has exceptional ganders at Mooselookmeguntic and Rangeley Lakes and the hundreds of acres of woods that surround. One of the state's better private camping areas, **Stephen Phillips Memorial Preserve** (207-864-2003), is located right on Mooselookmeguntic, with primitive, walk-in sites on the lake and on a couple of undeveloped islands in the middle of it.

To the northeast of Rangeley is Stratton, on the shores of artificially created Flagstaff Lake. This is the spot where the town of Flagstaff was sunk in the 1930s, when the Dead River was dammed. The Bigelow mountain range sprawls behind the lake, and it's one of the state's best hiking areas. And just beyond it on Route 27 is **Sugarloaf USA** (800–843-5623), the famed ski area, where there is lodging, dining, and adventuring year-round. Golfers are particularly fond of the Sugarloaf links, and the resort has mountain biking, moose safaris, and a host of other offerings during the warm-weather months.

For more information on the Rangeley area, contact the Rangeley Lakes Region Chamber of Commerce at (207) 864-5364 or (800) MT–LAKES or check www.rangeleymaine.com.

SCENIC DRIVES IN MAINE

It may seem strange, but only one of the 17 roads in Maine's Designated Scenic Highway program is along the coast. The 16 others wend and wind through the state's gorgeous interior, passing underneath mountains, skirting lakes, and wandering through the North Woods. The one piece of coastal pavement deemed worthy is State Route 182, a stunning alternative to Route 1 Down East, connecting the small towns Franklin and Cherryfield. (Of course, you never see the ocean on this short route either, and the lakes-and-forest landscape it passes looks a lot like the North Woods.) But there are plenty of other picturesque seaside drives the state might consider

should it ever decide to designate a few other highways scenic. They make for great detours and are often useful alternate routes.

State Route 103, Kittery Point to York Harbor

This two-lane road at the southern tip of Maine goes through the venerable, all-American village of Kittery Point, a white-clapboard place of fine old homes, before passing along Pepperrell Cove and through sections of the Rachel Carson National Wildlife Refuge, a pretty marshy area frequented by much birdlife.

State Route 24, Orr's and Bailey's Islands

The tip of rock at the end of this photogenic stretch of road in Harpswell is called Lands End, and that's just what it is—the road dead ends at the salty brine of Casco Bay. The views along the rolling road that lead to it are truly fine.

The River Road, Boothbay Harbor to Newcastle

A very pleasant backway between the resort of Boothbay Harbor and the Damariscotta/Newcastle area, the River Road follows the Damariscotta River for several miles. The road plays peekaboo with the salt water, passing sweet old homes all the while.

State Route 131, Thomaston to Port Clyde

This quiet road wanders through fishing village after fishing village, following the St. George River to the sea. It ends in the cool community of Port Clyde, home of the Marshall Point Lighthouse and jumping-off point for trips to Monhegan Island.

Blue Hill Peninsula

Any road down in these parts is a detour worth taking. The East Penobscot Bay villages of Castine, Brooksville, Deer Isle, and Stonington are all truly stunners. And the prospect from Caterpillar Hill in

In the 20 or so years since it was released, the *DeLorme Maine Atlas and Gazetteer* has become the bible of travel in Maine. The 78 maps it contains within its signature blue covers are more detailed than anything else available—showing old woods roads and overgrown farm byways as well as every piece of blacktop in the state—and you almost can't get lost if you follow them carefully. Most Mainers have a tattered old copy on the backseat of their cars and wouldn't go anywhere without it. You'll find the *Maine Atlas and Gazetteer* at a wide variety of shops and bookstores and you can order one online at www.delorme .com.

Sedgwick—the whole of Penobscot Bay spread out before you—is priceless.

Mount Desert Island

Home of Acadia National Park, Mount Desert is ringed with photogenic drives. Pick a road.

WHITE MOUNTAINS

It says something that one of the most favored destinations of the Maine Outdoor Adventure Club is the White Mountains of New Hampshire. No knock on Maine here, it's just that the Portland-based outing group is closer to the fabled Whites than they are to the mountains of Maine. Mount Washington is less than a couple of hours from the Forest City, and there is no end of things to do in the woods that surround New England's highest peak.

This is prime hiking country, some of the best woods to walk and mountains to climb in the nation. There are more than 1,200 miles of hiking trails—including the famous Appalachian Trail—and five areas designated as wilderness, the largest more than 45,000 acres. Outdoor enthusiasts will find 23 campgrounds, 14 picnic areas, and unlimited hunting, fishing, swimming, canoeing, and, in the winter, skiing. For a taste of the trail offerings, try the 20-minute hike in to the 66-foot Glen Ellis Falls (off State Route 16 in

Pinkham Notch, New Hampshire); the four-hour Boulder Loop round-trip, which gives some great views of Mt. Chocorua and the Swift River Valley (off Kancamagus Highway); or the Rob Brook Road trail (off Rob Brook Road), which takes you through some boggy areas where moose and bears have been known to hang out. For the ambitious climber, there is always Mount Washington. At 6,288 feet, it's the highest peak in the Northeast. Try the Tuckerman Ravine trail, the most direct—and one of the most popular— routes up the mountain. The trail begins at the Appalachian Mountain Club's visitor center on Route 16 in Pinkham Notch. Of course, plenty of the other Presidentials are good fun, too.

People who don't want to or can't hike enjoy the **Kancamagus Highway,** a 34-mile-long road that cuts right through the heart of the Whites. Those who want to rough it have options aplenty. Try the **Dolly Copp Campground** (Route 16, Pinkham Notch, New Hampshire) in the National Forest, near the base of Mount Washington. There are 176 sites, with a base rate of $20 per night. Or try **Wild River Campground** (Wild River Road, Gilead, Maine), which has 12 wooded sites on the Wild River in the Maine section of the forest. It's $16 a night. At the other end of the spectrum is the **Balsams Grand Resort Hotel** (State Route 26, Dixfield Notch, New Hampshire; 877-225-7267; www.thebalsams.com), a 130-year-old New England castle of sorts surrounded by the Whites. It's fancy enough that you can pretend you're in the Alps. *Ski America Guidebook* called the Balsams "one of the top ten romantic ski resorts in the country." See for yourself.

For more information contact White Mountains Attractions, Route 112, Kancamagus Highway, Woodstock, New Hampshire; (603) 745-8720 or (800) FIND–MTS; www.visitwhitemountains.com.

BOSTON

Mainers have always had a proprietary interest in the city of Boston, even if they like to make fun of Massachusetts in general. The city is only an hour and a half from Portland, close enough for an easy day trip. The Red Sox are our baseball team, just as the New England Revolution are our soccer team, and the Celtics our basketball team. (It's not uncommon to see a lot of Maine license plates on cars parked in lots at the big game.) The museums, the aquarium, and the Freedom Trail are where Maine schoolkids go for their field trips, and older kids and adults frequently drive down to the Fleet Center and sundry clubs to see the rock concerts that inevitably skip Maine. Many Pine Tree State residents even drive down to use Logan Airport when they travel, despite the fact that Portland Jetport has connecting flights. One has to look no farther than the Amtrak Downeaster rail service between Portland and Boston for evidence of the popularity of the city with Mainers—more than 20,000 riders make the trek every month.

What are they going to do and see? Everyone has different agendas, of course, but it's safe to say that all these travelers are looking for the sort of big-city entertainments that Maine lacks. Museums are particularly popular (a good resource is www.museumsofboston.org), and not just with those schoolkids. When big exhibits come through town, parents pack up the family and walk them through the **Museum of Fine Arts** (617-267-9300; www.mfa.org), the **Children's Museum** (617-426-8855; www.boston childrensmuseum.org), and the **Museum of Science** (617-723-2500; www.mos.org). (Some people go to the latter simply to see IMAX movies, too, something unavailable in Maine.) The **New England Aquarium** (617-973-5200; www.neaq .org) is also a large draw, with its penguin pool, shark wall, and auditorium shows.

History is another biggie. Maine was once part of Massachusetts, and Boston is rich with the heritage of those colonial times. From the architecture—places like the Old South Meeting House, Paul Revere House, and Fanueil Hall—to the well-preserved sites along the Freedom Trail to the decks of the Constitution, the chronicle of the past is easy to read and surprisingly popular.

And don't forget shopping. Newbury Street is a well-known high-end retail zone, as is Copley Square. People also enjoy the bookstores of Harvard Square in Cambridge, the cut-rate retail of Downtown Crossing, and the tourist-oriented shops of Quincy Market. It's easy enough to shop for CDs and books online, but when it comes to clothes, shoes, and furniture, you often want to see it first, and Boston is the nearest place Mainers can do just that in a big way.

Beantown's Convention and Visitors Bureau is a wealth of information on where to eat, what to see, and where to stay. Call 1-888-SEE BOSTON or visit its Web site—www.bostonusa.com—for ideas.

PORTSMOUTH, NEW HAMPSHIRE

Portsmouth is a truly fine city, with an appeal much like that of Portland, only on a much smaller scale (pop. 23,000). It too has the history, the sea, the progressive vibe, and a restaurant culture similar to the one found in its cousin to the north. In fact, like Portland, the city was recently named one of the 50 best places to live by *Money* magazine. Many southern Mainers—those from towns like Kittery, the Berwicks, and the Yorks—use the city as their hub, because it's closer than Portland. And many more pour in to buy big-ticket items, thanks to the fact that New Hampshire has no sales tax.

Portsmouth calls itself the nation's third-oldest city and it must be close, having been

i A few secrets when traveling to Boston. Do yourself a favor and take the train—driving in Beantown is always a major hassle, as the city was laid out in horse-and-cart days, and parking is inevitably a huge headache. The Downeaster is fast, relatively inexpensive, and drops you off right downtown, where you can easily connect to the T subway system. If you do drive, gas up before you leave the state, because there are no stations on the highway after Kennebunk. You'll be happier if you take Route 93 into town, rather than jumping for the first big Boston sign and U.S. Route 1—the old Atlantic Highway is stop-and-go from strip-mall Saugus all the way into the city.

settled in 1623. The architecture is beautiful. Check out the **Strawbery Banke Museum** (www.strawberybanke.org), a 10-acre, six-house study of a Portsmouth neighborhood over the course of 300 years. Spread across the city are a variety of other historic homes that scream "Early Americana" and are fascinating to visit. Try the **Jackson House** (76 Northwest Street; 603-436-3205), which was built in 1660 and is the state's oldest home; the **Moffat-Ladd House** (154 Market Street; 603-436-8221; www.moffatladd.org), which was built in 1760 and was owned by a signer of the Declaration of Independence; or the **Governor John Langdon House** (143 Pleasant Street; 603-436- 3205), a 1784 mansion that features a lot of classic furnishings.

For eats consider the **Blue Mermaid** (409 The Hill; 603-427-2583; www.bluemermaid.com), an acclaimed local favorite known for its grilled seafood; the **Dolphin Striker** (15 Bow Street; 603-431-5222; www.dolphinstriker.com), one of the oldest but best creative American places in town; **Radici** (142–144 Congress Street; 603-373-6464; www.radicirestaurant.com), an Italian place with an extensive vegetarian menu; or **Lindbergh's Crossing** (29 Ceres Street; 603-431-0887), a Mediterranean bistro in a 200-year-old building on the harbor.

CANADIAN MARITIMES

It doesn't get any more Down East than the coast of New Brunswick. The shore from the U.S. border at Calais and Lubec down into the Canadian Maritimes is very "Mainey." In fact, the small towns and the coastal country feel much like the Pine Tree State did back in, say, the 1950s or 1960s—not overly developed, with unspoiled fishing villages and large stretches of woods. Places like Labrador (admittedly far for a day trip) are seeing an influx of Maine sporting-camp owners, who are expanding their businesses north and east to find country more remote than Maine. Mainers thus feel right at home in the Maritimes, and many vacation here, especially in these days when the American dollar is greatly outpacing the Canadian dollar. Campobello is a fine place to begin an adventure.

Campobello

The New Brunswick island of Campobello, just across the border from Lubec, is the site of the former vacation home of President Franklin D. Roosevelt, which is part of an international park like none other in the world. Stop at the **Roosevelt Campobello International Park Visitor Centre** (506-752-2922; www.fdr.net) to get an overview of the things to do in the park's 2,800 acres. Next door is the focus of the park, the colorful old gambrel-roofed manse to which the Roosevelt family adjourned for fun in the sun. The 34-room "cottage" has been preserved to look much the same as it did when young Franklin and his siblings played on the water here—he spent every summer from 1883 to 1921 on the island, and, unfortunately, it was here that he contracted polio. The cottage is filled with family photos and memorabilia, and its grounds are made for strolling.

There's plenty to do in the park beyond the Roosevelt compound. Perhaps the best way to see the island is by hiking the 8.5 miles of trails, and you can begin right at the visitor center. Less than a mile away is the Friar's Head Picnic Area, which is a nice place to bring a basket for lunch right on the water (people also enjoy eating alfresco at Mullholand Point Picnic Area). Other options include the cliffy trail from Liberty Point and the perimeter walk, which traces the park's border right along the shore. Motorists enjoy drives along Cranberry and Liberty Points, which make fine loops from the visitor center, passing before stunning seascapes.

While on Campobello, don't miss the beach at Herring Cove and the East Quoddy Head Light, another Bay of Fundy sentinel that looks out over prime whale-watching seas. If you need more time, reserve a room at the pleasant **Owen House** (506-752-2977; www.owenhouse.ca), a nine-room bed-and-breakfast in the village of Welshpool, where you can get a room with a view for less than $150 U.S.

For more information call (506) 752-7043 or visit the Web site www.campobello.com.

RELOCATION

Realtors across Maine know the type: a handsomely dressed and starry-eyed person who arrives in their office at the end of the summer, raving rapturously about a piece of property seen while traveling through Maine. Most definitely from away, this individual would like to change that, having fallen truly, madly, deeply in love while on vacation. This scenario plays out scores of times across the state every year. And for good reason. As so many former visitors, retirees, kids, and just plain old Mainers know—this is a great place to call home.

Houses are affordable, considering the ridiculous prices to which real estate has escalated in other states, and the facts that our health care system is leading the way in several areas and our schools are holding their own. In recent years the state has been seeing waves of retirees who are setting up households here for their golden years and an influx of young families headed by natives who decided they want to come back home to raise their children Down East. And there are plenty of people who hate so much to leave at the end of their vacation that they decide to stay, too. Who can blame them?

REAL ESTATE

We already know Maine is a beautiful place, but its real estate remains relatively affordable compared to points south, especially in coastal sections east of Portland. The median selling price of a Maine home in 2007 was $194,000. Compare that to $415,000 in Seattle, $310,000 in Massachusetts, and $557,000 in places like Sedona, Arizona, and you can see why people get into such a lather about Maine. When it comes to coastal property, the discrepancies are even more dramatic—Down East in Washington County the median home price in 2007 was $110,000! Contrast that with Cape Cod's average home price of $346,900, factor in the fact that you don't have to wait in lines for hours to get to your place in Eastport, and Maine's looking pretty good. Like everywhere else, the market here cooled dramatically in 2008, so it's a good time to be looking.

The prices of coastal homes vary by community, of course, but there are some trends to note. In Kittery Point, which is commuting distance from Boston, homes are going to sell for much more than in the fishing village of Cutler, which

is in a fairly remote corner of the state far from any urban area and booming economic sectors. Just about anywhere in York County, which is the fastest-growing section of the state, is going to be more expensive than places up the coast, save for maybe Greater Portland. It's almost accurate to say that prices begin on the high end on the South Coast and fade as you head Down East. That's true for the most part, but there are a few anomalies, which the Portland and York figures show. Likewise, in Hancock County, where Bar Harbor and Acadia are located, the median price was higher than in neighboring Waldo County (home of Belfast) to the south. But as a general rule of thumb, it's true that the farther you go Down East, the lower prices of coastal property will be.

ⓘ Real estate ads have long been a specialty of *Down East: The Magazine of Maine.* Each summer there are dozens of pages of full-color advertisements showing homes up for sale across the state. It's a great resource, if only for the pictures alone. Pick up a copy at the newsstand.

Sales of Coastal Maine Homes by County, 2009*

	Total Units Sold	Median Sale Price
York	1,934	$235,000
Cumberland	2,949	$251,000
Sagadahoc	346	$200,000
Lincoln	370	$225,000
Knox	462	$218,000
Waldo	356	$175,000
Hancock	518	$205,000
Washington	55	$110,000

*from Maine Real Estate Information System

The state's largest city and its suburbs are increasingly desirable places to live, and they continue to experience development, with homes sprouting up even as the economy turns sour. Everyone in Maine knows that Cumberland and York Counties have been exploding with growth and sprawl; in fact, there was talk that in the late 1990s Portland, Maine, was one of the fastest-growing areas in the nation. These days the talk is how to control growth and minimize sprawl. But there were other booming pockets along the coast. Knox County, for example was up 3 percent in 2007 over 2006, the only county to see increased sales. The whole of the Midcoast has grown more popular, with places like Damariscotta seeing influxes of retirees as well as summer people who decided to move up full-time. There are a lot of reasons why, beyond cheap real estate. One is simply that people are realizing coastal land is going fast—and "they aren't making any more of it," as the joke goes. Cultural changes have weighed in, as well, with people looking for quiet, crime-free towns to raise their children in. The shock of 9/11 reverberated all the way up to the Maine coast, and Realtors found themselves fielding calls from New Yorkers anxious to get out of the city.

TAXES

You can't talk real estate in Maine without talking taxes. The Pine Tree State has a reputation for high taxes, and property taxes are part of the reason. Everyone has an opinion on taxes, and so sources vary in reliability and accuracy, due to political slant, but the Maine Municipal Association, a nonprofit, nonpartisan organization representing the interests of Maine's communities, has a wealth of information about the state's tax system on its Web site, www.memun.org/. A highlight for prospective buyers might be the property tax rates section, which lists each community by tax rate. It's a very handy resource.

REAL ESTATE AGENCIES

You can't drive more than a couple of miles on the coast of Maine without coming across a real estate agency. They're everywhere, and they come in all sizes and flavors. Some are housed in a trailer on the side of U.S. Route 1, some tucked away in an old home in a small village, others in fancy downtown offices in Portland. A good Realtor can make a huge difference in your shopping experience, and there are plenty in Maine who will go the extra mile to help you find what you want (and earn their commission).

Buyer's brokers—essentially personal Realtors—have become the way to go in Maine, especially for people from away, who can't zip around to anything that appeals and need a lot of help sifting through the options and narrowing down their lists.

It would be impossible to list all of the state's real estate agencies in a single space—try looking on the Web, searching by the town you're interested in, or by contacting the chambers of commerce in the region. Or visit www.maine realtors.com, where you'll find a listing of Realtors by town as well as wealth of links to helpful sites, from the Maine Real Estate Information System to a buyer database.

EDUCATION

In a 2006–2007 study by Morgan Quitno, Maine was ranked the "5th Smartest State" in the nation. Not bad for a state with a small, largely rural population. Rankings were based on 21 factors, including test scores, graduation rates, and education expenditures. From top-level colleges to schools private and parochial, Maine's educational system has begun to come into its own in recent years. According to *Education Week* magazine, Maine's primary school system is in the top 10 in the nation and has one of the best "school climates," which ranks student-to-teacher ratios, parental involvement, and school safety. The magazine also lauded the state for having 97 percent of its schools connected to the Internet.

Students who continue on to college have their choice of some of the nation's best small private schools in Colby, Bates, and Bowdoin; one of the nation's highest-ranking small public liberal arts colleges in the University of Maine at Farmington; and the school with the happiest students (the view is spectacular) in the College of the Atlantic in Bar Harbor. And, of course, there's always the giant University of Maine itself, a school of 10,000 in Orono, that's been the place to go for most Mainers for more than a century. A whole fleet of smaller state universities are spread across the state, and in recent years Maine has been seriously studying the addition of community col-

leges to the mix, transforming some of the state's technical schools into more traditional two-year colleges. The Pine Tree State is also home to a well-regarded divinity school—Bangor Theological Seminary. Anyone who wants to learn will find some exceptional places to do so Down East.

Public Schools

Maine's 707 public schools traditionally fare pretty well in national surveys. In a study in the late 1990s, the National Educational Goals Panel found Maine to be the state that had most improved its public education system. Proof of this might be that in 2005–2006 the state's eighth-graders were second in the national assessment tests for reading ability and fifth for the number of students above proficiency level in writing.

What does the state have going for it? Most schools are in rural or suburban areas where class sizes are small and where schools tend to be important parts of community life. There's been a lot of forward-thinking action at the state level as well, with first-in-the-nation moves like former governor Angus King's program to equip every seventh grader with a laptop computer and the establishment of magnet schools for gifted math and science students.

Maine's school system is divided into 70-some School Administrative Units (SADs) and 14 Community School Districts (CSDs) under local control. Many of these districts include two or more towns, which combine resources and expenses, and they're funded by the state and by local property taxes. In a few cases—like Lincoln Academy in Newcastle and George Stevens Academy in Blue Hill—towns pay for students to attend private schools, but these private schools usually accept every student in the area and function like public schools anyway.

The state has a very handy education directory online at www.state.me.us/education/, where you'll find a list of all schools in Maine broken down by community, private and public status, district, and more. There's also a set of useful school links, contact numbers for superintendents, financial information and more.

Homeschooling

Homeschooling has a pretty long history in the state, and Mainers have long been leaders in the homeschool movement. The Maine Department of Education is a lot more open to the idea than its equivalent in other states, and the hoops parents have to jump through are fewer. The **Maine Home Education Association** (350 Duck Pond Road, Westbrook 04092), a nonsectarian, nonprofit advocacy group, has a useful Web site—www.geocities.com/mainehomeed/—with links to all sorts of topics related to teaching kids at home.

Private Schools

There are more than 100 private schools in Maine, and they range from Catholic schools like Cheverus in Portland to Montessori to Ashwood Waldorf schools. A majority of these educational institutions are inland, but there are many along the coast. Some areas—Greater Portland and Camden-Rockport, for example—are particularly rich with alternatives to public schools.

Higher Eduation

In Bates, Bowdoin, and Colby Colleges, Maine has three of the better small, liberal arts institutions of higher education in the nation. The trio are the best and the brightest as far as Maine schools go, but there's no shortage of other choices, from the University of New England in Biddeford to the Maine Maritime Academy in Castine to the College of the Atlantic in Bar Harbor to the many schools of the University of Maine system (only the coastal representatives are listed here). Students have a lot of options and can go far with what they take in at Maine colleges.

BATES COLLEGE
Lewiston
(207) 786-6255
www.bates.edu

Founded in 1855, Bates is one of the nicest things about Lewiston, occupying 109 woody acres in the center of the city. Known for excellence in the sciences, the school has small student-to-teacher

---

Maine Media Workshops

Who would have guessed when this downtown Rockport school at 2 Central Street was founded in 1973 that it would become a world-renowned institution teaching the best of tomorrow's photographers and filmmakers? Over the years the Maine Media Workshops have grown exponentially, and there are now more than 250 one-week workshops and master classes to choose from. (Most of the hipsters you see walking or biking around Camden and Rockport are associated with the school.) Some of the biggest names in the industry teach courses in all aspects of film and photography, from writing the screenplay to doing final edits to darkroom techniques, all right here above Rockport Harbor. Rockport College, a spin-off of "the Workshops," was founded in 1996 and now offers associate's and master's degrees as well. All summer long there are free slide shows open to the public—check the Web site for dates and times—and while they can be hot and stuffy, where else do you get to see legends like Mary Ellen Mark discuss their work? There are also frequent gallery shows. For more information call (207) 236-8581 or (877) 577-7700 or visit www.theworkshops.com.

---

ratios (as low as 10:1) and is perennially ranked among the nation's best in college surveys. The school was number 25 in the *U.S. News & World Report*'s famed "Best American Colleges" issue among the top 217 liberal arts schools. And *Seventeen* magazine called it "cool" to boot. There are 1,700 students here, and they're a bright and active bunch. Most participate in some sort of student-run club or sport, and more than two-thirds go on to graduate school. Founded by abolitionists, the school prides itself on its diverse student body. Tuition and board run about $49,000.

The campus includes the Olin Arts Center (Russell and Bardwell Streets; 207-786-6135), where there are often films and performances open to the public, and the Bates College Museum of Art (Russell Street; 207-786-6158), an excellent small art collection. On Thursdays in the summer there are free concerts that are worth attending. Also a biggie in the summer is the Bates Dance Festival (207-786-6161), which attracts big names from the world of modern dance.

BOWDOIN COLLEGE
Brunswick
(207) 725-3000
www.bowdoin.edu

If you want to be a major political figure in the United States, you could pick a worse college to attend—Bowdoin has turned out scads of high-ranking officials, from presidents to governors (a dozen in Maine) to legislators. Founded in 1794, the liberal arts school has about 1,716 students and it accepts about 19 percent of its applicants. Tuition and fees are $38,190, and students graduate with Bachelor of Arts degrees in about 40 disciplines.

The 110-acre campus is a pretty place, with more than 80 buildings, the oldest of which date back to 1802. A famous stand of pines provides shade, adding a bit of class to the neighborhood, and there are a lot of fine squares and greens framed by all the brick. Downtown Brunswick is just down the hill, and Bowdoin's students help keep Main Street vibrant. Free guided tours are available from the admissions office.

COLBY COLLEGE
Mayflower Hill, Waterville
(207) 872-3000
www.colby.edu

The campus of Colby is huge—714 acres—and it's well apart from the rest of Waterville, its own brick kingdom of fine Georgian buildings. Coed since 1871, the school began life as a Baptist institution in 1813, and it is highly regarded for its liberal arts curriculum. There are 53 majors from which to choose—the top four being economics, biology, English, and government—and the school has become nationally recognized for its research- and project-based undergraduate programs. About a third of its applicants are accepted.

The campus of Colby was moved here from downtown Waterville in the 1950s, and it now consists of about 62 structures with an arboretum and bird sanctuary around them. In fact, most of the campus is considered a Maine Wildlife Management Area. There are 1,870 students wandering among all that wildlife going to classes with a 10:1 student-to-teacher ratio. Tuition and board cost about $49,000.

UNIVERSITY OF NEW ENGLAND
11 Hills Beach Rd., Biddeford
(800) 477-4UNE
www.une.edu

Another school with twin campuses, UNE has facilities in Biddeford and in downtown Portland (the site of the old Westbrook College). It is Maine's only medical school, and it has about 2,000 undergrads, 967 graduate students, and 500 medical students on its attractive campuses. The Biddeford campus has more than 4,000 feet of ocean frontage. And the school's level of prestige is rising fast—U.S. News & World Report has called it one of the best regional universities in the Northeast (81st), and has recognized UNE's College of Osteopathic Medicine for excellence in primary care, geriatrics, and rural medicine. The marine biology program is growing in repute as well, thanks to the new Marine Science Education Research Center.

MAINE MARITIME ACADEMY
Castine
(207) 326-4311 or (800) 227-8465
www.mainemaritime.edu

People see the cadets marching around Castine and automatically think of this nautical college as a military institution. It's not. About 60 percent of the school's 861 students are enrolled in the regimental program, which is quasi-military, but they're learning to be sailors in the merchant marine, not the navy. And students study a lot more here than simply commercial sailing. Majors include marine engineering, ocean studies, and marina management, among other things. The school is one of only seven merchant marine colleges in the nation, and it has a fleet of more than 90 vessels, most impressive of which is the *State of Maine,* a 498-foot training vessel that takes up blocks of the town's waterfront when it's not out on a tour. The 50-acre campus is an attractive centerpiece of the downtown of this historic community, all old brick and lawns, and the students here help offset the loss of the tourists and summer people in the fall. The school has a great record of job placement, too and was ranked 10th among baccalaureate colleges in the north by *U.S. News & World Report.*

COLLEGE OF THE ATLANTIC
105 Eden St., Bar Harbor
(207) 288-5015
www.coa.edu
Students have the choice of exactly one major at this progressive Bar Harbor school: human ecology. But the definition of that discipline is so hazy, they can study whatever they want. Within their degree focus they can concentrate on design, environmental science, landscape and building architecture, marine studies, natural history, museum studies, public policy, teacher ed, and various humanities. So there is a lot of wiggle room in human ecology, which the school describes as "emphasizing the interrelationships, specifically between humans and our natural, social, and technological environments." It's not for everyone, of course, and the school has a tiny student body—just 341. But in surveys of the nation's colleges they're always recognized as among the happiest in the country, and their campus, right on Frenchman Bay and minutes from Acadia, is often deemed the most beautiful. The school has come a long way since it was founded in 1969, and its list of alumni includes some cool folks.

For more information on the schools in the University of Maine system, log on to www.maineedu.com.

University of Maine System
There are seven universities in the UMaine system, serving 34,000 students. The University of Maine inland in Orono is the largest, with about 11,700 of those students. UMaine schools on the coast include the University of Southern Maine—which has campuses in Portland and Gorham and actually more students than Orono, but only half or so are full-time—and the University of Machias, with about 1,260 students way Down East. The biggest major at any of these schools is education, with health care and business, respectively, the second and third most popular.

UNIVERSITY OF SOUTHERN MAINE
P.O. Box 9300, Portland 04104
(207) 780–4141 or (800) 800–4USM
www.usm.maine.edu
Divided into two parts—one half in the leafy suburb of Gorham, the other in downtown Portland—USM was founded in 1878, and the two campuses are separated by about 8 miles. Thought of as something of a Maine commuter school, the university has students from 32 states and 15 foreign countries, so it's a lot more diverse than it's given credit for, and about 11,000 students are enrolled in undergraduate and graduate programs. The school confers degrees in close to 50 majors and has eight colleges: arts and sciences; business; applied science, engineering, and technology; nursing and health; education and human development; law; Lewiston-Auburn College; and the Muskie School of Public Service. Student-to-faculty ratio is kept small (about 13:1) and class sizes are, too, with an average of 22 students. The school was among the "Best Northeastern Colleges" in the *2007 Princeton Review.*

UNIVERSITY OF MAINE AT MACHIAS
9 O'Brien Ave., Machias
(207) 255-1200
www.umm.maine.edu

The easternmost college in the nation, UMM is a small school in a small town way Down East. The campus covers about 43 acres in Machias, a beautiful and historic Washington County community hard by the shores of Machias Bay. Of the 1,260 students, 60 percent are women. The school likes to bill the fact that it has a level of attention comparable to the good private schools—the student-to-faculty ratio is 14:1; average class size is 16—but with all the resources of the University of Maine system. It's a nice combination, and the setting is stunning if you can handle remoteness.

Other Educational Opportunities

If you're interested in fine furniture and how it's created, sign up for a one- or two-week course at the respected **Center for Furniture Craftsmanship** (25 Mill Street, Rockport; 207-594-5611; www.woodschool.com). Perhaps boats are more to your liking? Seek out the **Wooden Boat School** (Off Naskeag Point Road, Brooklin; 207-359-46513-; www.thewoodenboatschool.com), where traditional boatbuilders learn their craft from the best. Or maybe you fancy yourself an artisan? The **Haystack Mountain School of Crafts** (Deer Isle; 207-348-2306; www.haystack-mtn.org) is famous for its two- and three-week sessions in pottery, glass, fibers, and graphics.

HEALTH CARE

For such a small state in terms of population, Maine comes out at the top of a lot of surveys and polls when it comes to health care. Not too long ago, the cardiac unit at Maine Medical Center in Portland was deemed to be among the best in the nation, and more recently, the OB-GYN department at Miles Memorial Hospital in Damariscotta came out tops in the nation in patient satisfaction. So Maine doctors must be doing something right.

Hospitals

The state has about 40 hospitals spread throughout small communities and has large, state-of-the-art health care centers in Portland and Bangor. Wherever you go, from Kittery to Calais, excellent health care is not far away. Newly arrived Mainers take comfort in the fact that there are good hospitals within a reasonable drive, and Mainers in general have been taking advantage of them, too, turning to the state's hospitals for help close to three million times annually. The state's health care system is fairly hospital-centric, without a lot of the clinics you see in urban areas and with doctors generally being allied with one large center or another.

Visit the Maine Hospital Association at www.themha.org for a list of the state's hospitals.

Alternative Providers

When they aren't visiting hospitals, Mainers seem to be going to alternative health care providers, of which there are a growing number. In the past, Mainers, who tend to be a fairly skeptical lot, have looked askance at health care givers who worked outside the traditional fields of medicine. But today you'll see old-timers going to the acupuncturist or the chiropractor. Wellness centers have been popping up along the coast since the 1990s, and certain hospitals even have their own natural or homeopathic offshoots. Most of the major alternative disciplines are represented along the coast, with centers in southern Maine, Portland, and more forward-thinking coastal counties like Knox, Waldo, and Hancock.

For a list of providers pick up a copy of the *Maine Alternative Health Guide* or visit www.mainealternativehealth.net.

Churches

For a list of Maine's churches by county, click over to the Web site www.mainecouncilofchurches.org and go to the directory page.

Libraries

The Maine State Library in Augusta maintains a directory of all Maine libraries, with some fascinating stats. Visit its Web site at http://msl1.ursus.maine.edu to see the list.

Registering Your Car

The Maine Bureau of Motor Vehicles has a number of Motor Vehicle Branch Office locations. All are open from 8 a.m. to 5 p.m. Monday through Friday and are closed on all legal holidays. Call (207) 624-9215 and inquire about mobile locations before you head out—there might be one closer than the branch location. Information is also available at www.state.me.us/sos/bmv.

63 Portland Road, Suite 4, Kennebunk
(207) 985-4890

456 Main Street, Springvale
(207) 490–1261

704 Maine Mall Road, South Portland
(207) 822-0730

125 Presumpscot Street, Portland
(207) 822-6400

49 Topsham Fair Mall Road, Topsham
(207) 725-6520

212 New County Road, Rockland
(207) 596-2255

24 Church Street, Ellsworth
(207) 667-9363

376 North Street, Calais
(207) 454-2175

RETIREMENT

U sed to be Mainers of retirement age would head south for the winter, enjoying sun and golf while the rest of the state persevered through snow and ice. This pattern is still true for some, but in recent years, the Pine Tree State has seen more and more seniors stay put. Not only that, it has seen an actual influx of people who want to enjoy their golden years on the Maine coast, weather be damned. The state has grown exponentially in the retirement market—villages like Damariscotta and Camden are brimming with the older set—and senior communities have sprouted up all along the coast like mushrooms. They range from assisted-living facilities to simply condo villages where the common theme is age.

Many of these new Mainers have a history with the state, vacationing here for years and years and pining for the day when they could move north permanently. Others are simply drawn by the quality of life enjoyed Down East. The resort communities that cater to tens of thousands of vacationers in summer, with their shops and restaurants, are perfectly suited to serve retirees in winter. Crime is a nonissue, the climate is actually fairly hospitable (global warming?), the pace of life is easy and pleasant, and the state is made up of actual communities where it's not difficult to become involved and feel like you play an important part. Neighbors are still neighbors here, looking out for one another. And the health care system in Maine is now competitive with those found elsewhere. It's a nice place to grow old.

Of course, a lot of people who retire here have no intention of sitting around on their duffs. Many enjoy very active retirements, starting new businesses, exploring the outdoors, joining town boards and volunteering for worthy causes, and taking advantage of the excellent elder learning opportunities to be found here. Places like Bowdoin College in Brunswick allow seniors to audit courses for free, innumerable communities have great adult ed programs, fitness centers offer eldercize-type workouts, and on and on. The state park system can be enjoyed gratis by people over 65, and Audubon has a wealth of field trips geared toward older folks. A lot of people find themselves busier after leaving the 9-to-5 world behind than they were when they were working. There is no end to the things to do in Maine.

This chapter includes a list of retirement communities, information on elder education, and further resources for retirees.

i The state of Maine has a wealth of resources available to retirees, including the handy Web site of its Office of Elder Services—www.maine.gov/dhs/beas/. Here you'll find information on everything from Medicaid and prescription drugs to job possibilities and the senior farm-share program, which gets fresh produce to seniors for free.

RETIREMENT COMMUNITIES

Almost 50 retirement communities have been built in Maine, many of them along the coast. These are congregate housing where a meal or two is provided and services are clustered for ease of use. Many do feature an assisted-living option, where doctors and nurses are a more regular presence, but they feel more like elderly villages than anything else.

South Coast

SENTRY HILL
2 Victoria Court, York
(207) 363-5116
www.sentryhillatyorkharbor.com

Location, as they say in real estate, is every-thing, and that certainly applies to Sentry Hill. The sprawling retirement community sits within walking distance of York Harbor Beach, the York Golf and Tennis Club, and a nature preserve. The resort community of the Yorks—with all its restaurants and shops—are minutes away by car, and the nearest hospital is a half mile down the road. Sentry Hill offers seniors a whole raft of choices, from two-bedroom condo units to one- and two-bedroom apartments to assisted-living apartments where medical staff is at the ready. There's also a more traditional nursing home and even an option for those suffering from Alzheim-er's disease. Housekeeping, transportation, and as many as three meals a day are available, too. Units can be rented or purchased outright, and there are maintenance and entry fees. About 150 seniors have moved in already, and more are sure to follow.

ATRIA KENNEBUNK
1 Penny Lane, Kennebunk
(207) 985-5866
www.atriaseniorliving.com

Atria is a national chain of retirement com-munities, and this is its Maine facility. All of the amenities of the Kennebunks—from the sea to the shopping—are right out the doors of these assisted-living apartments (studio, one-bedroom, and two-bedroom). There are 66 units for rent, eight of which are for folks suffering from Alzheimer's. (Rental fees range from $3,075 to $4,250 per month, depending on the unit.) Three meals are served daily, and housekeeping hap-pens on a weekly basis. The facility has a library and a beauty salon on the premises, and the activity calendar is reportedly busy here. Private tours are available.

THE FARRAGUT AT KENNEBUNK
106 Farragut Way, Kennebunk
(207) 985-9740

"If you're not sixty, you'll wish you were." That's the slogan at the Farragut in Kennebunk, and it's easy to see why someone might have senior envy. Boston, Portland, and Portsmouth are all within an hour and a half of the retirement village's site along the Kennebunk River—and that's if you ever feel the need to leave the Ken-nebunks, one of Maine's oldest and best resort communities, with neat stores, fine restaurants, beautiful beaches, and superb scenery. Qualified residents here have the option of moving into a single-floor unit or a cottage that looks like a tasteful suburban home, and the amenities are many. On the Farragut's campus are an indoor pool,Jacuzzi, computer center, and library, and the facility offers the option of in-home health care and housekeeping. You don't pay for what you don't use, unlike some other places. And an emphasis is placed on being active, so you'll be up and about, and there will always be plenty to do. Units can be purchased—fees are anywhere from $200,000 to $259,000—and then there are monthly maintenance fees. You can even buy right on the saltwater river.

HUNTINGTON COMMON
1 Huntington Common Dr., Kennebunk
(207) 985-2810 or (800) 585-0533
www.huntingtoncommon.com

Both Portland and Portsmouth are handy to the folks living at Huntington Common, one of Maine's larger retirement communities, with more than 200 residents. From condos to Alzheimer's units, the place has a wide array of options for seniors. Most, however, live in independent apartments that are rented for anywhere from $2,175 to $5,600 a month. Three meals a day are served, and amenities include an exercise program, a beauty salon, a library, and an activities room. And then, of course, there's everything to do in the Kennebunks and you're right on the river.

ATLANTIC HEIGHTS RETIREMENT COMMUNITY
(207) 283-3022 or (800) 874-6990
www.atlanticheightsretirement.com

This place has been around only a couple of years and it's already one of the largest in the state with 231 residents tucked into its 46 cottages and 120 long-term and Alzheimer units. It's a full-service facility with all meals provided, a whole slate of programs, a beauty salon, and transportation to the many amenities in Biddeford and Saco. Purchase price is $290,000, and the place is still growing.

WARDWELL RETIREMENT NEIGHBORHOOD
43 Middle St., Saco
(207) 284-7061

One of Maine's oldest retirement communities, Wardwell was built in 1890 and now consists of 41 independent apartments and 46 assisted-living units right in downtown Saco. About 100 residents live here, and they enjoy three meals a day, an exercise program, a library, and a hair salon on the premises. Units are rented for $300 to $3,200 a month, and housekeeping and transportation are available.

Greater Portland

PIPER SHORES
15 Piper Rd., Scarborough
(207) 883-8700 or (888) 333-8711
www.pipershores.org

With 350-some residents, Piper Shores is Maine's largest retirement facility. And, as they say, 350 people can't be wrong—you have to assume the place is doing something right to attract and keep so many retirees. A nonprofit organization, Piper Shores has a continuum of care, with 200 independent apartments and cottages, 20 assisted-living units, and 40 long-term-care beds. And it offers 'most every amenity known to a retirement community— all meals, an exercise program, a pool, library, activities room, walking trail, beauty salon, movie room, even a wood shop. The shore is a short walk across the road, and Portland, with its symphony, museums, restaurants, and medical-care providers, is just minutes down the road.

THE ATRIUM AT CEDARS
640 Ocean Ave., Portland
(207) 775-4111
www.thecedarsportland.org

The Cedars began its life in 1929 as a home for elderly Jewish folks in Portland. Over the years it changed, adding a nursing component, before opening a nonsectarian retirement community at its present location on Ocean Avenue. The company likes to call the lifestyle it promotes at the Atrium "progressive living," and it certainly seems like the good life, with fine food at the formal dining room and at the cafe, an indoor pool and spa, a fitness center, proximity to all of the great restaurants of Portland, and comfortable apartments. Maintenance and housekeeping can be taken care of, making the hassles few.

THE PARK AT DANFORTH
777 Stevens Ave., Portland
(207) 797-7710
www.parkdanforth.com

The Park at Danforth is a big apartment building–style home with 160 units, most of which are set up for independent living, and three dozen of which are assisted-living spaces. The place has a fairly rich history, dating back to 1881 when a few Portland philanthropists opened a house for elderly mariners with no place else to go. Over the years, the mission of the home broadened to include any elderly residents of the Forest City, not just seamen, and today it's a completely modern facility with all the amenities. The rentals range from studio apartments to two-bedroom suites and rents range from $1,432 for a one-bedroom studio to $5,000 for an apartment in the assisted-living center. The activities calendar is particularly busy here, with something scheduled for every day. You won't want to miss Beano on Sunday or the trip to the Maine Mall on Friday. Students from the nearby University of Maine visit occasionally to help out and offer instruction in the computer room, and the activity room often hosts art classes or musical entertainment. (It also has a wide-screen TV for watching movies or the big game.) Friends and families are always welcome.

SEVENTY-FIVE STATE STREET

75 State St., Portland

(207) 772-2675

www.75state.org

State Street is hands down the oldest retirement community in Maine, predating the Civil War. It was founded as a home for three elderly Portland women and has grown from there, now housing 159 residents in as many apartments. Unlike many of the other senior housing options in the state—and else-where—this is a nonprofit organization, with all resident-derived income being reinvested to enhance the facilities and provide more services. So this building in the West End, one of the nicer residential neighborhoods of Portland, feels a little warmer than some of the operations that are obviously out for money first. The average age here is a little steeper than some other places—the last survey found most occupants to be in their 80s—but the amenities are many. The apartments are all rentals and come in a variety of layouts, from efficiencies to full suites, and they range in price from $2,100 to $4,700 per month. Concierge service is available seven days a week, as is nursing care.

THE WOODS AT CANCO

257 Canco Rd., Portland

(207) 772-4777

www.thewoodsatcanco.com

Not the woodsiest facility, but, hey, this is the Forest City; these Woods are operated by Holiday Retirement Corporation. There are 128 independent apartments—both one- and two-bedroom—and 13 cottages, and three squares a day. Amenities include a big-screen TV lounge, an activity room, library, and exercise room, and you're 5 miles from golf. All of Portland is available to you, thanks to regularly scheduled trips. Rent is $1,500 to $3,300.

GORHAM HOUSE

50 New Portland Rd., Gorham

(207) 839-5757

www.mainecare.com

Owned by the same people who run Sentry Hill in York, Gorham House is located in the peaceful Portland suburb of Gorham, a leafy college town not far from the city. Established in 1990, the facility offers an array of living choices for a continuum of care (these are rentals): 34 independent apartments, 29 assisted-living units, 52 long-term care beds, and 30 Alzheimer's units. The independent-living apartments are well outfitted with full kitchens and come in one- or two-bedroom layouts, and pets are allowed. One meal a day, housekeeping, grocery delivery, and trash removal are all provided free of charge, and there is a full activities calendar. RN care is available on a 24-hour basis. The assisted-living option brings the care right to your apartment, and help is offered with recreational and transportational needs.

OCEANVIEW AT FALMOUTH

20 Blueberry Lane, Falmouth

(207) 781-4460

www.oceanviewrc.com

OceanView is one of a trio of retirement villages owned by developer John Wasileski that advertises all over the place, from print to radio. "It's about life, it's about time" is their motto, and in many ways they live up to it. The OceanView campus is located on a side street in Falmouth, Portland's tony easterly neighbor, and includes 71 independent apartments in the Lodge, a large condo building, 107 cottages, and 38 assisted-living apartments. All units are purchased, and they come in pleasant one- or two-bedroom layouts. The complex sits on 45 acres within a few minutes' drive of Portland, so there is the quiet of the country but the convenience of being next to the state's largest city. And, as the name suggests, the water is not far. Activities are aplenty right at OceanView, however, so you needn't travel much. The retirement center offers workouts for the mind—a library and Internet access—as well as for the body—strength training, yoga, and tai chi. It also has an active calendar of social activities, from talks to musical performances to art shows. Best of all, though, are the services provided, from complete maintenance to grocery delivery to a hair salon. It's like living in a small Maine village where everything is taken care of.

BAY SQUARE AT YARMOUTH
27 Forest Falls Dr., Yarmouth
(207) 846-0044 or (888) 374-6700
www.benchmarkquality.com

Benchmark Quality is a big national corporation with dozens of assisted-living communities in New York and New England. The company's Maine offering is in the Greater Portland community of Yarmouth, 15 or 20 minutes north of the Forest City and just south of Freeport. Bay Square is a 60-unit assisted-living center housed in a big building it describes as a "grand seaside inn," and it has a specialized program for the memory-impaired. Studio, one-bedroom, and two-bedroom apartments are available for rent, and three meals are offered daily. The facilities are right on the Royal River and include a white-linen dining room, walking trails, a beauty salon, a library, a country kitchen, and a sunporch. Exercise programs are there to be enjoyed on a daily basis, and there is a full social calendar. The staff offers 24-hour nursing support as well as all the housekeeping and maintenance services anyone could want. There's a $2,300 entrance fee, and rents range from $4,300 to $5,900.

Midcoast

SUNNYBROOK VILLAGE
340 Bath Rd., Brunswick
(207) 443-9100
www.sunnybrookvillage.com

The newest of the retirement villages on the red-hot Brunswick retiree scene, Sunnybrook sounds like a Kate Douglas Wiggin book—you may wonder where Rebecca and the farm are—and it's privately owned rather than part of a soulless chain. There are already 60 people ensconced in its 12 apartments and 39 assisted-living units. Three chef-cooked meals a day, a beauty parlor and a barber shop, rose gardens, a computer center, and a calendar's worth of activities number among the many amenities. Plus, you're in Brunswick, which, among retirees, makes you one of the cool kids.

THORNTON OAKS
25 Thornton Way, #100, Brunswick
(207) 729-8033 or (800) 729-8033
www.thorntonoaks.com

The big Thornton Oaks campus went up in 1990 in Brunswick, home of Bowdoin College and Brunswick Naval Air Station, and it now has one of the highest populations of any retirement community in Maine. (The town was voted the best place to retire in New England by Money magazine in 2005.) Residential options run the gamut, from completely independent "private" homes to Alzheimer's units. The houses are on 29 acres, with a walking trail, and the owner can choose from a wide variety of floor plans. They all were built in a "New England cottage style" and feature large 14-by-25-foot living/dining areas and two bedrooms and three baths. The fancier models have fireplaces, central air, and whirlpools. While set up like any contemporary suburban development, these homes allow use of all of Thornton Oaks' facilities, including the dining room (catering is available in homes for parties), the arts and crafts room, the library, and the fitness center. Maintenance, of course, is provided. The apartments are in the campus's Matthews Terrace building and come in one and two-bedroom arrangements. Large windows, extensive lighting, and lots of closet space keep things comfortable. The activities calendar at Thornton Oaks is something to behold. Foreign affairs, religious, and book discussions are common, there's a lively arts program with classes in flower arranging and that sort of thing, and there are organized bridge and Scrabble competitions. Residents are welcome to audit courses and use the pool at nearby Bowdoin College. Excursions to the Portland Museum of Art, Portland Symphony Orchestra, and Maine State Music Theater are frequent.

THE HIGHLANDS
26 Elm St., Topsham
(207) 725-2650 or (888) 760-1042
www.highlandsrc.com

Topsham, just north of Brunswick, has undergone quite a building boom in the past few decades, and the Highlands was part of it, going up in

1989. Part of the Wasileski empire, it is one of the biggest retirement communities in Maine, with more than 300 residents, and the choices are many. There are 118 apartments, more than 125 cottage units, 44 assisted-living units, and 24 Alzheimer's units to provide a continuum of care. Many of these—the single- and duplex-home Estates, for example—can be customized to the owner's specifications. Others, like the six apartments in the 19th-century Benjamin Porter House, are more unique and character laden.

The Highlands campus sprawls across 75 acres, with walking trails wandering about, so there is something of a sense of rural living even though you're five minutes from the restaurants and cultural activities of Brunswick and less than 25 miles from all that Portland has to offer. Not that you need to go anywhere. The facility is very self-sufficient, with fine dining, a fitness center, library and media room, pool, bingo, bridge—even a bank—and regular outings to the Portland Symphony Orchestra, the Maine State Music Theatre, Portland Stage Company, Audubon events, and more. The Highlands van also whisks residents to Topsham, downtown Brunswick, Cooks Corner, Bath, and the Maine Mall for shopping.

ST. ANDREWS VILLAGE
145 Emery Lane, Boothbay Harbor
(207) 633-0920
www.standrewsvillage.com
St. Andrews Village has one of those nifty arrangements that are becoming common among retirement communities—buy into any one of the units on the campus and you can use all the amenities and services even if you live in one of the private cottages. Options here include 25 of these cottages, 30 independent apartments, 12 assisted-living facilities, 11 Alzheimer's units, and 30 long-term care beds. The setting is fine, with 60 acres of Boothbay Harbor out the door. The cottages have two-bedroom layouts, with kitchens, and one-and-a-half or two baths. The Saint Andrews Inn is where the apartments are located, as well as the dining room, library, and services. The calendar of activities is a busy one, with regu-larly scheduled exercise classes; transportation to town for shopping, eating out, and cultural happenings; and movies, coffees, book clubs, and birthday parties on a monthly basis.

SCHOONER COVE
35 Schooner St., Damariscotta
(207) 563-5523
www.mileshealthcare.org/schooner
Situated on the banks of the Damariscotta River, Schooner Cove has a lot going for it. The 59 residents have great views of the tidal river from their two-bedroom apartments, a fine dining room at which to sup, a well-stocked library, and access to medical services should they be needed, with Miles Memorial Hospital a stone's throw away. Chase Point Assisted Living Center and Cove's Edge Nursing Home are right next door, too, ready to serve if needed. There's plenty to do—classes and lectures, afternoon teas, and musical performances occur on a regular basis, and there are frequent trips into town and to points in the area for museum visits, nature walks, and shopping. Housekeeping and other services are taken care of—and the staff is second to none in Maine. This is one of the best.

BARTLETT WOODS
20 Bartlett St., Rockland
(207) 594-2745
www.bartlettwoods.com
Newly revitalized Rockland is the home of Bartlett Woods, an active retirement center with 14 cottage units and 34 independent apartments. The cottages are suburban homes clustered together in a woodsy area within walking distance of Rockland's historic downtown. Residents buy into a cooperative equal to the value of their home, which allows them to both create equity and vote on issues that concern all residents. The units are single-floor dwellings with two bedrooms, a full kitchen, a good-size living room, one and one-half baths, and an attached garage. Most have a sunroom. Snow removal, lawn care, and maintenance are all part of the package. Bartlett House is an apartment building with balconies, full kitchens, large living rooms, and one or two

bedrooms. All of the services of Bartlett Woods are right here—a library, dining room, wellness center, and even a hair salon. Pets are welcome.

CAMDEN GARDENS
110 Mechanic St., Camden
(207) 236-0154

Tiny in comparison to the many other retirement communities in Maine, Camden Gardens has just 12 residents living in its eight apartments and two cottages. But they have it good, being close to all of the excellent eateries, shops, outdoor areas, and services of Camden. Built in 1989, the facility has an exercise program, an activities room, and a library, and it provides one meal daily. Housekeeping and transportation are available. The units are rented for $2,500.

QUARRY HILL
30 Community Dr., Camden
(207) 230–6116
www.quarryhill.org

Quarry Hill offers the comforts of living in a resort community but the peace of being on your own 26-acre campus. Its 225 residents make it one of the biggest retiree villages in Maine, and folks live in 37 independent apartments, 45 cottages, 62 assisted-living units, and 24 Alzheimer units. You eat well, have all of the perks of Camden living— good restaurants, boutique shopping, fresh air, ocean, lakes, mountains, great classical concerts in summer, a fine library—and have your own little kingdom to return to. And you know that because it's in tony Camden it's going to be nice. Units range from $239,000 to $369,000 for purchase or $2,200 to $3,500 per month for rent, and there's a $1,000 maintenance fee.

HARBOR HILL
2 Footbridge Rd., Belfast
(207) 338-5307
www.sandyriverhealth.com

Part of the Sandy River Health empire of Farmington, Harbor Hill is an assisted-living and long-term care center with 85 residents. Those in the assisted-living program can maintain their independence but get help with meals, laundry,

and maintenance and enjoy the company of others. Health care is available at a moment's notice. The long-term care is more of a traditional nursing home service. Units are rented for $4,300 to $6,000 a month.

PENOBSCOT SHORES
10 Shoreland Dr., Belfast
(207) 338-2332
www.penobscotshores.com

Clustered onto 20 acres overlooking Penobscot Bay, the 28 apartments and 26 cottages of Penobscot Shores have fine views to go with their shingle-style architecture. This is an independent-living facility with its own cobblestone beach, library, fine dining room, hair salon, activity room, and fitness studio, and access to all that the cool city of Belfast has to offer. Wellness and health-care programs keep you happy and fit, and the maintenance services leave your mind at ease. Transportation is available, too. Penobscot Shores is affiliated with the excellent local Waldo County General Hospital and is only a quarter mile from its beds and services. Units are purchased for $135,000 to $360,000, and then a maintenance fee of $1,370 to $1,600 is paid on a monthly basis. The motto at Penobscot Shores is "the location you want and the lifestyle you deserve," and it certainly makes its case. Local residents have been overheard to say that they couldn't wait to reach retirement age so they can move in.

THE RESIDENCE AT TALL PINES
24 Martin Lane, Belfast
(207) 930-7031
www.tallpinesliving.com

Just over a year old, this new 30-unit facility in beautiful Belfast has already been voted "Best Retirement Community" in Waldo County by the readers of the local paper. Which says something in a town that already has the fine Penobscot Shores. (Perhaps voters are influenced by the newness factor?) One and two-bedroom apartments are tucked into a rambling grey place in a residential neighborhood and they come in both independent and assisted-living options.

The list of niceties and necessaries is long—from meals to an extensive activities calendar to a beauty shop, library, and walking trails—and the units are rented on a monthly basis for $2,100 to $4,100.

PARKER RIDGE RETIREMENT COMMUNITY
63 Parker Ridge Lane, Blue Hill
(207) 374-2306
www.parkerridge.com

One of the more gracious of Maine's retirement centers, Parker Ridge is a large complex on 90 acres overlooking Blue Hill Bay. The cottages are shingle-sided affairs with gables and pillars, and the Parker Inn is a sprawling, cupola-topped structure that has the feel of an old Maine seaside manse about it. Obviously modern, it has a shingle-style air even though its apartments have blocky balconies tacked onto them. There are 34 independent apartments here, along with 24 freestanding cottages and 13 assisted-living units. The latter enjoy three gourmet meals daily, help with laundry and housekeeping, and transportation into town and to Ellsworth. Residents of the two-bedroom cottages have the options of buying 10 or 20 meals a month in the restaurant-style dining room, and they too get help with repairs and maintenance and access to the on-staff nurse. The facilities and services include a library and wellness program and regular exercise and art classes, movies, and billiards contests. The lawns give way to walking trails, and the bay vistas are beautiful. Purchase prices range from $183,000 for a one-bedroom apartment to $265,000 for a two-bedroom deluxe cottage.

Acadia Area

BIRCH BAY VILLAGE
25 Village Inn Rd., Bar Harbor
(207) 288-8014
www.birchbayinfo.com

One of the newest, latest retirement communities in Maine, Birch Bay borders Acadia National Park. The cottage-style homes are terraced on the side of a hill, with outstanding views of the mountains of Mount Desert Island and the waters of Frenchman Bay. Each of the 20 cottages features two bedrooms, a fully applianced kitchen, a screened-in porch, and a terrace. Some have a den and a sunroom. Everyone who buys into the cottages has access to the Birch Bay Village Inn, the main lodge of the community and site of the 39 independent and assisted-living apartments. The inn's dining room and outdoor deck offer dramatic views of the bay and mountains, and inside residents will find a raft of amenities—library, fitness studio, hair salon, and arts and crafts and media rooms. A 1,200-square-foot cottage costs $300,000, with a monthly maintenance fee of about $1,200.

ELDER LEARNING

The sad thing about higher education is that it's generally taught to people when they're too young to truly appreciate it. By the time people hit their golden years, they often find themselves with both the time and the yearning to learn. Maine has a great **Senior College** program perfect for anyone in this boat, and compared to the fees young students pay, the cost is incredibly small. Eighteen schools and colleges affiliated with the University of Maine host classes for older learners across the state. They're all set up similarly.

Take the Coastal Senior College at the University College at Rockland, for example. Seniors pay an annual membership fee of $25, which allows them to take classes here or at any other Senior College location. The types of courses vary widely, just as at any other university; recent possibilities included classes in the arts, humanities, social sciences, sciences, technology, health, and finance. These classes might be anything from Irish film to photography to New England writers to alternative healing. They meet for two hours a week for eight weeks, and special events, field trips, lectures, and get-togethers outside of class are common. And you don't ever have to worry about passing in term papers or studying for exams. The fee for classes can be up to $50.

Senior College is open to any residents age 50 or older. Spouses, including those under 50, ℹ️ Did you run a company somewhere before retiring to Maine? If so, you could help the next generation of management by joining the Service Corps of Retired Executives. SCORE offers classes and counseling to young businesspeople. Contact SCORE's regional hub at (207) 772-1147 or visit www.scoremaine.com.

are welcome, too. Quite aside from all the learning going on, the Senior Colleges are a great way to get out and meet like-minded others and add a few dates to the social calendar. For an overview, click over to www.maineseniorcollege.org.

Other Education Options

Although the Senior College system is a fantastic resource, it's not the only way for older students to get back behind the desks at good schools across Maine. Mainers age 65 and older who are interested in a course at a University of Maine campus but can't seem to swing the tuition can apply to have the fee waived. (You'll still have to take care of books and lab fees.) For a more hands-on approach, try the state's community colleges (www.mccs.me.edu), where anyone age 65 or older can register for courses free of charge on a space-available basis.

SENIOR ADULT GROWTH EXCHANGE
CENTER FOR CONTINUING EDUCATION
University of Southern Maine 68 High St., Portland
(207) 780–5900 or (800) 787-0468
Much like Senior College, this USM-based program provides workshops for older area residents at reasonable prices. Students pay $35 ($53 per couple) to participate and then can select a lecture or discussion from the handful offered on the three dates when the SAGE program meets. These are single shots and might be anything from studying family history to genetic engineering in contemporary society.

SPORTS AND RECREATION

Maine has always been well suited to outdoor recreation, and seniors can find plenty of fun and exercise simply by taking to the hundreds of miles of hiking trails and walking paths across the state. Visiting the state parks, signing up with Maine Audubon, taking a class in boating, walking laps at the Maine Mall in the hours before it opens—the options are endless. Or try a more social outing or fitness program, like those sponsored by many coastal hospitals or community YMCAs. There are many, many possibilities for seniors all along the Maine coast. Here are a few ideas.

MAINE STATE PARK SYSTEM
Department of Parks and Lands
286 Water St., Augusta
(207) 287-3821
www.maine.gov/doc/parks/programs/park passes.html
The Department of Parks and Lands allows people age 65 or older to use the state's park system free, anytime. We're talking day use though, not camping. This privilege is particularly handy for folks who live near a park and would like to use it on a daily basis. Just call and they'll mail you out a free Senior Citizen Pass. Then, as they say, you're golden.

SENIOR GAMES
Southern Maine Agency on Aging
136 Route 1, Scarborough
(207) 396-6500 or (800) 427-7411
Maine has had its own Olympics for residents age 50 and older since the mid-1980s. Part of the national network of Senior Games, these contests take place every September and include both team and individual events. Participants can take part in basketball and softball as well as aquatics, canoe and kayak racing, bowling, cycling, field events, football throw, golf, horseshoes, racquetball, softball throw, table tennis, tennis, and track. And there is much opportunity for socializing as well. Gold-winning Mainers have gone on to compete in the nationals.

LIFELINE CENTER FOR FITNESS, RECREATION, AND REHABILITATION

University of Southern Maine
P.O. Box 9300, Portland 04104
(207) 780–4170
www.usm.maine.edu/lifeline

Based at the University of Southern Maine, Lifeline has been just that for generations of Mainers, helping people recover from physical trauma, quit smoking, improve their health and well-being, and simply find fitness. The center offers a host of programs and classes for seniors in the Greater Portland area, from simple walking and jogging sessions to aerobics, tai chi, and yoga. It also runs more academic health and wellness classes. They're a great resource.

CITY OF PORTLAND PARKS AND RECREATION

17 Arbor St., Portland
(207) 874-8793
www.ci.portland.me.us/rec/senioractivities
.asp

DEPARTMENT OF HEALTH AND HUMAN SERVICES

134 Congress St., Portland
(207) 756-8275

Portland's very active parks and rec department has a full slate of activities designed specifically for people over 55. These might include outings, luncheons, exercise, or educational programs. See the Web site or give a call for the full schedule. The city's Department of Health and Human Services sponsors a groundbreaking program called Eldercize, which incorporates movement from tai chi and dance to get people active.

i The Retired and Senior Volunteer Program (RSVP) encourages folks over 55 to use their life experience and skills to help their neighbors—from teaching kids to read to working in nursing homes and hospitals. Visit www.maine.gov/dhhs/oes/resource/volunt.htm.

SERVICES

THE AMERICAN ASSOCIATION OF RETIRED PERSONS (AARP)

1685 Congress St., Portland
(207) 775-7774
www.aarp.org/states/me

AARP has an active chapter in Maine, helping seniors in all aspects of life, from lobbying on political issues to setting up volunteer programs to distributing essential information. For the small annual fee of $12.50, anyone over age 50 can get access to a wealth of discounts on travel, lodging, food, and car rentals, as well as a home-prescription program, and they'll receive a subscription to the AARP newsletter. They get invites to social gatherings and events, they'll learn about issues facing seniors on the Maine coast, and they'll find out about community-service opportunities. It's probably the best $12.50 any retiree will ever spend.

AREA AGENCY ON AGING, SOUTHERN MAINE

(Serving York County and Greater Portland)
136 Route #1, Scarborough 04074
(207) 396-6500 or (800) 427-7411
www.smaaa.org

AREA AGENCY ON AGING, EASTERN MAINE

(Serving Penobscot, Piscataquis, Hancock, and Washington Counties)
450 Essex St., Bangor
(207) 941-2865 or (800) 432-7812
www.eaaa.org

The national Agency on Aging program is set up to help older people remain at home and independent, yet retain quality of life, and it has a few chapters in Maine. The agency provides an array of services to people from all walks of life, from health insurance and finance counseling to home repair to Meals on Wheels. Its Community Service Consultants visit homes and provide all sorts of information on helpful programs and benefits available to the elderly. The chapters organize volunteer programs and assist people in finding employment opportunities, too.

INDEX

INDEX

ABOUT THE AUTHOR

Andrew Vietze is a freelance writer and a registered Maine guide. As managing editor of *Down East: The Magazine of Maine*, he spent years traveling up and down the coast. He has co-authored a digital guide to adventure travel and written for a wide array of regional and national magazines, from *MaineBiz* and *Maine Times* to *Offshore, Hooked on the Outdoors, AMC Outdoors,* and *Time Out New York*. A seasonal ranger at one of the nation's premier wilderness areas, he's currently finishing his first novel, a thriller bout the North Woods of Maine during the lumbering era.